Snakes' Legs

snakes'

EDITED BY MARTIN W. HUANG

legs

Sequels, Continuations, Rewritings, and Chinese Fiction

University of Hawai'i Press   Honolulu

© 2004 University of Hawai'i Press
All rights reserved
Printed in the United States of America

09 08 07 06 05 04   6 5 4 3 2 1

Library of Congress Cataloging-in-Publication Data
Snakes' legs : sequels, continuations, rewritings, and Chinese fiction / Edited by Martin W. Huang.
   p. cm.
   Includes bibliographical references and index.
   ISBN 0-8248-2812-7 (alk. paper)
   1. Chinese fiction—History and criticism.
2. Sequels (Literature). I. Huang, Martin W.
   PL2415.S65 2004
   895.1'3009—dc22
                    2004004794

University of Hawai'i Press books are printed on acid-free paper and meet the guidelines for permanence and durability of the Council on Library Resources.

Designed by Leslie Fitch
Printed by The Maple-Vail Book Manufacturing Group

CONTENTS

Acknowledgments vii

Introduction 1
  MARTIN W. HUANG

1 Boundaries and Interpretations: Some Preliminary Thoughts on *Xushu* 19
  MARTIN W. HUANG

2 Transformations of Monkey: *Xiyou ji* Sequels and the Inward Turn 46
  QIANCHENG LI

3 In the Name of Correctness: Ding Yaokang's *Xu Jin Ping Mei* as a Reading of *Jin Ping Mei* 75
  SIAO-CHEN HU

4 Eliminating Traumatic Antinomies: Sequels to *Honglou meng* 98
  KEITH MCMAHON

5 *Honglou meng* Sequels and Their Female Readers in Nineteenth-Century China 116
  ELLEN WIDMER

6 Growing from the Waist: The Problem of Sequeling in Yu Wanchun's *Dangkou zhi* 143
  SHUHUI YANG

7 Rewriting the Tang: Humor, Heroics, and Imaginative Reading 159
  ROBERT E. HEGEL

8 Vindication of Patriarchy: Chen Tianchi's *Ruyijun zhuan* as a Critique of the Ming *Ruyijin zhuan* 190
  H. LAURA WU

9 The Voices of the Re-readers: Interpretations of Three Late-Qing Rewrites of *Jinhua yuan* 210
  YING WANG

10 From Self-Vindication to Self-Celebration: The Autobiographical Journey in *Lao Can youji* and Its Sequel   237
   MARTIN W. HUANG

Glossary   263

Bibliography   277

Contributors   299

Index   301

ACKNOWLEDGMENTS

It was during the AAS (Association for Asian Studies) conference in San Diego in March of 2000 that H. Laura Wu suggested to me the idea of organizing a panel on *xushu*. The panel, presented at the AAS conference in Chicago of 2001, and the audience's enthusiastic response to it, inspired the book.

I would like to thank Robert Hegel, the discussant for the original panel, for his insightful comments on the presentations by the panelists, for contributing to the volume himself, and for reading and commenting on earlier drafts of the introduction and my two chapters in the volume. David Rolston deserves special thanks for his support of this project and for his meticulous comments on the volume's manuscript, which have saved us from many errors. My gratitude also goes to David Wang for introducing potential contributors to me.

Portions of the introduction and my two chapters were written and revised during the academic year of 2001–2002, when I was on sabbatical leave funded in part by a grant from the Chiang Ching-kuo Foundation and in part by the School of Humanities at University of California, Irvine. I thank these two institutions for making this leave possible. My research was also aided by the grants I received from the Council on Research, Computing, and Library Resources, University of California, Irvine.

Finally, I thank all the contributors to this volume for being part of this project and for putting up with my constant "nagging" during the unexpectedly long process of putting this volume together. I hope this book will lead to more substantial studies on this important issue in the near future.

MARTIN W. HUANG

Introduction

IN HER study of eighteenth-century English fiction, Terry Castle asserts that "sequels are always disappointing" and that a sequel's own destiny is a "tragedy" in that "it cannot literally reconstitute its charismatic original."[1] This somber observation on English-language sequels by a modern scholar is reminiscent of an equally somber comment on *xushu* (the closest Chinese equivalent for "sequel") by the seventeenth-century Chinese writer Li Yu (1611–1680), who believed that *xushu* were invariably an unrewarding project for any writer.

> It is not that one could not revise *Xixiang ji* [The romance of the western chamber] or that one could not produce a sequel to *Shuihu zhuan* [Water margin, or The outlaws of the marsh].[2] The problem is that these two works are already well established in the minds of people and their position is as secure as Mount Tai and as solid as rock. It is highly improbable that you could force these works to yield their places of honor to you; not to mention whether a revised *Xixiang ji* or a sequel to *Shuihu zhuan* could ever live up to the standards set up in the original works. Even if they are indeed several times better than the original works, the best praise they could hope for is "a dog's tail used to substitute a sable's tail" or "the legs added to a snake *(xudiao shezu)*."[3]

However, Li Yu's dire warning apparently has failed to have its intended effect on many of his contemporaries. In fact, Li Yu's times witnessed the first boom of *xushu* for Chinese fiction. They became so popular that several decades later

Liu Tingji (b. 1653) devoted a much lengthier discussion in his *Zaiyuan zazhi* (Zaiyuan's random notes) to a dozen *xushu* works.

> Recently, authors and writers of fiction, whenever they see that the works of previous writers are prominently circulated, immediately appropriate the names [of those earlier works] and write sequels *(houshu)* to supplement *(fu)* them, in order to make their own works circulate more easily. Unfortunately, this has become a set pattern. . . . To sum up, as for their composition and the meaning invested in them, the original authors *(chuangshi zhe)* are always full of spirits, while even if the later works might be quite good, they are inevitably constrained [to start with]; very few sequels could aspire to the same level of excellence achieved by their parent works, not to mention surpassing them. It should be even more depressing in the case of those works, which are actually dog's tails [trying to pass themselves off as sable's tails]. They will naturally fail to rise above the lowest level of quality.[4]

A case often cited by modern scholars of Chinese fiction to illustrate the inevitable inferiority of *xushu* in comparison with its parent work is that of the eighteenth-century *Honglou meng* (Dream of the red mansion, better known in English as *The Story of the Stone*) and its numerous *xushu*. (Of course, some readers believe the last forty chapters of the novel's first printed edition are already a *xushu;* more discussion on this issue in chap. 1). *Honglou meng*'s unprecedented sophistication as a literary masterpiece seems to have only underscored the improbability of any satisfactory *xushu*.[5] Despite its "intimidating" achievement, this novel has managed to inspire the largest number of *xushu* in the history of Chinese fiction. According to one recent study, the number of *xushu* to *Honglou meng* has come close to one hundred and is still growing.[6] The most direct explanation for such a large number of *xushu*, as is the case for *xushu* to most other novels, is obviously the enormous popularity of the original work and the readers' yearning to know "what happens next," although there are many other, probably more subtle, factors at play, as some of the contributors to this volume explore.

Based on the titles listed in the recently published comprehensive catalogue of traditional Chinese vernacular fiction *(xiaoshuo), Zhongguo tongsu xiaoshuo zongmu tiyao* (A comprehensive catalogue of Chinese fiction with plot summaries),[7] Li Zhongchang estimates that approximately 13 percent of the works listed there are *xushu*. This certainly testifies to the prevalence of the *xushu* phenomenon in Chinese fiction.[8] The importance of this literary phenomenon is only now beginning to attract scholarly attention. To the best of my knowledge, Li Zhongchang's *Gudai xiaoshuo xushu manhua* (Random remarks on *xushu* and traditional fiction) is the only study focusing on this phenomenon, although there have been several monographs devoted to individual *xushu* works.[9] However, none of these studies, except for Li Zhongchang's short monograph, deals with *xushu* as a general issue.

This neglect is in large part due to the perception that *xushu* are too imitative and therefore not worthy of serious critical attention. However, without taking *xushu* into serious consideration, our understanding of Chinese fiction will remain vastly incomplete, not least because of the large number of *xushu* produced. Moreover, *xushu* should not be singled out for their presumed "derivativeness," because direct "textual borrowing" is a quality shared by almost all major works of the traditional Chinese vernacular *xiaoshuo*. After all, many of them were the products of repeated rewritings by multiple authors based on preexisting sources. The famous Ming novel *Jin Ping Mei* (The plum in the golden vase; also known in English as The golden lotus) is a classic example. Despite the great "originality" exhibited in this novel, its main plot is developed from an episode in the earlier novel, *Shuihu zhuan*. In addition, *Jin Ping Mei* "borrows" extensively from numerous other sources.[10] *Xushu* only highlight the second-degree nature shared by almost all literary works in the sense that each has its own literary precedents. *Xushu* as "discursive" practices reinforce the paradox that innovation is impossible without imitation. In fact, *xushu* are fertile ground for studying the intricate relationship between writer and reader in the *xiaoshuo* production process: the writer of a *xushu* is always self-consciously assuming the dual role of author and reader; the *xushu* writing process has to be a reception process of the precursor work(s) as well in the sense that the *xushu* are a continuation of and commentary on the earlier work(s).

This volume is a first collective scholarly step toward studying this important but long neglected phenomenon in Chinese literature. The *xushu* closely examined in this book range from the works produced during the late Ming (1368–1644) to those published in the late Qing (1644–1911). Two important questions explored by many contributors here are what prompted writers to produce *xushu* despite their bad reputation as a literary genre and what motivated readers to read them against the common presumption that they were bound to be disappointing in comparison with the original works.

While almost all contributors focus on the relationships between *xushu* and their parent texts, their approaches and emphases are quite different. Likewise, their understandings of the generic nature of *xushu*, given its complexities, are not necessarily always the same. Lin Chen, a historian of Chinese fiction, proposes two "definitions" of *xushu*, one broad *(guangyi)* and the other narrow *(xiayi)*. When broadly defined, the term "*xushu*," according to Lin, should refer to works that can be characterized as an expansion, abridgment, and rewriting of a previous work for the purpose of improvement. Cai Yuanfang's (fl. seventeenth century) *Dong Zhou lieguo zhi* (Chronicle of the eastern Zhou states), for example, should be considered a *xushu* since it was the result of a rewriting of Feng Menglong's (1574–1646) *Xin Lieguo zhi* (New chronicle of the states), which in turn was a rewriting of *Chunqiu lieguo zhi* (Chronicle of the states of the spring and autumn period), attributed to Feng's older contemporary, Yu Shaoyu (fl. 1580–1620). By the same token, Chu Renhuo's (b. 1635) *Sui Tang yanyi* (The romance of the Sui and Tang) should also be regarded as a *xushu* since it was based on earlier works such as *Suishi yiwen* (The forgotten tales of the Sui), attributed to other writers; however, *xushu*, when narrowly defined, refer to only what is usually understood as an "extension" *(yinshen)* or "further elaboration" *(yanyi)* of a previous work in terms of characters and plot development.[11]

Li Zhongchang proposes the concept of continuation and development *(xuyan)* to describe all those works subsumed in Lin Chen's two categories of *xushu*, which includes "continuations" *(xu)*, "supplements" *(bu)*, "rewritings" *(gai)*, and "imitations" *(fang)*. However, Li appears to have reserved the term *"xushu"* for use in its narrower sense as sequel: "*Xushu* are those extensions developed from their parent works by following the latter's veins and arteries (narrative logic)."[12] Elsewhere, Li offers an even narrower definition of *xushu* by emphasizing that a *xushu* must be structurally linked to its parent text (a *xushu* starts where its parent work ends) and that there must be causal connections between the plots of the two texts *(shouwei xiangxian, yin'guo xiangying)*.[13]

Some Western scholars of fictional narrative have proposed more precise and much narrower definitions of "sequel" (of course, "sequel" is not the exact equivalent for the Chinese term *"xushu,"* as many of the contributors here will demonstrate). Paul Budra and Betty A. Schellenberg have defined the sequel as a "chronological extension of a narrative" that "was originally presented as closed and complete in itself."[14] The French narratologist Gérard Genette also emphasizes the importance of the "closure" of the precursor work of a sequel by distinguishing a sequel from a "continuation": "The *sequel*... differs from a continuation in that it continues a work not in order to bring it to a close but, on the contrary, in order to take it beyond what was initially considered to be its ending."[15] Elsewhere Genette further defines "continuation" as a "completion" (to continue an unfinished work in order to bring it to an end) and "sequel" as a "prolongation."[16]

Apparently, if we are to follow the narrow definitions of "sequel" offered by these Western scholars, several of the novels explored by the contributors in this volume would have to be excluded from consideration as sequels. However, whether these same works can be considered *xushu* is open to debate. This certainly testifies to the complexities of the generic nature of *xushu* in Chinese literary tradition. Of course, one of the main goals of this volume is to explore such complexities. For the purposes of discussion here I offer only a minimum "working"—and therefore necessarily broad—definition of *xushu*: they are all "ensuing narratives"[17] regardless of the specific nature of their relationships to their precursor texts. I shall leave it to the contributors to explore the specific forms this "transtextual" relationship assumes in individual works of *xushu*.[18] Suffice it now to say that these complicated relationships defy easy categorization.

Except for chapter 1, which deals with some general issues in the history of *xushu*, the chapters in the volume are grouped into three parts: the first part (chaps. 2 through 6) examines many "classic" examples of *xushu* (many of them can be characterized as "sequels" with little qualification). The second part (chaps. 7 and 8) is concerned with those works that are usually not considered "sequels" but can still be regarded as *xushu* if we follow Lin Chen's broad definition; they should challenge us to rethink the generic nature of *xushu*. The third part (chaps. 9 and 10) focuses on several works of *xushu* produced during the last decade of the Qing dynasty, when this genre was undergoing important changes with the influx of Western influence. A close look at these late Qing *xushu* should tell us much about the direction *xushu* were going during the twentieth century.

In chapter 1, which is intended to be an overview of *xushu*, I examine this literary phenomenon in a larger as well as more historical context. I first attempt to demonstrate why "*xushu*," thanks to the "textual fluidity" often associated with works of Chinese fiction, has to be a much broader concept than "sequel" in English. Then I explore the close relationship between the rise of *xushu* during the seventeenth century and the simultaneous rise of "interpretation" in contemporary *xiaoshuo* discourse. This close relationship, I contend, was largely due to the increasing need for "serious" interpretations, a logical result of the canonization of several "masterworks" during the seventeenth century. *Xushu*, like the fiction commentary that began to flourish in the same period, were first of all an act of "interpretation" produced from a need to control the reading of the precursor texts. On the other hand, the prevalence of the *xushu* phenomenon may also have something to do with some historical factors that were not necessarily "literary." *Xushu* first began to flourish during the mid-seventeenth century, when China was undergoing a painful dynastic changeover. More than two hundred years later, at the turn of the twentieth century, when the last imperial dynasty was collapsing, *xushu* enjoyed another, even bigger, boom. There appears to be a "transitional" quality inherent in *xushu* as a narrative genre: it is a continuation of as well as a new departure from a previous work. It was this unique "liminal" quality that had rendered *xushu* so attractive to those who found themselves in the interstices between two historical "eras" and who were nostalgic about what had transpired before and, at the same time, anxious about what was happening or what was yet to come (see also chaps. 3 and 9, by Siao-chen Hu and Ying Wang, which touch on this issue from different perspectives). In addition to the mid-seventeenth century and the late Qing, another important moment in the history of Chinese *xushu* was the several decades immediately following the initial publication of *Honglou meng* in 1791. I suggest that many *Honglou meng* sequels can be considered "competing readings" of their common parent novel (cf. the essays on *Honglou meng* sequels in chaps. 4 and 5 in this volume, by Keith McMahon and Ellen Widmer). In fact, what abounds in these sequels are the symptoms of what I characterize as "*xushu* anxiety"—a high degree of readerly self-consciousness of the possibilities of other competing "readings" in the form of sequels. The appearance of a large number of *Honglou meng* sequels in a very short period of time only added to the need to justify *xushu*. A *xushu* writer in the wake of *Honglou meng* would feel even more pressure to combat the impression that a *xushu* was an act of redundancy or the superfluous legs added to a snake (*huashe tianzu*), as suggested by the common Chinese saying. While chapter 1 is by no means a chronological account of *xushu*, it does address what I consider to be some of the important issues in the history of this genre.

In chapter 2, Qiancheng Li concentrates on three *xushu* to the Ming classic *Xiyou ji* (The journey to the west), namely *Xu Xiyou ji* (A sequel to the journey to the West), *Hou Xiyou ji,* (The later journey to the West), and *Xiyou bu* (A supplement to the journey to the West, also translated as The tower of myriad mirrors). If we follow the definition that a sequel is the chronological extension of a completed work, then the famous *Xiyou bu* must be excluded from consideration, because *Xiyou bu*'s story is supposed to have taken place between chapters 61 and 62 of *Xiyou ji*. In his chapter, Li likewise disregards this strict definition of sequel. He also concludes that each sequel is a reinterpretation as well as a rewriting of the parent novel. If we read the original novel *Xiyou ji* as an allegorical journey of "mind," then in one way or another all three sequels continue as well as repeat this "journey." However, in the *continual* journeys of the mind presented in these sequel texts, Li notes a subtle process of "inward turning," an increasing focus on the inner workings of the human mind. This "inward" journey, according to Li, eventually reaches its "innermost destination" in the last sequel, *Xiyou bu,* a narrative characterized by its masterful exploration of "mind" in terms of its reactions to various subtle forms of desire. The "inward" journey exhibited in *Xiyou ji* and its three sequels, while reflecting a larger trend in the development of the Chinese novel during the seventeenth century, was also related to the neo-Confucian school of the mind *(xinxue)* movement that dominated the late Ming intellectual scene. If we accept the dating of these three sequels as works of the late Ming, they are the earliest *xushu* dealt with in this volume. The possible presence of cross-references among the three sequels (the author of *Xiyou bu* was probably taking aim at another sequel, *Xu Xiyou ji*), as some traditional commentators have called our attention to, could be a quite new *xushu* phenomenon that anticipated the kind of high degree of self-consciousness shared by many authors of the *Honglou meng* sequels in the nineteenth century, as I discuss in chapter 1.[19]

Xushu as a literary genre seems to have provided the seventeenth-century writer Ding Yaokang (1599–ca. 1670) with an important medium to search for the reasons behind the collapse of the Ming dynasty. In chapter 3, Siao-chen Hu seeks to demonstrate how Ding presents his own sequel *Xu Jin Ping Mei* as *the* correct reading of the parent novel *Jin Ping Mei.* To that end, Ding tried to drive home the painful message that it was the indulgence in excessive desire as reflected in many people's "misreadings" of *Jin Ping Mei* that contributed to the collapse of the Ming. By blaming the fall of the dynasty on the readers' failure to heed the kind of stern warnings delivered in *Jin Ping Mei* about the dire consequences of excessive desire (therefore, a "misreading"), Ding also tried to come to terms with his own dilemma as a subject under the new alien rule. While harboring certain nostalgic and even possibly loyalist sentiments toward the fallen dynasty, Ding seems to have come to acknowledge the inevitability of the cycle of history and the mandate the alien Manchu monarchy appeared to enjoy. Ding's sequel to the classic novel, Hu points out, was his desperate attempt to rationalize the painful dynastic transition in terms of the ruthless operations of karmic retribution—the fall of the Ming was heaven's severe punishment of its people for their massive moral failure to curtail their rampant desires. By assigning so much importance to the "correct reading" of a novel and by symbolically relating it to the tragic fall of the Ming, the author of *Xu Jin Ping Mei* also tried to elevate the status of his own *xushu* to new heights. Ding presented his novel as the most accurate interpretation of the popular morality book admired by the new Manchu ruler, the Shunzhi emperor—*Taishang ganying pian* (The supreme tractate of actions and retributions). Hu also explores in detail how the author of *Xu Jin Ping Mei* tries to come to terms with the parent text's eroticism in order to provide further justifications for his own sequel.

Given the sheer number of sequels *Honglou meng* has inspired, it is only appropriate that two contributors to this volume haven chosen to focus on several of these sequels, although their approaches and concerns are quite different. In chapter 4, Keith McMahon offers his readings of a dozen *Honglou meng* sequels (most of them produced in the nineteenth century) in terms of three areas: first, how these sequels attempt to "improve" Baoyu, the male protagonist of their common parent novel, by making him healthier, more sexually proper, and more compliant with the social expectations of an aristocratic male; second, how the sequels seek to vindicate Daiyu, the female protagonist in the parent novel, in various ways (having her become the first wife of Baoyu or the capable mistress of the household, etc., while her personality also becomes much more pleasant); and third, how these sequels try to provide resolutions for the love affair between Baoyu and Daiyu. Functioning as interpretations as well as rewritings of *Honglou meng,* these sequels, while adopting different strategies, all attempt to "simplify" the complex masterpiece by aiming at transparency (making what is obscure in the original novel more obvious or simpler to understand). Almost all these sequels share a common tendency toward "stability" as well as a strong desire for a more gratifying closure where all the "traumatic antinomies" are happily eliminated. At the end of his chapter, McMahon cautions us against dismissing these sequels too hastily merely because of their tendency toward "elisions" and "erasures." He observes, "The innovative attempts to work through *Honglou meng*'s intractabilities are also remarkable as the sequels insist on female agency within polygamy or expand upon scenarios of direct and pragmatic resolutions of youthful love affairs independent of adult direction." Here McMahon's interesting explorations of gender relationships within the institution of polygamy as they are constructed in these *Honglou meng* sequels can be considered a "continuation" (a sequel?) of his earlier admirable study on the issue of polygamy raised in other Ming-Qing fictional works.[20] McMahon's references to several sequels' new emphases on female agency lead us to Ellen Widmer's discussions of *Honglou meng* sequels in terms of the larger issue of fiction's female readership in the nineteenth century.

Due to the paucity of relevant data, there have been relatively few studies of the important question of readership and, especially, female readership of traditional Chinese fiction.[21] However, *Honglou meng* sequels, Widmer suggests in chapter 5, provide us with some important clues on this question. Widmer points out that because of its subject matter and unique narrative styles, *Honglou meng,* as evidenced in many sources (prefaces, collections of poems, etc.), appeared to have attracted an unusually large number of female readers.

This tendency toward a larger female readership continued and became even more pronounced for many of the *Honglou meng* sequels. As the "written-down" versions of their parent novel (a fact McMahon explores from a different angle in chap. 4), these sequels tended to target "an audience that was larger, less well educated, and significantly more female than the one Cao Xueqin had in mind." Several of these sequels project "a strong sense of women's importance as readers and critics, even more than was the case with *Honglou meng.*" Many female characters in these sequels are explicitly presented as readers and even critics of the parent novel and other earlier sequels (cf. my discussion of the high degree of *xushu* self-consciousness in several *Honglou meng* sequels in chap. 1).

The most important testimony to this large female audience for *Honglou meng* and many of its *xushu*, however, is a sequel titled *Honglou meng ying* (The shadows of dream of the red mansion), authored by the famous poetess Gu Taiqing (1799–1877). Here a woman was not only a "passive" reader but also an active participant in this phenomenon of *Honglou meng* sequels. The fact that the earliest extant Chinese novel by a female author was a sequel to *Honglou meng* was by itself very significant: it points to the dramatic impact of *Honglou meng* on female readership in part because it was one of the few popular fictional works deemed by a significant group of people as appropriate reading for women. At the same time, this fact also gives us enough reason to believe that *xushu*, with its relative "humble" generic status, probably made the idea of a female fiction writer much more acceptable to the public (including some female authors themselves) during a time when fiction by women was still relatively rare. Writing a sequel to a widely acknowledged "classic" rather than starting a novel on one's own was a much less "presumptuous" act, especially in the case of a woman. In other words, *Honglou meng* and its sequels provided not only "appropriate reading terrain" but also "appropriate writing terrain" for women. Widmer discusses several important features of *Honglou meng ying* in terms of their relationship to its author's unique female sensibility. Moreover, she relates them to other contemporary works authored by women in the poetic narrative genre *(tanci)* to present a more comprehensive picture of women's direct participation in the development of Chinese popular narrative during the nineteenth century. Widmer's findings in this chapter should go a long way in helping us better appreciate women's roles in the development of traditional Chinese fictional narrative.

Next to *Honglou meng*, *Shuihu zhuan* can perhaps boast the largest number of *xushu*.[22] Among all these *xushu*, Yu Wanchun's (1794–1849) *Dangkuo zhi* (The suppression of the bandits), the focus of Shuhui Yang in chapter 6, is arguably one of the most sophisticated as well as the most famous. Few *xushu* writers had taken writing *xushu* so seriously as Yu did (he spent almost two decades writing and revising *Dangkou zhi*). Ostensibly Yu wrote his *xushu* to *Shuihu zhuan* because he did not like its last part (in the 100- or 120-chapter versions), where the Liangshan bandits or rebels are granted amnesty by the Song imperial government. He was convinced that no rebels deserved amnesty. Consequently, his sequel, as its title explicitly reveals, was designed to show how these rebels were all finally executed rather than pardoned by the imperial government. Structurally speaking, *Dangkou zhi*'s acknowledged parent work was not the 100- or 120-chapter versions of *Shuihu zhuan*, since its plot starts right after chapter 71 of the latter. Rather, it is intended to be a sequel to Jin Shengtan's truncated edition of *Shuihu zhuan*, which contains the first seventy-one chapters of the "original" *Shuihu zhuan*. Yu was inspired by Jin's conclusion to his truncated version where the character Lu Junyi dreamed that all the "heroes" of the Liangshan were executed. Apparently feeling that Jin's truncation and added conclusion were not good enough, Yu wrote his sequel to turn this "dream" at the end of his acknowledged "parent text" into reality, further detailing how these rebels received their deserved tragic ends. In his chapter, Yang shows how Yu was trapped by his own *xushu*, or rewriting agenda. The original novel was so successful in exposing the corrupt and incompetent imperial government that it would be very difficult for Yu to be persuasive if he simply had the Liangshan rebels defeated and executed by governmental troops in his sequel. He had to go to the trouble of creating a group of entirely new characters like Chen Xizhen, who also took up arms due to persecution by corrupt officials and who, therefore, were able to maintain a measure of independence from the imperial government. In Yu's sequel, these are the people who later, with the blessing of the imperial government, defeat the Liangshan rebels. Instead of the Liangshan rebels helping the imperial government to suppress other rebels, as narrated in the last part of the original *Shuihu zhuan*, which Jin Shengtan had coyly designated a bad "sequel" by another writer, model characters like Chen Xizhen manage to quell the Liangshan rebels on behalf of this same government in Yu's "genuine" sequel. Consequently, despite Yu's painstaking efforts to differentiate his "new" characters from the Liangshan rebels, the former come very close to resembling the latter since in the original novel it is the Liangshan rebels who helped the imperial government to suppress other "bandits." These new characters eventually end up becoming the "replicas" of the bandits in the original novel, whom this sequel author set out to repudiate in the first place. As a sequel to a "formidable" precursor text, Yang points out, *Dangkou zhi* could not free itself from the original novel's powerful "mimetic" logic. While utterly repulsed by what he perceived to be the pernicious ideology of his precursor text, Yu was caught in a quandary as a *xushu* writer in that he was too "respectful" or "faithful" to the narrative logic of the original novel, despite his announced intention to repudiate its ideology. *Dangkou zhi* is an interesting case where a conscientious *xushu* writer struggled "heroically" but "tragically" within the constraints set up by its precursor. It is precisely this ambivalence on the part of its author—the combination of repulsion and fascination—that turns *Dangkou zhi* into such a compelling *xushu*. Yu Wanchun was a great storyteller and apparently an excellent student of the masterful narrative art exhibited in the original *Shuihu zhuan*. Artistically, *Dangkou zhi* is a sophisticated sequel not least because of its carefully wrought *xushu* structure. Yu's ambitious and yet implicit agenda was to rewrite the entire *Shuihu zhuan* (including the part Jin had already denounced as a bad "sequel"). He tried to show how, when persecuted, one did not have to rebel, as many characters had supposedly done in the original *Shuihu zhuan*. However, as Yang has persuasively argued, *Dangkou zhi*, constrained by the powerful "mimetic" logic firmly established in the original novel, ultimately fails to persuade us that this is ever possible. Rewriting ended up becoming repetition, a fascinating repetition nonetheless.

Among the fictional works examined in detail in this volume, the pseudonymous eighteenth-century *Shuo Tang quanzhuan* (Stories about the Tang, complete) and the nineteenth-century *Ruyijun zhuan* (The lord of perfect satisfaction) by Chen Tianchi (fl. early nineteenth century) are two novels that many readers would not readily associate with *xushu*. If we accept the Chinese scholar Lin Chen's broad definition of *xushu* to include rewriting, *Shuo Tang quanzhuan* can be read as a continuation to, as well as a rewriting of, several previous works in the so-called Sui-Tang romance series *(Sui Tang xilie xiaoshuo),* even though, strictly speaking, it is not a chronological extension of the plot of any of these works.

In chapter 7, Robert Hegel proposes that *Shuo Tang quanzhuan* can be read as an "outrageous" parody of the seventeenth-century *Sui Tang yanyi* by Chu Renhuo (ca. 1630–ca. 1705). Having elsewhere written extensively on several important works in the Sui-Tang romance series, such as *Suishi yiwen* and *Sui Tang yanyi*,[23] Hegel reminds us here about the intricate transtextual (he uses the term "intertexual") relationships among these texts. Focusing on the *Shuo Tang quanzhuan*'s "rewriting" of several important characters from its "progenitors" such as *Sui Tang yanyi,* Hegel is able to demonstrate how its author parodies lofty literati values in these precursor texts by turning those relatively "realistic" characters into "far larger than life theatrical types, at once both grotesque and wonderfully entertaining." Here in *Shuo Tang quanzhuan,* the "moral seriousness" typical of a literati historical novel such as *Sui Tang yanyi* is replaced with the "entertaining pleasure" of an adventure romance. *Shuo Tang quanzhuan* initiates an important alternative reading of "history" in the Sui-Tang romance series; in fact, it was to inspire many sequels of its own, such as the *Shuo Tang houzhuan* (Stories about the Tang, later collection). One of Hegel's important arguments is that *Shuo Tang quanzhuan* is a sophisticated work by a literati author rather than a work assembled from the scribes for professional storytellers, as earlier scholars have conventionally proposed.

The Qing novel *Ruyijun zhuan*'s relationship with the classical-language Ming novella of the same title is an intriguing one. Chen Tianchi, by adopting for his novel the same title as the famous Ming erotic narrative, was apparently attempting to make sure that his readers always kept in mind this Ming text when reading his own novel. After a careful comparison of these two novels in chapter 8, H. Laura Wu concludes that Chen Tianchi conceived his novel as a corrective rewriting of the Ming text. She demonstrates in detail how the author of the Qing *Ruyijun zhuan* carefully reversed everything from the Ming *Ruyijun zhuan* for the purpose of moral critique and censorship. What must have particularly disturbed the author of the Qing *Ruyijun zhuan* about the Ming text was the supposed "dominance by women"; consequently, his own novel was designed to be a story of "male dominance regained and patriarchy restored." Wu concludes her chapter with an argument as to why the Qing *Ruyijun zhuan* should be considered a *xushu*, albeit a quite unconventional one. Like any *xushu*, the Qing *Ruyijun zhuan*, she contends, should not be considered an autonomous text. Instead, it is a *secondary* text in that it would become a quite different work were it to be read without any reference to its Ming precursor, precisely what its author Chen Tianchi tried to avoid by adopting the earlier title for his own novel.

Obviously, the relationship between Chen Tianchi's *Ruyijun zhuan* and the Ming *Ruyijun zhuan* is quite different from that between *Shuo Tang quanzhuan* and its precursor texts. On the one hand, the setting and plot of the Qing *Ruyijuan zhuan* are concerned with people in the Ming dynasty while the Ming *Ruyijun zhuan* is about an empress from the Tang dynasty; on the other hand, *Shuo Tang quanzhuan* is presented as a different "version" of the same story (i.e., it is peopled by many of the same characters as in the precursor texts). However, both Hegel and Wu propose that these two works can be considered *xushu* because both texts are critical "readings" of previous texts in the form of rewritings. Hegel observes that "*Shuo Tang* is a sequel in the sense that it came *after* important and widely appreciated novels in the sequence and dramatically, even radically, *reinterprets* much of the material it adapts from them."[24] However, to approach this issue from a slightly different perspective, we might argue that the *xushu* status of these two works largely depends on the manner in which they are read. These texts are recognizable as rewritings only when the reader, in his or her reading, *recalls* their respective precursor texts. While a typical sequel compels the reader to recall its parent text by chronologically extending the plot of the latter, *Shuo Tang quanzhuan* and the Qing *Ruyijun zhuan* are able to make the reader do the same "recalling" only by constantly and explicitly parodying their precursor texts. As Hegel acknowledges at the end of his chapter, some readers may not choose to read *Shuo Tang quanzhuan* as a parody. That is to say, the novel will not acquire the status of a secondary text if the reader has not read or chooses to ignore its precursor texts such as *Sui Tang yanyi*.

Consequently, whether fictional works such as *Shuo Tang quanzhuan* or the Qing's *Ruyijun zhuan* can be considered a work of *xushu* (a secondary text) is largely an issue of "reading." Here a reader's "training" becomes a more important factor (whether he or she is familiar with the precursor text or sensitive enough to be aware of the possibilities of parody). In the case of a more typical sequel, its relationship with its parent text is so explicit that it can be read only as a secondary text. In fact, to make sure that their readers keep this secondary nature of sequels in mind through "recalling," some writers, such as the author of *Hou Honglou meng* (The later dream in the red mansion), even provided plot summaries of the parent texts at the beginning of their own sequels. In other words, without having read the parent *Honglou meng* or, at least, the summary of its plot, the reader would feel as if he or she were starting from the middle of a novel when beginning a sequel such as *Hou Honglou meng*.

Although *Shuo Tang quanzhuan* and the Qing *Ruyijun zhuan* are not typical sequels in the sense that they are not the chronological extensions of their respective precursor texts, the chapters in this volume by Hegel and Wu should position us better to appreciate the complexities of the *xushu* phenomenon and place in a broader perspective other contributors' explorations of many of those fictional works that can be defined more narrowly as sequels. In fact, *Shuo Tang quanzhuan*'s parent text, *Sui Tang yanyi* itself, as Hegel has convincingly demonstrated elsewhere,[25] is largely made up of an earlier text titled *Suishi yiwen* by Yuan Yuling (1599–1674) and a continuation probably by Chu Renhuo.[26] This is because the bulk of the first two-thirds of *Sui Tang yanyi* was copied from *Suishi yiwen* with little alteration, and the last third was another "text" added by Chu Renhuo. That is to say, *Sui Tang yanyi* might be considered a novel roughly composed of two large textual entities: the parent text plus a sequel. However, to further complicate the matter, *Suishi yiwen* was not the only major written source Chu Renhuo relied on in "compiling" his *Sui Tang yanyi*. He also substantially incorporated into the first half of his novel (though far less than *Suishi yiwen*) an earlier novel, *Sui Yangdi yanshi* (The romance of Emperor Yang of the Sui),[27] and, at the same time, this same text was already a source for *Suishi yiwen*.[28] More recently, Ouyang Jian has argued that the last third of *Sui Tang yanyi* was actually based on a little-known novel, *Hun Tang houzhuan* (Devastating the Tang: A later tale), while the title of the work suggests that it might have been conceived of as a *xushu* to another work considered the earlier story (*qianzhuan*).[29] If Ouyang Jian is indeed correct, then *Sui Tang yanyi* is basically a rewriting of three earlier texts—*Suishi yiwen, Sui Yangdi yanshi,* and *Hun Tang houzhuan*)—while *Hun Tang houzhuan* itself, in all likelihood, is a sequel to another work that is no longer extant. Moreover, *Sui Yangdi yanshi* and *Suishi yiwen* were also the "sources" from which the author of *Hun Tang houzhuan* must have derived some of the material for his novel, as openly acknowledged in the preface attached to the so-called Jiezi yuan edition of the novel.[30] Consequently, the textual "evolution" from the three earlier texts *(Suishi yiwen, Sui Yangdi yanshi, Hun Tang houzhuan)* to *Shui Tang yanyi* to *Shuo Tang quanzhuan* was also a *xushu* process in which rewriting and sequeling often became indistinguishable. Here I am suggesting a concept of a *xushu* continuum with rewriting and sequeling as the respective polarities at both ends of the continuum. While strict rewriting, such as editing, can hardly be considered an act of sequeling, more creative rewriting often overlaps with sequeling (rewriting and expanding a work at the same time). This should help us see a more general trend in the history of Chinese *xiaoshuo*—the *xushu* phenomenon of "sequel" was often, though not always, preceded by another, less explicit *xushu* phenomenon of rewriting. In other words, initially *xushu* often took the form of rewriting, and rewriting in turn led to sequeling (especially after the original work had achieved textual stability when it was attributed to a particular "author"), although the distinctions between these two forms of *xushu* were not always clear.

An important subgenre of *xushu* popular during the late Qing was what has been called fiction that imitates old works *(nijiu xiaoshuo)* or fiction that brings the new out of the old *(fanxin xiaoshuo)*. The titles of these sequels typically contain the character *xin* (new). By using devices such as anachronism, "misplacement," and especially parody, writers of such sequels often tried to take advantage of the medium of *xushu* to address their concerns with their rapidly changing contemporary society (a *xushu* phenomenon I discuss further in chap. 1). Two of the three sequels to the nineteenth-century classic *Jinghua yuan* (The destiny of flowers in the mirror) discussed by Ying Wang in chapter 9 can be classified as *fanxin xiaoshuo*. Both are titled *Xin Jinghua yuan* (New destiny of flowers in the mirror), one by Xiaoran yusheng and the other by Chen Xiaolu. Wang seeks to show how Xiaoran yusheng's *Xin Jinghua yuan* became a "vehicle" through which the author attempts to air his bitter disappointment over the contemporary "reform movement." Here the sequel becomes a "topical novel." Continuing the journey motif from *Jinghua yuan*, the author turns his own sequel into a novel of exposure *(qianzhe xiaoshuo)*, a genre that became extremely popular during the last decades of the Qing. At the same time, this self-reflexive sequel also satirizes this narrative genre for its overuse or abuse by many other writers (while the sequel itself participates in the very "abuse" it purports to satirize). Wang points out that the modern scholar Hu Shi and others of his generation were actually not the first to pay serious attention to the women's issues raised in *Jinghua yuan*. Both Chen Xiaolu's *Xin Jinghua yuan* and Hua Qingshan's *Xu Jinghua yuan* (A continuation of destiny of flowers in the mirror) could be read as two very different late-Qing attempts to "re-voice" the women's issues presented in their common parent text. While Chen Xiaolu, as an author of *fanxin xiaoshuo*, tried to reframe the women's issues in the late Qing context of his sequel by advocating "moderate feminist views," Hua Qingshan, apparently appalled by the nascent women's movement during the late Qing, tried to "correct" what he perceived to be the dangerous feminist tendency exhibited in *Jinghua yuan* by adopting various strategies of "inversions." Wang contends that such diametrically different responses to *Jinghua yuan* in the form of *xushu* could at least in part be attributed to the "indeterminacy" that characterizes the original novel and its self-conscious inclination to solicit rereadings as well as rewritings. After all, she affirms that sequels are invariably rereadings in the form of rewritings.

Another late-Qing *xushu* examined in detail in this volume is Liu E's (1857–1909) sequel to his own famous *Lao Can youji* (The travels of Lao Can). So far all the works of *xushu* explored in this volume are allographic (sequels written by someone other than the authors of the parent works), a focus reflecting the general situation of *xushu* in traditional China; autographic *xushu* (sequels written by the authors who wrote the parent works) were relatively rare prior to the twentieth century. The only extant autographic sequel prior to the late Qing period, to the best of my knowledge, was Fang Ruhao's (fl. early seventeenth century) *Chanzhen houshi* (The later tales of the true way), which was a sequel to his own *Chanzhen yishi* (The forgotten tales of the true way), although these two works are not that closely linked in terms of plot and characters.[31] The author of *Jin Ping Mei* was said to have also written a sequel to that famous work, but it is no longer extant.[32] Entering the twentieth century, with the professionalization of fiction writers (although Liu E was not a professional writer), autographic *xushu* became much more common. In chapter 10, I examine some of the features associated with autographic *xushu*. I note the increasingly explicit "autobiographical tendency" of the sequel in terms of "a journey from self-vindication (in the original) to self-celebration (in the sequel)." I attempt to demonstrate how this autobiographical explicitness in the sequel compels the reader to *reread* the parent novel from a *new* and more "autobiographical" perspective. Different from the rewriting of the original work attempted by an allographic sequel writer, Liu E's "rewriting" of his own previous work in the form of an autographic sequel is sanctioned and legitimized by the authority of the intention of a "single" author. This is an interesting example where an autographic sequel "reshapes" as well as "rewrites" its precursor text by making more transparent the latter's implicit autobiographical agenda. In other words, the sequel turns the precursor text into a work more autobiographical than it otherwise was. This is possible because its sequel is not only "autobiographic" but also "autographic." The chapter on Liu E's autographic sequel serves as a fitting conclusion to this volume on *xushu* produced during the Ming-Qing period in that the increasing popularity of autographic sequels was symptomatic of many changes that were happening to the *xushu* genre in the early twentieth century, reflecting the changing generic status of fiction and its authors in general.

Although this volume focuses on fictional works produced prior to the Republican period (1911–1949), here at the conclusion of my introduction it might be helpful to have a quick look at the direction *xushu* took in the several decades following Liu E's writing of his autoghraphic sequel. The first Chinese copyright laws were adopted by the Manchu government in 1910, but their impact on the practice of *xushu* was limited, and unauthorized *xushu* still remained quite common.[33] For example, soon after Zhang Henshui's (1895–1967) hugely successful romantic novel *Tixiao yinyuan* (Marriages in laughter and tears) was serialized between 1929 and 1930, there appeared a dozen unauthorized sequels. A publisher even put out an advertisement in a newspaper inviting people to submit their manuscripts for publication as sequels.[34] Zhang Henshui's reputation also caused many writers to produce fiction under his name *(maoming)*, and this, according to Zhang himself, was one of the reasons he decided, much against his previous pledge not to write any sequels to *Tixiao yinyuan*, to write one of his own, presumably in order to vindicate himself as the only legitimate author who could write an authentic sequel to his own novel.[35] Zhang had to compete with other writers in producing the "best" or most authentic sequel to his own *Tixiao yinyuan*. Someone even believed that the reason Zhang had many of his main characters die in the sequel was because he intended to make it much harder for others to produce more sequels. Consequently, his was an autographic sequel meant to prevent all other unauthorized allographic sequels.[36] Here, writing an autographic sequel became a means of asserting his ownership of the parent novel as the original author. One new facet of the *xushu* phenomenon during the first few decades of the twentieth century, when copyright laws, though adopted, were seldom rigorously enforced, was that now one had to compete with others in producing sequels to one's *own* works. In a way, there was more pressure for some writers, such as Zhang, to write sequels to their own works largely due to the radically new ways of circulation: the much quicker pace of publication and the coming of age of mass media in terms of newspapers, journals, radio, and even motion pictures.[37]

However, it is curious that in the first half of the twentieth century *xushu* was a phenomenon largely confined to the so-called old-style *(jiupai)* fiction writers such as Zhang Henshui. We seldom come cross a May Fourth writer (or a writer of the so-called "new literature") who wrote a sequel to his or her own work. It is equally rare that the work of such a writer would inspire allographic *xushu* by others. Even when May Fourth writers such as Ba Jin (b. 1904) felt the urge to write autographic sequels to their own works, they rarely chose to use the term *"xushu"* to refer to the sequels. Ba Jin, instead, much preferred the term *"sanbu qu"* (trilogy), as in the case of his *Jiliu sanbu qu* (The current, a trilogy), probably to underscore that these works should be considered an "organic" whole rather than attempts to exploit the success of a previous work for profit. For these "serious" writers of New Literature, *"xushu"* was a term often associated with traditional literature, from which they were supposed to break away. Writing *xushu* was a practice associated with those *jiupai* writers who sold their souls for money, against whom these May Fourth writers often defined themselves. Writing allographic *xushu* to classical novels continues even today, but many of them were written in the name of "scientific" reconstruction of the supposedly missing part of a text—as in the case of *Honglou meng*—known as the "study of the missing texts" *(tanyi xue)*. Writing a sequel is now considered part of literary research. Here, having come a full circle, literary interpretations are now explicitly presented as *xushu*. Interpretations and *xushu* become indistinguishable (a topic discussed in chap. 1).

While this volume is not meant to be a historical survey of *xushu* in Chinese literary history, it contains detailed discussions of representative individual works, many of which have so far received very little scholarly attention. As a whole this volume should help to shed light on the "contours" of the development of this important narrative genre in traditional China. Although there are many important questions that deserve further exploration (such as the relationship between *xushu* and the development of publishing in late imperial China and other motivating factors for reading and writing *xushu*), I hope that the chapters presented here serve as a good starting point for future studies of this important narrative genre.

NOTES

1. Terry Castle, *Masquerade and Civilization*, 133–134.
2. Throughout the volume, when referring to the title of a similar Chinese work, different contributors may provide different English translations as he or she sees fit in the context of his or her discussion.
3. "Ciqu bu shang," *Xianqing ouji*, in *Li Yu quanji* 3:29.
4. Huang Lin and Han Tongwen, eds., *Zhongguo lidai xiaoshuo lunzhu xuan* 1:384–385.
5. In his essay "Sequels to the *Red Chamber Dream:* Observations in Plagiarism, Imitation,

and Originality in Chinese Vernacular Literature," Lucien Miller apparently feels compelled to repeatedly apologize for the "disappointing quality" and "lack of originality" on the part of the three sequels he is discussing. The partial title of a recent book-length study of *Honglou meng* sequels is *"wucai ke butian"* (not talented enough to patch up the broken sky). This phrase is taken from the poem in the original *Honglou meng* referring to the piece of stone left unused by the goddess in her efforts to repair the broken sky. Borrowing this phrase from the original novel, the author of this study of *Honglou meng* sequels obviously tries to show how disappointing these sequel authors were in their attempts to provide continuations to the masterpiece. See Lin Yixuan, *Wucai ke butian: Honglou meng xushu yanjiu*.

6. Zhao Jianzhong, *Honglou meng xushu yanjiu*, 3. Zhao's estimate must have included many works that cannot be defined strictly as sequels, since he may have adopted a fairly broad concept of *xushu*, an issue to be explored further in this introduction and in chapter 1.

7. *Zhongguo tongsu xiaoshuo zongmu tiyao*. This catalog, however, does not cover many fictional works that are written in literary Chinese. Many Chinese scholars of Chinese fiction tend to use the term *"tongsu xiaoshuo"* (as it appears in the title of the catalogue) to refer to fictional works written in vernacular Chinese.

8. Li Zhongchang, *Gudai xiaoshuo xushu manhua*, 3. Elsewhere, Li broadens his concept of *xushu* to include "works imitating a precursor text" *(xufang)* and estimates that about 20 percent of works of traditional *xiaoshuo* could fall into this category. See Zhongchang, "Lun Zhongguo gudai xiaoshuo de xuyan xianxiang ji chengyin," 125.

9. Li's introductory study, however, was written as a brief book in a series that targeted high school students as the main audience. Those studies in English focusing on individual works of *xushu* include Widmer, *The Margins of Utopia*; Xiaolian Liu, *The Odyssey of the Buddhist Mind*; and Brandauer, *Tung Yüeh*. Studies in Chinese that concentrate on individual *xushu*, besides those two on *Honglou meng* sequels mentioned above, include Fu Shiyi, *Xiyou bu chutan*.

10. See Hanan, "Sources of the *Chin P'ing Mei*"; Zhou Juntao, *"Jin Ping Mei" sucai laiyuan*, and the many detailed notes provided by David Roy in his English translation of the first forty chapters of the novel, *The Plum in the Golden Vase*, vols. 1 and 2.

11. Lin Chen, *Mingmo Qingchu xiaoshuo shulu*, 117–119.

12. Li Zhongchang, *Gudai xiaoshuo xushu manhua*, 16.

13. Zhongchang, "Lun Zhongguo gudai xiaoshuo de xuyan xianxiang ji chengyin," 124.

14. Budra and Schellenberg, "Introduction," in Budra and Schellenberg, eds., *Part Two: Reflections on the Sequel*, 7.

15. Genette, *Palimpsests*, 206.

16. Ibid., 162.

17. Cf. the definitions given in the *OED* (1989): sequel is "the ensuing narrative" or "the following or remaining part of a narrative" or "that which follows as a continuation, especially a literary work that, although complete in itself, forms a continuation of a preceding one." See also my discussions in chap. 1.

18. "Transtextuality" is a term coined by Genette to refer to "all that sets the text in a relationship, whether obvious or concealed, with other texts," while he uses the more familiar term "intertextuality" in a much narrower sense referring to "quoting," "plagiarism," "allusion," etc.; see his *Palimpsests*, 1–2. For a list of "transtextual" relationships between *xushu* and their parent texts, see Li Zhongchang, *Gudai xiaoshuo xushu manhua*, 22–55.

19. Of course, this depends on the validity of the theory that *Xu Xiyou ji* predated *Xiyou bu*.

20. McMahon, *Misers, Shrews, and Polygamists*.

21. Fiction readership is an issue explored at length by Hegel's study, *Reading Illustrated Fiction in Late Imperial China*, although it does not focus on the particular question of female readership.
22. According to Li Zhongchang (*Gudai xiaoshuo xushu manhua*, 5–6), there are altogether fourteen *xushu* to *Shuihu zhuan*, and the number could reach seventy-four if the broad definition of *xushu* is adopted.
23. See Hegel, *The Novel in Seventeenth-Century China*, 84–142, 190–217.
24. Li Zhongchang (*Gudai xiaoshuo xushu manhua*, 45) regards *Shuo Tang quanzhuan* and other works in the Sui-Tang romance series as cases of flexible sequels *(huoxu)* in their relationship to their common parent text, *Sui Tang liangchao zhizhuan* (Chronicles from the courts: Sui and Tang), the supposed first work in the series. (There is still controversy concerning the dating of this work because the date of its earliest extant edition was rather late [1619].) They are like different fruits growing on the same vine.
25. For a detailed investigation into the question of how the bulk of *Sui shi yiwen* was copied almost verbatim into the first two-thirds of *Sui Tang yanyi*, see Hegel, "*Sui T'ang yen-i*: The Sources and Narrative Techniques of A Traditional Chinese Novel," 38–53. Hegel concludes that "it is wholly appropriate that Yuan Yuling's name should appear on the title page of *Sui Tang yanyi* as one of its authors" (53). In his postscript to the modern typeset edition of *Suishi yiwen,* Liu Wenzhong uses the term *"xudiao"* (a disappointing sequel) to characterize the last part of the novel supposedly written by Chu Renhuo himself (513).
26. In his commentaries to his own *Suishi yiwen,* Yuan Yuling often mentions how he has made changes with regard to "the old edition" *(yuanben)*. Consequently, *Suishi yiwen* resulted from the rewriting of an earlier text too!
27. See Hegel, "*Sui T'ang yen-i*," 53–69.
28. Hegel, "*Sui T'ang yen-i*," 63. In fact, elsewhere Hegel (*The Novel in Seventeenth-Century China*, 190) has made the observation that *Sui Tang yanyi* is in a sense a sequel to both *Sui Yangdi yanyi* and *Sui shi yiwen*.
29. Ouyang Jian, "*Sui Tang yanyi* 'zhui ji chengzhi' kao," 353–396, esp. 383–395. The degree of similarity between the last one-third of *Sui Tang yanyi* and *Hun Tang houzhuan* is indeed remarkable. However, to determine which text was the "source," one needs to date *Hun Tang houzhuan* more accurately. For example, scholars such as Sun Kaidi and others believe that *Hun Tang houzhuan* is the earlier source; see Tan Zhengbi and Tan Xun, *Guben xijian xiaoshuo huikao,* 227. While Ouyang Jian does provide some circumstantial evidence (mainly the use of taboo characters in the text) suggesting that *Hun Tang houzhuan* should predate *Sui Tang yanyi,* more convincing evidence is needed before this issue can be resolved with certainty.
30. "*Hun Tang houzhuan* xu," in *Hun Tang houzhuan*, 967.
31. Other possible autographic *xushu* are some of the sequels to *Shuo Tang quanzhuan,* such as *Shuo Tang houzhuan* and *Fan Tang yanyi zhuan*. Many of these sequels are attributed to Rulian jushi, while on the inner cover of the Yugu shanfang edition of *Shuo Tang yanyi quanzhuan* (an alternative title of *Shuo Tang quanzhuan*), Rulian jushi was also presented as the compiler. However, the 1783 edition of *Shuo Tang yanyi quanzhuan* was anonymous, and it listed only Yuanhu yusou as the editor or someone who did the collation *(jiaoding)*. At the same time, Yuanhu yusou also wrote a preface to *Shuo Tang houzhuan*. All of this makes one wonder whether Rulian jushi and Yuanhu yusou were the same person. It was possible that Rulian jushi was the author of *Shuo Tang yanyi quanzhuan* as well as many of its sequels, if the attributions of authorship are reliable. For relevant bibliographic information, see *Zhongguo tongsu xiaoshuo zongmu tiyao,* 490–494; and Xu Shuofang's prefaces to the *Guben xiaoshuo jicheng* series reprint of these works collected in his *Xiaoshuo kaoxin bian,* 545–550.

32. Shen Defu (1578–1642) reported that the author of *Jin Ping Mei* wrote a sequel titled *Yu jiao li*. See his *Wanli yehuo bian*, 25.652.
33. For the text of this copyright law (Zhuzuoquan lü) announced by the Manchu government, see Zhang Jinglu, *Zhongguo jindai chuban shiliao: Erbian*, 397–404. The Nationalist government adopted the copyright law in 1928. However, its exact effect is difficult to gauge mainly due to lack of relevant dada. See Alford, *To Steal a Book Is an Elegant Offense*, 50.
34. Wei Shaochang, *Wo kan Yuanyang hudi pai*, 103–105.
35. See Zhang Henshui, "Zuowan *Tixiao yinyuan* hou de shuohua" (1930) and "Zuozhe zixu" in the sequel (1933), *Tixiao yinyuan*, in *Zhang Henshui quanji*, 14:13–14, 369–370.
36. Shuohuaren, "Shuohua—ba," reprinted in Rui Heshi, et al. eds., *Yuanyang hudie pai wenxue ziliao*, 117.0
37. See my discussion of Zeng Pu's (1872–1935) novel *Niehai hua* (The flower in the sea of sins) in chap. 1.

MARTIN W. HUANG

1 Boundaries and Interpretations

Some Preliminary Thoughts on *Xushu*

SOME MAY conclude that the definition of *xushu* as "rewritings," as suggested by the Chinese scholar Lin Chen (discussed in the introduction), is too vague or too inclusive to be a useful generic concept. However, this "inclusive" understanding of *xushu* does highlight the intimate relationship between "rewriting" and *xushu* in Chinese literary history. To better understand the generic nature of *xushu* we have to take into serious consideration the ramifications of "rewriting," which had been the prevailing phenomenon in the history of Chinese *xiaoshuo*.

THE BOUNDARIES OF *XUSHU*

Almost all the important long works of vernacular *xiaoshuo* in traditional China have undergone in one way or another some complicated process of textual evolution and repeated rewritings. A major effort of modern scholarship has been to reconstruct such processes. These efforts to reconstruct all but confirm that full-length Chinese vernacular *xiaoshuo* were often circulated as "open" texts rather than as finished "products." *Xiaoshuo* was an open-ended discursive space where writers, editors, and commentators could collectively fashion a narrative text and where the roles of these three "participants" were often difficult to distinguish. The fact that many works of *xiaoshuo* were initially circulated in the form of hand-copied manuscripts before they were published might have contributed to their "openness." However, being in print did not necessarily prevent these texts from undergoing further textual transformations. This should, as we will see below, complicate the concept of sequel as developed by those Western scholars, since in their definitions the "completeness" of the parent work is a "precondition" for a sequel.

Like many traditional Chinese *xiaoshuo*, the eighteenth-century masterpiece *Honglou meng* is known for its complicated textual history. Most scholars accept that Cao Xueqin (ca. 1721–ca. 1765) was the author of the novel—at least the first eighty chapters—and that these chapters as we know them were based on the author's early manuscript, *Fengyue baojian* (The romance of the precious mirror). However, there are still quite a few scholars who are convinced that this early manuscript was by a different author.[1] Should this be the case, then Cao Xueqin was merely the author of a "rewriting" of another author's earlier work. Consequently, the novel as we have it now was already a *xushu* if we adopt Lin Chen's broad definition of *xushu* as "rewriting."

Even if, as most scholars believe, Cao Xueqin is indeed the sole author of the first eighty chapters of the novel, the authorship of the last forty chapters remains a more contentious issue. Since almost all the extant manuscript copies of the novel contain only the first eighty chapters (or less) and thus are all incomplete, and since the so-called first complete version of the novel (containing 120 chapters) was published in 1791 (several decades after the death of Cao Xueqin), many scholars have concluded that the last forty chapters were not the work of Cao. However, the editor and publisher of the 1791 edition, Gao E (*jinshi* 1788) and Cheng Weiyuan (ca. 1745–1820), claimed in their prefaces that the last forty chapters presented in their "completed" edition were simply the result of their editing what they had pieced together from several different sources, which, they were convinced, must represent different parts of the last portion of the "original" novel by Cao.[2]

Generally, there are three theories with regard to this issue: 1) Gao and Cheng told the truth, and these chapters were essentially the work of Cao Xueqin, and their role was only that of editor; 2) Gao and Cheng merely played the role of editor, but what they edited was work by someone other than Cao, and they might have unknowingly accepted it as part of the original novel; and 3) Gao and Cheng were being deceptive and actually were themselves the authors of the last forty chapters, which they tried to pass off as part of the original novel.[3] If we accept the second or third theory, then the last forty chapters of the novel should be considered a *xushu*. However, judged by Genette's definitions, the forty chapters are merely a "continuation" or a "completion" rather than a sequel or a prolongation, since the eighty-chapter *Honglou meng* has always been thought to be incomplete, while a sequel, by his definition, is an extension of a completed work. To make the matter even more complicated, some scholars believe that Cao had already completed his novel. If we are to entertain the possibility that Cao indeed had completed the novel, although the concluding portion of the manuscript is no longer extant, and if we are persuaded that the last forty chapters in the 1791 edition are the work of someone other than Cao himself, then this final third of the novel, according to Genette's definitions, is neither a sequel nor a continuation. While the last forty chapters were indeed an "addition" to a completed work, they were not intended to be an extension of the original work (and thus not a sequel) or an attempt to bring an unfinished work to its completion, since the parent work was complete (and therefore not a completion either). Instead, the last forty chapters would constitute an alternative conclusion to the novel, whether their author was aware of the existence of the original conclusion or not.

Moreover, if we are to accept the theories that Cao based his novel on another author's manuscript and that the last forty chapters were not Cao's work, then the so-called 120-chapter *Honglou meng* as we now have it is actually a work composed of an "original" work plus two *xushu*. It consists of an early manuscript titled *Fengyue baoqian*, the rewriting and expansion by Cao, and the last forty chapters by a third author, while the boundaries of these three "entities" are hopelessly murky. The case of *Honglou meng* only demonstrates how multiple authorship can complicate our understanding of *xushu*, since it tends to obscure the boundaries between a *xushu* and its parent work, especially when the latter appears to have never been "completed" by its author(s) in a seemingly endless process of constant rewritings and continuations *(xu)*.

The Chinese term *"bu"* (to make complete what is originally incomplete; to supplement or patch up) might, at first glance, correspond better to Genette's notion of "continuation." Indeed, if we accept the first and second theories cited above about the authorship of the last forty chapters of the first printed edition of *Honglou meng*, we can say these chapters were a "supplement" intended to bring an unfinished work to its completion. However, *"bu"* was also frequently used in the titles of those works that were written as formal "sequels" to the 120-chapter *Honglou meng*, such as *Bu Honglou meng* and *Honglou meng bu*, whose plots apparently move beyond the end of the parent work. In conclusion, we might say that *xushu*, even when narrowly defined, is a term vague and broad enough to cover both continuations and sequels.[4]

The late-Qing novel *Sanxia wuyi* (The three heroes and five gallants) is another example that throws into question any clear-cut concept of *xushu*. This novel has always been attributed to the legendary storyteller Shi Yukun (fl. 1810–1871). Many scholars believe that *Sanxia wuyi*, first published in 1879 (under the title *Zhonglie xiayi zhuan*), when Shi Yukun probably had already passed away, was based on the narrative *Longtu erlu* (The aural record of the Lord Bao Longtu), which was in turn based on various versions of the songbooks *(changben) Longtu gong'an* (The courtroom cases of the Lord Bao Longtu) or *Baogong an* (The courtroom cases of Magistrate Bao). These songbooks were believed to be the promptbooks used by Shi Yukun and his disciples when they performed their storytelling. Consequently, although the novel *Sanxia wuyi* was always attributed to Shi Yukun (presumably because Shi Yukun was thought to have "authored" and orally performed these stories, which later became the bases for the novel), it had undergone a complicated process of editing, assembling, and rewriting by many different hands.[5] Interestingly enough, at the end of *Sanxia wuyi*, the narrator "forecasts" what is going to happen in an upcoming sequel titled *Xiao wuyi* (Five young gallants).[6] One year later a sequel titled *Zhonglie xiao wuyi* was indeed published (but by a different publisher). The publisher claimed that this sequel was based on Shi Yukun's original manuscript *(yuangao)*, *Zhongyi xiayi zhuan*, which contained more than three hundred chapters in three volumes. While *Sanxia wuyi* comprised the first volume, his *Xiao wuyi* was made up of the chapters from the second and third volumes. The first volume was about the first generation of heroes and gallants (thus they were called *"da wuyi,"* or five old gallants), while the second and third volumes were about their descendents (thus *"xiao wuyi,"* or five young gallants). Hence the publisher was suggesting that *Xiao wuyi* was not a sequel but the "integral part" of the "original" work. However, this assertion is complicated by the fact that the plot of *Xiao wuyi* is substantially different from what is already forecast at the end of *Sanxia wuyi*. While the role of Shi Yukun in *Sanxia wuyi* is already vague enough, this gives us more reason to doubt whether Shi Yukun played any role in the "production" of *Xiao wuyi* and whether the same people who edited or rewrote *Sanxia wuyi* also may have edited or rewritten what became known as *Xiao wuyi*.[7] Here the distinctions between the allographic *xushu* (written by someone other than the author of the parent work) and autographic *xushu* (written by the same author of the parent work) become meaningless as well as impossible to determine.

Entering the twentieth century, the task of distinguishing many "original" works of *xiaoshuo* from their *xushu* remained an almost equally daunting task despite the availability of much more background information and the much shorter historical distance. Zeng Pu's (1872–1935) novel *Niehai hua* (The flower in the sea of sins) is a case in point. In 1905 Zeng published *Niehai hua* (in twenty chapters), which turned out to have been based on a text (in six chapters) written by his friend Jin Songcen (1874–1947). When Jin submitted his manuscript to Zeng, one of the founders of the Forest of Fiction (Xiaoshuo Lin) Book Company, Zeng was so enthusiastic that Jin simply asked him to finish the work. However, two of the six chapters had already been published in *Jiangsu* (a journal published by some Chinese students studying in Japan) in Tokyo in 1903. What Zeng eventually did was rewrite these six chapters and add a "continuation." Thus, strictly speaking, Zeng's original *Niehai hua* was already a *xushu*. In the publication announcement made by the publisher of the novel's first volume *(chuji)* in 1905, the attribution of authorship is interesting: "The original work *(yuanzhu)* by Jin Yi of Wujiang and completed with a continuation *(xucheng)* by the Sick Man of the Sick Nation." Here Jin Songcen is mentioned as the "original author" while Zeng Pu, whose pen name was "The Sick Man of the Sick Nation," is presented as the sequel writer.[8] Furthermore, when Zeng tried to remember many years later, he could not tell exactly who wrote what in the first six chapters of the 1905 edition.[9] In 1907, Zeng published a *xushu* in five chapters. No further *xushu* were published by Zeng until 1930, when he substantially revised the whole novel and produced a much more expanded version (with ten new chapters) totaling thirty-five chapters. By that time, Zeng had become the designated "original author," while Jin Songcen was left out as author in its various published editions. However, as early as 1912 another writer, Lu Shi'e (1878–1944), published his sequel, *Niehai hua xubian* (A continuation of the flower in the sea of sins). Following the plot plan forecast in chapter 1 of the 1905 edition, this sequel, which contains forty-two chapters, starts from chapter 21 without any references to Zeng's own five-chapter *xushu* (chaps. 21 to 25) published in 1907. In fact, two years earlier, in 1910, Lu Shi'e had already published another "sequel" titled *Xin Niehai hua* whose plot has little to do with *Niehai hua*, despite its title. It has been said that the publication of Lu Shi'e's "unauthorized" sequel soon provoked a lawsuit (most likely filed by Zeng or his friends), and sales of it were stopped not long after.[10] In 1943, another sequel, *Xu Niehai hua*, was published by Zhang Hong (under the pseudonym Yan'gu laoren), this time supposedly with the blessing of Zeng, who, however, had died in 1935. Despite Zeng's authorization, Zhang Hong started his sequel from chapter 31 and disregarded the last five chapters written by Zeng himself.

The complicated textual history of *Niehai hua*, which seems to have been composed of many rewritings and sequels by different authors, may also tell us something about the changing fate of *xushu* in the early part of the twentieth century. Lu Shi'e had to stop the sale of his "unauthorized" sequel because of the lawsuit, which might have been filed because he had produced this sequel based on the chapter titles revealed in the "original" novel before the original author could even produce his own continuation—an act more harmful to the original author than the common piracy violation of copyright laws. Lu Shi'e might have deprived the original author of his right and opportunity to continue his own work.[11]

AUTHORSHIP, INTERPRETATION, AND *XUSHU*

Thus far I have emphasized how the complicated textual histories of many *xiaoshuo* have made it difficult to draw the boundaries between a *xushu* and its precursor text. I would now contend that the initial boom of *xushu* in the seventeenth century was closely related to the rise of "interpretation" in *xiaoshuo* critical discourse. However, this intensified interest in interpretation was paradoxically signaled by the famous fiction commentator Jin Shengtan's (1608–1661) insistence on the distinction between an original novel and its *xushu* (here the English term "sequel" might actually be a more precise term, for reasons to be explored later). Conscientious effort to produce *xushu* or sequels often started by trying to define a precursor text as a "completed" narrative so that an extension could be added. A sequel writer had to assign "textual stability" to the original work in order to justify his own work as a proper addition or an appropriate interpretation, since a sequel usually has to have the parent work's conclusion as the point of its own departure. Jin Shengtan's "editing" of *Shuihu zhuan* (Water margin) and his extensive commentary on this novel should be a good example by default in this regard. Writers and commentators such as Jin Shengtan took advantage of *xiaoshuo*'s textual fluidity (including the blurred distinctions between a work and its *xushu*) to advance their own interpretative agendas.

Before examining in more detail how Jin Shengtan employed the concept of *xushu* in his interpretations of *Shuihu zhuan*, we have to revisit briefly the general issue of authorship in the history of *xiaoshuo* from a slightly different perspective.

A theory shared by many scholars of traditional Chinese vernacular *xiaoshuo* is that most works of *xiaoshuo* were anonymous or pseudonymous because the authors did not want their true identities associated with *xiaoshuo*, which was held in low esteem as a literary genre. People (writers as well as readers) usually did not care about *xiaoshuo* authorship as if it were always "authorless." However, to say that the "authorlessness" of *xiaoshuo* was always a result of its low prestige is not accurate, since anonymity and pseudonymity, as a long-established generic convention, continued to be widely practiced even after *xiaoshuo* achieved unprecedented prestige as a literary genre during the early twentieth century, when Western influence became pervasive. More significantly, anonymity and pseudonymity did not stop some fiction commentators from promoting the figure of "author" when, during the late Ming and early Qing, a significant group of literati writers attempted to assimilate *xiaoshuo* as a narrative genre into "high" literature. The emergence of "literati author" in *xiaoshuo* discourse during the seventeenth century was an important event related to the rise of *xushu* at that particular historical juncture.

In the West, the concept of "author" or "authorship" has remained relatively unproblematic until fairly recently, when Barthes and especially Foucault published their seminal essays on this issue. According to Foucault, the term "author" is much more than a simple reference to the individual human origin of a piece of writing. A private letter may be signed by a person, but it does not have an author; neither does a contract have an author. "Author" as a "function" emphasizing inventiveness, originality, and ownership began to emerge in Europe only after the Renaissance. Before then,

> [t]he word "author" was used interchangeably with its predecessor term "auctor," which did not entail verbal inventiveness as "author" did but the reverse—adherence to the authority of cultural antecedent.[12]

During the Middle Ages in Europe, authors were "for the most part content to repeat inherited materials, making their own primary contribution . . . in the area of decoration, and often content to remain anonymous."[13] Of course, this reverence for the past is only too familiar to students of traditional Chinese culture, although such reverence was never unambiguous. The closest equivalent in Chinese for the concept of "author" or "authoring" is *zuo* or *zuozhe*, which can be found in the Confucian classic *Liji* (Book of rites).

> There they who knew the essential nature of ceremonies and music could frame them; and they who had learned their elegant accomplishments could hand them down *(shu)*. The framer may be pronounced sage *(zuozhe zhi wei sheng)*, the transmitter, intelligent *(shuzhe zhi wei ming)*. Intelligence and sagehood are other names for transmitting *(shu)* and inventing *(zuo)*.[14]

Here *zuo* or "authoring" is not only sanctified as an act of which only a sage is capable, but it is also presented in contrast to *shu* (transmitting). Confucius was often considered the first individual "author" in ancient China, and yet it was

Confucius who famously insisted that what he had done was not "authoring/ innovation" but "transmission" *(shu er bu zuo)*.¹⁵ This disclaimer on the part of Confucius has given rise to many different and subtle interpretations. The neo-Confucian thinker Zhu Xi (1130–1200), for example, observed that

> Confucius edited *Shijing* [The classic of poetry] and *Shujing* [the classic of documents], finalized the principles of rites and music, commented on *Yijing* [The classic of changes] and compiled *Chunqiu* [The spring and autumn annals]. This was an act of transmitting what had already been authored by the former sagely kings and he did not author anything himself.... By the times [of Confucius], almost all the authoring had been accomplished. This was why the Master attempted a great synthesis *(ji dacheng)* of what all the sages had authored and struck a Mean. Thus his achievement was twice as valuable as that of "authoring/creating," even though it was "transmission."¹⁶

In fact, by insisting that there was almost nothing left to be authored by the times of Confucius, Zhu Xi was suggesting that "authoring" as an innovation was virtually impossible for anyone coming after the sagely Master. Consequently, the most "innovative" achievement one could hope to accomplish was "transmitting," and the best transmission was in the form of synthesis.¹⁷

This close association between "authoring" and "sagehood" *(shengren)* was precisely what Jin Shengtan appealed to when he tried to legitimatize his own unprecedented interpretative project on *xiaoshuo*. In a preface to his commentary edition of *Shuihu zhuan*, Jin presented a lengthy defense of his careful explanation of a work of *xiaoshuo* by referring to the associations of *zuo* with the authority of a sage. Following what was already suggested in the Confucian classic *Zhongyong* (The doctrine of the mean)—"One may have the virtue, but if he does not occupy the throne, he may not presume to make ceremonies and music"¹⁸—Jin insisted that only someone who was both emperor and sage would have the authority to author *(zuoshu)*. Even Confucius, who had the virtue of a sage, though not the position of an emperor, did not dare to claim that he had *authored* anything because his *Chunqiu* was based on other written records (thus, strictly speaking, his compilation was not an act of authoring). Then Jin calls attention to the following passage in *Mencius*.

> There were instances of regicides and parricides. Confucius was apprehensive *(ju)* and composed *(zuo)* the *Spring and Autumn Annals*. Strictly speaking, this is the Emperor's prerogative. That is why Confucius said, "Those who understand me will do so through the *Spring and Autumn Annals*; those who will condemn me will also do so because of the *Spring and Autumn Annals*."¹⁹

Jin elaborated that Confucius said this because he was worried that someone in the future might mistake him for an "author" and blame him for setting the example of "a commoner authoring books" *(shuren zuoshu)*. Many misguided people of later ages, Jin maintained, indeed presumed that they, like Confucius, had the authority to write all the books they wanted to write. Consequently, the world was full of harmful books that undermined the order and peace under heaven. Judged in this light, the notorious burning of books ordered by the first emperor of the Qin dynasty (259–210 B.C.), according to Jin Shengtan, despite its negative impact, also served a good cause by destroying many pernicious writings. Now as a commentator (presumably like Confucius), without the imperial authority to ban harmful books, Jin had to resort to "commenting" and "editing" in order to minimize their potential harm. Since very few were entitled to author (one had to be both sage and emperor), commenting on a book that was already "authored" was the best one could do.[20]

Beginning with his efforts to defend the authority of *zuo*, Jin ended up elevating the status of *shu* to a new height by appealing to the sagely authority of Confucius. Since the right of authoring, or *zuo*, according to him, had long been abused, the control of transmitting, or *shu*, became extremely important and, hence, an "authoritative" act, thus paradoxically helping blur the distinctions between *zuo* and *shu*. If we understand *xushu*—in addition to being a "creative" work on its own—as a commentary on a previous work, then it is indeed an "ambivalent" act since it is both *zuo* (authoring) and *shu* (transmitting and commenting). Like Jin's commentary, *xushu* was also an act of *shu* designed to "police" or control the readings of another work by others.

The ambivalence associated with the concepts of *zuo* and *shu* become more obvious if we recall the similar disclaimer of *zuo* or innovation made by Sima Qian (b. 145 or 135 B.C.) only a few hundred years after Confucius. In the postscript to his *Shiji* (Records of the historian), Sima Qian remarked, "My work is only a classification of the materials that have been preserved. Thus it is not innovation/authoring *(zuo)*, and it is a mistake to compare my work to the *Spring and Autumn Annals*."[21] Obviously, Sima Qian had in mind Confucius' famous disclaimer of innovation when he was making his own disclaimer, and hence a "subversive" mimicry of Confucius: Sima Qian was in fact trying to claim what he was ostensibly disclaiming by implying that Confucius' disclaimer was not to be taken literally—Confucius was an innovator despite his own disclaimer. Disclaiming was here turned into an act of claiming authorship. Significantly, Sima Qian was also the first Chinese "author" who explicitly associated the act of "authoring" with "immortality" by suggesting that the act of "authoring" could enable an author to transcend death by attaining cultural immortality *(buxiu)* by virtue of what he had authored.

Having offended Emperor Wu, Sima Qian found himself confronted with the painful choice between death and castration. He chose the latter, because, according to his own testimony, he had to opt for "life" so that he could finish writing his *Shiji*. Sima Qian had taken tremendous pains to explain why he had made such a humiliating choice, and his eloquent and elaborate apology gave rise to the influential theory that all great "authors," including Confucius, took to writing to express their anger and frustration *(fafen zhushu)*. Hence people were to infer that the *Shiji* authored by Sima Qian had to be a great work as a result of the traumatic sufferings its author had experienced.[22]

Sima Qian became the ultimate "author figure" (the "authority figure" as well) to appeal to when some literati writers tried to rescue vernacular *xiaoshuo* out of its "authorlessnes" during the late Ming and early Qing. To assert that *xiaoshuo* could stand side by side with other canonical works such as Sima Qian's *Shiji* or Du Fu's (712–770) poetry, many *xiaoshuo* commentators tried to seek "legitimacy" for their *xiaoshuo* on the theory of "great writers turned to writing to express their anger" because all these works, they insisted, were the result of the authors' great suffering in their lives. Li Zhi (1527–1602) was probably the first to make such an explicit association between this theory of authoring and a work of *xiaoshuo* in his preface to the novel *Shuihu zhuan*.

> Sima Qian once said: "'Shuinan' [The difficulty of persuasion] and 'Gufen' [A loner's anger] were works authored *(zuo)* by a virtuous man who wanted to express his anger." Thus we may say that the men of virtue in ancient times could not have authored those wonderful works had they not experienced great sufferings and frustrations *(bu fen ze bu zuo)*. Had they authored them without sufferings, hardship, and frustrations at first, they would have acted like someone who trembled when he was not cold or who groaned when he was not sick. Even if he did author something, what would be the value? *The Water Margin* is a work written as a result of great anger.[23]

Probably for the first time in the history of Chinese fiction, the "author" and his views began to matter in understanding a particular work. Chen Chen (b. ca. 1614), the author of *Shuihu houzhuan* (The later water margin) tried to justify his own sequel to *Shuihu zhuan* by taking as a point of departure Li Zhi's insistence that *Shuihu zhuan* was a "book of anger" *(fenshu)*. He argued that if *Shuihu zhuan* was indeed a book of anger, then his own sequel was a book for venting such anger, a book where anger could find its outlet *(xiefen)*.[24] What was also significant about *Shuihu houzhuan* as a sequel was the pervasive presence of "author" in the text (the assertion of an authorial personality backstage). In fact, before Chen Chen's times, very few fiction writers had devoted much energy to creating what Widmer has called "the authorial sphere" in a *xiaoshuo*.[25] It is no coincidence that *Shuihu houzhuan* as a *xushu* should be one of the first works of *xiaoshuo* where "author" figured so prominently. The rise of the "author" in *xiaoshuo* critical discourse was closely associated with the rise of *xushu* as a literary phenomenon during the seventeenth century. Obviously, Chen Chen was greatly influenced by the fiction commentator Jin Shengtan, who had put unprecedented emphasis on "author" and "authorial intention" in his commentaries on *Shuihu zhuan*.[26]

Sima Qian's theory of "great sufferings make great literature" also played an important role in Jin Shengtan's effort to reconstruct the "authorial intention" in his critical interpretation of *Shuihu zhuan*.[27] However, what is especially significant for our purposes here is Jin's justification of his truncating the novel by carefully fashioning the identities of two different "authors." His modification of *Shuihu zhuan* was an important event in the long textual evolution of the novel familiar to students of Chinese fiction. Jin justified his modification by asserting that the last part (after chapter 71) in what he had called the cheap, popular edition of the novel *(suben)* was actually a sequel authored by a different writer, Luo Guanzhong. Jin claimed that he reached this conclusion because the ancient edition (a *guben;* older and therefore closer to the "author's" original version of the novel) by Shi Nai'an in his possession contained only seventy chapters plus an "introduction." That is to say, the original novel concluded with chapter 71; consequently, the section after that chapter in the popular edition must be a sequel by someone other than the original author. The establishment of the "original" author's identity became an important task in Jin's overall interpretative project.

In the long textual evolution of *Shuihu zhuan,* Jin was the first to explicitly assert that the novel was *written* rather than *compiled* by Shi Nai'an. Jin chose the word *"zhuan"* (write) to describe Shi's involvement in the "production" of the novel rather than words such as *"jizhuan"* (assemble and write) or *"bianji"* (compile), which had so far been used to characterize Shi's role in many earlier editions.[29] To further support his attribution of the first seventy-one chapters to Shi and to "authenticate" his truncated version of the novel, Jin even resorted to forgery, fabricating a preface by Shi that he claimed to have found in the "ancient" edition he was reading. Before Jin, no one had paid so much attention to the novel's "author," although both Shi Nai'an and Luo Guanzhong had been attached to the different editions of the novel as "editors/compilers" prior to the appearance of Jin's truncated version (some editions mention only one of them as the editor/compiler).

Now Jin was making a clear distinction between the two writers who had often been associated with the novel by asserting that Shi was the original author while Luo was merely the author of a sequel. Here, separation of the text of a sequel from that of its parent novel hinged on the proper identification of the author of the latter. Despite the consensus among almost all modern scholars of the novel that Jin was using the excuse of "sequel" to censor the last part of *Shuihu zhuan* (presumably because he did not like the story of the rebels receiving amnesty from the imperial government as described in the last part), his truncation of the novel seems to have confirmed by default the fact that a sequel could be possible only when the precursor work was deemed complete in itself (thus, coincidentally, supporting the definitions of "sequel" offered by Genette and others). The portion after chapter 71 had to be a sequel because, Jin asserted, the novel had already reached its conclusion in chapter 71.[30] The determination of "authorship" was absolutely crucial to Jin's effort to distinguish a *xushu* from the parent novel since almost all *xushu* were allographic in traditional China.[31] To a large extent, it was this new emphasis on "author" that dramatically increased the possibilities of "interpretations" and "sequels."

Not surprisingly, in Chinese vernacular *xiaoshuo, xushu* became a noticeable phenomenon simultaneously with the emergence of "author" in *xiaoshuo* critical discourse during the late Ming and early Qing.[32] While commentators such as Jin and others were appealing to "author" to legitimize their own extraordinarily grand commentary projects—often based on the assumed presence of a mastermind behind every narrative detail of a great work of *xiaoshuo* such as *Shuihu zhuan*—[33] the seventeenth century also witnessed the first boom of *xushu* in China.[34]

Here Jin's reference to Confucius' concern that he might be blamed for starting the example of "a commoner authoring books" *(shuren zuoshu)* should also remind us of Foucault's insight that "speeches and books were assigned real author . . . only when the author became subject to punishment and to the extent that his discourse was considered transgressive."[35] Although what Jin did to *Shuihu zhuan* was not an attempt to literally "punish" its author, "authorship" indeed became an important issue in his "censoring" this novel, while his truncation itself was certainly a "violent" act of censorship. Significantly, *Shuihu zhuan* probably was also the first vernacular fiction in Chinese history to be banned by the imperial government.[36]

It is interesting that the first case in which an *author* was penalized for his work of *xiaoshuo* involved a *xushu* writer. Ding Yaokang was incarcerated for about four months in 1665 for authoring a *xushu* titled *Xu Jin Ping Mei*, (A sequel to the plum in the golden vase), presumably because of its anti-Manchu sentiments.[37] Like his contemporary Chen Chen, Ding Yaokang also painstakingly insisted on his authority as an author in his sequel, although his strategies were quite different. Several times in the novel he had "himself" appear as a character, and he even had a portrait of himself printed in the novel. All this insistence on "authorship" of vernacular *xiaoshuo* was not that common prior to the seventeenth century.[38] However, Ding paid dearly for his claim of authorship, since "author" often began to matter—in China as in Europe—when an individual was thought to be responsible for a transgressive work. If Jin Shengtan was one of the earliest readers to pay such serious attention to the authorship of *xiaoshuo* by insisting that the last part of the original *Shuihu zhuan* was a sequel by a different author so that he could censor it as he saw fit, the new Manchu regime apparently also focused unprecedented attention on a novelist, one who had to be imprisoned for authoring a seditious work. This was probably the first time in Chinese history that the imperial government took so seriously the authorship of a *xiaoshuo* work only for the sake of censorship. Thus both Jin and the Manchu regime aimed to police the reading of *xiaoshuo*. Of course, what adds to the irony is that Ding's sequel was itself an attempt to control the reading of another *xiaoshuo*, the late Ming classic *Jin Ping Mei*, just as Jin had done with regard to the original *Shuihu zhuan* through his editing and commentary.

Ironically, having anticipated the possible dangers involved in authoring a *xushu* that might be considered anti-Manchu, Ding deliberately stated in his preface that he wrote the *xushu* in order to illustrate the principles of karmic retribution in the morality book *Taishang ganying pian* (The supreme tractate of actions and retributions), a work just recently praised by the Manchu emperor.[39] Here the "policing" nature of *xushu* as an interpretative act was underscored by Ding's imprisonment for authoring a "wrong" reading of its precursor text.[40] Writing *xushu* and incarceration thus were both deliberate attempts to control "reading." The simultaneous "births" of *xiaoshuo* author and commentator as well as the boom of *xushu* during the seventeenth century pointed to the increasing importance attached to interpretation in contemporary *xiaoshuo* discourse, a key sign of *xiashu*'s maturity as an important narrative genre.

"Authorship" of some works of vernacular *xiaoshuo* began to matter in the seventeenth century because these works were now deemed important enough to need *interpretation*—whether for the purpose of literary appreciation, ideological control, or censorship—rather than just being read for enjoyment. Interpretation here was understood (by people such as Jin Shengtan) to be the "determination" of the intention *(zhi)* of an author, whose authority was appealed to for a systematic account of every detail in a "great" work of *xiaoshuo*. This desire for coherent "interpretation" gave rise to "author" as well as *xushu*. After all, *xushu* was first of all an interpretation of its parent work and an acknowledgement that the parent work deserved serious interpretations. By claiming that the last part of the original *Shuihu zhuan* was a sequel by another author, Jin Shengtan was insisting that that sequel was not only an interpretation but also a bad one (thus the need for another and more proper interpretation in the form of his extensive commentary). Therefore, the coincidence of the rise of "author" in *xiaoshuo* critical discourse with the rise of the *xushu* should not be regarded as merely a historical accident. Both were related to the increasing urge for appropriate "commentaries" during a time when several works of *xiaoshuo* such as *Shuihu zhuan* were canonized as "masterworks" *(qishu)* and canonical works had to be interpreted properly.[41]

Jin's truncation of *Shuihu zhuan* and his insistence that the novel had already reached its "end" with the grand reunion in chapter 71 also highlighted the importance as well as the difficulties of determining "the end" of a work, a crucial factor to consider in studying sequels. This is because the plot of a sequel often (though not necessarily always) starts to unfold after the conclusion of its parent work and because the long process of textual evolution of many traditional *xiaoshuo* had obscured their "endings" and even sometimes rendered them "endless" (with no formal closure or susceptible to countless added endings, as attested to in the complicated textual history of *Honglou meng*). This problem of textual "fluidity" was compounded by the fact that different readers might have different views as to where a narrative should end, especially when they are forced to choose between different endings presented in different editions of a "similar" work.[42] Jin's strategy was to influence many later writers and editors of fiction. For example, Ma Congshan, who once tutored in the house of the nineteenth-century fiction writer Wen Kang, mentions in his preface to Wen's novel, *Ernü yingxiong zhuan* (The tale of heroic lovers), that it originally contained fifty-three chapters, but only the first forty were published in that edition because the last thirteen were believed to be a poorly written *xushu* authored by another writer.[43]

Almost two centuries after Jin Shengtan published his shortened version of *Shuihu zhuan* and long after he apparently convinced most readers that his version was the best (since his seventy-chapter version of the novel eclipsed virtually all others and became the "standard edition" beginning in the late seventeenth century), Yu Wanchun decided that he had to write another sequel to further elaborate on what was being suggested in the conclusion worked out by Jin in his version. More specifically, Yu claimed that his sequel was intended to spell out what was only suggested in the character Lu Junyi's dream at the conclusion of Jin's edition, in which all Liangshan rebels were killed. Yu's sequel was supposed to be "corrective" of the last part of the original novel, which Jin had *already* censured as a sequel supplied by another writer. Apparently, Yu felt that Jin's shortened version was not good enough, and he had to write another counter-sequel to de-legitimate the "original" sequel. What complicated the matter was Yu's ambitious and yet hidden agenda to rewrite the entire "parent" novel (he was unhappy not only with the portion of the novel after chapter 71 as he had explicitly claimed, but also the seventy-one chapters of the parent novel themselves). Significantly, Yu's sequel also deliberately consisted of seventy chapters plus a "conclusion" *(jiezi),* the exact number of the total chapters of his acknowledged parent novel (Jin's edition of *Shuihu zhuan* contains seventy chapters plus a prologue *[xiezi]*). In his sequel, Yu wanted to demonstrate through his new protagonists that, unlike what was described in detail in the first part of the original novel, when persecuted by corrupt officials, one did not have to (and must not) rebel by joining the bandits *(guanbi min bufan)*.[44] Consequently, *Dangkou zhi* was an elaborate "rewriting" of the entire *Shuihu zhuan* (including the part deleted by Jin).[45] Both Jin's shortened version and Yu's rewriting became possible in large part thanks to the complicated textual history of the parent novel and its textual malleability.

Even though, formally, *Dangkou zhi* was written as a sequel to Jin's version, the parent work it purported to "rewrite" was the original version (including the part that Jin had censured as the sequel). The new conclusion in Jin's version provided *Dangkou zhi* only with a point of departure (as a typical sequel begins at the end of its parent work). Yet it was the conclusion of the original version (what Jin had *already* censured as a bad sequel) that motivated Yu to produce yet another sequel. However, Yu appeared to have been trapped by his own claim that he was following Jin's "correct" reading of the novel, since the validity of Jin's reading was predicated on his assertion the last part of the novel was a sequel, something imposed by another writer. The mere fact that *Dangkou zhi* was yet another sequel should invalidate itself as a proper "reading" of Jin's version of *Shuihu zhuan,* since Jin's truncated version sought justification in his theory that the original novel was ill served by a "sequel."

The above discussion should shed light on the fact that rewriting (often in the form of editing, omitting, and adding), commentary, and sequel are all attempts to control the "meaning" of an "original" work. While rewriting simply ignores the textual integrity of the original work, commentary and sequel often become possible and even necessary when the meaning of that original work seems to have achieved its stability thanks to the rise of the authority of an "author." That is why a *xushu* process often starts with rewriting, then commenting, and ends up with sequeling, although these steps are not necessarily always distinguishable from each other in practice.

EPOCHAL CHANGES AND THE "TRANSITIONAL" NATURE OF *XUSHU*

So far we have focused on the "interpretative nature" of *xushu*. And yet we can also approach *xushu* from a slightly different angle, which should bring our attention to some of *xushu*'s other "functions." It is generally agreed that there were two periods in the history of Chinese fiction during which *xushu* flourished (if we consider the phenomenon of *Honglou meng* sequels an exceptional case). The initial wave took place during the mid-seventeenth century, the other during the late Qing at the turn of the twentieth century. Interestingly enough, both waves took place during a period of important historical transition. The Ming dynasty collapsed and the Qing dynasty was founded during the mid-seventeenth century; during the late Qing, China bade farewell to the two-thousand-year imperial rule and entered the Republican era. Besides many other factors in the development of Chinese fiction as a narrative genre (some of which we have discussed above), there must be something inherent in *xushu* as a literary form that rendered itself so attractive to those writers and readers who were experiencing such rapid social and historical change. If *xushu* is understood as a sequel purporting to continue the "story" of a previous work, then we should not be surprised to find that many writers in an age of drastic social and political change could be drawn to this narrative genre.

First, *xushu* is often an attempt to prolong a narrative that is supposed to have already reached its "end" (Genette uses "prolongation" to characterize the sequel). To a large extent, *xushu* is a refusal to accept the closure provided by its parent work as "appropriate." On the one hand, *xushu* is an attempt to cling to (as well as rethink) "what has happened before"; on the other hand, *xushu*, by virtue of its intent to continue, is also an effort to try to relate "what happened before" to "what is happening since then." It is about making the connection between two "narrative entities" (or two "historical" periods). Despite its "nostalgic" inclination toward the past (what has already been narrated), it is also a narrative, paradoxically, about what happens beyond the "end" or the "past" and is thus future oriented as well. The raison d'etre of a *xushu* lies in the "interstices" (space/time) between "what has ended" and "what lies beyond that end."

One feature shared by several *xushu* novels produced during the mid-seventeenth century was the overriding obsession with the fall of the Ming dynasty. To name a few, *Xu Jin Ping Mei*, *Shuihu houzhuan*, and *Hou Shuihu zhuan* (A sequel to water margin) have all been considered works of the Ming loyalism *(yimin wenxue)* thanks to their persistent reflections on the collapse of the Ming and on the possible reasons behind such a catastrophic end to a long-reigning dynasty. Several of these works are set against the historical collapse of the Northern Song dynasty, and its relevance to the contemporary upheaval of Ming-Qing transition is difficult to miss. For Ding Yaokang, writing *Xu Jin Ping Mei* became an attempt to come to terms with the fall of the Ming dynasty as well as his personal dilemma as a subject under the new "alien" dynasty. As I mentioned earlier, Ding was in fact imprisoned for the supposed anti-Manchu sentiments found in his sequel. The historical setting for the conclusion of the parent novel *Jin Ping Mei* is the period during which the Northern Song monarchy began to collapse under the threat from the Jurchens. This provided sequel writer Ding with the perfect opportunity to explore the issue of dynastic transition in his "continuation." For this sequel writer, the continual stories of the characters from the parent novel had to be "contextualized" in the "national" crisis China was experiencing. As Siao-chen Hu argues in her discussion of *Xu Jin Ping Mei* in chapter 3 of this volume, Ding, while insisting that his own sequel was the correct reading of *Jin Ping Mei*, blamed the fall of the Ming on people's "misreading" of the parent novel—their failure to heed the warnings delivered in the novel against excessive indulgence in desire. In many ways, Ding's *Xu Jin Ping Mei* is a "continuation" designed to account for the sudden "closure" (discontinuation) of a dynasty.

In his sequel *Shuihu houzhuan*, Chen Chen took great pains to create a utopian land as an imaginary "alternative" to what had actually happened to the Ming monarchy.[46] With the help of the medium of a sequel, Chen Chen was able to symbolically extend the rule of the Ming monarchy by presenting a "continuation" that differed from the "conclusion" in reality. In Chen Chen's sequel, the "old" nation continued to exist (albeit on a remote island), thus keeping alive the hope that the Ming dynasty might one day be restored on the mainland. *Xushu* as a continuation of a previous narrative seems to have also allowed these seventeenth-century writers to retain a sense of "continuation" during an age of violent dynastic and social "discontinuity."

Almost two and a half centuries later, at the end of China's last imperial dynasty, the late Qing period witnessed another wave of *xushu*. If many mid-seventeenth-century *xushu* shared an obsession with the fallen Ming monarchy—an event of the past—a substantial number of *xushu* of the late Qing were primarily concerned with the issue of how the people in the "past" could adapt to the rapidly changing "present" and even prepare for the "future." In many works of *xushu* of this period, a character from the past (i.e., the parent novel) is suddenly thrown into the future and desperately tries to cope with the "new" environment. *Xushu* as a genre of transition helped to create a strong sense of the "epochal inevitability." Many *xushu* in this period have the word "*xin*" (new) in their titles to advertise their unique features as works of a new kind of *xushu*.[47] Several special terms have been coined by literary historians to describe these works, such as *"nijiu xiaoshuo"* (fiction that imitates the old), *"fanxin xiaoshuo"* (fiction that brings the new out of the old) and *"jieti xiaoshuo"* (fiction that thematizes one thing by talking about another thing).[48] The format of *xushu* seems to have provided these writers with a very effective discursive medium to explore the ramifications of the radical social change their contemporaries were experiencing at the turn of the twentieth century, when the imperial monarchy was quickly collapsing and when traditional Chinese culture was being seriously challenged by the influx of Western influence.

A character from the parent novel of a distant era (often from a well-known classic) is suddenly relocated into a "modern" environment or, even better, sent overseas as a student *(liuxuesheng),* as in the two sequels to *Honglou meng* that share the same title, *Xin shitou ji,* one published by Wu Jianren in 1905 and the other by Nanwu yeman in 1909. In Wu Jianren's *Xin Shitou ji,* while witnessing various social problems brought on by "modernization," Jia Baoyu (the famous male protagonist from *Honglou meng*) was also given the opportunity to get acquainted with many new scientific "inventions."[49] As in the case of the seventeenth-century *Shuihu houzhuan, xushu* as a unique narrative form, again, allows Wu to construct a utopian vision, which is apparently related to this author's dissatisfaction with his contemporary social environment.

Lu Shi'e, a prolific writer from the late Qing and early Republican periods, wrote many *xushu* in the form of *fanxin xiaoshuo* (he was also the author *Xin niehai hua,* as I mentioned before).[50] His *Xin Shuihu* (New water margin) begins with Lin Chong and other heroes from the Liangshan learning the news of "political reform" *(weixin)* in the capital. The entire *xushu* is about how these "old" characters from the parent novel are quickly adapting themselves to the new world by getting involved in various modern enterprises (from building railroads to running a shipyard).[51]

The impact of the radical "dislocation" (both in terms of time and space) on these "ancient people" from the parent novels was often the focus in these *new* sequels; what is underscored are the "discontinuities," or the radical differences between these sequels and their parent works and between the respective eras they reflect. If *xushu* are indeed continuations of previous narratives, then here they served as continuations produced to emphasize the "discontinuity." The "original" work was often an excuse (albeit an indispensable one) for a *xushu* that appeared to be merely tenuously tied to its precursor, while the emphasis was always on the "new" and the "different." Quite unlike the cases of *Xu Jin Ping Mei, Dangkou zhi,* or many *Honglou meng* sequels produced during the several decades immediately after the 1791 publication of the parent novel, in these "new" works of *xushu* interpretations of the precursor texts were apparently not their main focus, although they could still be read as a sort of "comment" on their parent works. The parent work now became the past to be "recalled" through devices such as anachronism and parody only to illustrate the radically different "present." For example, at the beginning of his *Xin Shitou ji,* Wu Jianren tried to justify his *xushu* effort by insisting that his sequel was "an expression of his own mind" *(zijia de huaibao)* rather than a slavish continuation of the original novel's story, implying that it had little to do with its acknowledged parent novel.[52] If we insist that these *xushu* are nevertheless interpretations or reinterpretations of their parent works, then they as *fanxin xiaoshuo* function even more effectively as "topical commentaries" on contemporary society.[53] Indeed, the turn of the twentieth century witnessed the quick emergence of a "new" subgenre of *xushu* that was radically different from its predecessors.

The above discussion is not meant to argue that there is an "automatic" linkage between *xushu* and dynastic change or radical historical discontinuity, since a great majority of *xushu* is not concerned with this issue at all and since *xushu* has been a near-permanent and constant fixture of traditional Chinese fiction since the seventeenth century. However, the fact that a substantial number of *xushu* do share this concern with historical transition or epochal change is strong testimony of its generic "fascination" with the issues of continuity and discontinuity, while an adequate understanding of this fascination, I believe, is crucial to a better appreciation of many *xushu* from the mid-seventeenth century, and especially those from the late Qing known as the *fanxin xiaoshuo*.

HONGLOU MENG SEQUELS AS COMPETING READINGS

In addition to the wave of *xushu* during the mid-seventeenth century and the late Qing, the production of numerous sequels to *Honglou meng* during the several decades after its initial publication in 1791 was another important "moment" in the history of Chinese *xushu*. Any general account of *xushu* in traditional China would remain incomplete without taking these sequels into consideration.[54] Lin Chen once characterized these *Honglou meng* sequels as "collections of criticism" devoted to the original novel.[55] Indeed, one is struck by how "interpretation" becomes a prominent issue in many of these sequels. One interesting aspect of the *Honglou meng* sequels is the rapidity with which these sequels were written and published and the short intervals between them. For example, the first sequel to the 1791 edition of *Honglou meng* was *Hou Honglou meng* (Later dream of the red mansion), which appeared in 1796.[56] Only three years after that, two more sequels, *Xu Honglou meng* (A sequel to dream of the red mansion) by Qin Zichen and *Qilou chongmeng* (The repeated dream of a beautiful mansion) were published. The year 1805 saw the publication of both Chen Shaohai's *Honglou fumeng* (The repeated dream of the red mansion) and *Xu Honglou meng* (A sequel to dream of the red mansion) by Haipu zhuren. Nine years later, *Honglou yuan meng* (The happy dream of the red mansion) was published, and *Bu Honglou meng* (A supplement to dream of the red mansion) was probably completed in the same year (the author's preface was dated 1814, although the earliest extant edition was dated 1820). The year 1819 witnessed the publication of a supplement to *Honglou meng*, *Honglou meng bu*. Five years later, the author of *Bu Honglou meng* published an additional sequel to his own work, this time titled *Zengbu Honglou meng*. (An additional supplement to dream of the red mansion). Consequently, within the three decades immediately after the initial 1791 publication of *Honglou meng*, there were at least nine sequels published. More sequels would come, although the pace slowed considerably during the following decades.

This unprecedented phenomenon of so many sequels to one novel being published in such a short period of time is testimony not only to the tremendous popularity of *Honglou meng* and the reading public's appetite for its sequels, but also to the efficiency of the publishing industry of the time. This speed or density gave rise to several important features unique to these sequels.

Unlike many other novels published during that time, almost none of these sequels was accompanied by commentaries *(pingdian)*, even though the practice of printing commentaries alongside the story proper of a novel (a practice that began during the late Ming) was already well-established by the beginning of the nineteenth century. This was obviously a result of attempts on the part of these writers and publishers to rush the publications in order to take advantage of the popularity of the parent novel.

As if to compensate for this lack of commentaries, comments on the parent novel and on other sequels abound in the texts of these sequels. In other words, there was an unusually high degree of "readerly" consciousness in these sequels. The author of *Hou Honglou meng*, Xiaoyaozi, claimed in his preface that he had discovered another thirty chapters written by the "original" author, Cao Xueqin. In this he was apparently mimicking Gao E and Cheng Weiyuan, the editor and publisher of the first-printed edition of the parent novel.

> After Mr. Gao published *Honglou meng* by Cao Xueqin, it has become so popular that almost every family has a set. It was rumored that Cao Xueqin had also written *Hou Honglou meng* in thirty chapters. People were rather disappointed that they could not find it after a long search. However, not long ago, Baiyun waishi and Sanhua jushi were able to locate the original manuscript and miraculously it was complete. . . . I was able to purchase the manuscript for a large sum of money and had it published with the help of my friends so that people could enjoy it together.[57]

Xiaoyaozi further claimed that to remain utterly faithful to the original manuscript by Cao Xueqin he did not alter a single word, implying he was much more respectful to the original author than Gao and Cheng in their handling of Cao's manuscript. To emphasize the authenticity of the "original" manuscript he purchased, Xiaoyaozi claimed that the seals of the original author were stamped on (the first page of) every chapter, and even the text of a letter from Cao's mother asking her son to write this sequel was also printed as part of Cao's "original" preface to the sequel.

Most scholars are inclined to believe that to convince his readers of the authenticity of the sequel, Xiaoyaozi was apparently trying to imitate the rhetoric of Gao E and Cheng Weiyuan in their earlier efforts to persuade their readers that the last forty chapters they presented were also written by the original author—but that Xiaoyaozi did a very poor job. One of Xiaoyoazi's contemporaries, Aisin Gioro Yurui (fl. 1803–1812), asserted that it was unheard of for any mother to address her own son by his courtesy name *(zi)*, as Cao's mother supposedly did in the letter presented as part of Cao's preface to *Hou honglou meng*.[58] However, I tend to doubt that Xiaoyaozi could be so incompetent as to make such a common-sense mistake. Gao E and Cheng Weiyuan's rhetoric of "authenticity" was mimicked with such deliberate exaggeration in this sequel that we have to seriously entertain the possibilities of a parody. This impression becomes even stronger when we start to read the novel proper. There the "original author" Cao Xueqin is made to appear repeatedly as a character who is said to be the uncle of the protagonist Baoyu. Cao even participates in a poetic competition with other characters. He is in fact the matchmaker for Baoyu and the female protagonist Daiyu. Daiyu is so grateful to him that she gives him a huge sum of money as a reward. Cao is said to have written both the 120-chapter *Honglou meng* (the parent novel) and the 30-chapter *Hou Honglou meng* at the direct request of Baoyu. Baochai (a cousin of Baoyu) and Daiyu are said to have written commentaries on both works in which they themselves are the main female characters. The reader is informed in *Hou Honglou meng* that Cao blames the inconsistencies of the original novel's plot on his following Baoyu's bad advice (1.922)! We are even told that whenever Cao finished writing a chapter of *Hou Honglou meng*, he would show it to Baoyu and sometimes Daiyu; Baochai would also read it (20.1043). Cao is even paid handsomely by the Jias for writing *Honglou meng* and the sequel. Here, "author," "characters," and "readers/commentators" all live in the same novelistic world.

All of this appears to be cases of self-conscious metafictional plays on the part of Xiaoyaozi. Here we should recall that it was in the last chapter of the 1791 printed edition where Cao appeared for the first time as a "character" in the novel, perhaps a ploy on the part of the author of the last forty chapters to "authenticate" his work as part of the original work (if we believe these chapters were the work of someone other than Cao). Apparently, here Xiaoyaozi was parodying the original novel's "conclusion" as provided in that edition. That is to say, the last forty chapters of the 1791 edition of *Honglou meng*, the "original" *xushu*, became the target of parody in another *xushu*, *Hou Honglou meng*, which, however, was presented as an autographic sequel (although nowhere in his prefaces or in the sequel proper does Xiaoyaozi explicitly express any doubt about the textual integrity of the 1791 edition).[59]

The "conclusion" of the 1791 edition became a target of parody in another sequel, *Bu honglou meng*. In chapter 120 of the 1791 edition we encounter the following curious passage.

> One day Vanitas the Taoist passed again by Greensickness Peak and saw the Stone "that had been found unfit to repair the heavens," lying there still, with characters inscribed on it as before. He read the inscription through carefully again and noticed a whole new section had been appended to the gatha at the back of the stone *(houmian)*. This new material provided several denouements and tied up various loose ends in the plot, completing the overall design of fate that underlay the original story.[60]

Here we are urged to assume that the last portion of the novel as we have it now was discovered by Vanitas only during his *second* visit, because in the first visit (at the beginning of the original novel), either he did not see the inscription at the back of the stone or at that time there was no inscription yet at the back of stone. Some scholars have concluded this should be the irrefutable "internal" evidence that the last forty chapters were a *xushu* authored by someone other than the original author, Cao Xueqin.[61] This appears to contradict directly Gao E and Cheng Weiyuan's claim that the last forty chapters were also by Cao. The question remains, if they were indeed trying to be deceptive, why would they conclude their own *xushu* in such a way so as to expose themselves? Scholars such as Zhao Gang and Chen Zhongyi have proposed that this can be explained only by the fact that the last forty chapters are an allographic *xushu* written by someone other than Gao and Cheng themselves; when they were editing these chapters, they must have failed, in their haste, to delete this passage. Had they done so, the novel's conclusion would have been more consistent with their *genuine* belief that these chapters were the work of Cao; this may be the best explanation one can come up with, although it is still difficult to believe. In other words, Gao and Cheng were absolutely honest in asserting what they thought was true about the authorship of the last forty chapters despite the fact that their unwitting blunder had left evidence invalidating their attribution of authorship.[62] Regardless of what Gao and Cheng believed, this internal evidence, it seems to me, does suggest that the last portion of the 1791 edition was an allographic *xushu* simply because it is unlikely that Cao, the "original" author, would have resorted to such a self-conscious *xushu* ploy as part of the conclusion of his novel had he himself been the author of its last forty chapters.[63]

Either way, the fact is that this *xushu* ploy of "discovering another manuscript by the original author" is parodied in Langhuan shanqiao's sequel, *Bu Honglou meng*. At the beginning as well as at the end of this sequel (1.2879 and 48.3121), we are told that Vanitas accidentally turned over the stone and found yet another inscription carved on the bottom, which, we are supposed to assume, he had apparently failed to copy down during his two previous visits there. Such a "metafictional" joke was probably adopted by Langhuan shanqiao in order to come to terms with what I would characterize as his own "*xushu* anxiety." His *xushu* anxiety appeared to be particularly strong compared with other *Honglou meng* sequel writers. This is understandable given the fact that as a latecomer in the field of *Honglou meng* sequels, he produced not one but two *xushu*. Consequently, he had to expend more energy defending his own *xushu* efforts as not redundant. No wonder a frequent topic among the characters in these two sequels is evaluating various works identified as "sequels" (to *Honglou meng* or to other literary works). Like their counterparts in *Hou honglou meng*, Baoyu, Baochai, and Daiyu also have a lot to say in this sequel about the parent novel. Furthermore, unlike their counterparts in *Hou honglou meng*, they also have a lot to say about other works of *xushu*.[64]

With so many sequels already published, some of the later sequel writers obviously felt more pressure to justify their continual efforts to produce even more *xushu*. Consequently, cross-references to other *Honglou meng* sequels became increasingly common in many of these sequels. Besides Langhuan shanqiao's *Bu Honglou meng* and *Zengbu Honglou meng*, cross-references to other *Honglou meng* sequels can be found in Qin Zichen's *Xu Honglou meng* (chap. 30) and Guichuzi's *Honglou meng bu* (chap. 1), where other earlier *Honglou meng* sequels are criticized. Disparaging other *Honglou meng* sequels often serves as justification of one's own. Related to this *xushu* anxiety was the increasing presence of the image of "reader" in these sequels. Often, the characters in the sequels themselves become the readers of their own lives as depicted in the parent novel as well as in other sequel novels, and, by virtue of such self-conscious readerly ploys, how to read (or interpret) the parent novel and how to interpret the other "interpretations" (the sequels) of this same work became a prominent issue for the characters as well as the "readers" of these sequels. It is in these *Honglou meng* sequels that we are compelled to confront the "interpretative" nature of *xushu* as well as the endless possibilities of "competing interpretations" (the endless process of *xushu*). All these features associated with the *Honglou meng* sequel phenomenon were unprecedented; they undoubtedly mark an important milestone in the history of Chinese *xushu*.

CONCLUSION

Given the complexities of *xushu* as a literary phenomenon, it is impossible to provide, even in a cursory fashion, a general history of this genre within the limited space of a chapter, and that is certainly not my goal here. However, I have chosen to dwell on what I consider to be some of the important "moments" in the history of *xushu*. This issue-oriented approach allows me to concentrate more on the "high points" in the development of *xushu*, even though my account is by no means chronological. I start with the "ahistorical" problem of how to define *xushu*, focusing on its shifting boundaries created by the kind of "textual fluidity" often associated with Chinese *xiaoshuo*. What are particularly intriguing about the rise of *xushu* as a self-conscious literary genre during the seventeenth century are precisely the attempts by several fiction writers and commentators to manipulate such shifting boundaries. A self-conscious *xushu* attempt (here very close to the meaning of sequel as defined by some modern Western narratologists) often had to begin with presenting one's own narrative as a "different entity" from its precursor text; consequently, the boundaries of the precursor text had to be stabilized. Jin Shengtan's shortening of *Shuihu zhuan* and his assertion that the last part of the original novel was an unnecessary sequel by a different author is certainly a good example by default—just like a formal sequel, Jin's systematic interpretative project had to be based on a work whose boundaries are adequately defined, and the interpretative device known as "author" became crucial in Jin's search for this textual stability. Consequently, the "ahistorical" problem of "the boundaries of *xushu*" leads to the discussion of the "historical" issue—the possible reasons behind the rise of *xushu* as a self-conscious genre during the seventeenth century. The simultaneous rise of *xushu*, fiction commentary, and *xiaoshuo* author, I argue, was related to the need for "interpretation," a result of the maturing of *xiaoshuo* as a narrative genre, when some of its works began to achieve their "canonical" status. The initial wave of *xushu*, which coincided with the violent dynastic transition of the mid-seventeenth century, also leads me to contemplate the significance of another wave of *xushu* almost two hundred years later during the late Qing, when Chinese society was undergoing yet another important transition. *Xushu* as a genre of "continuation" must have had a special appeal for people who were experiencing radical historical "discontinuities." Here *xushu*'s temporal "ambivalence" provided some writers and readers with a viable narrative space where they could come to terms with their own historical "dislocation." While the mid-seventeenth century and late Qing were indeed the periods when *xushu* flourished, the many *Honglou meng* sequels that appeared in the last decade of the eighteenth century and the first half of the nineteenth century—not long after the initial publication of their parent novel—constituted a unique historical phenomenon in the development of *xushu* that is worth a careful look. Never before did *xushu* writers become so self-conscious, and this self-consciousness helped in many ways to shape the fate of this genre in the following ages. There were so many *Honglou meng* sequels in such a short period of time that "redundancy" and "superfluousness" became the labels almost every *xushu* writer had to fend off, while the towering achievement of the parent novel only exasperated the reading public's disappointment at every sequel that was attempted. After all these *Honglou meng* sequels, a future *xushu* writer felt even more pressure to justify his writings.

If the textual fluidity associated with many full-length traditional *xiaoshuo* texts was indeed largely a result of the complicated rewriting process many of these texts went through, then studying *xushu* should help us appreciate better an important trend in the history of Chinese fiction—how *xiaoshuo* struggled to acquire its "respectability" as a narrative genre. As I have tried to show, rewriting and the sequel are two closely related and yet different forms of *xushu*. Rewriting ignores the textual "integrity" of the original, whereas a sequel is often testimony to the prestige of its parent work (attributable to an "author"). Rewriting thrives on "shifting textual boundaries" while the sequel acquires its status as a "prolongation" under the precondition that the parent work has indeed reached its "closure." The history of *xushu* is also a history of the "interactions" between rewritings and sequels: rewritings often led to sequels, as demonstrated in the cases of several works in the so-called Sui-Tang romance series (discussed in chap. 7 and the introduction) and the complicated textual history of *Honglou meng* and some of its *xushu*.

Of course, there are many other, "simpler" factors motivating a *xushu* writer or reader that I have not discussed here, such as many fiction writers' need to exploit the success of an original work for commercial reasons, or the fact that some fictional characters were so successful that they retained their "lives" even after the "closure" of the original work (i.e., a character was so popular among the readers that some of them felt that his or her story simply had to continue, an interesting issue touched on in chap. 6). However, despite such omissions, I do hope that my discussions above can help to demonstrate that *xushu* were not just a peripheral phenomenon, but were closely related to the character and development of traditional Chinese fiction as a whole.

NOTES

1. See, for example, Dai Bufan, *Hongxue pingyi waipian*, 1–82.
2. See Cheng Weiyuan's preface to the 1791 printed edition of *Honglou meng* and Gao E's preface to the 1792 edition in Yisu, *Honglou meng juan*, 31–32.

3. For a discussion of these theories, see Zhao Gang and Chen Zhongyi, *Honglou meng yanjiu xinbian*, 237–328.
4. This understanding will be reflected in my use of these terms in the remainder of this chapter.
5. For studies of the textual history of *Sanxia wuyi*, see Li Jiarui, "Cong Shi Yukun de *Longtu gong'an* shuodao *Sanxia wuyi*"; Yu Shengting, "Shi Yukun jiqi zhushu chengshu"; and Miao Huaiming, "*Sanxia wuyi* chengshu xinkao." See also Blader, trans., "Introduction," *Tales of Magistrate Bao and His Valiant Lieutenants*, xvi–xxiv; and her "A Critical Study of San-hsia Wu-I and Relationship to the *Lung-t'u kung-an* Song-Book," 4–9. The latter also contains a detailed discussion of the songbook *Longtu gong'an* and comparison with the novel *Sanxia wuyi*, 91–159.
6. References to an upcoming sequel can also be found at the conclusions of the seventeenth-century *Sui Tang yanyi*, the eighteenth-century *Shuo Tang houzhuan* (Stories about the Tang, later collection), which is a sequel in itself, and the early-nineteenth-century *Jinghua yuan* (The destiny of flowers in the mirror). This reference to an upcoming "sequel" might suggest a quite different notion of "closure" (what constitutes a "complete" work) on the part of the authors of these works.
7. For a discussion of sequels to *Sanxia wuyi*, see Hou Zhongyi, *Sanxia wuyi xilie xiaoshuo*, 97–129.
8. Wei Shaochang, "*Niehai hua* zuichu lianghui de yuanlai mianmu," in his *Wan Qing sida xiaoshuo jia*, 194. Ouyang Jian considers Jin Songcen the "original initiating author" (*yuanshi zuozhe*); Ouyang Jian, *Wan Qing xiaoshuo shi*, 189.
9. Zeng Pu, "Xiugai hou yao shuo de jiju hua," in Wei Shaochang, ed., *Niehai hua ziliao*, 129.
10. Both of Lu Shi'e's sequels were republished together under the title *Xin niehai hua* by Zhongguo wenlian chuban gongsi (Beijing) in 1989.
11. In his note to Zeng Xubai's "Zeng Mengpu nianpu" (*Niehai hua ziliao*, 182–183, n. 2), Wei Shaochang briefly mentions the lawsuit against Lu Shi'e regarding his "unautho-rizied" sequel, but Wei does not specify when this took place or who filed the suit and for what reason. At the same time, Wei might have confused Lu's sequel, *Xin niehai hua*, with his other sequel, *Niehai hua xubian*. See also Xiao Shi, "Houji," in Lu Shi'e, *Xin niehai hua*, 263. This book contains the texts of both *Xin Niehai hua* and *Niehai hua xubian*. See also my discussion of the case of the sequels to Zhang Henshui's *Tixiao yinyuan* in "Introduction."
12. Pease, "Author," 105. In his chapter Pease provides a brief genealogy of "author" in the West. See also Ede and Lunsford, eds., *Singular Texts/Plural Authors*, 76–93, for an account of "author" in the West from a somewhat different perspective.
13. Allen, *The Friar as Critics*, 59.
14. "Yueji," in Sun Xidan, ed., *Liji jijie*, 989; English trans., *Li Chi: Book of Rites*, trans. Legge, 100. Legge translates the first *zuo* as "frame"; but more literally, it can be translated as the act of "establishing or initiating rules or institutions" or as he presents it for the second *zuo*, "inventing."
15. Liu Baonan, ed., *Lunyu zhengyi*, 251. Note the word *"zuo,"* just like "author" in English, carries two different and yet related meanings: the act of producing a text as well as the act of creation or innovation. As in the case to be discussed below, Mencius referred to Confucius' writing of *The Spring and Autumn Annals* by using the word *"zuo,"* although he probably agreed with the Master himself that this work was a result of transmission; cf. the commentary collected in Liu Baonan, ed., *Lunyu zhengyi*, 252.
16. See *Lunyu jizhu*, juan 10, in Zhu Xi, ed. and annot., *Sishu zhangju jizhu*, 93. In fact, the phrase *"jidacheng"* was first used by Mencius to describe Confucius' contribution; see *Meng Zi jizhu*, juan 10, in Zhu Xi, *Sishu zhangju jizhu*, 315.

17. Zhu Xi's view would find support in the works of many later writers. For example, the early Qing neo-Confucian scholar Zhang Boxing (1665–1725) argued that all the important cultural figures after Confucius were merely great transmitters *(shuzhe)*. See his "'Shu'er buzuo' lun," *Zhengyitang wenji,* 9.7a–8a, in *Zhengyitang quanshu;* Jiao Xun (1763–1820) also believed that by Confucius' times, everything that could be created *(zuo)* had already been created; there was no longer any need for Confucius to create. See his "Shu'nan er," *Diaogu ji,* 7.12b–13a. See also Zhang Xuecheng (1738–1801), "Zhuanji," in his *"Wenshi tongyi" jiaozhu,* 248.
18. *Zhongyong zhangju,* in Zhu Xi, ed. and annot., *Sishu zhangju jizhu,* 36. See Legge, trans., *The Chinese Classics,* 1:424.
19. "Teng Wen'gong zhangju xia," *Meng Zi zhangju jizhu,* juan 6, in Zhu Xi, ed. and annot., *Sishu zhangju jizhu,* 272; English trans., *Mencius,* trans. Lau, 3b.9, 114.
20. See his "Xu yi," in *Jin Shengtan piping "Shuihu zhuan,"* 1–5.
21. Sima Qian, *Shiji,* 130.3299–3300.
22. "Bao Ren Shaoqing shu," in *Quan Shanggu, Sandai Qin Han San'guo Liuchao wen,* 1:501–503. For a discussion of the influence of Sima Qian's theory of *fafen zhushu,* see Wang Yingzhi, "Fafen zhushu shuo pingshu."
23. "Zhongyi Shuihuzhuan xu," in Huang Lin and Han Tongwen, eds., *Zhongguo lidai xiaoshuo lunzhu xuan,* 1:142. "Shuinan" and "Gufen" are the titles of two chapters in *Han Fei zi* (The works of Master Han Fei) attributed to Han Fei (280–233 B.C.E).
24. Qiao Yu (Chen Chen), "*Shuihu houzhuan* lunlüe," in Huang Lin and Han Tongwen, *Zhongguo lidai xiaoshuo lunzhu xuan,* 1:312.
25. See Widmer's detailed discussion of what she has called "the authorial sphere" in her *The Margins of Utopia,* 120–156.
26. See ibid., 110–120.
27. See his general comment on the "Xiezi" in *Jin Shengtan piping "Shuihu zhuan,"* 30; his interlineal comment on the character Lin Chong in chapter 6, 16; and his prechapter comment on chapter 18, 346. However, Jin was not consistent on this particular point. Elsewhere, he seems to argue just the opposite: the author wrote the novel merely out of boredom; see "Du *Diwu Caizi shu* fa," in *Jin Shengtan piping "Shuihu zhuan,"* 18. This assertion that *Shuihu zhuan* was not the result of its author's frustrations was probably part of his attempt to argue that the original title of the novel does not contain the reference to "loyalty" *(zhongyi).* This is related to his overall interpretation of the novel, namely that the rebels described in it are not meant to be characters who sincerely pledge loyalty to the emperor.
28. For studies of the textual evolution of *Shuihu zhuan,* see Irwin, *The Evolution of a Chinese Novel;* and Yan Dunyi, *"Shuihu zhuan" de yanbian.*
29. See Nie Gannu, "*Shuihu* wulun," in his *Zhongguo gudian xiaoshuo lunji,* 27–28.
30. Of course, Jin Shengtan used the same strategy to truncate the *Xixiang ji* in his commentary edition of the play by asserting that the original play already reached its end in scene 16.
31. As I have mentioned in the introduction, there were very few autobiographic sequels in traditional Chinese literature. This seems to be quite different from the situation in the West, where most "sequels" are autographic (cf. Genette's observation that "the continuation is in principle an allographic completion and the sequel an autographic prolongation," although he acknowledges that "there is no law that a sequel should be necessarily self-written." *Palimpsests,* 207).
32. In his recent study, *Reading Illustrated Fiction in Late Imperial China,* Hegel observes that "among the changes in novels produced during the last decades of the Ming dynasty was a

33. See Widmer's discussion of what she has called "the reconstruction of the 'author' in *Shuihu zhuan*" by Jin Shengtan in *The Margins of Utopia*, 83–91; and Rolston, *Traditional Chinese Fiction and Fiction Commentary*, 114–117.
34. Another factor, which I have not discussed here, is the possible role of commercial publishing in the rise of *xushu*. Hegel (*Reading Illustrated Fiction in Late Imperial China*, 155) regards the seventeenth century as the high point of fiction publication in late imperial China. However, due to the paucity of available data, I have not been able to find hard evidence that directly links the rise of *xushu* to the flourishing of commercial publication during that period. For a brief discussion of the relationship between *Honglou meng* sequels and commercial publishing, see Lin Yixuan, *Wucai ke butian: Honglou meng xushu yanjiu*, 29–35.
35. Foucault, "What Is an Author?" 124. See also Hegel, *Reading Illustrated Fiction in Late Imperial China*, 39–40.
36. It was formally banned in 1642. See Wang Liqi, *Yuan Ming Qing sandai jinhui xiaoshuo xiqu shiliao*, 16–17.
37. As was often the case with many incidents of literary inquisition during the Qing period, Ding Yaokang's troubles were initiated by someone who apparently bore a personal grudge against him. For a Chinese translation of some of the official documents in Manchu concerning Ding's case, see An Shuangchen, trans., "Shun Kang nianjian *Xu Jin Ping Mei* zuozhe Ding Yaokang shoushen an," 29–32.
38. Hegel notes that the late Ming publisher and editor Xu Xiangdou (ca. 1560–ca. 1630) sometimes printed his own portrait on the cover pages of the books he published to assert his "proprietorship" (*Reading Illustrated Fiction in Late Imperial China*, 138).
39. See his "*Taishang ganying pian wuzijie* xu," *Xu Jin Ping Mei*, in his *Ding Yaokang quanji*, 2:8.
40. Of course, it was condemned as a "wrong" reading not in the sense that the Manchu government believed Ding did not read *Jin Ping Mei* properly, but in the sense that this sequel contained what they considered to be anti-Manchu sentiments.
41. For a discussion on "Sequels and Imitations and Fiction as Commentary," see Rolston, *Traditional Chinese Fiction and Fiction Commentary*, 85–90. Elsewhere in his study, Rolston points out that one of the sequels to *Jin Ping Mei* titled *Sanxu Jin Ping Mei* (Third sequel to plum in the golden vase) was actually a sequel to Zhang Zhupo's commentary on *Jin Ping Mei* rather than the novel itself (71–72).
42. Some scholars believe that Jin Shengtan's shortened version was not completely "baseless" because the novel might have appeared in certain versions whose endings corresponded to the ending in Jin's truncated version, as suggested in certain late Ming sources. See Yuan Shishuo's preface to *Jin Shengtan piping "Shuihu zhuan*," 2–5.
43. See "Xu," in Wen Kang, *Ernü yingxiong zhuan*, 1; see also the reference to fifty-three chapters by Wuliaoweng (which is believed to be Wen Kang's pseudonym) in his original preface, 4. It is interesting to note that Wuliaoweng claims in his "original" preface that the novel was a result of his editing and rewriting *(buzhui chengshu)* of a book/manuscript titled *Zhengfayanzang wushi san can* (Fifty-three chapters of the hidden truth) that he purchased on the market. Here Wen Kang was actually claiming (albeit in a rather tongue-in-cheek manner) that he was merely a *xushu* writer—a claim, however, that would be invalidated by Ma Congshan. In his preface to the 1878 edition, Ma insisted that while Wen Kang was the original author of the first forty chapters, the last thirteen were a *xushu* by someone else. This would become even more interesting given that *Ernü yingxiong zhuan* was often considered by many to be an imitation *(fangshu)* of *Honglou meng*,

while, according to Lin Chen's broad definition (*Mingmo Qingchu xiaoshuo shulu*, 118), imitations, though strictly not sequels, should be regarded as a subgenre of *xushu*.

44. See "Jie *Shuihu quanzhuan*" and the prefaces to various editions of the sequel collected at the end of Yu Wanchun, *Dangkou zhi*, 1, 1039–1055.
45. For more detailed discussions of Yu's "rewriting" agenda, see chap. 6 in this volume and Wang, *Fin-de-siècle Splendor*, 125–137.
46. See Widmer, *The Margins of Utopia*, 13–77.
47. Based on the works listed in *Zhongguo tongsu xiaoshuo zongmu tiyao*, my estimate is that there are approximately thirty-five such *xushu* produced at the turn of the twentieth century that contain the character *xin* in their titles.
48. See Ouyang Jian, "Wan Qing 'fanxin' xiaoshuo zonglun."
49. Wang (*Fin-de-siècle Splendor*, 217–274) discusses Wu Jianren's *Xin shitou ji* under the rubric of what he has termed "Science Fantasy."
50. For a general discussion of Lu Shi'e life and works, see Chen Xi'nian, "Lu Shi'e jiashi shengping jiqi zhushu xinkao." There was an international conference on Lu Shi'e held recently in Shanghai (Oct. 8–11, 2000); see various papers published in *Ming Qing xiaoshuo yanjiu* 59.1 (2001).
51. For discussions of Lu Shi'e as a writer of *fanxin xiaoshuo*, see Hong Tao, "Lu Shi'e *Xin Shuihu* yu jindai *Shuihu* xindu"; and Tang Zhesheng, "Zhongguo xiandai xiaoshuo de yizhong wenti cunzai."
52. *Xin Shitou ji*, 1.2.
53. See Ying Wang's discussion of several late-Qing sequels to *Jinhua yuan* in chap. 9 of this volume. Two of the three sequels she discusses are titled *Xin Jinhua yuan* and are obviously works of *fanxin xiaoshuo*.
54. See also the chapters on *Honglou meng* sequels by McMahon and Widmer in this volume.
55. Lin Chen, "*Honglou meng* xushu zhi wojian," *Guangming ribao* (Feb. 26, 1985), referred to by Zhao Jianzhong, *Honglou meng xushu yanjiu*, 139, n. 1. Zhao's study contains, to the best of my knowledge, the most complete bibliographic information on *Honglou meng* sequels. My account here is largely based on this study.
56. The fact that all *Honglou meng* sequels from this period took as their parent text the 120-chapter printed edition rather than various manuscript editions is interesting. This may be accounted for by the novel's enormous popularity due to the much easier accessibility of the printed edition. The fact that the large number of sequels appeared only after the novel began circulating in printed form must also be related to the novel's textual stability because of this, since formal sequels usually depend on the textual stability of their parent texts to define themselves as an extension of an already completed work.
57. "Xu" (preface), *Hou honglou meng*, in Cai Yijiang, ed., *Honglou meng congshu quanbian*. Unless otherwise noted, all references in this chapter to *Honglou meng* sequels will be to this collection.
58. Yurui, *Zaochuang xianbi*, in *Lüyan suochuang ji Zaochuang xianbi*, 184.
59. However, there is subtle evidence that a few sequel authors from this period did express their doubts. For example, Xibei shanqiao, in his preface to *Honglou meng bu* (3126), asserts that the last forty chapters of *Honglou meng* are a *xushu* (this is probably why the plot of Guizuzhi's *Honglou meng bu* starts after chap. 97 rather than after chap. 120 of its parent text), while the author of *Honglou fumeng* noted that after chap. 80, the narrative of *Honglou meng* became quite unsatisfactory ("Fanli," in Chen Shaohai, *Honglou fumeng*, 1125). Of course, all this was presented as justification for producing more sequels.
60. *Honglou meng*, 120.1646; English trans. (modified), *The Story of the Stone*, trans. Hawkes and Minford, 5:374.

61. Ding Gan, "Cheng jiaben hou sishi hui shi zhenben ma?" esp. 121.
62. Zhao Gang and Chen Zhongyi, *Honglou meng yanjiu xinbian,* 322–323.
63. Of course, this might be remotely possible if we accept both Dai Bufan's theory that Cao Xueqin wrote/compiled his novel based on an earlier manuscript titled *Fengyue baojian* by someone else and the theory that Cao was also the author of the last forty chapters, as claimed by Gao E and Chen Weiyuan. In this scenario, Cao considered his own novel a *xushu* to an earlier text, and at the end he made a metafictional reference to this fact.
64. For the examples in *Bu Honglou meng,* see the comments on the sequel to the play *Baishe ji* on Jin Shengtan's theory that the portion after scene 16 in *Xixiang ji* was a sequel and on the sequel novels *Hou Shuihu* and *Hou Xiyou ji* (40.3077); see also Baochai's and Tanchun's comments on sequel plays (47.3115–3116) and the characters' extensive comments on other *Honglou meng* sequels (48.3119–3121). Similar examples can be found in *Zengbu Honglou meng,* 4.1747–1751 (the entire chap. 1) and 31.1885 (Baochai's comments on *Honglou yuanmeng*).

QIANCHENG LI

2 Transformations of Monkey

Xiyou ji Sequels and the Inward Turn

THIS CHAPTER studies three sequels to the novel *Xiyou ji* (The journey to the West), namely *Xu xiyou ji* (Sequel to the journey to the West), *Hou xiyou ji* (Later journey to the West), and *Xiyou bu* (A supplement to the journey to the West).[1] Liu Tingji, in the 1715 *Zaiyuan zazhi* (Zaiyuan's random notes), discussed the practice of writing sequels to famous novels and cited, among others, two sequels to *Xiyou ji*. He praised *Hou Xiyou ji* grudgingly, recognizing the author's virtuosity in composition. *Xu Xiyou ji* is, in his opinion, no more than "a dog's tail."[2] Liu argued that the original author had exhausted the artistic possibilities; later imitations, even of good quality, could not compare favorably with the original, let alone surpass it.

Liu Tingji's statement is a critique of the *Xiyou ji* sequels in particular, and an assessment of the sequel writing in general (discussed by Huang in the introduction). There is much truth in Liu's argument. However, he, assuming such a dismissive attitude, totally ignores, among other things, the lively, serious dialogue that these sequels have with the original novel as well as their thematic and structural innovations, thus failing to do justice to the works in question. Working within the tight constraints of the sequel genre, these authors had to deal with a different set of conventions and techniques. It is true that the two sequels to *Xiyou ji* mentioned by Liu are derivative and imitative, but one cannot say that they are devoid of originality. The one hundred-chapter text of *Xiyou ji* took centuries to evolve; its attributed author, Wu Cheng'en (ca. 1500– ca. 1582), or anyone else, should not have an exclusive claim of originality in the first place. As an open text, the novel in its final form has gone through the editorship and revision of many writers, editors, and commentators. The sequel authors, by contrast, were responsible for their own works and had to rely on their own creativity, since they were not reorganizing, rewriting, or editing earlier materials whose plot and structure had already taken shape.[3] It seems that they are more qualified to be called "authors." Moreover, the popularity of the parent work is, to the authors of *Xiyou ji* sequels at least, not necessarily an asset, for they must have been aware of the risks of competing with it. The author of *Xu Xiyou ji* was disturbed by the popularity of *Xiyou ji*, hence the wide circulation, in his opinion, of erroneous views. These authors, seemingly, did not write to take financial advantage of the parent work, but to correct what they perceived as gross wrongs or lapses there. These novels are all deliberate and self-conscious revisionist and corrective endeavors and continue the discourse started by *Xiyou ji*. The painstaking efforts of these authors are almost transparent. In short, they engaged the parent novel with a seriousness that has yet to be recognized.

The above considerations corroborate Huang's discussion (in chap. 1) about the relationship between the flourishing of sequel composition and the maturity of the vernacular novel as a genre, partly a result of appropriation by an increasing number of literati authors. These sequel writers were consummate literati authors, and their works were extremely "readerly" texts in that they relied on previous texts (not only *Xiyou ji*) for their compositions and in that they probably targeted better-educated readers (*Xiyou bu* is certainly a case in point).[4] Moreover, it seems that sequel writing and serious endeavors at criticism occurred simultaneously; just consider those writers and critics residing in Wucheng of Zhejiang Province: Huang Zhouxing (1611–1680), a prestigious literatus, refined the one hundred-chapter *Xiyou ji* and contributed a commentary; the resulting text, *Xiyou zhengdao shu* (Realizations of the Tao through the journey to the West), became the basis of most Qing editions. Among his friends, Dong Yue (1620–1686) wrote *Xiyou bu*, and Chen Chen (b. ca. 1614) wrote a sequel to *Shuhu zhuan* (The water margin) titled *Shuihu houzhuan* (The later water margin).[5]

The *Xiyou ji* sequels are interpretations as well as rewritings of the parent novel,[6] thereby giving it reorientations. I will pay special attention to how these authors read and interpreted *Xiyou ji*, how they consciously departed from it and changed its trajectory by their transformation of the central character, Monkey. I argue that among these sequels, there is an increasing tendency to internalize the journey. Since the centrality of the mind is a common feature among them (manifested in the proverbial mind-monkey, *xinyuan*), and since they, to a great extent, are fashioned by their authors' understanding of this ubiquitous mind, I will put these works within the context of the Ming cultural milieu, namely the "inward turn" in philosophy and literature.

In the traditional Chinese novel, the trend is a conspicuous one. As Hegel points out, "the literary novel in [seventeenth-century] China tends more toward an exploration of mind than an investigation of mere external reality."[7] In Plaks' formulation,

> In tracing the pattern of development from the sixteenth to the seventeenth-century novels, we can see a certain parallel to the "inward turn"

[die Verinnerung] of the Western novel described by Erich Kahler. That is, whereas the sixteenth-century novels were all based on pre-existing sources from the popular tradition, the seventeenth-century works come more and more to be based on personal experience, so that the public focus of the earlier work becomes increasingly one of private sensibility.[8]

It is certainly no accident that this period saw the development of an "interiority"—or "neo-Confucian interiority" in de Bary's words—in Chinese philosophy and literature.[9]

The literary "inward turn" can, to a great extent, be attributed to the intellectual and cultural background in which the authors found themselves writing, which can be characterized by a shift from the external world to the inner reality, or "psychology."[10] The inward turn in philosophy and religion is observable in all three influential teachings (sanjiao). It is in the human mind/heart that the three religions have converged; it is here that the syncretism is most fruitful. The culmination of this trend is certainly the Ming *xinxue* (learning of the mind/heart).[11] Integrating, among other things, Buddhist views of the world, the center of which is the mind, Chinese philosophers offered new interpretations of the Confucian classics; many of their doctrines were developed as commentaries on Confucian classics.[12] Lu Jiuyuan (Lu Xiangshan, 1139–1193), a precursor of this school of thought, directed his attention to the human mind rather than the external world and found the human mind to be the center of reality. As a result, the cultivation of the mind became increasingly important; it became the central issue to many of the Confucian thinkers from the Song times. Zhen Dexiu (1178–1235) even compiled passages about the mind from the Confucian classics into a book titled *Xin jing* (Heart classic), perhaps having in mind the Buddhist *Xin jing* (Heart sūtra).[13] According to Wang Shouren (Wang Yangming, 1472–1529),

> Man is the *xin* [mind] of Heaven and Earth and all things. The mind is the master of Heaven and Earth and all things. The mind is the word of Heaven; the mind suggests Heaven and Earth and all things. This is direct, simple, and intimate. So it would be better to say, for study one merely needs to develop the mind.[14]

Wang Yangming elevated and glorified the human mind. However, the consequent cultivation of the mind, paradoxically, resulted in increasing attention to what the thinkers regarded as negative qualities of the mind.[15] The most famous image for this mind is the mirror. Oftentimes the mind is not a bright mirror in its pristine state as it should be, emitting good intentions and reflecting the external reality; rather, the mirror is dusty, defiled. Wang Yangming wrote,

> The heart and mind of the sage cannot tolerate the least particle of dust and has naturally no need of polishing. The heart and mind of the average man, however, resembles a spotted and dirty mirror which needs thorough polishing to have all its dust and dirt removed. Then will the tiniest speck of dust become visible, and only a light stroke will wipe it

away, without our having to spend much energy. At this stage, one already knows the substance of perfect *ren*. When the dust is not yet removed, the mirror may still have certain bright spots, which allow us to detect falling particles of the dust and to rub them off. But whatever accumulates on top of the dirt and dust cannot even be seen.[16]

By *"ren"* Wang Yangming means the "original substance" of *xin*, or "mind-in-itself."[17] This passage certainly recalls the mirror metaphor/simile in Buddhism.[18] In literature, the bright spot only accentuates the dust that has accumulated. This polishing is the thematic thread that runs throughout the three *Xiyou ji* sequels.

The emphasis on the mind is a heritage of the parent novel. Before Xuanzang, also known as Tripitaka (Sanzang), sets out, the monks at a temple are anxious about his journey. He points his finger at his own heart and nods his head several times and explains, "When the mind is active, all kinds of māra come into existence; when the mind is extinguished, all kinds of māra will be extinguished" (*JW* 1:283; *XYJ* 13.152). Instances are numerous where the human mind/heart is singled out for emphasis. One conspicuous example is the position of the *Heart Sūtra* in the novel; its author, seemingly, takes it to be an exposition of the human mind, although the "heart" in the title means the central wisdom of Buddhism, its synopsis. Nevertheless, many tend to regard the *Heart Sūtra* as expounding on the intricacies of the human mind. The Ming thinker Li Zhi (1527–1602) wrote, "The *Heart Sūtra* is Buddha's elaboration on the most important principles of the mind" (or "a synopsis of the Buddha's teachings about the mind").[19]

The allegorical grid is not followed consistently in *Xiyou ji*, partly because the novel is, as Xiaolian Liu points out, a "discontinuous allegory," where only a part of the text follows a set pattern of symbolism, in contrast to the sequels, which are "continuous" allegories, where the entire plot is allegorical and is to be interpreted accordingly.[20] In the sequels, the allegorical schemes—mostly related to the manifestations of the mind—are meticulously adhered to. This is yet another manifestation of the seriousness with which the literati authors took up *Xiyou ji*, that is, for their philosophical discourses. They did not hesitate to explicate the allegorical significance of certain episodes or details, although they overdid it on occasion.[21] Brandauer rightly characterizes *Hou Xiyou ji* and *Xiyou bu* as didactic: they "show a serious and sustained teaching purpose," in contrast to the parent novel, which is "less overtly didactic."[22] His characterization is true of *Xu Xiyou ji* as well.

Before I discuss the sequels in detail, some preliminary discussions about their authorship and dates are in order. *Xu Xiyou ji* and *Hou Xiyou ji* were mentioned in Liu Tingji's 1715 *Zaiyuan zazhi*, but it is likely that they were published earlier. Nearly all scholars consider *Xu Xiyou ji* a Ming work, although we know practically nothing about its author. There are two candidates: Ji Gui (dates unknown) and Lan Mao (1397–1476). Ji Gui was a friend of Mao Qiling (1623–1716) and was mentioned by Mao in his collected works, *Xihe quanji* ("Ji Gui xiaopin zhiwen yin");[23] however, it is doubtful whether the title *Xiyou xu ji* refers to the novel in question or to a piece of a different genre.²⁴ Lan Mao was mentioned by Yuan Wendian (1726–1790) in *Diannan shilüe*.²⁵ Zhang Ying and Chen Su, who have collated and edited a typeset edition, suggest that *Xu Xiyou ji* is not a sequel to the Ming *Xiyou ji* attributed to Wu Cheng'en; rather, it is a sequel to an earlier edition, the *guben*. (Should this be the case, it would be completely unfair to compare it, disparagingly, with the Ming edition we know.) There is also the possibility, according to Zhang and Chen, that *Xu Xiyou ji* is by the same author of an earlier version of *Xiyou ji*. In the 1805 Jinjiantang edition, the character *you*ᵃ was used in place of *you*ᵇ, a convention of the last two reigns of the Ming dynasty. An alternative title of this 1805 edition is *Xinbian xiuxiang Xu Xiyou ji*, indicating that it is possibly an edition based on the one circulated at the end of Ming. For *Xiyou bu*, it is an almost established opinion among critics that it was written by Dong Yue in the year 1640, based on one of Dong's own poems,²⁶ although there are scholars who think that his father, Dong Sizhang (1586–1628), wrote the book.²⁷ Su Xing argues that it was written by Dong Yue during the Qing and reads it as a political allegory, one that champions Ming loyalists and chastises Manchu collaborators.²⁸ Most scholars date *Hou Xiyou ji* back to the Ming, among them Lu Xun, Xu Fuming, Su Xing, Zhang Ying and Chen Su, and Xiaolian Liu,²⁹ while others think that it was written during the Qing.³⁰ Yuan Wendian, in a long marginalia on the biography of Lan Mao in *Diannan shilüe*, mentioned Mei Zihe as the author of *Hou Xiyou ji* in the context of *Xu Xiyou ji*: the latter "propagates central teachings of Buddhism. It is based on events narrated in *Xiyou ji* by Qiu Chuji (1148–1227) and continues with stories about the return journey to the east. It, together with Mei Zihe's *Hou Xiyou ji*, forms a new category."³¹ Other candidates include Wu Cheng'en himself and Tianhua caizi, the commentator.³²

I do not intend to give precise dates or theorize and speculate about their authorship—the sequels, with the exception of *Xiyou bu*, are at least as reticent about their authors as the parent novel, if not more. Rather, I intend only to establish a working order. *Xu Xiyou ji* is perhaps the earliest sequel. The most difficult question is the place of *Hou Xiyou ji*. I follow Lu Xun, Xu Fuming, Su Xing, Xiaolian Liu, and others in regarding it as a Ming work. It is worthwhile to note that in the preface to *Xiuxiang Hou Xiyou ji zhenquan*, the above-mentioned convention with regard to the use of the character *you*ᵃ instead of *you*ᵇ was also observed.³³ However, in the text of the novel proper, this taboo was not heeded. No dates are given of this edition; Zhang and Chen think that it is from the Qing. The title from the caption to the text is *Xinke piping xiuxiang Hou Xiyou ji*, indicating that this is a new edition. A reasonable speculation is that the publisher copied the preface from an earlier, possibly late-Ming, edition, or used the same woodblock for the preface, since the type of the preface is different from the text proper. The order of my discussion is *Xu Xiyou ji*, *Hou Xiyou ji*, and *Xiyou bu*.³⁴ Given the dearth of indisputable evidence, this "chronological" order is only tentative. The order is based on another consideration: it points to how these works turn increasingly inward and probe deeper and deeper into the human mind in their attempts to internalize the journey.

XU XIYOU JI: JOURNEY TO THE EAST AND THE TAMING OF THE MIND/MONKEY

Xu Xiyou ji[35] is a severe criticism of the parent novel in general and Monkey in particular. In *Xiyou ji*, Monkey is belligerent from beginning to end. In the first chapter, he leaves Flower-Fruit Mountain in search of the Tao. His master, Subodhi, teaches him seventy-two transformations and the ability to cover 108,000 miles in one somersault. Before participating in the westward journey, he wreaks havoc in heaven, challenging the Jade Emperor and claiming that he has a right to the throne. He has many reasons to be proud of himself, because there is no one who can subdue him—except the Buddha. The Tang monk Tripitaka relies on him for the completion of the pilgrimage. In the end, he is apotheosized and becomes the Buddha Victorious in Strife.

Monkey's supernatural powers are always relished. His fight with monsters, his ingenuity, and his versatility have gripped readers' attention. For instance, on one occasion a monster threatens Monkey by mentioning the number of lesser monsters at his command.

> Pilgrim [Monkey] said, "Don't talk rot! And don't mention a few hundreds! Even if you have hundreds of thousands, just call them up one by one and I'll slay them. Every stroke of my rod will find its mark. I guarantee that they will be wiped out! Exterminated!"
>
> When the monster heard these words, he quickly gave the order and called up all the monsters before and behind the mountain, all the fiends in and out of the cave. Each holding weapons, they lined up thickly and completely barricaded the several doors inside the cave. When Pilgrim saw this, he was delighted. Gripping his rod with both hands, he shouted "Change!" and changed at once into a person having three heads and six arms. One wave of the golden-hooped rod and it changed into three golden-hooped rods. Look at him! Six arms wielding the three rods, he plunged into the crowd—like a tiger mauling a herd of sheep, like an eagle alighting on chicken coops. Pity those little fiends! One touch, and heads were smashed to pieces! One brush, and blood flowed like water! He charged back and forth, as if he had invaded an uninhabited region. When he finished, there was only one old monster left. (*JW* 2:92; *XYJ* 31.378)

The party's dependence on Monkey is not only for his physical prowess; he is also renowned for his intellectual acuity. In chapter 32, the Sentinel, a deity that accompanies and protects the pilgrims, tells him, "Those fiends do have great magic powers, and they know many ways of transformation. It's up to you to use all your cleverness, to exercise all your divine intelligence to guard your master carefully" (*JW* 2:103; *XYJ* 23.386).

In the parent novel, Monkey is constantly at odds with his master Tripitaka because of his tendency to kill at the slightest provocation. He is expelled by the master twice. However, he is eventually recalled because the master and his other disciples cannot deal with the demons that threaten them. Despite the overt paeans about the virtues of Tripitaka, it seems that Monkey has always been right; the master is uselessly merciful and virtuous, too naive to render any practical service. It seems that between *jing* (principle) and *quan* (expediency), *quan* always prevails.

The author of the sequel felt acutely the discrepancy between the master and Monkey, between the avowed Buddhist message and the actual unfolding of the plot, between the tenor and vehicle; it seems that the latter often subverts the former.³⁶ As Zhenfu jushi (Layman Zhenfu), the commentator, summarizes,

> The previous record is full of gross mistakes and absurdities, burlesque without rival. It mostly [elaborates on how to] subdue demons with the human mind; seventy-two forms of transformation are designed in order to show how this mind functions. . . . Most people of the world take delight in the book and propagate it. The author [of *Xu Xiyou ji*] is gravely concerned about its absurdity and profanity. Cleverness and schemes are too much relied upon, and increasing distractions arise. The book's teaching opposes the doctrine of emptiness and the practice [of the characters] strays from [Buddha's] impartial attitude toward all beings. The author therefore composed this book [*Xu Xiyou ji*] as a continuation in order to weed out all these wrongs (*ji zhuan shi bian, yigui chanxiao*).³⁷

Consequently, Monkey becomes the butt of satire in the sequel.

The sequel is set on the return journey: the pilgrims take another fourteen years to reach China. Theoretically, they should be able to go back to China with the scriptures in a matter of days, as they do in the parent novel, but the minds of the pilgrims, especially that of Monkey, are not ready, since they do not have good intentions. How can they become buddhas and bodhisattvas the way they do in *Xiyou ji*? They have not changed their minds, particularly Monkey, since he is still his old self toward the end of the novel. The concern with intentions and motivations is what characterizes this sequel's preoccupation with the human mind, in keeping with the trend in religion and philosophy of the Ming. In Ching's summary of Wang Yangming's moral philosophy, "the question of good and evil lies simply in following the 'principle of Heaven' or in deviating from it. . . . All depends on the intentions, and that which moves the intentions. If *xin* is correct, the desires and the acts which flow from them will also be."³⁸ As Plaks points out, "such things as . . . the reappraisal of the significance and consequence of moral action . . . have a very special relevance to the intellectual underpinnings of the novel. This . . . phenomenon is, no doubt, related to the widely observed sixteenth-century interest in the evaluation of personal behavior, taking on a variety of forms, from the so-called 'morality books' (*shanshu*) and 'registers of good and evil' (*gongguoge*) to instances of traumatic public confession."³⁹ Rolston has noted a parallel between what he calls "Getting (an) Inside" in fiction commentary and "a change of focus in morality books . . . from objective acts to intentions."⁴⁰

In chapter 2 of *Xu Xiyou ji*, while anticipating the arrival of the pilgrims, Buddha is especially concerned about the state of their minds. When they do arrive at the Western Paradise, Buddha asks them with what mind they have come. Tripitaka defines his as the most sincere mind *(zhichengxin)*, Zhu Bajie as the simple mind *(laoshixin)*, and Sha Monk (Shaseng) as the reverent mind *(gongjingxin)*. Monkey replies that he comes with a cunning mind *(jibianxin)*. *Jibianxin* also means a clever mind, a quick mind, a scheming mind, a tricky mind, a mind that adapts itself to all situations in an instant and finds the means to cope with them. Buddha is satisfied with Tripitaka, Bajie, and Sha Monk but is unhappy with Monkey for his cunning mind, because it is incompatible with the scriptures. Monkey retorts: But for this mind, how could they have managed to come this far?

> Your disciple's cunning mind, although inferior to my Master's sincerity, is superior to Bajie's simplicity. Even when it is cunning, it is adapting to different crises: it is not the mind of deception, mind of theft, mind of unrighteousness, mind of adultery, mind of treachery, mind of falsehood, mind of slyness, mind of cruelty, mind of treason, mind of disorder, mind of rebellion, mind of calumny, mind of chicanery, mind of avarice, mind of anger, mind of evil.

The list goes on. Zhu Bajie also joins in: "My elder brother's is not the mind of wolf, mind of tiger, mind of dog" (3.20). Monkey and Zhu Bajie together mention the word "mind" eighty-eight times; each mind will give rise to one calamity. Buddha refuses to give Monkey the scriptures. Monkey implores the Buddha for mercy, to which Buddha replies,

> My scriptures consist of one word only; there are not many branches and leaves. You alone are the cause of multitudinous [superfluous] thoughts. I am afraid that when you get the scriptures, there will be incidents caused by this cunning mind, and others will have to live with the consequence.[41] (3.20–21)

Monkey retorts that he can rely on his somersault and his rod. Buddha, however, accuses him of having slighted, with the rod, so many deities and spirits and destroyed so many lives. It merely helps to realize Monkey's evil intentions. Buddha orders that the rod be confiscated because it is incompatible with the scriptures, thereby depriving Monkey of his trademark weapon. The weapons of Zhu Bajie and Sha Monk are confiscated too.

The taming of the mind/monkey is the thematic concern of the sequel, as is summarized by the second half of the poem that opens the book—which elaborates on its purport, just as the poem in *Xiyou ji* does in its case.

> What is the purpose for the composition of the *Sequel to the Journey to the West?*
> It is to pinpoint the one spot of reality within the human being.
> . . .

> When the cunning mind is annihilated, all forms of māra are subdued.
> When divine understanding is achieved, the power of Tao maximizes.
> Look at Sun Wukong the pilgrim,
> He subdues demons, transforms, and is renewed. (1.1)

It is implied that while subduing demons, he is being transformed, reformed, and renewed in the process. Since it is Monkey's *jibianxin* that is lethal and perilous, that leads to acts of deception and violence, to renew him is to renew his mind. According to Zhenfu jushi,

> [Whether to use] the cunning mind is what distinguishes Buddha and demon. Seal it and it is silent; provoke it and it is active: suddenly it transforms itself; suddenly it becomes clever and crafty; suddenly one idea gives rise to another, one mind begets another.... The whole being is possessed by the demon, and it is out of the question to seek the wisdom of true emptiness.... With the cunning mind inside, the Great Tao is kept outside: this is absolute truth.[42]

Jibian is not a vice in Buddhism exclusively; it is also condemned in Confucianism and Taoism. According to Mencius, "He who indulges in craftiness [*jibian*] has no use for shame."[43] In *Zhuangzi* (chap. 12), Zigong, the disciple of Confucius, sees an old man irrigating his vegetable field with great effort. He stops to tell him about a more efficient, labor-saving device, another instance of the cunning mind.

> A look of indignation came into the gardener's face. He laughed scornfully, saying, "I used to be told by my teacher that where there are cunning contrivances [*jixie*] there will be cunning performances [*jishi*], and where there are cunning performances there will be cunning hearts [*jixin*]. He in whose breast a cunning heart lies has blurred the pristine purity of his nature; he who has blurred the pristine purity of his nature has troubled the quiet of his soul, and with one who has troubled the quiet of his soul Tao will not dwell. It is not that I do not know about this invention, but that I should be ashamed to use it."[44]

Note the similarity in diction and reasoning between this passage and Zhenfu jushi's preface quoted above.

Nor are the virtuous manifestations of the mind, like Tripitaka's sincerity (*zhichengxin*) and Sha Monk's reverence (*gongjingxin*), and, central to the novel, rectification of the mind, exclusively Buddhist or Taoist values; they are more relevant to neo-Confucianism. As is adumbrated in *Daxue* (Great learning), "Wishing to cultivate their persons, they [the ancients] first rectified their hearts. Wishing to rectify their hearts, they first sought to be sincere in their thoughts."[45] Elsewhere, "Sincerity is the way of Heaven. The attainment of sincerity is the way of men. He who possesses sincerity, is he who, without an effort, hits what is right, and apprehends, without the exercise of thought—he is the sage who naturally and easily embodies the *right* way. He who attains to sincerity, is he who chooses what is good, and firmly holds it fast."[46] Reverence is repeatedly reiterated in, for instance, the *Liji* (The records of rites): "The noble man is ever reverent *[junzi wu bu jing ye]* ("Aigong wen")."⁴⁷ *Jing* (reverence), like *cheng* (sincerity), is emphatically stressed by neo-Confucian philosophers.

Critics have objected to the addition of two new characters to the *Xiyou ji* saga, namely Monk Daobi and Master Lingxuzi. Of the entire book, they, in particular, are "snake's legs," as an anonymous critic of *Xiyou bu* comments.⁴⁸ This statement is true on one level. The cast of the original *Xiyou ji* is already complete, and the two additions are hence superfluous. However, in the sequel they are indispensable in dramatizing the novel's theme. In many ways Lingxuzi's reformation foreshadows that of Monkey. In the return journey, he serves as Monkey's foil, defining Monkey by contrast. As the commentator Zhenfu jushi puts it, Lingxuzi is another name of the mind-monkey.⁴⁹ The names of Daobi and Lingxuzi, the commentator suggests in the preface, signify the purport of the journey—that is, to reach the other shore by achieving emptiness of the mind *(zhu deng bi'an, huanfan lingxu).*⁵⁰

Structurally as well as thematically, the first chapter is a prelude to the whole novel. It opens, after Buddha's preparation for the transmission of the sūtras, with the character Lingxuzi. An *upāsaka* (a lay male disciple who remains at home and observes the first five precepts), he has stopped attending the meetings at the Spirit Mountain, devoting all his time and energy to practicing the art of transformation under his master Wan Huayin, an itinerant magician. Lingxuzi learns from him for three years, and his prowess at transformation is quite renowned.

The narrative then shifts to Buddha's assembly. But unlike those we are accustomed to, this one consists of practitioners who tend to be without much adventurous spirit, uninterested in acquiring supernatural powers. When asked to volunteer to protect the pilgrims on the return journey, all are reluctant to venture into the demonic realm, preferring to practice in the safe haven of Buddha's presence. Monk Daobi, who possesses great wisdom, volunteers, but Buddha does not know whether he has the power to subdue demons. The monk then recommends Lingxuzi. Lingxuzi's practice is a form of Taoism, his pursuits seen as straying from the right way, hence heretical.⁵¹ In order for him to be of service, the first thing is to bring him back to the Buddhist fold. Monk Daobi confronts Lingxuzi.

> If one's complete enlightenment is manifested, [such transformations] are known by neither heaven nor earth, comprehensible to neither ghosts nor deities. As for your transformations, they are only deceptions and illusions created by the human mind. You know that which is also known to others; you deceive yourself, but you cannot deceive others. (1.7)

In this sequel, Monkey's transformations also fall into the second category, a form of deception.

Daobi brings Lingxuzi to Buddha's presence, and Buddha blames him for indulging in the art of illusion. He asks Lingxuzi to demonstrate his power, telling him to transform into something big and small respectively. Buddha asks others whether they have observed Lingxuzi's transformations, and Daobi answers that he has seen Lingxuzi only twisting his body several times. Buddha smiles, saying, "I didn't see any of his transformations; I only saw his square inch [mind] within his inside stirring three or five times" (2.10). Lingxuzi renounces such practice; he is, however, permitted to transform for the sake of scriptures.

The comments by Monk Daobi and Buddha are not unlike Wang Yangming's when the Ming thinker wrote about such things.

> Stories concerning men of later generations who could ascend with their families into the air, transform objects, borrow corpses and return to life again, refer to deceptive and strange things belonging to the realm of secret magic and ingenious arts—what Yinwenzi called illusion, what the Buddhists call heterodoxy. If such actions are called real, you would be equally deceived.[52]

Indeed, Chinese philosophical writings provide a rich intertext with regard to Monkey's reformation. For instance, in chapter 3 of *Liezi*, Laochengzi studies magic under Master Yinwenzi for three years, but the latter teaches him nothing. Upon further inquiry, the master tells the disciple what Laozi has told him.

> The breath of all that lives, the appearance of all that has shape, is illusion. What is begun by the creative process, and changed by the Yin and Yang, is said to be born and to die; things which, already shaped, are displaced and replaced by a comprehension of numbers and understanding of change, are said to be transformed, to be illusions of magic. The skill of the Creator is inscrutable, his achievement profound, so that it is long before his work completes its term and comes to an end. The skill of a magician working on the shapes of things is obvious but his achievement shallow, so that his work is extinguished as soon as it is conjured up. It is when you realise that the illusions and transformations of magic are no different from birth and death that it becomes worthwhile to study magic with you. You and I are also illusion; what is there to study?"
>
> Laochengzi went home to practise Master Yinwen's teaching, and after pondering deeply for three months, was able to appear and disappear at will and turn around and exchange the four seasons, call up thunder in winter, create ice in summer, make flying things run and running things fly. He never disclosed his arts all his life, so that no one handed them down to later generations.[53]

In fact, the sequel may be regarded as a critique of stories of transformation, which culminate in Monkey's feats in *Xiyou ji*.[54]

Since Lingxuzi is enlisted to protect the pilgrims on their journey, he is the first to observe them. Surprisingly, he is impressed by Zhu Bajie and is appalled by Monkey for the latter's heroic ambitions: readers of *Xiyou ji* will remember how happy he is when there is a demon for him to quell. Daobi and Lingxuzi realize that, given Monkey's boastfulness, competitiveness, and versatility, it is no easy task to protect the pilgrims on their way back to China.

Like Lingxuzi in the first chapter, Monkey is changed on the fourteen-year return journey. On the way, he is divested of his ambitions and his limitless hubris. At the beginning, Monkey is still his old self, trying to resort to the methods he is familiar with to deal with crises on the road. He blames Tripitaka for his sincerity: the monk could have overcome all difficulties had he tried to be clever and cunning. But with his rod confiscated, Monkey cannot fight with the demons, who are, as the author repeatedly reiterates, caused by the pilgrims' own unclean minds, their evil intentions. The monsters here are not nearly as powerful as those in the parent novel. They will be converted to Buddhism in the end, rather than being annihilated by Monkey. For instance, in chapter 32, the Demon of Seven Emotions and the Monster of Six Desires are converted by Tripitaka when the monk recites the *Heart Sūtra*. The snake and turtle spirits in chapter 15 begin to practice the Tao instead, rather than continue to be demons. In chapter 48, Lingxuzi, emulating Buddha, offers himself to the reincarnation of the six-eared macaque killed by Monkey in the parent novel, so that the demon can have his revenge for what Monkey has done to him. The monster is so moved by this act that he leaves the forest (48.369). Many of the monsters are incarnations of demons or figures who have met violent deaths in *Xiyou ji*, such as the Dragon King killed by Wei Zheng and the six-eared macaque. One structural design of this sequel is to have them reincarnated and seek revenge initially. As the macaque puts it, "The ten-thousand-mile road from the west to the east is full of enemies of Pilgrim Sun. . . . They seek revenge everywhere" (48.365). However, they are converted eventually, testifying to the power of the scriptures.

Nor is Monkey as powerful as he used to be, with his weapon confiscated. Initially he has only his cunning mind to rely on, to outwit the demons. But the more the pilgrims exercise their mind—harboring evil intentions—the more demons they encounter. In chapter 30, when the pilgrims are fighting with demons, Lingxuzi transforms himself into an eagle and bites the finger of a demon in order to help the pilgrims. When Tripitaka sees this, he is overjoyed. It suddenly dawns on Lingxuzi: no wonder the pilgrims encounter demons always, because their minds are not set on benevolence (30.228). At the Sea-Pacifying Monastery, the monks try to snatch the scriptures away from the pilgrims so that they can make copies, but Monkey changes his hair into wasps to attack them (16.125). This is the cause of some reptiles breathing poison on them. They encounter a fox spirit, who, with good intentions, tells the pilgrims the whereabouts of the stolen scriptures. But Bajie still wants to beat her. This leads to the theft of the scriptures and Bajie's humiliation. In chapters 74–77 of *Xiyou ji*, Monkey fights with three monsters—the green lion, the white elephant, and the roc—who are finally subdued by Buddha and bodhisattvas. But two lesser monsters have remained and appear in the sequel (chap. 20). They originally intend to ask their subordinates to escort the pilgrims across the mountain, but the fox spirit incites them in her pursuit of vengeance. "These monks have an abundance of cunning minds and evil intentions," she says; "do they look like those who have renounced the world?" (20.151)

Thus deception leads to deception, and to bully others means to bully oneself. This is what Monkey painfully learns on the journey. One of the issues is his ability to change his hair into various beings or forms. He pays for such deceptions. Toward the end of the novel, a monster who is the hair of another monster subdued by Monkey in *Xiyou ji* appears and changes into Monkey's form, causing great inconvenience. This is regarded as a kind of retribution: "Who told Sun Wukong to exercise his cunning mind and pluck his hair? He has hair to pluck; will not the monster do the same?" (92.710) Monkey changes himself into a tiger to frighten the hunters, but he is almost harmed by them, a contrast to how he kills them off in the parent novel. As a result, Monkey stops this practice. Since the weapons of the pilgrims have been confiscated, they initially rely on the staffs Buddha has given them for carrying the boxes containing scriptures. But toward the end of the novel they have renounced the use of such. More strikingly, Monkey no longer exercises his cunning mind. Tripitaka wonders about this development: now Monkey recites Sanskrit spells to subdue the demons. Monkey explains that the more he uses his mind, the more demons he encounters; now as he is nearing China and his faith in the scriptures increases, demons vanish and no effort on his part is needed. Thus as long as the minds of the pilgrims are clouded, there will be demons, but when their minds are cleansed, no demons present themselves.

It is in the vicinity of the Temple of Five Villages (the setting of chaps. 24–26 in *Xiyou ji*) that Monkey has achieved the right mind. The journey thus ends hastily and abruptly. In the first half of chapter 100, the pilgrims are still on the road. In the second half, the journey is concluded. The hastiness may suggest how speedily the journey could have been accomplished had the characters simply had the right mind—the right intention.

The book pays a price for being a corrective endeavor, however: the sequel is not nearly as exciting as the parent novel.[55] Most readers of the parent novel are engrossed by the resourcefulness of Monkey, beginning with his birth. Here, with his weapon confiscated, he is not even allowed to exercise his mind! From one episode to another, it is stressed that the monsters will disappear so long as he sets his mind right. If *Xiyou ji* is repetitious, this sequel is more so, one example being the almost formulaic expression of "A mind of . . . arises" *(dong le . . . xin)* when one of the characters has an intention to do something, and "setting one's mind right," which is all he needs to do. Monkey is eventually tamed; he transforms from a larger-than-life figure with superhuman power into someone like us, but with the right mind. If Monkey, the soul of the journey and hence of the parent novel, is no longer what he used to be, we may wonder how much *Xiyou ji* is left: the novel departs from *Xiyou ji* so much that it can be called "Anti-*Xiyou ji*." Nevertheless, the issues the author raises are important ones, in particular the novel's avowed pacifism and the disdain of Monkey's transformations and his cunning mind.

HOU XIYOU JI: SECOND JOURNEY TO THE WEST AND THE LEARNING OF THE MIND

Hou Xiyou ji[56] mimics *Xiyou ji* in structure. Its frame is another journey to the West undertaken by the monk Dadian[57] and the descendants—by blood or spirit—of Monkey, Zhu Bajie, and Sha Monk.[58] However, the purpose of the journey is different; in a way, it is a remedy to the first journey. The scriptures brought from the West in the first journey have, unfortunately, become a means for selfish monks to attain fame and profit. Buddha therefore designs another mission to the West, this time for the true interpretation *(zhenjie)* of these scriptures. To some extent, the second journey is a negation of the first one. As such, the sequel questions many of the fundamental concepts of the parent novel.

The sequel opens with another Monkey King. The author follows the parent novel in presenting the sequence of the events. In chapter 1, many events from *Xiyou ji* are recapitulated, but set in a different context. Little Monkey King is born from a rock. An immortal informs him of his lineage; therefore, he humbly calls himself Lesser Sage Equal to Heaven (Qitian Xiaosheng) and names himself Sun Lüzhen. He, too, is disturbed by mortality when he has witnessed the death of an old monkey and, like his ancestor, sets out to search for the Tao.

Different from his ancestor, the Lesser Sage's search proves to be problematic and disappointing. He is admitted to a Taoist temple, where he successfully completes the course to still the mind *(dingxin)* and nourish the vital energy *(yangqi)*. But the Taoist patriarch, in contrast to Subodhi in *Xiyou ji*, proves to be an evil one, debauching on the pretext of Taoist physiological alchemical practice. Little Monkey therefore rightly leaves the place. He is not successful elsewhere. In a characteristic passage, he thinks to himself,

> I have been seeking here and there, and all I find is unorthodox ways and heretical practices. What use are these? While I was stilling the mind and nourishing the vital energy the other day, I sensed something happening within my self. Rather than roaming over endless rivers and mountains, I should turn my head and return [to where I came from], and work on this square inch [mind]. Maybe I can achieve something. (2.17–2.18)

He comes back to Flower-Fruit Mountain and enters the Leakless Cave (Wulou Dong). There, he meditates for forty-nine days, and, finally, in the radiance of the hallowed light that gathers in front of him, he sees the form of an elder monkey, Sun Wukong, who imparts to him the secrets of immortality. Immediately he transcends this world. He is about to ask further questions when the elder monkey and he suddenly become one. He understands: "Within one's mind and nature there is the real Teacher; only no one knows to seek him" (2.18–2.19). Later, he turns to himself—his own mind—so as to find his ancestor: "Since he and I are one, even if he is in the Heavens or in the Underworld, he is not away from my mind, this square inch" (19.197). It is at this time that he discovers he can use the rod the Great Sage has left behind, which he could not even budge previously.

Like his ancestor, the Lesser Sage also puts his newly acquired powers to the test. He becomes the second Monkey King and goes to the Underworld and questions the Ten Kings about the burning concerns felt by the populace at that time, questions about the moral order of the universe, in particular karmic retribution, which had been embraced as a workable substitute after the disintegration of official Confucianism.[59] Here Little Monkey discovers that someone—Judge Cui Jue—has changed Emperor Taizong's reign from thirteen years to thirty-three. The destiny of the Tang should be 289 years; Cui Jue's addition to Taizong's life brings it to 309 years, which is unacceptable. Little Monkey comes up with the idea to reduce the reign and life of the present emperor, Xianzong, from thirty-five and sixty-three years, respectively, to fifteen and forty-three years. Cui Jue will be reborn as a Taoist and will contribute to the premature death of the emperor by presenting alchemical pills to him.

More than two hundred years pass before Tripitaka and Sun Wukong return to Chang'an again to inspect what has transpired. They find that the monks make profit out of the scriptures, and even Tripitaka himself is commercialized. A selfish monk named Wuzhong (and styled Shengyou) calls himself the sixth-generation disciple and is reputed to be able to discourse on all the scriptures brought back by Tripitaka.

In a way, this is a severe criticism of the parent novel and its protagonists, who have brought the scriptures from the West. According to the author, sūtras are not to be relied on, and too much attention to words merely leads to absurdities. The author and the critic who penned the preface seem to have laid the blame on Buddha and the bodhisattvas themselves, who created the scriptures in the first place and had them brought to China. Consider the following statements: "The first culprit of absurd thoughts is the great compassion [of Buddha and Bodhisattvas]" and "What is the origin of all these evils? The establishment of words at the beginningless beginning is to blame."[60] Such notions were shared by the Ming literati; for instance, Li Zhi wrote, "Buddha Śākyamuni preached the Dharma for forty-nine years, but did not leave a single word to Kāśyapa. For no reason Kāśyapa asked Ānanda to organize the [first] assembly, so that teachings of three divisions (Tripitaka) are compiled, thus exerting a pernicious influence on myriad ages."[61]

The mistrust of words and texts can be, at the same time, construed as a criticism of the preoccupation with books among Confucian scholars. Many were disenchanted with the so-called learning of the Tao, particularly scholars obsessed with the words of the classics and offering lectures about them. Chen Xianzhang (1428–1500) even felt sympathy for the first emperor of the Qin, who burned Confucian books; to Chen, books are merely a hindrance to real learning.[62] The Confucian Six Classics, Wang Yangming argued, are an "inventory" of the storehouse, not the reality, which is the mind.[63] Li Zhi wondered whether Confucius had foreseen the harm of his writings.[64]

Thus the second journey to the West may be seen as a comment on the state of learning, allegorizing the crisis in the nation's intellectual life—that is, the overwhelming accumulation of materials about the classics, Confucian or otherwise, and the difficulties of dealing with it. The central issue is interpretation.

Buddha asks Tripitaka and Sun Wukong to travel back to Chang'an and find someone qualified for this mission, the same way that the bodhisattva Guanyin goes there to find Tripitaka. They disguise themselves as two deformed monks and reveal their identity to the emperor when the opportunity is right. They tell the emperor to send someone on another mission to the

West, to emulate them so as to obtain the true interpretation. Meanwhile, they have all the scriptures sealed. The emperor seeks a person that can accomplish such a task, but no one is willing to go except Monk Dadian, modestly styled by the emperor as Banji (half a *gāthā*),[65] a parody of the ambitious name of Tripitaka (Sanzang).

The first nine chapters can be regarded as preparation for the pilgrimage, like the beginning chapters of *Xiyou ji*. In chapter 9, Little Monkey goes to the Dragon Palace to obtain a dragon horse. In chapter 11, Bajie's son, Zhu Shouzhuo, styled Zhu Yijie by Tripitaka, joins the pilgrimage after a fight with Little Monkey. In chapter 15, Sha Zhihe, a disciple of Sha Monk, arrives. The pilgrimage begins here on the scale of *Xiyou ji*.

One of *Hou Xiyou ji*'s distinctive features is the predominance of monsters and demons from the Buddhist fold, such as Wuzhong (chaps. 5, 7, 8), Dianshi (chap. 11), Mingbao (chaps. 36–37), Bukong (chap. 40), and Wuqi (chap. 40). The journey results from the Buddhist clerics who have gone astray. In chapter 12, when Zhu Yijie joins the pilgrimage, he and Little Monkey have a fight with Monk Zili (Selfish, or Self-profiting). The author adds significance to the rake that Zhu Bajie carries. He lent it to Monk Zili to cultivate the Buddha field (Fotian), which refers to the Buddhist or neo-Confucian cultivation of the mind. Zili neglects the Buddha field and gets his provisions elsewhere, such as from donations and contributions. Zhu Bajie says, "The Buddha field, although of great magnitude, is as a matter of fact only a square inch [mind]. He who knows how to cultivate it will plant melons or peas and take care of the root of goodness, which will produce good fruits. He can enjoy such fruits all his life without ever exhausting them. . . . This Monk Zili, however, is ambitious and covetous. Unwilling to cultivate this square inch, he wants to cultivate the whole world" (12.115).

Confucians fare no better. Before Little Monkey sets out in search of Tao, the immortal at Flower-Fruit Mountain criticizes them: most of them "pay excessive attention to words. They look benevolent and decent on the outside, but inside they are lustful and covetous. Hence they can by no means become immortals" (2.12). Chapter 22 is about those scholars who care only about externalities and formalities: speaking the formulaic language as they do, they act against Buddhist monks for superficial reasons, at the instigation of the monster who styles himself the Heavenly King of Civilization (Wenming Tianwang). This monster, originally from China, is reincarnated in the West. He is born covered with gold coins and with a huge writing brush in his hand, both of which can be used as weapons. He puts the brush on the head of Little Monkey. It is as heavy as Mount Tai. This is obviously an attack on literati, especially those in power, who use their writing brushes for their selfish, unjust, and oppressive political agendas. As the monster threatens, he just needs to write a few characters like "evil monk" or "heretical monk" to have Banji condemned forever.[66] The author elaborates on the provenance of the monster, further highlighting his connection to Confucian China. The horse he rides is the reincarnation of Xiang Yu's steed. He also possesses the eight horses of King Mu of the Zhou dynasty (Zhou Muwang).[67] A parallel is deliberately maintained between these horses and Monk Dadian's—they are all related to some aspect of Chinese civilization. Moreover, the brush is the one Confucius used when writing *Chunqiu* (Spring and autumn annals). The monster is the reincarnation of the unicorn slain by woodcutters, an event that caused Confucius to bring the book to an abrupt end. Finally, the unicorn secludes himself waiting for the arrival of a new sage, and the writing brush is taken by the Kui Star (Kuixing), acting on the orders of the popular deity in charge of the fortunes of literati, Wenchang dijun. It seems that the author is so disenchanted with the current state of Confucianism that he courts Buddhism. The steed from the Dragons Palace, which Monk Dadian rides on the journey, is an example in point. After much threat and coercion on Little Monkey's part, the dragon kings give him the horse that carried the charts of the Eight Diagrams from the River in the legendary times of Fuxi, an event that inaugurated Chinese civilization. This suggests a convergence of Confucianism and Buddhism, although the dragon kings are also concerned about the appropriateness of their act, which tarnishes the purity of Confucianism. But the poem appended also suggests that the Confucian Tao has been in decline for such a long time that there is nothing for the horse to do; it can only join the Buddhist fold so as to contribute to civilization (9.89).[68]

Xu Xiyou ji advocates the power of sūtras for salvation, but in this sequel, except for one's mind, nothing else can be relied upon, neither sūtras nor Buddha himself. In chapter 27, when the Empress Dowager is saved by Little Monkey from the fox spirit who impersonates a Buddhist monk, she wants Dadian to administer penance to her. She is an ardent believer in Buddha and has a pavilion built, called Awaiting-Deliverance Pavilion (Daidu Lou). It is the desire to become a buddha that has caused a monster to appear and kidnap her. Dadian tells her, "You should repent of your mind for awaiting deliverance. Buddha is mind, and mind is Buddha; for whom do you wait to deliver you? When you wait for deliverance, the wild fox [unorthodox and impure practices] intervenes. I change the name of this pavilion from Awaiting-Deliverance into Self-Deliverance (Zidu Lou), and you can become a buddha instantaneously" (27.308). At the beginning of chapter 32, while they are near Spirit Mountain, the monk Dadian says that the road is becoming smoother due to proximity to the holy place. Little Monkey reacts strongly to this: it is because the elder's mind is peaceful that the road is peaceful. However, as the elder is now relying on Buddha and neglecting his own mind, the road, Little Monkey is afraid, will become troublesome (32.361–362). As it turns out, the pilgrims encounter new ordeals immediately.

As it is the human mind that produces obstacles, so it is by the human mind that they are removed. The best way is to keep the mind pure, not be stirred by outside stimuli. In chapter 30, the pilgrims encounter the Child Fortune (or Child Fate, Zaohua Xiao'er, suggesting fickleness of fortune). He knows that he cannot harm the pilgrims; all he can do is test them. He has one hundred rings, called ring of fame, ring of profit, ring of wealth, and so on. He asks Little Monkey to escape from them. Like the monkey in a circus, Little Monkey jumps out of the ring of fame, ring of profit, rings of wine, lust, wealth, and anger, and rings of greed, annoyance, folly, and love. Finally, the child encircles him with the ring of competitiveness, and this time Little Monkey cannot escape, even when he somersaults into the heavens, knocking Laozi down in a hilarious scene. There the Taoist patriarch enlightens him. Little Monkey can escape from other rings because the emotions these rings represent do not affect him. However, he is nothing if not combative and competitive. Laozi tells him that it is he himself that is restraining him. Hearing this, Little Monkey renounces his belligerence and is instantly freed from the ring.

In chapter 39, the pilgrims finally reach Spirit Mountain and pay homage to Buddha. However, in the ceremony an atmosphere of futility prevails. Buddha mentions that the evils in China are too rampant to eradicate; not even the scriptures are efficient—a marked contrast to the avowed confidence of *Xiyou ji* and *Xu Xiyou ji* in the efficacy of scriptures. The effect of the scriptures can last for only a moment. Even when true interpretations are provided, it is difficult to enlighten the myriad beings. It is best for the people there to forget knowledge and wisdom. Dadian beseeches Buddha for mercy, and Buddha grants his wish, giving him the true interpretation, but he is still skeptical: China with the true interpretation will not be much different from China without (39.467).

This is another manifestation of the mistrust of words and writings, a logical outcome of the emphasis on the mind in the *Xiyou ji* tradition. The emphasis on the mind inevitably subverts the physical pilgrimage. In the parent novel, the pilgrims are given blank "scriptures," a somewhat predictable end (although rejected), since there is nothing material to gain after all. However, the author of *Xiyou ji* has to compromise between the inner reality and the outward form of the pilgrimage. Since the journey is for the scriptures, the participants have to bring something back. The Tang emperor is waiting; the spirits suffering in the Buddhist hell are waiting. The denouement in a way accounts for the reconciliation of the two views on scriptures. The blank scriptures are returned for "authentic" ones, with words on them. In *Xu Xiyou ji*, it is repeatedly reiterated that it is the human mind that is of utmost importance: "Amitābha is in this mind, / Seek not endless words from outside. / If one sees the Spirit Mountain [inside], the scriptures are there. / There is no need for the arduous journey to the West"[69] (*XXYJ* 41.313). Here it seems that the author is equating *lingtai* (mind) with Lingshan (Spirit Mountain). As a result, the apotheosis is downplayed, taking approximately one page. In *Hou Xiyou ji*, the author maintains that of all things in the three thousand chiliocosms, only the human mind is Buddha. One should not think that Spirit Mountain is in the western regions (*HXYJ* 36.417). In this sequel, the tension between inner reality and outward pilgrimage manifests itself in two understandings of Buddha, or the "two faces" of Buddha—the face that has a form *(semian)* and the face that has none *(kongmian)*. When the pilgrims finally arrive at Spirit Mountain, the author hesitates as to whether to allow them to have an actual glimpse of the World-Renowned One, since Buddha is none other than their mind.[70] The pilgrims first see an empty hall, testifying to the Buddhist emptiness. Little Monkey discourses about this point: Buddhism is the gate of emptiness, and the awe-inspiring images are but illusions (39.462). He then transforms himself into the form of Buddha, teasing Zhu Yijie. However, the playfulness of this practical joke should not eclipse its significance, demonstrating as it does that Buddha is none other than one's mind (39.465).

Nevertheless, the author has to make a compromise about the physicality of Buddha, the same way the author of *Xiyou ji* before him had to decide whether or not to have the pilgrims bring material sūtras to China. In this sequel it has taken the pilgrims five years to reach Spirit Mountain for the true interpretation. Dadian is convinced of the formlessness of Buddha's existence, but he still wants to see Buddha with his own eyes because he has a "material" mission to accomplish (39.462). They are granted an audience with the Buddha. However, the setting of the audience—the Mustard Seed Monastery (Jiezi An) in Sumeru Park (Xumi Yuan)—blatantly suggests the human mind; that is, Sumeru Mountain is contained in the mustard seed. This hearkens back to the preface of this sequel: "The mind is only a square inch, so small that it can be contained in the mustard seed, yet it permeates the entire phenomenal world with ease."[71] The Mustard Seed Monastery forms a sharp contrast to the Thunderclap Monastery in the parent novel.

We can say that in this sequel the pilgrimage is further internalized. Indeed, the predominant setting for this novel—the mountains—supports this interpretation. Characters tend to enter the caves or caverns of these mountains. In chapter 2, Little Monkey enters the Leakless Cave, and it is there that he finds the secret to immortality during his meditation. The dark cave, with only a small opening into which no one else has entered (2.18), certainly is a graphic representation of the human mind. In chapter 12, the Mountain of Myriad Conditionings (Wanyuan Shan) suggests the world, but in the middle is the fertile Buddha field, which is the mind, and Little Monkey and Zhu Yijie go inside to have a look at it (12.117). In chapter 35, the pilgrims have to cross the Dividing Ridge (Zhongfen Ling), a trial that is to reveal whether they have any attachment to the world.[72] They find that the temple they have reached is none other than the one from which they have departed. In chapter 38, the pilgrims overcome the last obstacle by climbing over Cloud-Transcending Mountain (Yundu Shan), an event that is reminiscent of chapter 98 of *Xiyou ji*.[73] The mountain, filthy from the outside, is spotless inside. The distance between this mountain and Spirit Mountain is only a "square inch." But it is this distance that determines whether a man becomes a buddha or remains in the world deluded. In short, all these episodes suggest that the pilgrims walk in the corridors and passageways of the mind, and the episodes reveal a clear structural design.

The opening poem of chapter 39 sums up the author's self-conscious development of what has transpired in *Xiyou ji*.

> See clearly that there is no Buddha in the Buddha land,
> At the edge of the Western Paradise one can go further westward.
> Many seekers have achieved great wisdom,
> But in this area they are still somewhat beclouded. (39.456)

The events in chapter 39 can be regarded as the author's one more step westward, that is, further internalization of the journey. In the end, everything else should be put down, since only the mind is the true Buddha. *Xiyou ji,* in the sequel author's opinion, does not achieve this. Herein lies the difference between Tripitaka and Banji. As the author reads *Xiyou ji,* Tripitaka still holds on to something inessential, symbolized by the "alms bowl of purple gold" (*JW* 4:394; *XYJ* 98.1176). He is forced to surrender this as a "tip" to Kāśyapa and Ānanda. But Banji has nothing superfluous (*HXYJ* 39.467).

XIYOU BU: TOWARD A PSYCHOLOGY OF DESIRE

Xiyou bu further departs from *Xiyou ji* and represents a reorientation of the *Xiyou ji* saga. This short novel of sixteen chapters, unlike other sequels of the parent novel, has been carefully studied in both China and the West.[74] It is not a sequel in the narrowly defined sense of the word. It is supposed to be inserted between chapters 61 and 62, after Monkey's three attempts to borrow the palm-leaf fan so as to extinguish the fire of Flaming Mountain (all of the sequels amplify events in the vicinity of this mountain). Dong Yue inserts a new series of stories into the original *Xiyou ji.*

There are some uncanny parallels between certain episodes in *Hou Xiyou ji* and *Xiyou bu,* rapports that have thematic and structural significance, possibly suggesting that Dong Yue was responding to the sequel as well.[75] One possible affinity to *Hou Xiyou ji* is the representation of the monster. In *Xiyou ji,* Monkey is wont to enter the bellies of the monsters, the most famous episode being his entering Rakśasa's stomach. In chapter 34 of *Hou Xiyou ji,* the pilgrims find themselves in the midst of mirages produced by the Mirage Monster. Originally, the place is the sea of evil caused by the human mind. Buddha has filled it up with the sands of the Ganges. However, pheasants contained in the sands have become a monster, swallowing up whole cities and emitting mirages. At the outset of this episode, Little Monkey jumps into the air to see what is going on: he sees towns and cities, which then disappear. The local deity, who takes a long time to appear, to the dismay of Little Monkey (the deity appears again toward the end of the chapter), informs him that it is the working of the Mirage Monster. In this interval, the demon swallows the other pilgrims; their experiences inside the stomach of the demon and Little Monkey's attempts to save them constitute this chapter's plot. Predictably, Little Monkey and other pilgrims kill the demon.[76] In *Xiyou bu,* Monkey again enters the belly of the monster, the Qing Fish (Qingyu, or Mackerel). It is stressed by the author that Monkey is in the belly of the monster, in a question-and-answer section attributed to himself.[77] Moreover, the worlds Monkey finds himself in are the result of the Qing Fish "exhaling," the same way the Mirage Monster creates his worlds.[78]

Another possible affinity concerns the theme of *Xiyou bu.* In chapters 32–33 of *Hou Xiyou ji,* the pilgrims encounter Dame Never-Old (Bulao Popo), or Sister Forever-Young (Changyan Jiejie).[79] She is different from all other female monsters and demons in that she appears in a lovely form and does not harm human beings or other living creatures. She resides in Great Bo Mountain, corresponding to the hexagram *bo* ䷖, with one *yang* symbol above five *yin* symbols, hinting that she is to strip *(bo)* a man of his *yang* essence. She uses a pair of jade fire tongs *(yuhuoqian)*, suggesting the fire of desire *(yu)*. These tongs were originally used by Nüwa when melting stones to repair the rift in the firmament. Dame Never-Old wants to "fight" with heroes of the world, suggesting, in Taoist terminology, sexual intercourse. The weapons of all the heroes of the world are no match for hers. Upon hearing about Little Monkey and his rod, she wants to have a tournament with him. Zhu Yijie approaches her and is clamped by the tongs, signifying that he has an abundance of desire himself. In a scheme to trap Little Monkey, Dame Never-Old asks Zhu Yijie to tie a green silk thread, thinner than one's hair, on Little Monkey's head so as to drag him to her. The thread, in Little Monkey's words, is the dame's thread of desire *(qingsi)*. He pretends to be bound by this thread, but when the other pilgrims have escaped, he snaps it into pieces. "Your thread of desire," Little Monkey says, "can only bind ordinary people. I am a superior man without any desire *(taishang wuqing zhi ren)*. How can you treat me the same as others?" (33.387) Dame Never-Old, spurned by Little Monkey, destroys the tongs and commits suicide by casting herself against the mountain range. Little Monkey, however, feels uncharacteristically sorry for the woman (34.389), going so far as to make sure that she is properly buried.

Xiyou bu opens with a spring meadow with red peonies in full bloom and a group of girls and boys frolicking, a scene with blatantly emotional and even sexual connotations.[80] Monkey kills the girls and boys who tease the monk. However, like Little Monkey near Great Bo Mountain, he feels sorry for them and composes an elegy. Next, he sets out to beg alms: in a somersault he leaps into the heavens. It is at this moment that he is bewitched by the Qing Fish (Mackerel) Spirit and enters the eerie world created by this monster. There, he encounters a series of famous women lovers in Chinese history and characters like Dame Never-Old who do not look monstrous or demonic.

Xiyou bu's most conspicuous departure from the Xiyou novels is Monkey's experience of many forms of desire. In *Xiyou ji* and its other sequels, Monkey, or Little Monkey, despite his other weaknesses, is not susceptible to this brand of temptation. It is Zhu Bajie and his descendant who often fail such tests. In chapter 72 of *Xiyou ji*, Zhu Bajie is entangled in the cobweb woven by the Spider Monsters, who transformed into beautiful maidens, suggesting traps of emotional attachment.

> All at once the threads began to pour out of their navels, and in no time at all, Bajie was enclosed inside what appeared to be a huge silk tent. . . . All over the ground ropes and cords were strewn to trip him up. The moment he moved his legs, he began to stumble: he headed to the left and his face hugged the ground; he went to the right and he fell head over heels; he turned around and his snout kissed the earth; he scrambled up only to do a handstand. (*JW* 3:372; *XYJ* 72.876)

In the following chapter, the spiders play the same trick on Monkey, but to no avail. Monkey changes his hair into seventy little monkeys, each with a rod.

> They stood by the mass of silk cords and plunged the rods into the web; at a given signal, they all snapped the cords and then rolled them up with their rods. After each of them had rolled up over ten pounds of the cords, they dragged out from inside seven huge spiders, each about the size of a barrel. (*JW* 3:384; *XYJ* 73.886)

Monkey kills them all. In *Hou Xiyou ji,* the ring of desire is powerless to imprison Little Monkey. In his adventures at Great Bo Mountain, he calls himself a superior man without any desire, and the thread of desire cannot bind him. But in *Xiyou bu,* Monkey *is* entangled, and it takes great effort on his part to extricate himself, a sharp contrast to other works. Monkey is about to descend from the Tower of Myriad Mirrors when

> [o]utside the windows there was nothing but exquisite crimson railings arranged like cracked ice. Luckily the spaces in between were rather wide, and Monkey hunched up and scurried through one. Who'd have thought fate was against him, that the time was wrong, or that railings could bind a man? What were clearly railings arranged like cracks in ice suddenly became hundreds of red threads that tangled around Monkey so that he couldn't move an inch.
> Monkey changed into a pearl and the red threads became a pearl-net. When Monkey couldn't roll through he instantly changed into a blue-bladed sword. The red threads became a scabbard. Monkey had no choice but to return to his own form. He cried, "Master, where are you? Don't you know your disciple is in a lot of trouble?" And his tears fell like water from spring. (*TMM* 128; *XYB* 10.47)

This is rather uncharacteristic of the Monkey we have known, who had never experienced a debacle like this one.

Xiyou bu can be seen as a contrast to the *Hou Xiyou ji* episodes about Dame Never-Old. Indeed, an anonymous critic suggests that this work builds on such episodes and amplifies them *(jie qi yi).*[81] The same critic tries to forestall possible objections to this development: is it appropriate for Buddha Victorious in Strife to find himself helpless in various forms of human desire? The critic defends this new plot, saying, "Who does not have desire?" Dong Yue's book goes further than the chapters about Dame Never-Old, which almost amount to a rendezvous with desire for Monkey or his descendant. But even in these chapters, this encounter is disguised as a Taoist external alchemical practice.

This shift of emphasis has been noted by critics. As Hegel points out, "Monkey's adventures in *[Xiyou bu]* have, after all, made him much more human than he is in the 'parent' novel; for the first time this figure has to cope with physical desires, with family, with responsibilities in situations where even his magical powers are insufficient."[82] Madeline Chu writes, "[W]hile the journey of *Xiyouji* moves away from the world of shapes and sounds into that of serenity and enlightenment, the journey of *Xiyoubu* enters deep into the world of senses, emotions, attachments and desires."[83]

If *Xu Xiyou ji* constitutes one attempt to humanize Monkey by depriving him of his weapon and forcing him to unlearn all his supernatural powers, then *Xiyou bu* constitutes another attempt to humanize him, this time by making him undergo serious trials involving human desire. In this way, Dong Yue has brought Monkey closer to the reader. It is an exposure to desire that helps the protagonist to transcend them. As Dong put it himself,

> The forty-eight-thousand years are the amassed roots of desire. To become enlightened and open to the Great Way, one must first empty and destroy the roots of desire. To empty and destroy the roots of desire one must first go inside desire. After going inside desire and seeing the emptiness of the root of the world's desire, one can then go outside of desire and realize the reality of the root of the Way.[84]

The internalization of the journey in the *Xiyou* novels culminates in *Xiyou bu*, which devises a new way to represent the human mind, or the conflicts within the human mind. Since, in Tripitaka's words, all forms of māra are productions of the mind, it follows that all demons are manifestations of the mind. In a way, the pilgrims themselves *are* the demons, as Monkey finally realizes in *Xu Xiyou ji*. He tells Lingxuzi and Monk Daobi, "Except you and my master who are honest elders, the rest of us are all demons. Only when we bring the true scriptures to the east, accomplish complete success, and gain the true fruit, will we cease to be demons" (*XXYJ* 100.770). Zhenfu jushi asks, in his commentary, whether the two venerable elders are indeed demons also. He even suggests that *Xiyou ji* in its entirety is a record of the Buddha, but it is also a record of demons.[85] On a positive note, however, if the mind is Buddha, as *Xiyou ji* and all its sequels profess, then the objects of pilgrims' searches are their minds and, by extension, themselves. In other words, they *are* buddhas too. However, *Xiyou ji* and its other sequels all fall short of saying explicitly that the pilgrims themselves are demons or buddhas, or that the fights with the demons are staged within the mind of the pilgrims, with the exception of the episode about two monkeys in *Xiyou ji* (chap. 58). We can certainly make such an interpretation, but it is possible only on the allegorical, rather than literal, level. *Xiyou bu* brings the seeds in the *Xiyou* novels to fruition. The events are the activities of Monkey's mind. In other words, we can say that the protagonist is none other than Monkey's mind. *Xiyou bu* leads us further and further into the depths of his psyche. We may even say that this piece is literally a *psychological* study, even in the modern sense.[86]

This statement is supported by the configuration of the demons, the beings who deliver Monkey from the demons, and Monkey himself.[87] On the one hand, all the demons and demonic worlds are transformations or manifestations of the demon Qing Fish Spirit. On the other hand, the demon is none other than Monkey himself. As the Elder of the Void (Xukong Zhuren) tells Monkey: "There is no Qing Fish; / It is but Monkey's desire" (*TMM* 186; *XYB* 16.73).

Mind is where illusions are produced; it is also the seat of Buddha nature, or, on a *xinxue* note, of true knowledge *(liangzhi)*. When Sun Wukong is tightly bound by the red threads, a wise old man comes to his rescue. When Monkey inquires about his identity, he tells him that he is Sun Wukong. Monkey thinks that he has encountered the six-eared macaque again. However, it turns out to be his true spirit.

> The old man drew his sleeves and left. He shouted, "This is what's called saving one's self [by one's self]! Too bad you regard the unreal as real, real as unreal!"
> A beam of gold light pierced Monkey's eyes, and the old man's form vanished. Only then did Monkey realize that the apparition had been his own true spirit. He quickly made a deep bow to thank himself. (*TMM* 130, slightly modified; *XYB* 10.48)

This forms an interesting parallel with *Hou Xiyou ji*, when the Lesser Sage is taught by the Great Sage and they become one. In *Xiyou bu*, this scheme has become an integral part of the structural design.

There is a parallel between the philosophical inward turn and its literary counterpart. This trend is manifested in the increasing internalization of the journey in the three *Xiyou ji* sequels, whose authors probe deeper and deeper into the human mind.

All the sequels represent deliberate and self-conscious departures from the parent novel. *Xu Xiyou ji* satirizes Sun Wukong, thus parodying the parent novel in many ways. The belligerent Monkey, forever adapting himself to the changing situations by means of his cunning mind, reforms and learns to rely on scriptures only. Toward the end of the novel, he becomes a new person, with his mind rectified. If *Xu Xiyou ji* is characterized by a preoccupation with the motivation and intention of the characters, itself a result of the *xinxue* influence, then *Hou Xiyou ji* distinguishes itself by its mistrust of everything external. The author stresses that even Buddha is not to be relied on, let alone the scriptures. Since Buddha is the mind, an emphasis on the physical or historical Buddha to the neglect of the mind will lead only to disaster. The pilgrimage can be seen as a journey inward, and its criticism of the scriptural tradition is severe. The search for interpretation—which points to the human mind—may be seen as an allegory of learning at that time, for it was interpretation of the classics that was the burning concern of the literati class. Both *Xiyou ji* and *Xu Xiyou ji* suggest the oneness of Buddha and scriptures on the one hand and the oneness of Buddha and the human mind on the other, but it is *Hou Xiyou ji* that has developed this theme in a sustained and consistent manner, culminating in the penultimate chapter. *Xiyou bu* pits Monkey against a confrontation of desire, thus recasting Monkey and expanding the scope of mind under scrutiny. *Xiyou bu* explores the workings of human psychology and experiments with fictional representations of the human mind.

Notes

I gladly acknowledge my indebtedness to Professors Martin W. Huang and John B. Henderson, who read the manuscript and offered valuable criticisms and suggestions for its improvement.

I am also grateful to the anonymous readers for the University of Hawai'i Press for doing the same. Of course, any errors and inaccuracies that remain are solely my responsibility.

1. The following editions and translations are used: Wu Cheng'en, *Xiyou ji* (Beijing: Renmin wenxue, 1980), abbreviated *XYJ*; Anthony C. Yu, trans., *Journey to the West*, abbreviated *JW*; *Xu Xiyou ji*, (Shenyang: Chunfeng wenyi, 1986), abbreviated *XXYJ*; *Hou Xiyou ji*, (Hangzhou: Zhejiang wenyi, 1985), abbreviated *HXYJ*; Dong Yue, *Xiyou bu*, (Shanghai: Shanghai guji, 1983), abbreviated *XYB*; Tung Yüeh, *The Tower of Myriad Mirrors*, abbreviated *TMM*. For works in the Chinese original, both the chapter and page numbers are given in citations; for English translations the page number and, when relevant, volume number, are given. There are other punctuated typeset editions, as well as reprints of woodblock editions. Other typeset editions of the sequels include *Xu Xiyou ji*, in *Xiyou ji daxi* 2:1149–1878; *Xu Xiyou ji,* attributed to Ji Gui, (Shanghai: Shanghai guji, 1993), which preserves the commentary of the woodblock edition; *Xu Xiyou ji* (Nanjing), an abridged edition; *Hou Xiyou ji,* in *Xiyou ji daxi* 2:1879–2321; *Hou Xiyou ji* (Beijing). Woodblock reprints are listed in the bibliography; they will be discussed when relevant.
2. See Zhu Yixuan and Liu Yuchen, eds., *Xiyou ji ziliao huibian,* 316.
3. See Huang Yongnian, "Qianyan," 6–7. He argues that the late-Yuan and early-Ming stories about the westward journey are close to the one hundred-chapter edition. He is somewhat uneasy about the high esteem accorded to the "author" of the Ming edition, whoever it is. Zhang Nanquan's assessment of *Hou Xiyou ji* ("*Hou Xiyou ji* de sixiang yu yishu," 141–143) can be applied to other sequels too.
4. Cf. Wang Weimin, "Duiyu *Xiyou ji* de yizhong chanshi: *Xiyou bu* yu *Xiyou ji* de guanxi," 199.
5. Huang Yongnian, "Qianyan," 39; Rolston, *Traditional Chinese Fiction and Fiction Commentary,* 74. For a study of *Shuihu houzhuan* and its author, see Widmer, *The Margins of Utopia*.
6. Rolston studies the sequel as a form of commentary. See his *Traditional Chinese Fiction and Fiction Commentary,* 85–90.
7. Hegel, *The Novel in Seventeenth-Century China,* 232.
8. Plaks, "After the Fall," 553. Rolston has also dealt with this relationship; his discussions will shed much light on my discussion of *Xu Xiyou ji*. See his *Traditional Chinese Fiction and Fiction Commentary,* 213–216, esp. 213.
9. de Bary, introduction to *The Unfolding of Neo-Confucianism,* 13ff; Plaks, "After the Fall," 553ff.
10. Wang Gang, *Langman qinggan yu zongjiao jingshen,* 33; Zhao Shilin, *Xinxue yu meixue,* passim; and Song Kefu and Han Xiao, *Xinxue yu wenxue lungao*.
11. For studies of the relationship between *xinxue* and the traditional Chinese novel, see Plaks, *Four Masterworks of the Ming Novel,* 497–512; and Song Kefu and Han Xiao, *Xinxue yu wenxue lungao*. For *Xiyou ji* in the context of *xinxue,* see Plaks, *Four Masterworks of the Ming Novel,* esp. 240–276; and Song Kefu and Han Xiao, *Xinxue yu wenxue lungao,* 77–109. Guo Mingzhi ("Lun *Xiyou ji* xushu"), however, thinks that the three sequels to *Xiyou ji* constitute a reaction *against* the prevalent *xinxue*.
12. For a study of the Confucian exegetical tradition, see Henderson, *Scripture, Canon, and Commentary of Confucian and Western Exegesis*.
13. de Bary, *Neo-Confucian Orthodoxy and the Learning of the Mind-and-Heart,* 67–131.
14. Ching, trans., *The Philosophical Letters of Wang Yang-ming,* 113; "Da Ji Mingde," in Wang Shouren, *Wang Yangming quanji* 1:214.
15. Cf. the formulation in *Shujing* (Book of documents): "The human mind is precarious: the mind of the Way is subtle" ("Da Yu mo," "The Counsels of Yu the Great"); de Bary,

The Message of the Mind in Neo-Confucianism, 9. Zhu Xi's amplification on this, summarized by de Bary, is particularly relevant (10).

16. Ching, trans., *Philosophical Letters of Wang Yang-ming,* 9; "Da Huang Zongxian, Ying Yuanzhong," in Wang Shouren, *Wang Yangming quanji* 1:146.
17. Ching, trans., *Philosophical Letters of Wang Yang-ming,* 125.
18. Cf. Shenxiu (686–760) in *The Platform Sūtra:* "The body is the Bodhi tree, / The mind is like a clear mirror. / At all times we must strive to polish it, / And must not let the dust collect" (Yampolsky, trans., 130). For studies of the mirror in Buddhism and other beliefs, see Wayman, "The Mirror as a Pan-Buddhist Metaphor-Simile"; Demiéville, "The Mirror of the Mind"; Anthony C. Yu, *Rereading the Stone,* 137–151; and Ching, "The Mirror Symbol Revisited."
19. Li Zhi, "*Xin jing* tigang," in *Fenshu,* 100; see also Zuo Dongling, *Li Zhi yu wan Ming wenxue sixiang,* 146.
20. See Xiaolian Liu's discussions (*The Odyssey of the Buddhist Mind,* 8–11). Liu follows the classification by Murrin, *The Allegorical Epic.*
21. One of Su Xing's criticisms of *Hou Xiyou ji* can be summarized in this way: the sequel, in contrast to *Xiyou ji,* "tells" much and "shows" not enough. This, to different degrees, is true of other works under discussion. See his "Shilun *Hou Xiyou ji,*" 123.
22. Brandauer, "Violence and Buddhist Idealism in the *Xiyou* Novels," 131.
23. The Shanghai guji typeset edition is attributed to Ji Gui. For a study of Mao Qiling's life, see Pei-yi Wu, *The Confucian's Progress,* 173–186.
24. Liu Yinbo, ed., *Xiyou ji yanjiu ziliao,* 452; Liu Yinbo, "*Xu Xiyou ji* zuozhe tuikao," 106–107; Zhang Ying and Chen Su, "Guben *Xiyou* de yibu hanjian xushu," 783–784.
25. See Zhang Ying and Chen Su, "Guben *Xiyou* de yibu hanjian xushu," 783. In his "*Xu Xiyou ji* zuozhe tuikao," Liu Yinbo speculates that Lan Mao is its author and that it is a sequel to the *Xiyou ji* circulated during the Yuan. Su Shi, in "*Xu Xiyou ji* zuozhe wenti chutan," is of the same opinion.
26. This date was first established by Liu Fu, "*Xiyou bu* zuozhe Dong Ruoyu zhuan" (1927), 96.
27. Gao Hongjun, "*Xiyou bu* zuozhe shi shui," and Fu Chengzhou, "*Xiyou bu* zuozhe Dong Sizhang kao." Rolston takes Dong Sizhang's authorship very seriously, suggesting that the book is the labor of both; see his *Traditional Chinese Fiction and Fiction Commentary,* 176–178.
28. Su Xing thinks the book was written between 1649 and 1650. See his "*Xiyou bu* zhong po qinggen yu li daogen pouxi" and "*Xiyou bu* de zuozhe ji xiezuo shijian kaobian" in two installments. Su Xing is not the first to read the short novel as a work of social criticism and protest. Huang Ren in 1907 suggested that Dong Yue's book is a veiled attack on the Qing. See Zhu Yixuan and Liu Yuchen, eds., *Xiyou ji ziliao huibian,* 328–331.
29. Lu Xun, *Zhongguo xiaoshuo shilüe,* (Shanghai guji, 1998), 115–116; Xu Fuming, "Guanyu *Hou Xiyou*"; Su Xing, "Shilun *Hou Xiyou ji*"; Xiaolian Liu, *The Odyssey of the Buddhist Mind,* 275–289; Zhang Ying and Chen Su, "*Hou Xiyou ji* banben kaoshu"; and Guo Mingzhi, "Lun *Xiyou ji* xushu."
30. Among them Sun Kaidi (Liu Yinbo, ed., *Xiyou ji yanjiu ziliao,* 551–552), and Brandauer, "Violence and Buddhist Idealism in the *Xiyou* Novels," 137, n. 2. They, however, did not elaborate on this issue. Interestingly, Qi Yukun, in his *Mingdai xiaoshuo shi* (265–266), considers it a Qing work, whereas Zhang Jun, in his *Qingdai xiaoshuo shi* (99, n. 5), following Su Xing, considers it a late-Ming work.
31. This passage by Yuan Wendian was first noted by Sun Kaidi in his *Zhongguo tongsu xiaoshuo shumu.* See, among others, Liu Yinbo, ed., *Xiyou ji yanjiu ziliao,* 551; Xiaolian Liu,

The Odyssey of the Buddhist Mind, 276; Su Xing, "Shilun *Hou xiyou ji*," 117; Zhang Ying and Chen Su, "*Hou Xiyou ji* banben kaoshu," 238.

32. For discussion on the authorship of Wu Cheng'en, see Wu Yujin (1698–1777), *Shanyang zhi yi,* chap. 4; Su Xing, "Shilun *Hou Xiyou ji*"; Xiaolian Liu, *The Odyssey of the Buddhist Mind,* 275; Zhang Ying and Chen Su, "*Hou Xiyou ji* banben kaoshu." For discussions on the authorship of Tianhua caizi, see Xiaolian Liu, *The Odyssey of the Buddhist Mind,* 277–284; Zhang Ying and Chen Su, "*Hou Xiyou ji* banben kaoshu."
33. This edition is reprinted by Tianyi chubanshe. See "*Hou Xiyou* xu," 1b.
34. This is also the order in *Xiyou ji daxi,* and in Guo Mingzhi's discussion.
35. The only study of this novel in English is Brandauer's "The Significance of a Dog's Tail."
36. Cf. Brandauer, "Violence and Buddhist Idealism in the *Xiyou* Novels."
37. *XXYJ* 1–2 (separate pagination).
38. Ching, *To Acquire Wisdom,* 148.
39. Plaks, *The Four Masterworks of the Ming Novel,* 19. See also Ogawa Yōichi, "Mingdai xiaoshuo yu shanshu."
40. Rolston, *Traditional Chinese Fiction and Fiction Commentary,* esp. 213.
41. The text of the Shanghai guji edition (17) varies from this one, the result of different punctuation. After consulting the reprinted woodblock edition and the text in *Xiyou ji daxi,* I follow this version.
42. XXYJ 1 (separate pagination).
43. *Mengzi* 7A:7. Lau, trans., *Mencius,* 183.
44. Waley, *Three Ways of Thought in Ancient China,* 70. For another translation, see Watson, *The Complete Works of Chuang Tzu,* 134; Watson translates "*ji*" as machine.
45. *Daxue* 1.4. Legge, trans., *The Great Learning,* 1:357–358.
46. *Daxue* 20.18; Legge, *The Great Learning,* 1:413.
47. de Bary, *Neo-Confucian Orthodoxy and the Learning of the Mind-and-Heart,* 76.
48. "Xu [Du?] *Xiyou bu* zaji," *XYB* 3 (separate pagination). This piece is included in the 1853 edition of *Xiyou bu,* with a preface by Tianmushan qiao (Zhang Wenhu, 1808–1885). Su Xing thinks that this piece is by the nephew of the famous scholar Qian Xizuo (1800–1844); see his "*Xiyou bu de zuozhe ji xiezuo shijian kaobian* (shang)," 245. See *Xiyou bu, Shuoku* edition, "Zaji," 1a.
49. *Xu Xiyou ji,* Shanghai guji ed., 6. Here he also suggests that Wan Huayin and the character Subodhi in *Xiyou ji* are both identical and different.
50. *XXYJ* 2 (separate pagination).
51. For Buddhists' mistrust of magic, see, for instance, "The Prophecy of the Magician Bhadra's Attainment of Buddhahood," in Garma C. C. Chang, gen. ed., *A Treasury of Mahāyāna Sūtras,* 3–23.
52. Ching, *The Philosophical Letters of Wang Yang-ming,* 4–5; for Chinese, see Wang Shouren, *Wang Yangming quanji,* 1:805.
53. Graham, trans., *The Book of Lieh-tzu,* 65; for Chinese, see *Liezi* (*Zhuzi jicheng* ed.), 33–34.
54. For stories of transformation, see *Taiping guangji,* chaps. 284–287, 3:2262–2288.
55. Cf. Rolston's insightful remark about the sequel's limitations. "One reason is that many of the sequels are positioned as 'corrective.' This produces two problems: sequels of this kind are more 'reactive' than creative, and they often perversely set out to redo or eliminate precisely what is unique or of most value in the original" (*Traditional Chinese Fiction and Fiction Commentary,* 88).
56. Xiaolian Liu's monograph, *The Odyssey of the Buddhist Mind,* and Brandauer's article,

"Violence and Buddhist Idealism in the *Xiyou* Novels," are the only studies available in English.

57. Dadian (732–824) is a historical figure. That he developed some kind of friendship with Han Yu (768–824) when the latter was exiled to Chaozhou is also a historical fact. See, among others, Hartman, *Han Yü and the T'ang Search for Unity*, 93–99. Han Yu figures as a character in *Hou Xiyou ji*.

58. Descendants of characters in certain novels appear in later works. It reaches such a scale in *Hou Xiyou ji* that all the major characters are descendants of the protagonists of *Xiyou ji*, except for Monk Dadian. Cf. Rolston's discussions of this phenomenon, *Traditional Chinese Fiction and Fiction Commentary*, 199–200.

59. See Martin Huang's discussion on *Xingshi yinyuan zhuan* in *Desire and Fictional Narrative in Late Imperial China*, 153–157; and "Karmic Retribution and the Didactic Dilemma in the *Xingshi yinyuan zhuan*."

60. "*Hou Xiyou ji* xu," *HXYJ* 1 (separate pagination).

61. "Shijiafo hou," in Li Zhi, *Xu Fenshu*, 94.

62. See Jiang, *The Search for Mind*; Huang Tsung-hsi, *The Records of Ming Scholars*, 85–90.

63. "Jishan shuyuan Zunjing ge ji," in Wang Shuoren, *Wang Yangming quanji*, 1:254–256, esp. 255.

64. E.g., *Chu tan ji*, 2:245, 1:143–144.

65. Xiaolian Liu, *The Odyssey of the Buddhist Mind*, 130, notes the *locus classicus* of the term in Buddhist legend. Buddha, in his previous life, is willing to sacrifice his life for half a *gāthā*.

66. Su Xing, in "Shilun *Hou Xiyou ji*," 135, draws a parallel between this monster and figures like Geng Dingxiang (1524–1596), who slandered and persecuted Li Zhi in the name of Confucian orthodoxy, calling Li a heretic.

67. See *Taiping guangji*, 3529; and *Liezi*, chap. 3.

68. Cf. Li Zhi, *Chu tan ji*, 1:144: "These days, those who want to preach true learning of the Tao seek the world-transcending teachings of Confucianism, Taoism, or Buddhism, and escape from the harassment of the wealthy and powerful, absolutely have no other alternative but to take the tonsure and become monks."

69. It seems to be modeled after the following in the parent novel: "Seek not afar for Buddha on the Spirit Mount; / Mount Spirit lives only in your mind. / There is in each man a Spirit Mount stūpa; / Beneath there the Great Art must be refined." (*JW* 4:259; *XYJ* 85.1024).

70. Cf. Xiaolian Liu's discussion, *The Odyssey of the Buddhist Mind*, 103–109.

71. *HXYJ* 1 (separate pagination).

72. Cf. Xiaolian Liu, *The Odyssey of the Buddhist Mind*, 92–94.

73. Ibid., 94–103.

74. For studies of this short novel, see Hegel, *The Novel in Seventeenth-Century China*, 141–166; Brandauer, *Tung Yüeh*; Fu Shiyi, *Xiyou bu chutan*; C. T. Hsia and T. A. Hsia, "New Perspectives on Two Ming Novels; Kao, "A Tower of Myriad Mirrors: Theory and Practice of Narrative in the *Hsi-yu Pu*"; Andres, "Ch'an Symbolism in *Hsi-yu pu*"; I-Chun Wang, "Allegory and Allegoresis of the Cave"; Madeline Chu, "Journey into Desire"; Xu Fuming, "Guanyu *Xiyou bu* zuozhe Dong Yue de shengping"; Zeng Yongyi, "Dong Yue de qingyu shijie: Lüelun *Xiyou bu* de jiegou, zhuti he jiqiao"; Wang Tuo, "Dui *Xiyou bu* de xin pingjia"; Wang Weimin, "Duiyu *Xiyou ji* de yizhong chanshi: *Xiyou bu* yu *Xiyou ji* de guanxi"; He Lianghao, "*Xiyou bu* de qian yu ao"; and Qiancheng Li, *Fictions of Enlightenment*, 90–109.

75. My suggestions are tentative here.

76. Other details are significant too. In the belly of the monster, the pilgrims first think it is the Land of Ghosts (Guiguo) experience all over again: in chapter 20, a black wind blows the pilgrims to that place, ruled by the ghosts of Bull Demon and Jade-faced Princess. The ghosts there live a life of their own and inhabit a country of their own. The pilgrims manage to find a way out. Monkey's adventures in *Xiyou bu* may be regarded as paralleling those of the pilgrims in the Land of the Ghosts. The Dividing Ridge, created by Buddha in *Hou xiyou ji* to keep travelers from the reaching Spirit Mountain, may suggest the bronze wall erected to keep the pilgrims away from the West (*TMM* 48; *XYB* 13). In *Hou Xiyou ji*, the Lesser Sage visits the underworld and debates the ten kings about justice; in *Xiyou bu*, Monkey substitutes for the King of the Underworld and judges the Song traitor Qin Hui.
77. "*Xiyou bu* dawen," *TMM* 193; *XYB* 1.
78. See chaps. 1 and 16: *XYB* 1.1; 16.72. Cf. *HXYJ* 34.292–293. Another interesting detail is the enumerations of Tripitaka's "martial valor," one of which is "leaving . . . mirages at sea without form" (*TMM* 45; *XYB* 3.11).
79. Cf. Xiaolian Liu's discussion, *The Odyssey of the Buddhist Mind*, 177–192.
80. Cf. Andres, "Ch'an Symbolism in *Hsi-yu pu*," 31.
81. "Xu [Du?] *Xiyou bu* zaji," *XYB* 3 (separate pagination).
82. Hegel, *The Novel in Seventeenth-Century China*, 160.
83. Madeline Chu, "Journey into Desire," 656. See also He Lianghao, "*Xiyou bu* de qian yu ao," esp. 348.
84. "*Xiyou bu* dawen," *TMM* 192; *XYB* 1.
85. Cf., for instance, Manting guoke (Yuan Yuling, 1599–1674), preface to "Li Zhuowu"edition of *Xiyou ji*: "The demons are none other than the individual self." Plaks, *The Four Masterworks of the Ming Novel*, 270.
86. See Hegel, *The Novel in Seventeenth-Century China*, esp. 164.
87. See Wang Tuo, "Dui *Xiyou bu* de xin pingjia," 211–212; and Qiancheng Li, *Fictions of Enlightenment*, 103–104.

SIAO-CHEN HU

3

In the Name of Correctness

Ding Yaokang's *Xu Jin Ping Mei* as a
Reading of *Jin Ping Mei*

> Historical figures, past and present, are with no exception under
> the control of the providential abacus, being summed up, divided,
> accumulated, or separated.... What concerns humans is a period
> no longer than days and nights, but Heaven's calculation *(shu)* is
> based on a period of more than tens of hundred of years. What
> humans can see is no more than that of one man or one thing,
> but Heaven's calculation encompasses everything, from the past
> to the future.
> Ding Yaokang, *Tianshi*

DING YAOKANG (1599–1669) completed his novel *Xu Jin Ping Mei,* a sequel to *Jin Ping Mei,* in 1660,[1] sixteen years after the Manchus took over Peking. At the time, the Qing government was concentrating on the restoration of social and political order as well as economic prosperity, and probably more than half a century had passed since *Jin Ping Mei* first began to circulate.[2] Mostly thanks to its eroticism, *Jin Ping Mei* had become the most controversial narrative in Chinese literary tradition. Its sequel did not enjoy any better luck. The author got himself into trouble and was sent to jail in 1665,[3] and the novel was subsequently banned.[4] Considering that the Qing government, in the name of restoring moral and social order, was at that time engaged in banning "improper" works, and considering that the novel was viewed as the direct descendant of its "infamous" precursor, the banning of *Xu Jin Ping Mei* should have come as no surprise. What complicates the problem are the disagreements about the nature of *Xu Jin Ping Mei*. First, Ding was not accused of eroticism in his novel; there were obviously political factors behind the banning incident.[5] Also, modern critics tend to read the novel as a political critique. Second, Ding did not think of himself as continuing an erotic story. On the contrary, by writing the sequel, he claimed to have come up with a more respectable reading of *Jin Ping Mei* and to be offering a worldview that, because it was borrowed from popular morality books, was vital to humankind in a time of chaos. All this resists simplifying *Xu Jin Ping Mei* as merely a continuation of an erotic novel. The controversies imply continuities as well as discontinuities between the original and the sequel, and they encourage a reinterpretation of *Xu Jin Ping Mei*. To this end, I would like to ask the following questions: first, why did Ding choose to write a sequel to *Jin Ping Mei* instead of to another novel of the time? Second, in writing a sequel to *Jin Ping Mei,* why did Ding base his novel on the idea of karmic retribution and structure it in such a way as to incorporate popular morality books? And how did he argue that even *Jin Ping Mei,* not just his own sequel, was an anti-erotic novel? In short, why did he think it was important to read *Jin Ping Mei* correctly? Finally, what does *Xu Jin Ping Mei* tell us about Ding Yaokang and his time? I will explore these questions and thus hope to contribute to a better understanding of certain aspects of the general rhetoric of *xushu*, which, as many have observed, made up one of the predominant literary forms of expression in the seventeenth century. In addition, I will try to demonstrate how Ding interpreted the tumultuous historical events he was witnessing, that is, the transition from the late Ming to the early Qing.

Xu Jin Ping Mei develops along two plot lines. The first narrates the story of the original characters who are still living, such as Yueniang, Xiaoge, and Dai'an. The second plot line describes how characters such as Ximen Qing, Ping'er, and Jinlian, who died in the original, return to their next lives and pay their karmic debts. The two plot lines sometimes merge, and historical figures such as Emperor Huizong, Zhang Bangchang, and Qin Hui also appear in certain episodes. When the Jurchen army invades China, Yueniang and her son experience many difficulties while trying to escape. They return home to live in peace only after both mother and son have converted to Buddhism. In the meantime, the dead also continue their stories. Ximen Qing is reincarnated as the son of a wealthy family. He squanders all his fortune and dies a beggar. Ping'er in her next life is sold into prostitution. She commits suicide after being betrayed by her lover. Jinlian in her reincarnation marries an impotent cripple, who is the reincarnation of Chen Jingji. Jinlian becomes a "stone woman" after a demonic sexual encounter and decides to become a nun. Chunmei in her next life becomes the concubine of a Jurchen. She is tortured badly by the first wife and finally becomes a nun. The first wife turns out to be none other than the reincarnation of Sun Xue'e, whom Chunmei had mistreated and tortured in the original novel. Although the major characters of *Jin Ping Mei* continue their stories, either in this life or in the next, it is easily noticeable that the sequel diverges from *Jin Ping Mei* in its tone, style, and concerns. For example, although all the major characters of *Jin Ping Mei* are present, *Xu Jin Ping Mei* no longer tells its story in a domestic circle. Nor does it emphasize the revelation of domestic evils. Rather, in the sequel the characters are scattered around various places in China, and each is shown as having the fortune he or she deserves. In short, unlike *Jin Ping Mei*, the sequel does not even pretend to tell a story under the rubric of a domestic novel. Whereas the most eye-catching feature of *Jin Ping Mei* is its eroticism, the sequel writes against it in every possible way. This is a point that I will further elaborate on later. Actually, *Xu Jin Ping Mei*, given its radically new focus of interest, seems to have borrowed only the fame of the original. This allowed Ding to write his sequel not for the purpose of continuing the story of *Jin Ping Mei*, but to expose the corruption of the Ming government and criticize the cruelty of the Manchu troops that invaded China. The historical setting of the wars between the Song and the Jurchens was borrowed only to conceal Ding's true political intention.[6] Some critics have come to the conclusion that while the original novel emphasizes moral decline in the framework of a household, the sequel tends to emphasize social chaos and human suffering during wars.[7] I contend that the chaotic "social environment" at the end of *Jin Ping Mei* is much more than a convenient historical setting for Ding. It was chosen to help explain the transition of dynasties and the functioning of the universe. I also think that Ding's agenda in *Xu Jin Ping Mei* is more complicated than a political criticism of corruption and tyranny. It is actually a philosophy on the ties between individual and collective fates.

Considering the great length (at least one-sixth of the book) and intense emotion that are dedicated to the description of the dynastic fall, we must acknowledge that the author must have meant *Xu Jin Ping Mei* to be a reflection on the last decade of the Ming dynasty. Besides, when Ding wrote the sequel, less than twenty years had passed since the dynastic transition, and the memory of the mid-seventeenth-century crisis must still have been fresh in his mind. We have every reason to expect such a serious literary work to deal with the crisis in one way or another, consciously or unconsciously. Scholars in the past have argued that Ding decided to write a sequel to *Jing Ping Mei* not because it was a famous erotic novel with appeal to a large audience, but because the historical background of the Song-Jurchen wars was analogous to the conflict between the Ming and Qing.[8] However, this theory does not explain why he chose to write a sequel in the first place by confronting the erotic nature of the original and dramatically increasing the presence of supernatural retribution, which had already played a role in the original.[9] Ding may have had personal access to *Jin Ping Mei*,[10] but this hardly explains why he found it interesting enough to write a sequel. To answer these questions, especially why Ding wrote a sequel that diverged from the spirit of the original, I believe we have to start with the nature of the sequel as a literary form. I want first to propose two principles through which we can understand this form. First, a sequel basically represents its author's "reading(s)" of the original. Second, it also represents the author's understanding of the audience of the original. Taking *Xu Jin Ping Mei* as an example, we will consider how it functions along these lines.

Jin Ping Mei has always been a problematic work, and the consensus is that there are various ways of reading it. The seventeenth-century commentator

Zhang Zhupo's theory, as espoused in his essay "How to Read the *Jin Ping Mei*," is probably the most familiar. Zhang cautioned that "those who read it and find it enjoyable are a source of anxiety to the *Jin Ping Mei*."[11] Later, commenting on the "four masterpieces of novels," another seventeenth-century reader, Liu Tingji, argued that whether or not one knew "how to read" made immense difference. Those who read *Jin Ping Mei* and learned to pity were bodhisattvas, he insisted, and those who read and wanted to imitate were beasts. Liu was very pessimistic about ordinary people's reading capability and endorsed the Qing government's policy of banning dangerous books.[12] *Xu Jin Ping Mei* exhibits similar worries. The argument starts with this diversity of interpretations. The preface by Nanhai airi laoren starts off by saying,

> There are people who do not know how to read *Jin Ping Mei* correctly. The book intends to abstain from the obsession with desire, yet it turns them to such an obsession. The book intends to abstain from carnal lewdness, yet it turns them to carnal lewdness.[13]

The preface by Xihu diaoshi[14] says,

> There are myriad *xiaoshuo* [novel] works in this world, but only three are called masterpieces, i.e., *Shuihu*, *Xiyou*, and *Jin Ping Mei*. Why is that? . . . They all use the technique of explicit, exaggerated and indulgent language. Their intention, however, is to conceal, criticize and admonish (evils). Only those who do not know how to read will label these books as being weirdly supernatural, violent, or licentious and think they have violated the way of the sages. It is beyond their comprehension that novels are powerful enough to enhance the influence of the teachings of the sages and the classics.[15]

The prefaces argue for one correct reading of masterpieces like *Jin Ping Mei*. According to this view, any reading other than the correct reading is not only false, but dangerous, often leading to disastrous results on the reader's part. Certainly, similar arguments are often used to defend controversial works. What concerns us here, however, is the fact that they insist on one single way of reading.

Ding Yaokang shared this fear of an incorrect reading. Throughout *Xu Jin Ping Mei* he repeatedly expresses his worries on this issue. He also demonstrates a strong desire to unify the readings, establish the correct reading, and prevent false and dangerous readings. He begins his novel by offering his own reading of the original, taking it as a serious work that teaches the reader how to live. He also condemns those who misread *Jin Ping Mei*, saying they have committed a crime in doing so.

> The novel *Jin Ping Mei* intends to preach. It depicts how those who are debauched and greedy get proper retribution in this life. . . . (However), when people read about the episodes at the Kingfisher Feather Pavilion (Feicui Xuan) and the Grapevine Arbor (Putao Jia), their desires are aroused. When they read about Ximen being promoted, having children,

building houses, having women and enjoying song and dance, they forget that he dies from sexual exhaustion. Instead they call it seizing the moment to have fun and treat the chilling episodes such as the widows crying at the grave and Chunmei returning to the old establishment as less than common. There is no way to redeem their licentious and indulgent hearts. I have witnessed how this novel was turned into a guidebook for debauchery. . . . These people have turned the author's good intention into hell. What a great crime![16]

By condemning people who "misread" *Jin Ping Mei,* Ding also condemns in advance people who very likely will also "misread" his own work as no more than an erotic novel. Thus done, the legitimacy of his work is confirmed. Ironically, though, the "correct" reading proposed by Ding himself and his two friends never corresponds to the reading by those "censors," that is, the "official" reading delivered by the imperial government. The fortune of *Jin Ping Mei* tells that the official reading is precisely what these early critics would call the "wrong" reading. The political authority has proven itself to be an unqualified reader that does not know how to read, according to Ding's theory, and has actually committed a crime by misreading *Jin Ping Mei.* As we have seen, though, *Xu Jin Ping Mei,* as a "good" reading of its controversial precursor, did not have any better luck. Like its predecessor, it, too, was banned by the imperial government. Ding would no doubt argue that it was banned because it was misread, just as *Jin ping mei* was misread and subsequently banned. As I have said, *Xu Jin Ping Mei* should be understood as Ding's reading of *Jin Ping Mei;* ironically, it also repeats the fate of the original, though to a much less impressive degree.

Ding understood perfectly that "misreading" was inevitable. Words, according to him, always conceal the truth. This is shown in the novel's distinctive structure. Before the novel begins, Ding includes a "Fanli" (Editorial principles), a bibliography, a piece titled "*Taishang ganying pian* yinyang wuzi jie" (The interpretation without words of *Taishang ganying pian*)," and a preface to that piece. In the preface he states,

> I have heard that the way of Heaven should be concealed. If one tries to interpret it with language he only makes it shallow. I have also heard that the human heart is difficult. If one tries to confine it by rules he only pushes it away. The best way to interpret is to interpret without words.[17]

Thus said, Ding tries to develop his notion of the uselessness and even danger of language. *Taishang ganying pian* (The supreme tractate of actions and retributions), which had great influence on Ming-Qing society, is a popular morality book on karmic retribution. Ding was saying that his fear of language had to do with his belief in supernatural retribution. But surprisingly, the so-called "*Taishang ganying pian* yinyang wuzi jie" is in fact an exact "reprint" of text of the original morality book itself, with neither notations nor commentaries. If *Taishang ganying pian* stands for the way of heaven, as Ding claims, by adding no words of interpretation to it, he has managed to avoid making its truth shallow.[18] However, paradoxically, words are so fatally attractive to a writer that Ding ended up writing a novel of sixty-four chapters to interpret the way of heaven! By suggesting that *Xu Jin Ping Mei* itself serves as the annotation to *Taishang ganying pian,* Ding is undermining his previous denunciation of language, because after all his writing, too, is composed of words that conceal truth. It should come as no surprise, then, that his writing will inevitably surrender to others' mis/readings and mis/interpretations. Interestingly, though he puts so much emphasis on reading novels correctly, Ding himself has been accused of misreading the original. "Ding Yaokang was not a reader who truly understood the author of *Jin Ping Mei*," one modern scholar complained, presumably because his use of the idea of retribution and the divergence from the domestic framework set the sequel apart from the original.[19] Who could be considered *the* perceptive reader? Who has the interpretive authority? These questions concerned Ding and will always haunt *Jin Ping Mei* and its sequel.

Having related *Xu Jin Ping Mei* to the original on the question of reading, we also need to examine whether Ding tries to keep in line with *Jin Ping Mei* in terms of themes. Ding makes it clear that he has tried to be consistent with the plot of the original, though he may not always succeed. In the "Fanli" section of *Xu Jin Ping Mei* he makes the following apology.

> There are dates and events in my book that may not be consistent with the original. For example, Ying Bojue has been reported dead, but in my book he is brought to life again. I simply say there has been a false report of death and thus explain the inconsistency away. In the original, Xiaoge is already ten years old. In my book he is said to leave home at the age of seven. I have done this to emphasize the young boy's tender age and his widowed mother's loneliness. It is because I need to enhance the general effect that I ignore those minor inconsistencies. When I travel I do not have the original text with me and my time is limited. This is the reason I often make mistakes. I hope the reader will ignore them.[20]

Ding expresses his wish to continue the stories from the original, despite the fact that he cannot avoid some inconsistencies. But there is a very important aspect of *Jin Ping Mei* that no reader can ignore: its erotic or obscene elements. With a didactic intention in mind, Ding must have found this aspect difficult to handle. In the "Fanli" section he argues,

> This book of mine aims at admonishing lewdness. Yet still there are chapters called the "playful sections" *(youxi pin),* which will inevitably commit the sin of using erotic language. I do this for fear that the serious language of didacticism *(fayu zhi yan)* will be inconsistent with the original.... Therefore I try my hand at erotic language in these chapters. But I always turn to a moral argument right afterward, so that readers will regret and fear having been aroused.[21]

This is indeed a true dilemma! Ding's reading of *Jin Ping Mei*, no matter how moral he wants it to be, can never be so blind as not to see the eroticism in it. While obscenity causes much of the "false" reading of *Jin Ping Mei*, it worries the author of the sequel. But how does he manage to maintain consistency without "arousing sexual desire and spreading obscenity"?

Ding appears to be rather self-confident. He believes that the dilemma is in fact a great opportunity to demonstrate his writing skills. Here is his theory of writing a successful moral novel with erotic elements.

> Those who write to preach often discuss religious concepts through eroticism. Readers should pay attention not to take false as true. *Jin Ping Mei* describes how Pan Jinlian and Chunmei play sex games at the grapevine arbor, and readers to this day still have fun reading about it. But the novel also describes how Jinlian's sexual desire causes Ximen Qing's death over one night. She then quickly turns to Chen Jingji for an adulterous relationship, not mindful of Ximen Qing's love for her at all. As for Chunmei, who also has sex with Chen Jingji, she comes under the custody of Commander Zhou and, having given him a son, becomes his official wife. But she still cannot get rid of desire, so she entertains Chen Jingji again, and finally dies from having excessive sex. Their cases are clear and alarming. What a pity that readers ignore the latter half of the story and are constantly obsessed with the erotic episodes in the former half. If no one comes forward to explain what happens to these people in the next life, how can the desire that has been aroused be extinguished! Now I pick up the story and will describe their fortunes in the next life, and I will tell how much they enjoy and how much they suffer. If I do not describe it vividly, the reader will not be interested. Yet if I describe it too vividly, I will again arouse the reader's desire. Then they will say this person who writes the sequel to *Jin Ping Mei*, instead of preaching morality through the description of the mundane world, still arouses desire and spreads obscenity. My solution is to heat up for a while then cool down for a while, making the reader itch one moment and sore the next. This will demonstrate the creativity and flexibility of my brush.[22]

This long passage appears in the beginning of chapter 31, when Jingui (the reincarnation of Jinlian) and Meiyu (the reincarnation of Chunmei) are about to meet again and develop a lesbian relationship. As I have mentioned, throughout the book Ding is always conscious of his audience. This consciousness impels him to take a particular writing strategy, as he claims here. The major purpose of this "heat/cold" writing strategy is to keep the reader distant from the alluring power of the text: their being too involved is precisely the reason why *Jin Ping Mei* is repeatedly misread. According to his argument, the "correct" reading in fact depends on the "correct" writing. However, the "heat/cold" strategy can hardly be called Ding's invention. According to Zhang Zhupo's analysis, the first half of *Jin Ping Mei* is "hot" and the second half is "cold," but "in the first half there is 'cold' in the 'heat' and in the second half there is 'heat' in the 'cold.'"[23] And as Plaks explains, the cold/heat terminology appears in many critical writings, often referring to "the contrasting qualities of feverish activity or excitement and the corresponding 'coolness' of tranquility, loneliness, or unreality."[24] Elsewhere Plaks has convincingly argued that the shifts between temperatures in *Jin Ping Mei* itself are designed to reflect more abstract variables, and the humor in the description of sex scenes also aims to tone down the reader's possible excitement.[25] What, then, sets Ding's strategy apart from the "heat/cold" design of its precursor?

What Ding conceives as "correct" writing is based on two important principles. The first one is the emphasis on the notion of retribution. As pointed out, many novels of the mid-seventeenth century seem to be obsessed with retributive concepts.[26] This of course brings us to the relationship between *xiaoshuo* and *shanshu* (morality books). Not only did the popularity of novels coincide with that of morality books, but the texts of novels show many signs of influence from morality books.[27] *Taishang ganying pian*, which originated in the Southern Song and which serves as the major basis of Ding's novel, is one of the best-known texts in this genre. It was very popular in the Ming and Qing periods, particularly during the period of dynastic transition.[28] Originating from Daoist beliefs, *Taishang ganying pian* nevertheless preaches Confucian values of social order.[29] In general, the knowledge system of *shanshu* can be understood as a way of social control at the service of the elite class.[30] Works known as *gongguoge* (ledgers of merit and demerit) encourage individuals to stay in their proper roles for the sake of maintaining social order.[31] The theoretical basis of the *shanshu* and *gongguoge* is cosmic power, manipulation of fate, and supernatural retribution, all of which help to shape the moral framework of *Xu Jin Ping Mei*. In fact, belief in karmic retribution is so pervasive in *Xu Jin Ping Mei* that it is impossible to treat the notion of retribution as an insignificant facade that serves only to conceal the author's true message. Retribution is also a theme in Ding's other works as well. His *Tianshi* (The history of heaven), written around 1630, represents his cosmic views and historical perspectives. In the book he lists 195 serious crimes in history, comments on them, and explains the retributive consequence of each. In its appendix, "Guanjian," he dwells on concepts such as heaven's ordeal, fate and fortune, gods and ghosts, and supernatural retribution.[32] His dramas, such as *Chisong you* (The quest of Chisong the immortal), also contain retributive ideas.[33] All of this evidence leads us to believe that Ding was consistent in his belief in retribution throughout his writing career.[34] Ding's novel is therefore based on three foundations, as he states in the beginning of the book: "Now I will teach *fa* (the truth) for all the living things. I will follow the notion of retribution in the Buddhist scriptures, abide by *Quanshan lu* (Records of reformation) and *Ganying pian*, two works that have been promulgated by the emperor . . . and use the book *Jin Ping Mei*. I will then explain how retribution takes place in hell as well as in this world."[35] Among the three foundations, the Buddhist scriptures are the origin of the notion of retribution, *Taishang ganying pian* is the popular and still official version of how retribution works, and *Jin Ping Mei* is the text where he tries to enact the process of retribution. Moreover, *Jin Ping Mei* is the text that has been condemned, the text that has been misread, and the text that Ding tries to save. But it is also the text that will eventually challenge Ding's own novel internally. His religious beliefs, the controversial parent text, and his own sequel that aims to be erotic yet moral—these elements inevitably conflict with each other. What exactly, we need to ask, constitutes Ding's version of retribution and how does he present it in the novel?

Ding first impresses the reader with his strong belief in the eventual actualization of a providential plan. For example, in chapter 8 the narrator makes the following comment on the fortune of two villains: "Now, Lai'an and Xiaoqiao got the gold through an act of robbery. If they should have prospered from this, where are the principles of Heaven? Where are the gods and ghosts?"[36] Such beliefs compel the author to present the eventual downfall of the two villains. We must pay attention to how Ding presents this belief in retribution in the form of a precise calculation. The model of calculation has everything to do with the tradition of morality books, especially *Taishang ganying pian* and the ledgers of merit and demerit. In chapter 4 the narrator alludes to a long passage from *Taishang ganying pian* that appeals to supernatural power.

> Let me quote the *Ganying*. Heaven and Earth have installed a god in charge of people's sins. He will deduct from a person's destined life span *(rensuan)* according to the sins that he has committed. Once his share is deducted, he will be impoverished and diminished. He will often encounter worries and anxieties; other people will resent him, and disasters will follow him. Once his share is exhausted he will die. There is also a god called Ertai beidou shenjun above each person's head. He records the person's sins and mistakes, then deducts from his life span accordingly. There are also worm-gods that are called Sanshi shen in the midst of a person's body.[37] They report the person's sins and mistakes to Heaven periodically.[38] The more he speaks of a man's sins, the sooner he will die. On the last day of each month the god of the kitchen will do the same.[39]

For a modern reader, this may be no more than superstition. It was important and completely compelling, however, to many late Ming-early Qing intellectuals. Their obsession with retribution can be understood in different ways. Their desire to climb the ladder of success, anxiety at the failure of Confucian ideologies to maintain social and political stability, and concern about self-cultivation and individual responsibility—all these factors contributed to the intellectual preoccupation with the issue of karmic retribution.[40] Ding lists fifty-nine sources in his bibliography, including *shanshu*, Buddhist and Daoist scriptures, histories, *xiaoshuo*, essays, and popular songs. This bibliography delineates the framework of Ding's discourse; his plot, characters, and arguments are all determined by this symbolic context. The *Taishang ganying pian* is listed at the top of the bibliography, signifying its leading role. I think one important idea derived from *Taishang ganying pian* that dominates *Xu Jin Ping Mei* is that of *suan* (calculation, scheme), as we see in the quote above. In the context of that passage the word "*suan*" refers to the length of a person's life span, yet it also carries the meaning of "counting" and "calculation." Life is understood as something very concrete, something that can be put into mathematic terms and be counted, summed up, added to, or subtracted from. A very simplified version of life it may seem, yet only when this process of calculation works can

Ding tell his tale of retribution coherently and precisely. In writing the novel, he plays the role of God. He takes charge of human lives, diligently counting and judging their sins and evils, distributing punishments.

The author's playing the role of the calculating god is best demonstrated by the case of Yueniang's gold and jewelry. This episode extends from chapters 2 to 9, with threads and clues appearing intermittently. Yueniang packs up her jewelry and gold before she flees from the Jurchen troops. One of her servants, collaborating with an acquaintance, steals the jewels from her. When the robbery case is brought to the court it causes more avarice and henceforth more crime, but in the end everybody who has sinned gets the punishment he or she deserves. We can easily understand this episode as a critique of the corruption of both the human mind and the juridical system; however, Ding seems to have a different vision. In addition to his critical attitude, his story is told to demonstrate how the providential process of calculation works. He argues that heaven's principles cannot possibly allow Yueniang to keep the fortune, as it is obtained by Ximen Qing through illegal means.[41] The robbers, having acted against the principles of heaven, should definitely be executed;[42] and again, the greedy judges should also be punished accordingly.[43] Throughout the novel, each time a character receives his or her deserved punishment, Ding will remind the reader that heaven's calculations have worked again.

The emphasis on the precision of calculation throughout the novel has a distinctive characteristic—money and commodities, undoubtedly this-worldly, are always used as the metaphor for providential calculation. The most prominent example of this formula is the fate of Shen Jin'ge, alias Shen Huazi (Beggar Shen), the reincarnation of Ximen Qing. Before Jin'ge is born, his father, a miser, dreams of a piece of gold brick; therefore he names his boy Jin'ge (Golden Boy). However, the boy is born blind. During the Jurchen invasion, the Shen family loses their fortune and has to beg for food. At this time, the miser has a dream in which a messenger again delivers to him a piece of gold brick.[44] After the miser dies of hunger, his son gets to keep the brick and continues to live as a beggar. According to the novel, the gold brick is a gift from the king of hell before Ximen is sent for reincarnation.[45] Having nothing valuable other than the brick, Beggar Shen keeps it with him for every minute of his short life. When he dies at the age of nineteen, it is said that he has "used up the gold brick."[46] What Shen deserves in this life is metaphorically represented by the gold brick, and the metaphor reveals the author's view of fate and karmic retribution. In the novel we find many episodes about retribution that are based on the metaphor of money, including the case of Yueniang's gold and jewelry mentioned above. Another significant image of retribution that links the beginning and the end of the novel is a string of pearls, which is said to have been brought to the Ximen household by Li Ping'er from Hua Zixu's. The pearls, representing the debts that Ping'er and Ximen owe Hua, are used to link all the episodes together. The pearls cannot be returned to the sea until all debts are cleared.[47] In addition to these major images, there are also minor episodes about retribution that use the metaphor of money. For example, in chapter 5, in the nether world, Ximen Qing is rescued by Chang Shijie when Ximen is about to cross the river. The narrator explains that when he was alive, Ximen gave Chang fifty taels of silver and a coffin, so Chang has come back to repay him at this particular moment.[48] In chapter 12, a country scholar named Liu willingly offers help to the impoverished Yueniang only because he still owes the Ximen household a small amount of money. He gets rewarded in the end for this act of kindness. Also, in chapter 16 Shen San, the father of Shen Huazi, becomes a beggar because he has been making high-interest loans and causing others to suffer. Poverty is his punishment for unjustly manipulating money. Another example is associated with a historical figure, the minister Cai Jing. Chapter 17 describes how he has led an extravagant life, wasting an astonishingly great quantity of money and food. After he is executed, his mother is not even allowed by heaven to share a single grain of rice that a monk has saved from the leftovers of the former Cai household. Ding's theory about this incident is that each human being, from the emperor on down, has a predestined portion of prosperity. If one wastes too much and "overspends" his lot, misfortune will occur.[49] The novel inherits this viewpoint from the *shanshu*, especially the ledgers of merit and demerit. Good deeds can be accumulated, just as a merchant can accumulate money. Likewise, bad deeds can be accumulated, too. Here the result is the dwindling of one's "moral capital" and the diminishing of his fortune.[50] The perfect symbol for this process is the supernatural abacus, a recurrent motif in Ding's writings as well as many other seventeenth-century stories and works of fiction.[51]

All the examples of retribution in *Xu Jin Ping Mei* point to one theme: the precision of the retributive process. The theory, in accordance with *Taishang ganying pian,* states that everything that happens in the world can be explained rationally, and human beings should never question the rightness of the fates heaven metes out to them. This theory of precision is exemplified by the fortune that the author assigns to each of the major characters. Consider Yinping, the reincarnation of Ping'er, Jingui, the reincarnation of Jinlian, and Meiyu, the reincarnation of Chunmei. Yinping is brought up by the famous courtesan Li Shishi. She has a brief romance with a handsome young man, is soon abandoned, and then commits suicide (chap. 26). Jingui and Meiyu, on the other hand, being close friends, are brought up in poor families. Meiyu is taken as a concubine and is mistreated by the first wife; finally she becomes a nun (chap. 48). Jingui is born with uncontrollable sexual desire, but she suffers from a strange disease and is transformed into a *shinü* (a woman with defective sexual organs). She also becomes a nun in the end (chap. 47). The narrator fears the reader will get the wrong impression, so he eagerly indicates to the reader how precise these retributions are.

> My readers, you might say, "In the original Jinlian and Chunmei have committed too big a crime of licentiousness. We have not seen them pay the price, but now they escape by becoming Buddhist nuns! Ping'er, on the other hand, has committed a lesser crime of licentiousness. How come she receives a heavier punishment of death?" You have failed to understand that the crimes one commits in the last life and the lot one

enjoys in this life are both taken into account. In the past life Ping'er's first husband dies from too much anguish for her. She then snatches his money away to marry again. She has sinned just like Jinlian and Chunmei. In this life she is born to the rich household of General Yuan, and when she is led to Li Shishi's place, she is also cherished. She literally grows up among pearls, jades and silk. After that, she is adored by Zheng Yuqing. He takes care of her no matter how cold or hot the whether is, and has sex with her day and night. She has had everything: instruments to play, food to eat, and clothes to wear. She has enjoyed richness to the highest degree. On the other hand, Jinlian and Chunmei are born to families of low-ranking, poor officials. They are orphaned and widowed and have to wander everywhere. They are impoverished all their lives, without the opportunity to find husbands. They suffer from misfortunes, are struck by disease and deprived of sexual pleasures. Such suffering has paid most of their debts. They deeply regret what they have done. There are always adjustments in Buddhist retribution. Therefore they are given the chance to repent and prevent more calamities. They have to cultivate themselves to restore their original place. In the end, though Ping'er dies, she is immediately reborn as a male. But Jingui and Meiyu, though having become nuns, have to live three lives as women, before they can be reborn as men. If we want to distinguish between different degrees of licentiousness, we must trace the retribution for three lives.[52]

This argument tries to assure the reader of the precision of retribution and reinforce their belief in destiny. However, the fact that the author has to defend the dispensation also implies that there will always be questions about the operation of retribution. As he believes that only "correct" writing can ensure "correct" reading, Ding finds himself having to argue and explain constantly, whereas the text itself continues to generate doubts and questions. This is particularly apparent when Ding extends his theory of retribution to the account of national affairs.

Because the late Ming-early Qing intellectual preoccupation with retribution can be partly explained by sociopolitical chaos, Ding's effort to account for the fate of the nation in terms of retribution merits a close examination. *Xu Jin Ping Mei* is generally read as a loyalist text (the author has himself appear in the novel in a snow-white gown and a crimson-red cap, mourning the collapse of the Ming).[53] But it has also been argued that in "real" life Ding did not stick to loyalism and nationalism for too long after the Manchus took power. While most people looked at the dynastic transition from the perspective of national conflict, Ding considered it in terms of destiny and retribution.[54] I have no doubt that Ding felt great pain witnessing the fall of the Ming, yet I also believe that he was already prepared to accept the new ruler by the time he wrote *Xu Jin Ping Mei*.[55] Indeed, in the novel his efforts are more focused on how to understand dynastic transitions in history than on criticism of the foreign power. Ding's reflection on the fall of the Ming dynasty is based on one word—avarice—which is again related to the idea of money and commodity. The narrator tells the reader that greed has corrupted the human heart and as a result contributed directly to fall of the dynasty. Talking about natural and human calamities, the narrator explains that they happen because the emperor of heaven resents the avarice and extravagance of human beings. Hell has not enough room to accommodate these souls. He therefore creates predestined disasters, including wars, fires, floods, and banditry so that these greedy people will be swept away and the grand mission of retribution can be accomplished. Human beings, when undergoing these disasters, just take them as heaven's will. They do not even realize that the disaster is the result of the accumulation of everybody's crimes. The dynasty has brought itself to the end through its vanity, extravagance, and laziness. It is never fate![56]

The same process of calculation is again at work, just as when Ding explains individual fortune. For him, the collapse of the Ming dynasty is the result of a mathematical accumulation of crimes.

However, just as the question of individual fate may be raised, Ding also has to deal with doubts generated by his own argument about dynastic decline. Chapter 62, a borrowed episode that has little to do with the plot, deals directly with retribution on the national scale. It tells of a virtuous young scholar who has been summoned by the emperor of heaven to serve as the king of hell for one hundred days. Ding apparently has borrowed this episode from a text called *Huo Yanluoduan* (The verdict by the living king of hell), which is listed in his bibliography.[57] He borrows the story for the purpose of explaining the seemingly undeserved fates of Yue Fei and Qin Hui. If he wants to ensure the reader's confidence in the precision of retribution, he has to take up these two famous cases, which seem to contradict the principle of retribution. The narrator begins the chapter by telling the fate of Yue Fei and Qin Hui, saying that people have questioned and even given up their belief in retribution because of such obvious injustice, and human hearts have not been balanced ever since.[58] Ding then copies the story *Huo Yanluoduan* and makes him investigate the case of Yue Fei and the fall of the Song dynasty. The living king of hell, having looked through the files (*yinguoce*, the record of retribution), finds out that the fates of the Song and the Jurchens, as well as figures like Yue Fei, Qin Hui, and Jin Wuzhu, are predestined according to previous historical events. In other words, though it may look unfair that Yue was executed while Qin lived, these destinies are actually arranged by heaven and have abided by the principle of retribution.[59] The precision of retribution never fails; it is simply beyond human comprehension.

Ding's strategy to ensure "correct" writing and "correct" reading depends completely on the precision of retribution. As long as the reader is constantly reminded of the operation of retribution and the rigidity and precision of it, he will pay attention to the moral teaching in the novel without getting lost in the pleasure of reading. On the other hand, although the author requires belief in retribution, he is very aware of possible questions posed by rational reasoning. For fear that the reader's belief may be shattered by such questioning, Ding raises the questions beforehand, answers them, and tries to incorporate them into his stories of the exact workings of retributive justice. By doing so, he inevitably simplifies human sins and evils as crimes and mistakes, with clear causes (usually avarice) and just punishments. The depth and complexity of human evil is not considered in this theory. For Ding, it should always be easy to tell good from bad; and in the novel he cannot allow any ambiguity between good and evil. Ding appeals to rationalization to explain retribution, and as we know, the belief in rationality is always optimistic. As a result, despite all the gloomy descriptions of corruption and cruelty, the novel still provides the reader with a hopeful vision of future order. This is the correct reading that the author requires from his reader.

Ding's other major effort in *Xu Jin Ping Mei* is his strategy for dealing with erotic description and the problem of sexual desire. As I have mentioned, he is very proud of his writing skill and is convinced that he is able to dissuade the reader from the temptation of the pleasure offered by the erotic text. Two interrelated issues deserve a closer look here: transgression and reproduction.[60] We should begin by looking at Ding's description of sexual activity. In the novel almost all of the chapters that deal with sex are labeled *"youxi pin"* (the playful category), reminding the reader not to "take the false as truth." There are altogether ten chapters of *"youxi pin"* in the novel, including

- Chapter 5—it talks about the sexual desire that remains in the human heart even after death. The interaction between desire and death is another point.
- Chapter 20—it tells about the sex games played by Zheng Yuqing, Li Yinping, and Li Shishi.
- Chapter 23—it is about marriage and adultery. The characters involved are Master Chai, Zheng Yuqing, and Yinping.
- Chapter 32—it is about the sexual affair between two middle-aged women and their aged sexual partner. It is intended to underscore the relationship between sex and death. It also describes lesbian sex between Jingui and Meiyu.
- Chapter 39—it describes a collective orgy in a mysterious religious ritual.
- Chapter 40—it discusses sexual desirability and undesirability.
- Chapter 41—it is about lesbianism.
- Chapter 45—it is about money and sexual desirability.
- Chapter 47—it is about unfulfilled or suppressed sexual desire.
- Chapter 53—it describes the training, selection, and examination of desirable women.

We notice that the first four *"youxi pin"* chapters are arranged in such a way that each is kept at a distance from the other. This structural arrangement perfectly responds to the "heat/cold" strategy of which Ding is so proud. However, starting from the fifth chapter, the *"youxi pin"* chapters become closely linked. Will there be enough spatial and temporal gaps to help the reader cool down? Isn't the author giving the reader too much fun? Hasn't he broken his own rule about the "heat/cold" strategy? And, has he stopped worrying about "correct" writing and "correct" reading?

If we read the novel carefully, we will find that the first concrete description of sexual intercourse appears as early as in chapter 3. Yueniang and her maid Xiaoyu, escaping from the Jurchen troops, stay at a nunnery. During their short stay, the maid witnesses the nuns having sex with a visiting Buddhist monk.[61] This description of sexual intercourse is in exactly the same style as *Jin Ping Mei* and many other erotic novels: the voyeur happens to witness a sexual scene when she tries to go the bathroom. There is also a passage of parallel prose to describe the sexual intercourse using images of weapons, wars, and fatal destruction, all of which are conventional in erotic fiction. Also conventional is the detailed description of the scene of ejaculation. Such a "classic" description of sexual intercourse, significantly, is neither directly related to any of the major characters nor classified as *"youxi pin."* How do we understand the discrepancy between the ten cases of *"youxi pin"* and this exceptional episode?

Consider the ten chapters of *"youxi pin"* again. All of them are associated with sex, but only two—chapters 20 and 41—contain direct and relatively lengthy descriptions of sexual acts. Chapter 20 tells how Zheng Yuqing first approaches the famous courtesan Li Shishi, then seduces her foster daughter Yinping, and finally develops sexual relationships with both. The author again uses parallel prose to describe Yinping's first night with Yuqing,[62] yet the passage is much "milder" than the description of what the maid witnesses in chapter 3. Chapter 41 describes lesbian sex between Jingui and Meiyu. Interestingly, the author adopts more concrete and racier language to describe a lesbian relationship than that used in chapter 20 to describe a heterosexual one. Moxa burning on the human body, one of the typical sex games of *Jin Ping Mei*, also plays a role in chapter 41. If the author takes into consideration the effect of reading, does he believe that the description of lesbian sex gives more pleasure to the reader than heterosexual sex? This question will shed more light on Ding's strategy to guarantee "correct" reading.

Erotic fiction tends to deal with sexual activity in "transgression." Neither conjugal sexual intercourse nor legal market sex is considered an attractive topic for erotic works. It is usually adultery, homosexuality, or multipartner sex that is described in erotic fiction. This is also true in *Xu Jin Ping Mei*. Unlike *Jin Ping Mei*, however, the transgression of sexuality in the sequel goes in a different direction. Sexual desire in the sequel is more subversive and destructive than in the original if we consider the question of reproduction as a feature of sexual activity. According to the rhetoric of erotic literature, sex will eventually lead to death. This death, however, can take two different forms. One is death by exhaustion—sex means sheer loss of personal substance. The other one is death that will contribute to reproduction, and in this case sex means a particular kind of personal growth.[63] In traditional imaginings of sexuality, only successful, heterosexual sex can be reproductive. In *Jin Ping Mei*, although Ximen Qing dies from excessive sex, he does achieve "successful sex" with his beloved Ping'er and his legal wife Yueniang. He thereby produces children. Although

Ping'er's son dies young, Xiaoge survives and allegedly continues Ximen Qing's life. And it is not until the latter half of the novel that the theme of fatal excess is made manifest. *Xu Jin Ping Mei,* on the other hand, never takes up the issue of reproduction. If we examine the erotic scenes in the novel, we will see they are either unsuccessful and incomplete or not heterosexual.

In order to review the sex scenes in *Xu Jin Ping Mei,* we need to divide them into two categories: distorted sexuality and denied sexuality. The first category refers to topics such as sexual abuse. For example, chapter 7 describes how the souls of Ximen Qing, Ping'er, Jinlian, Chunmei, and Chen Jingji are punished in hell. One of the torture scenes, in which Chen Jingji, Jinlian, and Chunmei are put into a pot of boiling oil, is not only shocking, but also thrillingly sensual. The narrator uses phrases like "snowy, tender skin" and "powder-like buttocks" in contrast to phrases like "three piles of bones," "just like a bunch of fried dough twists," and "they must have been fried crisp and numbed, who would know how it feels?"[64] Chapter 36 also has a torture scene, this one involving the number-one courtesan Li Shishi. In a similar way, as the narrator describes how she is whipped by a Jurchen general, the language used is more sensual than anything else. Her buttocks are described as "snowy white, slippery smooth, alluringly fragrant and bouncingly firm," and they are "the roots of clouds and rain." During the whipping, her buttocks "spit out red rain" and her "snow-white skin is split," and she screams "more hotly and dearly than when she is on the pillow and under the blanket."[65] Both examples are descriptions with erotic implication and intense sensuality. The narrator even seems to take sadistic pleasure in the description. Nevertheless, as the scenes contain pain, the author could suppose that the reader will keep some distance from the sensual pleasure offered by the sadistic episodes.

The second category, denied sexuality, has abundant examples in *Xu Jin Ping Mei*. As mentioned earlier, the affair between Zheng Yuqing and Yinping is one of the few heterosexual relationships that is given concrete and detailed description. Their relationship, however, lacks the attraction to get readers involved. In chapter 26, Yinping elopes with Zheng, and they travel by boat. A man from a neighboring boat begins to persuade Zheng to exchange Yinping for another charming courtesan. Yinping is obviously put in a position similar to that of Du Shiniang, the famous courtesan who was betrayed and sold by her lover; however, in the end Yinping is deprived of the noble and moving death enjoyed by Shiniang. She dies a sad but silent death, disappearing into a void and signifying nothing.[66] The episode successfully juxtaposes the pleasure of sex and the emptiness it leads to. We will see more examples of the denial of sexual pleasure.

In *Xu Jin Ping Mei* the readers encounter other erotic scenes that may excite them. Chapter 5 tells how Jinlian and Chunmei meet Chen Jingji in hell. They continue their affair there, but never in the same way as before. Chapter 32 deals with an impotent old man, trying his best to please two insatiable middle-aged women. He tries very hard, only to hasten his own death. Chapter 33 tells how Jingui tries to seduce a young scholar, yet the virtuous young man never recognizes her feelings and desire. Chapter 42 describes how Jingui is haunted and has ghostly sex with a spirit. Chapter 47 tells how Jingui, having had sex with the ghost, develops an incurable disease and becomes a *shinü*, unable to have sex ever after. Significantly, she remains a virgin all her life, because neither her lesbian relationship with Meiyu nor her encounter with the ghost really takes her virginity away. These erotic episodes have the same characteristic, that is, insubstantiality. No matter what playful and seductive language the author uses, it will not change the fact that these sexual scenes are an illusion. The episodes about Jingui are the most symbolic. As the reincarnation of Jinlian, she is expected by the reader to be the major subject of the description of sexual activities. Admittedly, her relationships with Meiyu and the ghost have the author's keenest attention. The description of her sexual experiences is detailed and "vivid" (as Ding says about his writing strategy). Nevertheless, all the possible excitement of her transgressive sexuality is reduced to emptiness. Because of this unproductive emptiness, the author expects the reader to be distanced from the sexual pleasure the text originally promised to generate.

Having reviewed the erotic scenes in *Xu Jin Ping Mei*, we find that Ding is confident of his so-called "heat/cold" strategy as a means of dealing with the problem of sexual desire. As sex is either distorted or distanced, he believes that his novel keeps the reader at arm's length, thus resolving the danger of incorrect reading. However, has he successfully achieved "correct" writing? Or, in just the same way as he presents an overly rigid and precise calculation of retribution, will his writing challenge itself internally?

If we look at the problem in a broader context, we will find that erotic language and Buddhist teachings often coexist in late-Ming fiction. The fact that the discourse of desire and that of religion go hand in hand may seem incomprehensible, yet it reveals an important side of the intellectual milieu at that time. Religions, both Buddhism and Daoism, played a decisive role in many literati minds. *Jin Ping Mei* itself was written under the influence of both religions.[67] The manifestation of desire will finally show the nature of the world, which is emptiness, it is argued. *Xu Jin Ping Mei* should be understood in this context, and its author also states such intentions. However, intentions do not guarantee results. As I have discussed, Ding was aware of the problem and tried to accomplish his mission with a special form of writing. His intentions and strategies are clear, but what about the results? Let us take a look at one character in the novel.

Jingui is the most prominent example of distance and denial in Ding's "correct" writing. As a result, she gives rise to questions. Paradoxically, sexual desire in *Xu Jin Ping Mei* has a tendency to be internalized in the character to whom desire has been denied. In chapter 5, when the ghosts of Jinlian, Chunmei, and Chen Jingji meet each other in hell, their desire does not come to an end simply because they are dead. The narrator raises the question, "Now we will tell about ghosts having sex. I know people will definitely not believe in this and will regard it as a joke. They say ghosts have lost their flesh and skin; so even if they still have the thought, with what will they do it? People who say this have not read the Buddhist scriptures, which say when Heaven and humans come together, they can give birth to men and women just by exchanging looks. As soon as desire is aroused, bodies are no longer important. . . . This is the example of feeling (desire) without substance."[68] To reinforce this idea, the narrator mentions it again in chapter 23, saying, "Here I want to explain only that human desire is born from the original state of emptiness and transformed into our world of phenomena. Human beings are born from this; they also die from this. Birth and death alternate; they always remain in the cycle of retribution and incarnation."[69] Citing Buddhist ideas, instead of expelling them from the human mind, the author has defined desire as the very essence of human beings. Consequently, though the author succeeds in distancing the reader from the pleasure of reading about sex, he has on the other hand understood human interiority as desire itself.

Now consider the case of Jingui, the reincarnation of Jinlian and as a result the reincarnation of sexual desire. According to the story, she experiences several stages of life. At first she is described as a pretty, clever young girl, with a wild imagination of sexual pleasure.[70] However, it is not until chapter 38, in which she attends a mystic religious ritual that worships sexuality, that her deepest desire is completely brought out from her innerness. After this she is able to fathom the depth of desire even though she has not yet experienced any real heterosexual relationship. At this stage, she develops intimacy with Meiyu. When discussing their wild sexual activity, the narrator explains, "The two of them, . . . need neither form nor substance. Whenever there is touching there is communication."[71] Without any substance, the two women are mutually reflective of each other's innerness, which is desire.

Jingui's encounter with the ghost lover is further proof of her innerness as desire. As the narrator says, "If a person's mind is misdirected, all kinds of evils will follow. Evils do not come from outside; they are innate, as in the case of the evil of licentiousness, the evil of desire, the evil of love, and the evil of anxiety. Different states of mind lead to different evils. As for Jingui, she is the reincarnation of Jinlian. Her roots are deeply planted in sexual desire."[72] In other words, the ghost lover is the projection of her desire, or the exteriorization of her innerness. When sex becomes physically impossible for her, her innerness is henceforth blocked. Thus Jingui reaches her last stage. She has become a nun; moreover, she is a nun who cannot be seduced. In chapter 61, near the end of the novel, all the major characters that are still alive get together to worship the bodhisattva Avalokitesvara. In this scene, under the cliff there is a golden plum tree with a trunk as shiny as gold and flowers as pure as jade. The plum tree clearly stands for Jingui (gold) and Meiyu (plum). At this time, two petals fall from a blossom, they fly down slowly, and finally land on the gowns of Jingui and Meiyu.[73] This scene can be read as a symbol of salvation, suggesting that the two women finally get rid of the burden of desire. But it can also be read as the last and unchallengeable proof that their desire is innate and will continue.[74] Indeed, if desire is innerness, how can it ever be expelled?

Ding believes that his writing strategies have ensured "correct" reading. By developing the novel according to the principles of retribution and representing the pleasure of sex in a particular way, he not only keeps the reader mindful of the results of crimes of passion, but also prevents the reader from becoming obsessed with the eroticism in the text. Nonetheless, being the sequel to *Jin Ping Mei,* Ding's text cannot escape internally responding to what is problematic in the original; the inviting power of the text always returns and makes a perfectly "correct" reading impossible. *Xu Jin Ping Mei* is the result of a very self-conscious and deliberate reading of *Jin Ping Mei.* Despite all its attempt to direct reading by writing, *Xu Jin Ping Mei* will always be challenged by all kinds of "misreading" that Ding himself could not bear to see.

The popularity of morality books in the Ming and Qing had much to do with the development of *xiaoshuo.* Ding claims that his *Xu Jin Ping Mei* was written as an annotation to *Taishang ganying pian* and often cites morality books; as a result, some argue that the work is "not only a novel under the influence of *Taishang ganying pian,* but a version of *Taishang ganying pian* under the disguise of a novel."[75] However, when exploring the relationship between the *shanshu* text and the *xiaoshuo* text that coexist in the work, we find it to be extremely intricate and complex. The author diligently emphasizes such *shanshu*-related concepts as fate and retribution in order to prove his didactic intentions and prevent readers from misreading his work. He also attempts to demonstrate a correlation between emptiness and sexual desire. But in fact he can never get away from the different kinds of misreadings of both *Jin Ping Mei* and his sequel. There is a perpetual tension between *shanshu* and *xiaoshuo.* For a writer as self-conscious as Ding, language is inevitably powerful, even awesome. This is why he says, "I have been showing off to the world about the grandeur of my writing, but there's none of it that I can take to see *Yanluo* on my final day."[76] This statement points to the writer's moral anxiety. After the drastic transition, people often looked back at the late Ming and interpreted it as a period of corruption, avarice, desire, and transgression. In short, the late Ming stood for the breakdown of social and moral order. It was many people's understanding that the dynasty collapsed not only because of the invasion of foreign powers, but because of its own disorder and immorality. Writers of *xiaoshuo* also expressed such ideas in their works. In many people's minds, *Jin Ping Mei* came to be interpreted as the epitome of the late Ming—lust in disorder. Put more accurately, in Ding's view, it was not so much *Jin Ping Mei* as the collective misreading of it that corrupted the human heart, giving rise to lust and evils, disrupting social order, and finally bringing about the fall of the dynasty. This is why he began to reflect upon the dangers that writing might cause and why he developed deep regrets about his previous writings as well as great expectations of the moral influence of *Xu Jin Ping Mei.* We must also note that Ding claims he wrote the novel to echo the Qing emperor's resolve to reestablish moral value. We need to consider the fact that Ding personally experienced the crisis of Chinese civilization and the fall of the Ming, and he also witnessed human evils that permeated the society but whose cause and origin were hard to understand. But what finally shaped the problematic nature of *Xu Jin Ping Mei* is that Ding already had made his compromise and realized that he had to live under Qing rule. Reading, and writing a sequel to, the representative novel of the late Ming was his way of explaining the past era and justifying the current situation. As a force to maintain social stability, the *shanshu* was used by Ding as the basis of his novel and a means of resisting the potentially destructive power of fiction. He had serious doubts about language, but in order to explicate providential reason, he could not help but write a novel. For a writer like Ding Yaokang, who had a concern for morality, language has both to be questioned and relied on at the same time. Whether he was successful or not, Ding wanted *Xu Jin Ping Mei* to represent his reading of *Jin Ping Mei,* his soul-searching ponderings over the reasons behind late Ming decadence, and his vision of stability in years to come.

Notes

Epigraph. Ding Yaokang, "Shu," in the appendix "Guanjian " to *Tianshi.* See *Ding Yaokang quanji,* 136–137.

1. There has been some dispute on the dating of *Xu Jin Ping Mei*. Most scholars agree on 1660. See Shi Ling, "*Jin Ping Mei* de zuoqi ji qita," 335; Chan Hing-ho, "Hai'nei fenshu jin shiding," 24–28. Some scholars have proposed the year 1662. See Huang Lin, "Ding Yaokang ji qi *Xu Jin Ping Mei*," 56; and Lin Chen, *Mingmo Qingchu xiaoshuo shulu,* 347. Zhang Qingji, on the other hand, believes that *Xu Jin Ping Mei* was finished by 1658. See his *Ding Yaokang nianpu,* 93. Official trial files have confirmed 1660 as accurate. See An Shuangcheng, "Shun Kang nianjian *Xu Jin Ping Mei zuozhe* Ding Yaokang shoushen an."

2. *Jin Ping Mei* cannot be exactly dated. It is generally believed to be a late-Ming work, written between the Jiajing and Wanli reigns.

3. See Chan Hing-ho, "Hai'nei fenshu jin shiding," 24–28; and Zhang Qingji, *Ding Yaokang nianpu.*

4. Soon after the banning of *Xu Jin Ping Mei* in 1665, a revised version of it titled *Gelian huaying* (Shadows of flowers behind the screen), was published. It strategically deletes all the passages that have political associations, such as those concerning the Jurchen invasion. The narrator's discussions of karmic retribution are also omitted. In doing so, the editor of *Gelian huaying* actually moved away from the fundamental concepts of Ding Yaokang. However, before long it too was banned. Perhaps more interestingly, a new version titled *Jinwu meng* (Dream of the golden chamber) came out in 1915, less than four years after the last Manchu emperor abdicated the throne. This was a time when people were trying to promote nationalism and anti-Manchu sentiments. The editor Sun Jing'an therefore based his work on Ding's *Xu Jin Ping Mei* and restored all those "sensitive" passages related to history and politics. The retribution part is further reduced in this version, something understandable given the fact that this was a time obsessed with science and reason.

5. According to official files, Ding Yaokang was accused of using offensive terms such as "*ningguta*" and "*yupiguo*," which were associated with the origin of the Qing dynasty, and of describing the Manchus as barbarians who ate raw meat and slept with animals; see An Shuangcheng, "Shunkang nianjian *Xu Jin Ping Mei zuozhe* Ding Yaokang shoushen an." Liu Tingji (?–1676), in his *Zaiyuan zazhi* (147) also attributes the banning of *Xu Jin Ping Mei* to its political incorrectness.

6. Zhu Meishu, "Lun *Xu Jin Ping Mei* ji qi shangai ben *Gelian huaying* he *Jinwu meng*," 254–257; Lin Chen, *Mingmo Qingchu xiaoshuo shulu,* 348; Huang Lin, "Ding Yaokang ji qi *Xu Jin Ping Mei*," 58–59.

7. See, e.g., Fang Zhengyao, *Ming Qing renqing xiaoshuo yanjiu,* 74.

8. Huang Lin, "Ding Yaokang ji qi *Xu Jin Ping Mei*," 55–60.

9. Retribution is considered an important theme of *Jin Ping Mei*. For example, Xinxinzi (Master of Delight) says in his preface to the *Jin Ping Mei cihua* that the novel is "to

expound the secrets of flourishing and decay, failure and success, through the inexorable working of karmic cause and effect." Roy, trans., *The Plum in the Golden Vase*, 1:3–5.

10. As a young man Ding traveled to Jiangnan, where he met Dong Qichang, a famous member of the literati who owned a manuscript of *Jin Ping Mei*. See Huang Lin, "Qianyan," in Ding Yaokang et al., *Jin Ping Mei xushu sanzhong*, 3. Ding was also an acquaintance of the Qiu family, which that is said to have owned a copy of *Yujiaoli*, an early sequel to *Jin Ping Mei*. See Huang Lin, "Ding Yaokang ji qi *Xu Jin Ping Mei*," 55. Scholars have also gathered what Ding read to be probably the first *cihua* edition, which was already lost. See Hanan, "The Text of the *Chin P'ing Mei*," 54; Ye Guitong, "Cong *Xu Jin Ping Mei* kan *Jin Ping Mei* de banben yu zuozhe," 90–96.
11. See Roy, trans., "How to Read the *Chin P'ing Mei*," 237.
12. Liu Tingji, *Zaiyuan zazhi*, 104–106.
13. Ding Yaokang, *Xu Jin Ping Mei*, 2.
14. Shi Ling ("*Xu Jin Ping Mei* de zuoqi ji qita," 336) identifies Xihu diaoshi as Zha Jizuo.
15. Ding Yaokang, *Xu Jin Ping Mei*, 3.
16. Ibid., 2–3.
17. Ding Yaokang, *Jin Ping Mei xushi sanzhong*, 10.
18. Luo Derong contends that the *"wu"* represents Ding's understanding of the aesthetic value of novels, referring to a significance that transcends language. I think this is a good alternative interpretation. See his "*Xu Jin Ping Mei* zhuzhi suojie," 165.
19. Wang Rumei, "Ding Yaokang de *Xu Jin Ping Mei* chuangzuo," 160–161.
20. Ding Yaokang, "Fanli," *Xu Jin Ping Mei*, 5.
21. Ibid.
22. *Xu Jin Ping Mei*, 285–286.
23. Roy, trans., "How to Read the *Chin P'ing Mei*," 239.
24. Plaks, "Terminology and Central Concepts," 101–103.
25. Plaks, *The Four Masterworks of the Ming Novel*, 82.
26. *Jingshi yinyang meng*, *Xingshi yinyuan zhuan*, and *Xu Jin Ping Mei* are three good examples. See Martin Huang, "Karmic Retribution and the Didactic Dilemma in the *Xingshi yinyuan zhuan*," 399.
27. Ogawa Yōichi, "Mingdai xiaoshuo yu shanshu," 331.
28. See Sakai Tadao, *Chugoku zensho no kenkyu*. Other morality books and ledgers of merit and demerit were popular at that time. See Brokaw, *The Ledgers of Merit and Demerit*, 110–111.
29. Sakai Tadao, *Chugoku zensho no kenkyu*.
30. Brokaw, *The Ledgers of Merit and Demerit*, 112. See also Sakai Tadao, *Chugoku zensho no kenkyu*.
31. Zheng Zhiming, "Gongguoge de lunli sixiang chutan," 323.
32. See Ding Yaokang, *Ding Yaokang quanji*, 2:130–148.
33. Chan Hing-ho, "Hainei fenshu jin shiding: Ding Yaokang shengping ji qi zhuzuo," 17–18. See also Idema, "Coping with the Conquest," 21.
34. Some scholars believe Ding Yaokang also wrote *Xingshi yinyuan zhuan*, a tale of retribution. See Wang Sucun, "*Xingshi yinyuan zhuan* zuozhe Xizhou sheng kao"; Tian Pu, "*Xingshi yinyuan zhuan* zuozhe shi Ding Yaokang"; Zhang Qingji, "*Xingshi yinyuan zhuan* xinkao; and Feng Chuntian, "Xizhou sheng ji Ding Yaokang." This attribution of authorship remains far from conclusive. However, it is noticeable that both novels are deeply concerned with retribution.

35. Ding Yaokang, *Xu Jin Ping Mei*, 3.
36. Ibid., 74.
37. The Sanshi shen are also called Sanshi chong. The Daoists believe the three worm-gods reside in every human body, record the person's minutest mistakes, and report them to heaven on the *gengshen* days when the person is asleep.
38. The Chinese used Tiangan (The Ten Celestial Stems) and Dizhi (The Twelve Terrestrial Branches) to form a cycle of sixty. The *gengshen* day is the fifty-seventh day in the cycle of sixty.
39. Ding Yaokang, *Xu Jin Ping Mei*, 31.
40. See Martin Huang, "Karmic Retribution and the Didactic Dilemma in the *Xingshi yinyuan zhuan*," 400; and Brokaw, *The Ledgers of Merit and Demerit*, 3, 112.
41. Ding Yaokang, *Xu Jin Ping Mei*, 16–17. Here it refers to chapter 49 of the *Jin Ping Mei cihua*. A servant named Miao Qing murders his employer while traveling together and seizes his fortune. When the crime is revealed, the servant tries to bribe the judge through Ximen's mediation with three hundred taels of gold and one thousand taels of silver. Ximen, however, secretly keeps the gold for himself.
42. Ding Yaokang, *Xu Jin Ping Mei*, 74.
43. Ibid., 107.
44. Ibid., 142.
45. Ibid., 56.
46. Ibid., 473–477.
47. Ibid., 617–619.
48. Ibid., 44.
49. Ibid., 118.
50. "Moral capital" is a term used by Brokaw, *The Ledgers of Merit and Demerit*, 207.
51. For example, in his "Guanjian" he says the fortunes of all people are under the control of the grand abacus. In his drama *Chisong you* he also describes a ghost holding a huge abacus that signifies "the automatic and unfailing efficacy of retribution"; see Idema, "Coping with the Conquest," 21. McMahon (*Causality and Containment in Seventeenth-Century Chinese Fiction*, 16), in explaining the logic of cause and effect in seventeenth-century stories, points out that the idea of the "Great Abacus of the Heavenly Lord" is equivalent to the concept of causality.
52. Ding Yaokang, *Xu Jin Ping Mei*, 466.
53. Ibid., 636. Here the narrator tells about a Daoist immortal who appears as a wild crane with white feathers and red cap. As Ding Yaokang is also known as Yehe (Wild Crane), this episode clearly refers to himself. Red is the symbolic color of the Ming, as the family name of the Ming emperors is Zhu, meaning red. The white gown symbolizes mourning.
54. Chan Hing-ho, "Hainei fenshu jin shiding: Ding Yaokang shengping ji qi zhuzuo," 34–35.
55. His drama *Biaozhong ji* was written around 1656. In this work he clearly expresses his intention to serve the new government. See Chan Hing-ho, "Hai'nei fenshu jin shiding," and Wang Ayling, "Siqing huagong."
56. Ding Yaokang, *Xu Jin Ping Mei*, 119–123.
57. This motif of the living king of hell is also adapted in other stories of the seventeenth century. For example, Feng Menglong has two stories of this motif placed back-to-back in his *Gujin xiaoshuo* (Stories old and new). Story 31 tells the story of a scholar of the Eastern Han who is sent to hell after making many complaints about the injustice of heaven. Yanluo, the king of hell, tries to persuade him that his complaints are all due to human incomprehension of the divine will. The scholar, however, is not convinced and goes on

to investigate the "Four Cases" of the early Han, which refers to the unjust slaughters of Han Xin, Peng Yue, and Ying Bu by Emperor Liu Bang; Liu Bang's ill payback of Ding Gong's (Old Man Ding) good treatment; Empress Lü's torture of Lady Qi; and Xiang Yu's betrayal by his generals. The scholar gives each a fate in the next life that is based on the precise principle of retribution. The emperor of heaven approves his judgments, saying they reveal the ultimate justice of heaven and earth. Story 32 is again about a complaining scholar, this time of the Yuan dynasty. The king of hell summons him, trying to teach him the complicated operation of retribution that often takes place after a person's death. The scholar disagrees with the king because, he says, ordinary people will not be alarmed by afterlife rewards and punishments, and it is little wonder that there are far fewer good people than bad ones. In order to assure the scholar, the king sends him to hell to witness all types of torturous punishments. See Feng Menglong, *Gujin xiaoshuo,* 458–486. The recurrence of the living king of hell motif in the seventeenth century reveals a shared concern for karmic retribution and hidden doubts about the justice in its operation.

58. Ding Yaokang, *Xu Jin Ping Mei,* 624–625.
59. Ibid., 633–634.
60. Bataille, *Erotism,* 96.
61. Ding Yaokang, *Xu Jin Ping Mei,* 26–28.
62. Ibid., 190.
63. Bataille, *Erotism,* 96. Also, in explaining the Greek art of *aphrodisia,* Foucault points out that the sexual act prefigures "the death of the individual while assuring the survival of the species" and "[by expelling their semen,] living creatures did not just evacuate a surplus fluid, they deprived themselves of elements that were valuable for their own existence." Foucault, *The Use of Pleasure,* 125–130.
64. Ding Yaokang, *Xu Jin Ping Mei,* 61.
65. Ibid., 345.
66. Ibid., 249.
67. For its relationship with religions, see Yu Ke and Xie Qinglan, *Jin Ping Mei yu Fo Dao,* 1–13.
68. Ding Yaokang, *Xu Jin Ping Mei,* 47.
69. Ibid., 209.
70. Ibid., 287–292.
71. Ibid., 398.
72. Ibid., 408.
73. Ibid., 620.
74. This episode also reminds the reader of the "Tiannü sanhua" (Heavenly maiden scatters flowers) passage in the Vimalakirti sūtra, where the flowers land only on those who are still tied to the mundane world. See *Weimojie suoshuo jing,* 547–548.
75. Ogawa Yōichi, "Mingdai xiaoshuo yu shanshu," 338.
76. Yanxiadong yiyin, "*Xu Jin Ping Mei* ji xu," in *Xu Jin Ping Mei,* 1.
77. Early Qing narratives such as *Zuixing shi* and *Shuihu houzhuan* focus on the criticism of late-Ming social disorder.

KEITH MCMAHON

4 Eliminating Traumatic Antinomies

Sequels to *Honglou meng*

WE CAN see in the dozens of sequels to *Honglou meng* (Dream of the red chamber) the irresistible urge that authors felt to resurrect the mesmerizing world of Cao Xueqin's original novel. Readers and sequel writers debated the opposing virtues of Baochai and Daiyu. They loved to resent Baochai, Wang Xifeng, and Xiren for "stealing" Daiyu from Baoyu.[1] The unrelenting flow toward dissolution in the latter half of the novel left writers and readers craving a resolution in which the dead came back to life, wronged victims were vindicated, and villains were punished. Sequel writers also longed for stability and thus added chapters about the easygoing daily life of a highly placed family in which people ate well, played games, arranged marriages, and raised children. A number of them also took the opportunity to desublimate the "mind-lust" of the original Jia Baoyu by giving him or his reincarnation[2] multiple sexual partners. Only one of the sequels I have studied—the one known to be by a woman—concludes on something less than a positive note. At the end of *Honglou meng ying* (In the shadow of the dream of the red chamber), Baoyu sees Baochai, Daiyu, and two other women talking and laughing by a balcony railing, ignoring Baoyu, who discovers to his disappointment that the building the women are in lacks a stairway allowing him to reach them.[3]

The sequels in general evoke a nostalgia for the good times of the original novel.[4] Let us conceive of such nostalgia as a psychic mode that reproduces for the subject-reader the perspective of lost innocence. Sequel writers in this case presume that their readers will believe in the masterpiece's original world and will identify with that world in a way that excludes the intrusion of discordant, ironic distance. The sequels eliminate the traumatic antinomies—that is, unresolvable antagonisms—between male and female, adult and child, earthly sorrow and heavenly bliss, or life and death. Eliminating antinomies renders them transparent to each other, causing the boundaries between them to become permeable and traversable. Such an endeavor attempts to insert readers into a kind of eternal, mythic present with which they maintain a willfully naive fascination.

Of course *Honglou meng* itself is nostalgic in its celebration of idyllic premarital life in the Grand Prospect Garden, but in a different way. The particular mark of *Honglou meng*'s nostalgia is to take the untrammeled indulgence of innocent playfulness and infuse it with a subtler message, namely the vacuousness of normative adult social boundaries, in particular those of male and female roles and of the adult-dictated mission of marriage and family reproduction. Furthermore, *Honglou meng* undermines the idyllic world of the garden by introducing dystopic and traumatic elements, especially in the so-called "Precious Mirror" chapters.[5] In the sequels, on the other hand, nothing too drastic happens, and whatever happened that was drastic in the original *Honglou meng* is now repaired (e.g., Miaoyu, that is, Adamantina, is recovered; the Jia household becomes prosperous again). The nostalgia of the sequels, in other words, craves safety and stability and dreads too many of the realities of adulthood.

In line with the general idea of nostalgic recreation, I will arrange my discussion of these sequels according to three topics having to do with strategies by which the sequels sustain that psychic mode: the improvement of Baoyu, the vindication of Daiyu, and, most important, the resolution and simplification of the complex love affair of these two central characters. The sequels by no means uniformly represent nostalgia. *Qilou chongmeng* (Revisiting the silken chambers) for one creates a knavish Baoyu whose expertise about sex and the female body creates a sort of short circuit between the perspective of childlike innocence and the sexual awareness that the young man not so naively displays. It introduces a Baoyu who knows more about young women's bodies than the women themselves and thus evokes an implied male reader who is invited to enjoy the brazen pleasures of the precocious polygamist. *Honglou meng ying*, on the other hand, twists its recreation of the *Honglou meng* world in an opposite way by creating women whose realm is distinctly beyond that of the inadequate and melancholy Baoyu. In refusing to resurrect Daiyu or to allow Baoyu to "indulge his passion and desire to their fullest" (8.57),[6] the author in effect shows her disdain for the model of the coddled and indulged polygamist that is prominent in other sequels and in nonsequels that are less directly modeled after *Honglou meng*, like *Ernü yingxiong zhuan* (The tale of heroic lovers).

There are at least two other inviting approaches to the study of *Honglou meng* sequels besides mine: one would treat the post-*Honglou meng* formation of what can be called a vocabulary of *Honglou meng* qualities and characteristics.[7] The other is that of Widmer's 1997 contribution to *Writing Women in Late Imperial China* and chapter 5 in this volume, namely the meaningfulness of *Honglou meng* to female readers and the hypothesis that *Honglou meng* may have brought women closer to being able to write in the narrative form of the novel.⁸ More recently she has been studying the development of a female readership by the time of the decades in which most of the first sequels appeared, and she has proposed that authors of some of the sequels intentionally wrote with a mixed-gender reading audience in mind.⁹

My approach will stay within a framework linking *Honglou meng* and its sequels to the discourse of sexuality and romantic love that they share with other works of Ming and Qing literature focusing on the life of the elite household. The theme of female talent is particularly significant in that discourse. The remarkable woman became especially prominent in the Ming-Qing transition both as a real figure in herself, in particular as a courtesan, teacher, or writer, and as someone male writers elevated in their descriptions of both fictional and real heroines.¹⁰ The rise of the figure of the educated woman from the late Ming onward also contributes to the especially heightened way in which *Honglou meng*, its sequels, and numerous other works treat heroines and the theme of the feminine in general (including the feminized man).¹¹ I will focus on the talented woman in the context of polygamy, which I take to be a central issue in these works even though authors do not name it as such. All except one of the sequels I discuss turn Baoyu into a polygamist.¹² They also manifest numerous signs of the problems of polygamy in the form of jealousy, the ranking of wives, and the balance between chastity and eroticism. Although many of us might assume at a basic level that men are "for" polygamy while women are "against" it, I want to refrain from too strong an adherence to this dichotomy. By instead looking at the variety of male and female positions within polygamy and alongside the theme of female talent, we will discover an array of cases of both male and female agency, including, for example, marriages in which male agency is central but which still strongly evoke the themes of female talent, and, on the other hand, polygamy in which women (especially Daiyu) dominate, thus reflecting one of the main inheritances from the original *Honglou meng*.

In defining what constitutes a sequel to *Honglou meng*, I am eliminating novels that do not have obviously sequel-like titles but nevertheless hark back very clearly to *Honglou meng* (e.g., *Ernü yingxiong zhuan*, *Pinhua baojian*, *Qinglou meng*, and *Haishang chentianying*). Although novels with obviously sequel-like titles can be extremely unlike *Honglou meng*, I will confine myself to this group, in particular a dozen that were recently republished by Beijing University Press. The earliest of these—and the earliest of all sequels—is *Hou Honglou meng* (The later dream of the red chamber), which was completed no later than 1796, while the latest is *Honglou meng ying*, which appeared in 1877 but was written in the years before and after 1861, when a preface referring to its lack of completion was written.¹³ These sequels share the trait of claiming to be direct continuations of *Honglou meng* whether by using the same characters as in *Honglou meng* or by combining original characters, families, and settings with newly created takeoffs. They continue the original work from either chapter 97 (the death of Daiyu) or chapter 120. The first nine sequels, moreover, were published in fairly close succession up to 1824, after which three more appeared by 1877. Although many of these sequels were reissued throughout the nineteenth and early twentieth centuries, a gap in the production of new sequels ensued, with more finally appearing in the early 1900s and continuing up to the present.[14] These later works arguably constitute a separate group because of the interval between them and the first twelve and because of the large scale of changes that both China and Chinese fiction had undergone by that time.[15]

THE IMPROVEMENT OF BAOYU

In its primary sense, the improvement of Baoyu means that after he abandons his family at the end of the original *Honglou meng,* the Baoyu of the sequels returns happily and healthily to his family either as himself or in the form of a reincarnation or some other replacement. The new Baoyu no longer lacks the will to pursue studies and career.[16] He is no longer prone to useless or decadent activities such as associating with actors.[17] He is no longer "clinging" *(zhanzhi)* (*Honglou yuanmeng,* 3.16). He will no longer "drown himself in women's makeup rouge" *(ni yu zhifen)* (*Honglou huanmeng,* 2.21). In *Honglou meng ying* Baochai tells him, "You finally look like you will make something of yourself" *(ni jing you qiaodechu ren lai de rizi)* (6.43). In many of the sequels Baoyu is a successful official and in some cases a valiant martial hero (in *Qilou chongmeng* with the help of female warriors, in *Honglou yuanmeng* with the help of Qingwen and Daiyu).[18]

Depending upon the author, the new Baoyu is also more sexually proper. *Honglou fumeng* (Return to dream of the red chamber) goes so far as to create what amounts to a form of male chastity as a counterpart to female chastity.[19] Its preface, written in 1799 by Chen Shiwen, younger sister of the author Chen Shaohai, states that this is a book both men and women can read and that it is devoid of lewd contents (3–4). Even though the Baoyu of *Honglou fumeng* has twelve wives, he is fair to all, harboring no favorites.[20] Nor is he the busy and promiscuous sexual protagonist of *Qilou chongmeng* and *Honglou huanmeng* (The illusion of the dream of the red chamber). Reborn as Mengyu, he is all *qing* and no *se* ("sentiment" and no "lust"), as the narrator describes, such that when he consorts with his wives and maids, "he is not even aware that he is male and they are female. As far as he is concerned, someone else's body is mine, and mine is someone else's. . . . Even if one of the women is sponging herself or taking a bath, he comes and goes as he pleases and no one minds" (26.287).[21] With these conditions clearly laid out, the author of *Honglou fumeng* thus creates a Baoyu who is still intimate with women but in a chastely erotic way.[22]

Following upon the work of Widmer on female authorship and readership of fiction in the Qing, we should interpret the extreme adherence to chastity in *Honglou fumeng* and other sequels as a strong sign of female readership. Widmer believes that by the 1820s and 1830s educated women considered *Honglou meng* and its sequels to be appropriate reading material for women (who also probably read "inappropriate," including erotic, works as well). We should presume, moreover, that these authors envisioned reading audiences of both sexes.²³ In doing so they made the effort, as the *Honglou fumeng* author and his sister did, to spell out the particulars of Baoyu's behavior in order to make that behavior acceptable to both men and women. In effect the author took the so-called "mind-lust" (*yiyin*) of *Honglou meng*'s Baoyu and worked it into a purer but still mildly eroticized form—that is, retaining his physical intimacies but excising the sexual involvement with Qin Keqing and Xiren.

Hou Honglou meng's Baoyu is similarly polygamous in that he has three wives besides Daiyu, but his focus on Daiyu is far stronger than what the Baoyu of *Honglou fumeng* has for any one of his wives. He is intimate with Qingwen, for example, mainly by way of having her help him get through to Daiyu.²⁴ His goal is to persuade Daiyu to forgive him and finally allow him into her bed. *Hou Honglou meng* begins with a Baoyu who is "melancholy for days" (*menle haojitian*) (4.43) because Daiyu, now returned to life, will have nothing to do with him. He weeps, he later dreams of cutting his heart out for her (10.125; she "laughs at him coldly" [*lengxiao*]), he goes mad, then he finally sleeps with her for the first time only after Baochai, Qingwen, and Zijuan (Oriole) soften her for him by making her drunk (17.218–220).²⁵ Thus the new Baoyu is willing to commit ultimate acts of self-sacrifice. All such behavior achieves meaningfulness because of the prolonged nature of his quest, since it is after over half of the book has passed that he finally becomes reconciled with Daiyu. Even after that she never gives herself to him in the way the authors of *Qilou chongmeng* and *Honglou huanmeng* have her do.²⁶

In the explicitly erotic *Qilou chongmeng*, composed no earlier than 1797, Baoyu is reborn as Xiaoyu, the son of Baochai, while Daiyu is reborn as Shunhua, the daughter of Shi Xiangyun.²⁷ In this case, the supposed superiority of Baoyu manifests itself in a precociousness that goes far beyond that of *Honglou meng*. He is both a civil and martial *zhuangyuan* by age ten, at which time he accomplishes military feats with the aid of some of his future wives. He has five wives by age sixteen (chap. 43), including Shunhua, preceding which he has sexual relations with numerous young women except Shunhua. Before his marriage, he learns the trick of having sex with prepubescent girls, especially maids, so that none of them will be in danger of getting pregnant (Qingwen's reincarnation having already had an abortion, 33.215). Soon after this discovery, the boy learns erotic arts from a nineteen-year-old female acrobat, after which he practices these arts with a new group of twenty-four maids, of whom he takes four each night (chap. 35).²⁸ After his marriage, he continues having nonmarital relationships, his favorite kind, which he calls "the out-of-bounds ones" (*yede*) (1.4, 45.294). *Honglou huanmeng* (1843) likewise portrays a sexually and romantically successful Baoyu. A friend from southern China offers him an aphrodisiac to keep him from "harming himself" (*sunshen*) because of having so many wives (six in all, 19.288). He refrains from having sex with Daiyu, who at that time is too far in her pregnancy, but he and Baochai take the drug. "Ever since they had been sleeping together they had never experienced such pleasure" (19.289).²⁹

In both *Qilou chongmeng* and *Honglou huanmeng* Baoyu is like the sexually active polygamist of numerous Qing erotic novels in which a man has harmonious relations with multiple wives.[30] He thus exemplifies a correction of both a Ximen Qing-like profligate who cannot manage a bevy of women and an original Baoyu who, by implication, failed to be sexually active when he should and could have been.[31] Both attempt to achieve the difficult if not impossible goal of a type of pornographic art that tries to maintain a balance between a genteel love story and the explicit description of sex. In general in Ming and Qing fiction, the rule is that the more explicit the description, the more grotesque the detail and the less sublime the characters and their affair. Both sequels are examples of how explicit portrayals of sex depart from the aesthetic that emphasizes the rarefied effects of adumbrative portrayal that were so compelling to readers of the original *Honglou meng*, although *Honglou huanmeng* comes closer to *Honglou meng* than *Qilou chongmeng* in this respect. In other words, in *Honglou meng* Baoyu sniffing Daiyu's sleeves, threatening to tickle her, and otherwise trying to avoid hurting her feelings or making her angry are more compelling than actually getting in bed with her, which according to this aesthetic would derail the reader, male or female, who would rather imagine or leave unsaid what might have happened had Baoyu and Daiyu in fact become uncomplicated romantic partners. It is the sublime complications, in short, that empowered the original masterpiece and that inspired later works such as *Huayue hen* (Trace of moon and flowers) and *Pinhua baojian* (Precious mirror of boy actresses), which are in fact closer in spirit to *Honglou meng* than any of the sequels I have examined so far.

Honglou meng ying, on the other hand, contrasts with *Qilou chongmeng* and *Honglou huanmeng* by denying Baoyu the rewards of such sexual success. Its female author, Gu Chun (style name Taiqing, 1799–1877),[32] creates a melancholy Baoyu who, although married to Baochai, Xiren, and two others, still longs for Daiyu, who does not return to life as she does in other sequels; he likewise misses Qingwen and Fangguan (Parfumee). One area of nonmelancholy, however, shows the author inventing a new feature for *Honglou meng* and Jia Baoyu. *Honglou meng ying* contains two scenes of women giving birth, the first being Baochai, the second Ping'er (Patience, now married to Jia Lian). In the more detailed scene of Ping'er, we see "Mama Zhao uncovering Ping'er and taking a look, then hastily pulling off her last article of clothing. The baby and the placenta lay there in a heap, so she reached out and picked up the baby. Meanwhile Jia Lian saw that Zhao had no socks on and her hands were covered with blood. He was trembling but then said stupidly, 'Mama, why don't you put some socks on, you'll catch cold.'" An elder woman then cuts the umbilical cord and wraps the child, a boy, so that Ping'er can hold him (9.66–67).[33] In Baochai's case, just after the umbilical cord has been cut for her baby, Baoyu enters and exclaims, "I have never seen a baby before" (4.25).[34] A later scene shows Shi Xiangyun coming upon Baoyu holding his baby son and looking at peonies. Tanchun, also present, remarks that "He's even more capable now. He has learned how to hold a baby!" *(geng neng ganle, liande hui bao haizi le)* (10.75).[35]

The description of childbirth fills a gap in the attentive portrayal that *Honglou meng* gives of women by first simply foregrounding this momentous event in a woman's life, but then also by having men be present and having them open their eyes to the scene. The new Baoyu-Jia Lian can thus also be someone who participates in childbirth and child rearing, realms traditionally considered off-limits to a man. The portrayal of the woman's body in these scenes, moreover, gains sharper definition if we contrast it with the lurid attentiveness of *Qilou chongmeng*, which shows Baoyu's reincarnation repeatedly taking interest in young women's bodies, especially during ablutions. In one case, he delightedly inspects the vagina of a young woman who is having her first menstruation (20.131). He is able to explain what is happening to her because he has learned about this phenomenon from other female partners. We can also contrast the birth scenes in *Honglou meng ying* with the scene in *Xu Honglou meng* (Sequel to dream of the red chamber) that portrays Baoyu and Daiyu returning to life after death and taking milk from Baochai's breasts to help them gain strength. At first Baochai "squeezes the milk out" *(ji nai)* for him, but then he "takes the nipple in his mouth and learns how to suck on it himself" (18.228). The Baoyu of *Qilou chongmeng* knows more about women than women themselves, while the Baoyu of *Xu Honglou meng* happily suckles as he returns to a life in which he will be a polygamist doted upon and coddled by his wives. The difference between these two sequels and *Honglou meng ying* lies in the assignment of agency and in the assumed reader. *Qilou chongmeng* and *Xu Honglou meng* refrain from undercutting the privileged male and presume a reader who will enjoy the erotic teasing of scenes like those above. *Honglou meng ying*, as I have described already, ends precisely at a point in which women talk and laugh while paying Baoyu no attention. The novel thus conforms to the image of the marginal male of the original *Honglou meng* and creates women who live openly in a separate world that men have no possibility of entering or understanding.

THE VINDICATION OF DAIYU

Sequel writers as well as numerous critics and commentators have taken Baoyu's marriage to Baochai as the main injustice of *Honglou meng*. The majority of sequels vindicate Daiyu, having her return to life either as herself or in reincarnated form and marrying Baoyu. (*Honglou fumeng* alone favors Baochai over Daiyu,[36] drastically reducing her role in her reincarnation; although favored over Baochai, Daiyu does not return to life at all in *Bu Honglou meng*,[37] *Zengbu Honglou meng*, and *Honglou meng ying*.) She becomes a capable manager of the Jia household, better than Wang Xifeng or Tanchun *(Honglou meng bu)*. She becomes the primary wife of Baoyu's polygamous family, superior in rank to Baochai and other wives.[38] She reemerges fuller in flesh and happier in temperament, as in *Honglou huanmeng*, "completely abandoning her former pettiness and her tendency to dark melancholy" (3.31). She announces, "I should stop making cutting remarks" *(wo bugai yuyan jianli)* (4.53).[39] In two sequels her vindication includes the discovery of a half-brother, Qiongyu, smarter than Baoyu, who passes the metropolitan exam either at a higher level than Baoyu *(Honglou huanmeng)* or prior to him *(Xu Honglou meng gao).*

Granting Daiyu the prerogatives of running the household and managing the polygamy is a form of poetic justice that demotes Baochai in favor of Daiyu. If there is any statement about why Daiyu is better than Baochai or anyone else, it is mainly to say that Baochai was guilty of "false virtue" *(jia daoxue)* or that the inferior and illiterate Xiren and Wang Xifeng were part of a conspiracy to concentrate power in their hands.[40] The venom of such vindication is prominent in *Honglou yuanmeng* (The resolution of the dream of the red chamber), for example, in which "God" *(shangdi)* hates Baochai and Xiren and will thus have Daiyu return to life and marry Baoyu (1.2). Later Baoyu divorces Baochai by imperial order and marries Daiyu uxorilocally *(ruzhui)* (4.20–23).[41] *Honglou meng bu* (The dream of the red chamber revisited) and *Xu Honglou meng gao* (Draft sequel to dream of the red chamber) likewise have the emperor ordain the marriage of Baoyu and Daiyu, thus engineering what by implication should originally have occurred.

In her role as the primary wife, Daiyu enjoys the privilege of that highest rank, thus overturning her virtual expulsion in the original *Honglou meng.* In the first sequel, *Hou Honglou meng,* she disdains contact with Baoyu until he finally proves his dedication to her, at one point even creating the impression that she is seriously considering marrying another man (chap. 8). In a subsequent scene she still threatens to shut him out of her room and return to her earlier celibate meditations (chap. 23). She exerts control over Baoyu's polygamy by dictating the addition of Zijuan and Yinger (Caltrop) as concubines, doing so not for the sake of smoothing over Baoyu's dalliance with them, as it is said, but for the sake of fairness and unity (19.251). She calls a household meeting at which she announces strict regulations, including rules against luxury (chap. 19). She is also said to be Baoyu's number-one "soul mate" *(zhiji)* (19.256), which is proven when she demonstrates her understanding that Baoyu by temperament can serve only in the Hanlin Academy and could never assume a more demanding position in a local administration or central ministry.

Daiyu also expands the polygamy in *Honglou meng bu,* where she has Baoyu take Qingwen, Zijuan, Yinger, and Xiren as concubines.[42] She thus undergoes not only vindication, but a particular sort of improvement in the sense that she now conforms to the model of the virtuous and unjealous wife who tolerates and encourages the addition of concubines. In *Xu Honglou meng* she joins Baochai in a further twist that numerous Ming and Qing stories of polygamous families portray. They discuss the methods of keeping their husband in check by arranging the living quarters of the concubines so that none will be able to monopolize him (chap. 22). In other words, female management of polygamy is a matter of regaining a measure of control originally lost because of having to surrender to the condition of the man supposedly having his choice among multiple wives.

These combinations of unjealous deference with a sort of female directorship undo the portrait of Baoyu and Daiyu as lovers of deep passion and loyalty. In *Honglou huanmeng,* Daiyu pointedly states that their former difficulties arose because of the "selfishness of their love" *(sixin aimu)* (4.52), referring to the illicit tinge that their love had in the original *Honglou meng*. Now they are openly in love, but also share themselves with Baochai and the other wives. Authors nevertheless still take pains to hark back to that original deep-seated love. In *Honglou meng ying*, Baoyu deeply misses the dead Daiyu. On her birthday he sleeps in her bed, smells her fragrance, and dreams of having sex with her (8.60–62).[43] In *Hou Honglou meng*, as I have said, she is his number-one soul mate, a condition that now manifests itself in the vestigial form of her support of his disinterest in studying for the official exams. Even *Honglou huanmeng*, in spite of Daiyu's dismissal of their formerly "selfish" love, goes to extreme lengths to emphasize that Baoyu's love for Daiyu is profoundly different from his love for his other five wives, as I will show presently.

To generalize from these examples, instead of making her Baoyu's one and only love, these various attempts to uphold the primacy of Daiyu concentrate on making her the first among equals. The case of *Honglou huanmeng* is the most fine-tuned in this regard. Although the discussion and settlement of rank —especially between Daiyu and Baochai—occurs in numerous sequels (not to mention other novels in general), *Honglou huanmeng* subjects ranking to the most painstaking attention as Daiyu and Baoyu determine how he will divide himself between his wives. At first he says that of the ten portions of his heart, he will give four or five to Daiyu, then one and a half to Wanxiang (who is Qingwen reincarnated), one each to Zijuan, Xiren, and Baochai, and one-half to Yinger. Daiyu redraws the arrangement so that he gives her his entire "innate, original, and pure heart" *(xiantian benxing chizi zhi xin)*, which is actually their two hearts bound together. He should then divide his "external worldly heart" *(houtian de xin)* into ten parts, with Wanxiang getting three parts, Baichai two, Zijuan two, Xiren two, and Yinger one.[44] She then urges him to return to Baochai's apartments, for "he must be fair in every regard" *(yiqie dou yao gongping)*. He must not abandon Baochai, and, moreover, he must tell Baochai everything that Daiyu and he have discussed so that Baochai will not think that Daiyu is trying to "monopolize" him for herself *(longluo)*. Her ultimate goal is for "the three of them to be of one heart" *(sanren tongxin)* (4.54), which is born out in the eventual routine according to which Baoyu, Daiyu, and Baochai sleep together in the same bed each night.

That Daiyu is the one who determines how to divide up Baoyu's heart is a sign of deference to her as main wife, a deference that is required because of the weight of her high social position. Her parents are equal in status to his, in other words. In *Honglou huanmeng*, moreover, she has a half-brother who is superior in intelligence to Baoyu. But when it is a matter of two wives of high social status—that is, Baochai and Daiyu—then in *Honglou huanmeng*, as in many other works of Ming and Qing fiction, ambiguities arise that can only be treated in contradictory ways. For example, Daiyu is number one in Baoyu's heart, but Baoyu is nevertheless supposed to be completely fair to Baochai. The three of them will be of one heart, but Daiyu is nevertheless first. When later in the novel they do achieve the routine of all three sleeping together, the question of rank is dropped, as if resolved and in no more need of attention.

THE RESOLUTION OF THE LOVE AFFAIR BETWEEN BAOYU AND DAIYU

The deliberations about ranking of wives that occur in some of the sequels demonstrate the sensitive nature of ranking, but the truly sensitive issue is the relationship between just two people, that is, Baoyu and Daiyu. The original *Honglou meng* appealed to many readers precisely because of the fact that Baoyu's and Daiyu's love was so deep but was also so intractably bound to fail. The sequels in general cannot support intractability, of course, and instead resolve the affair in virtually magic ways by smoothing it out or replacing the original characters with new ones.

The sequels nevertheless have their idiosyncratic ways of reviewing and resolving the relationship between Daiyu and Baoyu. In abandoning the portrayal of tortured love in this or any other couple, these authors must invent other ways for Baoyu, Daiyu, Baochai, and other characters to be, and they choose between two broad alternatives. One is to deemphasize passion and sexual love and have the characters engage in other pursuits; the other is to make their characters more sexually romantic. Examples of the emphasis on the nonromantic can be found in *Honglou fumeng*, in which Baochai becomes a general and participates in the defeat of pirates (in *Honglou yuanmeng* Daiyu helps Baoyu quell bandits), and in which in general no woman plays a major role as a favored romantic partner (the role of Daiyu's reincarnation being extremely limited). In *Xu Honglou meng xinbian* (New sequel to dream of the red chamber) the women form a poetry club and enjoy hours of leisurely activity. Baoyu's replacement, who performs brilliantly in both the exams and service to the empire, takes no concubines. *Bu Honglou meng* and *Zengbu Honglou meng* (Patching the dream of the red chamber; Sequel to patching the dream of the red chamber) stage hours of men and women writing poetry and enjoying their leisure. In *Honglou meng bu* Baoyu and Daiyu practice philanthropy by distributing medicine, food, clothing, and coffins to the needy. In *Honglou meng ying* women write poetry and play games, while men engage in less worthwhile pursuits and sometimes get into trouble. In *Xu Honglou meng gao*, Baochai and Daiyu are both more learned than Baoyu, whom they help in his studies for the exams.[45]

On the other hand, the method of *Qilou chongmeng* and *Honglou huanmeng* (and to a certain extent *Xu Honglou meng*) is to eroticize the interactions of Baoyu, Daiyu, and his other wives, although these two works do so very differently. *Qilou chongmeng* extends the theme of Baoyu's connoisseurship of women to a degree that, as I have already indicated, makes him superior to women in knowledge about their bodies. *Honglou huanmeng*, on the other hand, emphasizes the romantic attachment between Baoyu and Daiyu, at the same time eroticizing both their bond and the bond between the female partners as well. Both sequels retain the themes of female talent and purity that are so prominent in *Honglou meng*, but in heavily sexualizing the relationships between the characters thereby enter the territory of erotic fiction that we usually think of as being written by and for men. I say "by and for men" because of the fact that the values of chastity normally exclude women from showing interest in sexual pleasure. Furthermore, erotic literature in the Ming and Qing is overwhelmingly focused on the sexual centrality of men. Promiscuous women never enjoy happy endings, while promiscuous men often do. Nevertheless, within the small universe of *Qilou chongmeng* and *Honglou huanmeng,* which like numerous other Qing novels portray happy and benevolent polygamists, we can make the distinction that while *Qilou chongmeng* focuses primarily on the agency of Baoyu, *Honglou huanmeng* grants women significant forms of agency in terms of both determining the direction of love relationships and expressing enjoyment in those relationships.

Qilou chongmeng in fact takes male agency to a new level in Chinese erotic fiction by granting Baoyu the knavish capacity to place himself at the very forefront of female bodily functions. By referring to Baoyu as knavish, I mean to call attention to the peculiar way in which *Qilou chongmeng* exaggerates the original Baoyu's empathy for women. If empathy means something like putting oneself inside someone else, then *Qilou chongmeng* both ingeniously and irreverently takes this gesture literally and engages in a relentless series of scenes in which Baoyu demonstrates his aptitude for knowing and manipulating female anatomy. His aptitude is so exaggerated that, however offensive the sequel was thought to be, the effect has something of a farcical tour de force, especially in the sheer repetitiveness of the portrayals of his knavish behavior. As soon as Baoyu is about to be reborn as Baochai's son, he expresses delight at the opportunity to "return to familiar territory" *(ye shi jiu you)* (1.3). When he is told he will have a wife and many concubines, he also begs for some "illicit" relations (1.4). After his rebirth, throughout his childhood he displays his precocious lust when he peeks at a naked girl (6.35), plays intimately with girls in bed (11.66, 13.91) or while bathing (20.130, 41.265–66), teaches a girl how to kiss (15.96), or has girls look at animals copulating (17.109). *Qilou chongmeng*'s parody of male connoisseurship of women occurs in Baoyu's numerous displays of precocious concern for women during illness or menstruation.[46] When a young female cousin is ill, Baoyu immediately knows she needs to sit on the chamber pot and helps her do so (9.53–54). He insists on "tending" to her *(cihou)* (54) and refuses the help of an old female servant. Later, when the same girl is ill again, he assists her in her ablutions with no fear of filth,[47] then helps her refasten her clothing (9.57). Similar tending occurs with a young woman possessed by a demon (27.174–75) and later one who accidentally burns her buttocks on a hot *kang* (38.248–250).[48]

The ultimate effect of this farcical repetition is the opposite of a sequel like *Honglou fumeng,* which attempts to hypersublimate male and female sexual differences in order to underplay and even erase the reality of actual sexual contact. *Qilou chongmeng* instead desublimates the original Baoyu's quality of "mind lust" and his theories of "muddy" men and "pure-as-water" women. The result is the hypernormalization of sexual promiscuity, turning the young male into the masterful and benevolent leader of women who automatically conform to his sensibility. The portrait of Baoyu the knave also has an ontological effect, which is to collapse the distance between female and male subjectivity by having the male entirely ventriloquize the female. In *Honglou meng*

Baoyu had empathy for women, but despite the fact that he gained their sympathy, he was always a fundamental outsider. *Qilou chongmeng* now makes him a virtual insider, removing all sense of sublime distance and mystery and thus eliminating the original sense of female agency that was foregrounded in *Honglou meng*.[49]

A contrasting attempt at seamless harmony occurs in *Honglou huanmeng*, which differs from *Qilou chongmeng* in its more serious effort to foreground female agency. *Honglou huanmeng* gives Daiyu the main role in her commanding position over the polygamous household. She also openly manifests her love for Baoyu and his other wives, especially Baochai and Qingwen.[50] She unashamedly enjoys sexual pleasure with him and engages in erotic play with Baochai and Qingwen.[51] *Honglou huanmeng*'s revision of *Honglou meng*, in other words, lies in its portrayals of happy lovers, the woman Daiyu in particular, who have overcome all former blockages and who manage their sexual and romantic relations in an unproblematic way.

Although such revision looks like little more than an attempt to idealize polygamy, it is worthwhile to consider at length the extent to which *Honglou huanmeng* attempts to make respectable the romantic and sexual role of Daiyu. Normative values forbid a proper woman like Daiyu from playing such a commanding role and especially from expressing interest in sexual pleasure.[52] Only courtesans or so-called "lascivious women" (*yinfu*) do such things. *Honglou huanmeng* instead domesticates what is normally condemned or else found only in the brothel, including the game of "drinking into the other's mouth" (*jing pibei*).[53] Such a domestication of sexual and romantic liaisons within the polygamous household is not new in Chinese fiction,[54] but in *Honglou huanmeng*'s case it represents a kind of experimental attempt to push further with what *Honglou meng* already implied or prestaged. As Epstein notes, before they were married even Baoyu and his female cousins already played "drinking games little different from those played by courtesans when entertaining their patrons."[55] *Honglou huanmeng* now actualizes these pursuits within the environment of the stable married family. Scenes like these are examples of how the sequel makes workable what could not be worked out in *Honglou meng*. In other words, in contrast to the numerous frustrated and ruined lovers in *Honglou meng*, we now have in *Honglou huanmeng* youths who in effect act as their own go-betweens.

For a particular example of female agency in *Honglou huanmeng*, let us look at a scene in which Baochai coaches a younger female cousin, Xiluan, who is in love with Daiyu's brother, Qiongyu.[56] Qiongyu has already been betrothed to Li Wan's younger sister, Li Wen, but then he and Xiluan fall in love. Neither knows how to communicate such feelings to the other or how to achieve recognition for their love. Baoyu, Daiyu, and Baochai finally figure out what is going on. Baochai takes charge by first getting Qiongyu to admit his love, then telling Baoyu, Daiyu, and Jia Zheng that she plans to have the two marry. Her last step is to ask Xiluan if she loves Qiongyu (9.130–132). Xiluan will not admit anything until Baochai finally presses her by saying, among other things, that she, Baoyu, and Daiyu know all too well the bitterness of frustrated love (131). She cuddles with Xiluan, praises her, and tells her how much she herself loves both her and Qiongyu (131, 132). "'Now, do you or don't you love him?' Xiluan answered right away, 'I love him'" *(Ni ke ai ta? Xiluan mang shuo, wo ai ta)* (132). Having finally gotten Xiluan to utter these "three important words" *(zhe sange zi)* (132), Baochai can now carry out her plan.[57]

This little scene amounts to a pragmatic working out of the kind of affair that was utterly blocked in *Honglou meng*. It may constitute a drastic simplification of the more subtle characterizations in *Honglou meng,* but it nevertheless plays on a utopian quality that *Honglou meng* likewise evoked, even if it did so in a finely suffused way. Central to this pragmatic working out of a problem is the direct declaration of love, which effectively cancels orthodox parental authority and thus realizes one of the key features of *Honglou meng*'s idealization of the paradise of youth in the Grand Prospect Garden. *Honglou meng* in contrast was as if too realistic or pessimistic to be able to realize such an effective enactment of love.

My point in concluding is that as strong as the tendency of the sequels may be to simplify and dull the complexity of the masterwork, the sequels nevertheless succeed in breaking the masterwork down into numerous elementary components. This breakdown is also a kind of undressing in which the masterwork's originally high intentions now appear in balder, more explicit ways. Bald in some cases means lurid or cynical. For example, no matter how we look at him, Baoyu was indeed a polygamist—or at least a pre-polygamist pressured and expected to be a full-fledged polygamist.[58] The sequels (with the exception of *Xu Honglou meng xinbian*) merely carry this assumption to fruition by mapping out variations of the polygamous arrangement. Likewise, Baoyu was indeed an obsessive admirer of women. The sequel *Qilou chongmeng* parodies that obsession by taking it to a perversely repetitious and unsubtle extreme in which Baoyu tends to women's physicality in a way that makes them beholden to him for their very entry into womanhood.

On the other hand, sequels like *Honglou huanmeng* and *Honglou meng ying* portray a Baoyu who cannot in the end take complete charge of his polygamous family. He cedes the power of directorship to one or more of the women who make up his harem, to the point of appearing to have virtually no control over how he distributes his affections and arranges his preferences. *Honglou meng ying* in particular demonstrates that Baoyu the polygamist necessarily fails to have any one woman conform to the way he wants her to be. The women he misses most—Daiyu, Qingwen, and Fangguan—no longer exist. Instead, women live a separate existence to which he has no access, as the final scene of the novel evokes. *Honglou meng ying*'s ultimate statement is that Baoyu cannot become one of the women; he cannot be among them without causing repercussions (jealousy and rivalry or suspicion of illicit involvement, all of which tend to cause more risk for women than for men). Another feature that the sequels reproduce and carry to extremes is the unrelentingly bland portrayal of the leisure activities of the elite family, especially as seen in *Bu Honglou meng* and *Zengbu Honglou meng*. Here it becomes a matter of how to sustain these activities: there can be no excesses of happiness or sorrow, hatred or love, and the household must meanwhile be run in ways that correct the errors of Wang Xifeng and other household managers in the original *Honglou meng*.

Sequel writing treads a fine line between critical revision, even travesty, and respectful recreation. A work like *Qilou chongmeng* is unconcerned about the accusation of travesty or offensiveness in general, hence its uniqueness. *Honglou meng ying* trespasses upon the grounds of *Honglou meng* in a different way by furthering the portrait of male venality while giving ultimate valorization to talented women. What these two hold in common with other sequels is the attempt to better *Honglou meng* and to do so by pushing to fruition what was missed or deflected in the original work: marrying two women, marrying twelve beauties, passing the exams, having healthy, successful children, especially sons, and so forth. Making possible what was impossible in *Honglou meng* amounts to imposing transparency where it could not have existed before. The best examples of such transparency are *Honglou fumeng*'s attempt to erase the divide between male and female, *Bu Honglou meng*'s (and other sequels') elision of the divide between supernatural and earthly worlds, and *Qilou chongmeng*'s farcical usurpation of female agency. Usurping female agency, in other words, makes the female subject transparent to the male. The elision of supernatural and earthly realms makes each transparent to the other by allowing a single eye to behold them both at once. Erasing the difference between male and female likewise demystifies all sexual taboo and creates a situation of transparent gender-oneness.

Instead of taking these elisions and erasures simply as reasons to dismiss the *Honglou meng* sequels, we should be fascinated with the variety of attempts to achieve a similar goal of eliminating traumatic antinomies: male/female, earthly/supernatural, or life/death. The attempts to work through *Honglou meng*'s intractabilities are also remarkable for their insistence on portraying female agency within polygamy and their emphasis on direct and pragmatic resolutions of youthful love affairs independent of adult direction. The will to carry out such attempts at elision and erasure draws these sequels into a composite whole. Nostalgic resuscitation of the original masterwork further grounds this composite wholeness, which in general involves reextending the eternal present of the favorite aspects of the *Honglou meng* narrative.

NOTES

1. Xiren is known as Aroma in the Hawkes-Minford translation. I will add the Hawkes-Minford translation of names in parentheses when appropriate. See Hawkes, trans., *The Story of the Stone*.
2. In some sequels the character who stands for Baoyu is either a reincarnation of him or a young man who represents a new Baoyu. For example, in *Xu Honglou meng xinbian*, Baoyu is named Mao and is not a true rebirth, but he does carry with him the precious jade of the original Baoyu.
3. See note 13 below for a list of sequels with dates and with titles translated
4. They resemble other cases in which stories that end badly are rewritten to end happily (e.g., "Cui Yingying zhuan" rewritten in *Xixiang ji* or *Dou E yuan* turned into *Jinsuo ji*). However, the mode of nostalgia distinguishes the *Honglou meng* sequels from these other

cases in terms of the sheer number of the sequels and the emotional intensity that they thereby establish.

5. See Epstein's discussion, "Reflections of Desire," 95–106.
6. In this chapter, all references to the *Honglou meng* sequels are to the editions published by Beijing daxue chubanshe.
7. Zhao Jianzhong's "*Honglou meng* xushu de yuanliu shanbian ji qi yanjiu" and Lin Yixuan's *Wucai ke bu tian,* both studies of *Honglou meng* sequels, already take major steps in this direction, which also include the discussion of narrative techniques as found in fiction and drama commentaries from Jin Shengtan (1596–1648) and Li Yu (1611–1679/80) onward, and general discussion of the comic ending in Ming and Qing drama and fiction.
8. Widmer, "Ming Loyalism and the Woman's Voice in Fiction after *Honglou meng.*" See also her "*Honglou meng ying* and its Publisher, Juzhen Tang of Beijing."
9. See Widmer's chapter in this volume.
10. Whom Li Wai-yee has recently examined in "Heroic Transformations: Women and National Trauma in Early Qing Literature."
11. The educated woman is examined in Ko, *Teachers of the Inner Chambers.* Other works besides *Honglou meng* include Pu Songling's *Liaozhai zhiyi* and later novels such as *Huayue hen* and *Pinhua baojian.*
12. The one that does not, *Xu Honglou meng xinbian,* instead concentrates on Baoyu's exam success and career.
13. *Hou Honglou meng* (The later dream of the red chamber), completed no later than 1796, is by Xiaoyaozi. The other sequels are *Xu Honglou meng* (Sequel to dream of the red chamber), written sometime between 1797–1798, published 1799 by Qin Zichen; *Qilou chongmeng* (Revisiting the silken chambers), completed no earlier than 1797, published 1805 by Wang Lanzhi of Hangzhou (*jinshi* of 1780); *Honglou fumeng* (Return to dream of the red chamber), preface 1799, by Chen *zi* Shaohai; *Xu Honglou meng xinbian* (New sequel to dream of the red chamber), preface 1805, by Haipu zhuren; *Bu Honglou meng* (Patching the dream of the red chamber), preface 1814, published 1820, and *Zengbu Honglou meng* (The sequel to patching the dream of the red chamber), preface 1820, published 1824, both by Langhuan shanqiao; *Honglou yuanmeng* (The resolution of the dream of the red chamber), published 1814 by Mengmeng xiansheng; *Honglou meng bu* (Dream of the red chamber revisited), published 1819 by Guichuzi; *Honglou huanmeng* (The illusion of the dream of the red chamber), published 1843 by Huayue chiren; *Honglou meng ying* (In the shadow of dream of the red chamber), preface 1861, published 1877 by Gu Taiqing (1799–1876); and *Xu Honglou meng gao* (Draft sequel to dream of the red chamber), unfinished, by Zhang Yaosun (b. 1807).
14. The most complete survey of *Honglou meng* sequels is in Zhao Jianzhong's *Honglou meng xushu yanjiu.*
15. Other sequels may have existed that do not survive, including one possibly by a woman (see Zhao Jianzhong, *Honglou meng xushu yanjiu,* 31–36). See also *Zhongguo tongsu xiaoshuo zongmu tiyao,* 631; and Sun Kaidi, *Zhongguo tongsu xiaoshuo shumu* (Beijing: 1982), 138–141. For general bibliography, surveys, and synopses of the sequels, see the following: Sun Kaidi, *Zhongguo tongsu xiaoshuo shumu,* 138–141; Yisu, *Honglou meng shulu,* 86–131; Ōtsuka Hidetaka, *Zōho Chūgoku tsūzoku shōsetsu shomoku,* 60–63; Feng Qiyong et al., eds., *Honglou meng da cidian; Zhongguo tongsu xiaoshuo zongmu tiyao;* Liu Shide et al, *Zhongguo gudai xiaoshuo baike quanshu;* Zhao Jianzhong, *Honglou meng xushu yanjiu;* and Lin Yixuan, *Wucai ke bu tian.* I have also derived information from the scholarly notes to the Beijing University Press (Beijing daxue chubanshe) and other recent editions. Through personal communication, Ellen Widmer has generously provided valuable information from her own study of *Honglou meng* sequels and has supplied me with a copy of Lin Yixuan's lengthy study of *Honglou meng* sequels. Other studies of *Honglou meng*

sequels include Chen Angni, "You *Honglou meng* ji qi xushu tantao Jia Baoyu zhi juese bianqian"; Huang Jinzhu, "*Honglou meng* de jindai xushu"; Li Zhongchang, *Gudai xiaoshuo xushu manhua;* Zhao Botao, "*Honglou meng ying* de zuoshe ji qita"; and Zhao Jianzhong, "*Honglou meng* xushu de yuanliu shanbian ji qi yanjiu."

16. In *Xu Honglou meng xinbian, Bu Honglou meng, Honglou meng bu,* and other sequels, he or his stand-in passes the *jinshi* exams; in the unfinished *Xu Honglou meng gao,* he makes advances in learning with the help of Baochai and Daiyu (perhaps if the author had finished his novel, he would have eventually intended that Baoyu pass the exams).

17. Thus targeting his fondness in *Honglou meng* for Liu Xianglian and Jiang Yuhan, especially the latter. In *Honglou huanmeng* Daiyu tells him that he must no longer "yearn for the company of actors" (4.53). In *Honglou meng ying* someone says that Baoyu might have had an affair with Jiang Yuhan (2.10). In *Honglou meng bu* he burns his racy books, *Feitian waizhuan, Wu Zetian,* and *Yang Guifei waizhuan;* and "his temperament completely changes from what it was in the old days."

18. In *Honglou fumeng* Baochai conquers pirates; in *Xu Honglou meng xinbian* the brilliant Baoyu serves in high office and has many glorious accomplishments.

19. It is the longest sequel at one hundred chapters and almost one million characters.

20. See Lin Yixuan, *Wucai ke butian,* 63–64, for a fuller discussion.

21. He is compassionate with all women, moreover, including old ones and ugly ones, for "King Yama of Hell dislikes men who pick a woman based on good looks only" (13.139). Chapter 13 contains the first major explication of his nature (13.139–140), including that the women "forget that he is a man."

22. He hugs them, he helps one put her shoe on (19.213), he is mesmerized as he watches a group of them (20.223), he licks the rouge off someone's lips (28.309–310).

23. See Widmer's chapter in this volume.

24. He pays little attention to Baochai, moreover (4.44). See also *Honglou meng bu* in which Baoyu feels indifference toward Baochai (7.75–76). Later, however, after she dies and then returns to life, he loves her again and she becomes a co-wife with Daiyu.

25. A similar delay occurs in *Honglou meng bu* in which it takes until chapter 25 (of forty-eight) before Baoyu and Daiyu marry. In *Honglou fumeng* they do not marry until chapter 91 (of a hundred).

26. For example, she later threatens to go back to her "old pursuits" *(jiu gongfu)* of celibate Daoist meditation (23.300).

27. First published in 1799, it also has an 1805 edition that refers to the two prior sequels, *Hou Honglou meng* and *Xu Honglou meng.* See Shi Changyu's entry in Liu Shide et al., eds., *Zhongguo gudai xiaoshuo baike quanshu,* 387. Yisu's entry on *Qilou chongmeng* mentions a nineteenth-century commentator who believes the author wrote the book as a roman à clef targeting, in the form of an enemy of his embodied in Xiaoyu. In other words, the lewdness of the book is by way of insulting his enemy (*Honglou meng shulu,* 99). Not enough information exists, however, to evaluate this interpretation in a meaningful way.

28. Later when a young woman of gentry status, Pei Quan, "goes three months without a period," Xiaoyu asks how can that be since, having learned "the erotic arts" *(fangshu),* he has learned how "to draw in his *qi* and return to the source, so that he knows how to keep from emitting semen too easily" (44.290).

29. Later he tries the drug with his other wives (chap. 20). The drug comes in "small Western porcelain bottles" (20.289) and is extremely fragrant. It is a "marvelous drug made according to a secret foreign formula" (21.294; there is no indication of what the drug contains, but opium comes to mind).

30. See McMahon, *Misers, Shrews, and Polygamists,* chap. 6.

31. *Xu Honglou meng* portrays a similar Baoyu but he is less prominently active than in *Qilou chongmeng* and *Honglou huanmeng*.

32. Gu Taiqing was a Manchu and a well-known writer of *ci* lyrics. She was married as a concubine, niece of the main wife, to a great-grandson of the Qianlong emperor Yihui (1799–1838). When the main wife died, Gu Taiqing became in effect the main wife for the last nine years of her husband's life (see Zhao Botao, "*Honglou meng ying* de zuojia ji qita," 243–251). She belonged to a poetry society with other female poets, including Shen Shanbao, who wrote the 1861 preface to Taiqing's novel. See also Widmer, "Ming Loyalism and the Woman's Voice in Fiction after *Honglou meng*," 393–396.

33. *Honglou huanmeng* portrays Daiyu giving birth to twins. Baoyu is frantic as he paces outside and hears Daiyu's cries of pain (22.324–325). The focus of attention is more on Baoyu outside the room than on Daiyu giving birth, about which the author provides little description besides her crying out and Baochai telling her to bite down on a piece of cloth (324). Qingwen later rubs Daiyu's stomach when it looks like Daiyu will have the second twin.

34. Cutting the umbilical is the only graphic detail given in Baochai's scene (4.25).

35. *Xu Honglou meng* (10.123) and *Bu Honglou meng* (9.78, which copies heavily from the former in much of the first half of the book) both portray Baochai and Ping'er nursing their babies. Qiaojie compares their breasts, noting that Ping'er's nipples are smaller.

36. The only sequel of the ones I study to do so. See Lin Yixuan, *Wucai ke butian*, 56–58.

37. In this sequel Baoyu and Daiyu meet as immortals but instead of being passionately in love have now reached what is termed an ultimate stage of "limpid" *(dan)* love (30.276–277).

38. As in *Hou Honglou meng, Xu Honglou meng, Qilou chongmeng, Honglou yuanmeng, Honglou meng bu, Honglou huanmeng,* and *Xu Honglou meng gao*.

39. See also *Honglou meng bu* in which she no longer suffers from insomnia or constant worries (4.39).

40. In the prologue to *Honglou yuanmeng* the words used to condemn Baochai and Xiren are "*jiadaoxue*" and "*yinxian*" (4).

41. Eventually Baoyu has Daiyu retrieve Baochai, but Xiren is never fully forgiven. She is delegated to serve in the shrine to Qingwen.

42. After Baochai dies and then returns to life (chap. 39), she and Daiyu become co-wives and arrange for the addition of Xiren and Ying'er (chap. 46)

43. Thus demonstrating that it was possible for a female author (an anonymous one pretending to be a man, to be sure) to refer directly to such a thing.

44. When Xiren later asks him who of Baochai and Daiyu is better in bed, he replies that Baochai is better because she is more voluptuous (she is "carved out of lamb's fat"; 5.58). Then he says that Daiyu is nevertheless better because when they make love, "it is marvelous beyond words" (5.58).

45. The erotic sequels also include a number of these nonromantic pursuits, but not to the exclusion of sexual interaction. *Honglou huanmeng*, e.g., also has Baoyu and Daiyu engage in philanthropy, while *Qilou chongmeng* has women engaging in battle.

46. *Honglou huanmeng* also features an instance in which Baoyu helps a young woman, Xiangling, when she has her first menstruation (16.244).

47. He "uses paper to wipe her front and back all clean" (9.57).

48. Other such examples can be found in 38.247–248, 39.257, 41.266, 45.291, and 296.

49. Early reactions to *Qilou chongmeng* are summed up by Baochai, who at the end of *Bu Honglou meng* (ca. 1814) describes the author of *Qilou chongmeng* as "a deranged maniac who has lost all sense of humanity" (48.430).

50. After Baochai tells Daiyu how much she loves her now, Daiyu responds, "I love you as much as he loves you" (5.55).
51. After she bears twins, she tells Baoyu why she figures she did so, recalling to him a night of pleasure in which they made love twice. The first time she climaxed first: "I felt your surging warm essence shoot into me, and then we fell into a deep sleep" (22.328). They later awoke and had sex again, in which they "had orgasm at the same time" (22.328). Thus, she concludes, the first session resulted in a boy, the second in a girl. On another occasion they whisper to each other about the pleasures of the night before (7.96). By chapter 12, the three of them routinely sleep together. For intimacy between Daiyu and Qingwen, see 16.237–238. Baochai sucks on Daiyu's breasts (19.279). Daiyu and Qingwen are said to be "just like female lovers," making reference to Li Yu's play *Lianxiang ban* (The fragrant companion), in which a man's two wives are lovers. See also the scene in which Qingwen and Daiyu cuddle in bed as they talk intimately (23.343)
52. For an actual example of a woman affirming sex as a part of love, see Ko's discussion of the *Three Wives' Commentary on Peony Pavilion* in *Teachers of the Inner Chambers*, 87.
53. That is, the game whereby one participant takes a drink and then transfers that mouthful to another (see 15.216–220 and 16.235).
54. The novel *Shenlou zhi* of about 1804 does the same, as do several other early and mid-Qing erotic novels. See McMahon, *Misers, Shrews, and Polygamists*, chap. 12.
55. Epstein, "Reflections of Desire," 93, referring to *Honglou meng*, chap. 63.
56. Xiluan is a distant cousin of Baoyu in the original novel. Grandmother Jia likes her and invites her to stay a while in the Jia mansion (*Honglou meng*, chap. 71).
57. Such intimate words are not unique to *Honglou huanmeng*. *Honglou fumeng* contains a scene in which one of Mengyu's wives, Zixiao, tells him just after their marriage that the reason she wanted to marry him was that she "wanted a husband for life who was a man of deep feeling" and that she was not motivated by a desire for "the love of pillow and mat" (28.310). She then asks him to spend the night of the next day in her room (311).
58. For more discussion of this point, see McMahon, *Misers, Shrews, and Polygamists*, 190–191.

ELLEN WIDMER

5

Honglou meng Sequels and Their Female Readers in Nineteenth-Century China

IAN WATT's classic study, *The Rise of the Novel,* charts a series of links between the English novel, its domestic subject matter, its female readers, and the emergence of fictions written by women.[1] Whereas his central preoccupation is with Defoe, Richardson, Fielding, and fictional realism, he also discusses ways in which women helped to shape the new genre. One important finding is the effect of extraliterary processes, such as mechanization, which in the eighteenth century began giving women more leisure time. Watt argues that despite all the artistry that went into its composition, the shaping of the English novel cannot be imagined without a cohort of newly liberated female readers whose interest was a necessary condition of this form's realistic and psychological turn. Against this background, the emergence of masterful women writers such as Austen takes shape as a plausible culmination of prior change.

It goes without saying that the novel's development in China, being completely outside the evolutions Watt discusses, evolved in very different ways. Except for *caizi jiaren* fiction (the so-called "scholar-beauty romance"), the Chinese novel prior to Western influence catered little to female readers, and there is scant evidence of any change in the amount of domestic leisure time. Furthermore, the most highly literate women subscribed to an ethos that, on the face of it, discouraged novel reading altogether. Even if these women, known as *guixiu* (gentlewomen), had enjoyed an increase in leisure, we would not have expected them to turn to popular fiction to fill the void. Many a *guixiu* abandoned all literary efforts once she took on domestic duties;[2] and the literary activity that was allowed her centered on poetry, not prose. At least this is the impression gleaned from works like Yun Zhu's *Guochao guixiu zhengshi ji* (Correct beginnings) of 1831, which downplays fictional interest in its various subjects' lives.[3]

This deemphasis affects Yun's own biography, as well as that of other women interested in *Honglou meng* (Dream of the red chamber). Yun's son Linqing was a good friend of *Honglou meng*'s second author, Gao E. Indeed, Gao wrote a preface to Yun's collected poems. Additionally, Yun herself once wrote poems on *Honglou meng* and its first sequel, *Hou Honglou meng* (Later dream of the red chamber).[4] Yet no signs of fictional interest appear in *Zhengshi ji*.[5] If Yun is any indication, we may eventually uncover further contrasts between ideal and actual *guixiu* practice. At any rate, by the late Qing, if not considerably earlier, a large audience of shopkeepers and women were consuming novels with avid interest, enough to disturb the moralists of the day.[6] This chapter uses the evidence of sequels to *Honglou meng* to build a case for a developing female readership well before that time.

Yun Zhu's ambivalent interest is not the only reason to view *Honglou meng* and its sequels as a fruitful field in which to explore the question of female audiences. The circumstances of this novel's composition and circulation are far from fully clear, but we understate when we say that the novel offers compelling female characters. We know, as well, that it was highly popular with women readers. Whether or not women constituted any part of Cao Xueqin's own intended readership, a number of women responded to his finished product in poetic form. The surviving writings of perhaps as many as twenty nineteenth-century women, all *guixiu*, contain references to *Honglou meng*.[7] Given the vulnerability of women's writings to time and other destructive forces, twenty is not an inconsiderable number to have come down to us since then. Evidence of another sort is found in the comments of literatus Chen Wenshu, whose *Xiling guiyongji* (In praise of gentlewomen of Hangzhou) of 1827 observes that women readers were captivated by *Honglou meng*.[8]

Meanwhile, with *Hou Honglou meng*, sequels to *Honglou meng* began emerging no later than 1796.[9] These would continue throughout the nineteenth century and beyond. Many of the authors of these sequels wrote under pseudonyms, but in recent decades the author of one of them has been identified as a woman. This is Gu Taiqing, who will be introduced immediately below. The combination of female characters, audiences, and at least one author in this series creates an analogy, however superficial, to the situation in England that Watt describes. Moreover, these interconnected data challenge the view that for inhibited *guixiu* readers, fiction was entirely out of bounds.

The argument that follows does not proceed in a straightforward manner. In unraveling the issue of female readership it is easier to proceed from the known to the unknown. This leads me to reverse the order of Watt's study, which begins with audiences and moves forward in time. Instead, I begin with a brief introduction to Gu Taiqing then search for evidence of audiences, and I focus first on Gu's sequel, *Honglou meng ying* (In the shadow of dream of the red chamber), even though it comes late in the series. After that, I backtrack to *Honglou houmeng* and the other sequels. Once I have explored this set of novels in some detail, I return to where I began, now having a basis from which to mark the distinctive traits of *Honglou meng ying*.

CHINA'S FIRST FEMALE NOVELIST?

The year 1877 marked the publication of *Honglou meng ying*, the first extant Chinese novel demonstrably by a woman. Widely known as a *ci* poet, *Honglou meng ying*'s author, Gu Chun (*zi* Taiqing) was born in 1799 and died in 1877, the same year her novel was published. Gu was a Manchu of the trimmed blue banner and the Xilin (or Xilinjueluo) clan. Her childhood is shrouded in mystery, and the fact that she acquired a Chinese surname has proven difficult to explain. We do know that she spent her adult years in Beijing. Gu used the pen name Yuncha waishi (Unofficial Historian of the Cloud Raft) for her novel rather than her real name or her regular pen names, thus helping to obscure her role as author. A preface by the ostensibly male Xihu sanren (Prose Writer of West Lake) does nothing to give her real gender away. The preface was written in 1861. Xihu sanren turns out to be the pen name of another woman writer, Shen Shanbao (1807–1862), the author's sworn sister and one of her best friends.[10]

The identity of Yuncha waishi and Xihu sanren was lost for many decades. An article by Zhao Botao in 1989 made the identifications, using poems by Gu that were preserved in manuscript in Japan.[11] These poems were not included in Gu's published collections and have only recently come out in printed form.[12] There is no doubt as to their authenticity. The identification of Gu as author depends in part on her use of the pen name Yuncha waishi for the "lost" poems. This overlap suggests that Gu did not aim fully to obscure her responsibility for *Honglou meng ying*.

The matchup further depends on a poem Gu wrote in mourning the death of Shen Shanbao. This poem is found among the poems in the manuscript in Japan. It contains the following lines.

> *Honglou*'s illusory landscape has no basis in reality.
> Occasionally I take up my writing brush and add a few chapters.
> [Shen's] long preface brought undeserved honor to my work.
> Frequent missives from her splendid pen demanded
> [that I complete the project].

Gu's own note to this poem observes,

> I have worked intermittently on a sequel to *Honglou meng* in several chapters, called *Honglou meng ying*. Shen wrote a preface to it. She asked to see it without waiting for me to relinquish the manuscript. She often chided me for my lazy nature and would tease me, saying, "You are almost 70 years old. If you don't finish this book quickly, I fear you will never succeed in doing so."[13]

In fact, Gu was sixty-two years old in 1861 when the preface was written. Shen died the next year, but Gu would live another sixteen years.

The long gap between the preface and the date of publication may mean that Gu wished her novel to be published posthumously. Blind in the last two years of her life, Gu could barely get around or write poems, much less transmit a manuscript to a publisher.[14] Thus some intermediary, possibly one of her children, has to be assumed.[15]

We know that the publisher, Juzhen tang, was situated in Beijing between about 1876 and 1896. One of the firm's special interests during this interval was vernacular fiction. Its main line of work was bilingual, Sino-Manchu books, a type of offering that continued before, during, and for some years after the seven or so years of offerings in Chinese.[16] It is plausible to assume that Gu's Manchu background entered into the publication process somehow,[17] and it is not impossible that the publisher knew her gender, even her full identity, although this cannot be proven. In any event, *Honglou meng ying*'s publication and hence preservation do not appear to have been completely accidental.

In twenty-four chapters, *Honglou meng ying* is not a long novel, but it is the product of considerable thought and artistic sensibility. Gu Taiqing would no doubt have been proud that it was preserved and that her authorship has been ascertained.

THE SEQUELS TO *HONGLOU MENG*

The sequels to *Honglou meng* emerged out of a wave of interest set in motion by the parent novel, yet each was an independent creative act with its own agenda, purposes, and intended readership. Taken as a group, they are an important index of how women reached out to fiction and how fiction was shaped by women's concerns. Additionally, they make a useful backdrop against which to assess *Honglou meng ying*.

No known sequel appeared until after the first printed edition of the Cao-Gao manuscript of 1792. The process of sequelization began between 1792 and 1796, during which time the first sequel, *Hou Honglou meng*, emerged.[18] *Hou Honglou meng* was closely followed by four other sequels (*Xu Honglou meng* in thirty chapters, *Xu Honglou meng xinbian* in forty chapters, *Qilou chongmeng*, and *Honglou fumeng*), all of which were in print no later than 1805.[19] This group of five early sequels helped to set the tone for later versions, both inspiring some of their specific features and establishing their generally high level of concern for women characters and readers. In this latter matter they continued and extended a trend set down by *Honglou meng*. The next twenty years saw the publication of four more sequels, (*Honglou yuanmeng*, *Honglou meng bu*, *Bu Honglou meng*, and *Zengbu Honglou meng*), all of which were in print by 1824.[20] After 1824, *Honglou meng* sequels appeared much more sporadically, though new ones continued to emerge into the Republican period, when *Honglou zhenmeng* (True dream of the red chamber, 1939) was published, and even later.[21] Besides the nine listed above and *Honglou meng ying*, I shall also consider *Honglou huanmeng* (The illusion of dream of the red chamber) of 1847 and *Xu Honglou meng gao* (Draft sequel to dream of the red chamber) after 1857. I do not count such apparent sequels as Wu Jianren's *Xin shitouji* (New story of the stone) of 1907, which parodies *Honglou meng* but with very new purposes and uses only two of its characters.[22] Besides these twelve, there is evidence of others that no longer survive, including another possibly authored by a woman.[23] But for the purposes of this discussion, I shall focus mainly on the eleven extant sequels that appeared before *Honglou meng ying*.

Reeditions and reprints are another gauge of the strength of the wave set in motion by *Honglou meng*. *Honglou meng* itself has been reprinted countless times, and many of the sequels also went through numerous reprintings. The most widely reprinted are the earliest, particularly *Hou Honglou meng*, which had inspired roughly twelve reeditions by 1900, most of which were themselves reissued several times.[24] *Hou Honglou meng*'s frequent reprints may have to do with its early date of publication; they may also be connected to such features as its conservative view of women.[25] The most highly regarded sequel in an artistic sense, *Honglou meng bu* (The dream of the red chamber revisited), on the other hand, is much less conservative in its attitudes.[26] It, too, was reprinted at least six times, although three of these reprints came out in the twentieth century and are hence beyond the scope of this study. *Honglou meng*'s twelve nineteenth-century sequels compare with only three to *Shuihu zhuan* (The water margin) all told, of which only one—*Dangkou zhi* (Quelling the bandits)—came out in the nineteenth century. *Dangkou zhi* was reprinted eleven times.[27] Multiplying the twelve *Honglou meng* sequels by their various reeditions and reprintings before 1900, one comes up with at least forty instances of new works or editions put out in print as sequels to *Honglou meng*. This crude measure leaves little doubt that sequels to *Honglou meng* and their reeditions constituted a prominent stream in nineteenth-century Chinese publishing. In addition, indirect sequels such as *Jinghua yuan* (Flowers in the mirror), which has over twenty reeditions plus some sequels of its own),[28] are manifestations of the same publishing trend.

The eleven sequels written between the 1790s and *Honglou meng ying* offer a wide spectrum of rationales for existing, plots, types of rhetoric, levels of artistic quality, and ways of connecting to the parent novel. Virtually every one justifies itself as a "correction" of some sort, whether because it resurrects Lin Daiyu to her former glory, punishes Wang Xifeng, or portrays the Jia family in a more civic-minded light than in *Honglou meng*. McMahon, in chapter 4 of this volume, develops these points in more detail. Sometimes the correction takes place within the plot and is justified as the result of a conversation between the author or the characters and Cao Xueqin or the stone; at other times a preface notes that it came about through the author's dissatisfaction with earlier sequels or with the way the parent novel ends.

In addition to the different rationales behind sequels, the plots can diverge significantly. This is true even of sequels that borrow ideas from one another. According to comments by the character Zhen Shiyin in the introductory chapter of *Zengbu Honglou meng* (Sequel to supplement to dream of the red chamber), *Honglou yuanmeng* (The resolution of dream of the red chamber; 1814) appropriated ideas from *Hou Honglou meng* (c. 1796). Moreover, the thirty-chapter *Xu Honglou meng* (Sequel to dream of the red chamber; 1799) is an important predecessor of *Bu Honglou meng* (Supplement to dream of the red chamber; preface 1814, published 1820). These last two novels share a conceit in their erection of parallel earthly and heavenly centers of activity, but after that, differences start to emerge. Moreover, *Bu Honglou meng*'s own sequel, *Zengbu Honglou meng* (1824), eventually branches out in the direction of barbarian relations, a plot line neither adumbrated in the parent novel nor developed in *Xu Honglou meng*.

As for rhetoric, here, too, the range is wide. The earliest sequel, *Hou Honglou meng*, is usually set at the conservative end of the spectrum, because it concludes with a resuscitated Daiyu setting down strict rules for household management. This is no doubt the reason it won Yun Zhu's approval, a point gleaned from her set of poems on this novel, mentioned above. On the liberal extreme lies *Honglou fumeng* (Return to dream of the red chamber; 1805), in which women pass exams and Baochai fights valiantly against an invasion of pirates and in which traditional hierarchies—class as well as gender—are questioned and (temporarily) overturned. Among the most overtly sexual are two later sequels, *Honglou yuanmeng* (1814) and *Honglou huanmeng* (1843).[29] In an earlier sequel, *Qilou chongmeng* (Revisiting the silken chambers; 1805), the author goes out of his way to inject scatological and erotic content into the story. Although this work, too, had several reprints, it frequently manages to offend.[30]

As far as connections to the parent novel are concerned, all sequels begin after either chapters 97 (the death of Daiyu) or 120 (the final chapter). Obviously the point of connection has a profound effect on the ways the subsequent plot line unfolds. Despite such vast differences, many of these works appear to be in conversation with one another. Even when the rhetoric of one is completely different from that of another, a minor detail or twist of plot raises suspicions that the author had read all or most of the sequels that had come out before his own. *Honglou meng ying*'s own points of indebtedness are discussed below.

Another point of interest is the broad geographic diversity of the sequels, in terms of place of publishing as well as where the fictional action unfolds. Although most of the early ones appear to have originated in the Jiangnan area, *Honglou fumeng* was written by a man from Canton, and both *Honglou yuanmeng* and *Honglou meng ying* were by authors with Manchu ties.[31] Furthermore, one of numerous books of criticism to spring up around the parent novel, *Du Honglou meng zaji* (Miscellaneous notes on reading *Honglou meng*; 1869), was by a writer from Anhui.[32] As for the site of the action, most sequels range broadly around China, including its border areas, and several venture onto foreign soil. Thus the forty-chapter *Xu Honglou meng* moves some of the action to Vietnam and Siam, some of *Zengbu Honglou meng* takes place in Hami and Tulufan (Turfan), *Honglou fumeng* has characters set in the Ryukyus, *Honglou yuanmeng* contains a few European characters, *Honglou huanmeng* has some female warriors from the Miao, and there are episodes involving Vietnamese and other "barbarian" evildoers in *Qilou chongmeng*. When foreign action is involved, it tends to be part of an effort to show the Jias in a good light by sending them to the defense of the dynasty, as if to compensate for their self-absorption in *Honglou meng*. Such geographical breadth is not confined to sequels to *Honglou meng*. One of *Shuihu zhuan*'s sequels, *Shuihu houzhuan* (Sequel to *Shuihu zhuan*) of 1664, is partly situated in Siam, and Hami is the site of some of the action of *Hou Xiyou ji* (Sequel to the journey to the West, Kangxi period).

The pattern of much Jiangnan or Beijing action complemented by outreach to other areas can be viewed as congruent with the situation in Yun Zhu's *Guochao guixiu zhengshi ji* of 1831, which was edited in the Jiangnan area but radiated out to distant frontiers. And it finds a mirror image in the extent to which foreign literary traditions looked to Chinese fictional sequels as material for adaptation into their own popular literatures. We will have occasion later in this chapter to consider developments in Korean and Japanese fiction by way of supplementing data from the Chinese fictional scene.

The extent, diversity, and ongoing richness of these responses to *Honglou meng* have something to do with the wave of interest among women readers that Chen Wenshu referred to in *Xiling guiyong ji*. It may also stem from a broadening of the reading community to include people of intermediate reading skills. An age- or gender-based explanation would be in keeping with *Bu Honglou meng*'s claim that the novel was widely known "among women and children,"[33] and it might further imply an expansion of the reading community in terms of class as well as gender and age. A question that can now be asked is whether the admittedly mediocre quality of many sequels is simply the result of the inherently derivative nature of sequel writing, or whether it is it better interpreted as an adjustment to its intended audience's lowered reading skills. To anticipate the ensuing discussion, it would appear that some *Honglou meng* sequels by highly literate authors are attempts to capitalize on *Honglou meng*'s popularity, but in terms the less well educated reader can enjoy.

Of course it is possible to explain the sequels without resorting to questions about their audiences. When Shen Shanbao's preface to Gu Taiqing's novel claims that regret over Daiyu's death was the primary motive behind all earlier sequels, her emphasis is as much on authors. A similar emphasis motivates a comment in the opening pages of Wu Jianren's *Xin shitouji* (1908) to the effect that every sequel writer proceeds from dissatisfaction with the sequels that came out up until his time.[34] Gu's autobiographical impulse, which comes up for discussion at the end of this chapter, would be another sign of the importance of author rather than audience in shaping sequels to *Honglou meng*.

In the ensuing discussion, I will focus largely on audiences but will pay some attention to authorial perspective. Both foci will ultimately help to link women to the production and consumption of fiction in new ways. This evidence is only partial, and it is often clouded by counterindications, all of which must be weighed in the balance as we go along. After I have worked through the purely gender-related aspects of this topic, I will return, briefly, to questions of class and age. These will ultimately lead to a summation of how the developing interactions of women and fiction affected both "parties" in the longer run. Once this series of steps is completed, I will return to *Honglou meng ying*.

HONGLOU MENG SEQUELS IN THE CONTEXT OF SCHOLAR-BEAUTY FICTION AND *TANCI*

McMahon has proposed that the scholar-beauty fiction of the mid-seventeenth century may have been written largely for and perhaps even by women.[35] If he is right, a female-centered fiction may have existed as much as one hundred years before *Honglou meng* first appeared. So far that case remains to be proven, though it is a promising avenue to pursue. We know that individual women did read this kind of fiction, and a very few responded to it in poetry.[36] It is even possible to find a stray female novelist or two, but almost none of their fiction survives.[37] This contrasts with the situation in *tanci* (prosimetric narrative), which were read by women in great numbers and which gave rise to a few poetical responses, but which appear to have generated a substantial literature in manuscript form. Beginning in the early nineteenth century, "women's *tanci*" went on to become a recognizable branch of published fiction under the initial leadership of Hou Zhi of Nanjing.[38]

Still another pattern is found with *Honglou meng*. The women who responded to the novel in their poems give us a prima facie basis on which to claim that women wrote about *Honglou meng* in significant numbers, very likely more than about any other novel. This could mean that it was the first novel to draw them in significant numbers as readers, thus disproving McMahon's hypothesis, or it could simply mean that it was the first novel to inspire them to craft responses in retrievable form. In the second case, McMahon's hypothesis is not disproved. Scholar-beauty fiction would then stand as a prelude to what later occurred with *Honglou meng*. We have also tentatively hypothesized that Gu Taiqing's demonstrated authorship of *Honglou meng ying* was a rare, though perhaps not unprecedented, turn of events among women writers. Additionally, I will argue below that *Honglou meng* sequels attracted women as readers and commentators. This evidence allows us to view these sequels as a new type of reading deemed suitable for women, whether or not Gu was the only proven author in this field.

In order to apply these rough observations to the question of sequels, we need to concentrate on the following questions: apart from Gu, can we identify other female authors in this branch of Chinese *xiaoshuo* fiction during the Qing? And are the narrators gendered in any way, as they are made to seem in "women's *tanci*?" If this literature were to resemble "women's *tanci*," with its "feminine" narrators and implied readership, one could safely assume that it was written exclusively for women (or for men who shopped on behalf of women). If not, another type of assumption must be brought in. Finally, what, if anything, do the sequels' array of characters allow us to infer about target audiences?

The data we have for answering these questions are not extensive, and the answers we have are only tentative. Yet the sequels do yield some answers, and they enlarge the context from which to understand *Honglou meng ying*.

Female authors

Other than *Honglou meng ying*, was any *Honglou meng* sequel authored by a woman? Among the twelve late eighteenth- or nineteenth-century sequels under discussion, five have authors identifiable as male.

1. Qin Zichen, *Xu Honglou meng*, thirty chapters, 1799. The author once held office in Shandong.[39]
2. Chen (first name unknown), *zi* Shaohai, *Honglou fumeng*, one hundred chapters, 1799. This work was edited by the author's sister, Chen Shiwen. The sister's editorial involvement gives us some ground on which to claim an infusion of feminine authorial talent, even though the lead author was male.
3. Wang Lan'gao, *Qilou chongmeng*, forty-eight chapters, 1805. Although the prefaces are not perfectly clear about the author's background, Yisu combs through other sources to confirm that this author had a modest official career.[40]
4. Guichuzi, *Honglou meng bu*, forty-eight chapters, 1819. The author once served in the army.[41]
5. Zhang Yaosun, *Xu Honglou meng gao* (Draft sequel to *Honglou meng*), twenty chapters, after 1857. The basic facts of Zhang's life are known.[42]

One other sequel is virtually certain to have had a male author: Xiaoyaozi's *Hou Honglou meng*, thirty chapters, before 1796.

The context in which Xiaoyaozi is discussed in the literature of his day suggests that this author enjoyed friendships with literati authors such as Zhong Zhenkui (who integrated the plot of *Hou Honglou meng* into his drama *Honglou meng chuanqi*) and Pan Zhao, another playwright who wrote on *Honglou meng*.[43] Nothing in the surviving record gives us reason to believe that these were friendships between a man and a woman. Until we have identified Xiaoyaozi for certain, however, the possibility of whole or partial female authorship cannot be eliminated altogether.

One avenue of approach to the remaining texts is to investigate certain features of fictional works that are known to have had female authors, then use these as a baseline against which to measure other sequels. The method is not without pitfalls, but it provides an avenue of access into the problem at hand. I propose that Gu Taiqing's *Honglou meng ying*, when set alongside Hou Zhi's *Zai zaotian* (Rebuilding heaven) of 1828, offers three suggestive common denominators in this regard: first there is a sustained interest in matters women knew a lot about, such as childbirth. Both *Zai zaotian* and *Honglou meng ying* offer detailed descriptions of this particular process, and each is otherwise immersed in the culture of the women's quarters. Second, there is a certain vagueness when it comes to the central features of masculine culture, such as the examination system, careers, promotions, and the world outside the home. For example, *Zai zaotian* is very much about affairs of state, but it views these affairs almost exclusively from the women's quarters; and *Honglou meng ying*'s chapters 11–12 mention Jia Zheng's expedition to the borders to fight against bandits, but it conveys very little sense of how these bandits were overcome. And, although chapter 17 of *Honglou meng ying* presents an exodus of characters from Beijing to the suburbs, it describes nothing of the landscape encountered along the way. And third, there is a strong sense of feminine propriety. For example, both *Zai zaotian* and *Honglou meng ying* celebrate fleshly sacrifice by females on behalf of ailing female relatives.[44] From a late-Qing reformist standard, this point would mark a conservative approach to female virtue. At the same time, a work like *Honglou fumeng,* which is rather liberal in its views of women, allowing them to don battle dress and fight pirates, could still pass the test that I have in mind. This is because it celebrates at least one virtue, filial piety, and also because the text is never vulgar in its descriptions of people and events. By contrast, a work that delves wholeheartedly into erotic territory cannot pass my test of propriety, no matter how "feminine-minded" it might seem in other regards. Because *Qilou chongmeng* and *Honglou huanmeng* elaborate on the characters' bedroom activities, they do not pass the test of propriety here proposed. *Honglou huanmeng* is the only anonymous work I eliminate from consideration as a feminine-authored novel on these grounds alone. (As previously indicated, we know that *Qilou chongmeng*'s author was male.)

There are many other attributes of our two female-authored fictions that draw them together, but the three selected have the advantage of conforming, in a commonsense way, to what we can safely assume about life in the women's quarters during the nineteenth century: women who lived there knew a lot about childbirth and other "womanly" matters, they did not know much about official careers and life outside the home, and they held (or were supposed to hold) high standards of behavior when it came to piety, chastity, and other forms of self-sacrifice. Another feature of *Honglou meng ying* that might appear to signal feminine authorship is contradicted by *Zai zaotian* and thus cannot be used. This is Gu Taiqing's self-effacing, relatively undidactic narrator, which is matched by Hou Zhi's much stronger rhetorical control. Whereas this difference might have more to do with genre than authorial gender, we so far have no reliable basis on which to conclude that any highly organized and manipulated *xiaoshuo* has to have been written by a man.

Applying these criteria to something as complicated as a novel is a very subjective matter, and one often encounters mixed signals. We will assess the value of our results in a moment, but for now, here is what happens when we apply our criteria to the sequels whose authorial gender is unknown.

Xu Honglou meng [xinbian] (Haipu zhuren, 1805, forty chapters) is very knowledgeable about the examination system, which it dwells on in great detail. It is also well informed about the career paths open to talented males. The men of the Jia family are now all extremely successful, and many chapters are spent on descriptions of official life—of appointments in such places as Shandong, Jiangxi, and overseas, of the droughts, floods, and pirates with which officials have to deal, and of their ascents up the career ladder. This is especially the case with Jia Zheng and his grandson Jia Mu, around whom the book revolves. Both men do well enough to come in close contact with the emperor, and Jia Mu even becomes prime minister. (Baoyu guides his son's successes from the immortal realm.) Although women do form poetry societies, the novel is not enthusiastic about their taking tutors (chap. 7), and it relegates their literary activities to a distinctly secondary role. It celebrates traditional womanly virtues, even seeing that an award is given to Baochai and Li Wan for their long years of chastity (chap. 39), but it is little interested in the psychological sacrifice that such chastity would have entailed. Nor is sexuality much at issue in this novel. Although the author has a somewhat shaky sense of world geography (Japan is just north of Siam), and although Jia Mu's birth is lovingly described, because of the heavy interest in officialdom, it is all but impossible to infer a female author behind the scenes.

Honglou yuanmeng (Mengmeng xiansheng, 1814, thirty chapters), along with *Honglou mengying*, is the second sequel by a Manchu. This novel is rather difficult to assess according to our criteria because of its overwhelming interest in the supernatural. On balance, it does not appear to have been written by a woman. The several instances of childbirth are described in perfunctory fashion. There is a good deal of military activity involving foreign women with big feet, all of which is highly fanciful. This may or may not suggest an interest in life outside the home. The novel cares about feminine propriety. This is especially visible in its attacks on Wang Xifeng and its praise for Lin Daiyu, but it is equally concerned with protecting the dynasty from its enemies, by means of fighters wielding magic pearls.

Bu Honglou meng (Langhuan shanqiao, forty-eight chapters, preface 1814, published 1820) and *Zengbu Honglou meng* (1824, thirty-two chapters) are both by the same author, Langhuan shanqiao, who may also have been responsible for reediting *Honglou fumeng*.[45] Since *Zengbu Honglou meng* is a continuation of *Bu Honglou meng*, the two works can be counted as two stages of a single idea. Both works feature instances of childbirth, but these are never elaborated on in detail. At the same time, the novels are precise about the ranks and positions to which the successful male characters are appointed.[46] *Zengbu Honglou meng*, furthermore, is quite explicit about relations between China and the Turfan and Hami peoples in chapters 28–30.[47] Although both works project a sense of female propriety and are interested in women who read fiction (see below), on balance the author of these two novels seems much more likely to be male.

Honglou huanmeng's (Huayue chiren, 1843) main emphasis is on the power of feeling. Feeling extends to sexual description, for example in chapter 19. By the standards here proposed, this means that the novel could not have been written by a woman. Also, although dozens of children are born, including many twins, the births are never described. Foreign combat is detailed, but in rather perfunctory fashion. This novel was issued under a different title, *Honglou houmeng*, in 1862.[48]

Admitting the limitations of our methodology, we come up with the answer that no anonymous sequel gives us sufficient reason to infer female authorship. Several, such as *Honglou yuanmeng* or *Bu Honglou meng*, offer somewhat mixed signals, but not enough fully to support such a claim.

This is not to say that our test criteria are free of problems. It is easy to imagine a discovery that would destabilize all that has been hypothesized so far. The worst problem with this methodology is the way it "essentializes" male and female writers. Were a woman other than a *guixiu*—or a *guixiu* who had abandoned her *guixiu* mind set, if such a thing were possible—to have written a sequel, its feminine authorship would not be detectable by the method at hand. And were a cloistered but curious woman to have consulted with male family members on details of the outside world, she might have been able to come up with a work like *Bu Honglou meng*. Conversely, although *Qilou chongmeng* has a male author, it has clearly researched the matter of childbirth, which it describes in what seems like "feminine" detail. Finally, we are met with the irony that the sequel with the most impeccably *guixiu* taste is *Hou Honglou meng*, whose author was almost certainly male. Although neither its narrative voice nor its actual author are female, it preserves attitudes about fidelity, motherhood, and piety that elicited favorable comment from a woman like Yun Zhu. Clearly, real texts present complexities that our simple scheme cannot account for. But insofar as it makes sense, this scheme suggests that Gu Taiqing is the only female author in this field.

Narrators

As we have seen, even *Honglou meng ying*, the one work definitely written by a woman, sustains an assumption of male authorship in both text and preface. This means that there is no clear-cut "feminine authority"[49] in any sequel to *Honglou meng*. Hou Zhi's narratives and other *tanci* by women offer a distinct contrast here. These constantly infuse autobiographical data to underscore the author's feminine gender, and they speak directly to feminine concerns. Additionally, no matter how great the proportion of female to male characters, there is never a constructed female recipient of narration within the sequels themselves, as there is in *Zai zaotian*. Thus the sense of fiction as a conversation between *guixiu* author and audience that characterize Hou Zhi's writings is completely absent from the sequels to *Honglou meng*.

Readers

Nevertheless, it is not surprising that many *Honglou meng* sequels find other ways of imagining their female readership, whether in prefaces or within the story proper. For example, even the very conservative *Hou Honglou meng* ends with Daiyu and Baochai exchanging critical comments on *Honglou meng*. In combination with "Cao Xueqin's mother's letter" preceding the novel, this conclusion suggests that intelligent women were imagined as part of the audience. Similarly, Chen Shiwen's editorial efforts on behalf of *Honglou fumeng* further the view that women's critical abilities had a place in works of vernacular fiction. And the concluding chapter of Qin Zichen's *Xu Honglou meng* features a discussion between Baoyu, Baochai, and Daiyu about the failings of *Hou Honglou meng*.

Bu Honglou meng is a particularly interesting example. Its concluding chapter presents a long sequence in which Baochai and others gather up all the sequels that have been written so far. Copies of some of these texts turn up in her own household, whereas others have to be sought from relatives and friends. Once the sequels have been gathered, Baochai spends a few days reading, then offers critical comments on where their good and bad points lie. Her motive is to ascertain her own fate and that of the other characters; yet the image of a woman reading fiction and issuing critical judgments about it sends another signal that *Honglou meng* sequels were fair game for women's critical powers. A similar process of sequel reading and evaluation occurs in *Zengbu Honglou meng*, but this time it is male characters who do the reading and make the judgments, not Baochai. Even so, *Bu Honglou meng*'s concluding sequence goes a long way toward encouraging women readers of both of these novels by Langhuan shanqiao. Like the critical comments by female characters and editors in other sequels, it forms a rough equivalent to the more visible implied female reader that Hou Zhi employed. In contrast, masterworks like *Shuihu zhuan, Sanguo zhi yanyi* (Romance of the three kingdoms), or *Xiyou ji* may indeed have been read by women, but they offer no built-in encouragement of this kind. Another contrast is to the covert reading of fiction by women that is portrayed in *Honglou meng*. What we are talking about is not covert; rather, we find women who read and judge fiction out in the open, not behind closed doors.

Apart from textual evidence, we have a few indications that historical women did actually read sequels to *Honglou meng*, both previously mentioned. One is Chen Shiwen's commentary to *Honglou fumeng;* the other is Yun Zhu's poems, written in response to *Hou Honglou meng*. One could also bring in the four poems of endorsement by women to *Jinghua yuan* in this regard, since they treat the latter novel as a welcome return to the type of reading experience they had found so enjoyable in *Honglou meng*.[50] Finally, The poems of Zhou Qi that were appended to her husband's edition of *Honglou meng* are obliquely relevant to the discussion. Here one could protest that it is the parent novel, not its sequels, to which Zhou appended her response, but Wang Xilian's edited edition does present itself as a reaction to the original *Honglou meng*.

The timing of the "Wang Xilian ping *Honglou meng*" (Wang Xilian's critical edition of *Honglou meng*) of 1832 allows us point to an interesting coincidence. The year 1828 was the date of *Jinghua yuan*'s final author-edited edition, whereas 1832 marked another important milestone: the first illustrated edition, with illustrations by Xie Yemei and preface by Mai Dapeng. This same four-year span also encompasses the first editions of Hou Zhi's *Zai zaotian* (1828) and Yun Zhu's *Guochao guixiu zhengshi ji* (1831). Scant though these examples are, the coincidence of their timing is striking. When viewed in combination with the fictional female critics of *Hou Honglou meng, Xu Honglou meng, Honglou fumeng,* and *Bu Honglou meng,* they leave little doubt that by the 1820s and early 1830s, if not earlier, well-read women regarded *Honglou meng* and all or most of its sequels as suitable reading terrain.

This is not to maintain that either *Honglou meng* or its sequels were ever directed solely at female readers. What seems much more likely is that authors visualized mixed audiences, although the more highly erotic sequels were most likely aimed only at men. (Certain woman may have permitted themselves to enjoy eroticism, but they do not appear to have been among the intended audiences for the erotic sequels. Such women are discussed by McMahon in chapter 4 of this volume and in recent writings by James Cahill.[51]) At this point we encounter an interesting chiasmus: the absence of images of female critics in the erotic sequels. In contrast, it is only non-erotic ones that create such images.[52] (*Xu Honglou meng xinbian* is the only novel that is neither erotic nor inclusive of criticism by women, on which see below.) This pattern can also be extended to *Jinghua yuan* on the non-erotic side, for *Jinghua yuan* does include reactions of women critics, as we have seen. Our finding suggests that early nineteenth-century authors may have made a distinction between fiction that was and was not thought suitable for women. The latter, no doubt, was sometimes read by women, and the former, no doubt, sought male as well as female readership. Such authors may even have preferred male readers. But the evidence at hand strongly identifies most sequels as suitable for women readers, even if they were not directed at them alone.

Characters and Issues

With or without female authors, narrators, or recipients of narration, the large number of female characters that people these sequels and the woman-centered plots give us further reason to infer female readership. A Daiyu who takes over leadership of the family and becomes Jia Zheng's close confidant *(Hou Honglou meng)*, a Baochai who leads an army *(Honglou fumeng)* or who holds down an earthly contingent of characters after the rest have moved on to heaven *(Zengbu Honglou meng)*—all suggest outreach to women who yearned for greater agency in their lives. Even compared to characters in *Jinghua yuan*, not to mention *Honglou meng* itself, the women that emerge in this literature are, for the most part, surprisingly resourceful, and they are often less obsessed with the tragedy of female existence.

At the same time, however, the erotic content of some of this fiction raises questions. *Qilou chongmeng* is positively awash in women characters, in far greater proportion to male characters than in *Honglou meng* itself, and some of them even pass examinations, but with the exception of a few high-minded *guixiu* set aside for marriage to the Baoyu-like hero, most of its female characters are subject to prurient scrutiny. A passage in which this hero inspects an ailing young woman and concludes, after a close-up of her private parts, that she has reached menarche is particularly unlikely to have been written with women readers uppermost in the author's mind (chap. 21). Similarly, deep kissing, groping, and hands under skirts force us to modify the assumption that all *Honglou meng* sequels featuring women were addressed to proper *guixiu*. The fictional Baochai's dismissal of this work as "insulting the eyes of those who read it" (*kanle wu ren yanmu*, 616) in *Bu Honglou meng* is completely understandable, given the regularity with which sexual activity is described. Throughout, *Qilou chongmeng* is deeply preoccupied with female anatomy, but not in a way that suggests the intimacies of the women's quarters that pervade *Zai zaotian* or *Honglou meng ying*.

Were *Qilou chongmeng* a spoof of more high-minded sequels, it might claim a certain artistic respectability, and this would give us another means of understanding the large number of ambitious and unconventional female characters.[53] Yet the work is not overtly humorous, though it is well written in places. Some traditional commentators view it as a mean-spirited attack on an enemy of the author, a verdict that does seem plausible, given the facts at hand.[54] Even if it was written out of spite and not for general audiences, *Qilou chongmeng*'s publication and its several reprints allow us to understand this text as part of the wave of popular publishing unleashed by *Honglou meng*. *Bu Honglou meng*'s Baochai may have disapproved of this book, but it was easily obtained, along with other sequels, from the bookshelves of her family members (616), who had no qualms about allowing her to read it. And while the uniqueness of its motivation sets it somewhat apart, the novel is rather traditional in the strictness of the distinction it makes between *guixiu* and other women. Alone among the large cast of female characters, the hero's future wives are exempt from sexual description. Except for its sexual interest, then, it creates a clear parallel to Yun Zhu's *Guochao guixiu zhengshi ji* of some twenty-five years later, which also put the *guixiu* on a pedestal while at the same time shielding her rhetorically from prying eyes.

A somewhat different picture is presented by the other sequel with erotic content, *Honglou huanmeng* of 1843. Revolving around the theme of "*qing*" (feeling), *Honglou huanmeng* is primarily concerned with punishing Wang Xifeng and elevating Daiyu. Eroticism per se is of less interest here than in *Qilou chongmeng*. Where this novel turns erotic, it is with the hortatory intent of pointing out the corruption and self-indulgence of the Jia family. At the end of the novel, the pursuit of sex for its own sake is abandoned, and the characters agree to reform themselves in other ways, as when they decide to donate their discarded outfits to the poor. Its descriptions of Baoyu, Baochai, and Daiyu's bedroom activities differ from what one finds in *Qilou chongmeng*, in that this time *guixiu* are not spared prurient scrutiny. Nevertheless, it again projects a sense that *guixiu* ought to hold themselves to a higher standard of behavior than other people, rather than lying around in bed so much of the time.

Works like *Qilou chongmeng* and *Honglou huanmeng* test without overturning the hypotheses advanced above. Not every *Honglou meng* sequel was designed for the proper woman reader, yet the category as a whole shows evidence of reaching out to women, and it mostly holds to a tone with which *guixiu* readers could feel at home. It was no doubt partly for this reason that the series of sequels gained currency as women's literature in Korea, as Pastreich has demonstrated, a point he bases on a collection of manuscript translations preserved in Naksonjae Palace.[55] In Korea, it was idle women (whether palace ladies or elite wives) who generated much of the demand for translations of

Chinese fiction, beginning in the eighteenth century.⁵⁶ The precise timing of the translations of *Honglou meng* sequels is only rarely known, but these may have been undertaken during the nineteenth century.⁵⁷ Translations for palace ladies were usually quite striking in their accuracy,⁵⁸ and they must have had to pass some test of appropriateness (if only in the minds of translators) before being put into Korean for this audience, who recirculated them by copying in an elaborate feminine hand. Given this readership of women, it is not surprising that such works as *Qilou chongmeng* and *Honglou huanmeng* were not among the ones translated.⁵⁹ In Korea, this series of works was grouped with translations of *caizi jiaren* novels, *tanci*, and other less exclusively "feminine" Chinese fictions that had previously reached readers of this kind.⁶⁰

Whereas Korean versions of these sequels may have seemed close in spirit to the *caizi jiaren* tradition, in China a distinction between the two categories can be made. No matter how contemptible they may be in an artistic sense, and no matter how their vulgar content may offend, most sequels to *Honglou meng* display a particular way of thinking about style. For example, *Honglou huanmeng*, which is far-fetched in the extreme when it comes to plot, is concerned throughout with a concept that Jin Shengtan termed "inserted speech" *(jiaxu fa)*, and it pays surprisingly great attention to the unspoken thoughts of characters. A much better pair of novels, *Bu Honglou meng* and its sequel *Zengbu Honglou meng*, focus heavily on stitching and construction, and they refer to the ideas and works of Li Yu and Jin Shengtan.⁶¹ Additionally, both are deeply interested in point of view, one of the key artistic features of *Honglou meng*. Taken as a whole, this collection of novels stands out not just as competing versions of how to conclude the parent novel, but also of active participation in a long-standing conversation about fiction that dates back at least to Jin Shengtan.⁶² We should also note, in this connection, that several of the twelve *Honglou meng* sequels draw inspiration from novels other than *Honglou meng*, among them *Shuihu zhuan, Xiyou ji, Jin Ping Mei* (The golden lotus), *Hou Shuihu zhuan,* and *Hou Xiyou ji*.⁶³

Evidence such as this provides a basis on which to argue that, within China at least, the sequels to *Honglou meng* occupy a somewhat different niche than the chaste fantasies of *caizi jiaren* fiction.⁶⁴ In terms of the texts to which they refer, if not their quality, they assert a conscious linkage to the great tradition of fictional masterworks, even when their orientation to women invites a feminine clientele. Their consistent portrayal of images of female readers, whether in the form of female editors, endorsers, or characters who read fiction, is a second point of contrast with *caizi jiaren* style.

NOVELS FOR WOMEN AND CHILDREN

To sum up, more than one *Honglou meng* sequel begins with a comment about the number of other sequels to which the parent novel has given rise. Naturally enough, the sequel making such a comment goes on to announce its own superior claims to sequel status, whether because of the worthier motivation behind its composition or because its subject matter makes a more appropriate follow-up to *Honglou meng*. Taken as a group, these comments provide yet another insight into the power of the wave set in motion by the parent novel, enough to give authors and publishers hope of significant advantage when they capitalized on its momentum, and enough to generate audiences wanting more of the characters, situations, and ambience of *Honglou meng*. More interesting still, the evidence provided by these sequels allows us to postulate a significant new look in the market for fiction during the decades after *Honglou meng* first appeared.

Some of this new look had to do with women. As far as *Honglou meng* sequels are concerned, there is only one case of proven female authorship, and not a single narrator or implied reader comes across as female. Yet the series as a whole gives rise to a multiplicity of female characters, and it projects a strong sense of women's importance as readers and critics, even more so than with *Honglou meng*. The evidence here considered suggests that *Honglou meng*'s enormous popularity among women readers, as documented by Chen Wenshu, women's own poetry, and other sources, helped to draw still more women into the fold of fiction readers. It is here that we find China's equivalent of the dynamic Watt described. This is not to claim that *Honglou meng* alone was responsible for such a change. It is just as possible, in fact probably more likely, that the spread of *Honglou meng* sequels was part of a larger process in which publishers, audiences, and seminal texts all played important roles.

Nor is it to suggest that fiction's new outreach in the nineteenth century was solely a matter of gender. As previously noted, class, too, is an area in which *Honglou meng*'s sequels appear to have reached out more fully than the parent novel. Compared to *Honglou meng*, most of the sequels are far more ordinary and plebeian, seemingly quite suitable for the shop clerks and women that read fiction during the late Qing.[65] Earlier we asked whether this rash of inferior writing was merely the understandable and unremarkable dilution of a masterwork in the process of reproduction and extension by lesser writers, or whether the audience for fiction extended downward for other reasons as well. The answer depends on which sequel one is talking about. In some instances, the sequel writer, though anonymous, comes across as barely aware of the subtleties of the parent novel. *Honglou yuanmeng* is an example along these lines.[66] At other times, the sequel comes much closer to achieving the moods and artistic accomplishments of the novel it succeeds. Here the best example is *Honglou meng bu*.[67] In a third category of sequel, the author appears to be highly literate himself and yet writes down to his audience, or at least writes a type of fiction that could pass muster as appropriate reading material for *guixiu* and other "lesser" readers, even as it satisfies other concerns. *Hou Honglou meng* exemplifies this type of situation. For whatever reason, we may hypothesize, most sequel authors aimed to reach audiences that were larger, less well educated, and significantly more female than the one Cao Xueqin had in mind.

A third type of outreach was to children. Several *Honglou meng* sequels present themselves in the context of widespread familiarity with *Honglou meng* among "women and children."[68] An orientation to young boys may help explain the huge geographic reach of such works as *Zengbu Honglou meng* and the forty-chapter *Xu Honglou meng*, which navigate their way through much of China and such places as central Asia, Siam, and Vietnam. These two works are much more adventure novels than novels about love. *Xu Honglou meng xinbian*'s unique position as the only novel in the set that is neither erotic nor accompanied by feminine commentary could suggest that it, too, targeted young male readers, perhaps more than women or girls. In any event, the role of sequels as chaste reading material for women, children, and members of the lower classes contrasts with a more erotic strain.

Faint though they are, the broad outlines of this picture show congruencies with a development in Japanese literature of about the same time. Just as the bulk of *Honglou meng* sequels was appearing, Takizawa Bakin (1767–1848) was rewriting works of Chinese vernacular fiction as *yomihon* (books for reading) and directing them at audiences that included women and children. His *Chinsetsu yumiharizuki* (Crescent moon; published in installments between 1807 and 1811) and *Nanso satomi hakkenden* (Satomi and the eight dogs; published in installments between 1814 and 1842) draw on *Shuihu zhuan* and *Shuihu houzhuan* most prominently, along with other Chinese sources. Bakin's work may also have drawn on *Honglou meng* and its sequels, but it is much more visibly dominated by *Shuihu*-like characters, themes, and concerns.[69] A samurai who had read widely in Chinese fiction, Bakin was able to use his adaptations to support himself between about 1790 and his death nearly fifty years later and to provide his readers with literature that was both entertaining and morally elevating.[70]

Does the Japanese reading market's ability to support an author who "wrote down" to readers have parallels on the Chinese side? Could deductions be made about the state of the Japanese economy and book trade that would apply to China of the same time? The limitations on the evidence available to date make it difficult to say. At any rate, like some of the Chinese authors we have been considering, Bakin wrote his adaptations for audiences whose reading abilities were far below his own.

Bakin's writings on *Shuihu zhuan* and *Shuihu houzhuan* (hereafter *Shuihu* and the *Houzhuan*, respectively) provide useful insight into the mechanics of "writing down." Both *Chinsetsu yumiharizuki*, which is heavily dependent on the *Houzhuan*, and a separate analytical essay about this novel titled "Hankan sōtan" (Windowside chats in a small room, which also takes up the *Houzhuan* and was published in booklet form in 1839) lend insight into the matter at hand.[71] They reveal that in addition to emphasizing chaste behavior, Bakin also worked toward happy endings even when the historical events on which his writing was based were not happy. We see this in his embrace of the *Houzhuan* as the way out of a dilemma posed by *Shuihu* (its moral rambunctiousness), which he did not want to pass on to naive readers in unadulterated form. Bakin is particularly critical of *Shuihu*'s "irresponsible" promotion of rowdies and murderers as heroes, but he also strongly rejected Jin Shengtan's solution of executing all of the heroes (if only in a dream) at *Shuihu*'s end.[72] The way the *Houzhuan* resolves this problem, in Bakin's mind, is through its tendency to honor only good characters and dishonor evildoers. On at least two occasions, he proposes that readers think of *Shuihu* and the *Houzhuan* as a single work, altogether 140 or 160 chapters long (100 or 120 for *Shuihu*, 40 for the *Houzhuan*).[73] The formula "beginning good, middle bad, end loyal *(shozen chūakū gochu)* is another way in which he characterizes the moral relationship between the two.[74] Bakin realized that a morally consistent universe was considerably at variance with reality, yet because of the censorship laws under which he operated, and because he expected to have women and children among his readers, he felt a responsibility to create a more perfect world. Bakin's well-elaborated thought processes give us a basis from which to explain the happy endings found in practically all sequels to *Honglou meng*. Explicitly or implicitly, most of the sequels reward positive behavior with positive outcomes and vice versa, on their way to turning out well.

Another reason for Bakin's interest in *Shuihu houzhuan* was its depiction of foreign travel. *Chinsetsu yumiharizuki,* the work most closely based on *Shuihu* and the *Houzhuan*, includes a well-researched foray into Ryūkyūan history and geography, as well as many excursions around Japan. The way in which foreign episodes are balanced against domestic ones is highly reminiscent of the *Houzhuan's* balance between chapters set in China and Siam,[75] and it could also be compared with *Xu Honglou meng xinbian's* Siam adventures, although in the latter case one finds less alternation between domestic and foreign scenes. With Bakin, travel may have been an idiosyncratic personal interest, but its depiction in his novels was also thought to be a selling point with readers.[76] As we have seen, the broad geographical reach of certain *Honglou meng* sequels makes sense along similar lines.

Having reviewed these various types of evidence, we can now sum up our findings about the confluence of literate women and fiction in China in the wake of *Honglou meng*. As far as women were concerned, the new availability of a sub-branch of fiction that welcomed their readership, criticism, and even authorship continued a process to which *Honglou meng* had given rise. As *Bu Honglou meng* helps to clarify, it was not unheard of for dignified families to store a full set of sequels in their bookcases or to lend them to virtuous and intelligent readers like Baochai. Whether the fates of their female characters were happy or grim, this literature had the capacity to interact meaningfully across a wide spectrum of women's lives. Compared to *caizi jiaren* fiction, where the main emphasis was on love and marriage, these works portray a much broader range of activities and states of mind. And compared to women's *tanci*, where narrator and recipient of narration were exclusively female, these works reached out to *guixiu* readers while accommodating younger or less well educated women and men.

On the other side of this confluence lies the issue of where *Honglou meng* sequels belong in the evolution of the novel during the nineteenth century. Earlier, I proposed that they may have extended a frontier opened by *caizi jiaren* novels as early as the seventeenth century; at least as likely, they expanded upon a new type of engagement with female readers set in motion by *Honglou meng*. In their apparent efforts to provide chaste reading material for the literate woman, *caizi jiaren* novels and chaste sequels share at least one common concern. Despite the dubious purity of certain individual sequels, the dominant impression of the set as a whole is of literature that *guixiu* might enjoy. The fact that this literature worked, via translation, as chaste reading material for Korean women is one measure of the success of its appeal. At the same time, *Honglou meng* sequels differ from *caizi jiaren* fiction in their more intense engagement with the great masterworks of fiction and with the ideas of Chinese fiction criticism to which these masterworks gave rise. Additionally, *Honglou meng* sequels yield evidence of a growing market for adventurous, idealistic, and accessible reading. This role finds parallels in Japan.

HONGLOU MENG YING IN THE CONTEXT OF OTHER SEQUELS TO *HONGLOU MENG*

With this groundwork now behind us, we can return to *Honglou meng ying* and explore it in more detail. We do this by placing it in two contexts: first in that of the other sequels, second in that of the life and work of Gu Taiqing.

When one sets *Honglou meng ying* alongside other sequels, it is obvious that Gu had read among them, despite the fact that she never quotes a single one by name. This is best seen in the details. For example, the name of Baoyu's and Baochai's baby, Jia Zhi, recalls that of their child in the forty-chapter *Xu Honglou meng,* where Zhige is the childhood name of Jia Mao. Jia Zhi has another antecedent in *Bu Honglou meng,* where Li Wan's son is given this name. Additionally, Ping'er's elevation from senior maid to legitimate wife of Jia Lian has a precedent in *Zengbu Honglou meng* (chap. 5). And, although Xiren (Aroma in Hawkes' translation) had previously married out of the Jia family, her marriage is undone and she returns to the family compound, exactly as happens in *Honglou meng bu.* Some of these duplications may have been coincidental, and others may derive from unfulfilled predictions in the parent novel, but they suggest a habit of looking to other sequels, which is characteristic of the sequel-writing process as a whole.

Turning now from details to larger patterns, *Honglou meng ying* is typical of many other sequels in its efforts to restore the Jia family's good fortunes and good name. This it does by retrieving Baoyu from his religious way of life and returning him to the family fold. He arrives home just in time for the birth of his son. Soon thereafter Ping'er, too, gives birth to a son, and Shi Xiangyun gives birth to a daughter. Near the end of the novel, Baoyu's son and Xiangyun's daughter are pledged to one another, and Ping'er's son finds an equally suitable mate among the family's circle of friends. Meanwhile Baoyu and others have performed brilliantly on the examinations, and Jia Zheng has carried out a successful mission against "hairy bandits" *(mao zei).* In gratitude, the emperor bestows many favors on the family. Events such as these combine with pardons (Jia She) or self-reform (Jia Lian) of the parent novel's less wholesome characters to effect a full reversal of the family's decline. When Shen Shanbao's preface points out that *Honglou meng ying*'s goods and bads are properly in alignment, she could be referring to adjustments of this kind.

Despite such indications of the role of earlier sequels in inspiring Gu's fiction, *Honglou meng ying* is very much her own. One important sign of her originality is identified by Shen Shanbao, who contends that Gu is the only sequel author to confine her attentions to characters still living at the end of *Honglou meng*. (For Shen to make such a claim in itself implies that she as well as Gu had read many sequels.) This claim is sustained by the sequels that survive. Virtually every other sequel resurrects Daiyu, or some stand-in for her.[77] Even *Bu Honglou meng* and *Zengbu Honglou meng*, which proclaim themselves offended when living and dead characters are mixed together (chap. 48 in the former, chap. 1 in the latter), get around this inhibition by opening several theaters of activity beyond the human realm. Because of this adjustment, Daiyu, Wang Xifeng, Grandmother Jia, and other highly memorable characters are still part of the fictional scene. By contrast, Gu's work is much more lifelike in completely closing down the stories of characters who died in *Honglou meng*. This means that her Baoyu is a rather dispirited character because he has no Daiyu to spark his interest, and the novel is subdued in contrast to the parent novel and to sequels that situate this couple's passion on center stage.

Other contrasts help to pin down *Honglou meng ying*'s distinctive tone. For example, Gu's narrator is noticeably weaker than that of other sequels. This is in part because it does not call attention to itself and has very little didactic function, but also because of the desultory way in which the plot unfolds. By contrast, a work like *Bu Honglou meng*, with its complex orchestration between different theaters of activity, projects a far greater sense of narrative control. Gu's interest in music also sets her sequel apart from others. *Bu Honglou meng* does have a number of musical moments (e.g., see chap. 41), but these are not as pervasive or as fully elaborated as in Gu's novel. *Honglou meng ying*'s interest in nature is also quite distinctive. Gu's keen eye for seasonal beauties and her express preference for the naturalness of nature, as opposed to man-made natural arrangements, harks back directly to *Honglou meng* (e.g., as expressed by Baoyu in *Honglou meng*, chap. 17). Yet along with her weak narrator, it enhances the lyrical tone.

Honglou meng ying's tendency toward autobiography further contributes to its distinctiveness. Gu's is probably not the only sequel to put a personal stamp on the action. If *Qilou chongmeng* is indeed a roman-à-clef, this would constitute individualization of a sort, and of course the parent novel's autobiographical bent makes a ready precedent for *Honglou meng ying*'s tendencies along these lines. Because we know nothing or next to nothing about the authors of other sequels, we cannot be perfectly sure when or even whether autobiographical details have crept in. Yet many other sequels, including several that were written anonymously, are so thoroughly plot-driven that it is difficult to infer much authorial self-presentation. By contrast, Gu's lyricism is in accord with her novel's autobiographical tone.

These autobiographical proclivities are highlighted when the novel is set alongside Gu's own poetical writings, many of which survive. Although much is obscure in Gu's biography, there is ample evidence that she was deeply involved in friendships with other talented women and that she often went on poetical outings with them. This is particularly the case during her later adulthood, after the early death of her "companionate husband," the Manchu prince Yihui. Just as in Gu's own life, her fictional heroines gather to celebrate holidays and to appreciate the changing natural scene. Whereas in *Honglou meng* such events take place largely in Daguan yuan, *Honglou meng ying* creates a second garden setting in Jia She's retirement home, located just outside Beijing. It is possible that the novel's second garden reflects the villa in the Beijing suburbs to which Gu moved after a sharp controversy with her in-laws following her husband's death in 1838. In the novel, women's poetry parties move from the first to the second location midway through.

Particularly interesting is the fact that one of Gu's own poem sets, nine poems in all, is fully replicated in this second garden, becoming the communal contribution of Shi Xiangyun and others to a poetry party celebrating the winter cold.[78] Like Gu herself, Shi is a widow in the novel, suggesting that Gu could have written some of herself into the picture in the form of this character, thus giving still clearer voice to autobiographical concerns. Finally, as a person who had experienced the sudden loss of a beloved partner, Gu may have empathized with Baoyu's painful yearning for Daiyu when she made his discomfort a centerpiece of her fictional scheme.

An autobiographical note of a different kind is struck by the various manifestations of Manchu culture in *Honglou meng ying*. For example, Zhao Botao observes that Manchu custom shaped the list of gifts Xue Baochai receives upon the birth of her son.[79] One of these, a kind of rocker, is customarily presented by Manchus, not Chinese. Another manifestation of Manchu culture can be found in the prince of Beijing's proposal of marriage to the Jia family on behalf of his daughter in chapter 15. The mores discouraging Manchu-Han marriages were especially strict when it came to Manchu women and Han men.[80] The prince's successful pursuit of this engagement for his daughter was most likely meant to bring out the Jia family's membership in the Chinese banner community. In *Honglou meng* the Jia family's banner identity is assumed but never highlighted to this degree. Here, as with the abundant horse riding, archery, and other signs of Manchu culture, Gu's own heritage is the likely reason for the change.

Cumulatively, this evidence points to a second way in which *Honglou meng ying* parts company with the fanciful and idealized plots of its predecessors. It is not only that Gu avoids bringing dead characters back to life, as Shen Shanbao maintains, but in implanting some of her own rather painful biography into her fiction, Gu contributes to its pessimistic and quotidian tone, a tone that persists even after the Jia family fortunes have been restored. This use of personal biography as material for fiction surely draws on *Honglou meng* itself; but Gu's feminine touch leads *Honglou meng ying* into new emotional territory. For example, its detailed scenes involving childbirth make for a kind of woman-to-woman conversation that is largely absent from *Honglou meng*, which puts Jia Baoyu at the center of its women's world.

It would be interesting to know whether Gu's self-referentiality derives only from antecedents in the parent novel, whether it was inspired by wider trends in nineteenth-century fiction, or whether it is best viewed as a natural extension of her work in poetical genres. Any one of these possibilities could explain *Honglou meng ying*'s shadowy but retrievable self-portrait of Gu Taiqing. Unfortunately, however, there is as yet too little outside evidence to allow us to reach a definitive answer at this time.

Honglou meng ying was not reprinted until 1988,[81] and we have so far found no sign that it influenced other fiction. This may be, in part, because of its very late arrival in the chain of sequels, which left few opportunities for direct emulation by later writers in this mode. Another deterrent may have been its general lack of robustness as a work of fiction. In terms of its chasteness, *Honglou meng ying* qualifies as a novel "suitable for women and children," and it makes a positive correlation between good behavior and success, as Gu's preface claims. However, alone among *Honglou meng* sequels, *Honglou meng ying* does not end particularly happily. Indeed, it hardly ends at all. The wrap-up in chapter 24, in which Baoyu encounters Daiyu and other women in a mirror only to be unable to reach them, is so abrupt as to seem like an afterthought.[82] Although this ending yields a potentially feminist moment, as analyzed by McMahon in chapter 4 of this volume, its abruptness also makes sense as a hasty response to pressure from Shen Shanbao.

Ironically, then, the definition of a literature "for women and children" to which our search for popular audiences led us in the first place is one that *Honglou meng ying* meets only partially. Neither blatantly optimistic nor conventionally entertaining, *Honglou meng ying* fails to qualify as popular literature in the purest sense of the term. Only now that we know of Gu's involvement do its artistry, its autobiographical proclivities, and its place in women's literature invite appreciation along other lines. *Honglou meng ying* may not compare with any work of Austen's, but it is a step beyond the *Honglou meng*s of Gu's acquaintance and a harbinger of future change.

Notes

1. Watt's work has undergone many challenges. See, e.g., DeJean, *Tender Geographies*.
2. See, e.g., Luo Qilan's statement to this effect, trans. Irving Lo in Kang-i Sun Chang and Haun Saussy, eds., *Women Writers of Traditional China*, 703–706.
3. For more on this source, see Mann, *Precious Records*.
4. Gao is one of several male prefacers to Yun's only extant collection of poetry, *Hongxiangguan shicao* (Draft poems of Hongxiang studio), which her son Linqing published as a surprise for her in 1814. Within the collection one finds other signs of Yun's interest in fiction, notably two sets of poems. One, "Xihe Daguanyuan jushe shi si shou" (Playfully following four poems on Daguan yuan's chrysanthemum club), parodies some among the set of poems on chrysanthemums in *Honglou meng* chap. 38; the other, "Fenhe Daguanyuan lanshe shi si shou" (Four poems after the Daguan yuan's orchid club), does the same with poems on orchids in *Hou Honglou meng* chap. 28. In the second case, the poems are most likely written to supplement a large set on the same subject by male endorsers of the novel. *Hongxiangguan shicao* is found in Tao Xiang, ed., *Xiyongxuan congshu* (jiabian).
5. For example, Liang Desheng's supplement to the *tanci Zaisheng yuan* is not mentioned in her entry. See 15/17a.
6. See the remarks of Xu Nianci dating from 1907 quoted in Hanan, *The Chinese Vernacular Story*, 11–12. Xu complains that youthful shop assistants were reading books like *Shuihu* and *Sanguo*, as well as erotic fiction, while women were reading *caizi jiaren* fiction. See also the similar sentiments expressed in Siqi zhai's *Nüzi quan*, 745, 758.

7. In addition to Yun Zhu's poems previously mentioned, see Wu Zao's poem on the novel, which is translated by Anthony Yu in Kang-i Sun Chang and Haun Saussy, eds., *Women Writers of Traditional China*, 611–612.
8. 15/10b.
9. In this chapter, references to all the *Honglou meng* sequels are to the editions published by Beijing daxue, except for Langhuan Shanqiao's *Bu Honglou meng*, for which I use the edition published by Hanyuan wenhua chubanshe (Taipei, 1993).
10. On sworn sisterhood, see Zhang Zhang, ed., *Gu Taiqing Yi Hui shici heji*, 169. For more on Shen, see Fong, "Writing Self and Writing Lives." I have written on Juzhen tang in more detail in "*Honglou meng ying* and its Publisher, Juzhen tang of Beijing."
11. Zhao Botao, "*Honglou meng ying* de zuozhe ji qita."
12. See Zhang Zhang, ed., *Gu Taiqing Yi Hui shici heji*. I am indebted to Lin Meiyi for supplying me with a copy of this work.
13. Zhao Botao, "*Honglou meng ying* de zuozhe ji qita," 247. See also Zhang Zhang, ed., *Gu Taiqing Yi Hui shici heji*, 169.
14. She discusses her blindness in a poem dated 1875. See Zhang Zhang, ed., *Gu Taiqing Yi Hui shici heji*, 176.
15. For information on Gu, I have relied on Nienhauser, Jr., ed., *The Indiana Companion to Chinese Literature*, 492; Wing-chung Ho, ed., *Biographical Dictionary of Chinese Women*: 52–54; Hummel, ed., *Eminent Chinese of the Ch'ing Period*, 386–387; Zhang Juling, *Qingdai Manzu zuojia wenxue gailun*, 231–245; Yan Dichang, *Qing cishi*, 555–559; Sun Wenliang, ed., *Manzu da cidian*, 205; Hu Wenkai, *Lidai funü zhuzuo kao*, 800; as well as Zhao Botao, "*Honglou meng ying* de zuozhe ji qita." See also the *nianpu* in Zhang Zhang, ed., *Gu Taiqing Yi Hui shici heji*, 719–754; and Zhang Juling, *Kuangdai cainu Gu Taiqing*, 1–30.
16. See Chong Yi, *Dao Xian yilai chaoye zaji*, 9, 19; and Sun Dianqi, *Liulichang xiaozhi*, 119–120, 139–140.
17. At least one other of the Chinese output had Manchu connections, e.g. *Ernü yingxiong zhuan* by the Manchu writer Wen Kang, which was published in 1878. See Sun Kaidi, *Zhongguo tongsu xiaoshuo shumu*, 151.
18. Yisu, *Honglou meng shulu*, 89.
19. Sun Kaidi, *Zhongguo tongsu xiaoshuo shumu*, 121–122; Ōtsuka Hidetaka, *Zōho Chūgoku tsūzoku shōsetsu shomoku*, 60–61.
20. Sun Kaidi, *Zhongguo tongsu xiaoshuo shumu*, 123; Ōtsuka Hidetaka, *Zōho Chūgoku tsūzoku shōsetsu shomoku*, 62–63.
21. *Honglou meng xinbu* (New supplement to Honglou meng) came out in 1984.
22. This novel's main hero is Baoyu, and Xue Pan is a fairly important character, but modernization is the main subject, not Baoyu's emotional life.
23. See, e.g., *Honglou zaimeng* (Another dream of the red chamber) and other titles listed in *Zhongguo tongsu xiaoshuo zongmu tiyao*, 631. Well before that, Tiefeng furen's *Honglou juemeng* (Awakening from the red chamber dream) had acquired a preface by the year 1844, but the work does not survive. For more on this work, see Zhao Jianzhong, *Honglou meng xushu yanjiu*, 31–36. The dating is based on a preface by Mei Shujun (1779–1844), which of course had to have been written before the author died.
24. See Sun Kaidi, *Zhongguo tongsu xiaoshuo shumu*, 121–123; and Ōtsuka Hidetaka, *Zōho Chūgoku tsūzoku shōsetsu shomoku*, 60–63.
25. *Zhongguo tongsu xiaoshuo zongmu tiyao*, 574; Yisu, *Honglou meng shulu*, 89–91, has other reactions.
26. *Zhongguo tongsu xiaoshuo zongmu tiyao*, 629, offers a judgment about this work's high quality.

27. Sun Kaidi, *Zhongguo tongsu xiaoshuo shumu*, 188–189.
28. Ōtsuka Hidetaka, *Zōho Chūgoku tsūzoku shōsetsu shomoku*, 152–155. For more on *Jinghua yuan* and its sequels, see chap. 9 in this volume.
29. Yisu, *Honglou meng shulu*, 111–114, 126–127; *Zhongguo tongsu xiaoshuo zongmu tiyao*, 618–619, 688.
30. *Zhongguo tongsu xiaoshuo zongmu tiyao*, 596–597; and Yisu, *Honglou meng shulu*, 100–101.
31. See preface by Liuru yisun, *Honglou yuanmeng*, 1.
32. Yisu, *Honglou meng shulu*, 174.
33. *Bu Honglou meng*, 615.
34. Yisu, *Honglou meng shulu*, 131.
35. McMahon, *Misers, Shrews, and Polygamists*, 102.
36. The woman dramatist Zhang Lingyi wrote her play *Mengjue guan* (Place of awakening from dreams) after reading the novel *Guilian meng* (Dream of returning to the lotus). See Hu Wenkai, *Lidai funü zhuzuo kao*, 509. See also note 6 above.
37. For example, Wang Duanshu's (1621–after 1701) semi-fictionalized portraits of Ming loyalists in her *Yinhong ji* (Red chantings), held in the Naikaku bunko; Wang Duan's (1793–1839) *Yuan Ming yishi* (Lost history of the Yuan and Ming), no longer extant. See also Zhang Hao, as described in Deng Hanyi's *Shiguan chuji* (Poetry survey, part one) section 12, of 1672, who is said to have written vernacular fiction. I am indebted to Tobie Meyer-Fong for information on Zhang. See her unpublished essay, "Collecting Knowledge about Women in Early Qing China," 9.
38. On numbers of *tanci*, see Toyoko Yoshida Chen, "Women in Confucian Society," 11–12. For one example of a poem on a *tanci*, see Gui Maoyi, *Xiuyu xucao*, 4:9b–10a. I have written on Hou Zhi in "The Trouble with Talent."
39. Zhao Jianzhong, *Honglou meng xushu yanjiu*, 84.
40. Yisu, *Honglou meng shulu*, 99.
41. *Zhongguo tonsu xiaoshuo zongmu tiyao*, 628.
42. Yisu, *Honglou meng shulu*, 130–131.
43. Ibid., 89. Zhong's note that he read *Hou Honglou meng* in 1796 is the basis on which it is dated.
44. *Zai zaotian*, chap. 8; *Honglou meng ying*, chap. 17.
45. See Ōtsuka Hidetaka, *Zōho Chūgoku tsūzoku shōsetsu shomoku*, 61. The editor is Langhuan zhai.
46. See, e.g, *Zengbu Honglou meng*, chap. 28.
47. The strategy of divide and rule outlined in this novel is described in more official sources. See Perdue, "Culture, History, and Imperial Chinese Strategy."
48. Ōtsuka lists *Honglou houmeng* as a separate publication, but its contents are actually the same as *Honglou huanmeng*'s. The copy of *Honglou houmeng* I viewed is in the Tokyo University Library.
49. Armstrong, *Desire and Domestic Fiction*, 30. Armstrong's definition of "feminine authority" includes a focus on women's experience, an intended audience of women, and perhaps critical commentary by women, as well as a woman narrator or author. I am using the term very narrowly here to mean only a woman narrator or a visibly female author.
50. *Jinghua yuan* has fourteen endorsements all told. Of these, four are by women.
51. Cahill, "A New Genre in Ming-Qing Figure Painting," in "Pictures for Use and Pleasure."

52. But not every non-erotic sequel, on which see below.
53. For more on the parodic quality of this piece, see chap. 4 in this volume.
54. Yisu, *Honglou meng shulu*, 99–100.
55. Pastreich, "The Reception of Chinese Vernacular Narrative in Korea and Japan," 27.
56. Ibid., 25.
57. Ibid., 103. On the possibility of earlier translation, see Zhao Jianzhong, *Honglou meng xushu yanjiu*, 39–40.
58. Pastreich, "The Reception of Chinese Vernacular Narrative in Korea and Japan," 28.
59. The sequels whose translations survive are *Bu Honglou meng, Honglou meng bu, Honglou fumeng, Hou Honglou meng,* and *Xu Honglou meng.* Pastreich's list on "The Reception of Chinese Vernacular Narrative in Korea and Japan," 28–29, does not clarify which *Xu Honglou meng* is implied. See also Zhao Jianzhong, *Honglou meng xushu yanjiu*, 39–40.
60. For example, *Sanguo zhi yanyi*, on which see Pastreich, "The Reception of Chinese Vernacular Narrative in Korea and Japan," 29.
61. See the discussion of various works of vernacular fiction in *Bu Honglou meng*, chap. 40, and chap. 1 of *Zengbu Honglou meng* where the discussion is continued. This second discussion refers to Jin Shengtan. *Zengbu Honglou meng* refers to the dramas of Li Yu on 118–119. See also the authorial comment at the end of *Qilou chongmeng*, which refers to Jin Shengtan.
62. I have not been able to consult all the *fanli* (general principles sections) that appear in some sequels. David Rolston informs me that some of these, too, establish connections between fiction and this type of fiction criticism.
63. *Xiyou ji* is cited intermittently in *Honglou huanmeng*, e.g., chaps. 6 and 9; *Zengbu Honglou meng*, chap. 11; and in *Honglou huanmeng*, chap. 17. *Hou Xiyou ji* is cited in *Bu Honglou meng*, chap. 40 and *Zeng bu Honglou meng*, chaps. 1 and 14. *Shuihu zhuan* is cited in *Bu Honglou meng*, chap. 40; *Zengbu xiyou ji*, chap. 11; and the concluding comment to *Qilou zhongmeng*. *Hou Shuihu zhuan* is cited in *Zengbu Honglou meng*, chap. 1. *Jin Ping Mei* is cited in the concluding comment to *Qilou chongmeng*.
64. Not every *caizi jiaren* novel is chaste. For information on erotic works in this vein, see McMahon, *Misers, Shrews, and Polygamists*, 126–149.
65. See note 5 above.
66. *Zhongguo tongsu xiaoshuo zongmu tiyao*, 619.
67. Ibid., 629.
68. For example, *Bu Honglou meng*, 615; *Zengbu Honglou meng*, 2.
69. His adaptations, borrowings from, and readings of Chinese fiction are discussed in Leon M. Zolbrod, *Takizawa Bakin. Jinghua yuan* is mentioned as one of the Chinese books that Bakin knew. See Zolbrod, *Takizawa Bakin*, 103. *Nansō Satomi Hakkenden* uses a conceit that may owe something to a device found in *Honglou yuanmeng* of 1814, magic pearls that are bestowed on a woman's children after her death and that help them run their lives. In *Honglou yuanmeng*, when Daiyu is resuscitated, she is wearing a pearl necklace that is said to represent congealed dragon tears. These are put to various useful effect as the story unfolds. Nowhere is it stated that Bakin knew *Honglou yuanmeng*, however.
70. See my "Island Paradises." See also Zolbrod, *Takizawa Bakin*.
71. Takizawa Bakin, *Chinsetsu yumiharizuki*. "Hankan sōtan" is reprinted in *Kokubungaku kenkyu* 27, 99–154. The original of this work is held in the Seikado bunko.
72. See Takizawa Bakin, "Hankan sōtan," 107.
73. For one of these, see Shiroaki Naoya, "Takizawa Bakin *Suiko gaden* 'kōtei gempon' choroku no kampon ni shu," 91. Shiroaki bases this observation on a line from Bakin's

Suikogaden of 1805. Bakin's own annotated copy of the *Houzhuan,* held in the Tenri Library, provides a second instance of this reasoning. It again refers to *Shuihu* as a 160-chapter novel, to which Chen's forty chapters are a fitting end.

74. Section seven of "Hankan sōtan" provides a good example of Bakin's thoughts about "blaming wrong." He argues that it is fitting that the *Houzhuan* begins with several officials being poisoned because Song Jiang's official suicide was by poison. He applauds this move even though, as he explicitly states, it runs counter to official history. See "Hankan sōtan," 107–108.

75. Both novels begin in the home country, then present a preliminary expedition by a small vanguard to the foreign land, which are islands in both cases. Many chapters later, the full contingent of heroes moves abroad. Near the conclusion, a small contingent returns to the mainland for a brief visit, then goes back to the island kingdom in which they now feel at home. For more on this sequel, see my *The Margins of Utopia*.

76. Zolbrod, *Takizawa Bakin*, 48–51.

77. *Qilou chongmeng* causes Daiyu to be reborn as someone else. Technically speaking, then, it does not resurrect Daiyu.

78. The poem set occurs in chap. 19 of *Honglou meng ying,* 154–156. Cf. Zhang Zhang, ed., *Gu Taiqing Yi Hui shici heji,* 145–147. Shen Shanbao's *Hongxuelou shicao* in *Hongxuelou shixuan chuji,* 8/16b–21a, has Shen's set of poems on the same theme with virtually the same rhymes. *Hongxuelou shicao* is found in the Nanjing Library. I am indebted to Grace Fong for supplying me with a copy of this source. The title to Gu's poems mentions that her set matches a set by Shen and by a third poet (Dong'e Shaoru), and since Shen's poems can be dated precisely to 1842, Gu's novel may date from that era.

79. Zhao Botao, "*Honglou meng ying* de zuozhe ji qita," 250. See *Honglou meng ying,* 29.

80. Ding Yizhuang, *Manzu de funü shenghuo yu hunyin zhidu yanjiu,* 335–342.

81. Beijing: Beijing daxue chuban she, 1988.

82. Zhao Botao, "*Honglou meng ying* de zuozhe ji qita," 249–250.

SHUHUI YANG

6

Growing from the Waist

The Problem of Sequeling in Yu Wanchun's *Dangkou zhi*

THE FAMOUS Ming-dynasty novel *Shuihu zhuan* (Water margin) is believed to have inspired the second-largest number of *xushu* (sequels) in the history of Chinese fiction, next only to *Honglou meng*. According to a recent study, there are fourteen bona fide *xushu* to *Shuihu zhuan*, seventy-four by a broader definition of the term.[1] Among all these *xushu*, Yu Wanchun's (1794–1849) *Dangkou zhi* (The suppression of the bandits) stands out not only for its literary sophistication, but also for its author's ultraconservative political position and the "loyalist fanaticism and loyalist paranoia"[2] with which he has all 108 members of the Liangshan band brutally killed in an attempt to crush the "rebellious spirit" of the original novel.[3] However, his project falls short of its purpose in spite of, or rather precisely because of, his extraordinary literary sensitivity and the great pains he took over twenty-two years in trying to make his sequel mimetically a natural outgrowth of the first seventy chapters of *Shuihu zhuan*. In rewriting the second part (or the last thirty or fifty chapters) of the original novel,[4] Yu ends up imitating it by modeling his chosen moral paragon Chen Xizhen after the very "brigands" that he condemns. This chapter intends to argue that by accepting the long-established narrative world of the original as his starting point, Yu is unable to rise above the law of "probability and necessity" prescribed by that world, as long as he intends his sequel to be mimetically convincing.

Yu Wanchun came from an official-scholar family in Shanyin (today's Shaoxing), Zhejiang Province. He acquired the preliminary academic degree of *zhusheng* early on in his life and was known as an intelligent and widely read scholar interested in all kinds of books, including Daoist teachings and vernacular fiction. It is not clear whether he tried but was never lucky enough to pass the provincial-level civil service examinations or whether he gave up his ambitions for an official position by choice and opted for a military career with his father in southern China. What is known is that he proved to be accomplished in martial arts as well, especially in archery, and, as his father's military assistant, he was granted an award by the Qing government for his "meritorious service" in one of the several crackdowns he was involved with on the armed rebellions in Guangdong and other areas of southern China of the time.[5]

Yu seems to have made full use of all his personal experiences mentioned above in writing his novel, which he started at the beginning of 1826 but did not finish until the end of 1847, after three extensive revisions. When the Taiping Rebellion broke out in 1850, government officials in Nanjing were already preparing for the publication of Yu's book in order to "safeguard public morals." When Nanjing fell to the Taiping rebels in 1853, the officials fled to Suzhou with the finished woodblocks of the novel and had it printed and published there. Authorities in the city of Guangzhou followed suit and published a pocket edition soon thereafter. When the Taiping leader Li Xiucheng took Suzhou in 1860, he ordered the destruction of the book—copies and woodblocks alike. But in 1871, after the suppression of the Taiping Rebellion, it was published again in a new edition.[6]

The eventful publication history of the book indicates how great an impact *Dangkou zhi* had on contemporary politics because of its author's avowed purpose of honoring the law and order of the empire *(dan ming guoji xie tianxiu).*[7] In his opening paragraph, Yu explains why he chose to express his loyalist views in fiction as a sequel to Jin Shengtan's seventy-chapter version of *Shuihu zhuan*.

> Gentle reader, why do you suppose the book was written? The fact is, Mr. Shi Nai'an's *Shuihu zhuan* does not present Song Jiang as a man of *zhongyi* [loyalty and righteousness]. Just observe how, throughout the novel, he devotes every word to descriptions of Song Jiang's vices. Where the words *zhong yi* are used in connection with Song Jiang, they are confined to verbal protestations only, from a man who is, at heart, nothing more than a vile bandit. Drawing such a contrast serves to show the iniquity in a clearer light. As Mr. Jin Shengtan put it, and in no uncertain terms, too, "Where do I see *zhong*? Where do I see *yi*?" In short, those who have *zhong* and *yi* will never allow themselves to be bandits. Those who take up banditry by no means qualify as men of *zhong* and *yi*. Now, there came along a certain Luo Guanzhong who suddenly whipped up a sequel to *Shuihu zhuan,* to present Song Jiang, of all people, as a man of true *zhongyi*. Henceforth, all later bandits under the sun have an example to follow: Do as Song Jiang did and claim to be *zhongyi* while remaining a bandit at heart. . . . Now that this book has already been printed and is in circulation, there is nothing I can do to stop it. But, Song Jiang, as a historical figure, far from being granted amnesty and given the mandate to quell the Fang La Rebellion, was captured and executed by Zhang Shuye. Since Luo Guanzhong resorted to

falsehood to wipe out historical facts, I might as well lay out the facts to debunk the myth, so that generations to come will be able to draw a clear distinction between bandits and men of *zhongyi*, a distinction that does not brook the slightest confusion.[8]

Clearly, Yu's sequel is meant to be more than a fictional account of a military crackdown on rebellious uprisings. It is also meant, as David Wang points out, "to be a *literary* campaign to 'terminate' a novelistic tradition—that of *The Water Margin*—allegedly responsible for thoughts of banditry and an ideology of treason" (the word "*jie*" in the other title of the novel, *Jie Shuihu zhuan*, means both to "complete" and to "terminate").[9] Wang is also right in saying that when it comes to the social effect of a fictional work, Yu should be regarded as "one of the progenitors of Yan Fu's and Liang Qichao's campaign for 'narrating' a modern nation half a century later."[10] But if we move beyond the Chinese vernacular novel as a specific literary genre to a broader sense of literature in general, be it highbrow or lowbrow, we can find that this tradition of (over)believing in the affective power of literature has a much longer history in China. The concept of literature as a means to achieve political, social, moral, or educational purposes has been a most influential one in traditional Chinese criticism since Confucius' time.[11] In Yu's case, his sequel is precisely a reaction in the same line of thought, as his opening paragraph indicates, to the overbelief in the affective power of fiction among generations of readers of *Shuihu zhuan*,[12] which seems to have taken on a life of its own in its hundreds of years of circulation. The distinction between fiction and fact, art and history, seems blurred not only for the majority of the reading public of *Shuihu zhuan*, but also for Yu himself, who, by relying on "historical facts" as he claims, is writing a fiction to "terminate" the social effect of another fiction that distorts "historical facts."

But *Dangkou zhi* is not meant to "terminate" the entire novelistic tradition of the *Shuihu zhuan* cycle. It is written as a sequel to "complete" the first part, that is, Jin Shengtan's seventy-chapter truncated version, which Yu attributes to Shi Nai'an, and to replace the second part, which he believes to be "falsehood" and to have been added by Luo Guanzhong. Yu's attribution of the two parts of *Shuihu zhuan* to Shi Nai'an and Luo Guanzhong, respectively, should not be taken seriously,[13] for it was just one of Jin Shengtan's unsupported assertions.[14] It simply means that he tries to follow Jin's interpretation of the novel as he understands it.

It is generally agreed that Jin's seventy-chapter edition was of his own making, based on the first seventy-one chapters of the Yuan Wuya 120-chapter version. In addition to providing analyses and evaluations to his text, Jin made some drastic changes. The most notable example was his "dismemberment at the waist" (*yaozhan*) of the novel, discarding the last forty-nine chapters of the version he used as his base text, which includes the Liangshan band's acceptance of amnesty and their tragic downfall after their successful but fatal mission against Fang La. Another thematically important change made by Jin was his exclusion of the word "*zhongyi*" in the title. Jin also used commentary and minor revisions to make Song Jiang seem more hypocritical than in the original text.

But opinions have been quite divided about Jin's intentions in making these changes and revisions and about his attitudes toward the Liangshan band in general, for his statements and explanations made on one page are frequently contradicted by himself on another.[15] Not surprisingly, Jin's commentary edition of *Shuihu zhuan* has provided fertile ground for a wide range of different interpretations, between Jin the advocator for rebellion and egalitarianism on the one hand, and Jin the staunch loyalist or reactionary on the other.[16] Yu Wanchun's position in this regard should undoubtedly be placed right at the most conservative extreme. He is apparently convinced that he shares exactly the same view with Jin on the Liangshan rebels, and by writing a sequel to exterminate them physically—not just symbolically in dreams, as in the seventy-chapter version—he is extending Jin's interpretation of the novel, carrying on the mission that Jin has accomplished only symbolically, or, twice symbolically.

To be sure, by choosing Jin's truncated version as the base of his own novel, as the starting point for his sequel, Yu faced a problem that did not quite bother other *Shuihu zhuan* sequel writers. In reviewing some of the most noticeable structural patterns that link the full-length *Shuihu zhuan* to *Jin Ping Mei* (The plum in the golden vase) and *Xiyou ji* (The journey to the West), Plaks points out that the text "follows the broad pattern of building up its central mimetic world gradually through the first half or two-thirds of the body of the text, followed by a lengthy final section devoted primarily to its accelerating dissolution."[17] In Jin's version, the latter phase is cut off, which means that not only does the story end where the Liangshan bandits are at the height of their power, but more important, the central mimetic world is fully established and has taken on a life of its own. In other words, Yu has to play the narrative game in his sequel by the same rules that inform that mimetic world, that is, the law of "probability and necessity." Yu cannot deny or ignore the existence of powerful evil officials like Gao Qiu and rampant official corruption in the Song dynasty society as described in the first half of *Shuihu zhuan,* nor the rebellions caused by official corruption and political persecution, nor the long-established Song dynasty's dual tactics of dealing with rebellions—*jiao* (crackdown by government troops) and *fu* (offering amnesty and enlistment to rebels), nor the knight-errant tradition among some rebels. Yu could and does have the three evil ministers, Tong Guan, Cai Jing, and Gao Qiu, punished toward the end of his sequel by executing the first two and sending the other into exile, but he could not eliminate them at the beginning. Had he done so, there would have been no motive for rebels such as Lin Chong to join the Liangshan band, and if the Liangshan band were not strong enough, there would be no need for Yu to write a sequel to eliminate them. In other words, Yu needs to keep the evil ministers alive and have them function as persecutors for a while to make his sequel a natural outgrowth of the original novel, just as he has to accept other social realities described in the first part of *Shuihu zhuan* to make his sequel mimetically convincing. If Jin cut the full-length *Shuihu zhuan* at the waist, Yu grows his sequel *from* the waist—the middle point of the structural pattern—

and follows the last part of the pattern to its final dissolution by continuing to stay in the same mimetic world until the end, although it is dissolved in a different way, with different protagonists.

Other well-known *Shuihu zhuan* sequels either start from a different point of this structural pattern or quickly enter an entirely different narrative world, or both, and consequently are less bound by the social realities and mimetic rules of *Shuihu zhuan*. Chen Chen (b. ca. 1613) starts his sequel, *Shuihu hou zhuan* (The water margin: A sequel), from the end of the full-length *Shuihu zhuan* when Song Jiang, Lu Junyi, and other major characters have all died. Some surviving members of the band carry on their rebellious spirit, sail overseas to Siam, and found a kingdom there, which means the central locale of the narrative is moved to a different mimetic world. Chen Chen got the idea for his sequel from a few lines in the penultimate chapter of the full-length *Shuihu zhuan* about what Li Jun is to become in the future (the ruler of Siam) when he leaves Song Jiang after the campaign against Fang La is over.[18] *Hou Shuihu zhuan* (A sequel to the water margin), written by pseudonymous writer Qinglian shi zhuren and published in the early period of the Qing dynasty, also begins after the death of Song Jiang and his principal associates. The protagonist of the sequel, however, is not a surviving member of the Liangshan band, but Yang Yao (ca. 1115–1135), an early Southern Song rebel who is described as a reincarnation of Song Jiang.[19] On the mimetic level, *Hou Shuihu zhuan* is really another story about another rebel leader, unrelated to and therefore unrestricted by the narrative world of the *Shuihu zhuan* cycle. Lu Shi'e's (1877–1944) *Xin Shuihu* (New water margin, 1909) does start after the grand assembly of the 108 heroes at the Liangshan stronghold from more or less the same point of the structural pattern as Yu Wanchun does. But it quickly moves into an entirely different world, the world of modern economy of the twentieth century. Tired of being rebels in an isolated area, the Liangshan heroes leave their stronghold voluntarily to devote themselves to economic activities in other parts of China. Jiang Jing, for example, sets up a bank with Shi Qian as his business partner in Xiongzhou, a prefecture known for its prosperous market economy, and becomes so successful that he is finally able to extend its branches to twenty other cities. Hu Sanniang runs a nightclub; Jin Dajian opens a bookstore; and Li Li and Li Jun set up a mining company while Tang Long and Liu Tang become managers of China's railway system.[20]

Yu Wanchun had more difficulties to overcome, if we take into consideration the fact that popular treatments of the Liangshan band, on stage or in simpler-text editions, tend to be sympathetic toward the rebels[21] and must have been in wide circulation among commoners for centuries.[22] This means that in the mimetic world of his sequel, Yu had to reckon with issues only implied in Jin Shengtan's version, but quite evident in popular accounts of the cycle, such as the possibility of granting amnesty to rebels who deserve it.[23] Yu can refuse Song Jiang amnesty, but he cannot deny in the mimetic world of the *Shuihu zhuan* cycle that the Song government's amnesty policy means that some rebels are more eligible for it than others.

In order to make his sequel a natural outgrowth from Jin's edition, Yu does indeed draw much of its structure and plot from the first part of *Shuihu zhuan*. Jin begins his seventy-chapter version with a *xiezi* (prologue) in which the three dominant images are a stone tablet, a serpent, and a tiger. Yu ends his sequel of seventy chapters, which are numbered from 71 to 140 instead, with a *jiezi* (epilogue) in which one can also find a stone tablet, a serpent, and a tiger.[24] Both texts conclude with two regulated verses in the same rhyming patterns. Mimetically, Yu's text begins exactly where Jin's ends: Lu Junyi wakes up from his dream in which all 108 members of the Liangshan band were executed by Zhang Shuye in a government crackdown. There are also some scenes in Yu's sequel that remind one of episodes in the first part of *Shuihu zhuan*. For example, Tang Meng's catching a monster leopard with his teeth in chapter 115 is probably meant to echo or outshine the famous scene of Wu Song beating a tiger to death with bare fists in the original novel. Sun Po's arranging an illicit love affair for her neighbors in chapters 96 and 97 clearly matches Ximen Qing's seduction of Pan Jinlian with Wang Po's help. The description of the archery duel between Chen Liqing and Hua Rong in chapter 125 bears strong resemblance to that of Yang Zhi's martial arts contest with other military officers in the northern capital of Daming. Also, Pang Yi's tug-of-war with a river monster in chapter 123 is as impressive as the way Lu Da, the Tattooed Monk, uproots a willow tree. And finally, Chen Xizhen's three attacks on the city of Yanzhou in chapters 106–110 appear to be modeled on the Liangshan band's three attacks on the Zhu Clan Village.

Similarly, quite a few of the stalwarts, whom Yu recruits in his sequel to deal with the Liangshan rebels, are either originally from Jin's version of the novel or are closely related to some characters in it. Zhang Shuye, who killed all the Liangshan heroes in Lu Junyi's nightmare in chapter 70, becomes the commander-in-chief of the government army. Hou Meng, who is mentioned in Jin's preface, which contains quotes from historical texts, only as someone who proposed granting Song Jiang amnesty, appears in Yu's sequel as an envoy sent by the emperor to offer amnesty to the Liangshan band. Wang Jin, who disappeared completely after the opening up of the text proper in chapter 1, shows up again in Yu's text to give Lin Chong a lecture. Wen Da and Li Cheng, who fled and disappeared without a trace after the fall of the city of Daming (the northern capital) to the Liangshan band in chapter 65, make a comeback in Yu's novel to participate in the military campaign against Song Jiang. Zhu Yongqing, Chen Xizhen's son-in-law and one of the archenemies of the Liangshan band, is the younger brother of Esquire Zhu, the head of the Zhu Clan Village. When Song Jiang was launching repeated attacks against the Zhu clan (chaps. 46–49), Zhu Yongqing, as he explains to Chen Xizhen in chapter 87, happened to be in the capital city away from home. Gai Tianxi, another archenemy of the Liangshan band, is the older brother of the boy that Li Kui brutally killed in a forest in order to force Zhu Tong to join the band (chap. 50), and Shi Gugong, who hates the rebels just as much, turns out to be the younger brother of Shi Wengong, who was captured and executed by the Liangshan band (chap. 67). But the best example that shows the care with which Yu tried to link his sequel to Jin's edition of the novel is the reappearance of Luan Tingyu, the martial arts coach of the Zhu Clan Village. In the final battle between the Liangshan band and the Zhu clan in chapter 49, there is no mention at all in the narrative whether Luan Tingyu fought to his death or simply escaped. The only information about him is found in Song Jiang's words: "Too bad such a worthy man was killed." To this Jin makes an interlinear comment, saying that Luan Tingyu's whereabouts after the battle is one of the three puzzles in the novel that the author devises in order to amuse himself by baffling his reader.[25] From here Yu picks up the narrative line and explains through Luan Tingyu's brother Luan Tingfang that Luan Tingyu was able to escape because the Liangshan band, thinking he was already dead, did not even bother to conduct a search (chap. 89).[26]

But Zhang Shuye, the commander-in-chief of the Song government army responsible for the crackdown on the Liangshan band, can be only a nominal leader because of Yu's sensitivity to the law of "probability and necessity" in the already fully established mimetic world of the *Shuihu zhuan* cycle, in which Zhang Shuye's characterization, sketchy as it is, is basically finalized and is not subject to further fictionalization.[27] Yu needed to create a new character as the protagonist of his sequel, someone who made no appearance in the *Shuihu zhuan* but was tangentially related to some other character in it. Chen Xizhen serves this purpose. Yu thus put Chen in charge of the suppression of the Liangshan band and presents him in the sequel as having been Gao Qiu's martial arts teacher before Gao gained power, and his brother as having been fatally wounded by Lin Chong in a martial arts contest. Yu may have had more freedom portraying Chen Xizhen than Zhang Shuye, but he still had to follow the mimetic rules in the *Shuihu zhuan* world as long as he wanted Chen Xizhen to be a believable character. As a result, I argue below, Yu ended up modeling Chen Xizhen on Song Jiang and other Liangshan rebels and imitating the last part of *Shuihu zhuan*, which he sets out to negate.

At the beginning of Yu's sequel, Chen Xizhen is a retired military officer who devotes himself to Daoist cultivation in the capital city. His only daughter Chen Liqing is a ravishing beauty well accomplished in martial arts, especially archery. They lead a quiet life until one day when Chen Liqing is seen in a temple by Young Master Gao, son of Gao Qiu, commander of the Imperial Guards. A lecherous man, Young Master Gao is beside himself with lust. He takes liberties with her, only to receive a sound beating by her on the street. Yet by dint of his powerful connections, he is not discouraged but insists on taking her as his concubine. Knowing full well that Gao will not let them off the hook unless they submit, Chen Xizhen pretends to accept Gao's proposal while making secret preparations to go into hiding with his daughter at his relative Liu Guang's place far away. They successfully make their escape from the city and arrive at Liu Guang's village safely after a long, arduous journey. But soon they learn that Gao Qiu has tracked them down and sent orders to arrest them. In a moment of desperation, they turn to the bandits of the nearby Ape Arm Fortress (Yuanbi Zhai) for help, and as a result, Chen Xizhen is made the leader of the band.

Chen Xizhen's experiences are almost a carbon copy of those of Lin Chong in *Shuihu zhuan*. Both start out as law-abiding, well-behaved government army officers, and both end up being forced to join a rebel band by exactly the same lecherous Young Master Gao and his father Gao Qiu. Chen Xizhen's experiences are also similar to those of Song Jiang and many other Liangshan rebels. Song Jiang repeatedly declines invitations to be a member of the Liangshan band until he has no other choice, having been arrested and sent to the execution ground by the local government in Jiangzhou but rescued just in time by the band.

This, however, does not mean that Yu approves of the popular notion of *guan bi min fan* or *bi shang Liangshan* (oppression by corrupt officials brings the rebel members together).[28] It is true that Yu seems to have no intention of denying the presence of rampant official corruption and official oppression in the world of *Shuihu zhuan*. But what he really wanted to advocate is the view that the oppressed should not rebel in spite of oppression and persecution by corrupt officials, and he tried to convey this message to his reader through some of the characters in his sequel. In chapter 98, when Song Jiang explains that what he is doing as a rebel leader is eliminating corrupt officials for the people, Yu has Master Bamboo-Shoot-Corona, a Daoist sage, retort, "Why should you be so concerned about corrupt officials? There is the emperor who rewards and punishes, there are the censors who press charges, and there are the inspectors who investigate. What posts are you holding now, to justify your eagerness to take on all these duties?"[29] In chapter 133, Yu has Wang Jin lecture Lin Chong for falling into Gao Qiu's trap and then becoming a rebel: "How come a talented man like you didn't know how to avoid traps [laid by Gao Qiu]?... And how come you didn't learn anything from your fall but debased yourself further by joining the underworld of 'the greenwood'?... Am I to believe that you had no choice but to become a bandit?"[30] And in chapter 109, Xu Hua, magistrate of Yuncheng, berates Lu Junyi sharply: "Even if you were wronged and wanted to avoid trouble, you could very well go into hiding in the mountains under concealed identities. How could you have ganged up in such a big way in defiance of all moral principles?"[31]

But this is easier said than done. Yu could have used these three characters as his mouthpiece without violating the law of "probability and necessity" in the mimetic world of *Shuihu zhuan* because their views, convincing or not, can be taken as the personal opinions of the characters. But when Chen Xizhen is physically placed in such a predicament in the sequel, he has to follow the same narrative pattern that many Liangshan rebels have gone through, rebels who started out as decent human beings just like Chen. When he is asked why he does not go and live in seclusion somewhere inaccessible to evil officials, Chen Xizhen replies, "I would be only too glad to go if there were such a good place under heaven."[32] In fact, Chen does choose to go to his friend Liu Guang's place to hide, but ends up having Liu's family implicated. As a result, Liu Guang is also forced to go to Ape Arm Fortress. So is Zhu Yongqing, by another evil official, Wei Fuchen, sometime later. Had Yu given the trio of Ape Arm Fortress leaders a place to hide so that they would not have to become rebels, he simply would not have been able to continue his sequel, because he would have no one eventually to carry out the task of suppressing the Liangshan band.

But this is only the first part of the structural pattern of the full-length *Shuihu zhuan* cycle. Yu had to move forward along the same narrative trajectory into the second part of the novel, where one can find a sharp distinction between good rebels and bad rebels.[33] Rebellion can not only be excused by an absence of evil intentions, but also justified by a strong loyalist desire to serve the emperor. Chen Xizhen is described in the sequel as a rebel leader who is intensely loyal to the government and who is simply biding his time until amnesty is granted. "Although he stays at Ape Arm Fortress, his heart is always with the emperor," as his friend Yun Long puts it.[34] Chen himself often claims that he, while in the greenwood, "would never dare to forget the lavish patronage of the emperor."[35] At the moment he is made the leader of Ape Arm Fortress, he proclaims with tears in his eyes, "I would never dream that such a calamity would befall me. Please allow me to bid farewell to the imperial court." He then kowtows in the direction of the capital and says, "Even though your unworthy subject finds himself temporarily in hiding from his nemesis, Your Majesty is never absent from his humble thoughts."[36] When trying to persuade Zhu Yongqing to join the Ape Arm Fortress band in chapter 87, Chen professes that he is "only taking temporary shelter" at the fortress while "awaiting an imperial pardon."[37]

This is exactly the same rhetoric that Song Jiang uses to talk captured government army officers into joining the Liangshan band. In chapter 55, Song says apologetically to Xu Ning, "I'm here in this marsh only temporarily, just waiting for an imperial amnesty so that I can repay our country with my utmost loyalty and strength."[38] In chapter 57 Song tells Huyan Zhuo in much the same words, "I've had to seek refuge in this marsh while awaiting an imperial pardon."[39]

But the parallel between Song Jiang and Chen Xizhen does not stop here. When he is made the chief of the Liangshan band after Chao Gai's death in chapter 59, Song changes the name of the Hall of Honorable Union (Juyi Ting) to the Hall of Loyalty and Honor (Zhongyi Tang) to emphasize his loyalty to the emperor and his desire to receive amnesty from the imperial court.[40] There is also a Hall of Honorable Union at Ape Arm Fortress,[41] and once he becomes the leader there, Chen Xizhen expresses the same feeling of loyalty by having a shrine for the emperor built named the Hall of His Majesty (Wansui Ting).[42] If Song Jiang's repeated claims of loyalty to the emperor in the first part of *Shuihu zhuan* invite suspicion and have often been deemed a utilitarian means to keep the band members together, as both Jin and Yu seem to suggest,[43] he is described in the second part as someone who would go to any lengths to gain imperial amnesty, even seek help from Gao Qiu, one of the mortal enemies of the Liangshan band. When Gao Qiu is captured in chapter 80, instead of taking revenge on him as the band does on Huang Wenbing (chap. 40/41), Song Jiang lavishes him with hospitality until Gao promises, "If you permit me to return to the capital, I and my whole family will be your guarantors before the throne. An amnesty will surely be granted and you will be given an important position."[44] In Yu's sequel, Chen Xizhen is depicted as equally eager to enlist anyone's help to obtain imperial amnesty, including his nemesis Gao Qiu. When the latter is besieged in Mengyin by the Liangshan band in chapter 101, Chen volunteers to save Gao's life by lifting the siege with his Ape Arm forces. Gao is moved to tears, saying, "Of all people it was you who saved my life. . . . Surely I will strongly recommend you to the emperor."[45]

Chen Xizhen has other ways to demonstrate or prove his loyalty to the emperor, much the same as what the Liangshan band does in the second part of *Shuihu zhuan*—that is, to fight against or help quell other rebels who have no desire to serve the emperor. In both the 100-chapter and 120-chapter editions, the Liangshan band launches a military campaign on the government's behalf against Fang La, a rebel leader who is unqualified for an imperial pardon/amnesty (*fu*) and therefore deserves to be suppressed (*jiao*). In Yu's sequel, Chen Xizhen repeatedly attacks the Liangshan rebels, who are described as defiant and treacherous. In chapter 87, Chen tells Zhu Yongqing that the suppression of the Liangshan rebellion will be the best gift he can present to the emperor.[46] In chapter 88, Chen's friend Luan Tingfang explains that attacking the Liangshan band is Chen's way of atoning for his sin of becoming a rebel himself.[47] In chapter 101, Chen says directly to Lin Chong, "In order to obtain an imperial pardon, I have no other choice but to do some damage to you heroes."[48] When the imperial pardon is granted, Chen, now the commander of a government army, keeps on fighting against the Liangshan band until all 108 members are either killed in action or captured and executed in the capital city by the government, much as what the Liangshan heroes do to the Fang La Rebellion in the second part of *Shuihu zhuan*. However, unlike Song Jiang, who is poisoned to death once his mission is accomplished, Chen Xizhen and his followers are awarded with promotions. But Chen resigns at this highest point of his official career and chooses to devote himself to Daoist cultivation as a recluse in Mount Song. Although Chen leaves the mundane world of Song-dynasty society in a very different way, his departure structurally marks the dissolution of the narrative world in *Dangkou zhi* much the same as Song's death does in *Shuihu zhuan*.

Thus Chen Xizhen has completed his five-phase journey in the mimetic world of the *Shuihu zhuan* cycle by following in the footsteps of Song Jiang and many other Liangshan rebels of the full-length editions, from oppression by corrupt officials, to rebellion, to imperial amnesty, to suppression of other rebels, and finally to dissolution. Yu may not have intended to portray his chosen paragon this way, but once he puts Chen into the mimetic world of the *Shuihu zhuan* cycle, he has to let Chen grow and develop on his own. It is not surprising that at the beginning of the sequel, Chen bears some resemblance to Yu himself, in terms of both social status and devotion to Daoism. But there is no way to engage such a withdrawn person in social and political activities unless he is forced to, and it is not likely for a person of such social status to rise to the top of the military in a short period of time, except through the rebellion-to-amnesty channel. In other words, Chen has to go through the first four phases of the five-phase journey in order to gain power and to carry out the formidable task of eliminating the Liangshan band that Yu assigns him. Without Gao Qiu's persecution, Chen would remain content in seclusion for the rest of his life. Without becoming a rebel, he would not qualify for an imperial pardon and therefore would not rise quickly to power. Yu cannot afford to let Chen miss any single link of this chain of causality if he wants to have the Liangshan bandits suppressed in his narrative, on the one hand, and to make his protagonist, who does the suppressing, a believable character, on the other.[49]

In writing his sequel, Yu not only follows the structural pattern of the full-length *Shuihu zhuan,* but also tries to model some of his heroes on the Liangshan rebels. For example, Yun Tianbiao is depicted as looking exactly the same as Guan Sheng, or Guan's ancestor Guan Yunchang, his family name "Yun" being the same ideograph as the "Yun" in Yunchang.[50] Chen Liqing's simple-mindedness reminds one of Li Kui,[51] and her indiscriminate killings in the city of Yizhou in chapter 84 are described in the same phrase *(yi jian yi ge, pai tou'er kan qu)*[52] as in Li Kui's case when he runs amok in the execution ground of Jiangzhou in chapter 39 *(yi fu yi ge, pai tou'er kan jiang qu).*[53] Chen Xizhen himself seems to be a composite character with features from four Liangshan leaders. He has Lin Chong's martial arts skills and shares Lin Chong's experiences as a victim of Gao Qiu's persecution. He also has Gongsun Sheng's supernatural magic power and Song Jiang's leadership capability. And when it comes to military strategy, he can hold his own with Wu Yong. At one point Chen even tries to rescue Liu Guang's mother by using the same stratagem that Wu Yong devises to rescue Lu Junyi from the prison of Daming.[54] Also, Yu's portrayal of Chen and other heroes as incarnations of thunder gods descending from heaven to help the Song emperor may have been inspired by the mythical idea in the initial narrative section of *Shuihu zhuan* that the 108 Liangshan heroes are all star spirits reincarnated, and therefore endowed with supernatural powers.

Similarly, Yu's negative portrayal of Song Jiang parallels the image of Fang La, who is categorized as a "bad rebel" in the second part of *Shuihu zhuan.* The best strategy at Yu's disposal to demonize Song Jiang and to justify a total elimination of all the Liangshan band members in a mimetic world where there is a sharp distinction between good and bad rebels is to reduce them to the "bad rebel" category by discrediting their claims of loyalty to the emperor as well as their activities avowedly in service of the emperor. The Liangshan heroes are "good rebels" in the full-length editions because, as Yan Qing says to the emperor in chapter 81, "Song Jiang and his band have 'Act in Heaven's Behalf' written on their banner and their hall is called Hall of Loyalty and Honor. They never attack any government seats or harm the people. They kill only corrupt and slanderous officials. They long for an early amnesty so that they can devote themselves to serving our country."[55] Fang La is a bad rebel because he does just the opposite of what Yan Qing says above. Fang rises in rebellion out of a belief that he is destined to be a king or emperor, and he loses no time in proclaiming himself king once he gains enough power over a large piece of territory containing twenty-five counties.[56] He rules like a despot, bringing such afflictions to the local people that complaints are heard everywhere. A man named Yuan in chapter 95/115 [57] says, "We are all good, loyal subjects of the Great Song Empire, but Fang La is crushing us with levies. If any man refuses to pay, he and his whole family are slaughtered."[58] An old man who volunteers to be a guide for the Liangshan army tells Song Jiang in chapter 97/117, "My family have been ordinary residents around here for generations, but Fang La is oppressing us cruelly and we have no place to hide."[59] Even an old Buddhist monk complains (chap. 98/118), "All the local people have been harmed by Fang La. There isn't one who doesn't hate him."[60]

In Yu's sequel, Song Jiang is described as a dangerous expansionist who, like Fang La in *Shuihu zhuan,* harbors ambitions for the throne. Not only do the Liangshan rebels attack government seats, but they also eagerly keep these cities in a bid to expand their territory.[61] To underline Song's military and political ambitions, interlinear comments in Yu's narrative observe that Song "intends to take the capital"[62] and is "trying to play the role of an overlord like Duke Huan of Qi and Duke Wen of Jin in the Spring and Autumn Period."[63] Yu also passes his view of Song to the reader through some of his characters, including Zhang Mingke, Zhang Shuye's nephew: "This sly Song Jiang harbors such high ambitions that he would neither be satisfied with the position of prime minister at court, nor with being the chief of a powerful rebel band in a regional area. He renamed his hall 'Loyalty and Honor,' and always claims that he is waiting for an amnesty. But this is just his strategy to keep his band members together."[64] Mimetically, Song is described as someone who would go to any lengths to prevent the emperor from granting him amnesty. When Hou Meng is sent by the emperor as an envoy to offer amnesty to the Liangshan band, Song has him assassinated on the way and puts the blame on Chen Xizhen. When it comes to doing harm to innocent people, Song Jiang in Yu's sequel outdoes even Fang La. The Liangshan rebels massacre the inhabitants of every city that they capture.[65] However, Song in his last days is punished for being a "bad rebel" by Yu the same way Fang La is in *Shuihu zhuan.* Like Fang, Song escapes when his stronghold falls to the government troops, but is captured before he is able to make it, taken to the capital city, and executed in the cruelest way—dismemberment by a thousand cuts *(lingchi).*

That Song is captured by two fishermen named Jia Zhong and Jia Yi, homophones of "phony loyalty" *(zhong)* and "phony righteousness/honor" *(yi)* brings out Yu's rationale for a total elimination of Song and his Liangshan band,[66] in keeping with Jin Shengtan's interpretation of Song as a hypocrite. To be sure, Yu is successful in reducing Song to the category of "bad rebels" like Fang La by depriving Song of his *zhong* and probably part of his *yi* as well, but he is not able to deny the Liangshan band some other aspect of *yi.* While *zhong* is mainly understood as loyalty to the emperor, the term *"yi,"* often translated in English as "righteousness" or "honor," has multiple meanings, two of which are particularly important in understanding *Dangkou zhi* as a sequel to or rewriting of *Shuihu zhuan.*[67] The first one refers to "justice" or "righteousness" or "appropriate moral conduct," as in the phrase *"zhengyi,"*[68] which Yu denies the Liangshan band by presenting them as doing great harm to innocent people, especially in chapter 81, when the first bloodbath takes place. The second one denotes "chivalric fraternity"[69] or dedication/unity/solidarity within a social group, as in such compounds as *jieyi* and *juyi*.[70] Ironically, in spite of his professed purpose of debunking the myth of both *zhong* and *yi* on the part of the Liangshan band, Yu has "surprisingly little to say against the spirit of dedication and sacrifice shared by the rebels."[71] David Wang is right that the Liangshan rebels' "dedication to their colleagues, combined with the desperate, defiant mentality" caused by Yu's denial of permission to get them amnesty, "gives rise to some of the most touching episodes in the novel."[72] But we also need to take into consideration Yu's literary sensitivity to the law of "probability and necessity" of the mimetic world of the *Shuihu zhuan* cycle. Without solidarity, the 108 rebels would not have become sworn brothers (*jieyi*) and would not have gathered together at Liangshan (*juyi*), or at least would have been quickly and easily dispersed by the government. Without a highly unified, powerful rebel band as is described in the grand assembly scene in Jin Shengtan's last chapter, there would be no need to write a sequel to have them all killed, and there would be no base from which Yu could grow his sequel.

To sum up, in order to present a dramatic account of the elimination of all 108 Liangshan band members without forfeiting too much of the reader's sense of credibility, Yu Wanchun has no other choice but to play by the same rules prescribed in the mimetic world of the *Shuihu zhuan* cycle. As a result, not only does his hero Chen Xizhen appear to be modeled after Song Jiang and other Liangshan bandits of the full-length editions, but his villain Song Jiang also bears much resemblance to Fang La. Ironically, Yu's *Dangkou zhi* does not seem to be a successful "termination" of the rebellious spirit of the *Shuihu zhuan* cycle, but rather thematically a new version of the original full-length novel, with Song Jiang replaced by Chen Xizhen and Fang La renamed as Song Jiang. It might not be an exaggeration to say that had *Dangkou zhi* been written and published by someone else three hundred years earlier, Yu would have probably found, in his crackdowns on the rebellions in southern China in the 1830s, some rebels claiming to have been emulating Chen Xizhen and his followers instead.[73]

NOTES

1. See Li Zhongchang, *Gudai xiaoshuo xushu manhua*, 3–4. For a discussion of different definitions of *xushu*, see Martin Huang's introduction to this volume.
2. David Wang, *Fin-de-Siècle Splendor*, 129.
3. Y. W. Ma, "Shui-hu chuan," 715.
4. According to Y. W. Ma, *Shuihu zhuan* as it existed before Jin Shengtan's redaction has six main sections: 1) from the escape of the baleful star spirits to the grand assembly of 108 heroes at the Liangshanbo stronghold; 2) events leading to the honorable surrender; 3) the expedition against the Liao Kingdom; 4) the campaign against Tian Hu; 5) the campaign against Wang Qing; and 6) the campaign against Fang La and the end of the group, 713. The Rongyu tang 100-chapter edition covers sections 1, 2, 3, and 6, while the Yuan Wuya 120-chapter version, which Jin's text follows most closely, contains all six sections. Jin's truncated version has only section 1.

5. Lin Wei, *Qingdai xiaoshuo lungao*, 47; Guo Yanli, *Zhongguo jindai wenxue fazhan shi*, 458–459; *Zhongguo tongsu xiaoshuo zongmu tiyao*, 605–606.
6. Dai Hongsen, preface, in Yu Wanchun, *Dangkou zhi*, 1–2.
7. This is the concluding line of Yu's sequel.
8. Yu Wanchun, *Dangkou zhi*, 1.
9. David Wang, *Fin de Siécle Splendor*, 126–127. The first and only mention of the term *"jie"* in the text (in Yu's opening paragraph), however, does not seem to mean "terminate" in its context; see Yu Wanchun, *Dangkou zhi*, 1.
10. David Wang, *Fin de Siécle Splendor*, 126.
11. James J. Y. Liu, *Chinese Theories of Literature*, 106; Lin Gang, *Ming Qing zhiji xiaoshuo pingdian xue zhi yanjiu*, 97.
12. For example, many Ming bandits fashioned sobriquets after the nicknames of the Shuihu heroes; Y. W. Ma, "Shui-hu chuan," 715. For more examples of rebels emulating Shuihu heroes, see Shi Zhengkang and Shi Huikang, *Shuihu zongheng tan*, 269–271; and Nie Gannu, *Zhongguo gudian xiaoshuo lunji*, 87–94. Two examples that Yu Wanchun personally witnessed are cited in his younger brother's preface to *Dangkou zhi*, 1049–1050.
13. Y. W. Ma, "Shui-hu chuan," 712.
14. See Jin's fourth preface on Song dynasty history, *Shuihu zhuan*, 17; Rolston, *Traditional Chinese Fiction and Fiction Commentary*, 117.
15. For examples of Jin's contradictions, see Rolston, *Traditional Chinese Fiction and Fiction Commentary*, 30, 40–42.
16. For a brief historical survey of the diametrically opposed readings produced by Jin's commentary edition of *Shuihu zhuan*, see Rolston, *Traditional Chinese Fiction and Fiction Commentary*, 37–39; for a detailed discussion of Jin's views of *Shuihu zhuan* and his attitudes toward the Liangshan bands, see Ouyang Jian, "*Dangkou zhi* jiazhi xinshuo," in his *Ming Qing xiaoshuo caizheng*, 420–455.
17. Plaks, *The Four Masterworks of the Ming Novel*, 311.
18. For a detailed study of Chen Chen's *Shuihu hou zhuan* in English, see Widmer's *The Margins of Utopia*.
19. Y. W. Ma, "Shui-hu chuan," 715; for a summary of the plot in Chinese, see *Zhongguo tongsu xiaoshuo zongmu tiyao*, 298–300.
20. Li Zhongchang, *Gudai xiaoshuo xushu manhua*, 129–131; *Zhongguo tongsu xiaoshuo zongmu tiyao*, 1145–1147.
21. Rolston, *Traditional Chinese Fiction and Fiction Commentary*, 27.
22. For examples of rebels emulating Song Jiang and other Liangshan heroes, see note 12. Jin's version of the novel may have eclipsed the longer versions, but obviously not popular versions of the cycle. Yu's mention of "Luo Guanzhong's sequel" in his opening paragraph indicates that even the full-length editions were quite available and influential in Yu's time.
23. Jin has self-contradicting statements about amnesty in his fourth preface, "Song shi gang, Song shi mu piyu," which contains quotes from historical texts. See Rolston, *Traditional Chinese Fiction and Fiction Commentary*, 36.
24. This can be understood as Yu's effort to follow Jin's comment on *Shuihu zhuan*'s broad structural pattern of both beginning and ending with a stone tablet (chapter comment for chap. 70). There is a stone tablet in Jin's last chapter as well.
25. *Shuihu zhuan*, 938.
26. Yu Wanchun, *Dangkou zhi*, 286–287.

27. This is pointed out in the chapter commentary on chap. 132: *Zhang Shuye bu ke duo fuhui*, Yu Wanchun, *Jie Shuihu quan zhuan*, 5:2526.
28. Y. W. Ma, "*Shui-hu chuan*," 714. Yu plays on the term *"bi shang Liangshan"* by setting its surface meaning "to become Liangshan rebels" against its general meaning "to become rebels." Chen Xizhen is described as adamantly refusing to join the Liangshan rebels as he is fleeing Gao Qiu's persecution. See *Dangkou zhi*, 65, 68, and 97.
29. Yu Wanchun, *Dangkou zhi*, 436–437.
30. Ibid., 930–931.
31. Ibid., 725.
32. Ibid., 281.
33. For a discussion of three kinds of peasant uprisings in both *Dangkou zhi* and *Shuihu zhuan*, see Ouyang Jianzhuo, "*Dangkou zhi* shi *Shuihu zhuan* zuozhe guandian de zaixian."
34. Yu Wanchun, *Dangkou zhi*, 464.
35. Ibid., 252.
36. Ibid., 204.
37. Ibid., 263.
38. Shapiro, trans., *Outlaws of the Marsh*, 912; *Shuihu zhuan*, 1052–1053.
39. Shapiro, trans., *Outlaws of the Marsh*, 937; *Shuihu zhuan*, 1081. Another excuse in the same line of thought that both Chen Xizhen and Song Jiang in the full-length *Shuihu zhuan* use to justify their attacks on governmental bastions is that they are to take revenge only on their persecutors; see Yu Wanchun, *Dangkou zhi*, 242.
40. Yu has the Hall of Loyalty and Honor burnt down by a heavenly fire right at the beginning of his sequel in an attempt to negate Song Jiang's claim of loyalty.
41. Yu Wanchun, *Dangkou zhi*, 284.
42. Ibid., 314.
43. See Jin's interlinear comments on what Song Jiang says to Xu Ning in chap. 55 and to Huyan Zhuo in chap. 57, *Shuihu zhuan*, 1053 and 1081.
44. Shapiro, trans., *Outlaws of the Marsh*, 1276; *Shuihu zhuan*, 1421.
45. Yu Wanchun, *Dangkou zhi*, 472–473.
46. Ibid., 263.
47. Ibid., 284.
48. Ibid., 470.
49. Yu could be regarded as a "pioneer in the technology of the Chinese military romance" (David Wang, *Fin-de-siècle Splendor*, 259) for his use of anachronisms such as *benlei che* (galloping thunder wagon) and *chenluo zhou* (underwater conch boat), but it should also be understood that Yu considers himself very much in the *Shuihu zhuan* tradition in using this kind of anachronism (*Dangkou zhi*, 14). Ling Zhen's prototypical cannon is one example from *Shuihu zhuan* (Shi Zhenkang and Shi Huikang, *Shuihu zongheng tan*, p. 190). For an argument that Yu puts these "modern" weapons in a traditional Daoist cosmological (as well as narrative) order, see David Wang, *Fin-de-siècle Splendor*, 259–265.
50. Gao Mingge, *Shuihu zhuan lungao*, 295. For a picture of Yun Tianbiao, see illustration 4, Yu Wanchun, *Jie Shuihu quan zhuan*, vol. 1.
51. Lin Wei, *Qingdai xiaoshuo lungao*, 57.
52. Yu Wanchun, *Dangkou zhi*, 217.
53. Shapiro, trans., *Outlaws of the Marsh*, 462; *Shuihu zhuan*, 753.
54. Yu Wanchun, *Dangkou zhi*, 206.

55. Shapiro, trans., *Outlaws of the Marsh*, 1289; *Shuihu zhuan*, 1432.
56. Shapiro, trans., *Outlaws of the Marsh*, 1436; *Shuihu zhuan*, 1767.
57. This refers to chap. 95 of the Rongyu tang 100-chapter edition and chapter 115 of the Yuan Wuya 120-chapter edition. See note 4 above.
58. Shapiro, trans., *Outlaws of the Marsh*, 1509; *Shuihu zhuan*, 1835.
59. Shapiro, trans., *Outlaws of the Marsh*, 1533; *Shuihu zhuan*, 1854.
60. Shapiro, trans., *Outlaws of the Marsh*, 1550; *Shuihu zhuan*, 1868.
61. Yu Wanchun, *Dangkou zhi*, 6.
62. Yu Wanchun, *Jie Shuihu quan zhuan*, 3: chap. 98, 1176.
63. Ibid., 1: chap. 77, 323.
64. Yu Wanchun, *Dangkou zhi*, 348.
65. Ibid., 165.
66. Ibid., 984.
67. For discussions of the various meanings of the term *"yi"* in the novel, see Plaks, *The Four Masterworks of the Ming Novel*, 168, 351–352; Wang Zengbin and Tian Tongxu, *Zhongguo gudai xiaoshuo tonglun zongjie*, 314–315; Ouyang Jian, "*Dangkou zhi* jiazhi xinshuo," 422; Ning Jiayu, *Shuihu zhuan qutan yu suojie*, 173–183; and Du Jinghua, *Yehua Shuihu*, 64–79.
68. Ning Jiayu, *Shuihu zhuan qutan yu suojie*, 173–174.
69. David Wang, *Fin de Siècle Splendor*, 131.
70. Ning Jiayu, *Shuihu zhuan qutan yu suojie*, 175–177.
71. David Wang, *Fin de Siècle Splendor*, 131.
72. Ibid., 133. Wang cites five examples: the heroic deaths of Wu Song, Lin Chong, Lu Zhishen, Gongsun Sheng, and Qin Ming.
73. Although Chen Xizhen is generally believed to be a far less appealing character than many of the Liangshan rebels, at least three episodes in *Dangkou zhi* were adapted for Beijing opera performances before 1949; see Gao Mingge, *Shuihu zhuan lungao*, 259, note 1.

ROBERT E. HEGEL

7

Rewriting the Tang

Humor, Heroics, and Imaginative Reading

BEGINNING IN the sixteenth century, China's readers were treated to a series of full-length novels, each recounting adventures and events from the Sui, Tang, and Five Dynasties periods, roughly the four centuries from 580 to 970. Several rewrote one or more predecessors to varying degrees; others were striking in the originality with which they developed convincing characters for historical figures from those periods. Most of these novels concentrated on political events, at court and on the battlefield. Martial heroes dominate a relatively late sequence of continuations produced during the Qing period that are sequels in the narrow sense of that term. Two among this series of novels have consistently delighted readers through the years; they have been reprinted numerous times since they first appeared. My concern here is with the second of this pair, a unique mid-Qing popular novel originally titled *Shuo Tang quanzhuan* (Stories about the Tang, complete; or, more literally, *Telling* stories about the Tang, 1736) that rewrote, revised, and thereby substantially subverted the narrative material of its predecessors, the older favorite *Sui Tang yanyi* (The romance of the Sui and the Tang, 1695) in particular.

My purpose in this chapter is to explore the ways that the *Shuo Tang* author, known only as Yuanhu Yusou (Old Fisherman of Mandarin Duck Lake), radically reinterpreted earlier texts. In short, by incorporating relatively raw material from the storytelling or theatrical traditions into elements of earlier written fiction, he took his novel in particular and the vernacular novel in general to new levels of entertainment writing. I conclude that *Shuo Tang* was intended, at least in part, to be an outrageous parody of seventeenth-century literati fiction, a literary game meant to amuse those readers who could appreciate his play. Furthermore, the artistic complexity involved in this parody suggests that this "Old Fisherman" must have been a writer of some sophistication who was intimately familiar with oral renditions of tales about late Sui-period warriors. Behind this pen name must have hidden a *wenren* (literatus) novelist similar in training to several of his predecessors, not the mere scribe for professional storytellers he has previously been made out to be.[1]

By *parody* I do not mean only the self-conscious imitation of an earlier writer's style. Instead I refer to the appropriation of characters and action from the source texts, deliberately misread and combined with elements probably exaggerated from their origins in professional oral presentations to degrees that surprise and amuse the sophisticated reader, in order to emphasize its differences from the older version. This cynical subversion of widely known narrative material produces expectations among readers that are explicitly left unfulfilled in the new text. Indeed, the derivative version frequently presents material that violently—and humorously—contradicts what the reader might be familiar with from the earlier fictional sources, while ironically undercutting the oral materials as well. Of course, I can only speculate on what any individual original reader or group of readers might have anticipated as they read this novel for the first time; presumably a range of responses greeted this work. Even so, because *Shuo Tang* can be read successfully as the vehicle for literary play, this suggests that the ideal intended reader for the work was sophisticated and that he (or she) was familiar with earlier works in the Sui-Tang sequence of novels. This perspective alone makes full sense of *Shuo Tang* as a deliberate parody rather than merely the jerky novel of exaggerated martial adventures replete with violence and trickery that it seems to be when read superficially. It also allows properly identifying the work as a sequel in the special sense of a thorough reinterpretation, even a comic deconstruction, of identifiable predecessor texts. In this, *Shuo Tang* may well be unique.[2]

OLDER NOVELS ABOUT THE TANG

Although it is not possible here to survey all extant novels in the Sui and Tang series (most are long and some are now quite rare), to understand the literary context of *Shuo Tang* requires a brief introduction to the range of narratives available to its author. The earliest of the series include *Tang shu zhizhuan tongsu yanyi* (Chronicles from *The History of the Tang*: A popular romance, preface dated 1553) and *Sui Tang liangchao zhizhuan* (Chronicles from the two courts, Sui and Tang, ca. 1600; extant edition 1619). Both explicitly acknowledge in their titles that they rewrite in chronicle format biographical information found in standard histories of the Sui and the Tang (not that these orthodox accounts are necessarily devoid of fictional, even fantastic, episodes, of course). The earlier of these texts is attributed to a Jinling (Nanjing) author and was published in Fujian by the printing house of Xiong Zhonggu (fl. 1570?); Xiong also penned a number of low-quality works of historical fiction, perhaps including this one. The Santaiguan (Fujian) edition attributes authorship to Yu

Ying'ao, probably a relative of Yu Xiangdou (ca. 1560–ca. 1637) of the famous Jianyang, Fujian family of printers.[3]

The second of these Ming novels may have been the first to inspire a sequel in the narrow sense of that term. *Sui Tang liangchao zhizhuan* rushes through 295 years of events until the year 878, part way through the reign of Xizong, without completing its coverage of the Tang. Yet its publisher's colophon urges readers to read the "complete text" *(quanshu)* as it continues in the novel *Can Tang Wudai zhizhuan* (Chronicles of the decline of the Tang and of the Five dynasties, ca. 1610). The first, very brief and synoptic, chapter of the sequel—now titled *Can Tang Wudai shi yanyi zhuan* (Historical romance and chronicles of the decline of the Tang and of the Five dynasties)—summarizes Tang history, and the second chapter begins at the first year of Xizong's reign. The rest of *Can Tang* is devoted to the decline of Tang power and the ensuing struggles for political stability that conclude, in its final chapter, with the founding of the Song.[4] In their continuity, then, the second is clearly a sequel to the first.

A different direction in novelistic fiction is exemplified by a prosimetric work attributed to an obscure scholar named Zhu Shenglin (fl. 1580–1600?), *Da Tang Qinwang cihua* (Poem tale of the great Tang's Prince of Qin). Zhu, according to the novel's preface (written early in the seventeenth century), developed his narrative on the basis of a narrative *guci* (drum song) then in circulation. Such comments confirm the hypothesis of May Fourth–era scholars (still accepted uncritically by some specialists) about the origins of the Chinese novel. With little supporting evidence, that generation asserted positivistically that vernacular fiction developed as a result of literati reliance on the creative imagination of China's working masses. They also speculated that these oral stories circulated in the form of *diben* (promptbooks)—even though none of these alleged sources has ever been found. Regardless of its varied relationships with written and oral traditions, *Da Tang Qinwang cihua*—like the popular chronicle *Tang shu zhizhuan tongsu yanyi*—narrates in detail the exploits of a single protagonist, here Li Shimin, who became the Tang emperor Taizong. It also develops characters essential to the later works in the series, the military heroes Qin Shubao, Shan Xiongxin, and Cheng Yaojin. It also introduces Luo Cheng, who was to become so important in Qing-period works in the series.[5]

The more noteworthy Ming novels in this series are *Sui Yangdi yanshi* (The merry adventures of the Sui emperor Yang, 1631) and *Sui shi yiwen* (The forgotten tales of the Sui, 1633). Both are elaborate recreations of historical figures introduced in *Tang shu zhizhuan tongsu yanyi* and *Sui Tang liangchao zhizhuan*. The first of these novels is anonymous, presumably because certain passages are erotic and others admit being read as an allegorical condemnation of the late Ming regime. The second, a fictional biography of the military hero Qin Shubao, was written by the poet, playwright, and (during the early Qing) civil administrator Yuan Yuling (Yuan Jin, 1599–1674). The central characters of these novels develop and progress, but in opposite directions: the Sui emperor generally becomes more widely reviled for his burgeoning excesses, while Qin Shubao develops from awkward youth to capable commander in the Tang armies. Neither protagonist is woodenly consistent, however; both express complex and conflicting motivations. The best known of the series, at least until the middle of the Qing period, was undoubtedly the still popular *Sui Tang yanyi*, compiled from a great number of earlier written sources by literatus Chu Jenhuo (ca. 1630–ca. 1705). Essentially this historical romance rewrites, reinterprets, and amplifies *Sui Tang liangchao zhizhuan* by incorporating other written fiction.[6]

A NEW KIND OF SEQUEL

Shuo Tang is a sequel in the sense that it came *after* important and widely appreciated novels in the sequence and dramatically, even radically, *reinterprets* much of the material it adapts from its sources. As such, it contrasts dramatically with subsequent works in the series of novels concerning events and figures of the Sui and Tang periods. A few years after the first *Shuo Tang* was published, a continuation appeared with the title *Shuo Tang houzhuan* (Stories about the Tang, later collection) (perhaps as early as 1738) that picks up chronologically where *Shuo Tang quanzhuan* left off. The earlier novel was thereupon renamed *Shuo Tang qianzhuan* (Stories about the Tang, former collection). *Shuo Tang houzhuan* in turn inspired further continuations, one of which was titled *Shuo Tang sanzhuan* (Third collection).

Both *Shuo Tang houzhuan* and *Shuo Tang sanzhuan* begin with characters introduced in *Shuo Tang quanzhuan;* both narrate further military campaigns led by Li Shimin and his commanders against challenges on the Tang frontiers posed by border peoples. *Shuo Tang houzhuan* is divided into two parts, "Luo Tong sao bei" (Luo Tong's northern sweep, fifteen chapters) and "Xue Rengui zheng dong" (Xue Rengui's eastern campaign, forty chapters). In the first part, the Tang ruler Li Shimin, with Qin Shubao as his commander, leads an expeditionary force northward, only to be entrapped by the northern commander Princess Tuhu. Luo Tong, the young officer who comes to rescue them, falls in love with the princess, and their liaison brings hostilities to an end. In the second, Li Shimin has a premonitory dream of the only warrior with the skills required for victory in their difficult campaign against the state of Liao in the east. This is Xue Rengui, whose efforts are central to pacifying the enemy in the second part, despite attempts by jealous rivals to take all the credit. Both of these *Shuo Tang* sequels also incorporate material from the oral and performing traditions.[7]

The title *Shuo Tang* (by which this middle Qing-period series is known) is apt: the degree of reference to the formally reliable historical record (as opposed to other intertextual relations) is far lower here for characters and incidents than in the earlier, and generally more historical, novels concerning the Sui and the Tang. *Shuo Tang* and its sequels are self-consciously fictional, and their purpose appears clearly more to be entertainment rather than pretended education for their readers. Their authors seemingly felt neither any compunction to accommodate all the figures mentioned in standard historical references nor even to base the exploits of their protagonists on recorded fact. Thus they freely adapted fantastic and romantic elements from theatrical and storytelling traditions (about their sources, more below). They also created new heroes and offspring for heroes from the parent novels to people successive generations in warrior families that could continue loyalties, and vendettas, through decades or even centuries. In the process of creation their authors also freely conjured up new rivalries and conflicts, new battles, and especially new weapons, new scenes of treachery, combat, victory, despair.

Shuo Tang and its sequels differ widely from earlier novels concerning Sui and Tang figures. Their models, in terms of structure and characterization, are older works of warrior fiction having sets of related characters dating from the middle Ming, when tales of the Yang family of generals first became popular. But their authors chose not to conform to earlier generic guidelines, either. These middle Qing-period novels range freely into established traditions of heroic, fantastic or demonic, and romantic fiction; their models seemingly included such works as *Shuihu zhuan* (known in English as *Outlaws of the Marsh* or *Water Margin*, ca. 1550–1610), *Fengshen yanyi* (The investiture of the gods, ca. 1600), and even *Haoqiu zhuan* (The fortunate union, ca. 1670) in these three categories.

Like Ming and early Qing novels concerning the Sui and the Tang, titles in the smaller *Shuo Tang* series quite obviously refer to their dependence on earlier narrative works, probably for legitimacy but perhaps only because it was conventional to do so. As Martin Huang has suggested in the introduction to this volume, sequels (including the reinterpretive *Shuo Tang*) may have been elicited by the "openness" of earlier historical fiction. Several having a chronologically lengthy sweep of narrative, such as *Sui Tang liangchao zhizhuan* and *Sui Tang yanyi,* end inconclusively, or, in these cases, with the suggestion that a continuation might be forthcoming.

But the approach of the *Shuo Tang* novels was quite unlike that of Chu Jenhuo, who slavishly copied major portions of earlier novels into his well-known and widely reprinted *Sui Tang yanyi.* The first *Shuo Tang* author, the "Old Fisherman," forged a new path away from all precedents to create a new, and in some ways more entertaining, work of fiction. In this regard he seems to have innovated, following the precedent of Yuan Yuling, the playwright who created an elaborate *Bildungsroman* for the historical general Qin Shubao. Yuan's novel *Sui shi yiwen* thus self-consciously demonstrated disregard for the generic conventions of the episodic and loosely organized historical romance. Yuan's character is psychologically and morally more complex, more likely to make mistakes, and more prone to introspection than his forerunners in earlier fiction.[8] *Shuo Tang* rewrote Qin Shubao and other protagonists to make them unsympathetic, unsophisticated, and considerably more violent. The Old Fisherman turned Yuan Yuling's literati practice of refining fiction on its head.

Reading for parody, seeking out narrative incongruities between early and later texts, can be justified by references to textual and reading practices of the early eighteenth century. My approach is based on several observations made in regard to other types of writing and other novels; it necessitates several assumptions, given the paucity of information, concerning the *Shuo Tang* author. Specifically, the author must have been conversant with literary practices that included appropriation of earlier texts through quotation, paraphrase, or parallel construction and comment. In the realm of poetic composition, intertextual practices generally promoted emotional and aesthetic identification between the author and the reader, both of them poets. Readers of fiction, as Zhang Zhupo (1670–1698) suggested in his commentary to the novel *Jin Ping Mei* (The plum in the golden vase; also known in English as The golden lotus), should seek a degree of imaginative identification with the author that allowed the reader to fancy himself the author of the text. Both practices involved very close textual readings, a broad familiarity with a variety of classical and popular writings, and the active engagement of the creative imagination on the part of the reader. For the reader of poetry, this experience was considered uplifting both aesthetically and morally; for the consumer of fiction, reading could be an entertaining, ongoing game of detection with lots of anticipation: could the reader *predict* what would happen next in the narrative? Could he imagine how this situation might be resolved (when the author is attempting to outwit the reader)? Could he catch the writer at his tricks?[9]

MODELS OF NARRATIVE APPROPRIATION

The sequence of novels concerning events of the Sui and the Tang began with some of the earliest examples of the form, written in the middle of the sixteenth century; the latest appeared in the nineteenth.[10] The first and, to my knowledge, only book devoted to the study of this series is Qi Yukun's *Sui Tang yanyi xilie xiaoshuo* (Novels in the Romance of the Sui and the Tang series), published in 1993. This is a book intended for general rather than scholarly readers; for the most part Qi's comments confirm standard interpretations about the development of vernacular fiction in China.[11] Although I disagree with Professor Qi's periodization and even some of his analyses, his comments can serve as a useful starting place for this investigation.

Qi Yukun sees the Sui-Tang series as having evolved through several stages. He groups these works into *lishi yanyi xiaoshuo* (historical novels) followed developmentally and chronologically by *yingxiong chuanqi xiaoshuo* (heroic romances). His first group ostensibly relies heavily on the relevant historical sources; these narratives took *Sanguo zhi tongsu yanyi* (Romance of the Three Kingdoms, 1522) as their model and are commonly characterized as *qishi sanxu* (70 percent fact and 30 percent fantasy). One novel so characterized in the Sui-Tang lineage is *Sui Tang liangchao zhizhuan*. It has a preface dated 1508, but there is no reason to accept as authentic either its attributed authorship or dating. In fact, it might have been compiled nearly a century later. Its prefacer attributes its "original version" to the reputed author of *Sanguo*, the playwright Luo Guanzhong (fourteenth century?). *Sui Tang liangchao zhizhuan* reads like a chronicle, with many figures and dates piled up in a dreary procession, having little of the moral seriousness of its precursor.

Another of the "historical novel" type is *Tang shu zhizhuan tongsu yanyi*, bearing a preface that is more likely to be accurately dated at 1553. Despite Qi's classification, to a great extent this novel fictionalizes events in the life of its central figure, Li Shimin. Just because these novels are presumably older than others does not necessarily make them any more historically accurate, and of course *Tang shu zhizhuan tongsu yanyi* may be around fifty years older than *Sui Tang liangchao zhizhuan*—during which time the novel was evolving rapidly. Zhu Shenglin's *Da Tang Qinwang cihua* may have been an experiment in adapting the materials of oral storytellers for readers, but it is more romantic than historical.

Two late-Ming novels that focus on the lives of single protagonists, *Sui Yangdi yanshi* and *Sui shi yiwen*, seem to have taken the opposite direction in cultural terms. The first relates with noteworthy sensitivity the inevitable downfall of a hedonistic and self-deluding monarch. In many ways *Sui shi yiwen* is artistically the most refined novel in the Sui-Tang series. Although it does refer to incidents of historical record, its purpose is to craft an incongruous background, the adventures of an awkward but promising teenager, for its central character, the mighty historical Tang general Qin Shubao. Yuan Yuling made his purpose clear in his preface and at the beginning of the first chapter: to fill in what most stories of individuals leave out, the early life of his hero.[12] Both of these works are literati novels. Their characterization is subtle; Yuan's hero is at one time or another foolish, lazy, filial, decisive, loyal, and courageous. Only when the central characters act in the public realm do these novelists revert to the outlines of recorded history to define their protagonist's activities. The complexity of both protagonists here distinguishes them from the more static characters straitjacketed by historical accuracy in earlier novels in the series.[13]

Clearly Chu Renhuo was impressed by Yuan Yuling's creativity; with only small modifications he appropriated the bulk of *Sui shi yiwen* for his own *Sui Tang yanyi*. He also grafted in major portions of *Sui Yangdi yanshi* and adapted numerous shorter narratives as well to create a highly derivative work that seems to have met popular tastes for more than three centuries, given the frequency with which it has been reissued.[14] In format and in focus, *Sui Tang yanyi*, like the middle Ming historical romances, seeks to chronicle the major events of a long period of time, nearly two hundred years. It, too, uses the reigns of monarchs to constitute its chronological backbone. In this, Chu's work contrasts with the first half of *Sui shi*, where events in its protagonist's life serve to structure the narrative. All three of these literati novels might separately be considered sequels to the extent that each refines and reinterprets its source texts. Even so, only Chu's work might be said to depend on familiarity with its predecessors for fullest aesthetic appreciation of its intertexual indebtedness.

Shuo Tang, a novel of sixty-eight chapters, appeared early in the Qianlong reign; its preface was signed by Rulian jushi (Layman Transcendent Lotus) dated during the first year of the period, 1736. This unidentifiable writer praises the work for clarifying distinctions between virtuous acts and their opposites in ways that are easily comprehended by all. This preface is correct: motivations of characters here are far more straightforward than in *Sui Tang yanyi* or the other literati novels. Partially this may be a function of having compressed most received material into fewer words, but scholars conclude that this was the Old

Fisherman's intention. *Shuo Tang* is less engaged with authentic records than are the historical romances; like *Shuihu zhuan,* its narrative framework is not the chronological development of a dynastic house, but instead the linked adventures of a series of individuals. These links interconnect as characters come in contact with one another, but the sequence of the novel's sections are not chronologically contingent upon each other.

Shuo Tang also introduces a new category of military figures, the *Sui chao haohan* (doughty warriors of the Sui), with a numerical rank assigned to each. (Not all of the sequence appear in the novel, leaving gaps that confuse Qi Yukun and other critics.) The basis for this ranking, to the extent that it is consistent, seems to be pure physical strength; those having the highest ranking swing weapons weighing hundreds of pounds each—and can defeat in battle every one lower than himself on the list. This ranking functions as a record, often predictive, of the pecking order among these grotesque fighters. Some characters, such as the evil commander Yang Lin and virtuous warriors Li Yuanba (the number-one doughty warrior) and Wu Yunshao (the fifth of this group) are totally fictitious. Important historical figures, including the rebel leader Zhai Rang, do not appear at all. Internal contradictions are numerous, and the distances between places with real names seem irrelevant to the movements of the characters; all journeys take *buzhi yiri* (more than just a day). Scenes of fighting abound, complete with detailed descriptions of armor, comments by the combatants, movements of their weapons (some of which also have names), number of clashes between the antagonists, and responses of their magnificent —and named—mounts. These exciting conflicts may have been the primary reason that the novel has been constantly in print since its first appearance.

It seems incontrovertible that the "Old Fisherman" drew most of his material from the popular *Sui Tang yanyi* rather than the already rare *Sui shi yiwen* or other texts.[15] In *Shuo Tang,* the dramatic and blatantly obvious inversion of major figures and events from literati fiction, especially given the continuing popularity of *Sui Tang yanyi* throughout the Qing period, reveals a close relationship between these two novels, given the writing and reading practices outlined above. *Shuo Tang*'s appropriation of oral story material also suggests literati writing practices. One might even read this novel superficially, "for the plot" only, as it were, and never be aware of its highly derivative nature and its use of irony. This could produce an enjoyable reading (to which I will return at the end), but it would miss much of what *Shuo Tang* truly has to offer, especially its crude humor.

READING AGAINST THE SOURCE TEXTS

It has been common practice among Chinese critics to see the novel as having greater value as entertainment than as didactic fiction. Qi Yukun echoes previous scholars who assess *Shuo Tang* as fundamentally "popular" in contrast to novels catering more to the tastes of the educated, such as *Sui shi yiwen* and even *Sui Tang yanyi*. He declares,

Shuo Tang quanzhuan is fiction in the storyteller's format *(shuoshuti xiaoshuo).* In order to attract listening and reading audiences, its plot is discontinuous and active and its language is popular and brisk; the book embodies strength and roughness. In a classic way it embodies the classic vulgar literary style that matches the psychology and tastes of China's working masses. Consequently it has been widely welcomed by readers.

For the most part, it was compiled from stories "current among the masses" *(minjian gushi),* Qi concludes.[16] At first glance, such sources might seem impossible to trace, by their very definition: what was exclusively transmitted orally ceased to exist, except in memory, the moment the tale was concluded. This may be why Qi makes no attempt to do so. But certain features of oral performance can still be seen in the text, in particular the characteristics of its heroes and the burlesqued interactions between them. Likewise, given the great amount of story material shared between the oral and written traditions of late imperial China, virtually every story has left some sort of textual trail. The obvious area to search for possible *Shuo Tang* performance sources are plays about the Sui and the Tang current in the burgeoning popular theater during the Qing. This approach is facilitated by the names given some sections of the novel.

A case in point is the play first known in its Yuan-Ming *zaju* (variety play) version by the title *Laojun tang* (The Laozi temple). In this play, and in chapter 42 of *Shuo Tang,* during a moonlit ride the Tang prince Li Shimin spies a white stag and shoots it. The deer runs away carrying the arrow, with the prince in pursuit. Soon the prince discovers himself at the gate of a great fortification. This turns out to be the stronghold of his rival Li Mi, self-styled prince of Wei. Two of Li Mi's generals, Qin Shubao and Cheng Yaojin, are patrolling the perimeter; they hear the jingling of Li Shimin's harness bells and give chase, thinking that he is a spy. Upon hearing their bells, the Tang prince dashes away into the mountains. When Cheng catches up and challenges him, Li Shimin gives his name and begs to be released. This makes Cheng furious: the warrior is adamant about seeking vengeance for the beating he suffered at the hands of Li Shimin's younger brother Li Yuanba. Li Shimin gallops away at top speed, only to find that his path ends at a temple dedicated to the Daoist saint Laozi. Quickly he takes refuge within, but Cheng easily discovers his hiding place and aims a great blow of his mighty hammer directly at the prince. Only because Qin Shubao deflects the blow is Li Shimin's life spared. Qin does so, he reports, because he saw a golden dragon circling protectively above the prince's head; surely he is mandated by heaven to be emperor and they must ultimately serve him. Cheng acquiesces, taking Li Shimin to be incarcerated in the Wei fortress. The Tang prince is freed only later when Li Mi decrees a pardon for all prisoners, with the explicit exception of Li Shimin. Military adviser Wei Zheng hits upon the idea of changing the decree from "I do not pardon" to "I first pardon" Li Shimin by adding a stroke to the negative *"bu"* to create *"ben."* On the authority of this falsified document Wei and strategist Xu Maogong send Li Shimin on his way back to the Tang.[17]

Later, when Xu Maogong, Qin Shubao, and Cheng Yaojin discuss shifting allegiance to the Tang, the happy Cheng shouts out, "If we go swear allegiance over there, that will make sure we have a great future!" It will be fine for the two of them, Qin observes, but he cautions Cheng about his own prospects: "How can it be that you don't remember

> Taking an Ax to the Laozi Temple,
> Pursuing the Prince of Qin in the Moonlight?"

These two lines *(Fu bi Laojuntang; Yuexia gan Qinwang)* rhyme, of course, making them a couplet that stands out from its prose context. Phrasing it this way is a clearly self-conscious hint to the reader about how the author views his material—as discontinuous segments, separate stories—that the reader (and, incongruously, the relevant characters as well) should keep in mind as the novel progresses.[18]

By contrast, the dispositions of the armies are far more complicated in *Sui Tang yanyi,* and the scene lasts much longer: on entering the temple, Li Shimin prays for aid; because he is the destined True Ruler the god blows up a wind to obliterate the prince's tracks and covers the gate with a spiderweb to make it appear that no one had entered. The golden dragon visible to Qin Shubao in *Shuo Tang* here restrains Cheng's deadly blow, however, but Qin must explain the significance of this ominous event to the ignorant Cheng. In *Shuo Tang* it is foolish Cheng who reminds Li Mi to exclude Li Shimin from the pardon; Wei Zheng has to explain how he will change the character to make the alteration harder to recognize. In *Sui Tang* the jailer observes, correctly, that changing this word would make the line read awkwardly and the falsification would be instantly detected. Better to let him spirit Li Shimin away as he goes to his next post. All the heroes agree with the jailer, and so the escape is accomplished by a more plausible means.[19]

Throughout this episode the Old Fisherman of *Shuo Tang* has avoided the carefully rational Confucian turns of events of *Sui Tang* in preference for the simpler, even illogical, version given in texts more closely related to the popular oral tradition. His choices must have been deliberate, given his summaries of *Sui Tang* events for other sections of his novel (such as those concerning Qin Shubao in chaps. 1–10); *Shuo Tang* revises *Sui Tang* "backward" and thus away from orthodox rationalism, to use the developmental model proposed by May Fourth–era literary historians. As with the impossibly strong *Sui chao haohan,* the Old Fisherman calls into question the neat narrative linkages of his literati fiction source by annihilating contingency in favor of arbitrary events and impossible feats.

The "game" the Old Fisherman is playing here with his sources is rendered yet more amusing by the fact that the doggerel couplet cited above comes soon after another story familiar to theater audiences, the surrender to the Tang and subsequent rebellion of the Wei ruler Li Mi. In *Shuo Tang* he sends Luo Cheng and Qin Shubao to capture Wei Zheng and Xu Maogong for their treasonous act; they fail to do so, and Li Mi orders them executed. When Cheng Yaojin pleads for their lives, Li Mi dismisses all three of them from his presence, and ultimately they all join the Tang. In addition to these losses, Li Mi's food supplies have been carried away by strange winged creatures resembling large rats. He has no alternative; Li Mi must follow the suggestion of his close friend and adviser Wang Bodang to throw himself at the mercy of Li Shimin. But he still wants to be independent; thus when Li Shimin posts him away from the capital, Li Mi makes plans to rebel. His new wife, a member of the Tang royal house given him by its founder Li Yuan, objects, and he slays her. He and Wang Bodang flee, only to fall in a rain of Tang arrows. Appropriately, the text had long before identified this as a dishonorable death.

The northern play titled *Shuang tou Tang* (A pair cast their lot with the Tang) presents the background for this situation in considerably more simple terms. There, Wang Bodang has failed to capture the generals who released Li Shimin, but Li Mi cannot doubt his loyalty. "If I misjudge your good heart, may I die in a hail of arrows!" he declares ominously. Using the retrieval of a goose Li Shimin has shot as an incongruously lame introduction, Li Mi and Wang Bodang give themselves up. When he rebels, Li Mi kills his royal wife, blaming it all on destiny. For his part, Wang bewails his fate to serve a man who betrays his commitments. In contrast to these rather mechanical justifications for actions in the play, the Old Fisherman has woven other references to these events into the fabric of his *Shuo Tang*. The stolen Wei grain stores, for example, reappear magically—and utterly incongruously—in chapter 65 to stave off starvation for General Yuchi Gong and his men when they are marooned on a city wall surrounded by water. Furthermore, Cheng Yaojin is also incorporated here as a means to develop his character further.[20]

Qi Yukun and other scholars have explained the obvious connections between the novel and popular plays by suggesting that *Shuo Tang* served as their *source*, but I conclude that the opposite relationship is the case. That is, this novel, like at least one of it predecessors in the Sui-Tang series, refers frequently—and explicitly, by identifying the names of popular plays—to the theater, rewriting plays to produce a consistent parodic distance. Regardless of its sources, this novel presents all major characters in a low mimetic light, as worthy, at least part of the time, of ridicule. In effect, the *Shuo Tang* text both fantastically romanticizes its protagonists and reduces them to a level of foolishness that evokes the reader's laughter. To me, and I am certain to any reader familiar with the *Sui Tang yanyi* versions of these stories (i.e., the more widely read and most likely better-educated reader), *Shuo Tang* can only come across as a parody, glittering with wit and ironic reversals of characters' personalities, their motivations for action, and their dilemmas.[21] This is effected by the ironic manipulation of materials apparently originating in the oral tradition. Scenes involving two major characters, Cheng Yaojin and Shan Xiongxin, demonstrate this reading with particular clarity.

CHENG YAOJIN: BLUNT RUSTIC BECOMES SMUG RUFFIAN

Perhaps the clearest example of these ironic transgressions of the earlier, more somber, and morally complicated material is in the characterization of Cheng Yaojin. In both novels he is introduced as the son of the woman who sheltered the infant Qin Shubao and his mother when Qin's father, a general, was killed during the Sui conquest. After that brief scene, Cheng disappears from *Sui Tang yanyi* until much later in Qin's adventures, when Qin has taken an important position in military administration and is lying low because he has slain the sadistic rapist Yuwen Huiji in the capital.[22] In the parent novel, Cheng reappears as a grown man, but he has become a rough and tough character. Even so, he is generally referred to by his formal name, Cheng Zhijie (which suggests moral steadfastness rather than the brute strength of Yaojin, literally "Metal Biter.") And in truth, the character as he appears in *Sui shi yiwen* and *Sui Tang yanyi* is to a noteworthy degree a man of simple virtue in addition to being a powerful warrior.

By contrast, in *Shuo Tang* Cheng Yaojin makes a yet more dramatic reappearance as a pardoned murderer who refuses to give up his imprisonment, and thus the story veers wildly away from the historical record. This is how he is introduced:

> Once the amnesty was announced, it pardoned a parasite. This fellow was extraordinary. He was a salt smuggler, feared by everyone for his utter ruthlessness. He was physically tall and strong and undaunted in his courage. While a salt smuggler he had beaten a salt inspector to death, but the examining official had taken pity on him for a doughty warrior *(haohan)* and determined that it was a case of accidental homicide. He had been sentenced to exile, and was waiting in prison. So when the amnesty was received there, he was pardoned and released. This fellow had raised havoc in Shandong and knew no restraint. He had lived in a rural village named Pigeon Shop Market under the jurisdiction of Licheng County in the Jinan District. His surname was Cheng, and his formal name was Zhijie. He was eight feet tall, with a tiger's body and a dragon's waist, his face was like green mud, and his hair the color of cinnabar. His strength was extraordinary, and he was terribly fierce.
>
> His father Cheng Youde had died when the child was only seven, leaving him with just his mother for support. Who would have thought that when Emperor Wen's armies destroyed the Northern Qi the fires set by the soldiers would reach to them, leaving Mrs. Cheng to earn a living for the two of them as best she could. At nine he studied together with Qin Shubao, but as he grew he never learned a single character, and by the time he was an adult they went their separate ways. His mother then sent him out to do a little business. Yet because they had no capital he and a group of ne'er-do-wells began trading in illegal salt, so it turned out that he did earn some money to give to his mother. Since one way or another he would get into fights and because he was utterly ruthless, everyone feared him and all called him "Tiger Cheng."
>
> Who would have thought that suddenly one day he would get into a fight with a newly appointed salt inspector he happened to bump into. Cheng's anger flared and in no time he had beaten this supervisor of the Salt Patrol to death. Two local constables were sent to arrest him. Fearing

that the others might be implicated as well, he turned himself in to the county court, admitted his guilt, and was sentenced to death. The county magistrate who tried the case, an upright man, remanded him to prison, where he had remained for three years. By that time Emperor Yang had ascended the throne, and he was covered by the amnesty.

When Cheng Yaojin heard this news, he thought it over half the night. "If I get out, I won't be able to eat my fill," he mused. "What'll I do?" You might ask why this Cheng Yaojin would not want to get out of prison. After all, it was because there he had everything he wanted to eat, everything he needed to use, and whenever a new prisoner came in he shared their wine and food. It was just like he was the head of the prison. But after a few days, seeing that the prison gate was wide open, one after another the prisoners all left and the jail was deserted. Only Cheng Yaojin sat there stupidly, not making a move. The warden came in to him, saying, "Master Cheng, the Imperial Court has demonstrated its benevolence by granting a general amnesty. All the other criminals are gone; what are you lazing around in here for?" Hearing the words "lazing around," a storm arose in his heart, and he flew into a rage. He rushed forward spreading his five fingers to strike as if with an iron fan. Knowing how fierce he was, all the jailers came forward to calm him down.

"Motherfuckers!" *(runiang zei)* Cheng Yaojin said. "If you want me to leave, you'd better invite me to drink, and when I'm good and drunk, then I'll see." Being conscientious jailers, they knew it was no good to provoke him. Fearful that he'd fly into a rage, they had no choice but to buy him half a keg of wine and even more pure water to warm it in while he watched; they also bought some chitterlings and invited him to eat as a way to redeem themselves for insulting him.

By then that Cheng Yaojin was parched: with nary a care that three sevens might be twenty-one, he straightened his throat and began to eat like a whirlwind. Standing up, he said, "Well, the wine's all gone, and the meat's all gone, so I'm leaving. If you've got any clothes and a hat, bring them here and lend them to me. If you won't lend them to me, my privates will be all hanging out, so how can I face anybody on the outside?" Alarmed, the warden said, "Now that's no easy task." Aloud he could only say, "Master Cheng, you know that all we have are the clothes on our backs. We're on duty every day; so when would we have time to get anything else?" Yaojin glared at him and was just about to beat him up, but having no choice, the warden said, "All I have that I'm not using is a funeral robe made out of plain cotton and a funeral hat made of rough hemp. Master Cheng, you take them."

"You motherfucker!" Yaojin said. "You'd try to fob off funeral clothes on me? Well, it doesn't matter. Bring them here."[23]

Even from this brief passage, several important features of *Shuo Tang* can be discerned. First, of course, is its use of the vernacular language, even vulgar slang, to enliven the scene. Cheng is the character to whom the most colloquial style is allotted, often with humorous effect when he substitutes slang for the formal terminology used by other characters. Dialogue is lively, and the characterization is made more vivid thereby.

Although some consider this style of language evidence of the novel's origins in the oral tradition, other elements of the scene are far more reliable guides to this conclusion. As Ong has pointed out, oral storytelling across cultures relies on monumental or "heavy" characters, memorable figures who serve as a focus for organizing experience in ways that can be easily remembered, or constructed, and presented effectively to listening audiences. Such characters are generally agonistic, pursuing struggle at every turn, engaging in name calling and quickly resorting to gross physical violence when thwarted.[24]

For our purposes here, the more important feature of this characterization is the absurdity with which it imbues the whole scene. The fellow who is too stupid to learn a single character after years of study becomes the bully who is clever enough to boss around the local law enforcement personnel and bend them to his will. Those constables, we must infer, are yet more benighted than he. All Cheng does is sit around in prison, and yet he has worn out his clothes to the extent that they are all in tatters, apparently without his even noticing. He spends the whole night contemplating his options and produces no more long-range plans than how to bully the guards into giving him a good meal and something to cover his nakedness. All of these elements of characterization make this Cheng Yaojin the fictional equivalent of the *chou* (clown) characters on the popular stage. Such characters, also termed *"sanhualian,"* stood out from the other figures on stage because they wore comic facial paint, and although most were fools, some were very clever. All were people of low status. Unquestionably, the scene is amusing even when viewed totally out of literary context for its spectacular bathos that is reminiscent of, if not simply borrowed from, the popular theater.

The bathos intensifies as the scene continues, piling absurdity upon absurdity. This Cheng is a giant; as a *haohan,* he is of course much bigger in stature than the warden from whom he borrows the clothing. This means that when the funeral robe is pulled down in front, it rides up in back. Worse yet, "On his lower body, his one pair of pants wore out over the three years, and all that was left of them was a piece of tattered cloth. If he covered his testicles, he exposed his butt; if he covered his butt then he exposed his gonads." Even so, thinking only of seeing his mother again, he covers himself as best he can and rushes away.[25]

Once at home he and his starving mother try to make ends meet: she weaves baskets, which he sells in the nearby Pigeon Shop market town. But his appearance is so frightening that potential customers avoid him; Cheng succeeds in his business only when he bullies potential customers into buying his wares. Incidents of this sort soon force both shoppers and all the other merchants to abandon the market, and Cheng is left with no income at all. In his frustration he runs amok, beating those who refuse to buy and demanding food and wine without paying for them. Before long he is located by the underworld boss You Junda, who recruits him to assist in the theft of silver bound for the imperial coffers. The boss tries, unsuccessfully, to teach him the techniques of fighting with the ax; alas, Cheng is too stupid to remember them. It takes the local earth god to teach him in a dream before Cheng is able to master most—but not all—of the sixty-four moves of ax fighting. When he awakens, he is so excited that he rides a stool around the courtyard like a hobbyhorse practicing what he has just learned.[26]

In *Sui Tang yanyi* Cheng is simple-minded and only occasionally rash. But he is not the malicious fool the Old Fisherman made him into. Of the events narrated above, only his recruitment into banditry is borrowed from earlier fiction. His introduction in chapter 21 of *Sui Tang yanyi* is accomplished through indirect narrative. When the underworld boss seeks an accomplice for this major heist, his retainers mention the name of Cheng Yaojin. Cheng had been involved in salt smuggling, they tell him, but he had been arrested and sent into exile at the frontier. He had returned after the amnesty was announced. You Junda finds him in a tavern, where the narrator describes him in verse: indeed, Cheng is a ferocious-looking character. However, in contrast to the Old Fisherman's version, this Cheng Yaojin initially is given no distinctive personality; readers see him from a distance, as it were, through the mock-heroic lens of poetic description. Not surprisingly, his actions are generally colorless as well.[27]

Qi Yukun has observed that Chu Renhuo emphasized the heroic and democratic qualities of Cheng Yaojin. In *Sui Tang yanyi* his great strength makes him a successful bandit, and he handily assembles a large force of highwaymen. But the incipient fall of the Sui court makes all such outlaws potential contenders for the throne. Cheng is unwilling to merge his bandit gang with the powerful rebel force at Wagang. Instead, he observes that with Qin Shubao in his own lair, all they need is to recruit Shan Xiongxin and their combined abilities would allow them to pose a serious challenge to the Wagang band itself. "If brother Zhai [Rang] has been able to become an emperor [in the Wagang camp], how could it be that brother Qin and second brother Shan could not also become emperors?" To Qi Yukun, this negates the idea of a heavenly mandated ruler and supports the egalitarian idea that anyone could become an emperor.[28] From Qi's perspective, this is a progressive political stance on Chu Renhuo's part, likely to enhance the stature of the character in the eyes of his readers. Yet *Sui Tang yanyi* adheres comparatively closely to the historical record concerning Cheng and his political allegiances; thus it is *Shuo Tang* that comes closer to popular values in its rewriting of the character, Qi concludes.[29]

Perceiving Chu's novel as intended to be entertainment for the educated casts this character in a different light, however. Every serious student of Chinese history, whether now or during the early Qing, is painfully aware that virtually anyone *could* become an emperor, whether by conquest or by inheritance. China had had its share of rulers who were mentally or morally incompetent or were derelict in their duties; royal families and even dynastic founders included those who were rude, hedonistic, and violent. It is hard to imagine that any knowledgeable and reflective Chinese reader of history—or of historical fiction—might believe that heaven had chosen all of China's monarchs. In the context of *Sui Tang yanyi*, Cheng Yaojin's comment is not extreme: to this point in the narrative both Qin Shubao and Shan Xiongxin have been presented as conscientious, moral, and courageous men quite worthy of great responsibilities.

Cheng's *Sui Tang yanyi* comment is literalized in *Shuo Tang quanzhuan* for comic effect: in the later novel Cheng himself becomes an emperor, albeit temporarily. The stage for this is set when his partner in crime You Junda reports on how corrupt the Sui emperor Yang has become. "Ah, ya ya!" Cheng declares. "If that dog's head is so unloyal, unfilial, unvirtuous, and unjust as all of that and is still Emperor, why don't we just kill him and have somebody else be Emperor?" Later, when Cheng and his men take over the Wagang fortress, a curious earthquake opens a great cavern in the parade ground. Xu Maogong identifies it as a divine cave; only the appointed may enter. The rebel leaders draw lots to see which it is. Cheng gets the short stick, and so he descends. There he finds wondrous armor and regal robes; quickly he puts them on. Cheng also witnesses a battle between a green dragon and a bizarre beast that has a dragon's tail but the head of a boar. These creatures represent Li Yuan, future emperor of the Tang, and the Sui emperor Yang. A sheet of paper with writing on it (which Cheng cannot read) that he discovers in this cavern predicts that he will rule for three years with the title Demon King who Roils the World (Hunshi Mowang). And so his followers recognize him as emperor. Appropriately, and absurdly, he adopts the attitudes, even the first-person pronoun, commonly assumed by historical emperors.[30]

Because Cheng regularly plays the fool in *Shuo Tang quanzhuan,* his adviser Xu Maogong is amused by his gullibility and plays tricks on him. Later, however, Cheng tires of the duties that accrue to his exalted position. One morning at court he declares,

> "Please, brothers, do not bow to me. I can't bear the trouble of being your Emperor any more—I have to get up so early in the morning, and late at night I still can't go to sleep. How hard that is! I'll give the throne to any one of you who is willing to take it. Now hurry up, hurry up!"

He removes his crown and robe and throws them to the floor, insisting, "I won't do it any more, I won't, I really won't!" Soon thereafter he explains to Li Mi, whom he has just freed from an imperial prison cart, "I don't want to be an emperor; you're a lot more honest than I am." Cheng thereby happily relinquishes his title to Li Mi, who becomes the (short-lived) prince of Wei. Not only is this episode silly enough to be amusing in its own right, but it is even more so when the reader knows how this text distorts its source. The reader is to learn, however, that Cheng is not only the object of mirth in *Shuo Tang;* he can also be a malicious prankster.[31]

SHAN XIONGXIN: GENEROSITY DISPLACED BY OBSESSION

Cheng Yaojin is not the only major character to have been appropriated from the popular tradition and twisted by the Old Fisherman into a caricature of his former identity. Through his development in these several Sui-Tang novels,

Shan Xiongxin comes to embody the virtue *yi* (brotherly generosity), a characteristic of the *Shuihu zhuan* heroes. Time and again Shan provides shelter as well as financial and emotional support for heroes in difficulty—and for their families. Yet like the other martial heroes of *Shuo Tang*, Shan's single-minded charity becomes warped into something quite bizarre in the Old Fisherman's hands.

The Shan Xiongxin of *Shuo Tang* suggests the morally shallow but showy *jing* (villain) role from the theater rather than the man of powerful passions and deep commitments in Chu Renhuo's more literary novel. This Shan is not just a wealthy landowner who is generous to men of valor; he is the center of all bandit activity in a vast region. Every highwayman for miles around must give him half of their take, and all knights-errant in the region must respond to his summons. Shan's generosity serves only to buy their loyalty, his "gifts" more arbitrary largesse than selfless contributions to the less fortunate. An enormous man of ugly mien, this Shan has a voice like thunder. In earlier novels he was quick to lend a hand; here he is exceedingly quick to anger. A doughty warrior in his own right, Shan is ranked as eighteenth (and last) among the Sui-period *haohan*. Here he is the incarnation of a green dragon from the celestial realm (*shangjie qinglong*) instead of his former presentation as a man of strong, but convincing, passions.

The Old Fisherman's Shan Xiongxin is also extremely vulgar in his speech, nearly as much so as Cheng Yaojin, and inveterately suspicious of his fellows. Thinking he has been robbed of some imperial loot he desires, he charges the offender, Luo Cheng, brandishing his weapon and shouting, "You donkey-fucker, Luo, I'll fuck your jailbird mother!" (*Lüqiu rude: Luo Zi ru nide guai qiuniang!*) Later, when commiserating with Qin Shubao about being beaten because he has failed to apprehend two robbers, he says, "Truly they have no sense of honor, fuck their mothers, the whores!" (*Zhenzheng mei tianli de. Ru ta jia liangge langniang!*)[32] Thus in contrast to the modest benefactor at the celebration for the sixtieth birthday of Qin's mother in the literati novels, here Shan gets in his cups and allows himself to be deeply offended by one of Cheng Yaojin's pranks.

In the earlier novels, *haohan* from near and far assemble in a local stalwart's home the day before the celebration. There Cheng admits to the robbery that has caused Qin so much trouble: because Qin is in charge of the investigation, he was severely punished when he failed to locate the culprits. Shan suggests various ways to extricate Qin from this perilous situation, but Qin burns the warrant, refusing to sacrifice his childhood friend to save himself. For his part, Cheng offers to take sole responsibility for the theft, leaving the mastermind You Junda to care for his mother. Other stalwarts leap forward to help: in the end, the stolen silver is repaid, liberal bribes facilitate Qin's transfer to other duties without having solved the robbery, and Cheng remains free. Qin's burning of the warrant is seen as an extraordinarily magnanimous act, but Cheng also receives respect for his quick response. At the birthday celebration itself, held at the Qin residence, various among the assembled stalwarts offer congratulatory comments and drink to the old lady's health. Unable to come up with a flowery statement, Cheng simply downs three penalty drinks in her honor, to the amusement of all present. Then Mother Qin retires, to allow the men to drink to their satisfaction without needing to stand on ceremony. They do, and the following morning all go their separate ways.[33]

In *Shuo Tang* these scenes move more quickly, with considerably less dialogue and with very significant plot changes. When Qin refuses to arrest his childhood friend, Xu Maogong questions whether he is in earnest. "From ancient times it has been said that a man should die for his friend, and that he should die without regret," Qin declares, as he burns the warrant. This act so impresses the assembled stalwarts that all thirty-nine of them swear brotherhood with each other on the spot. The ceremony involves mixing a bit of each brother's blood into the wine shared by all. But when it is Shan's turn, all he can squeeze from his arm is green water, which Xu calculates as proof of his true identity as the green dragon star. (Since Shan never swears allegiance to the Tang, it is appropriate that he cannot join his blood with the others, the narrator confides to the reader.)[34]

Since the birthday guests are so numerous and so physically large in *Shuo Tang,* they cannot all fit comfortably in the Qin residence; Qin arranges with the caretaker of the local earth-god temple to have them convene there. The birthday celebration concluded, which involved a number of gifts of precious metals and tangible symbols of longevity (rather than mere refined statements, as in *Sui Tang yanyi*), the stalwarts repair to the temple for wine and conversation. There, Qin puts Cheng in charge of the wine before returning home with his mother.

Looking around at the assembly, Cheng says to himself, "It appears that of all these friends here, the only ones that are really tough *(lihai)* are that gang boss Shan Xiongxin and the young guy Luo Cheng. Why don't I just get them into a fight with each other and see how they do." To Shan, he whispers that Luo despises him because he is smug about his wealth and power and shows no respect for Luo's own situation. "This is what I heard him say, and I tell you with the best of intentions: you should watch out for him." Then Cheng confides to Luo, "Brother Luo, you know what? Shan Xiongxin wants to rip your nuts off" *(louchu nide niaozhu)* because the younger man has shown him no respect. At first Luo laughs it off as a prank, but the more he thinks about it, the angrier he becomes—especially because Shan is now glaring at him. When the others go out for a walk, these two happen to bump into each other.

> Luo Cheng was the stronger, and with a "boom" he knocked Shan Xiongxin backward, and he fell to the floor inside the temple. Everyone was startled, not knowing what was behind this. Enraged, Shan picked himself and cursed at Luo Cheng: "You son of a thief, how dare you knock me down?!" "You green-faced bandit," Luo said, "So what if I hit you?" and charged up the slope toward him. Xiongxin's foot flew out in a kick, but Luo Cheng grabbed it and, like a little child, with a *"putong"* tossed him into the air. Everyone rushed up to calm them down, but Cheng Yaojin shouted out, "Don't stop them, let them fight!"

The conflict comes to an end when Qin races back to make peace between them. But when Qin scolds him, Luo gallops off in a rage—and Cheng volunteers to bring him back for Qin. Fortunately, Cheng runs into the villainous Sui official Yang Lin with another load of imperial treasure before he can exacerbate the friction between Luo and Shan. After a brief battle, Yang captures both Cheng and his accomplice You Junda, which absolves Qin from any consequences of having burned the warrant and delays the resolution of the quarrel until later in the narrative. This personal grudge also prevents Shan from joining the Tang because Luo is on that side, all because of the cruel prank played by Cheng.[35]

Perhaps the most dramatic demonstration of Shan's one-dimensional and obsessive personality—and of the Old Fisherman's reconceptualization of the character—comes when Li Shimin, accompanied only by his adviser Xu Maogong, happens to wander into a deserted imperial pleasure garden not far from the Zheng headquarters in Luoyang. There Shan spies on them and charges the prince. Xu desperately grabs hold of Shan's robe as he chases Li Shimin around an artificial hill. "Brother Shan, for my sake, spare my lord's life!" he cries. "What are you saying, brother Maogong! They killed my older brother, and his death has not been avenged—it's on my mind both day and night!" Xu holds on to Shan's robe for dear life to slow him down, until Shan cries in exasperation, "Xu Ji! If I didn't remember that day in Jia Liu's shop when we swore brotherhood, I'd cleave you in two with my sword! Enough—I'll just cut off my robe and consider this an end to my obligations to you!"[36] Thus this irascible Shan can no longer even brook friendship—if it comes between him and the object of his vengeance.

The several versions of Shan's death demonstrate just how the character is to be read differently in *Shuo Tang* from the Shan Xiongxin of earlier novels. Generally following the same outline of events and motivations, *Da Tang Qinwang cihua* narrates the scene in fewer than 100 characters; *Tang shu zhizhuan tongsu yanyi* devotes around 350. Yuan Yuling (*Sui shi yiwen*, chap. 59) developed the scene in around 1,500 characters, but Chu Renhuo narrated Shan's end using about 3,400 characters.[37]

The general outline of the event in the older novels is this: Li Shimin, the Tang prince of Qin, has been successively eliminating all Tang's potential rivals for power, among them the state of Zheng to which Shan has sworn allegiance. He has become Zheng's leading general. When Tang forces overrun their capital, Shan is imprisoned along with his ruler. Despite repeated attempts by a number of Shan's friends and colleagues to dissuade him, Li Shimin insists that Shan is to be executed rather than recruited to the Tang. This is because the Tang ruler Li Yuan had mistakenly killed Shan's brother, and Li Shimin fears that Shan is determined to get revenge. Thus the state of Tang must be rid of this implacable enemy. In chapter 60 of *Sui Tang*, Shan waits impatiently for the decision on his fate. All doubts are dispelled when his erstwhile comrades, now all Tang generals, arrive with parting draughts of wine. Cheng Yaojin and Qin Shubao cannot swallow for weeping; Shan alone downs three large bowls before marching off to his death. Qin hurries ahead to have the heads and bodies of the other prisoners removed and the area put in order. Shan strides on to the execution ground holding Cheng's hand. Once there, Qin's mother thanks him for saving her son so many years before, and then Shan takes leave of his wife and daughter. However, Shan nearly loses his composure before the women, and, to preserve his heroic demeanor, he has them sent away. As a final gesture of friendship, Cheng, Qin, and Xu Maogong slice pieces of their own flesh, roast them over a fire, and offer them to Shan to eat. If we fail to care for your family, let us be consumed like these slices of flesh, they vow. Then Qin has his son come forward to bow to Shan as his father-in-law; the boy has been betrothed to Shan's daughter. With a laugh, Shan stretches out his neck to receive the executioner's ax. The blow falls; thereafter his friends sew his head back on to his body and bury the corpse with honor.[38]

Thus Chu Renhuo's character progresses through a range of emotions as Shan gradually admits to himself that there will be no reprieve and that his end is near. He had been determined to seek revenge throughout the struggle between Zheng and Tang, and yet the earlier texts suggest that, unlike Qin, Shan has found no convenient way to extricate himself from his commitment to the Zheng ruler Wang Shichong. For the literati novels' Shan, therefore, revenge was at least in part a convenient excuse for him. In *Sui Tang yanyi*, for Qin, and for Cheng as well, joining the Tang could be justified in terms of filial obligation: both of their mothers had been given shelter and support by Li Shimin. But for Shan, family obligations militate against such a move: his only brother had been killed by the Tang prince. Thus he remains adamant when Li Shimin offers him a pardon in return for a change of allegiance. It is on his unwavering integrity, readers of *Sui shi yiwen* and *Sui Tang yanyi* are led to believe, that Shan in this climactic scene pins his hopes for a last-minute reprieve. As his doom becomes clear, Shan plucks up his courage, despite his friends' sorrow, only to have his determination undermined by the final gratitude of Qin's mother and his own concerns for his daughter's future. And again, family concerns complicate adherence to the simple heroic image Shan has cultivated. This is a powerful scene not only for the narrator's description of the words and complex feelings of all concerned, but also because it draws to a climax Qin's extended maturation. Thus Qin's dreams of brotherly devotion cherished since his youth are sacrificed here to satisfy the overpowering interests of the state to which he now owes all loyalty. This conclusion is thus convincing on both personal and political levels.

The end of Shan Xiongxin is considerably more expeditious in *Shuo Tang quanzhuan*; it also begins, not surprisingly, with an emotional response rather than an act having overt political significance. In chapter 56 the state of Zheng, headquartered in Luoyang and headed by Wang Shichong, is clearly doomed. All efforts to recruit new warriors have been thwarted, and even Shan's most trusted aide has been captured and beheaded. With resignation he takes leave of his wife. In a scene reminiscent of Xiang Yu's final separation from his concubine Yu Ji in Sima Qian's (145–186? B.C.E.) classic history *Shiji* (*Records of the Grand Historian;* recently immortalized in film),[39] Shan goes to his wife, a princess, to share a farewell cup of wine. "'Princess! Today I drink this wine with you; hereafter, I fear, I will never again see your face. If we meet again, it will only be in the next life.' As he finished speaking, without realizing, tears rolled down his face." Like her historical predecessor, she vows to protect her chastity should he fail. To that end he gives to her his sword with which to take her life if need be. Pushing her away, he strides off with never a backward glance. Shan hastily returns to his encampment, bids his ruler farewell, dons his armor, and rides off toward the enemy fortifications, declaring, "By heaven, this will be the day I take my revenge!"

Alone he charges into the Tang camp, slaying left and right like a madman, but Li Shimin cautions his generals to take Shan alive, in hope of winning his allegiance. Cheng confronts him.

> "Hey, Little Shan you scrounging mutt, what kind of business are you up to that you break into our camp? Your old man Cheng is here." In anger, Xiongxin shouted back, "Hey, Cheng Yaojin you mongrel, today I'm going to change that expression on your face!"

Then Shan attacks with his spear. Fearing for his own life, Cheng flees, only to lead Shan around and around the encampment and ultimately to the center of the fortress where Li Shimin is resting. Then Cheng runs away. By then Shan is exhausted, but knowing heaven's will cannot be changed, he continues to fight. For their part, his many friends among the Tang generals fall back before his onslaught until finally Xu Maogong and the powerful youth Luo Cheng capture him. Brought before the prince, Shan refuses to kneel, instead shouting,

> "You Tang brat, if I can't eat your flesh in this life, I'll suck up your ghost after death!" He never stopped cursing.
>
> Smiles covering his face, the Prince of Qin personally loosened Shan's fetters. The moment his hand was free, Shan grabbed the sword he noticed the Prince was wearing and swung it at him. Guards from both sides stepped forward to save him, but more than twenty of them were cut down. The Prince retreated into his antechamber, and Maogong hurriedly ordered them to use a horse bridle to bring him to the ground and tie him up as before.
>
> "Do not hobble him," the Prince commanded as he stepped out from his place of hiding. "Brother Shan, you've let off enough steam for now. That event long ago on Hawthorn Ridge really was not intentional. You chased me all around the Imperial Orchard, and that should count as the revenge you desire. Today we want to treat you with fullest ceremony to urge you to surrender." And then he knelt before him.
>
> "You Tang brat, if you want me to swear allegiance to you, you'll wait until the sun rises in the west!" Xiongxin declared.

Because he is so adamant, Xu advises the prince to execute Shan. To honor their vows of brotherhood, Xu, Cheng, and Qin are given permission to make "offerings to the living" (*huoji*), including incense and candles. Xu offers Shan a cup of wine with the words, "Brother Shan, even Jie's dog bit Yao; each has his own master. I've filled this cup in remembrance of our feelings of brotherhood in the past. May you quickly join the Immortals!" But Shan fills his mouth with the wine only to spit it in Xu's face. "You cow-nosed Daoist! You put our fine realm all in sixes and sevens, and you still want to talk about brotherly feelings! How about the feelings of your mother's ass! Who asked you for any wine?" "Even if you will not drink it, I will complete my ritual," Xu said. The others drink him a toast, but Shan refuses to participate until Cheng approaches him. "When I meet you in hell, I'll say that you're a doughty warrior who'd rather die than switch allegiance—and that you're ten times better than those who did it just to save their miserable lives. As your younger brother I salute you with this wine. I've been straightforward all my life. Drink it or not, as you please; I won't urge you again." In the end Shan drinks Qin's offerings and Cheng's as well, vowing to get revenge in the next life. Then others urge him again to drink, including the hated (thanks to Cheng' earlier lie) Luo Cheng. "Luo Cheng, you son of a thief!" he cried. "You turned your back on honor when you joined the Tang. If I can't kill you in this life, I'll kill your whole family in the next. And I'll fuck your mother!" At that, Luo struck him in two with his sword.⁴⁰

As with the characterization of Cheng, here, too, the Old Fisherman is at pains to recreate the vitality of a storyteller's performance, whether or not a storyteller provided this outline of the episode. Its oral style can be discerned in the numerous antagonistic exchanges between Shan and the Tang heroes, their regular use of fixed, but not particularly informative, epithets ("cow-nosed Daoist" *[Niu bizi Daoren]*; "Tang brat" *[Tang tong]*; "scrounging mutt" *[goucai]*), to say nothing of the earthy language with which Shan curses his captors. The narrator here also engages in a fictive dialogue with his audience. ("Readers, how much ability could Shan Xiongxin have, that he could fight his way from east to west, from south to north in such a great Tang encampment? There was a reason for this.") Even so, these appropriations of oral narrative practices do not preclude a highly literate author, suggested especially by the appearance of well-constructed ironies throughout the novel.⁴¹

OVER-THE-TOP UGLINESS

Comparisons of the ways that Shan Xiongxin meets his fate show just how the Old Fisherman endeavored to replace refined and upright heroes with rude and irascible warriors for his version of their adventures. Some scenes, such as Shan's capture and execution, are violent and crude, striking primarily in the degree to which the literati novel characters—and their genteel manners—have been subverted. These contrasting presentations, and the ironic distance between them, are perhaps at their most comical in chapter 24, in which the nearly forty heroes assemble to celebrate the sixtieth birthday of Qin Shubao's mother. The reader sees the scene through her reaction.

> The matron had just come to the doorway and was still behind the door screen when, ah, ya ya! Look that that bunch of guys: Some were dark-green faced, some were red faced, some were purple faced, some were blue faced; some had melon-skin green faces; some had scarlet hair with

red sideburns; some had big mouths with fierce fangs. Seeing these strange faces, the old lady stopped dead in her tracks, startled, and refused to go in. From his side of the screen, in a low voice Shubao pointed out, "That one with the dark-green face is Shan the Second from Luzhou; the one with the blue face is First Master Cheng; this one is the scholar Chai Shao, he's the Duke of Tang's Commandant. They all are my good friends, so there's no reason that you shouldn't go out."

Clearly here the novelist is trying to familiarize Qin's mother, and the reader, with what should be grotesque and terrifying monsters, reading them back into the narrative as presented by Chu Renhuo and his other literary sources. This, too, is ostensibly a storyteller's technique, here inserted for its comic effect.[42]

Mother Qin's vision seems like a response to a *lianpu*, a register of ferocious face patterns for the *jing* role types in traditional theater. The *jing* roles required rough speech (both in content and delivery), projection of a strong martial spirit, and conflicting personality traits. All wore complex facial paint, each color of which suggests an attribute or a collection of attributes. Even for those unfamiliar with the specific references, these colorful facial patterns appear on the stage as gigantic warriors made to look larger than life with high-soled boots, padding on the shoulders, and lofty headgear. Here the Old Fisherman seems to have self-consciously tapped his readers' theatergoing experience to turn the more realistic—and courteous—figures of *Sui Tang yanyi* into monstrous theatrical types, at once rude and grotesque, frightening and yet wonderfully entertaining. In short, *Shuo Tang quanzhuan* has converted the drama of the earlier novels into a spectacle of a theatrical sort by exaggerating the characteristics of heroes in an oral performance. When compared with the genteel manners of the characters having these names in literati fiction, the incongruity of this sort of spectacle becomes extremely amusing.

HOW TO READ A HEROIC ADVENTURE

Although I have endeavored to demonstrate that the intertextual reliance of *Shuo Tang* on earlier novels in the series enables reading the novel as a parody of its immediate predecessor, *Sui Tang yanyi*, I am under no illusion that this is the only, or even a particularly common, way to read it. Its brisk pace, its earthy and overblown characters, its wildly exaggerated battles between titans, its exoticism—all parallel the standard features of a theatrical performance. In their textual reincarnation, these elements contribute to a ludic reading, for the reader's enjoyment primarily if not exclusively.

Theorists demonstrate that reading for pleasure depends for the most part on the predictable appearance of familiar generic conventions of fiction. That is why, in our own day, there are thousands of mystery fans, spy novel devotees, passionate consumers of romances of the sort termed "bodice rippers," science fiction, or fantasies set in some enchanted variant on the European Middle Ages. The majority of works in each of these genres is conventional in structure and substance; it is their very predictability that ensures their welcome among the consumers of printed fiction.

Here I have argued for a type of *un*conventionality in *Shuo Tang quanzhuan*. Which way is it, after all? Can one novel both create humorous subversions of familiar material and remain predictable to readers? Can one and the same text reflect the conventions of performance and the writing games of idle literati? Reading *Shuo Tang* as a parody has required a kind of transgeneric interpretation: I have read *Shuo Tang* against its progenitor(s) and the very different conventions followed by the historical novel *Sui Tang yanyi* written for literati on the one hand and the performances for general audiences on the other. I have argued that it is only when viewed against this complex cultural context that the comic incongruities of the Old Fisherman's innovations become readily apparent. Those who read the novel as I have would surely concur with me on the clever manipulation of received materials I have discerned there.

But those who customarily read—or listened to professional renditions of—adventure stories might have quite a different response. *Shuihu zhuan* and related oral or dramatic narratives, for example, have always had a considerable audience among the uneducated. Twentieth-century scholars have lauded it for that reason; this is also why commentators of late imperial China often warned against its potentially pernicious effects on public order. And in fact *Shuihu zhuan* was banned numerous times at a variety of locations throughout the empire during the Ming and Qing. Apparently *Shuo Tang quanzhuan* was also banned, probably because both novels romanticize rebels and bandits; China's administrators often feared that reading (or *seeing*) such works might provoke unruly or even disloyal behavior among the masses (which were the most serious crimes during the Ming and Qing).[43] Thus to potential censors and other critics, *Shuihu zhuan* and *Shuo Tang* were seen as related generically—in terms of the potential threat to civil authority they posed, if not in more specifically literary ways. And of course parallels can be found between the fantastic battles in the late Ming *Fengshen yanyi* and the duels of magic in *Shuo Tang*. Cloud transport for Li Jing and other characters here was surely inspired by the great *Xiyou ji* (Journey to the West, ca. 1580)—which has itself been read both as fantastic adventure and as religious classic. Likewise, *Shuo Tang* inspired sequels on the model of stories about the Yang family of generals, *Yang jia jiang tongsu yanyi* (Popular romance of the Yang family generals, ca. 1550?), and perhaps even the Qing fictional life of the Song-period general Yue Fei, *Shuo Yue quanzhuan* (Complete tales of Yue [Fei], 1798). Thus when read along with books from this list, as making intertextual references to these novels of romantic adventure and heroic combat, *Shuo Tang* is not so different. Readers seeking diversion and entertainment from such books might have less interest in historical romances such as *Sui Tang* and might avidly have immersed themselves in its episodic and stirring narrative.

Although to my knowledge no critic during late imperial times identified in any detail a way of reading that would make such fiction politically subversive, danger could seemingly exist if the reader were to imaginatively project himself into the story. Ludic reading depends on visualization of the scenes and characters in the narrative; *Shuo Tang* encourages this through its colorful references to physical attributes of the heroes, hints about the course of combat, suggestive but still vague names for weapons, fighting techniques, and battle arrays. Professional storytelling, generally performed with a minimum of realistic action or stage properties, invoked just this sort of imaginative interaction from the audience. And what is the point of visualization if not to make oneself a part the picture, if only as a vicarious onlooker, the narratee to whom the narrator speaks directly? Does not the fiction thereby take on a kind of personal reality, at least in the mind of the reader?

And is this so different from the "literati reading" I've outlined above? Ludic reading might involve seeing oneself in a distant past, galloping along at breakneck speed on a marvelous courser among gigantic warriors of unbelievable strength equipped with enormous weapons, bound to them by oaths of brotherhood and a common code of valor. Literati reading practices also involve imaginatively projecting oneself into the narrative. But, to follow the suggestions of the seventeenth-century critics Jin Shengtan and Zhang Zhupo, the sophisticated reader reads more slowly, projecting himself into the narrative not as a *protagonist* of the fiction or even as a bystander, but as *its creator*. Intellectual and emotional identification with the writers of past times had been recognized as the proper way to appreciate poetry for many centuries. Readers trained in the reading of poetry would undoubtedly follow the same practices in reading other works for enjoyment, at least to some degree. For them (as for me) pleasure would come as they delight in each new inversion of every sensitive *Sui Tang* hero into his foul-mouthed *Shuo Tang* opposite. To such ideal readers, these comic incongruities more than adequately compensate for the resultant infelicities in plot and unconvincing characterization in the later novel. Yet for the reader who speeds through the book to see what happens next, incongruities and infelicities might simply be passed over without notice.

One could conclude, then, that *Shuo Tang* is a very successful rewriting of *Sui Tang yanyi* and other novels. It does not compete with them for readers; it complements earlier fiction concerning Sui and Tang figures by encouraging new types of reading and other varieties of enjoyment. By using imaginative material appropriated from oral and theatrical performances, it builds on the strengths, and the weaknesses, of its predecessors to create new heroes and new adventures that transcend all bounds of conventions that guided Chu Renhuo and the other historical romancers. And like any other good book, it admits several types of reading, some perhaps overlapping, to satisfy a diverse aggregate of readers.[44]

Notes

1. The edition I will refer to here is Yuanhu Yusou *jiaoding, Shuo Tang quanzhuan* (hereafter *Shuo Tang*). Another well-edited edition is the 1998 Beijing *Shuo Tang quanzhuan*. For a survey of early imprints, see Ōtsuka Hidetaka, *Zōho Chūgoku tsūzoku shōsetsu shomoku*, 207–209. Given his intimate familiarity with the characteristics, and probably the content, of oral narratives concerning these figures, we might hypothesize that the *Shuo Tang* author was an educated man from a not-so-educated family who was thus familiar with the ways of thinking and of organizing narratives that were distinctive to oral cultures. For

a comparison of ways of organizing material between oral and literate cultures, see Ong, *Orality and Literacy*, 7–10, 22–26, and 118–132; see also Goody, *The Interface Between the Written and the Oral*, 260–261, 269, and, for his discussion of writing and power relations within a society, 281–283.

2. For studies of parody in Western literature, see Rose, *Parody//Metafiction* and her more recent *Parody: Ancient, Modern, and Post-Modern*, esp. 20–53; here Rose lists signals for identifying parody on 37–38 and explores the reactions of a range of hypothetical readers to parody on 41–42, including those of the "ideal" reader who recognizes the "comic discrepancy, or comic incongruity" between the parody and its source "text-world." Chartier, "Representations of the Written Word," 17–18, explores the shift in medieval Europe from "intensive" to "extensive" reading; clearly the reader for whom reading was challenging would not have enough experience with literature to grasp irony; only an experienced, "extensive" reader would appreciate *Shuo Tang* at the level I propose.

3. The Santaiguan edition (published in Jianyang, Fujian, ca. 1600) of *Tang shu zhizhuan* was reprinted as no. 6 in the series *Taiyaku Chūgoku rekishi shōsetsu senshū*. The only premodern edition of *Sui Tang liangchao zhizhuan* exists in only one copy, in the Sonkeikaku Library, Tokyo. There have been two modern editions, a photo-reprinted version in the *Guben xiaoshuo jicheng* and a typeset edition in *Mingdai xiaoshuo jikan*, 3d. series, vol. 1. Both use the alternative title *Sui Tang liangchao shizhuan*. I am grateful to Martin Huang for this second reference.

4. See the *Sui Tang liangchao zhizhuan* colophon, 12.55b; the two titles are obviously intended to be interpreted as paired. For a modern edition of its sequel, see *Can Tang Wudai zhizhuan*. I give its first edition the tentative date of ca. 1600 because it carries a "Li Zhuowu" commentary, probably written by the early seventeenth-century writer Ye Zhou. There is no reason to associate this commentary with the historical Li Zhi (1527–1602), but other novels having commentary attributed to him began to appear around 1600; see appendix 2, in Rolston, ed., *How to Read the Chinese Novel*, 356–363; Plaks, *Four Masterworks of the Ming Novel*, 513–517; and esp. Ye Lang, *Zhongguo xiaoshuo meixue*, 280–302. Wang Zhongmin tentatively dates the novel in the 1570s; see his *Zhongguo shanben shu tiyao*, 401–402, but I am more persuaded by recent scholarship on Ye Zhou. Curiously, although the parent novel seemingly quickly went out of print, *Can Tang Wudai zhizhuan* was frequently reissued during the Qing period. See Ōtsuka Hidetaka, *Zōho Chūgoku tsūzoku shōsetsu shomoku*, 218–219.

5. For a modern photo-reprint edition of *Da Tang Qinwang cihua*, variously identified (suggesting, perhaps, that the printing blocks changed hands among several printing houses) as *Tang Qinwang cihua* (Ballad tale on the Tang prince of Qin) and *Tang Qinwang benzhuan* (The basic biography of the Tang prince of Qin), see Zhu Shenglin, *Da Tang Qinwang cihua*. *Tang shu zhizhuan tongsu yanyi* has virtually the same story; the relationship between these two works and *Sui Tang liangchao zhizhuan* will be the subject of a later study. For bibliographic notes on *Da Tang Qinwang cihua*, see Sun Kaidi, *Riben Dongjing suo jian Zhongguo xiaoshuo mu*, 32–34. Luo Cheng in *Shuo Tang* seems to be a conflation of that character from the earlier novels, the son of a regional commander, and a violent youth of poor background befriended by Qin Shubao in *Sui shi* and *Sui Tang* named Luo Shixin. On the limited use of secret notebooks of story outlines and information shared by members of a single storytelling "family," see Børdahl, "Narrative Voices in Yangzhou Storytelling," 7–8; and Hrdlicková, "The Professional Training of Chinese Storytellers and the Storytellers' Guilds," 233–234.

6. Several scholars have speculated that in its present form, *Sui shi* is a rewritten version of a now lost earlier, probably less refined, fictional biography of Qin Shubao. This is because the unsigned commentary refers in several places to how this novel differs from the *jiuben* (older version) or the *yuanben* (original version), which is hard to explain otherwise. Beyond these few references, there is no mention in any other source. Consequently I wonder whether the commentator here, perhaps the novelist or a close friend, might

simply be referring to Yuan's earlier *draft* of the novel. I base this speculation on the author's preface to *Sui Tang yanyi* in which Chu Renhuo complains that he loaned an incomplete draft of his novel to friends, who returned it only years later, thus delaying its completion and publication. See *Sui Tang yanyi* (Sixuecaotang ed.), "Fafan," p. 1b. Yuan might have done the same. For noteworthy recent editions of these three works, see Qidong yeren, *Sui Yangdi yanshi;* Yuan Yuling, *Sui shi yiwen* (a Taiwan photo-reprint of the 1633 edition); Yuan Yuling, *Sui shi yiwen,* ed. Liu Wenzhong; Yuan Yuling, *Sui shi yiwen,* ed. Song Xiangrui (hereafter *Sui shi*); Chu Renhuo, *Sui Tang yanyi* (hereafter *Sui Tang*). Except as indicated, all are modern typeset editions.

7. See *Shuo Tang houzhuan;* its major part is commonly reprinted with the title *Xue Rengui zheng dong;* for the "Third collection" or *Xue Dingshan zheng xi,* see *Shuo Tang zheng xi zhuan,* a reprint of a Shanghai lithographic edition of ca. 1900. Wu Qiong summarizes the novel and its printing history in his "Qianyan," 1–2.

8. The narrative of *Sui Tang,* 774, ends with the admission that events of the reigns of thirteen emperors remain to be told and that they should form another novel *(dang ling ju biebian),* a "continuation" *(xukan).* Of the Ming novels mentioned above, *Tang shu zhizhuan* is less "open" than *Sui Tang liangchao zhizhuan* or *Sui Tang yanyi:* it is essentially the narrative of the career of Li Shimin, from his initial rising against the Sui in the 617 to the consolidation of his border defenses and the peace won through campaigns led by Xue Rengui.

9. For discussions of reading and critical practices in late Imperial China, see Kao, "Aspects of Derivation in Chinese Narrative," 1–36; Xiao Chi, "Lyric Archi-Occasion," 17–35; Rolston, *Traditional Chinese Fiction and Fiction Commentary.* Likewise, the Old Fisherman had a fine model for literary parody in the writings of Li Yu (1610–1680). However, for the most part Li Yu's source works were rewritten only in part, for example his send up of Confucian ideas in rewritten lines from *Mengzi* in his erotic novel *Rou putuan,* chap. 1; see my *The Novel in Seventeenth-Century China,* 172–174. For a broad study of Li Yu, see Hanan, *The Invention of Li Yu;* Hanan's translation of *Rou putuan* appeared as Li Yu, *The Carnal Prayer Mat.*

10. For studies of early vernacular fiction, see Idema, "Some Remarks and Speculations Concerning *p'ing-hua,*" 69–120; and, more recently, Breuer, "Orality and Literacy in Early Chinese Vernacular Literature." English-language surveys of the development of Chinese vernacular fiction can be found in Idema and Haft, *A Guide to Chinese Literature,* 198–230; Hanan, "The Development of Fiction," 115–143; and in my *Reading Illustrated Fiction in Late Imperial China,* 21–71. For Chinese readers, the standard version is, of course, Lu Xun's (1881–1936) magisterial *Zhongguo xiaoshuo shilue,* trans. Yang Hsien-yi and Gladys Yang as *A Brief History of Chinese Fiction,* with which I will take issue below.

11. Qi Yukun, *Sui Tang yanyi xilie xiaoshuo.* (My thanks to Martin Huang for providing me with a copy.)

12. The preface appears unpaginated at the beginning of all recent editions. Portions of it are translated in my *The Novel in Seventeenth-Century China,* 129; see also *Sui shi,* 1–2.

13. For suggestions about how to distinguish literati novels from more popular fiction, see my "Distinguishing Levels of Audiences for Ming-Ch'ing Vernacular Literature."

14. For the textual histories of these last three novels, see my *The Novel in Seventeenth-Century China,* 241–246, 250–253; and my "*Sui shi yiwen* kaolüe." There I trace the degree to which Chu Renhuo copied the earlier novels into his own. Recently Ouyang Jian has documented the remarkable degree of similarity between *Sui Tang* chaps. 68–100 and the entire contents of a now rare novel generally known as *Hun Tang yanyi* (Devastating the Tang: A romance). Based on a comparison of taboo characters in the two texts, Ouyang concludes that *Hun Tang yanyi* predates the Kangxi period and hence *Sui Tang* as well, for which it may have served as a source. For his discussion of this dating problem, see Ouyang Jian, "*Sui Tang yanyi* 'Zhui ji cheng zhi' kao," 353–396, esp. 383–395. Taking the opposing view, Sun Kaidi reportedly considered *Hun Tang yanyi* to be heavily indebted

to *Sui Tang;* Tan Zhengbi and Tan Xun, *Guben xijian xiaoshuo huikao,* 227, agree. I concur. Qi Yukun, *Sui Tang yanyi xilie xiaoshuo,* 8, misdates *Sui Tang* as 1719, apparently basing this date on Sun Kaidi's and Liu Ts'un-yan's preference for a late misreading of the cyclical characters for the date on the preface to Chu's first (Sixuecaotang) edition; see Sun Kaidi, *Zhongguo tongsu xiaoshuo shumu* (rpt. Hong Kong, 1967), 44, and Liu Ts'un-yan, *Chinese Popular Fiction in Two London Libraries,* 99, 257. (Liu refers to the correct date of 1695 for *Sui Tang* on 134, then concludes that his sources, Sun Kaidi and Zheng Zhenduo, are incorrect!) It suits Qi's argument to make *Sui Tang* and *Shuo Tang* more nearly contemporaries, which probably induced him to rely on this later date. Qi characterizes the content of *Sui Tang* as *za* (varied), 48. With virtually all other scholars, I base my dating, 1695, on the unambiguous date given in its first edition.

15. See Qi Yukun, *Sui Tang yanyi xilie xiaoshuo,* 59–76. *Sui shi yiwen* appeared in only the one Ming edition of 1633 and was not reprinted again until 1975; see Ōtsuka Hidetaka, *Zōho Chūgoku tsūzoku shōsetsu shomoku,* 203–204. Zheng Zhenduo, "Zhongguo xiaoshuo tiyao," 352–353, argues that the "source" for *Shuo Tang* was *Sui Tang liangchao zhizhuan* and that *Shuo Tang* must predate *Sui Tang.* Other scholars agree with him, although Sun Kaidi, the primary bibliographer among May Fourth–era scholars of fiction, sees the dating of the preface as relevant and concludes that *Shuo Tang* was based on *Sui Tang.* See his *Zhongguo tongsu xiaoshuo shumu* (rpt. Hong Kong, 1967), 44–45. Xu Shuofang's prefatory comment to the *Guben xiaoshuo jicheng* series reprint of *Shuo Tang,* included in his *Xiaoshuo kaoxin bian,* 545–546, notes the references in notes there and in *Sui shi yiwen* that refer to "older versions" and concludes that both were based to some degree on earlier manuscript texts. Contradicting the positivistic formulation that "cruder" versions inevitably lead to "more refined" versions, Xu interprets this relationship as indicative of the flexibility with which new texts were derived from older ones, regardless of their provenance.

16. *Shuo Tang,* preface, 1; Qi Yukun, *Sui Tang yanyi xilie xiaoshuo,* 8, 73.

17. For the text of *Laojun tang,* see *Yuan quxuan waibian,* 530–544; this episode occurs in *Shuo Tang,* 250–251. For the parallel scene, see *Sui Tang,* chaps. 50 and 51, esp. 380–391.

18. *Shuo Tang,* chap. 45, 267.

19. On changing the edict, compare *Shuo Tang,* 254, with *Sui Tang,* 392. There is also a *zaju* perhaps dating from the Ming on the changing of the pardon. In *Wei Zheng gai zhao, Guben Yuan Ming zaju,* 3:2061–2096, Wei Zheng changes the pardon and then takes full responsibility for that act. Like the version given in *Sui Tang,* this is a rational explanation that constitutes a morally significant action.

20. *Shuo Tang,* chaps. 43–44, 256–259; the earlier reference to dying in a hail of arrows occurs in chap. 9, 51, and the grains reappear in chap. 65, 389. For the text of a *jingju* (Beijing opera) version of *Shuang tou Tang,* see *Guoju dacheng,* 5:359–372; the quotation is from 361. An earlier theatrical version is preserved as *Si ma tou Tang, Guben Yuan Ming zaju,* 3:2127–2167. Compare this episode in *Sui shi,* chap. 53, 459–461, where Qin and Cheng honorably join the Tang after providing a fitting burial for these two comrades, and especially in *Sui Tang,* chap. 54, 410–413, where Cheng Zhijie (i.e., Cheng Yaojin) joins the Tang on his own initiative, to be with his mother. In this regard Chu Renhuo makes this character more filial; his mother plays a smaller role in *Shuo Tang.* I make comparisons of this scene between the plays and the various novels in "Distinguishing Levels of Audiences for Ming-Ch'ing Vernacular Literature," esp. 117–132.

21. In a recent study of *Shuo Tang* sources, Peng Zhihui posits the existence of a number of storytellers' "prompt books" to suggest a lost *pinghua* version of Sui and Tang stories. Lacking any textual evidence, Peng suggests that disciples of the late Ming professional storyteller Liu Jingting (also known as "Pockmarked" Liu, Liu Mazi) would have expanded on the Sui-Tang tales for which he was famous and that they are likely to have produced stories much like those now incorporated into *Shuo Tang.* Peng's reconstruction is as hard

REWRITING THE TANG 187

to refute as it is to verify; certainly the Liu school would logically have developed their master's narrative materials rather like Yangzhou *pinghua* artist Wang Shaotang expanded the *Shuihu zhuan* tales of his father and grandfather. (See Wang Shaotang, *Wu Song* and *Song Jiang*; and Børdahl and Ross, *Chinese Storytellers*, 60–72, 102–125, 169–259.) Peng Zhihui considers *Shuo Tang* to be the intermediary in a direct evolutionary line between early prosimetric oral narrative such as the late Ming *Da Tang Qinwang cihua* and the northern *pingshu* versions of the Sui-Tang material by contemporary raconteurs such as Chen Yinrong, *Xing Tang zhuan*, 4 vols. See Peng, "Lun *Shuo Tang quanzhuan* de diben," 181–187. I agree that the Old Fisherman appears to have been inspired by storytelling and theatrical narratives. But I submit that its clearly subversive engagement with literati novels is at least as important as its appropriation of oral material for understanding the novel's significance and that searching for his specific sources is less fruitful than exploring how, and to what end, he used these easily identifiable earlier printed fictional texts.

22. I have explored the rather more detailed *Sui shi* chap. 22 version of this rape scene in my *The Novel in Seventeenth-Century China*, 113–119. Chu Renhuo deleted its graphic detail from *Sui Tang* chap. 18 to retain Qin's retaliation and subsequent flight from punishment from Yuan's novel.

23. *Shuo Tang*, 118–119. Later the reader learns that Cheng can in fact read one character, "ren" (person); see 126. *Sui Tang* and its parent novel *Sui shi* consistently refer to him using the simpler character for "zhi."

24. Qi Yukun and Peng Zhihui echo the usual interpretation of this racy language as proof of the novel's oral origins and that it was intended for unlettered readers. Needless to say, a reader of any level of sophistication can appreciate slang and vulgarity, but less experienced readers might well miss the literary play in their use. For summary statements on the characteristics of oral narrative, see Ong, *Orality and Literacy*, 37–56, esp. 44, 57, 70.

25. *Shuo Tang*, 119. As an anonymous reviewer pointed out, on the Beijing opera stage Cheng Yaojin was sometimes performed by a *chou* (clown) actor and at other times by a *jing* (painted-face) actor. Needless to say, this scene could not be presented on stage, although it may have formed part of a professional storyteller's repertory, another example of the gross physicality available in oral performance.

26. *Shuo Tang*, 123–126.

27. *Sui Tang*, 151, 153. Compare *Sui shi* chap. 27, 215–221. In both novels, You merely demonstrates ax-fighting techniques from horseback, and Cheng is able to master them quickly.

28. See *Sui Tang* chap. 45, 341. Qi Yukun goes to great pains to demonstrate the degree to which Cheng embodies the masses' antifeudal and democratic principles; see *Sui Tang yanyi xilie xiaoshuo*, 63–65. Probably without realizing it, Qi even describes Cheng's youthful economic plight with a phrase from *The Internationale (Guoji ge)*: "[Qilai,] jihan jiaopo de [nuli]" ([Arise, ye] prisoners of starvation), 63. In a lengthy examination of *Shuo Tang*, Ouyang Jian takes great pains to show how the novel meets popular, specifically *pingmin baixing* (common people's), tastes. To Ouyang, the influence of the "older version" is visible here; he places it firmly within the *Shuihu zhuan* tradition of romantic fiction in contrast to its predecessors in the Sui-Tang series of novels. He hews to the idea that the most important attribute of a hero is *yi*, ignoring the role played by pure physical strength, so well explored by Qi Yukun. See Ouyang Jian, "*Shuo Tang*—pingmin de Sui Tang yingxiong pu." The unexamined agendas of these two critics can be easily discerned from these comments.

29. Qi Yukun, *Sui Tang yanyi xilie xiaoshuo*, 55.

30. The quotation is from *Shuo Tang*, 125; Cheng becomes emperor in chap. 28, 165–167. Later he complains when Li Mi disregards his suggestions that Li Mi has no respect for him, even though he would not have become an emperor if not for Cheng (256). See Qi Yukun's comments, *Sui Tang yanyi xilie xiaoshuo*, 64–65.

31. *Shuo Tang*, 172, 215–216. In *Sui Tang*—as in fact—the first ruler of Wagang was Zhai Rang, who later repents having yielded the throne to Li Mi, but as soon as he learns of this change of heart Li Mi has him executed; see *Shuo Tang*, 321–323, 345–348. Cheng Yaojin's excursion in the underground palace has its source in *Sui Tang* as well. In chap. 32, 245–247, the mighty swordsman Di Quxie (who makes no other appearance in the novel) sees a vision of a giant rat in the cavern; a deity explains that this is the real form of the Sui emperor Yang, who is doomed to die in five years. It is a witty twist to combine the figures, knight-errant and enormous rat, into the single, very ugly, bully emperor Cheng Yaojin.

32. Shan is introduced in *Shuo Tang*, 26–27; Shan has a register of all the bandits in the realm, a *xiangma dan*. The first quotation appears at the end of chap. 23; see *Shuo Tang*, 138, 142.

33. *Sui Tang* chaps. 23–24, 166–180. In *Sui Tang*, Cheng Yaojin is rude to Qin Shubao because the latter does not recognize him; this is because, the narrator explains in an aside (172), that Cheng had not previously been so ugly: because he had encountered a "strange man" (*yiren*) who had given him, for no explicit reason, an elixir (*danyao*), subsequently Cheng's face had turned dark, his hair red, and his beard yellow. It would appear that the Old Fisherman accommodated this anomalous bit of afterthought (or theatrical convention?) by simply making Cheng ugly from the start and modifying the reason for the nonrecognition to be more realistic: the two have not seen each other for many years. Compare *Shuo Tang*, 141–142.

34. See *Shuo Tang*, 143. Such explanatory asides, reminiscent of storytellers' practices, are another way in which the novelist draws the reader into a compact involving a complicit reading. Other such asides are numerous; see 13, 33, 45, 48, 50, 52, 58, 63, 65, 83, 86, 89, 92, 98, 99, 100, 135, 137, 147, 154, 159, 191, 212, 220, 223, 235, 237, 246, 248, 252, 256, 270, 286, 287, 299, 303, 305, 306, 343, 353, 356, 359, 366, 370, 376, 377, 382, 389, 403, and 407. In many of these asides, the narrator addresses his audience as *Liewei*. The narrator refers to himself with the first-person pronoun *wo* on 171, 248, and elsewhere. See n. 42 below.

35. *Shuo Tang*, 142–147. Thereafter Luo Cheng does boast of his abilities (he is higher in the ranking of *haohan* than Shan) with the purpose of irritating Shan, in which he succeeds. Cheng later exacerbates further this already obsessive grudge on Shan's part; see chap. 39, 229–233. Such agonistic relations seem also to have originated in oral performance conventions; see Ong, *Orality and Literacy*, 44.

36. *Shuo Tang* chap. 51, 303–305; Qi Yukun also draws attention to this episode (*Sui Tang yanyi xilie xiaoshuo*, 70). The source for this is *Sui Tang* chap. 57, although there the prince chases a beautiful pheasant to where a mysterious monk saves him from pursuit. Shan's response in the literati novel refers more to political realities than to personal loyalties: now we each have our separate rulers, and past personal feelings should be put aside, Shan insists; see *Sui Tang*, 440–441. Readers of erotic novels might know about a more famous anecdote in which an emperor cut off a part of his robe to avoid disturbing his sleeping lover. See Hinsch, *Passions of the Cut Sleeve*, 52–53.

37. These are Qi Yukun's figures, 57–58.

38. *Sui Tang*, 461–464. *Sui shi* has Shan respond to his friends' weeping with the retort, "Stop acting like women!" (*Buyao zuo ci ernü tai!*) An original note on that page, most likely penned by Yuan Yuling himself, comments, "He's a real man" (*Shi zhangfu*). *Sui shi*, 509. The rejoining of head to the corpse is intended to counteract the ostensibly unfilial act of causing one's body, the gift from one's parents, to be mutilated. Such acts were performed in reality as well as in fiction for this purpose; here the heroes are again acting as surrogate family for their sworn brother Shan. *Jiu Tang shu* (Bona edition), 67.9b, the biography of Xu Maogong (i.e., Li Ji, using the imperial surname that was granted to him by Li Shimin and deleting from his formal name, Shiji, the taboo character in common with Li Shimin) records that it was only Xu who cut a piece of flesh from his thigh. His wish was that at least this piece of him might accompany his friend Shan into the grave.

39. Xiang Yu's leave-taking appears in *Shiji* 7, 1:333–334. For a translation, see Sima Qian, *Records of the Grand Historian,* trans. Watson, Han Dynasty 1:44–45. The film I refer to is, of course, *Bawang bie ji* (Farewell my concubine, 1993) directed by Chen Kaige and starring the late Leslie Cheung, Gong Li, and Zhang Fengyi. This scene is a favorite in traditional operas, such as the *Jingju* version around which Zhang's film revolves.

40. *Shuo Tang,* 333–337. The scene concludes with Shan's spirit streaking off to another land where it takes the form of General Kaesomun, who will invade the Tang in days to come—suggesting a sequel.

41. See Ong, *Orality and Literacy,* 44. Some of the most vulgar expressions, such as *"Ni niang de biqing,"* were partially expurgated from the Shanghai Guji edition of *Shuo Tang,* 336; the Beijing Shiyue wenyi edition retains all of these expressions, however; see 448. In a private communication, July 30, 2002, Martin Huang insightfully observed, "The version of this incident in *Sui Tang* where words in the chapter title 'cutting off his robe' (to sever his relationship with his sworn brother) is very telling. In a word, this is not entirely the 'innovation' of the author of *Shuo Tang.* I tend to believe that Chu Renhuo has reinserted this detail into his novel to show that Shan is in fact the first to disregard *yi,* thus making more excusable Qin Shubao and others' later failure to keep their words when they fail to die with Shan as they have promised in their swearing of brotherhood. Chu's efforts to 'alleviate' Qin's guilt can also be seen in his expanding the scene of Shan's death in his novel (emphasizing more the attachment among the sworn brothers). . . . In fact, if Qin and others had tried really hard, they might have been able to save Shan. This is at least the impression I got from reading the version in *Sui shi.* Furthermore, this episode, though not seen in *Suishi yiwen,* is not Chu Renhuo's 'innovation' either, since it can be found in Chapter 61 of *Sui Tang liangchao zhizhuan.*"

42. *Shuo Tang,* 144. On the rhetorical use of questions here, compare Børdahl, "Narrative Voices in Yangzhou Storytelling," 9: "The storyteller-narrator's narratee may be identified as the real audience. However, the narratee must be defined specifically as the storyteller's narratee, i.e., his audience in its specific social role as audience at a storytelling performance. The difference is manifest, for example, in the way the audience reacts to his simulated dialogue: the storyteller asks many questions during his recitation, but he never expects to get an answer from his audience. The audience likewise is not prepared to enter into a dialogue. If someone from the audience would raise his voice from the benches and answer the storyteller's question, it would be completely out of place." Even more ironically, these heroes even look ugly to each other. In chap. 27, Cheng rides against the Wagang Fortress for the first time. A young warrior named Ma Zong rides out to challenge him to battle. "Ah ya, where in the world did such a weird looking character come from?" he says to himself. And to Cheng he shouts, "Hey, you ugly devil, who are you anyway? Tell me your name and be quick about it!" Enraged, Cheng responds, "Yer old man's no other: I'm the Cheng Yaojin who smuggled salt, bumped off an official, grabbed a dragon robe, sold bamboo baskets, and raised hell in Shandong, that I am!" See *Shuo Tang,* 162–163.

43. On banned books, see Wang Liqi, *Yuan Ming Qing sandai jinhui xiaoshuo xiqu shiliao;* for the various attacks on *Shuihu zhuan,* see 204–210, etc. An Pingqiu and Zhang Peiheng, eds., *Zhongguo jinshu daguan,* include *Shuo Tang* on their list of books banned during the Qing (649–715); see 695. Okamoto Sae, *Shindai kinsho no kenkyū,* does not, however. For the crimes of sedition, see Jones, *The Great Qing Code,* 237–239. Wang Liqi (*Yuan Ming Qing sandai jinhui xiaoshuo xiqu shiliao,* 18–21) quotes the general Qing legal restrictions concerning the sale of banned books.

44. Chartier writes convincingly about the many ways cultural products might be used within a single society; see his "Popular Appropriation," esp. 89, 92–93.

8

H. LAURA WU

Vindication of Patriarchy

Chen Tianchi's *Ruyijun zhuan* as a
Critique of the Ming *Ruyijun zhuan*

About three hundred years after the Ming *Ruyijun zhuan* (The lord of perfect satisfaction) was produced, a novel bearing the same title was in circulation in manuscript form among a small circle of readers. The two *Ruyijun zhuan* are diametrically different in terms of language, content, authorial stances, and reader responses. Yet the common title sets the two texts within a context of a reciprocally influencing reading and interpretative framework: titles, especially titles that allude to another text or other texts, by their very nature are anticipatory, recapitulative, and reflective. Such a title often rereads another text and insists on "the memory of one text as a prior, ongoing, and reflective means of comprehending another. More than that, a work that bears another work's title or subject makes linear reading into contrapuntal reading." To miss the link set by the title or titles is "to thin out the texture of works";[1] misreading may occur as a result.

My chapter aims at a contrapuntal reading of the two *Ruyijun zhuan*. It will start with a brief description of the two texts but will concentrate more on the obscure later work, trace the thematic parallels and links between the two texts, and then hypothesize that the Qing *Ruyijun zhuan* is a special kind of *xushu*, one that is a critical response to the earlier Ming work.

THE TWO *RUYIJUN ZHUAN*

The better-known Ming *Ruyijun zhuan* is a classical Chinese tale whose date of production and authorship are still issues of much debate.[2] This story purports to relate Empress Wu Zetian's (r. 690–705) erotic adventures, thereby depicting a picture of disruption and decadence in the sociopolitical order. It has been received primarily as a dirty little book of debauchery.[3] Allegedly the author wrote the story as a vicarious quest for sexual gratification for both author and reader.[4] There have been some iconoclastic, or perhaps more perceptive, readers who interpret *Ruyijun zhuan* as a moral remonstration under the guise of sensual enticement, but even these readers defend the story in an apologetic manner. Huang Xun, in his "Du *Ruyijun zhuan*," the earliest extant critique of the novella,[5] proclaimed that the text was less a censure of Wu Zetian's depravity than a veiled attack against the problematic moral standard set by Emperor Taizong (r. 627–649), founder of the Tang dynasty. However, Huang still deemed the book utterly unworthy, asserting that "to speak of it is to pollute one's mouth and tongue, to write of it is to pollute the stationery on which it is written; it is fit for burning."[6]

Most modern studies of the Ming *Ruyijun zhuan* focus on its textual relations to the Ming classic *Jin Ping Mei* (The plum in the golden vase).[7] A couple of recent examinations follow more closely Huang Xun's precedent, scrutinizing the politics of sex and the mechanisms of politics and sex.[8] Yet their authors seem to query the "effectiveness" of the strategies to politicize sex and to sensualize power in order to deliver moral admonishment.[9] The Ming *Ruyijun zhuan*'s erotic content has apparently been seductive but repulsive and problematic all at once.

The later *Ruyijun zhuan*, however, heads in a very different direction in many aspects. Its production is meticulously dated by various prefatory writings. Its author, Chen Tianchi, most likely finished writing the novel before 1833 and spent the next fifteen years or so revising the manuscript and circulating it among friends and potential patrons in order to have the novel printed.[10] However, very little is known of Chen Tianchi except that he had a famous forefather, Chen Tingjing (1639–1712). Chen Tingjing had a successful official career. He received his *jinshi* degree in 1658, apparently at a relatively young age. During his lifetime, he filled various posts in many government departments and eventually reached the top position of grand secretary of the Hall of Literary Profundity (Wenyuange da Xueshi). Chen Tingjing was also Emperor Kangxi's (r. 1662–1722) favored minister: when Chen fell seriously ill, the emperor sent his personal physicians to treat this loyal subject. Upon Chen's death, the emperor wrote an elegiac poem and also had his third son and many high-ranking officials attend Chen's funeral, an honor granted only to a privileged few.[11] It seems that Chen Tianchi used his ancestor as a model in his fictional production; his novel therefore can serve as a celebration of his own family's glorious past. However, Chen Tianchi himself failed to emulate his famous ancestor. He took the provincial examination once but did not pass. After this unsuccessful attempt, he gave up any pursuit of officialdom and relied on tilling a few *mu* of rather barren farmland to make a living. He had to turn to tutoring and writing to subsidize farming.[12] Seen from this biographical and autobiographical light, Chen Tianchi's *Ruyijun zhuan* takes on certain therapeutic function of wish fulfillment.

Thematically the Qing *Ruyijun zhuan* advocates order and orthodoxy, be they political, social, familial, or sexual, via celebrating the perfect success and happiness in the long life of the protagonist, Tian Jinsheng, or Lord of Perfect Satisfaction. In Chen Tianchi's story, Tian is marked from the very beginning for an extraordinary life. He is endorsed with divine seed, being the human incarnation of Jintong to bodhisattva Guanyin. His fall from grace, the only blemish in an otherwise impeccable life, is due to a harmless and thus excusable misdemeanor: he is amused at seeing all the deities from the Three Teachings gathering together to celebrate Buddha's nirvana and the birthday of Taishang Lao jun and cannot help smiling at his counterpart, Yunü. This mischief leads to our hero's exile from heaven, yet far from being doomed to suffer from purgatory affliction and distress, he is showered with all the imaginable luck and happiness that a human being could ever dream of enjoying.[13]

Tian has the good fortune to be born into a prominent family that can trace its roots to the legendary sage King Shun and boasts of many eminent ancestors. His father retires from the important and prestigious post of grand secretary of the Hall of Literary Profundity. Tian himself is a prodigy who demonstrates an extraordinary ability to learn at the tender age of three; his pursuit of officialdom starts at age twelve. To the full credit of his incredible talent and profound learning in both literary and military matters, he wins first place in both the civil and military examinations at the district, provincial, and metropolitan levels. Upon winning the civil and military *zhuangyuan* title at about fifteen or sixteen *sui*, Tian is appointed grand secretary *(da xueshi)* and then vice minister of war *(bingbu shilang)*. Within a year he has top posts in all six ministries and has been granted the honorary title of Grand Mentor *(taifu)*, thus inaugurating a successful career as a capable and loyal minister. In his official capacity, Tian recognizes the talented and loyal under his charge and recommends them for positions of importance and responsibility, the historically famous Wang Yangming (1472–1529) being one of those under his patronage. Tian also plays a strategic role in the downfall of the evil eunuch Liu Jin (d. 1510), thereby purging detrimental influences at the emperor's side. As a warrior-general, Tian leads successful campaigns against the invading Tufan, thus pacifying China's western border. For his diligently delivered services, he received countless imperial favors from three emperors, among them marriage to a princess, a princely residence, frequent and numerous gifts, and the title Prince of Pacifying the West (Pingxi Wang).[14]

Tian is an ideal family man, too. He is a filial son who looks after his parents personally, imitates the filial Lao Laizi in amusing them, and dutifully celebrates their birthdays and mourns their deaths. He is a fair patriarch of the Tian clan and a very protective patron of the less fortunate in his native place and home district. He finances the clan's school, charity burial ground, and ancestral worship ceremonies. He donates money and property to famine relief programs and initiates development projects to cultivate farmland and utilize natural resources to benefit local people. He is blessed with conjugal bliss. Being a handsome and puissant man, he can easily satisfy the needs of his many consorts. He fathers sixteen sons and eleven daughters and is a kind and responsible parent to his children. He invites leading scholars of his day such as Kang Hai (1475–1541), Shao Bao (*jinshi* 1484), and Li Jingchen[15] to tutor his sons. As a result, on a single occasion five sons take the metropolitan examination and all gain the most sought-after *jinshi* degree.[16] He also arranges appropriate matches for his offspring, with one daughter becoming an empress, three daughters marrying princes, and two more marriages to Confucius' descendants. At the conclusion of the novel, Tian and his princess wife celebrate their centennial birthdays, attended by all his siblings, children, and many high-ranking officials. By then the old couple have thirty-six grandsons, four great-grandsons, and one great-great-grandson. Even the ruling monarch sends him gifts, including an inscribed board bearing the imperial tributes: "An all-around paragon of his time, perfect contentment in all domains, excellence in five virtues, and full possession of three esteems." Tian Jinsheng, or Lord of Perfect Satisfaction, is indeed success and happiness personified.[17]

In artistic and technical terms, the Qing *Ruyijun zhuan* is a much more ambitious work. This vernacular novel is much longer and tries to accommodate as many generic varieties as possible.[18] It patches together elements of military romance, talent-beauty love story, court case story, and spirit-demon fantasy. It parades abstruse knowledge and trivia of sundry disciplines and topics, aping the novel of erudition. It incorporates metafictional discourse and literary criticism into the narrative. It peppers the story with historical and autobiographical references to give the novel a touch of *shizhuan* (history and biography). To contain the all-inclusive conglomeration of myriad ingredients and to match its thematic perfection, the later *Ruyijun zhuan* is a structurally tidy and orderly work, with the normative features of the *qishu ti* (style of the novelistic masterworks).[19] Comments on the Qing *Ruyijun zhuan*'s structural pattern by a critic of the time bear testimony to the novel's neat construction.

> This book of seventy-two chapters begins with the fall from heaven due to mischief and ends with the pleasure trip to the mountains, which indeed posits a grand correlation *(da zhaoying)* between the opening and the denouement. The middle can be subdivided into several sections, too. Chapter one narrates the protagonist's reincarnation on earth and chapter ten is about his marriage; this ten-chapter cycle makes a small, unifying block *(xiao jieju)*. Chapter eleven tells that the hero is enfeoffed, and here he is first addressed as Lord of Perfect Satisfaction. In chapter twenty, he has successfully pacified the west, been made a prince, and [been] granted retirement from office, thus another small, unifying block. From chapter twenty-one to chapter thirty, the joys of the husband and wives are depicted, another small, unifying block. In chapter thirty-one the protagonist takes a long journey and returns from Mount Hua only in chapter forty, thus another small, unifying block. Chapters forty-one to fifty detail the pleasure of friendly gatherings and marriages of the children, another small, unifying block. Chapters fifty-one to sixty start with the parents' funeral and end with the daughters-in-law taking over the management of family affairs, another small, unifying block. Chap-

ters sixty-one to seventy tell of the successful career of the younger generation and celebration of the old couple's birthday, another unifying block. The last two chapters, seventy-one and seventy-two, wrap up the after-ripples, which echo back to the beginning and at the same time conclude the whole book. The narrative structure is meticulously ordered. The reader should pay close attention to it and then he will notice it.[20]

Superimposed on this ten-chapter rhythm is a tripartite framework, or as the critic calls it, "the three places of pivotal importance" *(san da guanjian chu)*. These are the *qianbu* (the first segment; chaps. 1 to 30), about the hero's great achievements during his youth; the *zhongbu* (the middle segment; chaps. 31 to 50), on the hero's retirement life since his prime; and the *houbu* (the concluding segment; chaps. 51 to 70), on his happy old age. The three segments function as the ordering scheme that endows the aforementioned seven blocks with thematic coherence, logical continuity, and structural order.[21] Thus a story of complete success is also exquisitely constructed: perfect order in life is matched with perfect order in its literary representation.

However, responses from readers of the time varied. Some thought very highly of the author and the work, while others needed much persuasion, even being pestered into finishing a perusal of the novel.[22] But eventually all seemed to be won over especially by the content of the novel. One reader believed that Chen's *Ruyijun zhuan* was most remarkable because "it succeeds in conveying the spirit (mind/heart) and principles *(xinfa)* of Yao and Shun, [teachings on] human nature and the Dao *(xingdao)* by Confucius and Mencius, instructions *(jiaoyan)* of the Cheng brothers and Zhu Xi, and code of proper behavior advocated in *The Mean,* all in folksy language *(liyan).*"[23]

PARALLELS IN THE TWO *RUYIJUN ZHUAN*

Interestingly, two works of such radically different orientations share some easily discernible parallels. First of all, we find a common setting for both stories, that is, the imperial context. The Ming *Ruyijun zhuan* is set in the Tang court, and most fictional events occur within the confines of the imperial palace. Based on historical records, fanciful legends, and malicious gossip, the novella portrays Empress Wu as being intimately related to three Tang emperors—Taizong, Gaozong (r. 650–683), and Zhongzong (r. 685, 705–709)—via sex, incest, marriage, and blood relations. She is also sexually involved with numerous men of various social status and walks of life, some of her paramours being illiterate and of dubious origin. Sexual orgies are described in graphic detail, but very often and with increasing intensity intertwined with politics, especially the paramount issue of imperial succession. The male protagonist Xue Aocao, a mere sex plaything of the empress with no official status, is presented as a wise counselor and loyal subject who plays an important role in the restoration of Tang rule. Because of his foresight, opportune counsel, loyalty, and superb services, he is showered with favors by the empress and rewarded with immortality by the novelist at the very end of the story.[24]

Similar motifs appear in the Qing *Ruyijun zhuan* as well, but very often with a thematic twist. The later novel also places its male protagonist, Tian Jinsheng, in an imperial context. He is the royal son-in-law and a capable, trusted minister. During his long and successful official career he serves three Ming emperors—Xiaozong (r. 1488–1505), Wuzong (r. 1506–1521), and Shizong (r. 1522–1566)—and wins countless imperial favors. At the end of the novel, Tian, along with his princess wife, also rises up to heaven and joins the pantheon of deities and immortals. In sharp contrast to Xue Aocao, Tian obtains his prerogatives through conventional and honorable means. He definitely does not, and moreover has no need to, solicit imperial favors through sex.

However, Tian is a sexually puissant man. He has ten consorts whose social backgrounds form a hierarchical spectrum from the highest to the lowest and humblest, with a princess as the principal wife, daughters from eminent families as secondary wives, and maidservants as concubines. Even a fox fairy enters his harem. These women, regardless of their different social backgrounds, all have their own admirable talents in literary, military, administrative, or other practical matters, and they, each in her own way, contribute to the well-being of the Tian family.

There are occasional sexual orgies alluded to and once explicitly narrated in the novel. Yet no graphic details are given even in the explicit depiction, and the tone in these parts of the novel is always playful, never enticing or sadistic. Tian is shown to fulfill successfully his sexual duties to his ten consorts, and he and his women seem to enjoy conjugal sex and happiness.[25]

The setting of sexual and other acts among the Lord of Perfect Satisfaction and his women is mostly the Tian residence, the Guansheng cheng, or Township of the Royal Son-in-law. The novel devotes substantial parts to detailing location selection, construction, completion, physical layout, defense, and management of the township.[26] The fictional fortress complex resembles the imperial court both in physical features and in administrative hierarchy and thus apparently is intended as a miniature imperial court *(xiao chaoting).*[27] The *xiao chaoting* ploy is a favored textual strategy that writers of Chinese vernacular fiction frequently resorted to for special and specific rhetorical effects. For instance, the Ximen household in *Jin Ping Mei* is made to mirror the empire and the imperial household, hence adding a layer of social and political protest to the novel's multilayered significance.[28] *Shuihu zhuan* (Water margin) very often labels its warriors as "a 'junior' *(xiao)* or 'sick', i.e. deficient *(bing)* copy of an earlier hero" so as "to poke fun at the small-time status of some of the *Shui-hu* warriors,"[29] thus contributing to the novel's overall design of "deflation of heroism."[30] The Qing *Ruyijun zhuan*'s "junior" or pseudo-imperial setting can very well be seen as a thematic echo to the Ming *Ruyijun zhuan,* but the marked twist perhaps alludes to another narrative topos—the *suwang* (uncrowned king) in the Chinese cultural tradition[31]—and thus lends more moral weight to and elevates the axiological status of the novel's protagonist.

The most obvious link between the two *Ruyijun zhuan* is undoubtedly the title "Ruyijun," or Lord of Perfect Satisfaction. Similarities in the descriptions of the entitlement circumstances occur in the two texts. In the Ming *Ruyijun zhuan*, the title character is first mentioned to the sexually frustrated empress because of his fame or the notoriety of his private member. Upon hearing of Xue Aocao's prodigious natural endowments *(biaozi weiyi)*, the empress immediately issues a decree and sends for the recommended talent of "high moral standing" *(xianshi)*. Once Aocao enters the imperial harem, the empress requests to verify his endowment by first inspecting it and then personally testing it. The empress is perfectly satisfied, and therefore she immediately grants imperial endorsement, naming him "Ruyijun," or Lord of Perfect Satisfaction.

Tian Jinsheng, the protagonist in the Qing *Ruyijun zhuan*, gains access to the imperial presence also through reputation, though of an entirely different nature. He is a prodigy who can recite and interpret poems as well as write beautifully at the tender age of four. Upon hearing of Tian's precocity and talents, Emperor Xiaozong issues a decree granting an audience with the *enfant chéri*. The emperor is so impressed by the child's natural endowments and cultivated talents that he showers him with many presents. Later on, the emperor handpicks Tian as the royal son-in-law,[32] which eventually leads to his entitlement as Lord of Perfect Satisfaction.

The entitlement procedure of widespread fame, imperial audience, tests, and endorsement as well as other parallels[33] in the two texts are too obvious to be random coincidences. The Ming *Ruyijun zhuan* was in fact quite well known and well circulated during the late Ming and the Qing times. It was often cited in fictional and nonfictional works. For instance, when the male protagonist in *Rou putuan* (The carnal prayer mat) finds it necessary to educate his naive and sexually inexperienced wife, he purchases some sex manuals and erotic stories. One of the three titles explicitly mentioned is *Ruyijun zhuan*.[34] Similar motifs also surfaced in other literary works.[35] The story generated quite a few rewrites and imitations, too.[36] Due to its explicit, erotic content, it was blacklisted several times in official lists of banned books.[37] Chen Tianchi, author of the later *Ruyijun zhuan*, was a well-read and well-connected scholar, so it would be difficult to imagine that he could have been unaware of the existence and notoriety of the Ming work.[38] By appropriating the title of the earlier text in spite of its ill repute, Chen apparently intended the two texts to be read in tandem. Moreover, when Chen was circulating his novel among friends and patrons, some of these first readers suggested three other titles. Most of the preface writers preferred to use the other titles, referring to the novel as *Di yi kuaihuo qishu* (The first remarkable book of joy and happiness), *Di yi kuaihuo shu* (The first book of joy and happiness), *Wuhen tian chuanqi* (The remarkable tale of heaven of no regrets), or a combination of the three.[39] Chen preferred *Ruyijun zhuan* and persistently used it in his own preface to the novel and in his correspondence to a friend whereby he elaborated on his motivation for writing the novel and described his efforts in producing it. The authorial preference of and insistence on calling his work *Ruyijun zhuan* serve as "the contractual index,"[40] confirming a close link between the two texts.

THE QING *RUYIJUN ZHUAN* AS A *XUSHU*

What, then, is the link? What is the nature of these transtextual relationships?[41] Or what is the Qing *Ruyijun zhuan* to the Ming *Ruyijun zhuan*?

The link between the two texts is not one of mere intertextuality, if intertextuality is understood as borrowing, quoting, alluding, or even local plagiarizing,[42] as *Jin Ping Mei* is to *Shuihu zhuan*[43] or as *Honglou meng* (Dream of the red chamber) is to earlier classics like *Shuihu zhuan, Jin Ping Mei,* and *Xiyou ji* (The journey to the West).[44] The link between the two *Ruyijun zhuan* is so fundamental and prevalent and yet more concealed that I would venture to call the Qing *Ruyijun zhuan* a sort of *xushu* to the Ming text of the same title. Next I will examine the construction of sexuality in the two *Ruyijun zhuan* in order to demonstrate in what ways the Qing text functions as a *xushu* to the Ming story.

Regulating Sexuality

Sex or the description of sexual acts in the Ming *Ruyijun zhuan* has been seen as denoting different things. It can be and has been treated as simple promiscuity *(yin)* because it details the promiscuousness of a female who cannot get enough sex. Consequently, the book is deemed dirty and pornographic, an advocacy of debauchery *(xuanyin)*. It can be read as a display of sexual abnormality because the erotic scenes are not between compatible golden couples but between a woman in her seventies and much younger men who usually have nothing to recommend them but the size of their penis[45] or who mean very little to the empress except as a source of sexual pleasure. Moreover, the empress is deemed perverse because she herself enjoys sadistic sex and inflicts pains on herself and her partners. She is depicted more like a sexual vampire who thrives on sex, but men become emaciated after sexual encounters with her, and some simply die of depletion.[46] Because sex is portrayed as abnormal, absurd, and grotesque in the Ming *Ruyijun zhuan,* some critics rightly believe that erotica is merely a pretext for moral remonstration and/or political criticism.[47] Whichever view a reader chooses to uphold, she or he cannot but notice that the Ming work parades sex and does it with excessive and overly graphic particulars. Hence, disproportionate eroticism tends to eclipse whatever moral or sociopolitical message could have been hidden behind the juicy sex story.

The Qing *Ruyijun zhuan* seems resolute in redressing the excessive eroticism in its hypotext.[48] It opts for the opposite extreme. Not only is illicit sex purged or assigned only to minor, negative characters and mentioned in passing, but even conjugal and thus appropriate sex is devoid of any impropriety. The Lord of Perfect Satisfaction has taken ten consorts, and in between these ten wedding events the lord has gone through vital changes, from a teenager to a man in his prime and thus sexually maturing and mature. Such experiences no doubt provide ample opportunity to depict scenes of lovemaking in erotica and even in a romance. Yet the Qing *Ruyijun zhuan* properly hushes up each bridal night, with only a perfunctory mentioning of the consummation of marriage.[49] Clearly there are insinuations to sex, the most obvious being that the lord has fathered numerous children with his ten consorts. The text demonstrates no interest in the sexual acts that result in these children's conception but seems obsessed with their status in the extended household: the children's biological mothers and order of birth are meticulously documented. Details with more explicit sexual overtones occasionally surface, but immediately afterward a moral dressing-down follows. For instance, after the lord acquires his ninth consort, the princess proposes a fair way of sharing the husband among the nine women. Each woman will have her own sleeping corner for her private use when she has her periods, after childbirth, or when she is not inclined to have sex. In the north wing, which is also the locale of dominance and authority, there is a communal bedroom with a master bed and eight single beds in it. The master bed is big enough to accommodate the husband and all the women at once; its sole purpose seems to be for the husband and wives to have sex or group sex.[50] A reader familiar with erotic fiction and having a vivid imagination, or perhaps a lewd mind-set, could certainly conjure up some wild scenes. Thus as a preemptive measure, the author has the princess deliver a sermon on maintaining harmony in polygamy, presumably also a declaration of the rationale behind introducing such a "problematic" motif.

> We have here eight or nine persons and naturally there will be eight or nine minds. Human nature is different just as human faces are unlike. I indeed have no clue what you may harbor in your heart. However, although we are all entitled to our own thoughts, we must know to whom we all belong, and our heart should also go to that man. It goes without saying that even with one man and one wife there are bound to be disagreements, but that situation is easier to handle. In our case, there is one man but eight or nine women. As for that matter [sex with the husband], we have already had an arrangement and I do not need to repeat it. In my view, the eight or nine of us must be of one heart/mind. Our eight or nine bodies can be seen as the transformations of one single mind and body, like Sun Wukong's. We should never bear a grudge against one another or speak ill of one another. We should never keep a false facade and flatter others but, turning around, curse and wish ill of them. Ever since antiquity, there have been countless wives and concubines like that. For us, we should reason in this manner: "Her body is what my man loves most, and thus it should be just like my own skin and flesh. If she is injured, I'll feel the pain." Then our hearts are linked together like one piece and we can truly love one another and treat the others benevolently. If we are of one mind in this matter, we can live together. If anyone is found out to have two minds and gossip around, I will immediately throw her out and give her away to a turtle [i.e., brothel runner]. If that happens, you should not complain about my lack of compassion.[51]

On another occasion, the lord and his ten women are inspecting imperial gifts sent to the princess. Two trunks are reported to contain various sexual paraphernalia, including erotic paintings, sex manuals, sexual implements, and stimulants. This time, it is the Lord of Perfect Satisfaction's turn to censure. He takes to task master painters who stooped so low as to paint erotic pictures. In his eyes, those painters have led people astray with artifacts and caused depletion and corruption. Sexual implements and stimulants are even worse, since

> [l]ove between a man and a woman has its natural beauty, therefore there is no need to resort to artificial help to invoke licentious desires. If we just do the real thing *(shishi)*, that will be joy and pleasure enough. These things cause harm to one's health and therefore should not be kept. Take them out, throw them into the ditch, and let them flow away with water. I remember in the past whenever there was an examination, there would be many ruffians sweet-talking the young into purchasing erotic stimulants. Those young profligates would fall for it and go wild. It definitely did not do them any good but a lot of harm. They became emaciated and enervated. Since they damaged their innate essence, how could they pursue their study so as to achieve great deeds and fame? This indeed causes tremendous harm. I will firmly exhort local officials to get rid of these ruffians and their goods so that morality and mores will not be contaminated.[52]

If sexuality in the Ming *Ruyijun zhuan* is constructed and construed in such a manner that death or total eradication of sexual desires becomes the only resolution for managing sex and morality,[53] then the Ming text is indeed very conservative. Its conception of and attitude toward sexuality lean "closer to traditional, rational Neo-Confucianism than to subjective, radical reappraisals of the sixteenth century."[54] If the Ming text is conservative in essence, then the Qing *Ruyijun zhuan* is puritan and uncompromising. As can be inferred from the above quoted passages, appropriate sexuality means conjugal sex only. Conjugal sex can and should be enjoyable. Its pleasure originates from the fusion of five essential elements—sincerity, moderation, gusto, enticement, and opportune timing *(cheng he qu dong shi)*—as is advocated in a discourse on *gou* (intercourse) in the novel. However, this discourse propagates that sex and sexual pleasure are by no means the end but more a means to reach the ultimate goal, that is, sex is the effective way to impregnate a woman with a son *(zhongzi rongyi zhi fa)*.[55] Apparently, the sexuality presented in the Qing *Ruyijun zhuan* is solely for the purpose of procreation.[56]

RECTIFYING PATRIARCHY AND REESTABLISHING ORDER

Regulating sexuality by redefining it as procreative serves the purpose of rectifying patriarchy because it assigns the husband the active, central, and dominant role in sex. In this aspect, the Qing *Ruyijun zhuan* is a total reversal of its prior text.

The Ming *Ruyijun zhuan* delineates a radically unconventional sex relation in which the female usurps the traditional male role. Empress Wu is the senior partner in every sense of the term. She is much older in age, much more experienced in sex, and ranks much higher in the sociopolitical hierarchy than Xue Aocao. She initiates the relationship, deflowering and depleting him.[57]

Also, it is the empress who imposes sadomasochistic practice and grants favors. In contrast, Xue Aocao as the Lord of Perfect Satisfaction is so named because he is able to satisfy perfectly the needs of and cater obediently to his female sovereign. He is actually reduced to a sex object, the phallus.[58] The unconventional dispenser-receiver pattern thus fully reveals the role of dominance or submission in their relationship. If sex-role distribution mirrors and reveals power structure, then this displacement of male and female roles in sexuality represents a reversal of the established power and control mechanism in a sex relation.[59] Furthermore, sex and politics are intimately intertwined in the Ming *Ruyijun zhuan,* as Stone competently argues and demonstrates,[60] hence chaos in the sex-power structure in the imperial harem is a disruption in the sociopolitical institutions, especially the polity of court and governance.

Then to Chen Tianchi, author of the Qing *Ruyijun zhuan,* this reversal apparently signals a dangerous disturbance of the proper order of things and thus must be rectified. His novel is a conscious and diligent endeavor to restore male power in family, sex, and male-female relations. The establishment of perfect order in the family *(qijia)* is of paramount importance, and his novel offers conventional and conservative wisdom in this matter. For instance, to prevent detrimental influences on the young masters from nursemaids, maids, and pages *(rumu shinü shutong),* these three groups of servants are not allowed to gain access to male children in the Tian household once sons reach the age of ten. Daughters are to be taught proper womanly works *(fugong),* and their literary education is limited to teachings of proper female behavior and virtues *(fuxing fude).* Segregation of the sexes is to be strictly implemented. Contact among male and female family members and relatives is thus forbidden until both parties reach a mature age and accomplish proper moral cultivation. Since monks and nuns are by nature and by circumstances lustful, they should never be admitted to a respectable household. The Lord of Perfect Satisfaction even petitions the emperor to allow only those who are facially disfigured, handicapped, or extremely destitute to enter monastery life; all others must be made to resume a secular life.[61]

Inside the inner quarters, male dominance *(fugang)* reigns supreme, even when the principal wife is a princess. In fact, Chen Tianchi has the princess herself emphasize repeatedly the necessity of rectifying patriarchy *(zhen fugang).* For instance, upon being informed of the prerogatives a princess enjoys after marriage, the principal wife accepts all the rites and rules but orders that the old practice that requires the royal son-in-law to bow to the princess be abolished. She reasons that once married, a princess is no longer royalty but a wife and daughter-in-law. As such, she must practice the earthly way of wifely behavior *(didao qidao).* And the essential female virtue and propriety are to yield to the husband and follow him obediently *(kunde yi shuncong wei zheng).* As a gesture of respect for *fugang,* the princess willingly gives up the title "her royal highness" *(huanggu)* and addresses her husband as master *(xiansheng),*[62] apparently intended as an outward sign and constant reminder of who is the boss in the household.

Proper order exists and must be maintained in sex relations between the husband and the women as well as among the women. The princess has seniority in social status and naturally enjoys seniority in the pecking order of sex. Therefore it is suggested that in a given month the princess be entitled to sleep with the lord for ten days; the four secondary wives each have three days, and the four concubines must be content with sharing the remaining eight days. Yet all the women must yield to the husband, even sexually. The Qing *Ruyijun zhuan* only once explicitly depicts a sex scene. It is set on the night of the mid-autumn festival and after a hearty banquet. Perhaps husband and wives are all under the influence of wine because the consorts, except for the princess, playfully challenge the lord's sexual puissance. In order to put right the order of things and put these women in their proper place, the lord enlists the princess as referee and engages the other nine women in a sexual battle. The scene of group sex is depicted in military similes and metaphors but in a teasing and lighthearted tone, definitely with no lewd and licentious details and references. The lord defeats all the women in quick succession; the easiest conquest takes only a few thrusts, and the last and longest fight against the most sexually potent and sophisticated woman lasts about a hundred rounds. But eventually all women surrender, and the husband proves to be the real master of his domain. Perfect satisfaction is his to enjoy.[63]

Now, here we have two Lords of Perfect Satisfaction, one dominated by a woman and the other towering over his women; one a feminized male with diminished status and the other a male exemplar with an expansive and expanding sphere of influence. We also have two accounts of the Lords of Perfect Satisfaction, one purportedly exposing the unnatural essence and dangerous consequences of female dominance and the other striving to rectify patriarchy and restore order and orthodoxy. In such a juxtaposition, the later text is more likely a response to and a commentary on the prior text. Thus the Qing *Ruyijun zhuan* can be seen as a *xushu* to the Ming *Ruyijun zhuan*.

CONCLUSION: WHAT KIND OF *XUSHU* IS THE QING *RUYIJUN ZHUAN*?

As a *xushu*,[64] Chen Tianchi's *Ruyijun zhuan* is highly unconventional, though the tenets of the novel are ultraconservative. It is unique in a couple of ways. First of all, *xushu* writers of imperial China usually identified their work as such. They tended to insert words like *"xu"* (sequel), *"bu"* (supplement), *"hou"* (continuation), *"xin"* (a new version), and so on in the title and use them as an identification tag. Yet Chen's work lacks such telltale generic markers,[65] although he did try to manipulate the title to direct his readers' attention to an earlier work and encourage them to establish a link between his novel and the Ming *Ruyijun zhuan*.

A further complication lies in the fact that conventional *xushu* works, marked or unmarked, as a rule bear various yet observable relations to their generating texts. They very often have "clear links to the originary text in terms of character, storyline, and the world created by the author. The sequel need not have all three elements, but it usually contains at least two of them."[66] That is, *xushu* texts usually have structural, thematic, and/or causal links with their parent texts. However, we do not find any migration of characters from the world of the Ming *Ruyijun zhuan* to that of the Qing novel. Nor are there structural links or causal connections between the two. What we find in the two are the common title and numerous and various thematic resonances.[68]

There is, therefore, another kind of *xushu*—those in the broad sense *(guangyi)*.[69] This second category encompasses transtextual relationships of expansion, compression, correction, rewriting, inversion, imitation, and other forms of textual transformation. An umbrella term for this group of *xushu* is suggested: *yan,* or what Genette would call hypertext.[70] Or a *xushu* in the broader sense refers to a text that "has certain relations to an originating text. It is essentially an offshoot of the originating text and is inspired by that text. In terms of content, the two works may not have very much in common and the later text may bear no relationship of continuation or supplement to the earlier one. Yet, without the prior text, the posterior text could never have come into being."[71]

A *xushu* hypertext and its hypotext, when linked by a tenuously defined hypertextual relationship, broaden up and also complicate the configuration of an original text and its derivative writing(s). "Texts and authors can be seen as adopting (voluntarily or involuntarily) certain affective attitudes towards the past, announcing their affiliations, selecting their burdens of narrative memory."[72] Consequently, stances espoused in a *xushu* to its precursor text manifest in complex patterns of influence, borrowing, emulation, complication, correction, resistance, refutation, contestation, and even subversion. Chinese scholars sum up such a spectrum as *xu bu gai fang fan fan xin.*[73] Chen Tianchi's *Ruyijun zhuan* falls right into the *fanfan* (reversal and subversion) tradition.[74] It forms an Oedipal relationship with the Ming *Ruyijun zhuan:* the Qing novel borrows from, interprets, and responds to its originary text, but at the same time disagrees with and severely criticizes it. We can say that this particular *xushu* functions more as literary criticism and ethical censorship in the form of a novel,[75] and as such it is "both a tribute and a betrayal"[76] of its parent text.

Chen's *Ruyijun zhuan* can be read in isolation, just as *Ulysses* can be read without reference to the *Odyssey,* as Gennete suggests. However, Gennete also argues that "[t]he hypertext thus always stands to *gain* by having its hypertextual status perceived," because

> hypertextuality is more or less mandatory, more or less optional according to each hypertext. But the fact remains that it cannot be overlooked without voiding the hypertext of a significant dimension, and we have often seen that authors went to great trouble—at the very least by means of paratextual clues—to guard against such loss of meaning or of aesthetic value. "The entire beauty of this play," Boileau said of *Chapelian décoiffé,* "consists in its relation to that other one *(Le Cid)*." "The entire beauty" may be overstating things a little in many cases—but in part, at least, the beauty of the hypertext always does consist in such a relation.

Indeed, "the entire beauty" of reading the Qing *Ruyijun zhuan* consists in a "*palimpsestuous* reading."[78] This perfectly ordered narrative about the perfect life of a perfect Confucian figure, when read in isolation, makes a very dull and frustrating reading.⁷⁹ Only when set in a dialogical relation to the generating text does the Qing novel take on new significance: it now becomes a multi-dimensional elaboration on and a vengeful, parricidal transposition of the Ming *Ruyijun zhuan*.

Notes

I am very grateful to Professor Patrick Hanan for lending me his own copy of Chen Tianchi's *Ruyijun zhuan*.

1. Seidel, "Running Titles," 36–38.
2. For instance, Liu Hui believes that the Ming *Ruyijun zhuan* was most probably written between 1514 and 1520, which were the years the preface and postscript to the novella were respectively dated; see Liu Hui, "*Ruyijun zhuan* de kanke niandai jiqi yu *Jin Ping Mei* zhi guanxi," 56. Charles Stone disputes Liu Hui's claim. He thinks that the preface dates to 1634 and the postscript to 1760. He speculates that the author of the earliest critique of *Ruyijun zhuan*, Huang Xun (1490–c. 1540), could very well be the author of the novella and thus speculates that *Ruyijun zhuan* was probably written between 1524 and 1529; see Stone, "The *Ruyijun zhuan* and the Origins of the Chinese Erotic Novel," 166–194, 232–233.
3. Modern scholars, as a rule, classify *Ruyijun zhuan* as erotica or even pornography. For instance, Sun Kaidi places the book in his bibliography under the category of *yanfen lei weixie zhi shu*; see Sun Kaidi, *Zhongguo tongsu xiaoshuo shumu*, 215 and 227. Wu Liquan in his history of *yanqing* (romance and erotica) fiction discusses *Ruyijun zhuan* in the *huiqing* section; see Wu Liquan, *Zhongguo yanqing xiaoshuo shi*, 233–235. Stone's "*Ruyijun zhuan* and the Origins of the Chinese Erotic Novel" is so far the most recent and important work in English on the novella. His scrutiny includes not only a critique of the novella, but a comprehensive study of its production, publication, sources, reception, and annotated text of the novella as well as an English translation.
4. For instance, Wu Liquan believes that *Ruyijun zhuan* depicts and details sexual intercourse in an appreciatory tone and thus that the author intended his work to be entertaining and self-entertaining. See Wu Liquan, *Zhongguo yanqing xiaoshuo shi*, 232.
5. Liu Hui asserts that Huang Xun's essay was written at the latest before 1540, the year Huang probably died, and it could date back as early as 1525, the year Huang successfully passed the provincial examination. See Liu Hui, "*Ruyijun zhuan* de kanke niandai jiqi yu *Jin Ping Mei* zhi guanxi," 56. Stone believes that the latest possible date for Huang's piece on *Ruyijun zhuan* is 1538; Stone, "*Ruyijun zhuan* and the Origins of the Chinese Erotic Novel," 174.
6. Cited in Liu Hui, "*Ruyijun zhuan* de kanke niandai jiqi yu *Jin Ping Mei* zhi guanxi," 52. The English translation is Stone, "*Ruyijun zhuan* and the Origins of the Chinese Erotic Novel," 177.
7. For instance, Hanan, "Sources of the *Chin P'ing Mei*," and Liu Hui, "*Ruyijun zhuan* de kanke niandai jiqi yu *Jin Ping Mei* zhi guanxi."
8. See Kang Zhengguo, *Chongshen fengyue jian*, 81–95; and Stone, "*Ruyijun zhuan* and the Origins of the Chinese Erotic Novel," esp. the introduction, chaps. 1 and 10, and the conclusion.
9. Stone, "*Ruyijun zhuan* and the Origins of the Chinese Erotic Novel," 18.
10. Chen Tianchi's preface to the *Ruyijun zhuan* is dated 1833. In a letter to a friend dated 1838, Chen claimed that he had spent more than a decade polishing the novel and revised it no less than five times; see Chen Tianchi, "Yu youren shu," 11. Also see Liu Xiangheng,

"Chen Tianchi *Ruyijun zhuan* xu," 1–2, and Tian Shu, "Xu," 1–2. The prefatory writings, individually paginated, were all written between 1833 and 1848.

11. See *Qingshi liezhuan,* 31–34 and Tu Lien-chê, "Ch'ên T'ing-ching."
12. See Liu Xiangheng's and Tian Shu's prefaces to *Ruyijun zhuan.*
13. Tian's initial fall from paradise is told in chaps. 1 and 2. This tale of his fall is also in sharp relief to other prologue tales featuring the same theme of offense and punishment. The "original sin" in other tales is usually of a more serious nature, ranging from wreaking havoc in the heavenly paradise (e.g., Monkey in *Xiyou ji*) to negligence of duty and work (e.g., Flower Fairy in *Jinghua yuan*) to unwholesome sexual liaisons (e.g., the banished deities in *Longfengpei zaisheng yuan*).
14. Chen Tianchi, *Ruyijun zhuan,* chaps. 2–4, 5, 7–10, 13, and 18–20.
15. Kang Hai and Shao Bao were both well-known scholar-officials of the mid-Ming. However, I fail to find references to Li Jingchen and so do not know if Li was a historical figure or a fictional creation.
16. Apparently this detail alludes to the Chinese expression *"wuzi dengke"* (five sons obtain the *jinshi* degree all at once), a cherished but unobtainable goal dreamt by parents in imperial China.
17. Chen Tianchi, *Ruyijun zhuan,* chaps. 5, 9, 12, 15–17, 21, 23, 28, 31, 35, 37–38, 48–50, 52–53, 55–56, and 70. One novel that invites comparison with Chen's *Ruyijun zhuan* is Xia Jingqu's (1705–1787) *Yesou puyan* [The humble words of an old rustic], an earlier and better-known novel. These two works both celebrate the perfect career of a perfect Confucian statesman and are both set in the same period of Chinese history (c. 1500), and both advocate, in large part, the same set of values and ideals. However, although the two texts share much in common, they do not seem to have any direct influence on each other. *Yesou puyan* was produced about half a century before the Qing *Ruyijun zhuan,* but the earlier work was not in print until the 1880s, decades after Chen Tianchi wrote his novel. There might have been a holographic version of *Yesou puyan* in circulation when Chen was writing and revising his work, since an 1837 list of banned books had both the Ming *Ruyijun zhuan* and *Yesou puyan* on it (see Wang Liqi, *Yuan Ming Qing sandai jinhui xiaoshuo xiqu shiliao,* 134, 136; Chen Qinghao and Wang Qiugui date this list as issued in 1837; see "*Ruyijun zhuan* chuban shuoming," 16). Yet a fictional work's manuscript or holographic version tended to circulate first among a group of closely related readers (relatives, friends, and acquaintances) who were living or active in a particular locale. Xia Jingqu was a native of Jiangyin in the Jiangnan region, and Chen Tianchi hailed from Yangcheng of Shanxi Province. Xia wrote his novel during the last years of his life, after he had retired from a life of being private secretary to officials and had settled down in his native place. Chen lived a much more secluded life and seldom ventured out of his home province. So the south-north divide would not warrant them a common group of first readers. I therefore doubt that Chen Tianchi could have access to Xia's novel. Apparently he did not write his *Ruyijun zhuan* as a response to or an imitation of Xia's *Yeshou puyan.* All the thematic similarities in the two novels could very well be a happy coincidence, though they certainly signal common interests, beliefs, and even an intellectual/ideological trend of conservative leaning around the turn of the eighteenth and nineteenth centuries. It will be very interesting and worthwhile to answer the question, Why were fiction writers from the period around 1800 so keen on portraying the perfect statesman? A search for this answer is beyond the scope of this chapter. However, I am grateful to the anonymous reader for calling my attention to *Yesou puyan.* For Xia Jingqu's life and writing of *Yesou puyan,* see Sun, "Xia Erming yu *Yesou puyan,*" 238–247; Zhao Jingshen, "*Yesou puyan* zuozhe Xia Erming nianpu," 433–447, and "*Yesou puyan* yu Xia shi zongpu," 448–449; and Martin Huang, *Desire and Fictional Narrative in Late Imperial China,* 237–238, n. 1.
18. The Ming *Ruyijun zhuan* is a short novella of about 9,000 words (Liu Hui, "*Ruyijun*

zhuan de kanke niandai jiqi yu *Jin Ping Mei* zhi guanxi," 49), and the Qing *Ruyijun zhuan* boasts seventy-two chapters of about 400,000 words (Chen Tianchi, "Yu Youren shu," 11).

19. The term "*qishu ti*" is coined by Plaks; see Pu Andi (Plaks), *Zhongguo xushixue*, 23. The generic characteristics of the *qishu ti* novel include "the paradigmatic length of one hundred chapters, narrative rhythms based on division into ten-chapter units, further subdivision into building blocks of three- or four-chapter episodes, contrived symmetries between the first and second halves of the texts, special exploitation of opening and closing sections, as well as certain other schemes of spatial and temporal orderings, notably the plotting of events on seasonal or geographical grids." See Plaks, *The Four Masterworks of the Ming Novel*, 497–498.

20. Li Heng, "Du *Ruyijun zhuan* lüeyan," 25–26. Translations in this article are mine except where indicated otherwise.

21. Ibid., 26–27.

22. For instance, some of the preface writers, who were also Chen Tianchi's friends or patrons and thus bound to pile flattering praises on the work, reacted quite negatively while writing about their first encounter with the novel. Lu Lianzhu, one of the preface writers, describes his reading experience thusly: "[Chen Tianchi] presented his *Ruyijun zhuan* to me. Another title for this story is *The First Remarkable Book of Joy and Happiness (Di yi kuaihuo qishu)*. Hence, it only talks about contentment and happiness, nothing else. There is no contour and flex, no twists and turns, no literary manipulation and variation, just a straight and direct account. I first thought that there was nothing really remarkable about it and thus put it down on the desk." He made a couple of attempts to read but could not finish. Chen repeatedly urged this friend-cum-patron to read his novel and even offered to read aloud the entire text for him. It was only after this desperate and rather pathetic offer that Lu reluctantly agreed to listen to the reading. He then professed that he actually loved it, stating, "I jumped up and held his hands in mine, saying to him: 'Remarkable! I almost missed reading your book because I was fooled by its appearance.'" See Lu, "*Diyi kuaihuo qishu* xu," 3–4.

23. Xu Ao, "Chen Tianchi *Diyi kuaihuo qishu* xu," 2.

24. See Xu Changling, *Zetian huanghou Ruyijun zhuan*.

25. Chen Tianchi, *Ruyijun zhuan*, chaps. 5, 21–27, and 41.

26. Ibid., chaps. 7–8, 11, 13. These parts in the novel read like an imitation of the building and inspection of Prospect Garden in *Honglou meng*.

27. There seems to be a real-life model for the description of the Guansheng cheng. Chen Tingjing, the author's famous ancestor, had a mansion built for the Chen family. According to a recent newspaper report, this impressive building complex is located in the Huangcheng cun, or Village of the Royal Villa of Yangcheng County, Shanxi Province. It has a *waicheng* (outer compound) and a *neicheng* (inner compound), with a total of sixteen courtyards of 640 rooms. In the news story, the Chen mansion is billed as an imitation of the Ming-Qing Forbidden City complex and has recently been restored, becoming a tourist attraction. See *Renmin ribao (haiwai ban)*, June 3, 2000, 1. The fact that Chen Tianchi used his own ancestral house as a prototype for the fictional Tian residence, which happens also to be in Shanxi Province, lends some external support to the hypothesis that the Tian household is intended as a miniature or replica of the imperial court.

28. See Carlitz, *The Rhetoric of Chin P'ing Mei*, 3, 28, 38, 41–44, 45, 132, and 145.

29. Plaks, *The Four Masterworks of the Ming Novel*, 320.

30. Ibid., chap. 4.

31. The term "*suwang*" refers to a sagely person who, like Confucius, is a commoner but has the virtues of a benevolent ruler. According to Martin Huang, the term first appeared in *Zhuangzi* and began to be associated with Confucius in the Former Han dynasty. See

Martin Huang, *Literati and Self-Re/Presentation,* 192, n. 16. An antecedent example is the Qing novel *Yesou puyan.* This novel portrays its hero in the light of the *suwang* tradition, giving him, for most of the story, no official capacities yet letting him function like a powerful minister and later a de facto ruler. And this character is properly named Wen Suchen, literally meaning the "unappointed minister." For a discussion of Wen Suchen as a Confucian *suwang*-like hero extraordinaire, see Martin Huang, *Literati and Self-Re/Presentation,* 114–122.

32. Chen Tianchi, *Ruyijun zhuan,* chaps. 3 and 5.
33. For instance, there are also similar wordings in the two texts when depicting how their respective protagonists get the title of Lord of Perfect Satisfaction; see Xu Changling, *Zetian huanghou Ruyijun zhuan,* 1:21 and 22–23; and Chen Tianchi, *Ruyijun zhuan,* chap. 2:15.
34. See Kang Zhenguo, *Chongshen fengyue jian,* 291.
35. For instance, both the novel *Xiuta yeshi* [The embroidered couch] and the play *Hongmei ji* [The story of red plum] have their characters read *Ruyijun zhuan.* See Chen Qinghao and Wang Qiugui, "*Ruyijun zhuan* chuban shuoming," 15–16.
36. "Wu Zhao zhuan" in *Xing shui bian* is an abridgment of the Ming *Ruyijun zhuan,* and the Qing novel *Nongqing kuaishi* quotes, verbatim, the bulk of the earlier novella. The Ming *Ruyijun zhuan* also leaves an indelible mark on many erotic stories and novels, e.g., *Chipozi zhuan, Su'e pian, Sengni niehai, Xu Jin Ping Mei,* and *Taohua ying.* It even influences the erotic classic *Jin Ping Mei.* See Chen Qinghao and Wang Qiugui, "*Ruyijun zhuan* chuban shuoming," 15–16, and Stone, "The *Ruyijun zhuan* and the Origins of the Chinese Erotic Novel," 235–251.
37. It was banned in 1810, 1837, 1844, and 1868 by central or local governments. See Chen Qinghao and Wang Qiugui, "*Ruyijun zhuan* chuban shuoming," 16. Significantly, the two years (1837 and 1844) when the Ming *Ruyijun zhuan* appeared on the list of banned books were also when Chen Tianchi, the author of the Qing *Ruyijun zhuan,* completed his novel and was busy revising and circulating his manuscripts.
38. Chen Tianchi claimed that he had read and referred to several hundreds of works of various natures and kinds when he was writing *Ruyijun zhuan.* See Chen Tianchi, "Yu youren shu," 11. All those who wrote prefaces, poems, and editorial principles for the Qing *Ruyijun zhuan* were local officials and members of the local elite (degree holders or students). They would know of, if they had not read, the Ming *Ruyijun zhuan.* So even if Chen had not heard of the earlier work, some friends or patrons would have told him, hence Chen's use of the title could not be an innocent oversight.
39. See Chen Tianchi, *Ruyijun zhuan,* vol. 1. By suggesting and favoring other titles, these preface writers could very well be demonstrating a certain unease with Chen's choice of a title.
40. Genette, *Palimpsests,* 9.
41. Genette defines "transtextuality" or "transtextual relationship" as "all that sets the text in a relationship, whether obvious or concealed, with other texts." *Palimpsests,* 1.
42. Genette believes that intertextuality refers essentially to quoting, plagiarism, and allusion; see *Palimpsests,* 1–3.
43. *Jin Ping Mei* starts with the story about Wu Song, Pan Jinlian, and Ximen Qing and even plucks a sizable part from *Shuihu zhuan,* using it as its own beginning, which we could call a case of "plagiarism."
44. For instance, Zhang Xinzhi (fl. 1828–1850), a Qing commentator, described the relationship between *Honglou meng* and the other three novels as follows: "The *Honglou meng* grows out of the *Hsi-yu-chi* [The Journey to the West], takes a trail blazed by the *Chin P'ing Mei,* and takes its spirit from the *Shui-hu chuan* [The Water Margin]." Quoted in Plaks, "How to Read the *Dream of the Red Chamber,*" 327.

45. The text has Empress Wu comment on the male member of her sexual partners and her own sexual pleasure or lack of it. See Xu Changling, *Zetian huanghou Ruyijun zhuan*, 32–33.
46. The text describes several times the youthful appearance of the empress; see Ibid., 13, 33.
47. See Stone, "The *Ruyijun zhuan* and the Origins of the Chinese Erotic Novel," esp. the introduction, chaps. 1 and 10, and the conclusion.
48. The term is Genette's and designates a preexistent text upon which a hypertext or a derivative text is "grafted in a manner that is not that of commentary." Genette, *Palimpsests*, 5.
49. The bridal night usually merits a one-sentence narration and goes like, "[the two brides] and the royal son-in-law went through the wedding ceremony and got married, which needs no further mentioning." Or "there is no need to describe the wedding night." Or "at night, the four [maids] were sent to the east and west wings respectively and the royal son-in-law was asked to go there to consummate the marriage." And for the last wedding, the text says, "Xixian got married in that wing of the building and lived there for three days. After the third day, she returned to the north wing and joined the other consorts in their turns of duty." Chen Tianchi, *Ruyijun zhuan*, chap. 9:89, chap. 20:76, chap. 21:88, and chap. 24:116.
50. Ibid., chap. 22:93–94.
51. Ibid., chap. 23:100–101.
52. Ibid., chap. 25:3–4.
53. See Kang Zhenguo, *Chongshen fengyue jian*, 94–95.
54. Stone, "The *Ruyijun zhuan* and the Origins of the Chinese Erotic Novel," 50, 52–53, and 62–67.
55. Chen Tianchi, *Ruyijun zhuan*, chap. 41:43–48.
56. *Yesou puyan* also advocates a similar conservative, Confucian sexuality. For discussions on *Yesou puyan*'s view on sexuality, see McMahon, *Misers, Shrews, and Polygamists*, 150–175; Huang, *Desire and Fictional Narrative in Late Imperial China*, 236–251; and Epstein, *Competing Discourses*, 229–248.
57. The text actually specifies that Xue Aocao is still a virgin when he first meets Empress Wu. This is because his extraordinarily huge penis has scared away all women, even the "old and promiscuous ones" *(lao er yin zhe)*; Xu Changling, *Zetian huanghou Ruyijun zhuan*, 12, 20.
58. See Stone's discussion of the object *ruyi* and its connotations, including erotic connotation, in "The *Ruyijun zhuan* and the Origins of the Chinese Erotic Novel," 151–158.
59. See Kang Zhenguo, *Chongshen fengyue jian*, 91–92.
60. See Stone, "The *Ruyijun zhuan* and the Origins of the Chinese Erotic Novel," introduction, chaps. 1 and 10, and conclusion.
61. Chen Tianchi, *Ruyijun zhuan*, chap. 31:62–63, and chap. 38:15–16.
62. Ibid., chap. 5:46, and chap. 12:112–113.
63. Ibid., chap. 22:91–92, and chaps. 25–26:5–11.
64. This part touches on issues of definition, classification, boundaries, and functions of *xushu*. These issues are discussed in detail in the introduction and chap. 1 of this volume.
65. There are other "unmarked" *xushu*. *Shuo Tang quanzhuan*, discussed by Hegel in chap. 7 of this volume, is an example. On the other hand, not all marked stories are *xushu*. For instance, the 1910 *Xin Xihu jiahua* relates a romance between a courtesan and a scholar, yet the Ming *Xihu jiahua* is a collection of *huaben* stories; the only common element shared by the two texts is their setting: Xihu, or West Lake. See *Zhongguo tongsu xiaoshuo zongmu tiyao*, 1199 and 362. Obviously the later text is not a *xushu* to the earlier one, though it appropriates the conventional identification tag of a *xushu*.

66. Gillies, "The Literary Agent and the Sequel," 134.

67. A Chinese literary critic describes these connections as *"shouwei xiangxian, yinguo xiangying."* Zhongchang, "Lun Zhongguo gudai xiaoshuo de xuyan xianxiang ji chengyin," 124–125.

68. The Qing *Ruyijun zhuan* is not the only case of an unconventional *xushu*. *Xin Jinghua yuan* by Chen Xiaolu of the late Qing is the same kind of *xushu* as the Qing *Ruyijun zhuan*. Chen Xiaolu establishes a link between his novel and the parent work, *Jinghua yuan*, through the title and many thematic/topical parallels, but Chen's *xushu* features no character and plot appropriation. Ying Wang discusses *Xin Jinghua yuan* in chap. 9 of this volume.

69. For a discussion of the narrow and broad definitions of *xushu*, see the introduction to this volume

70. Zhongchang, "Lun Zhongguo gudai xiaoshuo de xuyan xianxiang ji chengyin," 124; and Genette, *Palimpsests*, 5.

71. Li Zhongchang, *Gudai xiaoshuo xushu manhua*, 16.

72. Zeitlin, "Donald Barthelme and the Postmodern Sequel," 163.

73. See Li Zhongchang, *Gudai xiaoshuo xushu manhua*, 18; and Ouyang Jian, "Wanqing 'fanxin' xiaoshuo zonglun," 257–258.

74. Li Zhongchang proposes an eight-term classification, covering *xushu* of both the narrow and broader senses. These categories are *shunxu* (forward continuation), *nixu* (backward continuation), *jiexu* (interpolational or paraleptic expansion), *lianxu* (sequel), *taoxu* (imitation of narrative form and techniques), *fanxu* (thematic subversion), *huoxu* (sequence or series), *leixu* (imitation of content or form), and *fangxu* (imitation). See Li Zhongchang, *Gudai xiaoshuo xushu manhua*, 22–55. Following this classification, the Qing *Ruyijun zhuan* combines *fanxu* and *leixu*. The former refers to a *xushu* text that completely reverses the values and judgments of the prior text, and the latter is a *xushu* text that has a certain analogy with the precursor text in thematic content and/or narrative structure but no logical continuity in plot or returning characters. See Li Zhongchang, *Gudai xiaoshuo xushu manhua*, 42–42, 48–50. Li's classification is by no means exhaustive or precise. There are gray areas and overlaps; for instance, the differences among *taoxu*, *leixu*, and *fangxu* are not very clear. Also, Li follows in the footsteps of traditional Chinese critics and commentators when he coined the terms and defined them. That is, he tends to use similes and analogies and casts them in colorful language. So when defining *taoxu* and *jiexu*, he illustrates the former as *"jiuping xinjiu chengshang qixia"* and the later as *"jiewai shengzhi meihua xiecha."* Neither is actually very helpful in fathoming what the term really refers to. I have to rely more on the examples Li provides to make sense of his terms. For instance, examples given for the *taoxu* type are *Xiyou ji* as the parent text and *Hou Xiyou ji* as the *xushu*. Then in the *taoxu* group, the *xushu* text takes over the prior text's basic narrative form, yet the content or the story itself is vitally different, as if new wine were poured into an old bottle. Examples for *jiexu* are *Shuihu zhuan* and *Yan Poxi yanshi*. This type of *xushu* is supposed to borrow an episode from the parent text, elaborate on it, and create a new work from the borrowed episode. In translating Li's terms, I refer to Gennete's discussion of types of hypertexts. Some of the terms—for instance, forward and backward continuations, paraleptic expansion—are Gennete's. See Genette, *Palimpsests*, 177, 181.

75. The fusion of narrative and criticism was not something new when Chen Tianchi wrote his *Ruyijun zhuan*. Rolston notices increasing occurrences of blurred boundaries between narrative and critical discourses in Chinese fiction since mid-seventeenth century. See Rolston, *Traditional Chinese Fiction and Fiction Commentary*, esp. 269–348. Zhao Jianzhong explicitly states that "all the *Honglou meng* sequels are in essence literary criticism, in imagery, of the original novel [i.e., the first eighty chapters] and its last forty chapters.

Therefore they should be treated as *Honglou meng* commentaries (Honglou meng *pinglun ji*) rather than mere novelistic texts." Zhao Jianzhong, "*Honglou meng* xushu de yuanliu shanbian jiqi yanjiu," 331–332.

76. Taylor, "The Curious Eye and the Alternative Ending of the *Canterbury Tales*."
77. Genette, *Palimpsests*, 398.
78. Ibid., 399.
79. See H. Laura Wu, "A Fantasy of Perfect Order and Success." As a matter of fact, most *xushu* are rather disappointing when read on their own.

YING WANG

9

The Voices of the Re-readers

Interpretations of Three Late-Qing Rewrites of *Jinghua yuan*

IN CHAPTER 48 of Li Ruzhen's (c. 1763–1830) *Jinghua yuan* (The destiny of flowers in the mirror, 1828), Tang Guichen, a flower fairy incarnated as a mortal being, arrives at Little Penglai, a Taoist paradise. In the Pavilion of Lamenting the Female Talents (Qihong Ting), she is presented with an enigmatic text. The text is written in the "tadpole" *(kedou)* calligraphic style on a jade tablet and contains details about the "one hundred talented women" (flower fairies banished from heaven for upsetting the seasonal order). However, this text is intelligible only to a very few of the "destined" ones.[1] To learn of their own destinies, the novel's characters have to re-read this text. After several failures, their deciphering and interpreting efforts escalate to an elaborate discussion in chapters 89 and 90. In these chapters the Taoist female deity Magu, in a long poem, presents the contents of the inscription to all of the talented women. Although the women are now able to identify some of the events in the poem because they are familiar with these experiences, the majority of the women fail to be enlightened.

The enigmatic inscription on the jade tablet represents the novelized text, while the frustrated characters mirror the novel's implied readers.[2] Li wrote his novel with the expectation that readers would have to re-read it, hence *Jinghua yuan* may remind us of Vladimir Nabokov's famous paradox, "One cannot read a book, one can only re-read it."[3] The frustration of re-reading, depicted in the novel, is an experience that has haunted the readers of *Jinghua yuan* for almost two centuries. Because of the novel's multidimensional content, dense intertextuality, and ambiguous ideological orientation, its readers will have to admit that a single reading of *Jinghua yuan* is not sufficient, nor does it do justice to the novel. The literary and structural designs of classic Chinese novels, especially those of *Jinghua yuan,* are intended to be read circularly, retrospectively, and holistically. An initial linear reading gives readers a chaotic and episodic impression of the structure and causes them to misread. It is imperative to re-read to grasp the underlying meaning of the novel.[4]

The necessity of re-reading *Jinghua yuan* has always been recognized by its readers. Since its publication in 1828, intense efforts to re-read *Jinghua yuan* have occurred at different historical moments. In chronological order, the earliest endeavor appeared in the late Qing, which produced three rewrites of *Jinghua yuan* by Xiaoran yusheng, Chen Xiaolu, and Hua Qinshan. This was followed by Hu Shi and Lu Xun's oft-quoted interpretations of the book in the May Fourth period and the subsequent studies done by modern scholars in response to these two leading Chinese critics.[5] Recently, renewed interest in reinterpreting *Jinghua yuan* was inspired by feminist reader-oriented criticism and gender studies.[6]

However, the way that literary texts influence each other is a two-way street. Unlike the "historical" past, the "aesthetic past is altered by the present as much as the present is directed by the past."[7] Various rewritings and literary commentaries lead a reader back to the originals to double-check, reinforce, and revise the conclusions of earlier, provisional stages of interpretation. More important, these later critical re-readings provide new angles, unexpected possibilities, and additional layers of meaning to the models that have inspired them in the first place.

This concept of "reverse influence,"[8] in which later texts (literary and/or critical) influence earlier ones (literary models and/or the texts to be criticized), brings our attention to the three late-Qing rewrites of *Jinghua yuan,* including two works with the same title, *Xin Jinghua yuan* (New destiny of flowers in the mirror) by Xiaoran yusheng and Chen Xiaolu respectively, and a third work, *Xu Jinghua yuan* (A continuation of destiny of flowers in the mirror) by Hua Qinshan. For the past century, the critics of *Jinghua yuan* have overlooked these *xushu.*[9] However, by presenting their criticisms of *Jinghua yuan* in the form of re/writings, these narratives, as my study will show, clearly reveal the reversible nature of literary reading. Their interpretations of *Jinghua yuan* are "influential" in the ways they reshape our reading and understanding of the novel.

This chapter offers a close reading of these three rewritings of *Jinghua yuan.* I will focus on their different ways of recalling and restructuring *Jinghua yuan* and show how these works pass judgment on Li's vision of utopia and his representation of women. I emphasize that these pieces, written either in the form of *fanxin xiaoshuo* (fiction that brings new out of the old)[10] or the mixed form of continuation and *fanxin xiaoshuo,* are intended to be a double-edged critique: to create a parodic reflection on the original while providing the reader with commentary on the contemporary society of the late Qing.

THE RE-VISIONING OF LI RUZHEN'S POLITICAL IDEAL

In 1907 a writer using the pseudonym Xiaoran yusheng published a parodic reworking of *Jinghua yuan* titled *Xin Jinghua yuan* in the fiction periodical

Yueyue xiaoshuo (All-story monthly, 1906–1908). Written in the form of *fanxin xiaoshuo*, this twelve-chapter rewrite borrows original characters and continues the journey motif in *Jinghua yuan*. After Emperor Zhongzong's (r. 684, 705–710) re-enthronement, Tang Xiaofeng (the son of Tang Ao, the male protagonist in the parent novel) is demoted[11] and decides to search for his father and sister, who in the original novel have renounced the world and devoted their lives to the pursuit of Taoist ideals and immortality at Little Penglai. Tang Xiaofeng's companions include two voyagers from the original novel, Lin Zhiyang and Duo Jiugong. However, instead of reaching their destination, a storm takes them to a foreign land called The Country of Reform (Weixin Guo), a metaphor for late-Qing China.

The novel treats reformers satirically, with the literary technique that was overused by many of the author's contemporaries. However, in this work Xiaoran yusheng combines parody with the kind of exposé often seen in *xianxing ji xiaoshuo* (a popular fictional form in the late Qing)[12] to recreate the utopia described by Li Ruzhen in *Jinghua yuan*. Like Li Baojia's (1867–1906) *Guanchang xianxing ji* and *Wenming xiaoshi* (Modern times, 1906) and Wu Jianren's (1866–1910) *Ershi nian mudu zhi guai xianzhuang* (Eyewitness reports on strange things from the past twenty years, 1910), the author provides the reader with an eyewitness account of bizarre events resulting from the national campaign for reform. The travelers' first experience in this "Country of Reform" is being arrested as revolutionaries for simply talking about reform in a tea shop. They then meet a two-faced police chief whose ferocity immediately changes to servility when he realizes that his prisoners are foreigners. They see students shouting "Equal rights! Freedom!" only to learn later that their intention is to disrespect their teachers. They learn that the military of this country is good only at killing its own people and that the soldiers will run for their lives the minute they see real invaders. They meet merchants who are interested only in selling lottery tickets and fake diplomas. They are disgusted to discover that government officials are eager to learn survival skills from prostitutes. However, for the newcomers, their most shocking experience is when they are stopped in the Country of Reform by foreign officials who ask them to pay customs duties.

Holding a posture of moral critique, this rewrite echoes other exposé novels that reveal the self-delusion and futility of the national campaign for reform and ridicule the new breed of opportunists and swindlers produced by contemporary society. Xiaoran yusheng suggests that one of the main reasons for the failure of reform and for the rise of various social foibles is that people have sacrificed the "fundamental for the incidental" *(qiumo quben)*: to have superficially imitated the West without changing the substance of the old and corrupt China. He also implies that such blind worship of anything foreign, a cultural frenzy of mimicry, might eventually lead to China's downfall. At the end of the novel, a government-banned book titled *Weixin guo miewang lun* (On the demise of the country of reform) is brought to the reader's attention expressing a fear that was very real to the author. Xiaoran yusheng's novel was written after the aborted Hundred Days Reform in 1898 and the Boxer Rebellion in 1900, at a time when the debate on building a constitutional government amounted to nothing but empty talk. His work not only reflected his disappointment with the reform campaign and his suspicion of Western culture, but also promoted the ideas of the Guocui Pai (the school promoting Chinese national essence), a group of Chinese intellectuals whose goal was to address the problem of over-Westernization.[13]

Although the techniques of exaggeration, disfiguration, and carnivalesque inversion are all at work here, this novel does not particularly impress the reader with its literary representation as other kindred works do. Notably, however, the novel demonstrates a sense of self-consciousness and self-reflexivity as a work of *xianxing ji xiaoshuo* by presenting the reader with a panorama of character exposures—a collection of various reform imposters and tricksters. Exposé fiction was quite popular and overused at the turn of the twentieth century. As a new form of fiction when "newness" was fetishized, it came instantly into fashion and became an object of pursuit for Xiaoran yusheng's contemporary writers. These writers plagiarized sensational materials in the most fashionable writing styles to such an extent that many works duplicated each other and ultimately bored their readers.[14] By stringing all sorts of *xianxing ji* together in one book, Xiaoran yusheng makes *xianxing ji xiaoshuo* a target of exposure. He clearly pokes fun at the worn-out conventions and the overabundance of this type of writing in the market.[15]

The relations between Xiaoran yusheng's rewrite and Li Ruzhen's original are emphasized by various rhetorical devices in the former. In the prologue, for instance, the author provides the reader with information about his writing and the publishing of his novel, which explicitly links the rewrite to Li's *Jinghua yuan*. The reader is told by the narrator that White Ape, to whom Tang Guichen entrusted the task of finding a writer for the stone inscription in the original,[16] presents the finished text of *Jinghua yuan* to Tang, who now has already resumed her divine status as the Fairy of the Hundred Flowers in the world of immortals. She finds that the novel does not provide closure and therefore urges White Ape to ask the original author to write a *xubian* (continuation). The author refuses to do so, using exhaustion as an excuse. The ape then embarks on a series of searches for the right person for the continuation. White Ape encounters writers who feel that to write a continuation will degrade them, and he also meets those who are eager to do it purely for economic gain. Finally he is able to find a penniless and frustrated scholar whose writing skills are not great, but passable. Of course, his novel is still a "dog's tail replacing a sable" (*gouwei xudiao*).[17]

In Xiaoran yusheng's work the writer-hunting episode from the end of the original is turned into a target of parody. The self-promoting gesture of Li Ruzhen, in mentioning himself in the same breath with three compilers of Tang histories (Liu Xu, Ouyang Xiu, and Song Qi), is parodied in Xiaoran yusheng's self-mockery as he arrays himself with the pretentious and profit-driven writers of the late Qing. Xiaoran yusheng's parody cuts both ways: his critical irony not only points at the self-elevated "author" image created by Li, but it also betrays his own inferiority complex as a *xushu* writer by labeling his own work as a "dog's tail replacing a sable."

More interestingly, this self-reflexive representation of the search for an author in Xiaoran yusheng's rewrite brings to light the self-consciousness and textual fluidity of its precursor. The Fairy of the Hundred Flowers' account of *Jinghua yuan*'s begging for continuation is not altogether without basis, for the book indeed ends in a way that anticipates a continuation. In the very last paragraph of *Jinghua yuan,* the narrator claims the novel is only half complete and makes a promise that the author will write a continuation later. He even titillates the reader by saying, "If you want to see the complete reflection in this mirror (to read the whole story), you have to wait for a later *Destiny* [of flowers in the mirror] (a continuation)."[18]

The anticipation of rewrites at the end of *Jinghua yuan* was also recognized by Chen Xiaolu and Hua Qinshan, the authors of the other two sequels to *Jinghua yuan.* Like Xiaoran yusheng, Chen and Hua legitimized their *xushu* by considering *Jinghua yuan* an "incomplete" novel.[19] It is still debatable whether *Jinghua yuan* is indeed "unfinished" and needs a continuation. However, by claiming its own "incompleteness," *Jinghua yuan* is certainly open to textual extensions and new possibilities.[20] It may be true that Li wanted to write a continuation to his own novel; it may also be plausible that this strategy was really the author's way of soliciting *xushu* from others, a gesture that reflects the self-conscious, dialogical, and mutually promoting relationship between *xushu* and their parent works in the nineteenth century.[21]

Another rhetorical device that invokes the original in Xiaoran yusheng's rewrite is anachronism.[22] By choosing *Jinghua yuan* as the basis of his rewrite and by placing the original characters such as Tang Xiaofeng, Lin Zhiyang, and Duo Jiugong outside their preprojected temporal and spatial settings, the novel achieves a twofold purpose: 1) the effect of *jiegu fengjin* (borrowing the past to criticize the present); and 2) disturbing the linear and singular literary representation to provide a new paradigm for writing and reading fiction.

The anachronism in the rewrite produces the effects of contrast and parallelism. Since two historical periods—the late Qing in the foreground and the high Tang in the background—coexist in the textual space, the reader cannot help but make comparisons between them. In the eyes of the Tang travelers, the Country of Reform, an allegorical reference to late-Qing China, is a decadent and disastrous world beyond repair, a place much worse than the politically "chaotic" but economically and culturally prosperous Tang China. As outsiders and representatives of the Tang culture, the travelers are placed in a superior position to the inhabitants of the land they are visiting, and they become the policy advisers and critics of the status quo in the Country of Reform. Their superior morality and political wisdom, in contrast to the corrupt and degenerate late-Qing society and culture, suggests that the author favors the prosperous and strong historical past over the disappointing present.

In terms of imperial politics, a parallel is drawn between Wu Zetian's usurping of imperial power and Empress Dowager Cixi's (1835–1908) reclaiming the regency²³ and between the two powerless emperors, Zhongzong and Guangxu (r. 1875–1908). Such an analogy, a rhetorical device used by many of the author's contemporaries in fictional and historical writings, obviously serves as an indirect criticism of Cixi's control of the government.²⁴ In chapter 1 the narrator relates how Wu Zetian is keen on building imperial palaces and gardens and continues to spend even when the state treasury is empty. This anachronistic detail reminds the reader of the accusation that Cixi built the Summer Palace (Yihe Yuan) by diverting navy funds.²⁵ The narrator then heightens the reader's sense of anachronism by describing how Wu Zetian teams up with Empress Wei to persecute Xu Chengzhi, Luo Chengzhi, Tang Xiaofeng, and other anti-Zhou heroes (who helped Zhongzong regain power in Li Ruzhen's original novel). The fate of these Tang loyalists best reflects the misfortune of the so-called Baohuangdang (the party loyal to the emperor) of the late Qing. Here, the author's criticism simultaneously points at Wu Zetian and Cixi, the two female usurpers-cum-tyrants separated from each other by over one thousand years (more on Wu Zetian and Cixi later).

By now it has become very clear what Xiaoran yusheng achieved by using anachronistic rhetoric: although his feelings about the historical past (the Tang dynasty) are ambivalent, as he mixes nostalgic sentiment with conservative, male-oriented criticism, his condemnation of and disillusionment with the present (the late Qing) are quite clear. The preprojected Tang time in Li's original is intentionally invoked and revised in Xiaoran yusheng's rewrite to mirror the late-Qing society. Xiaoran yusheng did not lose hope completely for China, for he wrote an incomplete novel titled *Wutuobang youji* (The journey to utopia, 1906). In this novel he tried to envision a better future for his homeland, very different from the utopia of Li Ruzhen.

Xiaoran yusheng parodied Li's utopian vision in his rewriting. In *Jinghua yuan,* particularly from chapter 8 to chapter 40, Li explored and envisioned his political ideal by presenting the reader with both a Taoist/Confucian utopian realm and ghostly paradises. As contrasts to the Country of Gentlemen, Li's ghostly paradises anticipate Xiaoran yusheng's panorama of character exposures—the inhabitants of the Country of Reform possess the traits of the characters from Li's dystopian realms. Li's political ideal, on the other hand, is clearly undermined in *Xin Jinghua yuan.*

The story of the Country of Gentlemen, the embodiment of Li's Taoist/ Confucian utopian vision, is delineated in chapters 11 and 12 of *Jinghua yuan.* While chapter 11 presents a harmonious picture of *haorang buzheng* (people yielding to one another without strife), chapter 12 validates the Confucian concept of *ren* (humanity toward others) by criticizing the social ills of China. Li describes what Tang Ao and his companions observe when they first step on this land.

> When they came to the market they heard a soldier talking to a shopkeeper. He was holding something in his hand and saying, "What a lovely thing this is! But you are charging too little for it! How could I deprive you of it? Please do me the favor of making it more costly,

so that I may buy it with an easy conscience. If you refuse, it will only mean that you do not consider me your friend." . . .

The Shopkeeper replied, "You know that we are not allowed to haggle here. All prices are one! I am afraid I shall have to ask you to shop elsewhere if you insist on paying more than the fixed price, for I cannot oblige." . . .

"Really," thought Tang Ao, "customer and shopkeeper have changed places. Each is saying what the other would say in other countries."

Not only do the commoners of this utopian country value social harmony and show indifference to material gain, but so do the king and government officials. The king, for instance, forbids ministers and subjects from presenting pearls and jewels to the court. In order to remind people of his principle, he has an inscribed board hanging on the gate of the country that reads *"Weishanweibao"* (kindness is the only treasure of all). The two prime ministers of the country, Wu Zhihe and Wu Zhixiang (whose names signify harmony and auspiciousness), enjoy idyllic lives. They live in a dwelling with a door made of firewood, a fence twined with green wisterias, and a yard decorated by a lotus pond and surrounded by bamboo woods. These details remind the reader of the Taoist utopia portrayed by Tao Qian (365–427) in his *Taohua yuan ji* (Record of peach blossom spring), which describes a fisherman's adventure in a paradise inhabited by people from an ancient civilization. The inhabitants of *Taohua yuan ji* enjoy peace and harmony, as they are spared wars, political turmoil, and economic disasters. Li Ruzhen clearly shares the sentiment of *fanpu guizhen* (returning to simplicity and restoring innocence) with Tao Qian, and his utopian vision reflects a regressive or escapist ideology, which people would consider Taoist. The Little Penglai in Li's work can be seen as another mirror image of Tao Qian's *Taohua yuan,* which represents a paradise that is either already lost or simply exists in people's imaginations. The protagonists of the novel, Tang Guichen and her father Tang Ao, eventually renounce the world and join the Taoist order at Little Penglai, again evidencing that Li has an inclination for dealing with the disappointments of life and politics in a Taoist way.

As many critics have indicated, Confucian humanitarianism is also strongly present in the story of the Country of Gentlemen. In chapter 12, the Wu brothers, as ministers of the country, are portrayed as "sensible, frugal, and humanitarian Confucians."[27] They express indignation and disapproval at the uncivilized customs and social problems of Tang China. The Wu brothers are advocates for social reform. Their suggestions for improvement reflect Li's desire for change and progress.

With a mixture of Confucian and Taoist thought, Li's utopian vision appears to be ambivalent, self-contradictory, and regressive and progressive at the same time. By paying homage to Confucianism and Taoism, Li proves himself to be a scholar who is incapable of disloyalty to the Chinese cultural tradition. Culturally conservative, Li seeks a restoration of the old civilization when Confucian and Taoist values "held undisputed sway."[28] However, his remedies for social ills could not have impressed late-Qing satirists like Xiaoran yusheng in their age of cultural decay. In Xiaoran yusheng's *Xin Jinghua yuan,* neither Taoist nor Confucian idealism holds the same influence as it did in *Jinghua yuan.* The fictional world of the Country of Reform is a world where paradise is lost, dreams become nightmares, traditional values and ideologies are shattered, and even new hopes and ideas are abandoned before they capture people's minds and imaginations. In this place morality and ethics are worthless, people are materialistic and profit driven, government and its officials are corrupt, and the entire society is in utter disarray. Chapter 6 of the rewrite conveys a parody ridiculing the Wu brothers' successful and appreciated counsel to the Tang travelers in the original novel. Having heard from the police chief that revolutionaries have become a substantial threat to the government and the country's social stability, Tang Xiaofeng offers three suggestions to help return order.

> First, [the government] needs to immediately get rid of the dictatorship and establish a constitutional system so as to demonstrate that it is trustworthy. Second, [the government officials] should be selfless so as to show their fairness and sense of justice. Third, [the rulers] ought to be humanitarian and benevolent so as to exhibit their morals and kindness. If the government adopts these policies, the [revolutionary] party members will be extinguished of themselves.[29]

Tang Xiaofeng's brand of political soundness is a blend of Western democracy and Confucian humanitarianism. However, contrary to the Tang travelers' appreciation of the Wu brothers' advice in the original, here the police chief immediately rejects all of Tang Xiaofeng's suggestions. As he explains, "building a constitutional government" would serve only to silence the masses. The officials are naturally selfish and have every intention to keep their class privileges and maintain social inequalities. The commoners are slavish in nature, and a humanitarian policy will only induce rebellion. Cynical as they are, the police chief's comments on Tang Xiaofeng's proposal reveal a dark side of human nature, which in turn ironically reflects Li's naïveté and overly idealistic sociopolitical agenda.

Late-Qing intellectuals like Xiaoran yusheng might not have completely abandoned Confucian teachings, but most likely they were not enchanted by Li's dream of Taoist immortals. They clearly understood that traditional ideologies were not ready-made remedies for their contemporary social and political problems. To them, it was inconceivable to think or even imagine fixing contemporary problems by restoring ancient civilizations and antiquities. Their utopian visions were very different from that of Li, the Taoist recluse-cum-humanitarian Confucian. In his four-chapter unfinished *Wutuobang youji,* Xiaoran yusheng shows the reader a glimpse of his utopian imagination: on a flying-ship en route to the utopian land, people enjoy a lifestyle that is materialistically rich, technologically advanced, and sociopolitically democratic. Xiaoran yusheng's viewpoint was reiterated by many late-Qing writers, including the famous Wu Jianren. Wu also wrote a rewrite of *Honglou meng* titled *Xin Shitou ji* (New story of the stone, 1908) in which he has Jia Baoyu travel to Wenming Jingjie (The Civilized World)—a utopia in the minds of late-Qing intellectuals. The Civilized World resembles neither Tao Qian's Peach Blossom Spring nor Li's Country of the Gentlemen. "The Civilized World is a country strong in military power, political structure, scientific advancement, educational institutions, and moral cultivation. It is a tremendous technocratic empire that in every aspect leads its time."[30]

Xiaoran yusheng's *Xin Jinghua yuan* targets the political failures and social problems of his time, but it does so by parodying Li's *Jinghua yuan* and ironically reflecting Li's utopian vision. As a parody, Xiaoran yusheng's work holds up a mirror to both social reality and the literary model that he imitated, and his irony cuts both ways. Although it is considered to be a mediocre exposé, a reader familiar with *Jinghua yuan* would enjoy reading Xiaoran yusheng's rewrite because, as Palmer states in his commentary on Chaucer's *Book of the Duchess*, "reading a text of this kind is thus simultaneously a re-reading of an absent, yet present other."[31]

THE RE-VOICING OF WOMEN'S ISSUES

In 1908, one year after Xiaoran yusheng serialized his *Xin Jinghua yuan* in *Yueyue xiaoshuo*, Chen Xiaolu published his rewriting of *Jinghua yuan* (also titled *Xin Jinghua yuan*). Two years later, in 1910, Hua Qinshan completed his *Xu Jinghua yuan*. Both Chen's and Hua's rewrites focus on women's issues, the same subject that attracts different generations of readers to Li's novel, while generating conflicting views and opposing interpretations. So far, Hu Shi has been credited or discredited for his emphasis of *Jinghua yuan* as a work with a feminist agenda. However, such an emphasis had already been anticipated by the rewrites of Chen and Hua a decade earlier—at a time that saw a countrywide women's movement that opposed foot binding while promoting the education of women.

Chen Xiaolu was a Shanghai fiction writer whose background we know very little about. Chen took the theme of talented and gallant women from *Jinghua yuan*, intending to write a new version of female heroes *(nü haojie)* who not only travel overseas, but also become students in foreign countries. Although Chen's rewrite is also considered *fanxin xiaoshuo*, unlike Xiaoran yusheng's *Xin Jinghua yuan*, which borrows characters and continues the journey motif from *Jinghua yuan*, there is no character or plot appropriation that links Chen's rewrite to the original. What Chen did borrow from Li are the stereotypes, traits, and concepts of talented and gallant women.[32] Reversing the China-centered centripetal structure of the original, Chen's novel proposes an opposite narrative development—"from family to society, to school, to the whole country, [and then] to the whole world,"[33] attempting to distinguish between the old and new ethics, and particularly those concerning women's roles in family and society.[34]

The author's ambitious plan was aborted before the novel's main plot was set into motion, which left readers with undeveloped characters confined to their domestic spheres—at home and within China. The extant fourteen chapters center around the intellectual pursuits of two sisters, Huang Shunhua and Huang Shunying, who attend a school for women when their plan to study abroad is temporarily suspended. The two sisters become associated with twelve other equally talented women who share their views on fundamental moral issues. These women's meetings, discussions, and debates on different occasions and in different settings set forth the central theme of the novel: how to assume a new womanhood through modern education, an issue that was of deep concern to, and heatedly debated by, late-Qing reformers and intellectuals.

Chen's idea of new womanhood is revealed and articulated in two of the most elaborate discussion scenes of the novel, chapters 9 and 11. In chapter 9 the Huang sisters, having invited their two newlywed sisters-in-law and ten classmates to organize a women's association, call their first meeting. Their discussions present two views on women's education. The first view emphasizes that women should be educated only on subjects that will benefit them in their roles as good wives and mothers. The second view asserts that women ought to study all subjects as men do so as to be equal to men in their social standing. Chen promotes the former, and his proclivity can be detected as he speaks through his characters to emphasize the importance of having different curricula for men's schools and women's schools and the impracticability of women studying all subjects of modern education. He evidently is unconvinced by the more radical reformist view that equal rights between men and women are conditioned by equal education.

For the late-Qing period, Chen's viewpoint reflects a moderate reformist concept of women's education that is supported by a belief that the rectification of people's *(guomin)* hearts and the expansion of their talents should begin with their maternal instruction at an early age. Consequently, education for women was understood to be key to national survival or extinction. Reformer Liang Qichao (1873–1929) summarized this view in his announcement of the foundation of the first Chinese-run girls' school in Shanghai: the new woman "above, will be a helpmeet to her husband, below, a source of instruction for her sons; in her immediate surroundings, she will give ease to the family, and in a wider sphere, she will improve the race."[35] Around this same period, the Qing government issued conservative regulations for girls' schools. What distinguishes the reformist view from that of the Qing government is that the reformers placed an emphasis on the citizen consciousness *(guomin yishi)* of women and did not completely deny women a role in the social and political arena.[36] On the other hand, the Qing government's goal was to merely improve Chinese women within the framework of traditional virtue in the home. Additionally, some reformers believed that limited women's education could develop into a broader curriculum that would eventually lead Chinese women to full public and social engagements similar to those that Western women went through in their various stages of reforming educational systems and fighting for women's rights.[37]

Echoing this school of moderate reformers, Chen repeatedly emphasizes women's significant role in the betterment of the nation: "I really hope that in this extremely competitive twentieth century, Heaven will endow China with more heroines who could redress the humiliation of two hundred-million men (*nanzihan*) who were enslaved and treated as cows and horses [by foreigners]."[38] The urge for reforms and Chen's realization of women's role in social and national advancement motivated him, along with many of his fellow reformers, to fantasize and create an idealized woman "at a time when Chinese men were experiencing political impotence."[39] Thus it is no surprise that the discussion of heroism in women becomes another focus of the novel. Interestingly, chapter 11 switches from the female voice that dominates in chapter 9 to the male voice that delineates the ideal image of a female hero, mirroring the author's tendency to fantasize about heroic women. Having heard that the women's association members are scared of traveling at night, the younger brother of the Huang sisters, Zhenfu, comments that it is important for modern women to have both literary talents and chivalric dispositions. He then cites a long list of historical heroines who not only possess a combination of literary and chivalric traits, but are also regarded as Confucian paragons of self-sacrifice for high moral causes. Among those on his list are the famous women warriors Hua Mulan and Liang Hongyu, but the most impressive and elaborate of all stories is that of a late-Ming woman named Shen Yunying.

Shen Yunying is the daughter of Shen Yuxu, a distinguished degree holder of the military examination in the Chongzhen period (1628–1644). At a tender age, she demonstrates exceptional literary talent by mastering abstruse Confucian classics. Coming from a military family, she also excels in horsemanship and archery. When she is twenty years old, her father is killed in a battle with bandits, and their enemies take away his body. Upon hearing the grievous news, Yunying immediately takes charge of her father's troops and leads ten cavalrymen to break into the enemy's camp. They kill more than thirty bandits, and she carries her father's body home on her back. However, Yunying's misfortune does not end here. Her husband, who is sent to guard the south gate of Jingzhou City, is also killed in the line of duty. Overcome by grief and out of a sense of chastity, Yunying tries to drown herself but is saved by her mother. She then spends the rest of her life teaching Confucian classics to the younger members of her clan. Yunying is an extraordinary woman not only because she possesses both literary and martial talents, but, more important, because she strikes the reader as the embodiment of Confucian womanly virtues with her self-sacrificing filial devotion and chastity. To the readers of *Jinghua yuan*, Yunying conjures up the familiar image of one hundred talented and gallant women who are recognized for their exceptional loyalty and filial piety.

Because *Jinghua yuan* is criticized for its celebration of feminine virtue and talent in strict accordance with traditional morality,[40] one might not be impressed by the fact that Chen borrows images of the talented and gallant women from *Jinghua yuan* as models of his idealized women. The reader is probably even more disappointed by Chen's repetition of the literary formula combining "good house wife" with "woman warrior," because the combination represents a male-oriented fantasy that cancels out or neutralizes the potential threat of unfettered womanhood. Although such a borrowing pays homage to the old models, it is also a renewing or a redefining that distinguishes itself from the original's stereotypes, patterns, and conventions. A re-reading or rewriting never repeats the exact same message or image that is delivered by the original author. Thus it is no surprise for us to see that the stereotypes of female knights-errant from the Chinese classic novels were appropriated and refashioned as female revolutionaries and women nihilists by late-Qing writers in works such as *Nüwa shi* (The stone of the goddess of Nüwa, 1904) and *Nüyuhua* (A flower of the women's prison, 1904). The formula for "heroism and love" *(yingxiong ernü)* proposed by Wen Kang in *Ernü yingxiong zhuan* (The tale of romantic heroes, 1878) was taken and retoned as a new blend of "revolution and love" *(geming jia lian'ai)* in late-Qing novels such as *Dong Ou nühaojie* (Heroines of Eastern Europe, 1903). In Chen's case, his new image of the idealized woman is someone who has benefited from both Chinese and Western education, who takes the role of family educator and manager seriously, but who has the courage and disposition to participate in political and military actions if they are called for. As he emphasizes in the prologue, the idealized woman is different from the radical revolutionary Qiu Jin (1875–1907), who abandoned her family roles as a docile wife, a good mother, and a filial daughter in pursuit of revolutionary ideals. Rather, "she" (the idealized woman) resembles the fictional character Xu Pingquan from *Nüyuhua,* a moderate feminist who believes that equality between men and women can be achieved through women's education and continued negotiation with men.[41]

Some important issues about women from *Jinghua yuan* are revoiced by Chen in his rewrite. These issues include women's education, their roles in family and sociopolitical arenas, and the image of the idealized woman. As a moderate reformist deeply concerned with women's reforms, Chen embarked on the task of creating a new (or renewed) literary image of women and found *Jinghua yuan* to be his best reference. His re-reading of *Jinghua yuan* was one with a feminist agenda, although its goals were modest. Such a re-reading is interesting and significant, as it offers an earlier interpretation of *Jinghua yuan* than the critique by Hu Shi while it anticipates and reinforces the latter. A common characteristic shared by the re-readers of the late Qing and those of the May Fourth period is that they all lived in historical times that witnessed the pervasive sociocultural impacts from women's movements; consequently, their interpretations of *Jinghua yuan* were colored by this reality. Chen's re-reading, similar to that of Hu Shi, can be seen as a creative reading that rewrites the original to comment upon contemporary society.

If the moderate reformist Chen Xiaolu tried to refashion *Jinghua yuan* into a novel that promoted progressive ideas on women's issues, then the conservative writer Hua Qinshan intended to do just the opposite by taking a polemical stand against the original and writing an antifeminist novel. As is the case for the two previous writers, Hua and his book are also virtually unknown to readers of Chinese literature. From the prologue of the novel and two other prefatory writings we know that Hua, whose pseudonym was Zuihua sheng (Scholar of Drunken Flowers), was a discontented scholar who withdrew from worldly affairs *(bu wen shishi)* and buried himself in fiction and unofficial histories. Distinguished from the rewrites of Xiaoran yusheng and Chen Xiaolu,

Hua's reworking of *Jinghua yuan* mainly takes the form of continuation or plot derivation, while it also demonstrates some characteristics of *fanxin xiaoshuo*.⁴² As described in one of the prefaces, "He started off from reopening the civil service examinations for women, and took as his main plot the line from the original that went 'the talented female scholar Lu Zixuan will assist the new female king to be a worthy ruler.'"⁴³

Hua's novel works out two different textual relationships with its parent work, a linear one and a circular one. Linearly, the novel continues what is left undeveloped in Li Ruzhen's novel regarding the fates of Wu Zetian and her followers after the collapse of the Zhou dynasty and the story of the Women's Kingdom after Yin Ruohua and her three aides return and seize power. The continuation also regressively traces the original's plot from the male-reclaimed Tang court to the male-women *(xiong nüren)*⁴⁴ dominated "Women's Kingdom," and then back to the mythical realm where the Star of Literature transforms from a female to a male appearance, indicating that the inverted *yin* and *yang* hierarchy has been restored. In so doing, Hua's rewrite completes a circle that ends exactly where *Jinghua yuan* begins.⁴⁵ It provides the reader with a re-inversion to what has been inverted in the original, a mirror image of *Jinghua yuan*'s fictional world, and a betrayal and correction of Li Ruzhen's intended messages. This strategy of re-inversion is revealed by the author at the very beginning of the novel in a couplet: "Gazing flowers in the mirror, their bewitching beauty is doubled; Setting a mirror in front of the flowers, their splendor is tripled."⁴⁶ "Flowers in the mirror" is used here as a pun to refer to a realm of literary creation in general and Li's novel in particular. Hua describes his recreation as holding up a mirror to Li's literary work, a metaphor that reveals the hypertextuality as well as the critical function of his work.

Hua is obviously dismayed by the image of Wu Zetian that Li created and intends to override it. He brings back two anti-Zhou heroes, Song Su (whose original name is Li Su, a Tang prince) and Wen Song, who disappeared in the four military passes in the original, to launch another political and military crusade against Wu's remaining confederates and Empress Wei, who emulates Wu in usurping imperial power. As the result of this political battle, Wu is startled to death, and then her head is cut off; Empress Wei's body is chopped into pieces, and both the Wu and Wei clans are wiped out. The brutal punishments of the two female usurpers in the rewrite, undoubtedly, reveal Hua's strong objection to Li's lenient treatment of Wu as well as his contentious view that women cannot legitimately become rulers and take part in state politics. Interestingly, Hua's counteraction not only puts him in the camp of the conservatives and the defenders of patriarchal order, but it also highlights the subversive and defiant side of the original.

In *Jinghua yuan*, Li's attitude toward Wu Zetian is ambivalent. On the one hand, he disapproves of her political usurpation; on the other hand, he applauds her policies to improve women's living conditions and to allow women to take part in the imperial examinations. Li's condemnation of Wu's overstepping her female role can be seen on a symbolic level, in the contrived trinity of the Heart-Moon Fox, the female king of Women's Kingdom, and Wu Zetian. With the Heart-Moon Fox and the female king both symbolizing lust, transgression, and disorder, Wu is indirectly presented as a destructive woman whose inversion of the *yin-yang* order is disruptive and irregular and therefore needs to be rectified.[47] However, Li's criticism is understated and restrained, in contrast to Wu's stereotypical image as the oversexed and ruthless female tyrant one usually sees in other fictional writings such as *Ruyijun zhuan* (The lord of perfect satisfaction),[48] *Sui Tang yanyi* (The romance of the Sui and Tang, 1695), and *Wu Zetian waishi* (The unofficial history of Wu Zetian, n.d.). Li clearly distances himself from the popular views and offers a kind of indeterminacy that the reader rarely sees from other fictional representations of this historical figure.

This indeterminacy is further attested to by Li's ironic treatment of the anti-Zhou heroes who reclaim and restore the rule of the male emperor (Zhongzong) after dethroning Wu Zetian. The conventional view would take such a plot as hard evidence of Li's disapproval of Wu, but a careful reading does not support this interpretation. In the last five chapters (chaps. 96 to 100), which deal primarily with the anti-Zhou political and military campaigns, the rebel troops led by the Tang loyalists Luo Chengzhi, Xu Chengzhi, and Song Su are trapped in four military passes that are guarded by Wu's male relatives. The "four passes" are a metaphorical remaking of the "four vices"—wine, women's charms, money, and wrath *(jiu se cai qi)*—which are presented as the embodiment of Wu's evil power, and yet they turn out to be illusions. The anti-Zhou "martyrs" are, in fact, trapped and destroyed by their inner weaknesses—their drunkenness, licentiousness, greed, and irascibility. As what a Taoist nun describes, those who are caught in these "traps of self-destruction" *(zizhuzhen)* have no one but themselves to blame. The underlying message here is that what the so-called anti-Zhou heroes are fighting against is really the self-indulgent human nature that brings about their self-destruction. Wu, a stereotypical representative of the dark side of femininity, is conveniently blamed for such destruction.[49]

What complicates Wu's image in *Jinghua yuan* is her proclamation of the twelve statuses to improve the lot of women and her promotion of the imperial examination for women. It would be naive to believe that Li credits Wu with being the spokesperson for women's welfare and education, since she serves only as the author's mouthpiece for his Confucian humanitarian concerns, as do the two prime ministers of Junzi guo in chapter 12. However, *Jinghua yuan* does include some approving comments and favorable accounts of Wu that are too significant to ignore. For instance, in chapter 8 Tang Ao and Duo Jiugong, at the beginning of their adventure, encounter a rare animal, Dangkang (literally "it will be prosperous"), at the East-Mouth Mountain (Dongkou Shan). The reader is told that the appearance of Dangkang is an auspicious omen for peace and prosperity. This detail ought to be taken as a positive comment on Wu's reign, as this is a rhetorical device that Chinese historians and historical fiction writers often use in their writings. In chapter 40 Tang Ao's younger brother, Tang Min, makes a similar comment praising Wu's political achievement after her enthronement.[50] More important, even the Tang loyalists must recognize the fact that the omen of heaven favors Wu Zetian.

> [When the surprised loyalists were watching the star of Wu Zetian—The Star of the Heart-Moon-Fox—emitting a wondrous light,] Xu Chengzhi asked: "What kind of good government can so move Heaven and Earth?" . . . Wen Song said: "On her Seventieth birthday, Wu issued a decree to reduce taxes and criminal punishment. And she also issued twelve decrees especially for women. . . . All these are unprecedented. As soon as the decrees were issued, the officials implemented them at once, thus rescuing numerous lives and saving many more from poverty. . . . [S]uch deeds must have touched Heaven."[51]

Li's ambivalent depiction of Wu is reminiscent of the famous historian Sima Qian's (c. 145–c. 85 B.C.) portrayal of Empress Lü (r. 188–180 B.C.) of Western Han (206 B.C.–A.D. 25), another female regent who was also severely criticized by many for seizing imperial power after the death of her husband, Emperor Gaozu (r. 206–195 B.C.). In his *Shiji* (Records of the grand historian), Sima Qian, in making a moral judgment, criticizes Empress Lü for her usurpation and for her ruthlessness and cruelty in power struggles. He provides horrific details of the killings and bloodshed that she engineered. However, as a conscientious historian he is able to offer multiple perspectives and a broader vision in order to judge Empress Lü's rule and political career. Not only does he place Empress Lü in the category of "basic annals" *(benji)* with other male emperors,[52] but he also makes the following remarks about her reign.

> In the reign of Emperor Hui and Empress Lü, the common people succeeded in putting behind them the suffering of the age of Warring States and ruler and subject alike sought rest in surcease of action. Therefore, Emperor Hui sat with folded hands and unruffled garments and Empress Lü, though a woman ruling in the manner of an emperor, conducted the business of government without ever leaving her private chambers, and the world was at peace. Punishments were seldom meted out and evildoers grew rare, while the people applied themselves to the tasks of farming, and food and clothing became abundant.[53]

History, committed to "truth-claiming," has to work with various and conflicting interpretations and perspectives. "Where the traditional poet must confine himself to one version of history, the *histor* can present conflicting versions in his search for the truth of fact."[54] The latter can be found in both Sima Qian and Li Ruzhen. As we know, Chinese fiction has a close relationship with historiography, thus it is not surprising that Li takes history as his model when writing about a complicated and controversial historical figure like Wu Zetian.[55] Whereas for Sima Qian such a conflicting representation reflects his broad outlook and his capacity to encompass different facts and perspectives, for Li an ambiguous depiction certainly provides artistic complexity and the re-readability of his novel.

Hua Qinshan, as a careful and conservative re-reader/rewriter, is clearly disturbed by Li's ambivalence toward Wu Zetian and finds that the ambiguity in *Jinghua yuan* might have provided an excuse for women's transgressions and their interference in state politics. In order to present his polemical stand toward Li, Hua works out another set of re-inversions. The elimination of the Wu and Wei clans in the Tang court drives Wu Jinglian, one of Wu Sansi's sons, and Wei Lizhen and Wei Baoying, two young men from the Wei clan, into desperation, and they disguise themselves as women to take refuge in a remote village. Preordained by heavenly design, with the help of the female immortal Yan Zixiao they go to the Women's Kingdom. While Wu Jinglian becomes the imperial consort of the female king, Yin Ruohua, Wei Lizhen and Wei Baoying respectively marry the two prime ministers, Lu Zixuan and Li Hongwei. As a result, the three male refugees-turned-imperial "ladies" become the inverted Wu Niangniang and Wei Niangniang (Queen Wu and Ladies Wei).

The men-turned-Wu Niangniang and Wei Niangniang in the Women's Kingdom are the mirror images of Empress Wu and Empress Wei of the Tang court. They are portrayed as idealized imperial consorts and wives of ministers according to Hua's standard. They not only learn to behave exactly like women, but they also carefully preserve womanly virtues (*jin shou fude*). For instance, the male Wu Niangniang is not jealous of the female king's multiple consorts; "she" even urges the king to go to other imperial concubines on the third day of their wedding. "She" is docile and benevolent, but most important, "she" has no political ambition and never oversteps "her" role as an inner helper to the female king. "She" also gives birth to a son, providing an heir for the throne. Similarly virtuous, the two Wei "ladies" dutifully fulfill their womanly responsibilities in times of peace and go to war to defend their kingdom when the country's security is at stake, repeating the pattern of "good house wives"-cum-"women warriors." The author's portrayal of the model behaviors of these three male-women is clearly intended to reinforce the same message he delivers in the Wu Zetian and Empress Wei saga, only this time he provides the reader with exemplary characters.[56]

One may wonder why Hua is obsessed with the image of Wu Zetian and why he tries so hard to correct the "wrong" message that Li might have delivered. The puzzle is resolved when we treat Hua's novel as a social commentary —when we read his criticism of Wu as a commentary on Empress Dowager Cixi, a domineering and authoritarian woman who became regent to the throne for a third time in 1898. As a political conservative, Cixi was rigorously attacked by reformists such as Kang Youwei (1858–1927) and Liang Qichao, who accused her of crushing the Hundred Days Reform, causing the turmoil of the Boxer Rebellion in 1900, and conspiring to dethrone Emperor Guangxu. As a female ruler, Cixi was also harshly treated by historians and fictional writers as a usurper and transgressor whose interference in court politics brought China one calamity after another. In this period, it was common to condemn the Empress Dowager by comparing her with/to Wu Zetian and by drawing a parallel between Cixi's reclaiming the regency and taking power from Emperor Guangxu in 1898 and Wu's dethroning of her son, Emperor Zhongzong, in

684. Xiaoran yusheng and Hua both employed this analogy in their rewrites. In the latter's case, Zhongzong was killed in a coup d'état planned by his wife Empress Wei and Wu's infamous nephew, Wu Sansi. This fictional recreation interestingly coincides with a rumor spread after the aborted Hundred Days Reform that Empress Dowager Cixi took over the government by force and that Emperor Guangxu died during the armed conflict.[57]

Although Hua and Chen Xiaolu are politically opposite in their ways of interpreting *Jinghua yuan* and describing women's issues, they are alike in that they both reconstruct the image of the idealized women provided in the original. If Chen presents the reader with the image of a moderate feminist like Xu Pingquan, Hua provides us with his recreation of feminized "male-women" who exhibit the most feminine qualities and exert the Confucian womanly virtues to the fullest.

In contrast to Li, who focuses on the story of talented women, Hua shifts his focus to six male-women. The four returning female characters from *Jinghua yuan,* Yin Ruohua and her three capable assistants Lu Zixuan, Li Hongwei, and Zhi Lanyin, become mere puppets in Hua's rewrite, and the story revolves around their male-wives and the two male-women warriors, Hua Ruyu and Mei Fengying. In portraying these male-women and projecting the author's sexual ideology, one striking literary device employed by Hua is the feminization of these characters. Such feminization is meticulously and painstakingly rendered in their appearance, clothing, mannerisms, and moral behaviors, often in a language typical of Ming-Qing erotic fiction. In the imperial wedding scene, Hua describes Wu Jinlian's[58] feminine beauty as seen through the eyes of the female king.

> The palace maid rolls up the pearl curtain and hastily assists the Queen [Wu Jinlian] in getting off the imperial chariot. [The Queen] gently moves "her" lotus steps and enters the palace. The King [Yin Ruohua] gets off the throne. They stand side by side and worship heaven and earth. The King then sits on the throne again. Jinlian makes a deep bow and kneels down in front of the King, making a formal salute as a subject. After that, a banquet is served in the palace and the King and the Queen drink wine from each other's cups. Ruohua takes a look at Jinlian and sees that Jinlian's eyebrows resemble spring-mountains. "Her" eyes contain autumn-water. "Her" face is like peach blossoms dripped with raindrops, and "her" waist is as light as a delicate willow that stands in the wind.[59]

Interestingly, the language Hua uses to describe Jinlian's feminine beauty is taken almost verbatim from the scholar-and-beauty romances and erotic novels. The linguistic borrowing is a deliberate effort on the author's part to re-invoke and reinforce the femininity that is predetermined by men (according to men's fantasy and the codification of Confucian teaching), a femininity that seems to have disappeared in Li's depiction of his female scholars-cum-warriors.

In writing about his characters' sexuality, Li intentionally abandoned stereotypical terms and expressions. His female characters are androgynous but not "feminine" in a conventional sense. Possessing both literary and military talents, they are not only misplaced in masculine spaces, but also are supposed to fulfill family and public duties in place of men. Sometimes Li's women warriors remind the reader of the Liangshan heroes in Shuihu zhuan. For instance, Luo Hongqu is a woman warrior and tiger killer whose first appearance in the novel is reminiscent of the "macho" tiger killer Wu Song, while Wei Ziying, a skillful shooter, conjures up the image of the genius archer Hua Rong. More important, in Jinghua yuan, Li creates a fictional world in which the very notions of femininity and masculinity are often questioned and the boundaries between the two become blurred. Gender distinctions, associations, and normative roles prescribed by society as shown in previous literary works are played with and tossed around by Li—so much so that the conventional gender norms become completely arbitrary, fluid, and mutable. Aside from the gender transgression and transcendence of the female characters, Lin Zhiyang's experience of being taken into the imperial harem in the Women's Kingdom presents the most bizarre and revealing example of gender displacement. In this oft-studied episode, Lin, a man in Tang society, is not only identified as a woman according to the gender rules of the Women's Kingdom, but is also feminized physically and mentally by force under imperial order. Written in the mode of satirical comedy, Lin's forced gender switch reveals the arbitrariness and changeable nature of sexual categorizations, poking fun at the gender conventions and stereotypes endorsed by society and literary models of the past.

By substituting his feminized male-women for Li's androgynous women as the ideal heroines, Hua intends to redraw the gender boundaries and reset the norms of femininity that are undermined and subverted by Jinghua yuan.[60] However, ironically, Hua re-endorses the conventional gender rules and sexual qualifications by creating literary images that are the very representation of the arbitrariness of these rules and qualifications. The gender-reversing motif Hua appropriated from Li produces a subversive rather than sustaining effect for his agenda. The bizarre image of male-women, biologically male but representing femininity, is purely a literary construct that causes enormous linguistic and conceptional confusion and is therefore more damaging to the traditional sexual ideology that Hua was trying to defend. As a mirror image of Li's heroines, Hua's ideal women represent only a sign of a preexisting sign. The ghost of the original seems to have constantly haunted Hua as a rewriter.

As a critique of contemporary reality, Hua's novel targets the late-Qing feminist movements that fundamentally changed the old concepts of women and helped to give rise to an image of the new woman. For instance, in chapter 31 the author is unable to hide his indignation at the changes in women's appearances and behaviors that he witnessed during the transitional period of the late Qing and the early Republican eras. As a foil to the idealized Women's Kingdom, the author presents Baimin Guo as a country that undergoes social "destruction."

> "Unbinding feet" has become a trend, and many people are following suit. This started with female students. The female not only releases her feet from the bindings, but also abandons wearing her hair in a "cloud bun," and instead, wears her hair in long braids. On her face, there is a pair of gold-framed glasses. A high collar surrounds her neck. On her upper body she wears short and close-fitting clothes. On her lower body she wears pants instead of a skirt. On her feet there are a pair of leather shoes that resemble those worn by men. Clothes are not like clothes, and shoes are not shoes; both clothes and shoes are grotesque in shape and appearance. The books that she is reading are neither "Neize" [regulations for household] from the *Book of Rites (Liji)* nor the *Biographies of Eminent Women (Lienü zhuan)* by Liu Xiang, but something that is taken from the streets or vulgar folk songs; things that are completely fabricated by someone.... [A]s a result, man and woman cannot be distinguished from each other.... I do not know how many girls from good families are ruined by this. Even worse, some girls find husbands for themselves, and elope with their men without telling their parents.... [S]ome of the female students also go to theater where they play roles in operas and befriend actresses *(yu nüling weiwu)*. There are all kinds of immoral behaviors; I am simply unable to name them all.[61]

Here Hua's criticism directly points to the image of new/modern women, the movement in favor of natural feet, and the establishment of women's schools at the turn of the twentieth century.

As a conservative who set out to attack the feminist movement in the late Qing, Hua found the images of Wu Zetian and androgynous women in *Jinghua yuan* offensive and subversive. Thus he adopted a contentious attitude toward the original and tried to restore the traditional gender order by reversing what Li Ruzhen had done. Although diametrically opposed in their political stands, both Hua and Chen Xiaolu interpreted *Jinghua yuan* as a novel that could have an important impact on women's issues; both embarked on the task of re-voicing these issues and recreating an ideal image for women. It is fascinating to see that resonating interpretations have emerged over and over again by different generations of critics, including literary historians and theoreticians from the May Forth period and modern feminist critics.

CONCLUSION

The three late-Qing *xushu* in question, written at a time marked by drastic historical and social change, are different attempts to come to terms with the "epochal inevitability" that people were confronted with during that time.[62] They all demonstrate a keen interest in the pressing issues of the late Qing: political reform, Western influence, women's rights, commercialization of society, and technological advancement. This active engagement with contemporary sociopolitical and sociocultural changes is one of the trademarks of the late-Qing *xushu*, although these writers could have come from very different ideological backgrounds. A common strategy shared by late Qing *xushu* is *jiegu fengjin*, and their criticism is double-edged, directed at both their parent works and the sociopolitical problems of late-Qing times. In the case of Xiaoran yusheng, his criticism targets both Li Ruzhen's Taoist/Confucian utopian vision and the failed national campaign for reform. For Chen Xiaolu and Hua Qinshan, their re-voicing of women's issues and recreations of the image of the ideal woman either reinforce or undermine what has been proposed by Li Ruzhen while responding to the women's movements of their time with opposing ideologies.

Besides deep social concerns, another common characteristic of these three *Jinghua yuan* rewrites is that they are representative in signaling a fictional renovation, and they are revealing of the "repressed modernities" that are embedded in different cultural discourses at the turn of the twentieth century.[63] As parodic doubles or mirror images of the classic novel *Jinghua yuan*, the three rewrites present a heterogeneity of voices, yet one can still discern a shared aspiration among them to pursue a narrative format different from that of their predecessors. Both Xiaoran yusheng's and Chen Xiaolu's *Xin Jinghua yuan*, for instance, are written in the style of *fanxin xiaoshuo*, a *xushu* subgenre that emerged in the late Qing. Hua Qinshan's *Xu Jinghua yuan*, although a formal continuation, combines the elements of the traditional *xushu* and *fanxin xiaoshuo*.

If the traditional *xushu* are "faithful" (or at least pretend to be faithful) to their originals—that is, if they imitate the latter in subject matter and narrative techniques and provide the "correct" interpretation and "authentic" (or truthful) closure or continuation of the original—then the *fanxin xiaoshuo* are deliberately "unfaithful," and their agenda is to transform the old model into a new work. While such a transformation is often achieved through temporal and spatial displacement and ironic inversion, as in the cases of Xiaoran yusheng and Hua, for Chen, the effect of *fanxin* is realized by refashioning the original's image of talented and gallant women in his own contemporary setting. Whereas Xiaoran yusheng and Hua's *xushu* are scornful ridicules of the parent novel, Chen's rewrite pays homage to *Jinghua yuan*, renewing the theme of talented and gallant women with new characters and plots.

The multiple and at times conflicting voices of these three re-readers/rewriters further attest to the re-readability and malleability of their model text. Their re-readings/rewritings of *Jinghua yuan* offer new perspectives, unexpected possibilities, and additional layers of meaning to this nineteenth-century masterpiece. Their different versions of reworking the same text bring to the fore the openness, multiplicity, and indeterminacy of this work. *Jinghua yuan* is a novel that demands repeated re-readings and rewritings. Li Ruzhen himself offered the best metaphor for his novel as one that was ultimately plural and playful. In citing the famous anecdote of "*xuanji tu*," a palindrome created by the talented female poet Su Hui, Li's narrator tells the reader that by design the 841-character maze contains over two hundred poems. To please

Wu Zetian, two talented girls at court succeed in unraveling hundreds more poems than the poetess intended. *Jinghua yuan,* indeed, resembles Su Hui's palindrome as the novel haunts and seduces its readers of different generations into reading, re-reading, and rewriting the novel time and time again.

Notes

1. Besides Tang Guichen, White Ape, a supernatural character in the novel, is also described as a "destined one" who can read and understand the enigmatic inscription. But even in Tang Guichen's case, the understanding of the text comes only after repeated re-reading.
2. Antecedent examples of this motif can be found in both *Shuihu zhuan* and *Honglou meng.* In the prologue of *Shuihu zhuan,* an unintelligible text is imprinted on the front of a stone tablet, while four large characters are written on the back that read *"yu Hong er kai"* (open when Hong comes). This detail suggests that the inscribed text (the story of *Shuihu zhuan*) will be unfolded by the "destined" character Marshal Hong. In *Honglou meng* the story of the novel is inscribed on the magic stone abandoned at the foot of Greensickness Peak (chaps. 1 and 120). The fates of *Honglou meng*'s characters are repeatedly revealed to Baoyu as riddles, poems, and songs in his dream to the Land of Illusion (chap. 5), but he fails to be enlightened. His enlightenment is frustrated and suspended until he returns to the Land of Illusion a second time in his dream at the end of the novel (chap. 116).
3. Nabokov, *Lectures on Literature,* 3.
4. In his book *Traditional Chinese Fiction and Fiction Commentary,* Rolston discusses the necessity of re-reading to appreciate the classic Chinese novel. On the seemingly disjointed narrative structure that demands multiple re-readings, see 266; on the *pingdian* tradition that projects re-reading, see 127; on the implied and dramatized re-reader, see 344 and 348. Anthony Yu also indicates that *Honglou meng* self-reflexively postulates the necessity of its own misreading, knowing that the fiction will be taken for fact and the fact for fiction. See Yu, *Rereading the Stone,* 50.
5. Hu Shi believes that *Jinghua yuan* is a novel that shows serious concern for women. He asserts that in writing this novel, Li criticizes the subordination of women, foot binding, and the double standard of chastity that existed in the patriarchal society, demanding a new social system that allows women to be educated as well as participate in state politics. See Hu Shi, "*Jinghua yuan* de Yinlun." Brandauer, Evans, and Qingyun Wu all followed Hu Shi in emphasizing the sociocultural impacts of the novel. See Brandauer, "Women in the *Ching-hua yüan*"; Evans, "Social Criticism in the Ch'ing"; and Qingyun Wu, "Separation from the Patriarchal World." Lu Xun, on the other hand, classifies *Jinghua yuan* under the rubric of *caixue xiaoshuo* (the novel of erudition) and thinks that Li wrote this novel for his own amusement. See Lu Xun, *A Brief History of Chinese Fiction,* 317–336. Lu's categorization is reiterated by Hsia, Roddy, and several Chinese scholars such as Zhang Jun. For detailed discussions, see Hsia, "The Scholar-Novelist and Chinese Culture"; Roddy, "The Philological Musings of *Jinghua yuan*"; and Zhang Jun, *Qingdai xiaoshuo shi,* 316–321.
6. For feminist studies on *Jinghua yuan,* see Edwards, "Domesticating the Woman Warrior"; and Qingyun Wu, "Separation from the Patriarchal World." For a reading inspired by gender studies, see Epstein, *Competing Discourses,* 249–263.
7. Calinescu, *Rereading,* 54.
8. Ibid., 55.
9. Throughout this chapter I will use the original Chinese word *"xushu"* or the broad English terms "rewrite" and "rewriting" for the genre. *Xushu,* as I see it in Chinese tradition, designates a rather broad category of works that covers almost the entire range of variants

of what Genette calls "hypertextuality," including continuation, supplement, sequel, parody, travesty, etc. By "hypertextuality" Genette means the relationship uniting a text B (which he calls the hypertext) to an earlier text A (which he calls hypotext), upon which it is grafted in a manner that is not that of commentary. See Genette, *Palimpsests*, 5. For a detailed discussion on the nature and complexities of *xushu* and the important historical developments of this literary phenomenon, see chap. 1 of this volume.

10. The term *"fanxin xiaoshuo"* is used to refer to a group of rewrites of fictional masterpieces in the form of parody. For discussions on this subject, see Ouyang Jian, "Wan Qing 'fanxin' xiaoshuo zonglun," and chap. 1 of this volume.

11. Xiaoran yusheng's *Xin Jinghua yuan* begins with the disappointing situation of Zhongzong's re-enthronement: not only has the expected political reform not been implemented, but imperial power is still in the clutches of Wu Zetian, the Empress Dowager. Worse still, Empress Wei (wife of Zhongzong), following in the footsteps of Wu, interferes with court politics. Zhongzong becomes a complete puppet while evil characters run rampant in the government. Xu Chengzhi, Luo Chengzhi, and Tang Xiaofeng, together with the other nineteen anti-Zhou heroes from Li's original novel, hold a meeting to discuss countermeasures. They are all demoted by Zhongzong, who believes Wu's and Empress Wei's lies that the heroes intend to overthrow the government. See chap. 1.

12. *Xianxing*, or to reveal one's original shape, is a Buddhist term that is often used in *shenmo xiaoshuo* (the novel about gods and devils) to describe a demon or a deity showing its true form. In the late Qing there appeared a large group of works with titles including *"xianxing"* (exposure), such as *Guanchang xianxing ji* (Exposure of officialdom, 1903), *Xuesheng xianxing ji* (Exposure of the world of education, 1906), *Shangjie xianxing ji* (Exposure of the world of business, 1906), *Piaodu xianxing ji* (Exposure of the worlds of prostitution and gambling, n.d.). See David Wang, *Fin-de-siècle Splendor*, 244, 247.

13. Guocui Pai was influenced by a Japanese nationalist school of thought that emerged in the Meiji period. They opposed the conception of complete Westernization and advocated the idea of studying Chinese civilization and preserving Chinese national essence.

14. For detailed discussions of late-Qing writers' plagiarism, see David Wang, *Fin-de-siècle Splendor*, 186–187; Lee and Nathan, "The Beginnings of Mass Culture," 363.

15. Xiaoran yusheng's panorama of exposures is reminiscent of a similar treatment in *Xin Xiyou ji* (1909) by Zhumeng in which Pigsy visits the modern Shanghai. Using his thirty-six-transformation magic, Pigsy constantly changes and renews his status to adapt to his ever-changing circumstances. By transforming Pigsy into a student, a government official, a policeman, a guest in a brothel, and a prostitute, the story reveals the ugly side of each transformation. This episode also simultaneously presents a caricature of modern opportunists and a parody of *xianxing ji xiaoshuo*. See Ouyang Jian, "Wan Qing 'fanxin' xiaoshuo zonglun," 267.

16. In chap. 100 of *Jinghua yuan*, Li self-reflexively concludes his narrative with White Ape hunting for someone who will turn this inscription into a novel. Entrusted by the Fairy of the Hundred Flowers, White Ape first took the inscription of Qihong ting to Liu Xu (887–946), who compiled *Jiu Tangshu* [Old history of the Tang dynasty], and asked him to write a *baiguan yeshi* (fiction/unofficial history) based on the inscription. Liu refused to do it because he was not in a leisurely and carefree mood *(xianqing yizhi)* to write for entertainment at a politically unstable time. White Ape then waited until the Song dynasty to beg Ouyang Xiu (1007–1072) and Song Qi (998–1061), the compilers of *Xin Tangshu* [New history of the Tang dynasty], for help. Neither of them agreed to write the novel, claiming they were exhausted. White Ape finally found a descendant of Laozi (suggesting Li Ruzhen himself, who shares Laozi's surname) in the peaceful time of the sacred dynasty *(shengchao taiping zhi shi)* and left the inscription in his care. This descendant of Laozi (Li Ruzhen) then worked the inscription into a one-hundred-chapter novel titled *Jinghua yuan*.

17. Sable, an expensive commodity, was historically used as decoration on the hats of high-ranking Chinese officials. The expression "a dog's tail replaces a sable" means that the quality of the original will be lost when a genuine and/or high-quality product is replaced by a fake and/or inferior one. The term was originally used when the government hired incompetent officials. Later, it referred to literary rewrites that were considered artistically inferior to their precursors.

18. Li Ruzhen, *Jinghua yuan*, 435. The English translations in this chapter are mine except where indicated otherwise.

19. In his preface, Hu Zongyu, a friend of Hua Qinshan's, describes how Hua decided to write a continuation for *Jinghua yuan*. "Mr. Hua used to say to me: 'Shi Nai'an's *Shuihu zhuan* did not require a continuation but some village pedant did it anyway. Wang Shifu's *Xixiang ji* was complete but there was still someone who was interested in reworking it. Cao Xueqin's *Honglou meng* was perfect the way it was; however, more than ten follow-up works were written after its publication. Li Songshi's [Li Ruzhen] *Jinghua yuan* was obviously only half complete, begging for continuation, but no one has done anything so far.' I then said to Mr. Hua: 'You are both talented and erudite. Why don't you provide what was left out and finish the second half of the *Jinghua yuan*? Wouldn't it be a great pleasure to satisfy the later generation of readers who would consider themselves lucky to be able to read the complete work!' Mr. Hua said: 'Yes, I will do it.' He then revealed what was not fully elaborated in the original." See Hu Zongyu, "Xu *Jinghua yuan* quanbian xu." Chen Xiaolu also indicates that Li did not provide closure for the talented women in *Jinghua yuan*; see Chen, "Xin *Jinghua yuan* zuoyi shulüe."

20. For further discussion on textual fluidity of traditional *xiaoshuo*, see chap. 1 of this volume.

21. Interestingly, *Xin Tangshu* is actually a rewrite of *Jiu Tangshu*. The former not only continues and supplements the latter, but also views it critically, providing the reader with the "correct" ways of arranging events and judging characters. See "Chuban shuoming" [Words from publishers], Ouyang Xiu and Song Qi, *Xin Tangshu*, 1–7. Here, Li might have intentionally drawn a parallel between the relationship of these two historical works and that of his work and its expected continuation.

22. David Wang, in identifying the characteristics of "repressed modernity" of some late-Qing works such as *Dangkou zhi* (Quelling the bandits, 1871), indicates that by using anachronism and displacement, the myth of linear temporality in (literary) history is disturbed and the fictional narrative is no longer presented as singular and irretrievable, signaling progress for the modernization of Chinese fiction. See Wang, *Fin-de-siècle Splendor*, 22. Anachronism and displacement are indeed two of the important rhetorical devices in *xushu*. As early as the seventeenth century, Dong Yue (1620–1686) employed similar techniques in his *Xiyou bu* (The tower of myriad mirrors, 1641), in which the New Tang, a reference to the author's own era, is put next to the historical Tang time, and Xiang Yu (233–202 B.C.), a hegemony contender, coexists with Qin Hui (1090–1155), a Southern Song traitor in Monkey's (the novel's protagonist) dream. Anachronism has also been incorporated into *Jinghua yuan*. In contrast to Xiaoran yusheng, who asserts the superiority of Tang China, the narrator/implied author of *Jinghua yuan* is often dismayed by the backward and barbarous customs and social mores of the "Tang dynasty," an allegorical reference to Li Ruzhen's time.

23. Cixi claimed regency in the late Qing court three times in her more than fifty-year political career. After Emperor Xianfeng (r. 1851–1861) died in 1861 and Cixi's six-year-old son, Emperor Tongzhi (r. 1862–1874), was enthroned, she allied herself with Empress Ci'an and Prince Gong and got rid of her political enemies and shared the regency with Empress Ci'an. In 1875, after the sudden death of her son, she installed her four-year-old nephew, Emperor Guangxu. Once again, the two dowager empresses governed from behind the curtain. In September 1898, right after the aborted Hundred Days Reform,

Cixi resumed the task of *xunzheng* (giving instruction in the art of governance) and acted as regent for the third time in her life. In the case of Wu Zetian, she had Zhongzong replaced by his younger brother Ruizong (r. 684–690, 710–712) in 684, only six weeks after Zhongzong's accession. Wu Zetian acted as regent from 684 to 690. Many late-Qing writers and later historians thus viewed Cixi as an example in the "Wu Zetian," or usurping empress, tradition.

24. Examples of this analogy can be found in unofficial historical writings like *Shiye yewen* (Ten leaves of unofficial anecdotes, 1917) by Xu Zhiyan. See "Kou taijian" and "Konghe zhenwen," *Shiye yewen*, 70–72, 82. A similar comparison is also made in fictional writings such as *Xu Niehai hua* (A sequel to Flower in the sea of sins, 1943) by Zhang Hong. See Zhang Hong, *Xu Niehai hua*, 346.

25. It is believed that Cixi originally wanted to rebuild Yuan Ming Yuan (the Old Summer Palace) but settled for Yihe Yuan (the New Summer Palace) after failing to secure funds. She diverted funds intended for the Chinese navy in order to carry out the work. Cixi was severely criticized for her plan to rebuild Yuan Ming Yuan. In one of her edicts issued in 1888, Cixi defended herself by proclaiming that "the costs of construction have all been provided for out of the surplus funds accumulated as a result of rigid economies in the past. The funds under the control of the Board of Revenue will not be touched, and no harm will be done to the national finances." See Elder, *Old Peking*, 253–254. For more discussions of this matter, see Xu, "Yuan ming yuan xiufu yi," *Shiye yewen*, 8–13.

26. Li Ruzhen, *Jinghua yuan*, 37. Trans. Evans in "Social Criticism in the Ch'ing," 61.

27. Hsia, "The Scholar-Novelist and Chinese Culture," 301–302.

28. Ibid., 273.

29. Xiaoran yusheng, *Xin Jinghua yuan*, 420.

30. David Wang, *Fin-de-siècle Splendor*, 273.

31. Palmer, "Rereading Guillaume de Machaut's Vision of Love," 169.

32. This is not an isolated case in the genre of *fanxin xiaoshuo*. Two versions of *Xin ernü yingxiong zhuan* (New tale of heroes and lovers), one by Chucang and another by an anonymous writer, are written in the same fashion. Lu Shi'e's (1877–1944) *Xin Niehai hua* (New Flower in the sea of sins, 1909) also belongs to this group. This group of *fanxin xiaoshuo* has a much looser relationship with their parent works. Usually the authors create a new set of characters instead of recycling the old ones, and they do not pick up the plot or story line from the originals either. However, *"fanxin"* is an appropriate term for these rewrites because these texts not only grow out of their models, but aim at renewing them. In Lu's *Xin Niehai hua*, for instance, the two courtesan romances—the romances between the infamous Sai Jinhua and her two lovers (the Qing official Jin Jun and the German general Count Waldersee)—are refashioned into a modern romance between a female schoolteacher, Su Hui'er, and a returning overseas student, Zhu Qichang. For Lu's characters, however, the free love not only develops into a marriage, but also generates mutual trust and respect between the lovers. This is a new type of relationship between a man and a woman that is absent in Sai Jinhua's romances. Rather than being satirical or scornful, this type of rewriting pays homage to its originating narrative by renewing it with fresh images and opening it up to new possibilities. See Lu Shi'e, *Xin Niehai hua*; and Ouyang Jian, *Zhongguo tongsu xiaoshuo zongmu tiyao*, 1125, 1253.

33. Chen Xiaolu, *Xin Jinghua yuan*, 220.

34. In his preface Chen expresses his disappointment in both classic Chinese novels and translated Western novels for the ways they portray women. According to him, many Chinese novels are "impure" or "indecent," especially those that write about women and *qing* (desire, love). *Jinghua yuan* is an exception, but it is too "hollow" and does not provide "closure," thus it also fails to represent women with extraordinary splendor. The translated Western novels, however, are either too extreme or too individualistic and irrational.

It would be a grave mistake for women to take the female characters in these foreign novels as good examples of "civilized behavior." In an attempt to correct all of these problems, Chen decided to write a new *Jinghua yuan* to be distinguished from the old one by Li Ruzhen. See Chen Xiaolu, "*Xin Jinghua yuan* zuoyi shulüe."

35. Liang Qichao, "Changshe nü xuetang qi," 561. Trans. Borthwick in "Changing Concepts of the Role of Women from the Late Qing to the May Fourth Period," 72.

36. See Xia Xiaohong, *Wanqing wenren funü guan*, 79–101.

37. For detailed discussions on late-Qing women's movements, see ibid.; and Borthwick, "Changing Concepts of the Role of Women from the Late Qing to the May Fourth Period."

38. Chen Xiaolu, *Xin Jinghua yuan*, 220. Here, "foreigners" refers to English, Japanese, Russian, and those who fought against China and signed unequal treaties with the Qing government.

39. David Wang, *Fin-de-siècle Splendor*, 168.

40. Hsia holds the view that *Jinghua yuan* is "far less ambiguously a celebration of feminine virtue and talent in strict accordance with traditional morality." See his "The Scholar-Novelist and Chinese Culture," 266. In analyzing Lin Siniang (a woman warrior praised by Jia Baoyu in *Honglou meng*) and Yan Ziqiong (a character from *Jinghua yuan*), Edwards also states that the causative and rationalizing moral principles for these characters to fight a war are either filial piety or loyalty. See Edwards, "Domesticating the Woman Warrior," 99.

41. For detailed discussion on Xu Pingquan and *Nüyuhua*, see David Wang, *Fin-de-siècle Splendor*, 170–174.

42. The old characters, for instance, are thrown into the author's contemporary social setting and have to deal with late-Qing sociopolitical problems. A territory dispute between the Country of Dog Head (Quanfeng Guo) and the Country of Giants (Daren Guo), described in chap. 14, and the war fought between the Country of Scholars (Shushi Guo) and the Women's Kingdom (Nüer Guo), from chaps. 15 to 27, are anachronistic treatments of the chaos during the late-Qing period. Chap. 31, which describes women's moral degradation in the Country of People with White Complexion (Baimin Guo), is obviously a satire of the sociocultural changes that happened in China at the turn of the twentieth century. See Hua Qinshan, *Xu Jinghua yuan*, 133–141, 142–264, 299–308. Hua also used the rhetorical device of reversal or inversion, a trademark of *fanxin xiaoshuo*. More on this later.

43. Hu Zongyu, "*Xu Jinghua yuan* Quanbian xu," 3.

44. "Male-woman" (*xiong nüren*) is a term used by Hua to refer to a biological man who is identified socially as a woman in the Women's Kingdom. "Female-man" (*ci nanren*) is another term he uses to identify a biological woman who functions socially as a man in the same fictional world.

45. *Jinghua yuan* starts off from the metamorphosis of Star of Literature (transforming from a male body to a female body). The story is then followed by the three Tang travelers' journey to more than thirty overseas countries, including their visit of the Women's Kingdom dominated by female-men. The novel ends at the male-reclaimed Tang court (Zhongzong's re-enthronement). Although Li did end his novel with Wu Zetian's abdication of the throne, he left the reader with the impression that Wu was still powerful. Furthermore, according to her edict, another female imperial examination was to be carried out the next year. Thus the reversed *yin* and *yang* order was not really restored in Li's original.

46. Hua Qinshan, *Xu Jinghua yuan*, 3.

47. See Epstein, *Competing Discourses*, 263–264.

48. There are two opinions regarding *Ruyijun zhuan*'s dates. Liu Hui suggests that the novel

was written between 1514 and 1520, while Stone believes it was completed between 1524 and 1529. For further discussion on the dates of *Ruyijun zhuan* and on its negative portrayal of Wu Zetian, see chap. 8 of this volume.

49. This episode is reminiscent of a similar treatment in Dong Yue's *Xiyou bu*, which also creates a world of self-delusion. Monkey, as a metaphor for the human mind, is trapped by sex and passion and becomes his own villain. The deluded self is the real evil in Dong's Buddhist allegory tale, not an outside agent or force. See Hegel, "Self as Mind or as Body"; and chap. 2 of this volume. The same underlying meaning emerges in Li Ruzhen's episode as well.

50. Tang Min says, "The Empress Dowager became an emperor from an empress, this was rare since ancient times. It has been more than ten years since she was enthroned, and there have been many good harvests and the country now is at peace." See Li Ruzhen, *Jinghua yuan*, 164.

51. Ibid., 244. Trans. Qingyun Wu in "Separation from the Patriarchal World," 92.

52. Watson argues that Sima Qian did not include Emperor Hui in the "Basic Annals" but wrote one for Empress Lü instead because Emperor Hui was a powerless figurehead set up by Empress Lü. According to Watson, Sima Qian realistically ignored the de jure monarchs but included the accounts of their brief reigns in the chapters about the person who wielded the real power, including Empress Lü and Xiang Yu. See Watson, *Ssu-ma Ch'ien*, 112.

53. Sima Qian, "*Shi ji* 9," 284.

54. Scholes and Kellogg, *The Nature of Narrative*, 243.

55. Li must have consulted historical writings when he wrote *Jinghua yuan*. Not only did he include a number of historical figures in his novel, but he also faithfully, although briefly, related some of the historical events, such as Xu Jingye and Luo Binwang's rebellious expedition against Wu Zetian (chap. 3) and Zhang Jianzhi and Li Duozuo's support of Zhongzong's bid to reclaim his power (chap. 100). The fate of Luo Binwang in the novel (he is not killed but is said to have disappeared) is in accordance with the account in Ouyang Xiu and Song Qi's *Xin Tangshu*. Moreover, at the end of *Jinghua yuan*, Li presents a detail about White Ape, a fictional incarnation of the implied reader/author, visiting the compilers of *Xin Tangshu* and *Jiu Tangshu*. Both books, written by Liu Xu and Ouyang Xiu and Song Qi, respectively, used Sima Qian's "The Basic Annals of Empress Lü" as a reference for writing the official histories of Wu Zetian. See Zhu Meishu, *Li Ruzhen yu Jinghua yuan*, 58; also see Ouyang Xiu and Song Qi, *Xin Tangshu*, 1:113; and Liu Xu, *Jiu Tangshu*, 1:133.

56. A reader of my chapter might suspect that Hua is being playful in creating the image of male-women, but my reading of Hua's novel suggests otherwise. To me, it seems that, unlike Li, who is obviously being comical in his writing about the gender reversals in the Women's Kingdom in *Jinghua yuan*, Hua is deadly serious.

57. See Chung, "The Much Maligned Empress Dowager," 181.

58. Wu Sansi's son, whose original name is Wu Jinglian. He changes his name to the feminine sounding Wu Jinlian after arriving at the Women's Kingdom.

59. Hua Qinshan, *Xu Jinghua yuan*, 95.

60. As analyzed in my preceding discussion, I see Li's ambivalent attitude toward Wu Zetian and his description of gender fluidity and demystification of sexual categorizations as something more than aesthetic gestures. Intentionally or not, *Jinghua yuan* provoked a debate to which both Chen and Hua—and later literary historians and critics—responded on how women should be represented and what literary impact such a representation would have on a reader.

61. Hua Qinshan, *Xu Jinghua yuan,* 302–303. Here, the narrator/author stands out and addresses the reader directly to comment on the social "destruction" of the Baimin Guo.
62. I agree with Martin Huang that "the raison d'etre of a *xushu* lies in the 'interstices' (space/time) between 'what has ended' and 'what lies beyond that end,'" and that in the late Qing "*xushu* as a genre of transition helped to create a strong sense of the 'epochal inevitability.'" See chap. 1 of this volume.
63. In his book, David Wang argues that late-Qing fiction is not a mere prelude to "modern" Chinese literature, but a most active stage that precedes its rise. However, the "modern nature" of late-Qing fiction was somewhat repressed by the May Fourth writers' monolithic discourse of realism and was thus neglected in research of the past. See Wang, *Fin-de-siècle Splendor,* 13–52.

MARTIN W. HUANG

10 From Self-Vindication to Self-Celebration

The Autobiographical Journey in
Lao Can Youhi and Its Sequel

EVER SINCE Lu Xun (1881–1936) identified it as a novel of exposure of the late Qing in his pioneering historical study of Chinese fiction, Liu E's (1857–1909) *Lao Can youji* (The travels of Lao Can) has been read by many, not without justification, as a work that exposes the seamy aspects of late-Qing society (especially the ruthless behavior of the so-called "honest officials" [*qingguan*]).[1] However, what sets *Lao Can youji* apart from other late-Qing novels of exposure *(qianzhe xiaoshuo)* such as Li Baojia's (Li Boyuan) *Guanchang xianxing ji* (The true portraits of the bureaucrats) is, among other things, its persistent autobiographical agenda and its focus on the individual self in relation to a chaotic social environment. The inadequate critical attention to this aspect of the novel is partly the result of critics' long-standing neglect of the author's own sequel—known as *Lao Can youji erbian* (The travels of Lao Can: The second part)—which was published approximately three years after the original novel (later known as *Chubian* [the first part]) was first serialized in 1903. The sequel, as a continuation as well as a "commentary," compels the reader to *re*think the autobiographical dimension of the original novel. In this chapter I argue that the original novel becomes a rather different work (much more autobiographical and "personal") when read in the context of the sequel and when it is reframed by the "new" closure of the sequel (even though the sequel itself lacks a formal closure and ends abruptly in chap. 9).[2]

Any discussion of the relationship between the original novel and the nine-chapter sequel has to start with a look at their textual histories. According to Liu Dashen, the fourth son of Liu E, his father initially started to write the original novel in order to help financially his friend Lian Mengqing, who was having problems supporting his family after being forced to flee by a government displeased by his (or his friends') published newspaper writings. Lian was given the royalty for the novel when he gave Liu's manuscript to the bimonthly journal *Xiuxiang xiaoshuo* (Illustrated fiction). The serialization was abruptly stopped at chapter 13 (actually the fourteenth chapter in Liu's manuscript; the editor, well-known writer Li Baojia, had expurgated all of chap. 11) by Lian when he found out that Li had failed to abide by their verbal agreement that no word in the manuscript was to be altered and made substantial changes to the novel.[3] Scholars used to believe that the rest of the original novel was later completed by Liu and re-serialized in its entirety in the *Tianjin riri xinwen* (The Tianjin daily news) in 1904.[4] Recently, however, some scholars have found evidence suggesting that the original novel was probably not finished until late 1905 or even early 1906.[5] Since the only extant complete copy of the *Tianjin riri xinwen* edition of the original novel—in the possession of Liu Houze, the grandson of Liu E—was undated,[6] we will probably never know with certainty when the original novel was finished and when its serialization was completed, although there was evidence in Liu E's own diary that it was not completed at least as late as late 1905. In the three entries during October and November in his diary of the year of *yisi* (1905), Liu E mentioned that he was writing *juan* (chapters) 10, 15, and 16. Liu Houze believed that his grandfather was referring to the sequel rather than the original novel and that his father Liu Dashen was probably mistaken in asserting that the sequel contained fourteen chapters.[7] According to Liu Delong (the son of Liu Houze and Liu E's great-grandson) and others, the main problem with Liu Houze's theory that Liu E was already writing the sequel during 1905 was how to account for the fact that Liu E should have waited almost two years to have the sequel serialized in the *Tianji riri xinwen*[8] and why he should have waited so long to produce his *zixu* (self-preface) to the original novel—which, according to Lu Xun, was dated 1906—if its serialization was already completed in 1904, as Liu Houze and others have believed.[9]

The dating of the original novel is relevant to the topic of this chapter since Liu E's own experiences during the period between his completion of the original novel and his writing of the sequel must have played a role in shaping some of the latter's obvious departure from the former. A quick comparison of the original novel and its sequel should give the reader the initial impression that the concerns for *public* injustice and the well-being of the common people that dominate the original novel have all but disappeared in the sequel, which instead focuses on the *personal* enlightenment of the individual. While the preface to the original novel dwells on "weeping" and the need for weeping, the preface to the sequel now focuses on the Buddhist message that life is a dream.[10] The sequel can almost be read as an attempt to come to terms with the anger and frustration that permeate the original novel. Despite the uncertainty over the question as to exactly when the original novel (hereafter *Chubian*) was completed, it is probably safe to believe that the series of setbacks the author suffered in his personal life during the period approximately from late

1905 to early 1907 must have contributed to many of the "inconsistencies" between the novel and its sequel.[11]

FROM SIGHTSEEING TO CRUSADE FOR PUBLIC JUSTICE

As suggested by its title, the original novel's plot is structured around the protagonist Lao Can's travels. With the exception of Shen Ziping's trip to Peach Blossom Mountain (chaps. 8–11), the novel's plot unfolds as Lao Can travels around Shandong Province; most of the novel is about what he witnesses or hears during his journeys. At the beginning of the novel, the reader is supposed to assume that Lao Can does not have any particular destination since he is an itinerant doctor *(zoufang langzhong)*. He once claims that "where my footsteps will lead me after that even I myself do not know" *(Chubian* 7.83; Shadick, 77).[12] He *wanders*—going wherever he could make a living as a doctor *(zhibing hukou; Chubian* 1.2). However, as the reader is explicitly urged to see, Lao Can's medical expertise is to be understood allegorically as the skills and ability that qualify him to "cure" the *national* "disease." The patient whom Lao Can has successfully cured in chapter 1 used to suffer from an illness whose symptoms are said to resemble the flooding of the Yellow River that has plagued the central part of China for a thousand years. The patient's name, Huang Ruihe, is supposed to be a pun on the Yellow River. Curing one's illness obviously symbolizes the "curing" of the river (an autobiographical reference to the author's own successful work on river control in He'nan Province). Thus Lao Can's wandering is actually a "crusade" with a goal or destination—to look for opportunities to offer his knowledge and advice to those in power in order to save the nation (e.g., his advice to Governor Zhuang on how to control the flooding of the Yellow River in chap. 4). Yet despite his successful curing of Huang Ruihe's illness, his service at a more important level will be rejected, as prophesied in his allegorical dream in chapter 1, where he is even accused of being a traitor after he tries to deliver a compass to the people on a rapidly sinking ship, which is meant to symbolize China, a nation in deep crisis.[13]

Chapter 1 comprises the brief story of Lao Can's success as a doctor and a detailed account of his allegorical dream, during which he and his friends watch many people struggling on a sinking ship and his offer of help is rejected by those on the ship. Chapter 2 fits the novel's title most perfectly since this chapter is a *youji* (travelogue) in the fullest sense of the word. Here the reader is invited go along with the protagonist as he tours many sightseeing spots in the provincial capital as an ordinary tourist. However, beginning in chapter 3 this sightseeing trip is gradually turned into an "investigative" journey *(chafang; Chubian* 4.45) that seems to have a "destination"—the search for injustice in order to combat it. The couplet title of chapter 3 itself reveals this subtle change in the nature of Lao Can's travels: "From Golden Thread eastward seeking the Black Tiger / A cloth sail goes to west in search of the Gray Falcon." Obviously Golden Thread and Black Tiger are the names of two famous springs in the city Lao Can is visiting, while Gray Falcon refers to the "incorruptible" official Yu

Xian, whose cruel treatment of the common people is becoming clear to Lao Can. However, the Black Tiger soon carries different implications: as the reader finds out, in novels the tiger often symbolizes an oppressive government and its harsh officials. Of course, the classic association of an oppressive government with a tiger, as explicitly mentioned in the novel (*Chubian* 6.67), can be found in the Confucian classic *Liji* (The book of rites): "Oppressive government is more terrible than tigers *(kezheng meng yu hu)*."[14] Elsewhere in chapter 9, the reclusive wise man Yellow Dragon (Huang Longzi) compares officials directly to tigers (*Chubian* 9. 113), and in chapter 8, during his journey to Peach Blossom Mountain, Shen Ziping's insistence that he would rather be robbed by bandits than confronted by a tiger (*Chubian*, 8.96–97) can also be read as a symbolic condemnation of oppressive officials.[15] Consequently, our novelist, by virtue of the double meaning of Black Tiger, is able to subtly underscore the changing nature of Lao Can's travel from sightseeing to moral crusade. After seeing the Black Tiger Spring (i.e., hearing about the cruel deeds of the oppressive official), Lao Can, of course, is no longer in any mood for sightseeing *(youxing yizu)* and resumes his journey by picking up his string of bells *(chuanling)* again (*Chubian* 3.28; more about the symbolic implications of the string of bells later). He is once again an itinerant doctor, only this time with the destination set.

Lao Can's next patient happens to be a concubine of Mr. Gao, who is a secretary in the provincial government. After successfully curing her illness, he is brought to the attention of Governor Zhuang by Mr. Gao and others. Though he fails to heed Lao Can's suggestions on flood control, the governor is so impressed by Lao Can that he tries to recruit him. This association with the governor will prove to be important, since the success of Lao Can's future crusade to save the wrongly prosecuted will largely depend on such connections. Lao Can's ongoing journey will lead him to confront several cases of injustice done to common people by those presumptuous, "honest" officials. This special relationship with the governor adds another quality to his "investigative" journey—he is assuming the role of self-appointed "imperial commissioner" *(qinchai dachen)*. Occasionally he even acts as an "official" imperial commissioner after he is formally commissioned by Mr. Bai, the governor's subordinate, as a detective charged with capturing the culprits in the the Jia family murders. The exchange between Mr. Bai and Lao Can is revealing.

> "You are too flattering," Mr. Bai answered. "I have only done the first and easy part of the job. The second and more difficult part will have to be Mr. Bucan's [Lao Can] responsibility." Lao Can said, "What do you mean? I am neither a great official personage nor am I a minor yamen runner. What has it got to do with me?" Mr. Bai said, "Well then, who wrote the letter to the Governor?" "I did," Lao Can said. "How could I watch people die without helping them?" "You're right," Mr. Bai said, "but if it is one's duty to help someone who is not yet dead, shouldn't you seek justice for people already dead? Just think! Can an ordinary yamen runner handle this sort of extraordinary case? There is no

alternative but to ask the help of a Sherlock Holmes like you!" Lao Can laughed, "I haven't enough perseverance to be that, but if you want me to go I'm willing. Ask His Excellency Mr. Wang to give an appointment as head of the yamen runners and draw up a warrant, and I'll go!" (*Chubian* 18.226; Shadick, 206)

This conversation highlights the substantially changed nature of Lao Can's "travels" almost at the end of the novel. Lao Can's string of bells is burnt in a fire in chapter 15. Now, five chapters later, as an officially appointed government detective, Lao Can has his string of bells remade and resumes his "wandering." The difference is, of course, that before Lao Can was a self-appointed investigator; now he is an officially appointed detective, although he still "wanders" ostensibly as an itinerant doctor. Being a doctor before gave him access to the governor, while being a doctor now will give him access to the common folks in order to gather important information on the culprits in the murder case. This is one of the few moments in the novel when Lao Can, with his official appointment, appears to be in danger of losing his carefully maintained status as an outsider. What saves Lao Can from becoming an insider (becoming too involved in the official world) is his profession as an itinerant doctor—he can always run away when necessary. On the other hand, he cannot remain an outsider completely (with absolutely no connections to the official world); otherwise he would not be able to protect those common people from being persecuted. Throughout the novel, Lao Can is able to remain effective in his moral crusade for justice in large part due to his success in maintaining the ambiguities of his status as an outsider who is nevertheless able to enjoy the advantages of an insider by having good connections *inside* the official world.

Although Lao Can is extremely careful in distancing himself from the world of officials, paradoxically, almost all of his close friends, from Shen Dongzao to Huang Renrui to De Huisheng, are officials. When invited by the governor to join his staff, and when people consequently begin to treat him differently as an "official," Lao Can warns himself, "I was planning to stay here a couple of days more, but with things as they are I fear that these meaningless entanglements will get worse and worse. 'Of thirty-six plans, to get out is the best'" (*Chubian* 4.44; Shadick, 44). In chapter 15, both the prostitute Cuihuan's bedding and Lao Can's string of bells are burnt in a fire that breaks out during the middle of the night; consequently, Lao Can feels compelled to accept Cuihuan's offer to share her bed. He also has to seriously consider taking an official position since he cannot be an itinerant doctor without his trademark bells. This leads Cuihua to congratulate herself and Lao Can on their eventual union: "Cuihuan from now on is to be a virtuous girl *(congliang)*. Mr. Tie from now on is to be an official. This fire certainly was a fire of good luck and of profit." Lao Can's reply is revealing: "According to what you say, she is to become virtuous *(congliang)* and I will become degraded *(congjian)*" (*Chubian* 1.189; Shadick, 170, translation modified). Obviously, Lao Can takes every opportunity to demonstrate his disdain for the official world despite the fact that he would be an ineffective doctor without help from his official friends.

As a visitor and a commoner, Lao Can does not run the risk of getting bogged down in any place. He can distance himself from what he is observing because he is an outsider everywhere he visits. More important, he has the distinct advantage of being able to leave whenever his involvement in a place becomes too deep. Consequently, many of his "official" friends express their envy of Lao Can for his outsider *(fangwai ren)* status. When explaining to Wang Zijing why Lao Can is able to intervene in the murder case while they themselves cannot, Huang Renrui drives home an important point: "In my opinion all you need do in the matter of your Qidongcun case is to ask Mr. Bu to write a letter to the Governor.... All of us are officials and colleagues so that it's not very good for us to offend him, but Mr. Bu is an *outsider (fangwai ren)* and need not be so cautious" (*Chubian* 15.186; Shadick, 167). Obviously, Lao Can cherishes his status, and this is why he becomes so fastidious when it comes to dressing. He insists on dressing causally (*bianyi*; 3.33) when being introduced to the governor. Here the word "*bianyi*," understood as "plain clothes" (as opposed to dressing in formal attire), emphasizes Lao Can's determination to keep his distance from the official world. Read in this light, Lao Can's refusal (twice) of the fox-fur gown as a gift from his friends (*Chubian* 6.73 and 15.188) becomes all the more significant. Lao Can explains that he is not just being polite. He asks his friend Shen Dongzao, who is trying to convince him to accept his gift, "Has there ever been an itinerant bell ringer who wore a gown lined with fox fur?" This puzzles Shen Dongzao.

> "You didn't have to shake that string of bells of yours in the first place. Why must you go to such extremes in feigning vulgarity?... Last night I heard you say that you despised those who 'live in lofty seclusion claiming to be high-minded.' You said, 'The world produces a limited number of gifted men; it is not good to belittle oneself unreasonably!' I prostrate myself in admiration of those sentiments! But your actions rather contradict your words. The Governor really wants you to come out of seclusion and be an official, but you run off in the middle of the night, determined to get away and shake your string of bells." (*Chubian* 6.73; Shadick, 69)

It is true that with the invitation from the governor, Lao Can indeed has no need to make a living as an itinerant doctor. Shen Dongzao, however, fails to realize that the status of an itinerant doctor is precisely what Lao Can is trying to cling to. He needs to dress in such a way that no one would mistake him for an insider (in the world of the rich and powerful). Even Shen Dongzao has to acknowledge that as an official he himself does not have access to the common people as Lao Can does. "The ears and eyes of men of my kind are fenced off from the world. But you traveling about as you do in cotton clothes *(buyi youli)*, must get to know the true state of the world" (*Chubian* 6.69; Shadick, 64). Later, Huang Renrui is able to convince Lao Can to rescue Cuihuan from prostitution by accepting her as a concubine by arguing that as an official he himself could not be seen associating with a prostitute. As a commoner *(buyi)*, however, Lao Can does not have to worry about this (*Chubian* 17.211).[16] Indeed, dressing as a commoner is crucial to Lao Can's success in his moral crusade. This is why the string of bells becomes so important to him: it is a symbol of his ambiguous identity as an itinerant doctor who enjoys the advantages of both an insider and an outsider while at the same time being neither.

Many readers have been dissatisfied with the novel's last part (chaps. 19 and 20), in which Lao Can assumes the role of detective, and especially the episode in which Lao Can revives the thirteen murdered people with the magical drug he acquired from Green Dragon (Qing Longzi).[17] I believe, however, that we should not read this section too literally. It makes more sense when it is interpreted as part of an allegory. After all, most of Lao Can's travels in the previous eighteen chapters could certainly be read as types of "detective" journeys to find the culprits who have committed gross injustices. Therefore, structurally the last two chapters are only a part of this long "detective" journey. What helps to alert the reader to the possibility of an allegorical reading is the way Lao Can's trip to the Black Pearl Grotto at the end of the original novel is described. He is supposed to get there to acquire the magic drug from Green Dragon in order to revive the murder victims. The conversation between Lao Can and a farmer on how to get to the destination is particularly interesting.

> "But the path is not easy. If you know the way, then it's a good level path; if you don't know it, then it's terrible! There are boulders of all sizes and no end of thorns. It would take a lifetime to get there! I don't know how many people have lost their lives on it." Lao Can laughed and said, "You don't mean it's worse than the road followed by the Tang monk when he brought back the Scriptures?" The farmer colored up, "Yes, about as bad as that!"

Then the farmer elaborates further.

> "The paths in these mountains are like the nine fold whorls of the pearl: every step or so a bend. If you go straight forward you are certain to walk into a tangle of thorns; but neither must you purposely turn aside, for if you do, you will fall into a deep pit and you will never get out. But I'll tell you the secret since you are willing to take advice. The path in front of you always grows out of the path you have already covered, so when you've done a few steps, if you will turn round and look back along the path you have come by, you can't go wrong." (*Chubian* 20.248–249; Shadick, 227)

This is a peculiar "talk" about a "path" that cries out for an allegorical reading. Its message becomes even more significant given that the fact that the entire novel focuses on "travels," as its title explicitly emphasizes. According to the farmer, one must know the way. Otherwise one could not reach the destination even in a lifetime ("many people have lost lives" trying to travel through this path). This is a pilgrimage for acquiring the wisdom of "truth," just like the pilgrimage undertaken by Tripitaka and his disciples to acquire the Buddhist scriptures from India, the central story of *Xiyou ji* (The journey to the West). Lao Can should not purposefully turn aside merely because there appear to be many obstacles before him. Since the paths Lao Can has so far covered are all "correct," he just has to keep doing what he has been doing and will eventually succeed in reaching his destination. This is an implicit confirmation of the virtue of Lao Can's deeds up to this point. What is then the symbolic implication of the magical drug that could revive the dead? It is the ultimate moral wisdom enabling one to tell the virtuous from the evil as Green Dragon has characterized it: "Its effect will depend on whether the nature of the individual is good or bad. If it is good, he will come to life as soon as it is lighted; if evil, you must go on heating it for a long time, and in the end he will revive" (*Chubian* 20.250; Shadick, 228). At the end of the original novel, precisely at the moment when Lao Can's traveling is supposedly becoming most "public"—he is carrying out his official duty trying to capture the culprits in a murder case and to revive the murdered—the reader is cautioned against reading this episode too literally and is reminded through references to Lao Can's individual moral qualities that this public journey might have deep personal implications, which will be fully articulated in the more autobiographical sequel.

FROM PUBLIC JUSTICE TO PERSONAL SALVATION

At the end of the original novel, it is suggested that Lao Can is now a "pilgrim" who has acquired the "scriptures" or who has attained the ultimate moral discrimination. The travels Lao Can has so far undertaken are now to be seen as part of a long journey, which is not only a moral crusade for public justice but also a personal pilgrimage of self-cultivation. This impression of the changing nature of the "travels" in the original novel will be reinforced if the reader relates it to the conclusion in chapter 9 of the sequel: there, Lao Can dreams that his body radiates a special fragrance, a sign that he has become enlightened. What is only subtly suggested at the end of the original novel will bear itself out more fully in the sequel.

Lao Can continues to travel in the sequel; however, the narrative focus is now *explicitly* on self-cultivation and personal enlightenment. Unlike the original novel, which starts with Lao Can wandering as an itinerant doctor seeking to cure people's illnesses (redressing public injustice), the sequel begins with Lao Can's journey back to Jiangnan, or the lower Yangtze region (presumably a journey toward the autobiographical protagonist's hometown, thus more personal). The journey in the sequel also starts out with sightseeing. Lao Can and the family of his friend, De Huisheng, are touring Mount Tai. Repeating the pattern of the original novel, the sightseeing nature of the journey gradually changes to something more serious: it is now a journey to seek personal enlightenment. The central event in Lao Can's Mount Tai trip is the encounter with the charismatic nun/courtesan Yiyun in the famous convent Doumu Gong.[18] The main story of the first six chapters of the sequel is how this nun has attained her "awakening."

The reader learns that a local bully has threatened to shut down the convent if one of the nuns does not accede to his demands. All this enrages Lao Can and De Huisheng. However, this time Lao Can's intervention is not necessary since

De Huisheng is an official from the central government *(jingguan)*. Instead of Lao Can writing letters to the governor, as is often the case in the original novel, De Huisheng sends a letter directly to the magistrate. Later the matter is easily resolved when De Huisheng threatens to report the matter to his superior. However, the casual manner in which the whole incident is mentioned and quickly resolved only serves to underscore how the sequel's narrative focus has shifted to something different. Furthermore, in the sequel the subtle balance between the stance of an insider and that of an outsider, which Lao Can tried so hard to maintain in the original novel, is no longer that important, since the main concern is now with seeking individual enlightenment. Significantly, in the sequel Lao Can no longer travels as an itinerant doctor. He is now mainly addressed as Second Master Tie (Tie Er laoye). Here the bipolar concept of outsider and insider, if still relevant, seems to have acquired new significance: the reader is supposed to realize that the distinction between insider and outsider is something one is supposed to transcend when the ultimate enlightenment is achieved, as in the case of the young nun Yiyun.

One thing Lao Can continues to do in the sequel is "listen to stories." In the original novel Lao Can has to be a good listener during his investigative journey. He is the audience to long stories about the river flood (its disastrous impact on the families of Cuihua and Cuihuan) and the murder case of the Jia family. Cuihua's and Huang Renrui's telling of these stories during that night, which is once interrupted by a fire, takes up almost four chapters in the original novel (chaps. 13–16; Hsia considers it "the longest night in traditional Chinese literature").[19] Here in the sequel (hereafter *Erbian*) the reader is again invited to listen to a long story along with the characters, although this time it is a much more personal story, a nun's monologue on her unfulfilled love, which takes up almost three chapters (*Erbian*, chaps. 3–5). As if to underscore the similarity between the "listening" in the original novel and here in the sequel, there is also much fuss about whose bedding should be where before the storyteller and the listeners finally settle down for the night. However, here the issue of bedding no longer implies a possible arrangement between a prostitute and her client.

Like the two prostitutes who tell Lao Can their stories in the original novel, Yiyun, as a nun, is in the equally questionable profession of entertaining male customers. The candidness with which she reveals the secrets of her private life —her abortive love affair—to two new acquaintances is amazing for a woman at that time. This could only be considered a testimony to the "awakening" she has achieved. Unlike Cuihua's story in the original novel, which is about a girl from a good family being forced into prostitution, Yiyun's story is about how a young nun is able to stay out of "prostitution" by keeping herself "clean" in a compromising environment and eventually achieves her ultimate awakening. However, her unfulfilled love must be a precondition to this achievement. Yiyun once was infatuated (*shangmo; Erbian* 3.281–282) with Ren sanye (Third Master Ren), but she could not marry him because of his mother's objections and because of other factors (among them the fact that he already had a wife and concubine). For an extended period of time, Yiyun did not know what she should do. During a long, emotional roller-coaster ride, she weighed every option available but found none that worked. Yiyun's long "confession" of her unfulfilled love is full of words such as *"xiang"* (think or imagine), *"youxiang"* (think again or imagine again) and *"meng"* (dreaming). Her story is virtually a monologue on the workings of her own subjective mind, her constant imagining and reimagining of what others would do if she did or did not do certain things.

What her audience and the novel's reader are presented with is a subtle psychological picture of a woman whose mind is in "turmoil" *(xinluan)*, a picture of the "the monkey of the mind and the horse of the will" *(xinyuan yima)* running wild, to use the Buddhist proverbial phrase. All of Yiyun's problems seem to have resulted from the confusion in her own mind. Then she had a dream in which an old man told her,

> "Yiyun! Yiyun! You originally have great potential but you've lost it and become bedeviled because of your mortal desires and passions. Today the light is shining on you and your wisdom is reemerging. Why don't you take up the sword of wisdom to sever your mortal devilish ties."
> I replied quickly: "Yes, yes! But my name is Huayun [Beautiful Clouds] not Yiyun [Ethereal Clouds]." "That was your name when you were deluded but when you are awakened you should be called Yiyun," the old man said.
>
> I was so shocked that I was in a cold sweat. I woke up and suddenly felt that all the desires and passions were swept away from me. From that time on, I changed my name to Yiyun. (*Erbian* 4.297)

Yiyun was suddenly enlightened *(dunwu)*, and the essence of her story seems to have been captured in the famous Buddhist aphorism, "realizing the emptiness of reality via experiencing reality *(youse rukong)*," as suggested by the title of chapter 3, "The Initial Chan Buddhist Truth Is Acquired via Sexual Passion."[20] Although a woman, Yiyun as a novelistic character may have autobiographical implications for the author. Many scholars have called attention to Liu E's close ties to the syncretic religious movement during the late Qing known as the Taigu school (Taigu xuepai). The story of Yiyun's religious enlightenment can be read as an illustration of the teachings of this school as understood by Liu E. For example, when Cuihuan decides to follow Yiyun's example to become a Buddhist nun, Lao Can's congratulatory remark is interesting: "I congratulate you on transcending this mundane life and entering the holy way *(chaofan rushing)*" (*Erbian* 6.315). Here "transcending the mundane life and entering the holy way" was one of the four "instructions" *(xunyan)* a master/teacher of the Taigu school could give to his disciple during the elaborate ritual of "paying homage to the teacher" *(yeshi li)* when he formally accepted students. This phrase was supposed to represent the highest "evaluation" the teacher/master could make with regard to a new disciple. The other three instructions (representing relatively lower evaluations) are also mentioned indirectly in the sequel. It was said that Liu E himself had received the highest evaluation as instruction from his teacher/master Li Longchuan (1808–

1885) when he went through this ritual.²¹ In fact, Yiyun's lengthy account of her "confused" mind reminds people of Li Longchuan's Buddhist characterization of the disturbance of the human mind as the source of erroneous thinking *(xin shi wangxiang).*²² Consequently, Yiyun's and Cuihuan's entering the way could also be read as a "metaphorical" reference to the author's pride at his own achievement in pursuit of religious enlightenment.

Interestingly enough, Lao Can is not part of the audience when Yiyun is telling her long story of her awakening. His absence here in the sequel forms an interesting parallel to his more conspicuous and much longer absence in the original novel where Shen Ziping travels to Peach Blossom Mountain. In the original novel, Shen Ziping undertakes the trip to the mountain in order to meet the martial art specialist whom Lao Can has recommended for the position of constable. The account of this trip, which takes up approximately four chapters, forms a distinct part that does not appear to be well integrated with the rest of the novel. This is also the section where Lao Can as the novel's sole protagonist is conspicuously absent. Many critics have considered this section a main structural flaw in the novel. Obviously, this is not part of Lao Can's travels as the title of the novel suggests. Hsia has come up with an interesting explanation. He considers Lao Can and Yellow Dragon as representing two different aspects of the authorial self: one more practical, the other more reclusive and more philosophical. The author, Hsia suggests, tries to avoid having these two characters confront each other directly in the novel. This, according to Hsia, is the reason our novelist takes the trouble to have Shen Ziping instead of Lao Can himself undertake this trip.

> To maintain the continuity of Lao Can's travels, as I have earlier suggested, the author could have easily dispensed with the character Shen Ziping and assigned his hero the journey to the Peach Blossom Mountain. But he could not do [so] because he did not want a confrontation of the two aspects of his self [referring to Lao Can and Yellow Dragon] that are in unreconciled conflict. A more naïve person without the mature experience of Lao Can will be far more receptive to the discourses of the Yellow Dragon and Yugu.²³

Basically agreeing with Hsia's interpretation, Leo Ou-fan Lee elaborates,

> But the most important contribution of Lao Can, although it is rendered indirectly, lies in expounding his own philosophical beliefs. It seems to me that the real self of Lao Can and of Liu E is revealed in the middle chapters—truly the heart of the narrative. This is where Liu E lays bare the inner essence of his being—a religious sense of serenity and spontaneity derived from the syncretic teaching of the Taigu school and explained through personas of Yugu and Yellow Dragon. I fully endorse Professor Hsia's insight that Yellow Dragon represents the author's ideal self, but I disagree with his thesis that the two portraits of the self—Lao Can and Yellow Dragon—are in "unreconciled conflict." Yellow Dragon's prophetic faith in Chinese culture and Lao Can's despondency over the

fate of China are not necessarily in contradiction. On the contrary, one might argue that in an era fraught with uncertainties it was more imperative for Liu E to affirm his "spiritual essence" in the face of external adversities. The more Lao Can ponders the fate of China, the more he needs Yellow Dragon's spiritual faith. Lao Can and Yellow Dragon represent, it seems to me, two *complementary* sides of Liu E's fictional self—one "outer" and the other "inner."[24]

The sequel seems to have both confirmed and complicated the above analyses offered by Hsia and Lee. Artistically, these chapters on Shen Ziping's trip are indeed a structural "flaw," and this should become more apparent since in the sequel the author is able to avoid repeating this kind of "mistake." Lao Can's absence in this section of the sequel is much more plausible as well as more natural since it would be unlikely for Yiyun to tell such a personal story about her private love to a male audience, although Mrs. De would later relay the story to Lao Can. Yiyun's story, though quite long, does not disrupt the narrative flow of the sequel. The reader probably even does not notice the absence of Lao Can until the narrator mentions how he has learned of the story through Mrs. De.

In the original novel, Shen Ziping's encounter with Yugu and Yellow Dragon indeed provides the author with the opportunity to reveal the other side of his self—his close ties to the so-called Taigu school. While I agree with Lee that Lao Can and Yellow Dragon may indeed represent two complementary sides of the author, there is still tension (though not necessarily "irreconcilable") between these two sides. It is telling that the novelist has to go out of his way to devise Shen Ziping's trip in order to avoid a direct encounter between Lao Can and Yellow Dragon. The implications of Yellow Dragon as an autobiographical character, however, will be complicated in the sequel with the appearance of his "younger brother" Red Dragon, or Chi Longzi.

> "I have heard," replied Yiyun, "that there were three brothers, of whom this Red Dragon is the youngest and the most romantic *(fangdan buji)*. His brothers, Green Dragon and Yellow Dragon, are austere characters, although they are really very kind at heart. One can tell immediately from their appearance that they are pious souls. As for this Red Dragon, you cannot make head or tail of him, for he gambles and eats and drinks and indulges in philandering with women. He mixes with all classes of people, from officials and scholars to merchants and common people. . . . People respect him because he studied under the same master as Green Dragon and Yellow Dragon, but very few people really understand him. . . . I asked him, 'I hear that you have quite a few sweethearts in the brothels, and I suppose it is all a shadow without the substance, as it is between you and me?' And he said, 'I observe rules in the spirit and not in the flesh. What I do all depends on the person I am dealing with. For instance, if you are pure, then I am pure with you, and if you are impure, then I am impure with you. But I cannot do anything that will injure others or myself—this is my spiritual asceticism. On the other hand, if

both parties think it is all right, then no harm is done anybody and so why not? That is why I do not observe physical asceticism.'" (*Erbian* 5.306–307)[25]

As some critics have pointed out, the brief mention of Red Dragon in the sequel is fraught with autobiographical significance.[26] The relationship between Red Dragon and his brothers parallels that between Liu E and his senior comrades of the Taigu school, Huang Baonian (1845–1924) and Jiang Wentian (ca. 1845–1909). Liu, Huang, and Jiang all were disciples of Li Longchuan, who was in turn a disciple of Zhou Gu (d. 1832; also known as Zhou Taigu), the founder of the semireligious Taigu school.[27] In the first chapter of the sequel (*Erbian* 1.261), Lao Can, quoting Yellow Dragon, mentions that the three brothers Yellow Dragon, Green Dragon, and Red Dragon are all disciples of Zhou Er (apparently a pun on Zhou Taigu). Red Dragon is born in the year of *dingsi* (1857), Green Dragon the year of *yisi* (1845). This is significant since Liu E himself was also born in 1857, while both Huang Baonian and Jiang Wentian were born in 1845.[28] What is implied here is that Red Dragon, like the author himself, is a "free spirit," while Yellow Dragon and Green Dragon, like Huang and Jiang are "austere characters," although all three are "faithful" disciples of their common teacher/master.[29]

Furthermore, Liu E had claimed elsewhere that he and Huang were declared by Li Longchuan to be the "chosen two" to transmit the *dao*, despite the fact that Huang was twelve years Liu's senior.[30] However, the relationship between these two "brothers" was not always free of problems, as attested to by some of the extant correspondence between them. In one of his letters to Liu E, Huang accused Liu of being arrogant *(feiyang bahu)* and "running wild" for ten years *(kuangben shicai)*. More specifically, Huang believed that during the ten years since they last saw each other all Liu did was satisfy his various personal desires *(dayu)* for material comforts and sensual pleasures.[31] Elsewhere, Huang even specifically referred to Liu as a "negative" model, warning his own disciples against committing similar mistakes.[32] In his own defense, Liu, it seems, avoided answering some of the specific charges, such as the accusation regarding his pursuit of sensual pleasures. Instead, he insisted that all his entrepreneurial efforts were for the purpose of "nurturing the people" *(yang tianxian)*. These efforts, he insisted, although quite different from what Huang was doing—"educating the people" *(jiao tianxia)*—served the same purpose and was consistent with the teachings of the Taigu school. In his defense, Liu appealed to the authority of Confucius by quoting his remark that "[t]he Gentleman agrees with others without being an echo *(junzi he er butong)*."[33] Interestingly enough, in chapter 10 of the original novel, the reader, along with Shen Ziping, is treated to the harmonious music played by three fairy-like girls; this is probably meant to be a literalization of *he er butong* (being harmonious without being identical).[34] However, presented in the original novel as the personification of the idea of "nurturing the people," Lao Can as an autobiographical character is not an effective "vindication" of Liu E's own "free" lifestyle. In the original novel, Lao Can is never shown expressing interest in women or wine:

he agrees to take Cuihuan as a concubine reluctantly only to rescue her from prostitution.

To the extent that Red Dragon is another autobiographical character in the sequel, he is presented here to further vindicate the author and defend his "romantic" lifestyle. Yiyun's extravagant praise of him should be read in this context. According to her, Red Dragon is the youngest among the three brothers (just like Liu E was the youngest among Li Longchuan's three favorite disciples) and the most romantic *(fangdan buji)*, but very few people truly understand him.[35] Yiyun also mentions that although she and Red Dragon have slept in the same bed, nothing actually happened between them. Deeply impressed, Mrs. De compares Red Dragon to Liuxia Hui, the moral paragon who could remain undisturbed even with a beautiful woman sitting on his lap. Yiyun, however, much to the astonishment of everyone else, insists that Red Dragon would feel insulted if he were compared to Liuxia Hui (*Erbian* 5.305–306). The implied message is that while Liuxia Hui may be "asexual," Red Dragon is far superior morally precisely because he feels attracted to women and yet is able to be "pure" when needed. Red Dragon is able to exercise both "spiritual asceticism" and "physical asceticism" according to the situation. Philandering and drinking wine did not necessarily prevent Red Dragon from achieving "buddhahood."[36]

THE GENDERED AWAKENING AND SELF-CELEBRATION

What, then, are the implications of the story of Yiyun's awakening in relation to this image of Red Dragon? Both Yiyun and Red Dragon share the ability to adapt perfectly to specific situations despite, or because of, their enlightened status.

> Recently I have decided to divide my personality into two beings. The first is called "the Yiyun of this world" *(zhushi de Yiyun)*. As a nun in this Doumu kong I will do whatever I ought to do and talk to whoever wants to talk with me. If he wants me to drink with him at dinner, then I drink with him, and if he wants to hug or embrace me, I will let him hug and embrace me, no matter who he is—except in the matter of sleeping with a man, where I draw the line. The other self is called "the Yiyun of the other world" *(chushi de Yiyun)*, who likes to spend her leisure hours associating with the great founders of Confucianism, Taoism and Buddhism, and feels contented and happy watching the changing drama enacted by the sun and the moon and forces of the universe. (*Erbian* 5.300)[37]

Here Yiyun, like Red Dragon, has acquired a "double identity" that enables her to be both an "insider" and an "outsider" because ultimately the difference between the two is meaningless to the enlightened such as Yiyun.

> *The Diamond Sutra (Jingang jing)* says "no consciousness of self and no consciousness of [any] others *(wu woxiang wu renxiang)*." All the

troubles of this world come from this distinction between self and others.... All our sorrows and our sufferings come from the idea that we are women. If we only see that there is no difference between men and women, we shall have already enjoyed the bliss of paradise. (*Erbian* 5.298)³⁸

However, compared with Red Dragon, Yiyun, it seems, has to set a limit for her theory of "no distinctions" when it comes to actual practice. She has to draw the line when it comes to sex, while Red Dragon does not appear to be constrained by such a limit at all. No matter how enlightened Yiyun has become, she cannot change her gender identity, and she has to remain "clean" as a virgin to "authenticate" her status as the awakened despite her insistence that there is no difference between men and women. Red Dragon, as a man, is entitled to the benefit of "spiritual asceticism," which, however, does not prevent him from being sexually involved with women. How wonderful this idea of *fangbian* (*upaya* or expediency) is for men such as Red Dragon! He can ascend to the Western Paradise while enjoying sex and wine to his heart's content. Strictly speaking, Yiyun, as a woman, could also exercise "spiritual asceticism," but she has to resort to "physical asceticism" when it comes to "real sex." Here the reader may recall Yugu's talk about desire in chapter 9 of the original novel. Criticizing the Song neo-Confucian "repressive" view of desire and citing the first love poem in the Confucian classic *Shijing* (The book of songs) as evidence, Yugu asks, "Can we really say this only illustrates heavenly reason *(tianli)* and not a mere human desire *(renyu)?*" (*Chubian* 9.110; Shadick, 101) However, in the sequel, the reader finds that the first half of the couplet title of chapter 5 reads, "The wise Yiyun has completely eradicated her desires." It seems that Yugu's talk about the "legitimacy" of desire applies only to men such as Red Dragon, while Yiyun, as a woman, is supposed to fall into a different category. That is why Yiyun is repeatedly praised for her "cleanness" and "non-desire" and is regarded as a "marvel" given the brothel-like environment of the convent she finds herself in.

> "Why it is like finding a wild orchid in a secluded valley," said Lao Can. "It is hardly believable that one should find such a cultivated person in such a place, much less to find it in a young nun who looks almost like a prostitute. It is indeed true that the lotus flower grows out of mud, as the ancient people say." (*Erbian* 5.306)³⁹

Yiyun's enlightened status has to be authenticated with her virgin body, or she has to change herself to an "asexual" being in order to become enlightened, while men such as Red Dragon and Lao Can have only to subscribe to the rules of "spiritual asceticism" and still enjoy sexual bliss. Their male sexuality remains an important part of their identity as the enlightened. Consequently, Yiyun, as an "autobiographical metaphor" for the author, apparently has its gendered limitations, which, in turn, betray the "hypocrisy" inherent in the author's overall agenda of "self-vindication."

Read in this context, Cuihuan's decision to take the Buddhist order may also have "autobiographical" implications. Obviously, Cuihuan gives Lao Can an opportunity to assume the role of a civilian knight-errant *(wenxia)*. Yet his agreeing to take Cuihuan as a concubine merely for the purpose of rescuing her from prostitution is meant to differentiate him from the stereotypical image of a traditional knight-errant, who would never accept his female beneficiary's expression of gratitude in the form of offering herself through marriage (such as Tie Zhongyu in the early Qing novel *Haoqiu zhuan*).[40] However, the author apparently felt that Lao Can, despite his "indifference" to his self-image as a knight-errant, has to be vindicated further in the sequel. Cuihuan's decision to become a nun after being so impressed with Yiyun conveniently "immunizes" Lao Can against any accusation that he has taken a prostitute as concubine under the excuse of saving her.[41] Compared with Cuihuan, who needs others to save her *(tali)*, Yiyun has been able to save herself from "prostitution" on her own *(zili)*, consistent with the Chan Buddhist spirit the latter is supposed to embody.[42]

While some scholars have emphasized that the Taigu school was a syncretistic religious movement,[43] several descendents of members of this school have argued that it was mainly a school of Confucianism that also incorporated elements from Buddhism and Taoism, rather than a syncretistic religion.[44] However, both of these understandings of the teachings of the Taigu school, it seems to me, have found expression in the novel: in her "lecture" to Shen Ziping, Yugu first quotes her father as saying, "The three schools—Confucianism, Buddhism, Taoism—are like the signboards hung outside three shops. In reality they are all sellers of mixed provisions; they all sell fuel, rice, oil, salt. But the shop belonging to the Confucian family is bigger" (*Chubian* 9.103; Shadick, 97–98). Then she makes a fine discrimination among the "three schools."

> Their similarity consists in encouraging man to be good, leading man to be unselfish. . . . Only Confucianism is thoroughly unselfish. . . . Now the Buddhists and Taoists indeed were narrow-minded. They feared lest later generations should not honor their teachings, so they talked a lot about heaven and hell in order to frighten people. This is partly intended to spur people to well-doing and to this extent they were unselfish. But when they teach that even to say that you believe their teachings is to have all your sins blotted out, while not to believe their teachings is to be possessed by devils and when dead to go down to hell—in this they are narrow and self-interested. (*Chubian* 9.103–104; Shadick, 98)

Here Confucianism is obviously presented as "the best" while both Buddhism and Taoism are found "imperfect." This, however, begins to change in the sequel, which is increasingly dominated by the ideology of Chan Buddhism, as the phrase *"zheng chuchan"* in the title of chapter 3 clearly suggests.[45] This should not come as a surprise since the original novel, as I have argued, is mainly about Lao Can's crusade for public justice (it is more "this worldly," or *zhushi*, to use Yiyun's term) and thus is more "Confucian," while the sequel focuses more on personal salvation and enlightenment and, therefore, is more Buddhist and more *chushi*, to use Yiyun's words again.

In chapter 1 of the sequel, when asked by Lao Can if heaven and hell exist, Yellow Dragon launches into a lecture. The gist of his theory is that this is actually a question of whether one is enlightened enough. One will witness the existence of heaven and hell when he has achieved tranquility and has emptied his mind (*xuxin jingqi*; *Erbian* 1.262). Here the reader is presented with a view of heaven and hell rather different from that of Yugu as mentioned before. Of course, the last three chapters of the sequel are about nothing but the netherworld, a very un-Confucian view of life after death.

These last three chapters are a lengthy account of Lao Can's dream journey in the underworld. In his dream he finds his self divided into two beings. Seeing his body still lying in bed, Lao Can comes to the realization that "[t]he person who is standing is my true self *(zhenwo)*, while what is lying there in bed is [just] my body" (*Erbian* 7.322). This parallels the double identity of Red Dragon as well as of Yiyun. Later, when Lao Can is being tried before King Yama, he is asked whether he has committed any sins of debauchery *(fan yinlü)*. Lao Can confesses, "Yes. Because I traveled a lot, I went to brothels quite often whenever I felt bored" (*Erbian* 7.326). This is, however, inconsistent with the Lao Can the reader has encountered in the original novel, in which he claims "I have never done this kind of thing before" when his friend Huang Renhui insists on sending Cuihuan's bedding to his room (*Chubian* 13.164).

Obviously, this inconsistency is the result of the enhanced autobiographical agenda of the sequel. Patronizing brothels is an important issue in Lao Can's underworld journey, and he is surprised to find that there are also prostitutes in the underworld. The explanation his friend gives him is, to say the least, ironic: these prostitutes in their previous lives were all women from good families. Knowing that their husbands had been patronizing brothels, these women, instead of trying to reform their husbands through wifely virtue, began to cuss at and berate the prostitutes and their husbands. The very fact that the husbands and prostitutes were already cussed at and berated in their lives will make them less "sinful," while the wives, as punishment for their outbursts, were sentenced in their next lives to be prostitutes to atone for the sin of cursing. Lao Can further asks if patronizing brothels in the underworld is considered a sin. The answer is that it is only a minor offense that can be easily redeemed or even canceled out (*Erbian* 9.343–344). Consequently, patronizing prostitutes is less "sinful" than cursing or berating prostitutes or those husbands who patronize them!

This discourse on "prostitution" becomes even more bizarre: Lao Can is further told that enjoying the services of a courtesan in the underworld is actually considered an act of compassion or mercy *(cibei)* since it will grant that prostitute an opportunity to atone for her sin of cursing her husband in her previous life (*Erbian* 9.345)! Here the reader begins to wonder if he or she is reading a chauvinistic "apology for patronizing brothels" *(piaoji bian)* and to doubt if at this moment the novelist might have been totally overwhelmed by his own wish to celebrate his autobiographical image as a romantic. It seems that the author's autobiographical urge for vindication got the better of his position as novelist in the last three chapters of the sequel, where Lao Can is literally put on trial and his "innocence" is resoundingly vindicated. According to King Yama, a sin much more serious than patronizing prostitutes is the so-called "oral crime" *(kouguo),* or "slandering." Lao Can even witnesses the excruciating torture a *kouguo* "criminal" is being put through. King Yama offers Lao Can a lengthy explanation as to why this "sin" merits the most severe punishment (*Erbian* 8.329–335). Obviously, King Yama's anger at "slandering" is meant to be a veiled reference to the author's own fury at his being repeatedly "slandered" by others. Liu E, because of his involvement with foreign companies and diplomats, had been accused by many of being a *hanjian* (traitor), a fact already alluded to in the allegorical dream in chapter 1 of the original novel, where some people on the sinking ship called Lao Can a traitor when he tried to help them. Here again in an allegorical dream almost at the end of the sequel (as we have it now), the author's exasperation at being "slandered" finally boils over.[46] Obviously, in the sequel the author feels that he has to "fight back" against those slanderers. The narrator cannot help taking a shot at those *liuxuesheng* (students who were studying in Japan; *Erbian* 8.329). Presumably this is because some of these students once accused the author of being a "traitor" who sold out China's natural resources to foreigners after they learned about the controversy surrounding Liu E's involvement in a foreign company's mining project in Sanxi Province.[47]

However, our novelist's self-vindication does not stop here. At the end of this nine-chapter sequel, Lao Can is congratulated because it is said there is a special fragrance radiating from his person, and he is told that he is soon going to ascend onto the Western Paradise. His friends tell him that as someone who has attained buddhahood, he is sure to bring bliss to them with his visit! Here self-vindication is simply turned into unabashed self-celebration (no wonder some of Liu E's descendants were reluctant to have the last three chapters republished).[48] The original novel starts with Lao Can's dream, and the sequel ends with another of his dreams. While self-vindication is indeed an implicit agenda in the dream at the beginning of the original novel, the main concern is the fate of China. In the "final" dream of the sequel, however, the overriding concern is personal vindication and even self-glorification. This "journey" from the public to the personal and from self-vindication to self-celebration tells the reader much about the nature of these nine chapters as an autographic sequel.

Despite many of their apparent differences, Liu E's autobiographical strategies remind us of those of Cao Xueqin, the author of *Honglou meng,* and his thinly veiled self-celebration in the sequel reminds us of Xia Jingqu's (1705–1787) much more exaggerated self-glorification in his own *Yesou puyan* (The humble words of an old rustic). Both *Honglou meng* and *Lao Can youji* have a single "autobiographical" protagonist, and yet the representation of the authorial self does not confine itself to that of the protagonist. That is to say, several other characters are also "appropriated" to represent different aspects of the complex authorial self. In *Lao Can youji,* for example, besides the apparent autobiographical protagonist Lao Can, Yellow Dragon, Red Dragon, and even Yiyun might be capable of functioning as "metaphors" for the different aspects of the authorial self. While we do not see in him the kind of strange mixture of romantic *daoxue* (an orthodox neo-Confucian) as in Xia Jingqu, Liu E, as an autobiographical novelist, exhibits almost the same zeal for self-celebration, albeit on a much smaller scale and in a less exaggerated manner.[49]

The ever-present autobiographical agenda in *Lao Can youji* sometimes makes one wonder how accurate is Liu Dashen's oft-referred to testimony that his father never took the writing of the novel seriously. According to Liu Dashen's account in his essay "Guanyu *Lao Can youji*"—which, because of the paucity of relevant information, has been regarded as the most important and "authoritative" source of "facts" on the writing of the novel—Liu E wrote this novel merely as a way to offer financial help to a friend in financial distress. We learn further from Liu Dashen that the friend, Lian Mengqing, stopped the serialization of the novel in *Xiuxiang xiaoshuo* when he found out that the editor had failed to abide by their mutual agreement not to change any words in the manuscript. Why should Lian Mengqing care so much if the original author took his work so lightly? Or did Liu E himself get upset, or was Liu E the person who asked his friend to stop the serialization (Liu Dashen did not inform us what role, if any, was played by Liu E in the abrupt end to the serialization)? Did Liu Dashen's open "disdain" for *baiguan* (fiction; a term he used[50]) affect his account of some of the "facts" associated with his father's writing of the novel (he acknowledged he had objected to the republication of the sequel)?[51] Liu Dashen's attitude seems to have changed when he was approached by Harold Shadick, an American scholar who was interested in translating his father's novel into English. One of the immediate reasons for Liu Dasheng to break his long silence and write the lengthy article about his father and his novel, he seems to suggest, was a foreigner's *(yangren)* expressed interest in his father's casual writing *(youxi bimo)*.[52]

Even if we accept Liu Dashen's account of Liu E's initial motivation for writing the novel, the latter might have become more "serious" about his novel after it had unexpectedly won great popularity. Nothing appears more serious than his own preface to the original novel, which is about "sadness" and "weeping" and which he wrote sometime after he had finished many chapters of the original novel.[53] Of course, the strongest evidence against the view that *Lao Can youji* was a "casual" work was the tremendous pains with which the author wrote his own "life" into the novel and with which he tried to rewrite that "life" by erasing his memory of failures and frustrations, as I have so far sought to demonstrate. This is a novel about "memory" and the frustrations of "being unable to forget" *(buneng wang)*, as the author explicitly confessed at the end of his preface to the sequel (*Erbian* p. 258).[54] It is this desperate urge to "forget" that turned the last part of the sequel (chaps. 7–9) into a "dream" of self-celebration. This is especially ironic when the reader learns in hindsight that the author had to *travel* thousands of miles only to die in forced exile in Xinjiang just two years after he wrote the final "dream journey" undertaken by his autobiographical protagonist Lao Can (his ascendance to Western paradise as a Buddhist saint).[55] What has probably saved this "almost-too-happy conclusion" from turning the novel into a mockery of the author himself are that Lao Can is only *dreaming* of ascending to the paradise, as well as the sequel's Buddhist sentiment emphasized in its preface that life is nothing but a dream.

In *Lao Can youji* there are indeed a few moments of self-mockery on the part of the autobiographical protagonist, and yet they never develop into the sort of serious effort at self-examination *(ziwofanxing)* or self-scrutiny *(ziwo jiepou)* that we encounter in Lu Xun's fictional works some years later.[56] Through the voice of Cuihuan, the author satirizes those who habitually complain about their talents being neglected in their poems (a perennial theme in traditional literati literature); the character Huang Renrui even declares that poems are nothing but lies (*Chubian* 13.160–163). However, Lao Can continues to "produce" poems in the novel, apparently believing his poems are a different sort. In the sequel, during his visit to his sister, he is soon invited by his brother-in-law to compose poems on a flower that is in full blossom. Lao Can "invents" an excuse for continuing the show of his poetic talents: "Human dung could usually serve as manure to aid the growth of plants. But human dung might be too strong for this kind of delicate flower. Why don't we compose some poems as if they were just farts that could be used as manure for the flower?" (*Erbian* 7.320–321) Although this sort of humorous self-mockery might have saved the autobiographical protagonist from appearing too conceited, unfortunately it never helps to create between the implied author and the protagonist Lao Can a distance significant enough to sustain serious self-reflection, which could have otherwise turned *Lao Can youji* into an even more compelling autobiographical novel.

Erbian, as an autographic sequel, continues as well as accentuates the autobiographical trend in the original novel. While making the original novel's autobiographical agenda more transparent, the sequel also compels the reader to reevaluate many of its autobiographical implications. That is to say, *Erbian,* by virtue of its being an autographic sequel, forces the reader to re-read the entire original novel. An autographic sequel is a *xushu* that literally "rewrites" its precursor text by virtue of the fact that both texts are supposed to have been authored by the same person. Unlike the "rewriting" performed by an allographic sequel, this rewriting project is carried out in an autographic sequel with the full legitimacy of a "single" authorial intention. What makes *Erbian* particularly interesting as a work of *xushu* is that it is not only autographic, but also autobiographical, while the former is the precondition of the latter. This should become significant if we compare Liu E's autographic sequel with some of the allographic sequels to *Lao Can youji* produced by other writers.[57] While a detailed comparison is out of the question here, suffice it to say that these allographic sequels, as re-readings or rewritings of *Chubian,* tend to downplay the autobiographical implications of the parent novel.[58] Written by the same author who had produced the original novel, an autographic sequel is almost guaranteed a total "victory" in competition with allographic (and therefore unauthorized) sequels. This is the main reason that Liu E's *Erbian* continues to be widely read, while all allographic sequels by other writers have long been forgotten, not necessarily because the latter are of lower quality. On the other hand, what makes *Erbian* a less typical sequel is the fact that the original novel lacks a clear closure thanks to its unique "picaresque" structure of a journey that does not have an ultimate destination—its protagonist can always resume his journey. Consequently, Liu E could afford to pay less attention to the "continuities" between the "first part" and the "second part," and he was allowed more freedom to pursue his new interest in his sequel.

As an autographic sequel, *Erbian* is significant in the history of Chinese *xushu*. It pointed to the changing fate of *xiaoshuo* in twentieth-century China, when many fiction writers became "professional" (although Liu E was not a professional writer) and when the social status of the fiction writer became much higher.

NOTES

1. Lu Xun, *Zhonguo xiaoshuo shilüe* (rpt. in *Lu Xun quanji*), 282–295. Using a broader concept in his essay "*The Travels of Lao Ts'an:* An Exploration of Its Art and Meaning," 41 and 50, Hsia argues that it is "China's first political novel." Hsia's essay hereafter will be referred to as "An Exploration."
2. Judging from the conclusion of chapter 9 of the sequel, which ends with the formulaic phrase "If you want to know what happens next, please listen to the story of the next chapter," *Lao Can youji*, 345, the sequel is supposed to continue. The discovery of the fifteen-page fragment of the manuscript by the author (known as *Waibian* or *Waibian cangao*) confirms his intention to "continue" the story of Lao Can. In this chapter I use the edition of *Lao Can youji* annotated by Yan Weiqing. It contains the text of the original novel, the sequel, and the fifteen-page manuscript that was posthumously published. I refer to the first twenty chapters of the original novel as *Chubian* and the nine-chapter sequel as *Erbian*, with chapter and page numbers in parentheses. According to the testimony of Liu Dashen, the son of Liu E, the sequel contained altogether fourteen chapters, although the extant *Tianjin riri xinwen* clipping shows that only nine chapters were serialized in that newspaper in 1907. See Liu Dashen, "Guanyu *Lao Can youji*"; Wei Shaochang, ed., *Lao Can youji ziliao*, 58; and Liu Houze's (Liu Dashen's son) note 8, *Lao Can youji ziliao*, 93–94. Given the information available so far, we probably will never be able to determine exactly how many chapters Liu E wrote or planned to write for his sequel. See also Liu Delong, Zhu Xi, and Liu Deping, *Liu E xiaozhuan*, 175; and Wong, "Notes on the Textual History of the *Lao Ts'an yu-chi*," 26–29.
3. Liu Dashen, "Guanyu *Lao Can youji*," 57–58.
4. See, e.g., Hsia, "An Exploration," 42.
5. See also Liu Delong, Zhu Xi, and Liu Deping, *Liu E xiaozhuan*, 167–170; and Wong, "Notes on the Textual History of the *Lao Ts'an yu-chi*," 29–32.
6. Liu Houze mentioned a complete two-volume *Tianjin riri xinwen* edition (in the book form, or *danxingben*), which, however, was undated; see Wei Shaochang, ed., *Lao Can youji ziliao*, 95, n. 11. A Ying also reported that he had in possession one volume of the *Tianjin riri xinwen* edition in the form of bound newspaper clippings (containing the first ten chapters), which, he speculated, was dated 1904, although there was no hard dating evidence, since the back of each page was covered with advertisements. A Ying, "Guanyu '*Lao Can youji*' erti," 279–289.

7. See Wei Shaochang, ed., *Lao Can youji ziliao*, 94, n. 9.
8. The extant copy of the nine-chapter sequel in the form of newspaper clippings indicated that the serialization started from the tenth day of the seventh month (*qiyue*) and ended the sixth day of the tenth month (*shiyue*) of the thirty-third year of the Guangxu reign, or 1907. One extant copy is in the library of Kyoto University. Liu Houze also mentioned a copy of the nine-chapter sequel in the form of clippings once in the possession of his relatives; see Wei Shaochang, ed., *Lao Can youji ziliao*, 92.
9. Lu Xun, *Zhonguo xiaoshuo shilüe*, 288. However, Lu Xun did not provide evidence for his dating. The one-volume copy in A Ying's possession contained a preface, although A Ying did not give any evidence to support his 1904 dating; "Guanyu '*Lao Can youji*' erti," 279. See also Wong's discussion of the question when the original novel was probably completed, "Notes on the Textual History of *Lao Ts'an yu-chi*," 29–32.
10. Hsia commented on Liu E's preface to the original novel, "Jin Shengtan's preface to *Shuihu zhuan* has set the fashion for novelists to compose autobiographical statements tinged with melancholy, and Liu E's essay on weeping is a particularly famous product of that tradition." See Hsia, "An Exploration," 42. Hsia's observation is not completely accurate here. First, such mention of "melancholy" or "frustrations" as a reason for a novelist to write his book was already made by Li Zhi, as I discuss in chap. 1 of this volume. In fact, Jin Shengtan, in one of his prefaces to *Shuihou zhuan*, insisted on just the opposite: Shi Nai'an's writing of the novel had nothing to do with "melancholy" (although Jin did mention melancholy as a factor behind the writing of the novel elsewhere in his commentaries on the novel). See his "Du *Diwu Caizi shu* fa" and his general comment on "Xiezi," in *Jin Shengtan piping Shuihu zhuan*, 18 and 30; see also his interlineal comment on the character Lin Chong in 6.16, and his pre-chapter comment on 18.346. Furthermore, one thing Hsia has failed to point out is that the musings over the quick passage of time and life being like a dream in Liu E's preface to his sequel indeed bear great resemblance to Jin Shengtan's similar musings in his prefaces to his commentary edition of *Xixiang ji*. See "Xuyi" and "Xu'er," *Guanhua tang pi diwu caizishu Xixaing ji*, in *Jin Shengtan wenji*, 336–341.
11. During this period, many of his large-scale entrepreneurial projects failed miserably, and some of them landed him in political hot water. For example, in 1906 his textile factory went bankrupt, and the North Sea Trading Company he had set up for manufacturing fine salt for distribution in Korea also went under. He was also accused of involvement in criminal activities. Because of a land dispute, Liu E was accused by others of being a traitor who purchased the land at Pukou for foreign interests. See Liu Huisun, *Tieyun xiansheng nianpu changbian*, 112–139.
12. All the English translations of the *Chubian* quoted, unless otherwise noted, are from Shadick, trans., *The Travels of Lao Ts'an*. It is referred to parenthetically as "Shadick" followed by page number. I have converted all Wade-Giles romanizations in translations into *Hanyu pingyin*.
13. Cf. Holoch, "*The Travels of Laocan*: Allegorical Narrative."
14. "Tan'gong," in Sun Xidan, anno. and ed., *Liji jijie* 292; and Legge, trans., *Li Chi*, 1:190–191.
15. There are other symbolic references to the tiger as associated with the official world in the novel (*zhuadihu xuezi*, or the "tiger boots" [4.42]; *hubao feng*, or "the wind of tiger and leopard" [6.70]; and *ruhu*, or the "mother tiger" [10.124]). See also Hsia's brief discussion of the implications of the tiger image in the novel in "An Exploration," 56–57.
16. Cuihuan's name would later be changed to Huancui (as she is consistently called in the sequel) by Lao Can after she becomes his concubine. To be consistent I will refer to this character by her old name throughout this chapter.
17. See, e.g., Yan Weiqing's preface to his annotated edition of the novel, 37–38; Hsia, "An Exploration," 44; and Lee, "The Solitary Traveler," 285–286.

18. For a discussion of the tradition of *huachan* (Buddhist nuns serving as prostitutes) and especially the famous nuns of Mount Tai during the late Qing, see Cai Hongsheng, *Nigu tan,* 122–138.
19. Hsia, "An Exploration," 45.
20. Of course, the most famous discourse on achieving enlightenment (the realization of the emptiness of reality) via the full experience of reality *(youse rukong)* can be found in the first chapter of the eighteenth-century classic *Honglou meng;* see *Honglou meng* 1.6. Wai-yee Li suggests that this could be traced back to the cryptic passage on *se* and *kong* in the famous Heart sutra; see his *Enchantment and Disenchantment,* 177, note 32.
21. See Liu Delong, Zhu Xi, and Liu Deping, *Liu E xiaozhuan,* 80–81.
22. Li Longchuan, *Guanhai shanfang zhuisui lu,* ed. Huang Baonian, rpt. Fang Baochuan, comp., *Taigu xuepai yishu* (diyi ji), 3:26. More on Liu E's relationship with the so-called Taigu school later.
23. Hsia, "An Exploration," 53.
24. Lee, "The Solitary Traveler," 287. See also Shuen-fu Lin, "The Last Classic Chinese Novel," for a discussion of "harsh reality" vs. "lyric vision" in the novel.
25. English translation (with modification) from "The Nun of Taishan," in Lin Yutang, trans., *Widow, Nun and Courtesan,* 162–163.
26. See Wang Xuejun, *Liu E yu Lao Can youji,* 109–113; and "Liu E de zibian zhuang—*Lao Can youji,*" 394–408. Wang provides a detailed analysis to show on what specific issues the author is trying to vindicate himself in the novel.
27. For a study of Zhou Taigu's life and thought, see Chen Liao, *Zhou Taigu pingzhuan.* Chen (3–5) argues that Zhou Taigu was born in 1762. This study also contains extensive discussions of various important disciples of Zhou Taigu.
28. The fact that Liu E was very conscious of the significance of these years of "birth" is confirmed in his letter to Huang Baonian in which he quoted their teacher as saying that the two born in the years referred to with the character *si* are destined to transmit his *dao (ersi chuandao);* see "Zhi Huang Baonian," in Liu Delong, Zhu Xi, and Liu Deping, *Liu E ji Lao Can youji ziliao,* 300. However, Liu E's interpretation of Li Longchuan's words *"ersi chuandao"* has been questioned by some scholars. In his "'Ersi chuandao' kaobian: Liu E yu Taigu xuepai guanxi lunkao zhiyi," Wang Xuejun argues that by *"ersi"* (the two born in the year of *si*) Li Longchuan must have meant Huang Baonian and Jiang Wentian. Other scholars, however, have argued that Wang's suggestion cannot be possible, since Jiang Wentian was born in 1843 rather than 1845. For example, Chen Liao believes that Jiang was born in 1843; see his "Jiang Wentian pingzhuan," in *Zhou Taigu pingzhuan,* 155. Consequently, the determination of the birth year of Jiang Wentian becomes a crucial issue. For a brief review of different views on this issue, see Fang Baochuan, "Jiang Wentian ji qi zhushu," in *Taigu xuepai yishu* (di'er ji), 4:1–2; and for Wang Xuejun's rebuttal, see his "Jiang Wentian yu Li Longchuan," esp. 91–94.

    Curiously enough, it is also mentioned here in the sequel that Yellow Dragon is born in the year of *jisi,* which could be either 1809 or 1869. However, since Red Dragon (born in 1857) is said to be the youngest among the brothers, then 1869 has to be excluded. At the same time, if Yellow Dragon is indeed born in 1809, then he is too old to be a brother to Red Dragon and Green Dragon. Significantly, Li Longchuan, the teacher of both Huang Baonian and Liu E, was born in 1808, only one year earlier than the year of *jisi.* This "inconsistency" with "facts" is probably part of a deliberate ploy on our novelist's part to try to make the autobiographical reference here less "explicit."
29. Liu Dashen ("Guanyu *Lao Can youji,*" 64) observes that "initially there was no symbolic significance attached to the character Yellow Dragon, later [in the sequel?] the author used this character to allude to *(yingshe)* Huang Guiqun [Huang Baonian]."
30. See Liu E's letter, "Zhi Huang Baonian," in Liu Delong, Zhu Xi, and Liu Deping, *Liu E ji*

Lao Can youji ziliao, 300. Liu E's much younger age is one clue that leads Wang Xuejun to conclude that Liu E could not be one of the "chosen two."

31. Huang's letter in its entirety is reprinted in Liu Delong, *Liu E sanlun*, 221–222.
32. See Huang Baonian, *Guiqun caotang yulu*, rpt. in Fang Baochuan, comp., *Taigu xuepai yishu* (diyi ji), 5:19.
33. "Zhi Huang Baonian," in Liu Delong, Zhu Xi, and Liu Deping, *Liu E ji Lao Can youji ziliao*, 299–300. The English translation of Confucius' remark follows that in Lau, trans., *The Analects*, 13.23, 122. For a discussion of Liu E's understanding of the idea of "nurturing the nation" and its relationship to the teachings of the Taigu school, see Liu Delong, Zhu Xi, and Liu Deping, *Liu E xiaozhuan*, 85–91.
34. Cf. Wang Xuejun's discussion, *Liu E yu Lao Can youji*, 75.
35. In his letter to Huang Baonian, Liu E complained that "although among my comrades, many are forgiving and care about me but very few really understand me." "Zhi Huang Baonian," in Liu Delong, Zhu Xi, and Liu Deping, *Liu E ji Lao Can youji ziliao*, 300.
36. For a general study of the relationship between Buddhism and sexuality, see Faure, *The Red Thread*; see esp. his discussion of what he has termed "The Ideology of Transgression" (98–143).
37. Translation (with modification) from Lin Yutang, trans., "A Nun of Taishan," in *Widow, Nun and Courtesan*, 151–152.
38. Ibid., 148–149.
39. Ibid., 161.
40. *Wenxia* is a term used by Lee ("The Solitary Traveler," 286) to describe Lao Can as a knight-errant who does not engage in physical fighting as a *wuxia* usually does. Of course, Lao Can "fights" with his pen, which he uses to write letters to the governor whenever there is a case of injustice. For a discussion of Lao Can as a new knight-errant, see David Wang, *Fin-de-siècle Splendor*, 146–154.
41. Liu E's biographer Jiang Yiyun believed that Liu E wrote about Lao Can's rescue of Cuihuan from prostitution as a way to justify his own taking of concubines as "saving" women. "Liu Tieyun nianpu," in Wei Shaochang, ed., *Lao Can youji ziliao*, 177.
42. For discussions of the concepts of *tali* (the strength of another) and *zili* (one's own strength), see Chen Yangjiong, *Zhongguo Jingtuzong tongshi*, 122–125, 419; a concept close to *zili* in Chan Buddhism is *zixing* (one's own nature); see Du Jiwen and Wei Daoru, *Zhongguo Chanzong tongshi*, 186.
43. For example, Wang Xuejun and most Western scholars such as Hsia, Lee, and Wong.
44. Among them, Liu Huisun's view is the most representative. See, e.g., his "Taigu xuepai zhengzhi sixiang tanlüe" and "Taigu xuepai yishu," rpt. in Liu Delong, Zhu Xi, and Liu Deping, *Liu E ji Lao Can youji ziliao*, 591–602, 603–630; see esp. 593, 629.
45. Cf. Wang Xuejun, "*Lao Can youji* de chan zhihui—Yiyun shilun."
46. David Wang (*Fin-de-siècle Splendor*, 174) suggests that there might be an analogy between the descriptions of Yama's court here in the sequel and the courtroom scenes in the original novel, and therefore they could be read ironically. But he believes that this is an ironic reading Liu E himself, as the author, may not have been aware of.
47. See Liu E's own self-defense, "Kuangshi qi," published in the newspaper *Zhongwai ribao*, Nov. 24, 1903, rpt. in Liu Delong, Zhi Xi, and Liu Deping, *Liu E ji Lao Can youji ziliao*, 131–133, where he explicitly mentioned the anger of those students studying in Japan. For background information on this mining controversy, see Liu Delong, Zhu Xi, and Liu Deping, *Liu E xiaozhuan*, 24–34; for a different view of this controversy by a scholar who is not a descendant of Liu E, see Wang Lixing, "Liu E yu *Lao Can youji*," 74–76. In evaluating Liu E and reading various historical accounts of his controversial life, I believe we

have to take into consideration the fact that most of these accounts were written by Liu E's own family members or descendants (e.g., Liu Dashen is Liu E's fourth son, Liu Huisun and Liu Houze are his grandsons, and Liu Delong and Liu Deping are his great-grandsons). Of course, some of the "negative" essays written by people such as Zhang Bilai during the 1950s and 1960s were also biased due to the political atmosphere in China at that time. For a bibliography of the articles on Liu E published in this period, see Liu Delong, Zhu Xi, and Liu Deping, *Liu E ji Lao Can youji ziliao*, 546–558.

48. Liu Houze offers a different explanation as to why only the first six chapters were republished by some of Liu E's family members in the Liangyou ed. in 1935; see Wei Shaochang, ed., *Lao Can youji ziliao*, 94, note 4.

49. Cf. my discussions of the "autobiographical" strategies adopted in the eighteenth-century literati novels (especially *Honglou meng* and *Yesou puyan*) in *Literati and Self-Re/Presentation*.

50. Liu Dashen, "Guanyu *Lao Can youji*," 62.

51. Ibid., 55. Ma Youyuan has characterized Liu Dashen's attitudes toward the public's interest in information on his father and his novel as "hoarding" *(qihuo keju)*; see his "Xiaoshuo yanjiu de diandian didi," in *Zhongguo xiaoshuo shi jigao*, 11. Expressing doubt on Liu Dashen's explanation of the immediate cause behind Liu E's writing of the novel, Hsia speculates that Liu E "agreed to write a novel more for the fun of engaging in friendly competition with Lian, who had already begun one." See "An Exploration," 63, note 22.

52. Liu Dashen, "Guanyu *Lao Can youji*," 55. Liu Dashen uses the phrase *"youxi bimo"* to characterize the novel on page 90.

53. Wang Lixing has argued that the fact that Liu E initially wrote the novel as a way to offer financial assistance to his friend does not necessarily mean that he did not take his work seriously; "Liu E yu *Lao Can youji*," 88.

54. According to the testimony of Liu E's nephew Liu Dajun, who lived with his uncle, Liu E often rewrote what he had written when he was writing the sequel; see Liu Dajun, "*Lao Can youji* zuozhe Liu Tieyun xiansheng de yishi," in Wei Shaochang, ed., *Lao Can youji ziliao*, 106. This should complicate Liu Dasheng's characterization of Liu E's attitudes toward his own novel as "casual."

55. No wonder Liu Dashen compared his father to Christ and Confucius, whose tragic lives were the result of their being too much ahead of their own times. "Guanyu *Lao Can youji*," 79.

56. Lao Can as a novelistic character is of course different from the traditional image of a literatus *(wenren)* or that of a modern intellectual such as those represented in Lu Xun's fiction. Wong argues that the image of Lao Can has a lot to do with the *fangshi* (diviners) tradition in China. See Wong, "Liu E and the *Fang-shih* Tradition," 302–306.

57. For brief accounts of some of the allographic "sequels" to Liu E's *Lao Can youji* produced during the early decades of the twentieth century, see Liu Dashen, "Guanyu *Lao Can youji*," 73–76; and the Liu Delong, "*Lao Can youji* banben gaishuo," 59–60. Liu Dashen called these sequels *fangzuo* (imitations), while Liu Delong considers them *fangxu ben* (imitative sequels).

58. In this regard, Liu E's grandson Liu Huisun's sequels to *Lao Can youji* might be exceptions to a certain extent. Liu Huisun completed his sequel, *Lao Can youji bupian* (in eleven chapters), in 1989, and its first two chapters were initially serialized in the Shanghai newspaper *Jiefang ribao*. It was later published in book form by the publisher Wenhua yishu chubanshe in Beijing in 1992. Only three years later Liu Huisun published yet another sequel, *Lao Can youji waipian,* in twenty chapters, which is supposed to have been based on his grandfather's handwritten, fifteen-page incomplete manuscript left in his possession. This second sequel was published by Yanshan chubanshe in Beijing in 1995, together with his previous sequel *Lao Can youji bupian* and Liu E's original novel (including Liu E's

autographic sequel known as *Erbian* in nine chapters and the content of the fifteen-page manuscript fragment), under the title *Lao Can youji quanbian* (The complete Lao Can's travels). Liu Huisun's first sequel is in fact a fictionalized biography of his grandfather, while the second sequel is a fictionalized "genealogy" of the Liu clan, tracing their common ancestors to the famous general Liu Guangshi (1089–1142) of the Song dynasty. It can almost be considered a sort of prequel to his grandfather's *Lao Can youji*. Writing sequels or prequels to his famous grandfather's novel—published almost ninety years ago—must have been a gratifying act of filial piety on the part of Liu Huisun.

GLOSSARY

Aigong wen 哀公問
Aisin Gioro Yurui 愛新覺羅裕瑞
Ba Jin 巴金
baiguan 稗官
baiguan yeshi 稗官野史
Baimin guo 白民國
Baishe ji 白蛇記
Banji 半偈
"Bao Ren Shaoqing shu" 報任少卿書
Baochai 寶釵
Baogong an 包公案
Baohuangdang 保皇黨
Bawang bie ji 霸王別姬
ben 本
benji 本紀
bianji 編輯
bianyi 便衣
Biaozhong ji 表忠記
biaozi weiyi 標資偉異
bing 病
bingbu shilang 兵部侍郎
bo 剝
Bona 百衲 edition
bu 不
bu 補
bu fen ze bu zuo 不憤則不作
Bu Honglou meng 補紅樓夢
bu wen shishi 不問世事
Bukong 不空
Bulao popo 不老婆婆
buneng wang 不能忘
buxiu 不朽
Buyao zuo ci ernü tai 不要作此兒女態
buyi youli 布衣遊歷
buzhi yiri 不只一日
buzhui chengshu 補綴成書
Cai Jing 蔡京
Cai Yuanfang 蔡元放

caizi jiaren 才子佳人
Can Tang Wudai zhizhuan 殘唐五代志傳
Cao Xueqin 曹雪芹
chafang 察訪
Chai Shao 柴紹
Chang Shijie 常時節
changben 唱本
Changyan jiejie 長顏姐姐
Chanzhen houshi 禪真後史
Chanzhen yishi 禪真逸史
chaofan rusheng 超凡入聖
Chaozhou 潮州
Chen Chen 陳忱
Chen Jingji 陳經濟
Chen Kaige 陳凱歌
Chen Shaohai 陳少海
Chen Shiwen 陳詩雯
Chen Tianchi 陳天池
Chen Tingjing 陳廷敬
Chen Xianzhang 陳獻章
Chen Xiaolu 陳嘯盧
cheng 誠
cheng he qu dong shi 誠和趣動時
Cheng Weiyuan 程偉元
Cheng Yaojin 程咬金
Cheng Youde 程有德
Cheng Zhijie 程知[智]節
Cheung, Leslie 張國榮
Chipozi zhuan 痴婆子傳
Chisong you 赤松遊
Chongzhen 崇禎
chou 丑
Chu Renhuo 褚人穫
chuangshi zhe 創始者
chuanling 串鈴
Chubian 初編
Chucang 楚傖

chuji 初集
Chunmei 春梅
Chunqiu 春秋
Chunqiu Lieguo zhi 春秋列國志
chushi 出世
chushi de Yiyun 出世的逸雲
ci nanren 雌男人
Ci'an 慈安
cibei 慈悲
cihou 伺候
Ciqu bu shang 詞曲部上
Cixi 慈禧
congjian 從賤
congliang 從良
Cui Jue 崔珏
"Cui Yingying zhuan" 崔鶯鶯傳
"Da Huang Zongxian, Ying Yuanzhong" 答黃宗賢應原忠
"Da Ji Mingde" 答季明德
Da Tang Qinwang cihua 大唐秦王詞話
da xueshi 大學士
Da Yu mo 大禹謨
da zhaoying 大照應
Dadian 大顛
Dai'an 玳安
Daidu lou 待度樓
Daiyu 黛玉
dan 淡
dan ming guoji xie tianxiu 但明國紀寫天庥
dang ling ju biebian 當另具別編
Dangkang 當康
Dangkouzhi 蕩寇志
danxingben 單行本
danyao 丹藥
Daobi 到彼
daoxue 道學
Daren guo 大人國
Daxue 大學
dayu 大欲
Di yi kuaihuo qishu 第一快活奇書
Di yi kuaihuo shu 第一快活書
Diannan shilüe 滇南詩略
Dianshi 點石
diben 底本

didao qidao 地道妻道
Ding Yaokang 丁耀亢
dingsi 丁巳
dingxin 定心
Dizhi 地支
dong le ... xin 動了…心
Dong Qichang 董其昌
Dong Sizhang 董斯張
Dong Yue 董說
Dong Zhou lieguo zhi 東周列國志
Dong'e Shaoru 棟鄂少如
Dongkou shan 東口山
DongOu nühaojie 東歐女豪杰
Dou E yuan 竇娥冤
Doumu gong 斗姥宮
"Du *Diwu Caizi shu* fa" 讀第五才子書法
Du Fu 杜甫
Du Honglou meng zaji 讀紅樓夢雜記
"Du *Ruyijunzhuan*" 讀如意君傳
Du Shiniang 杜十娘
dunwu 頓悟
Ernü yingxiong zhuan 兒女英雄傳
Ershi nian mudu zhi guai xianzhuang 二十年目睹之怪現狀
ersi 二巳
ersi chuandao 二巳傳道
Ertai beidou shenjun 二臺北斗神君
fa 法
"Fafan" 發凡
fafen zhushu 發憤著書
fan 反
fan 翻
Fan Tang yanyi zhuan 反唐演義傳
fan yinlü 犯淫律
fanfan 翻反
fang 仿
Fang Ruhao 方汝浩
fangbian 方便
fangdan buji 放誕不羈
Fangguan 芳官
fangshi 方士
fangshu 仿書
fangshu 房術
fangwai ren 方外人
fangxu 仿續

fangxu ben 仿續本
fangzuo 仿作
fanli 凡例
fanpu guizhen 返樸歸真
fanxin xiaoshuo 翻新小說
fanxu 反續
fayu zhi yan 法語之言
Feicui xuan 翡翠軒
Feitian waizhuan 飛天外傳
feiyang bahu 飛揚跋扈
Feng Menglong 馮夢龍
Fengshen yanyi 封神演義
Fengyue baojian 風月寶鑒
"Fenhe Daguanyuan lanshe shi si shou" 分和大觀園蘭社詩四首
fenshu 憤書
Fotian 佛田
fu 副
fu 撫
Fu Pi Laojuntang; Yuexia gan Qinwang 斧劈老君堂, 月下趕秦王
fude 婦德
fugang 夫綱
fugong 婦工
Fuxi 伏羲
fuxing 婦行
gai 改
Gao E 高鶚
Gaozong 高宗
Gaozu 高祖
Gelian huaying 隔簾花影
geming jia lian'ai 革命加戀愛
Geng Dingxiang 耿定向
geng neng ganle, liande hui bao haizi le 更能幹了, 練的會抱孩子了
gengshen 庚申
Gong Li 鞏俐
gongguoge 功過格
gongjingxin 恭敬心
gou 媾
goucai 狗才
gouwei xudiao 狗尾續貂
Gu Chun (Taiqing) 顧春 (太清)
Gu Taiqing 顧太清
guanbi min bufan 官逼民不反
Guanchang xianxing ji 官場現形記

Guangming ribao 光明日報
Guangxu 光緒
guangyi 廣義
Guanhai shanfang zhuisui lu 觀海山房追隨錄
Guanhua tang pi diwu caizishu Xixiang ji 貫華堂批第五才子書西廂記
Guanjian 管見
Guansheng cheng 館甥城
Guanyin pusa 觀音菩薩
guben 古本
guci 鼓詞
Gufen 孤憤
Guichuzi 歸鋤子
guiguo 鬼國
Guilian meng 歸蓮夢
Guiqun caotang yulu 歸群草堂語錄
guixiu 閨秀
Gujin xiaoshuo 古今小說
Guocui pai 國粹派
Guoji ge 國際歌
guomin 國民
guomin yishi 國民意識
Haipu zhuren 海圃主人
Haishang chentianying 海上塵天影
Han Fei 韓非
Han Fei zi 韓非子
Han Yu 韓愈
hanjian 漢奸
Haoqiu zhuan 好逑傳
haorang buzheng 好讓不爭
he'er butong 和而不同
Honglou fumeng 紅樓復夢
Honglou houmeng 紅樓後夢
Honglou huanmeng 紅樓幻夢
Honglou juemeng 紅樓覺夢
Honglou meng 紅樓夢
Honglou meng bu 紅樓夢補
Honglou meng chuanqi 紅樓夢傳奇
Honglou meng pinglun ji 紅樓夢評論集
Honglou meng xinbu 紅樓夢新補
"*Honglou meng* xushu zhi wojian" 紅樓夢續書之我見
Honglou meng ying 紅樓夢影
Honglou yuan meng 紅樓圓夢

Honglou zaimeng 紅樓再夢
Honglou zhenmeng 紅樓真夢
Hongmei ji 紅梅記
Hongxiangguan shicicao 紅香館詩詞草
Hongxuelou shicao 鴻雪樓詩草
Hongxuelou shixuan chuji 鴻雪樓詩選初集
hou 後
Hou Honglou meng 後紅樓夢
Hou Shui hu zhuan 後水滸傳
Hou Xiyou ji 後西游記
Hou Zhi 侯芝
houbu 後部
"Houji" 後記
houmian 後面
houshu 後書
houtian de xin 後天的心
Hu Shi 胡適
Hu Zongyu 胡宗垿
Hua Mulan 花木蘭
Hua Qinshan 華琴珊
Hua Rong 花榮
Hua Zixu 花子虛
huaben 話本
huachan 花禪
Huang Baonian 黃葆年
Huang Ren 黃人
Huang Ruihe 黃瑞河
Huang Shunhua 黃舜華
Huang Shunying 黃舜英
Huang Xun 黃訓
Huang Zhouxing 黃周星
Huangcheng cun 皇城村
huanggu 皇姑
huashe tianzu 畫蛇添足
Huayue chiren 花月痴人
Huayue hen 花月痕
Huayun 華雲
hubao feng 虎豹風
huiqing 穢情
Hun Tang houzhuan 混唐後傳
"Hun Tang houzhuan xu" 混唐後傳序
Hun Tang yanyi 混唐演義
Hunshi mowang 混世魔王
Huo Yanluoduan 活閻羅斷
huoji 活祭

huoxu 活續
ji dacheng 集大成
Ji Gui 季跪
Ji Gui xiaopin zhiwen yin 季跪小品制文引
ji nai 擠奶
ji zhuan shi bian, yigui chanxiao 繼撰是編, 一歸鏟削
jia daoxue 假道學
Jia Lian 賈璉
Jia Zheng 賈政
Jia Zhi 賈芝
Jiang Wentian 蔣文田
"Jiang Wentian ji qi zhushu" 蔣文田及其著述
"Jiang Wentian pingzhuan" 蔣文田評傳
Jiang Yiyun 蔣逸雲
Jiang Yuhan 蔣玉函
Jiangnan 江南
Jiangsu 江蘇
Jiangyin 江陰
jiao 剿
jiao tianxia 教天下
jiaoding 校訂
jiaoyan 教言
jiaxu fa 夾敘法
jibianxin 機變心
jie qi yi 借其意
"Jie Shuihu quanzhuan" 結水滸全傳
Jiefang ribao 解放日報
jiegu fengjin 借古諷今
jieti xiaoshuo 借題小說
jiewai shengzhi meihua xiecha 節外生枝 梅花斜插
jiexu 截續
jieyi 結義
jiezi 結子
Jiezi an 芥子庵
Jiezi yuan 芥子園
Jiliu sanbu qu 激流三部曲
Jin Ping Mei 金瓶梅
Jin Shengtan 金聖嘆
jin shou fude 謹守婦德
Jin Songcen 金松岑
Jin Wuzhu 金兀朮

jing　敬
jing　淨
jing　經
jing pibei　敬皮杯
Jingang jing　金剛經
jingguan　京官
Jinghua yuan　鏡花緣
Jingju　京劇
Jingshi yinyang meng　警世陰陽夢
Jingui　金桂
Jingzhou　荊州
Jinjiantang　金鑒堂
Jinlian　金蓮
jinshi　進士
Jinsuo ji　金鎖記
Jintong　金童
Jinwu meng　金屋夢
"*Jishan shuyuan Zunjing ge ji*"　稽山書院尊經閣記
jishi　機事
jiu gongfu　舊功夫
jiu se cai qi　酒色財氣
Jiu Tang shu　舊唐書
jiuben　舊本
jiupai　舊派
jiuping xinjiu chengshang qixia　舊瓶新酒 承上啟下
jixie　機械
jixin　機心
jizhuan　集撰
ju　懼
juan　卷
Junzi guo　君子國
junzi he er butong　君子和而不同
junzi wu bu jing ye　君子無不敬也
juyi　聚義
Juzhen tang　聚珍堂
Kaesomun　蓋蘇文
Kang Hai　康海
Kang Youwei　康有為
Kangxi　康熙
kanle wu ren yanmu　看了污人眼目
kedou　蝌蚪
kezheng meng yu hu　苛政猛於虎
Konghe zhenwen　控鶴珍聞
kongmian　空面
Kou taijian　寇太監
kouguo　口過
kuangben shizai　狂奔十載
"*Kuangshi qi*"　礦事啟
Kuixing　魁星
kunde yi shuncong wei zheng　坤德以順從為正
Lai'an　來安
Lan Mao　藍茂
Langhuan shanqiao　瑯嬛山樵
Langhuan zhai　瑯嬛齋
Lao Can youji bupian　老殘遊記補篇
Lao Can youji erbian　老殘遊記二編
Lao Can youji quanbian　老殘遊記全編
Lao Can youji waipian　老殘遊記外篇
"*Lao Can youji* zuozhe Liu Tieyun xiansheng de yishi"　老殘遊記作者劉鐵雲先生的佚事
lao er yin zhe　老而淫者
Lao Laizi　老萊子
Laochengzi　老成子
Laojun tang　老君堂
laoshixin　老實心
Laozi　老子
leixu　類續
lengxiao　冷笑
Li Baojia　李寶嘉
Li Boyuan　李伯元
Li Duozuo　李多佐
Li Ji　李勣 (Li Shiji 世勣)
Li Jing　李靖
Li Jingchen　李景沉
Li Longchuan　李龍川
Li Mi　李密
Li Ruzhen　李汝珍
Li Shimin　李世民
Li Shishi　李師師
Li Songshi　李松石
Li Wan　李紈
Li Yu　李漁
Li Yuan　李淵
Li Yuanba　李元霸
Li Zhi　李贄
Li Zhongchang　李忠昌
Li Zhuowu　李卓吾
Lian Mengqing　連夢青

Liang Desheng 梁德繩
Liang Hongyu 梁紅玉
Liang Qichao 梁啓超
Liangyou 良友
liangzhi 良知
lianpu 臉譜
Lianxiang ban 憐香伴
lianxu 連續
Liao 遼
Lienü zhuan 列女傳
Liewei 列位
Liezi 列子
lihai 利害
Liji 禮記
Lin Chen 林辰
Lin Meiyi 林玫儀
Lin Siniang 林四娘
Lin Zhiyang 林之洋
lingchi 凌遲
Lingshan 靈山
lingtai 靈台
Lingxuzi 靈虛子
Linqing 麟慶
lishi yanyi xiaoshuo 歷史演義小說
Liu Dajun 劉大鈞
Liu Dashen 劉大紳
Liu Delong 劉德隆
Liu E 劉鶚
Liu Guangshi 劉光世
Liu Houze 劉厚澤
Liu Huisun 劉惠孫
Liu Jin 劉瑾
Liu Jingting 柳敬亭 (Liu Mazi 麻子)
"Liu Tieyun nianpu" 劉鐵雲年譜
Liu Tingji 劉廷璣
Liu Xiang 劉向
Liu Xianglian 柳湘蓮
Liu Xu 劉昫
Liuru yisun 六如裔孫
Liuxia Hui 柳下惠
liuxuesheng 留學生
Liyan 里言
Longfengpei zaisheng yuan 龍鳳配再生緣
longluo 籠絡
Longtu erlu 龍圖耳錄

Longtu gong'an 龍圖公案
louchu nide niaozhu 摟出你的鳥珠
Lu Jiuyuan 陸九淵
Lu Shi'e 陸士諤
Lu Xiangshan 陸象山
Lu Zixuan 盧紫萱
Lunyu jizhu 論語集注
Luo Binwang 駱賓王
Luo Cheng 羅成
Luo Guanzhong 羅貫中
Luo Qilan 駱綺蘭
Luo Shixin 羅士信
Luo Tong sao bei 羅通掃北
Lüqiu rude, Luo Zi ru nide guai qiuniang! 驢囚入的, 羅子入你的怪囚娘
Ma Congshan 馬從善
Magu 麻姑
Mai Dapeng 麥大鵬
Manting guoke 幔亭過客
Mao 茂
Mao Qiling 毛奇齡
mao zei 毛賊
maoming 冒名
Mei Shujun 梅樹君
Mei Zihe 梅子和
Meiyu 梅玉
meng 夢
Meng Zi jizhu 孟子集注
Mengjue guan 夢覺關
Mengmeng xiansheng 夢夢先生
Mengzi 孟子
menle haojitian 悶了好幾天
Miao Qing 苗青
Miaoyu 妙玉
Mingbao 冥報
minjian gushi 民間故事
mu 畝
Nanhai airi laoren 南海愛日老人
Nanwu yeman 南武野蠻
nanzi han 男子漢
neicheng 內城
Neize 內則
ni jing you qiaodechu ren laide rizi 你竟有瞧的出人來的日子
Ni ke ai ta? Xiluan mang shuo wo ai ta 你可愛他? 喜鸞忙說我愛他

"*Ni niang de biqing*" 你娘的屄情
ni yu zhifen 溺於脂粉
Niehai hua 孽海花
Niehai hua xubian 孽海花續編
"*Niehai hua zuichu lianghui de yuanlai mianmu*" 孽海花最初兩回的原來面目
nijiu xiaoshuo 擬舊小說
Ningguta 寧古塔
Niu bizi Daoren 牛鼻子道人
nixu 逆續
Nongqing kuaishi 濃情快史
nü haojie 女豪杰
Nüer guo 女兒國
"number one doughty warrior" 隋朝第一條好漢
Nüwa 女媧
Nüwa shi 女媧石
Nüyuhua 女獄花
Ouyang Xiu 歐陽修
Pan Jinlian 潘金蓮
Pan Zhao 潘炤
Pei Quan 佩荃
Piaodu xianxing ji 嫖賭現形記
piaoji bian 嫖妓辯
pingdian 評點
Ping'er 瓶兒
Ping'er 平兒
pinghua 平話 (prose narratives)
pinghua 評話 (Yangzhou oral narrative form)
pingmin baixing 平民百姓
pingshu 評書
Pingxi wang 平西王
Pinhua baojian 品花寶鑑
Pu Songling 蒲松齡
Putao jia 葡萄架
Qi Yukun 齊裕焜
Qian Xizuo 錢熙祚
qianbu 前部
"*Qianyan*" 前言
qianzhe xiaoshuo 譴責小說
qianzhuan 前傳
Qiao Yu 樵餘
Qiaojie 巧姐
Qihong ting 泣紅亭

qihuo keju 奇貨可居
qijia 齊家
"*Qilai, jihan jiaopo de nuli ...*" 起來，饑寒交迫的奴隸
Qilou chongmeng 綺樓重夢
Qin Hui 秦檜
Qin Keqing 秦可卿
Qin Shubao 秦叔寶
Qin Zichen 秦子忱
qinchai dachen 欽差大臣
qing 情
qingguan 清官
Qinglou meng 青樓夢
qingsi 情絲
Qingwen 晴雯
Qingyu 鯖魚
Qiongyu 瓊玉
qishi sanxu 七實三虛
qishu 奇書
qishu ti 奇書體
Qitian xiaosheng 齊天小聖
Qiu Chuji 邱處機
Qiu Jin 秋瑾
qiumo quben 求末去本
qiyue 七月
quan 權
Quanfeng guo 犬封國
Quanshan lu 勸善錄
quanshu 全書
ren 人
ren 仁
Renmin ribao (haiwai ban) 人民日報 (海外版)
rensuan 人算
renyu 人慾
Rou putuan 肉蒲團
ruhu 乳虎
Ruizong 睿宗
Rulian jushi 如蓮居士
rumu 乳母
runiang zei 入娘賊
Ruyijun 如意君
Ruyijun zhuan 如意君傳
ruzhui 入贅
Sai Jinhua 賽金花
san da guanjian chu 三大關鍵處

sanbu qu 三部曲
Sanguo zhi tongsu yanyi 三國志通俗演義
Sanguo zhi yanyi 三國志演義
sanhualian 三花臉
sanjiao 三教
sanren tongxin 三人同心
Sanshi chong 三尸蟲
Sanshi shen 三尸神
Santaiguan 三台館
Sanxia wuyi 三俠五義
Sanxu Jin Ping Mei 三續金瓶梅
Sanzang 三藏
se 色
semian 色面
Sengni niehai 僧尼孽海
Sha Zhihe 沙致和
Shan Xiongxin 單雄信
Shangdi 上帝
shangjie qinglong 上界青龍
Shangjie xianxing ji 商界現形記
shangmo 上魔
shanshu 善書
Shanxi 山西
Shanyang zhi yi 山陽志遺
Shao Bao 邵寶
Shaseng 沙僧
Shen Huazi 沈花子
Shen Jinge 沈金哥
Shen San 沈三
Shen Shanbao 沈善寶
Shen Yunying 沈雲英
shengchao taiping zhi shi 聖朝太平之世
shengren 聖人
Shengyou 生有
Shenlou zhi 蜃樓志
shenmo xiaoshuo 神魔小説
Shenxiu 神秀
Shi Changyu 石昌渝
Shi Nai'an 施耐庵
Shi Yukun 石玉崑
Shi zhangfu 是丈夫
shihua 詩話
Shiji 史記
Shijiafo hou 釋迦佛後

Shijing 詩經
shinü 石女
shinü 使女
Shiroaki Naoya 白木直也
shishi 實事
Shiye yewen 十葉野聞
shiyue 十月
shizhuan 史傳
Shizong 世宗
shouwei xiangxian 首尾相銜
shouwei xiangxian, yin'guo xiangying 首尾相銜, 因果相應
shozen chūakū gochu 初善中惡後忠
shu 數
shu 述
shu er bu zuo 述而不作
"*Shu'er buzuo' lun*" 述而不作論
Shu jing 書經
"*Shu'nan er*" 述難二
Shuang tou Tang 雙投唐
Shuihu zhuan 水滸傳
Shuihu houzhuan 水滸後傳
"*Shuihu houzhuan* lunlüe" 水滸後傳論略
"*Shuihu* wulun" 水滸五論
Shuihu zhuan 水滸傳
"*Shuinan*" 説難
Shujing 書經
Shun 舜
Shunhua 舜華
shunxu 順續
Shuo Tang houzhuan 説唐後傳
Shuo Tang qianzhuan 説唐前傳
Shuo Tang quanzhuan 説唐全傳
Shuo Tang sanzhuan 説唐三傳
Shuo Tang yanyi quanzhuan 説唐演義全傳
Shuo Yue quanzhuan 説岳全傳
"*Shuohua—ba*" 説話—八
Shuohuaren 説話人
Shuoku 説庫
shuoshuti xiaoshuo 説書體小説
shuren zuoshu 庶人作書
Shushi guo 淑士國
shutong 書童
shuzhe 述者

shuzhe zhi wei ming 述者之為明
Si ma tou Tang 四馬投唐
Sima Qian 司馬遷
sixin aimu 私心愛慕
Sixuecaotang 四雪草堂
Song Qi 宋祁
Song Su 宋素
Sonkeikaku 尊經閣 Library
Su Hui 蘇蕙
Su'e pian 素娥篇
suan 算
suben 俗本
Sui shi yiwen 隋史遺文
Sui Tang liangchao shizhuan 隋唐兩朝史傳
Sui Tang liangchao zhizhuan 隋唐兩朝志傳
Sui Tang xilie xiaoshuo 隋唐系列小説
Sui Tang yanyi 隋唐演義
Sui Tang yanyi xilie xiaoshuo 隋唐演義系列小説
Sui Yangdi yanshi 隋煬帝艷史
Suichao haohan 隋朝好漢
Suikogaden 水湖畫傳
Sun Jing'an 孫靜庵
Sun Lüzhen 孫履真
Sun Xue'e 孫雪娥
sunshen 損身
suwang 素王
taifu 太傅
Taigu xuepai 太谷學派
"Taigu xuepai yishu" 太谷學派遺書
"Taigu xuepai zhengzhi sixiang tanlüe" 太谷學派政治思想探略
"*Taishang ganying pian wuzijie* xu" 太上感應篇無字解序
"*Taishang ganying pian* yinyang wuzijie" 太上感應篇陰陽無字解
Taishang Lao jun 太上老君
taishang wuqing zhi ren 太上無情之人
Taizong 太宗
tali 他力
"Tan'gong" 檀弓
Tanchun 探春
tanci 彈詞
Tang Ao 唐敖

Tang Emperor Taizong 唐太宗
Tang Guichen 唐閨臣
Tang Qinwang benzhuan 唐秦王本傳
Tang Qinwang cihua 唐秦王詞話
Tang shu zhizhuan tongsu yanyi 唐書志傳通俗演義
Tang tong 唐童
Tang Xiaofeng 唐小峰
tanyi xue 探佚學
Tao Qian 陶潛
Tao Xiang 陶湘
Taohua ying 桃花影
"Taohua yuan ji" 桃花源記
taoxu 套續
Tian Jinsheng 田金生
Tiangan 天干
Tianhua caizi 天花才子
Tianjin riri xinwen 天津日日新聞
tianli 天理
Tianmushan qiao 天目山樵
Tianshi 天史
Tie Er laoye 鐵二老爺
Tiefeng furen 鐵峰夫人
Tixiao yinyuan 啼笑因緣
Tōhō gaku 東方學
Tongzhi 同治
Tufan 吐蕃
Tuhu (Princess) 屠護公主
Wagang 瓦崗
Waibian 外編
Waibian cangao 外編殘稿
waicheng 外城
Wan Huayin 萬化因
Wang Bodang 王伯當
Wang Duan 汪端
Wang Duanshu 王端淑
Wang Lan'gao 王蘭皋
Wang Lanzhi 王蘭沚
Wang Shichong 王世充
Wang Shifu 王實甫
Wang Shouren 王守仁
Wang Xifeng 王熙鳳
Wang Xilian ping Honglou meng 王希廉評紅樓夢
Wang Yangming 王陽明
Wanxiang 婉香

Wanyuan shan　萬緣山
Wei (Prince of)　魏王
Wei Baoying　韋寶應
Wei Lizhen　韋利楨
Wei Niangniang　韋娘娘
Wei Zheng　魏徵
Wei Zheng gai zhao　魏徵改詔
Wei Ziying　魏紫櫻
Weishan weibao　惟善為寶
weixin　維新
Weixin guo　維新國
Weixin guo miewang lun　維新國滅亡論
Wen Kang　文康
Wen Song　文菘
Wen Suchen　文素臣
Wenchang dijun　文昌帝君
Wenming jingjie　文明境界
Wenming tianwang　文明天王
Wenming xiaoshi　文明小史
wenren　文人
wenxia　文俠
Wenyuange da xueshi　文淵閣大學士
wo bugai yuyan jianli　我不該語言尖利
Wu Cheng'en　吳承恩
Wu Jianren　吳趼人
Wu Jinglian　武景廉
Wu Jinlian　武錦蓮
Wu Niangniang　武娘娘
Wu Sansi　武三思
Wu Song　武松
wu woxiang wu renxiang　無我相無人相
Wu Yujin　吳玉搢
Wu Yunshao　伍雲召
Wu Zao　吳藻
Wu Zetian　武則天
Wu Zetian waishi　武則天外史
Wu Zhao zhuan　武曌傳
Wu Zhihe　吳之和
Wu Zhixiang　吳之祥
wucai ke butian　無才可補天
Wucheng　烏程
Wuhen tian chuanqi　無恨天傳奇
Wuliaoweng　吾了翁
Wulou dong　無漏洞
Wuqi　烏漆

Wutuobang youji　烏托邦遊記
wuxia　武俠
Wuzhong　無中
wuzi dengke　五子登科
Wuzong　武宗
Xia Jingqu　夏敬渠
Xianfeng　咸豐
xiang　想
Xiang Yu　項羽
Xiangling　香菱
xiangma dan　響馬單
Xiangyun　湘雲
Xianqing ouji　閒情偶記
xianqing yizhi　閑情逸志
xiansheng　先生
xianshi　賢士
xiantian benxing chizi zhi xin　先天本性赤子之心
xianxing ji xiaoshuo　現形記小說
Xianzong　憲宗
xiao　小
xiao chaoting　小朝廷
xiao jieju　小結聚
Xiao Penglai　小蓬萊
Xiao Shi　曉式
Xiaoge　孝哥
Xiaoqiao　小橋
Xiaoran yusheng　蕭然鬱生
xiaoshuo　小說
Xiaoshuo lin　小說林
"Xiaoshuo yanjiu de diandian didi"　小說研究的點點滴滴
Xiaoyaozi　逍遙子
Xiaoyu　小鈺
Xiaozong　孝宗
xiayi　狹義
Xibei shanqiao　犀背山樵
Xie Yemei　謝葉梅
xiefen　泄憤
xiezi　楔子
"Xihe Daguanyuan jushe shi si shou"　戲和大觀園菊社詩四首
Xihe quanji　西河全集
Xihu　西湖
Xihu diaoshi　西湖釣史
Xihu jiahua　西湖佳話

Xihu sanren　西湖散人
Xilin　西林
Xilinjueluo　西林覺羅
Xiluan　喜鸞
Ximen Qing　西門慶
xin　新
Xin Ernü yingxiong zhuan　新兒女英雄傳
Xin jing　心經
Xin jing tigang　心經提綱
Xin Jinghua yuan　新鏡花緣
Xin Lieguo zhi　新列國志
Xin Niehai hua　新孽海花
xin shi wangxiang　心是妄想
Xin Shitou ji　新石頭記
Xin Shuihu　新水滸
Xin Xihu jiahua　新西湖佳話
Xin Xiyou ji　新西遊記
Xinbian xiuxiang Xu Xiyou ji　新編繡像續西游記
xinfa　心法
Xing shui bian　醒睡編
xingdao　性道
Xingshi yinyuan zhuan　醒世姻緣傳
Xinke piping xiuxiang Hou Xiyou ji　新刻批評繡像後西遊記
xinluan　心亂
Xinxinzi　欣欣子
xinxue　心學
xinyuan　心猿
xinyuan yima　心猿意馬
xiong nüren　雄女人
Xiong Zhonggu　熊鐘谷
Xiren　襲人
"Xiugai hou yao shuo de jiju hua"　修改後要説的幾句話
Xiuta yeshi　繡榻野史
Xiuxiang Hou Xiyou ji zhenquan　繡像後西遊記真銓
Xiuxiang xiaoshuo　繡像小説
Xixian　西仙
Xixiang ji　西廂記
Xiyongxuan congshu　喜永軒叢書
Xiyou bu　西游補
Xiyou bu dawen　西游補答問
Xiyou ji　西游記

Xiyou ji daxi　西游記大系
Xiyou xu ji　西游續記
Xiyou zhengdao shu　西游證道書
Xizong　僖宗
xu　續
"Xu"　序
"Xu [Du?] Xiyou bu zaji"　"續[讀?]西游補雜記"
Xu Honglou meng　續紅樓夢
Xu Honglou meng gao　續紅樓夢稿
Xu Honglou meng xinbian　續紅樓夢新編
Xu Jin Ping Mei　續金瓶梅
Xu Jingye　徐敬業
Xu Maogong　徐茂功
Xu Nianci　徐念慈
Xu Niehai hua　續孽海花
Xu Pingquan　許平權
Xu Xiyou ji　續西游記
"Xu yi"　序一
Xu Zhiyan　許指嚴
xuanji tu　璇璣圖
xuanyin　宣淫
Xuanzang　玄奘
xubian　續編
xucheng　續成
xudiao　續貂
xudiao shezu　續貂蛇足
Xue Aocao　薛敖曹
Xue Dingshan zheng xi　薛丁山征西
Xue Rengui zheng dong　薛仁貴征東
"Xu'er"　序二
Xuesheng xianxing ji　學生現形記
xufang　續仿
Xuji　續集
xukan　續刊
Xukong zhuren　虛空主人
Xumi yuan　須彌園
xunyan　訓言
Xunzheng　訓政
xushu　續書
xuxin jingqi　虛心靜氣
xuyan　續衍
"Xuyi"　序一
yan　衍
Yan Poxi yanshi　閻婆惜艷史

Yan Weiqing　嚴微青
Yan Ziqiong　燕紫瓊
Yan'gu laoren　燕谷老人
yanfen lei weixie zhi shu　煙粉類猥褻之書
Yang family of generals　楊家將
Yang Guifei waizhuan　楊貴妃外傳
Yang jia jiang tongsu yanyi　楊家將通俗演義
Yang Lin　楊林
yang tianxian　養天下
Yangcheng　陽城
yangqi　養氣
yangren　洋人
yanqing　言情
Yanxiadong yiyin　煙霞洞曳隱
yanyi　演義
yaozhan　腰斬
ye shi jiu you　也是舊遊
Ye Zhou　葉晝
"Ye Zhou pingdian *Shuihu zhuan* kaozheng"　葉晝評點水滸傳考證
yede　野的
Yehe　野鶴
yeshi li　謁師禮
Yesou puyan　野叟曝言
yi　義
yi fu yi ge, pai tou'er kan jiang qu　一斧一個, 排頭兒砍將去
yi jian yi ge, pai tou'er kan qu　一劍一個, 排頭兒砍去
Yihe yuan　頤和園
Yihui　奕繪
Yijing　易經
yimin wenxue　遺民文學
yin　淫
Yin Ruohua　陰若花
yinfu　淫婦
Ying Bojue　應伯爵
Yinger　鶯兒
yingshe　影射
yinguo xiangying　因果相應
yinguoce　因果冊
yingxiong chuanqi xiaoshuo　英雄傳奇小說
yingxiong ernü　英雄兒女

Yinhong ji　吟紅集
Yinping　銀瓶
yinshen　引申
Yinwenzi　尹文子
yinxian　陰險
yiqie dou yao gongping　一切都要公平
yiren　異人
Yiru jushi　嶷如居士
yisi　乙巳
yiyin　意淫
Yiyun　逸雲
yomihon　讀本
you^a　繇
you^b　由
You Junda　尤俊達
youji　遊記
youse rukong　由色入空
youxi bimo　遊戲筆墨
youxi pin　遊戲品
youxiang　又想
youxing yizu　遊興已足
yu　慾
yu hong er kai　遇洪而開
Yu Ji　虞姬
Yu Ji　虞集
Yu Jiao Li　玉嬌李
yu nüling weiwu　與女伶為伍
Yu Shaoyu　余邵漁
Yu Xiangdou　余象斗
Yu Ying'ao　余應鰲
Yuan Ming yishi　元明逸史
Yuanmingyuan　圓明園
Yuanmingyuan xiufu yi　圓明園修復議
Yuan Shishuo　袁世碩
Yuan Wendian　袁文典
Yuan Yuling　袁于令 (Yuan Jin 晉)
yuanben　原本
yuangao　原稿
Yuanhu yusou　鴛湖漁叟
yuanshi zuozhe　原始作者
yuanzhu　原著
Yuchi Gong　尉遲恭
Yue Fei　岳飛
"Yueji"　樂記
Yueniang　月娘

Yueyue xiaoshuo 月月小說
Yugu shanfang 漁古山房
yuhuoqian 玉火鉗
Yujiaoli 玉嬌李 (麗)
Yuncha waishi 雲槎外史
Yundu shan 雲渡山
Yunü 玉女
Yupiguo 魚皮國
Yuwen Huiji 宇文惠及
za 雜
Zaisheng yuan 再生緣
Zaiyuan zazhi 在園雜志
zaju 雜劇
Zaochuang xianbi 棗窗閒筆
Zaohua xiao'er 造化小兒
Zeng Xubai 曾虛白
"*Zeng Mengpu nianpu*" 曾孟樸年譜
Zeng Pu 曾樸
Zengbu Honglou meng 增補紅樓夢
Zha Jizuo 查繼佐
Zhai Rang 翟讓
Zhang Bilai 張畢來
Zhang Fengyi 張豐毅
Zhang Hao 張昊
Zhang Henshui 張恨水
Zhang Hong 張鴻
Zhang Jianzhi 張柬之
Zhang Juling 張菊玲
Zhang Lingyi 張令儀
Zhang Shuye bu ke duo fuhui 張叔夜不可多附會
Zhang Wenhu 張文虎
Zhang Xinzhi 張新之
Zhang Yaosun 張曜孫
Zhang Zhang 張章
Zhang Zhupo 張竹坡
zhanzhi 粘滯
zhe sange zi 這三個字
Zhejiang 浙江
Zhen Dexiu 真德秀
zhen fugang 振夫綱
Zhenfu jushi 真復居士
Zheng (state of) 鄭國
zheng chuchan 證初禪
Zhengfayanzang wushisan can 正法眼藏五十三參
Zhengyi 正義
Zhengyitang wenji 正誼堂文集
zhenjie 真解
zhenwo 真我
Zhenzheng mei tianli de. Ru ta jia liangge langniang 真正沒天理的。入他家兩個浪娘。
zhi 志
Zhi 跖
"*Zhi Huang Baonian*" 至黃葆年
zhibing hukou 治病餬口
zhichengxin 至誠心
Zhige 芝哥
zhiji 知己
Zhong 忠
Zhong Zhenkui 種振奎
zhongbu 中部
Zhongfen ling 中分嶺
Zhonglie Xiao wuyi 忠烈小五義
Zhonglie xiayi zhuan 忠烈俠義傳
Zhongwai ribao 中外日報
Zhongyi 忠義
"*Zhongyi Shuihuzhuan* xu" 忠義水滸傳敘
Zhongyong 中庸
Zhongyong zhangju 中庸章句
zhongzi rongyi zhi fa 種子容易之法
Zhongzong 中宗
Zhou Er 周耳
Zhou Gu 周谷
Zhou Muwang 周穆王
Zhou Qi 周綺
Zhou Taigu 周太谷
Zhu Bajie 豬八戒
zhu deng bi'an, huanfan lingxu 助登彼岸, 還返靈虛
Zhu Shenglin 諸聖鄰
Zhu Shouzhuo 豬守拙
Zhu Xi 朱熹
Zhu Yijie 豬一戒
zhuadihu xuezi 抓地虎靴子
zhuan 撰
zhuangyuan 狀元
Zhuangzi 莊子
"*Zhuanji*" 傳記
Zhumeng 煮夢

zhushi 住世
zhushi de Yiyun 住世的逸雲
"Zhuzuoquan lü" 著作權律
zi 字
Zidu lou 自度樓
Zigong 子貢
zijia de huaibao 自家的懷抱
Zijuan 紫鵑
Zili 自利
zili 自力
ziwo jiepou 自我解剖
ziwo fanxing 自我反省
Zixiao 紫簫

zixing 自性
zixu 自序
zizhuzhen 自誅陣
zoufang langzhong 走方郎中
Zuihua sheng 醉花生
Zuixing shi 醉醒石
zuo 作
zuoshu 作書
"Zuowan *Tixiao yinyuan* hou de shuohua" 作完啼笑姻緣後的說話
zuozhe 作者
zuozhe zhi wei sheng 作者之為聖
"Zuozhe zixu" 作者自序

BIBLIOGRAPHY

A Ying 阿英. "Guanyu '*Lao Can youji* erti'" 關於老殘遊記二題 (1936). Rpt. in *A Ying wenji* 阿英文集. Hong Kong: Sanlian shudian, 1979, 279–280.

Alford, P. William. *To Steal a Book Is an Elegant Offense: Intellectual Property Law in Chinese Civilization*. Stanford: Stanford University Press, 1995.

Allen, Judson Boyce. *The Friar as Critic: Literary Attitudes in the Later Middle Ages*. Nashville: Vanderbilt University Press, 1971.

An Pingqiu 安平秋 and Zhang Peiheng 章培恆, eds. *Zhongguo jinshu daguan* 中國禁書大觀. Shanghai: Shanghai wenhua, 1990.

An Shuangcheng 安雙成. "Shun Kang nianjian *Xu Jin Ping Mei* zuozhe Ding Yaokang shoushen an" 順康年間續金瓶梅作者丁耀亢受審案. *Lishi dang'an* 歷史檔案 (2000, no. 2):29–32.

Andres, Mark F. "Ch'an Symbolism in *Hsi-yu pu*: The Enlightenment of Monkey." *Tamkang Review* 20.1 (autumn 1989):23–44.

Armstrong, Nancy. *Desire and Domestic Fiction*. New York: Oxford University Press, 1987.

Bantly, Francisca Cho. "Buddhist Allegory in the *Journey to the West*." *Journal of Asian Studies* 48.3 (Aug. 1989):512–524.

Bataille, Georges. *Erotism: Death and Sensuality*. San Francisco: City Light, 1986.

Blader, Susan. "A Critical Study of *San-hsia Wu-i* and Relationship to the *Lung-t'u kung-an* Song-Book." Ph.D. dissertation, University of Pennsylvania, 1977.

———, trans. *Tales of Magistrate Bao and His Valiant Lieutenants: Selections from "Sanxia wuyi."* Hong Kong: The Chinese University Press, 1998.

Børdahl, Vibeke. "Narrative Voices in Yangzhou Storytelling." *CHINOPERL Papers* 18 (1995):1–31.

Børdahl, Vibeke, and Jette Ross. *Chinese Storytellers: Life and Art in the Yangzhou Tradition*. Boston: Cheng and Tsui, 2002.

Borthwick, Sally. "Changing Concepts of the Role of Women from the Late Qing to the May Fourth Period." In David Pong and Edmund S. K. Fung, eds., *Ideal and Reality: Social and Political Change in Modern China 1860–1949*. Lanham, Md.: University Press of America, Inc., 1985, 63–91.

Brandauer, Frederck P. "The Significance of a Dog's Tail: Comments on the *Xu Xiyou ji*." *Journal of the American Oriental Society* 113.3 (1993):418–422.

———. *Tung Yüeh*. Boston: Twayne, 1978.

———. "Violence and Buddhist Idealism in the *Xiyou* Novels." In Jonathan N. Lipman and Stevan Harrell, eds., *Violence in China: Essays in Culture and Counterculture*. New York: State University of New York Press, 1990, 115–148.

———. "Women in the *Ching-hua yüan*: Emancipation toward a Confucian Ideal." *Journal of Asian Studies* 36.4 (Aug. 1977):647–660.

Breuer, Rüdiger. "Orality and Literacy in Early Chinese Vernacular Literature: The Example of Song and Yuan Dynasties Pinghua." Ph.D. dissertation, Washington University, 2001.

Brokaw, Cynthia. *The Ledgers of Merit and Demerit: Social Change and Moral Order in Late Imperial China.* Princeton, N.J.: Princeton University Press, 1991.

Budra, Paul, and Betty A. Schellenberg, eds. *Part Two: Reflections on the Sequel.* Toronto: University of Toronto Press, 1998.

Burton, Watson, trans. *The Complete Works of Chuang Tzu.* New York: Columbia University Press, 1968.

Cahill, James. "New Genre in Ming-Qing Figure Painting: Paintings for Women?" Chapter of unpublished manuscript titled "Pictures for Use and Pleasure: Urban Studio Painting in High Qing China."

Cai Hongsheng 蔡鴻生. *Nigu tan* 尼姑譚. Guangzhou: Zhongshan daxue, 1996.

Cai Yijiang 蔡義江, ed. *Honglou meng congshu quanbian* 紅樓夢叢書全編, 4 vols. Taiyuan: Shanxi guji, 1998.

Calinescu, Matei. *Rereading.* New Haven, Conn.: Yale University Press, 1993.

Can Tang Wudai zhizhuan 殘唐五代志傳. Beijing: Baowentang, 1983.

Cao Xueqin 曹雪芹. *Honglou meng* 紅樓夢. Beijing: Renmin wenxue, 1985.

Carlitz, Katherine. *The Rhetoric of Chin P'ing Mei.* Bloomington: Indiana University Press, 1986.

Castle, Terry. *Masquerade and Civilization: The Carnivalesque in Eighteenth-Century English Culture and Fiction.* Stanford: Stanford University Press, 1986.

Chan Hing-ho 陳慶浩 (Chen Qinghao). "Hai'nei fenshu jin shiding: Ding Yaokang shengping ji qi zhuzuo" 海內焚書禁識丁─丁耀亢生平及其著作, presented at the Third International Sinology Conference, Academia Sinica, June 29–July 1, 2000.

Chang, Garma C. C., gen. ed. *A Treasury of Mahāyāna Sūtras: Selections from the Mahāratnakūṭa Sūtra.* University Park: Pennsylvania State University Press, 1983.

Chang, Kang-i Sun, and Haun Saussy, eds. *Women Writers of Traditional China: An Anthology of Poetry and Criticism.* Stanford: Stanford University Press, 1999.

Chartier, Roger. *Forms and Meanings: Texts, Performances, and Audiences from Codex to Computer.* Philadelphia: University of Pennsylvania Press, 1995.

———. "Popular Appropriation: The Readers and Their Books." In Chartier, *Forms and Meanings,* 83–97.

———. "Representations of the Written Word." In Chartier, *Forms and Meanings,* 6–24.

Chen Angni 陳昂妮. "You *Honglou meng* ji qi xushu tantao Jia Baoyu zhi juese bianqian" 由紅樓夢及其續書探討賈寶玉之角色變遷. *Guowen tiandi* 國文天地 9.7 (1993):33–44.

Chen Chen 陳忱. *Shuihu houzhuan* 水滸後傳. Shanghai: Gudian wenxue, 1955.

Chen Liao 陳遼. *Zhou Taigu pingzhuan* 周太谷評傳. Nanjing: Nanjing chubanshe, 1992.

Chen Qinghao 陳慶浩 and Wang Qiugui 王秋桂. "*Ruyijun zhuan* chuban shuoming" 如意君傳出版說明. In *Si wu xie huibao* 思無邪匯寶, com. Chen Qinghao and Wang Qiugui. Taipei: Taiwan Encyclopedia Britannica, 1995, 15–21.

Chen Shaohai 陳少海. *Honglou fumeng* 紅樓復夢. Beijing: Beijing daxue, 1988.
Chen Tianchi 陳天池. *Ruyijun zhuan* 如意君傳. Shanghai: Shanghai Wenji shudian, 1936.
———. "Yu youren shu" 與友人書. In Chen Tianchi, *Ruyijun zhuan*.
Chen, Toyoko Yoshida. "Women in Confucian Society: A Study of Three T'an T'zu Narratives." Ph.D. dissertation, Columbia University, 1974.
Chen Wenshu 陳文述. *Xiling guiyong ji* 西泠閨詠集 (1827; in Harvard-Yenching Library).
Chen Xiaolu 陳嘯廬. *Xin Jinghua yuan* 新鏡花緣. In *Zhongguo jindai xiaoshuo daxi* 中國近代小說大系. Nanchang: Baihuazhou wenyi, 1996, 2:215–307.
———. "*Xin Jinghua yuan* zuoyi shulüe" 新鏡花緣作意述略. In *Xin Jinghua yuan* 新鏡花緣. In *Zhongguo jindai xiaoshuo daxi* 中國近代小說大系, 2:215.
Chen Xi'nian 陳希年. "Lu Shi'e jiashi shengping jiqi zhushu xinkao" 陸士諤家世生平及其著述新考. *Ming Qing xiaoshuo yanjiu* 明清小說研究 14 (1989, no. 4): 190–199.
Chen Yangjiong 陳揚炯. *Zhongguo Jingtuzong tongshi* 中國淨土宗通史. Nanjing: Jiangsu guji, 2000.
Chen Yinrong 陳蔭榮. *Xing Tang zhuan* 興唐傳, 4 vols. Beijing: Zhongguo quyi, 1984.
Ching, Julia. "The Mirror Symbol Revisited: Confucian and Taoist Mysticism." In Steven T. Katz, ed., *Mysticism and Religious Traditions*. Oxford: Oxford University Press, 1983, 226–246.
———. *To Acquire Wisdom: The Way of Wang Yang-ming*. New York: Columbia University Press, 1976.
———, trans. *The Philosophical Letters of Wang Yang-ming*. Canberra: Australian National University Press, 1972.
Chong Yi 崇彝. *Dao Xian yilai chaoye zaji* 道咸以來朝野雜記. Beijing: Guji, 1982.
Chu, Madeline. "Journey into Desire: Monkey's Secular Experience in the *Xiyoubu*." *Journal of the American Oriental Society* 117.4 (Oct.–Dec. 1997):654–664.
Chu Renhuo 褚人穫. *Sui Tang yanyi* 隋唐演義. Suzhou: Sixuecaotang 四雪草堂, 1695.
———. *Sui Tang yanyi* 隋唐演義. Shanghai: Shanghai gudian wenxue, 1956; rpt. Hong Kong: Xuelin, 1966.
Chung, Sue Fawn. "The Much Maligned Empress Dowager: A Revisionist Study of the Empress Dowager Tz'u-hsi (1835–1908)." *Modern Asian Studies* 13.2 (May 1979):177–196.
Dai Bufan 戴不凡. *Hongxue pingyi waipian* 紅學評議外篇. Beijing: Wenhua yishu, 1991.
de Bary, Wm. Theodore. *The Message of the Mind in Neo-Confucianism*. New York: Columbia University Press, 1989.
———. *Neo-Confucian Orthodoxy and the Learning of the Mind-and-Heart*. New York: Columbia University Press, 1981.
———. *The Unfolding of Neo-Confucianism*. New York: Columbia University Press, 1975.
DeJean, Joan E. *Tender Geographies: Women and the Origins of the Novel in France*. New York: Columbia University Press, 1991.

Demiéville, Paul. "The Mirror of the Mind," trans. Neal Donner. In Peter N. Gregory, ed., *Sudden and Gradual: Approaches to Enlightenment in Chinese Thought*. Honolulu: University of Hawai'i Press, 1987, 13–40.

Deng Hanyi 鄧漢儀. *Shiguan chuji* 詩觀初集. In Naikaku bunko, Tokyo.

Ding Gan 丁淦. "Cheng jiaben hou sishi hui shi zhenben ma" 程甲本後四十回是真本嗎? *Honglou meng xuekan* 紅樓夢學刊 (1994, no. 4):97–123.

Ding Yaokang 丁耀亢. *Ding Yaokang quanji* 丁耀亢全集. Zhengzhou: Zhongzhou guji, 1999.

———. *Xu Jin Ping Mei* 續金瓶梅. In *Jin Ping Mei xushu sanzhong* 金瓶梅續書三種. Jinan: QiLu shushe, 1988.

Ding Yizhuang 定宜莊. *Manzu de funü shenghuo yu hunyin zhidu yanjiu* 滿族的婦女生活與婚姻制度研究. Beijing: Beijing daxue, 1999.

Dong Yue 董說. *Xiyou bu* 西遊補. In Wang Wenru 王文濡, ed., *Shuoku* 說庫. Shanghai: Wenming shuju, 1915. Photoreprint. Hangzhou: Zhejiang guji, 1986.

———. *Xiyou bu* 西遊補. Shanghai: Shanghai guji, 1983.

———. *Xiyou bu*. Photoreprint. Ming Chongzhen 崇禎 ed., *Beijing Tushuguan cang zhenben xiaoshuo congkan* 北京圖書館藏珍本小說叢刊, series 1, no. 15. Beijing: Shumu wenxian, 1996, 9605–9914.

———. *Xiyou bu. Xiyou ji daxi* 西游記大系, 2:2323–2413.

Du Jinghua 杜景華. *Yehua* Shuihu 夜話水滸. Beijing: Beijing tushuguan, 1997.

Du Jiwen 杜繼文 and Wei Daoru 魏道儒. *Zhongguo Chanzong tongshi* 中國禪宗通史. Nanjing: Jiangsu guji, 1993.

Dudbridge, Glen. *The Hsi-yu chi: A Study of Antecedents to the Sixteenth-Century Chinese Novel*. Cambridge: Cambridge University Press, 1970.

Ede, Lisa, and Andrea Lunsford, eds. *Singular Texts/Plural Authors: Perspective on Collaborative Writing*. Carbondale: Southern Illinois University Press, 1990.

Edwards, Louise P. "Domesticating the Woman Warrior: Comparisons with *Jinghua yuan*." In Edwards, *Men and Women in Qing China: Gender in the Red Chamber Dream*. Leiden: Brill, 1994, 87–112.

Elder, Chris. *Old Peking: City of the Ruler of the World*. Hong Kong: Oxford University Press, 1997.

Epstein, Maram. *Competing Discourses: Orthodoxy, Authenticity, and Engendered Meanings in Late Imperial Chinese Fiction*. Cambridge: Harvard University Asia Center, 2001.

———. "Reflections of Desire: The Poetics of Gender in *Dream of the Red Chamber*." *Nannü* 1.1 (1999):64–100.

Evans, Nancy J. F. "Social Criticism in the Ch'ing: The Novel *Ching-hua yüan*." *Papers on China* 23 (July 1970):52–66.

Fang Baochuan 方寶川, comp. *Taigu xuepai yishu* (diyi ji) 太谷學派遺書 (第一輯). Yangzhou: Jiangsu guangling guji keyin she, 1997.

———. *Taigu xuepai yishu* (di'er ji) 太谷學派遺書 (第二輯). Yangzhou: Jiangsu guangling guji keyin she, 1998.

Fang Zhengyao 方正耀. *Ming Qing renqing xiaoshuo yanjiu* 明清人情小說研究. Shanghai: Huadong shifan daxue, 1986.

Faure, Bernard. *The Red Thread: Buddhist Approaches to Sexuality*. Princeton, N.J.: Princeton University Press, 1998.

Feng Chuntian 馮春田. "Xizhou sheng ji Ding Yaokang: *Xingshi yinyuan zhuan* jizhuzhe zheng" 西周生即丁耀亢—醒世姻緣傳輯著者證. *Shumu jikan* 書目季刊 32.2 (1999):38–44.

Feng Menglong 馮夢龍. *Gujin xiaoshuo* 古今小說. Nanjing: Jiangsu guji, 1993.

Feng Qiyong 馮其庸 et al., eds. *Honglou meng da cidian* 紅樓夢大辭典. Beijing: Wenhua yishu, 1990.

Fong, Grace S. "Writing Self and Writing Lives: Shen Shanbao's (1808–1862) Gendered Auto/Biographical Practices." *Nan Nü* 2.2 (2000):259–303.

Foucault, Michel. "What is an Author." In Foucault, *Counter-Memory Practices: Selected Essays and Interviews*, ed. Donald Bouchard, trans. Donald Bouchard and Sherry Simon. Ithaca, N.Y.: Cornell University Press, 1977, 113–138.

———. *The Use of Pleasure*, trans. Robert Hurley. New York: Vintage Books, 1985.

Fu Chengzhou 傅承洲. "*Xiyou bu* zuozhe Dong Sizhang kao" 西游補作者董斯張考. *Wenxue yichan* 文學遺產 (1989, no. 3):120–122.

Fu Shiyi 傅世怡. *Xiyou bu chutan* 西遊補初探. Taipei: Xuesheng, 1986.

Galef, David, ed. *Second Thoughts: A Focus on Rereading*. Detroit: Wayne State University Press, 1998.

Gao Hongjun 高洪均. "*Xiyou bu* zuozhe shi shui" 西游補作者是誰. *Tianjin Shida xuebao* 天津師大學報 (1985, no. 6):81–84.

Gao Mingge 高明閣. *Shuihu zhuan lungao* 水滸傳論稿. Shenyang: Liaoning daxue, 1987.

Genette, Gérard. *Palimpsests: Literature in the Second Degree*, trans. Channa Newman and Claude Doubinsky. Lincoln: University of Nebraska Press, 1997.

Gillies, Mary Ann. "The Literary Agent and the Sequel." In Paul Budra and Betty A. Schellenberg, eds., *Part Two: Reflections on the Sequel*, 131–143.

Goody, Jack. *The Interface Between the Written and the Oral*. Cambridge: Cambridge University Press, 1987.

Graham, A. C., trans. *The Book of Lieh-tzu*. London: John Murray, 1960.

Gu Taiqing 顧太清. *Honglou meng ying* 紅樓夢影. Beijing: Beijing daxue, 1988.

Guben xiaoshuo jicheng 古本小說集成. Shanghai: Shanghai guji, 1990–1995.

Guben Yuan Ming zaju 孤本元明雜劇, ed. Zhao Yuandu 趙元度. Beijing: Zhonghua xiju, 1958.

Gui Maoyi 歸懋儀. *Xiuyu xucao* 繡餘續草 (1832; in Harvard-Yenching Library).

Guichuzi 歸鋤子. *Honglou meng bu* 紅樓夢補. Beijing: Beijing daxue, 1988.

Guo Mingzhi 郭明志. "Lun *Xiyou ji* xushu" 論西游記續書. *Xuexi yu tansuo* 學習與探索 109 (1992, no. 2):120–125.

Guo Yanli 郭延禮. *Zhongguo jindai wenxue fazhan shi* 中國近代文學發展史, vol. 1. Ji'nan: Shangdong jiaoyu, 1990.

Guoju dacheng 國劇大成, ed. Zhang Bojin 張伯謹. Taipei: Zhenxing Guoju yanjiu fazhan weiyuanhui, 1970.

Haipu zhuren 海圃主人. *Xu Honglou meng xinbian* 續紅樓夢新編. Beijing: Beijing daxue, 1990.

Hanan, Patrick. *The Chinese Vernacular Story*. Cambridge, Mass.: Harvard University Press, 1981.

———. "The Development of Fiction." In Raymond Dawson, ed., *The Legacy of China*. New York: Oxford University Press, 1964, 115–143.

———. *The Invention of Li Yu*. Cambridge, Mass.: Harvard University Press, 1988.
———. "Sources of the *Chin P'ing Mei*." *Asia Major* 10.1 (1963):23–67.
———. "The Text of the *Chin P'ing Mei*." *Asia Major* 9.1 (1962):1–57.
Hartman, Charles. *Han Yü and the T'ang Search for Unity*. Princeton, N.J.: Princeton University Press, 1986.
Hawkes, David, and John Minford, trans. *The Story of the Stone*. 5 vols. Harmondsworth, England: Penguin Books, 1977–1986.
He Lianghao 何良昊. "*Xiyou bu* de qian yu ao" 西游補的謙與傲. *Wuhan daxue xuebao* 武漢大學學報 54.3 (May 2001):345–354.
Hegel, Robert E. "Distinguishing Levels of Audiences for Ming-Ch'ing Vernacular Literature." In David Johnson, Andrew J. Nathan, and Evelyn S. Rawski, eds., *Popular Culture in Late Imperial China*. Berkeley: University of California Press, 1985, 112–142.
———. *The Novel in Seventeenth-Century China*. New York: Columbia University Press, 1981.
———. *Reading Illustrated Fiction in Late Imperial China*. Stanford: Stanford University Press, 1998.
———. "Self as Mind or as Body: Fictional Examinations of Identity." In Hegel, *The Novel in Seventeenth-Century China*, 141–187.
———. "*Sui shi yiwen* kaolüe" 隋史遺文考略. In Yuan Yuling, *Sui shi yiwen*. Taipei: Youshi wenhua gongsi, 1975, 1–15.
———. "*Sui T'ang yen-i*: The Sources and Narrative Techniques of a Traditional Chinese Novel." Ph.D. dissertation, Columbia University, 1973.
Henderson, John B. *Scripture, Canon, and Commentary of Confucian and Western Exegesis*. Princeton, N.J.: Princeton University Press, 1991.
Hinsch, Bret. *Passions of the Cut Sleeve: The Male Homosexual Tradition in China*. Berkeley: University of California Press, 1990.
Ho, Clara Wing-chung, ed. *Biographical Dictionary of Chinese Women: The Qing Period, 1644–1911*. Armonk, N.Y.: M. E. Sharpe, 1998.
Holoch, Donald. "*The Travels of Laocan*: Allegorical Narrative." In Milena Doleželová-Velingerová, ed., *The Chinese Novel at the Turn of the Century*. Toronto: University of Toronto Press, 1980, 129–149.
Hong Tao 洪濤. "Lu Shi'e *Xin Shuihu* yu jindai *Shuihu* xindu: Lun shidai cuozhi wenti" 陸士諤新水滸與近代水滸新讀: 論時代錯置問題. *Ming Qing xiaoshuo yanjiu* 明清小説研究 59 (2001, no. 1):73–84.
Honglou meng 紅樓夢. Beijing: Renmin wenxue, 1982.
Hou Xiyou ji (*Xinjuan piping Hou Xiyou ji* 新鐫批評後西遊記, or *Xinke piping xiuxiang Hou Xiyou ji* 新刻批評繡像後西遊記, comment. Tianhua caizi 天花才子). Rpt. Taipei: Tianyi, 1975.
Hou Xiyou ji (*Xiuxiang Hou Xiyou ji zhenquan* 繡像後西遊記真銓, or *Xinke piping xiuxiang Hou Xiyou ji* 新刻批評繡像後西遊記, comment. Tianhua caizi 天花才子). Rpt. Taipei: Tianyi, 1975.
Hou Xiyou ji 後西遊記, ed. Xu Yuan 徐元. Hangzhou: Zhejiang wenyi, 1985.
Hou Xiyou ji, ed. Gu Liang 固亮. Beijing: Baowentang, 1989.
Hou Xiyou ji. *Xiyou ji daxi* 西游記大系 2:1879–2321.
Hou Zhi 侯芝. *Zaizaotian* 再造天. (n.p.) Guangyi shuju, 1936.

Hou Zhongyi 侯忠義. *Sanxia wuyi xilie xiaoshuo* 三俠五義系列小說. Shenyang: Liaoning jiaoyu, 1992.

Hrdlicková, Vena. "The Professional Training of Chinese Storytellers and the Storytellers' Guilds." *Archiv Orientalni* 33 (1965):225–248.

Hsia, C. T. "The Scholar-Novelist and Chinese Culture: A Reappraisal of *Ching-huan Yuan*." In Andrew H. Plaks, ed., *Chinese Narrative: Critical and Theoretical Essays*. Princeton, N.J.: Princeton University Press, 1977, 266–305.

———. "*The Travels of Lao Ts'an*: An Exploration of Its Art and Meaning." *The Tsing Hua Journal of Chinese Studies,* new series 8.2 (1969):40–66.

Hsia, C. T., and T. A. Hsia. "New Perspectives on Two Ming Novels: *Hsi Yu Chi* and *Hsi Yu Pu*." In Tse-tsung Chow, ed., *Wen-lin: Studies in the Chinese Humanities*. Madison: University of Wisconsin, 1968, 229–245.

Hu Shi 胡適. "*Jinghua yuan* de yinlun" 鏡花緣的引論. In Hu Shi, *Hu Shi wencun* 胡適文存. Taipei: Yuandong tushu gongsi, 1975, 400–433.

Hu Wenkai 胡文楷. *Lidai funü zhuzuo kao* 歷代婦女箸作考. Shanghai: Shanghai guji, 1985.

Hu Zongyu 胡宗堉. "Xu *Jinghua yuan* quanbian xu" 續鏡花緣全編序. In Hua Qinshan, *Xu Jinghua yuan* 續鏡花緣, 3.

Hua Qinshan 華琴珊. *Xu Jinghua yuan* 續鏡花緣. Beijing: Shumu wenxian, 1992.

Huang Jinzhu 黃錦珠. "*Honglou meng* de jindai xushu 紅樓夢的近代續書." *Taibei Shiyuan xuebao* 9 台北師院學報 (1996):171–196.

Huang Lin 黃霖. "Ding Yaokang ji qi *Xu Jin Ping Mei* 丁耀亢及其續金瓶梅. *Fudan xuebao* 復旦學報 (1988, no. 4):55–60.

Huang Lin 黃霖 and Han Tongwen 韓同文, eds. *Zhongguo lidai xiaoshuo lunzhu xuan* 中國歷代小說論著選, vol. 1. Nanchang: Jiangxi renmin, 1982.

Huang, Martin W. *Desire and Fictional Narrative in Late Imperial China*. Cambridge, Mass.: Harvard University Asia Center, 2001.

———. "Karmic Retribution and the Didactic Dilemma in the *Xingshi yinyuan zhuan*." *Hanxue yanjiu* 15.1 (1997):397–440.

———. *Literati and Self-Re/Presentation: Autobiographical Sensibility in the Eighteenth-Century Chinese Novel*. Stanford: Stanford University Press, 1995.

Huang Tsung-hsi. *The Records of Ming Scholars,* trans. Julia Ching. Honolulu: University of Hawai'i Press, 1987.

Huang Yongnian 黃永年. "Qianyan" 前言. In *Xiyou zhengdao shu,* annot. and comt. Huang Zhouxing, 1–46.

Huang Zhouxing 黃周星, annot. and comt. *Xiyou zhengdao shu* 西游證道書. 2 vols. Beijing: Zhonghua, 1993.

Huayue chiren 花月痴人. *Honglou huanmeng* 紅樓幻夢. Beijing: Beijing daxue, 1990.

Hummel, Arthur W., ed. *Eminent Chinese of the Ch'ing Period*. Taipei: Chengwen, 1967[1943].

Hun Tang houzhuan 混唐後傳. *Mingdai xiaoshuo jikan* 明代小說輯刊, series 3, vol. 1.

Idema, Wilt L. "Coping with the Conquest: Some Preliminary Comments on Three Plays by Ding Yaokang." Unpublished paper.

———. "Some Remarks and Speculations Concerning *p'ing-hua*." In Idema, *Chinese Vernacular Fiction: The Formative Period*. Leiden: Brill, 1974, 69–120.

Idema, Wilt L., and Lloyd Haft. *A Guide to Chinese Literature.* Ann Arbor: University of Michigan, Center for Chinese Studies, 1997.

Irwin, Richard Gregg. *The Evolution of a Chinese Novel: "Shui-hu-chuan."* Cambridge, Mass.: Harvard University Press, 1953.

Jiang, Paul Yun-Ming. *The Search for Mind: Ch'en Pai-sha, Philosopher-Poet.* Singapore: Singapore University Press, 1980.

Jiao Xun 焦循. *Diaogu ji* 雕菰集 (*Baibu congshu jicheng* 百部叢書集成 ed.)

Jin Ping Mei cihua 金瓶梅詞話. Hong Kong: Taiping shuju, 1993.

Jin Shengtan 金聖嘆. *Jin Shengtan wenji* 金聖嘆文集. Chengdu: Bashu, 1997.

Jin Shengtan piping "Shuihu zhuan" 金聖嘆批評水滸傳. Ji'nan: QiLu, 1991.

Jones, William C., trans. *The Great Qing Code.* Oxford: Clarendon Press, 1994.

Kang Zhengguo 康正果. *Chongshen fengyue jian: Xing yu Zhongguo gudian wenxue* 重審風月鑒: 性與中國古典文學. Taipei: Maitian, 1996.

Kao, Karl S. Y. "An Archetypal Approach to *Hsi-yu chi.*" *Tamkang Review* 5.2 (1974): 63–97.

———. "Aspects of Derivation in Chinese Narrative." *Chinese Literature: Essays, Articles, Reviews* 7 (1985):1–36.

———. "A Tower of Myriad Mirrors: Theory and Practice of Narrative in the *Hsi-yu Pu.*" In Tse-tsung Chow, ed., *Wen-lin.* Madison: University of Wisconsin Press, 1989, 205–241.

Ko, Dorothy. *Teachers of the Inner Chambers: Women and Culture in Seventeenth-Century China.* Stanford: Stanford University Press, 1994.

Langhuan shanqiao 瑯嬛山樵. *Bu Honglou meng* 補紅樓夢. Beijing: Beijing daxue, 1988.

———. *Bu Honglou meng* 補紅樓夢. Taipei: Huayuan wenhua chubanshe, 1993.

Lau, D. C., trans. *The Analects.* Harmondsworth, Eng.: Penguin Books, 1979.

———, trans. *Mencius.* Harmondsworth, Eng.: Penguin books, 1970.

Lee, Leo Ou-fan. "The Solitary Traveler: Images of the Self in Modern Chinese Literature." In Robert E. Hegel and Richard Hessney, eds., *Expressions of Self in Chinese Literature.* New York: Columbia University Press, 1985, 282–307.

Lee, Leo Ou-fan, and Andrew Nathan. "The Beginnings of Mass Culture: Journalism and Fiction in the Late Ch'ing and Beyond." In David Johnson, Andrew J. Nathan, and Evelyn S. Rawski, eds., *Popular Culture in Late Imperial China.* Berkeley: University of California Press, 1985, 360–395.

Legge, James, trans. *The Chinese Classics.* Vol. 1: *Confucian Analects, The Great Learning, The Doctrine of the Mean.* Rpt. Taipei: SMC, 1998.

———, trans. *The Chinese Classics.* Clarendon Press, 1893 (rpt. Taipei: Wenshizhe, 1972).

———, trans. *Li Chi: Book of Rites.* Oxford University Press, 1885 (rpt. New Hyde Park, N.Y.: University Books, 1967).

Li Heng 李恆. "Du *Ruyijun zhuan* lüeyan" 讀如意君傳略言. In Chen Tianchi, *Ruyijun zhuan,* 25–29.

Li Jiarui 李家瑞. "Cong *Shi Yukun de Longtu gong'an* shuodao *Sanxia wuyi*" 從石玉崑的龍圖公案說到三俠五義. *Wenxue jikan* 文學季刊, vol. 2 (April 1934):393–397. Rpt. in Wang Junnian 王俊年, ed., *Zhongguo jindai wenxue lunwen ji (1919–1949): Xiaoshuo juan* 中國近代文學論文集 (1919–1949): 小說卷. Beijing: Zhongguo shehui kexue, 1988, 323–329.

Li, Qiancheng. *Fictions of Enlightenment: "Journey to the West," "Tower of Myriad Mirrors," and "Dream of the Red Chamber."* Honolulu: University of Hawai'i Press, 2004.
Li Ruzhen 李汝珍. *Jinghua yuan* 鏡花緣. Ji'nan: QiLu shushe, 1995.
Li Shiren 李時人. *Xiyou ji kaolun* 西游記考論. Hangzhou: Zhejiang guji, 1991.
Li, Wai-yee. *Enchantment and Disenchantment: Love and Illusion in Chinese Literature.* Princeton, N.J.: Princeton University Press, 1993.
——. "Heroic Transformations: Women and National Trauma in Early Qing Literature." *Harvard Journal of Asiatic Studies* 59.2 (1999):363–443.
Li Yu 李漁. *The Carnal Prayer Mat,* trans. Patrick Hanan. New York: Ballantine Books, 1990.
——. 李漁. *Li Yu quanji* 李漁全集. Hangzhou: Zhejiang guji, 1991.
——. *Rou putuan* 肉蒲團. Tokyo? 1705. Rpt. Hong Kong: Lianhe chubanshe, ca. 1976.
Li Zengpo 李增坡, ed. *Ding Yaokang yanjiu* 丁耀亢研究. Zhengzhou: Zhongzhou guji, 1998.
Li Zhi 李贄. *Chu Tan ji* 初潭集. Beijing: Zhonghua, 1974.
——. *Fenshu, Xu Fenshu* 焚書, 續焚書. Beijing: Zhonghua, 1975.
Li Zhongchang 李忠昌. *Gudai xiaoshuo xushu manhua* 古代小說續書漫話. Shenyang: Liaoning jiaoyu, 1992.
Liang Qichao 梁啟超. "Changshe nü xuetang qi" 倡設女學堂啟. In Li Youning and Zhang Yufa, eds., *Jindai Zhongguo nüquan yundong shiliao* 中國近代女權運動史料. Taipei: Zhuanji wenxue she, 1975, 561.
Liao Zhaoheng 廖肇亨. "Wan Ming qing'ai guan yu fojiao jiaoshe chuyi" 晚明情愛觀與佛教交涉芻議. Paper presented at "Concealing to Reveal: An International Scholarly Conference on the 'Private' and 'Sentiment' in Chinese History and Culture." Taipei: Center for Chinese Studies, August 20–22, 2001.
Liezi 列子. *Zhuzi jicheng* 諸子集成, vol. 3. Shanghai: Shijie, 1936.
Lin Chen 林辰. *Mingmo Qingchu xiaoshuo shulu* 明末清初小說述錄. Shenyang: Chunfeng wenyi, 1988.
Lin Gang 林崗. *Ming Qing zhiji xiaoshuo pingdian xue zhi yanjiu* 明清之際小說評點學之研究. Beijing: Beijing daxue, 1999.
Lin, Shuen-fu. "The Last Classic Chinese Novel: Vision and Design in *The Travels of Laocan.*" *Journal of American Oriental Society* 121.4 (2001):549–564.
Lin Wei 林薇. *Qingdai xiaoshuo lungao* 清代小說論稿. Beijing: Beijing guangbo xueyuan, 2000.
Lin Yixuan 林依璇. *Wucai ke butian: Honglou meng xushu yanjiu* 無才可補天: 紅樓夢續書研究. Taipei: Wenjin, 1999.
Lin, Yutang, trans. *Widow, Nun and Courtesan.* New York: The John Day Company, 1950.
Liu Baonan 劉寶南, ed. *Lunyu zhengyi* 論語正義. Beijing: Zhonghua, 1990.
Liu Dashen 劉大紳, "Guanyu *Lao Can you ji*" 關於老殘遊記. In Wei Shaochang, ed., *Lao Can youji ziliao,* 54–104.
Liu Delong 劉德隆. "Guanyu *Lao Can youji* zuozhe suoyu zhi yishi" 關於老殘遊記作者所語之異事. In Liu Delong, *Liu E sanlun,* 158–170.

———. "*Lao Can youji* banben gaishuo" 老殘遊記版本概說. In Liu Delong, *Liu E sanlun,* 49–67.

———. *Liu E sanlun* 劉鶚散論. Kunming: Yunnan renmin, 1998.

———. "Liu E de mengshuo" 劉鶚的夢説. In Liu Delong, *Liu E sanlun,* 20–31.

Liu Delong, Zhu Xi 朱禧, and Liu Deping 劉德平. *Liu E ji Lao Can youji ziliao* 劉鶚及老殘遊記資料. Chengdu: Sichuan renmin, 1985.

———. *Liu E xiaozhuan* 劉鶚小傳. Tianjin: Tianjin renmin, 1987.

Liu E 劉鶚. *Lao Can youji* 老殘遊記, annot. Yan Weiqing 嚴薇青. Ji'nan: QiLu shushe, 1981 (1985 printing).

Liu E 劉鶚 and Liu Huisun 劉惠孫. *Lao Can youji quanbian* 老殘遊記全編. Beijing: Yanshan, 1995.

Liu Fu 劉復. "*Xiyou bu* zuozhe Dong Ruoyu zhuan" 西遊補作者董若雨傳. In Dong Yue, *Xiyou bu*. Shanghai: Shanghai guji, 1983, 77–129.

Liu Hui 劉輝. "*Ruyijun zhuan* de kanke niandai jiqi yu *Jin Ping Mei* zhi guanxi" 如意君傳的刊刻年代及其與金瓶梅之關係. In Liu Hui, *Jin Ping Mei lunji* 金瓶梅論集. Taipei: Guangya, 1992, 47–60.

Liu Huisun 劉惠孫. *Lao Can youji bubian* 老殘遊記補編. Beijing: Wenhua yishu, 1992.

———. *Lao Can youji quanbian* 老殘遊記全編. Beijing: Yanshan, 1995.

———. *Tieyun xiansheng nianpu changbian* 鐵雲先生年譜長編. Ji'nan: QiLu shushe, 1982.

Liu, James J. Y. *Chinese Theories of Literature*. Chicago: University of Chicago Press, 1975.

Liu Shide 劉世德 et al., eds. *Zhongguo gudai xiaoshuo baike quanshu* 中國古代小説科全書. Beijing: Zhongguo da baike quanshu, 1993.

Liu Tingji 劉廷璣. *Zaiyuan zazhi* 在園雜志. Taipei: Wenhai, 1969.

Liu, Ts'un-yan. *Chinese Popular Fiction in Two London Libraries*. Hong Kong: Lung Men, 1967.

———. "The Prototypes of *Monkey* (*Hsi-yu Chi*)." *T'oung Pao* 51 (1964):55–71.

Liu Xiangheng 劉象衡. "Chen Tianchi *Ruyijun zhuan* xu" 陳天池如意君傳序. In Chen Tianchi, *Ruyijun zhuan,* 1–2.

Liu, Xiaolian. *The Odyssey of the Buddhist Mind: The Allegory of* the Later Journey to the West. Lanham, Md.: University Press of America, 1994.

Liu Xu 劉昫. *Jiu Tangshu* 舊唐書, vol. 1. Beijing: Zhonghua, 1975.

Liu Yinbo 劉蔭柏. *Xiyou ji fawei* 西遊記發微. Taipei: Wenjin, 1995.

———. "*Xu Xiyou ji* zuozhe tuikao" 續西游記作者推考. *Yunnan shehui kexue* 雲南社會科學 (1984, no. 3):101, 106–107.

———, ed. *Xiyou ji yanjiu ziliao* 西遊記研究資料. Shanghai: Shanghai guji, 1990.

Liu Zuolin 劉作霖. "Chen Kequan *Wuhen tian chuanqi* xu" 陳可泉無恨天傳奇序. In Chen Tianchi, *Ruyijun zhuan,* 7–8.

Lu Jiuyuan 陸九淵. *Lu Xiangshan quanji* 陸象山全集. Taipei: Shijie shuju, 1966.

Lu Lianzhu 盧聯珠. "*Diyi kuaihuo qishu* xu" 第一快活奇書序. In Chen Tianchi, *Ruyijun zhuan,* 3–5.

Lu Shi'e 陸士諤. *Xin Niehai hua* 新孽海花. In Lu Shi'e, *Xin Niehai hua,* 200–260.

———. *Xin Niehai hua* 新孽海花. Beijing: Zhongguo wenlian, 1989.

Lu Xun 魯迅. *A Brief History of Chinese Fiction*, trans. Yang Hsien-yi and Gladys Yang. Beijing: Foreign Language Press, 1959.

———. *Zhongguo xiaoshuo shilüe* 中國小說史略. 1930; rpt. Hong Kong: Sanlian, 1958.
———. *Zhongguo xiaoshuo shilüe* 中國小說史略. Shanghai: Shanghai guji, 1998.
———. *Zhongguo xiaoshuo shilüe* 中國小說史略 [1924]. Reprinted in Lu Xun, *Lu Xun quanji*, 魯迅全集, vol. 9. Beijing: Remin wenxue, 1982, 285–295.
Luo Derong 羅德榮. "*Xu Jin Ping Mei* zhuzhi suojie" 續金瓶梅主旨索解. In Li Zengpo, ed., *Ding Yaokang yanjiu*, 164–175.
Ma, Y. W. "*Shui-hu chuan*." In William H. Nienhauser, Jr. et al., eds., *The Indiana Companion to Traditional Chinese Literature*. Bloomington: Indiana University Press, 1986, 712–716.
Ma Youyuan 馬幼垣. *Zhongguo xiaoshuo shi jigao* 中國小說史集稿. Taipei: Shibao wenhua, 1980.
Mann, Susan. *Precious Records: Women in China's Long Eighteenth Century*. Stanford: Stanford University Press, 1997.
McMahon, Keith. *Causality and Containment in Seventeenth-Century Chinese Fiction*. Leiden: Brill, 1988.
———. *Misers, Shrews, and Polygamists: Sexuality and Male/Female Relations in Eighteenth-Century Chinese Fiction*. Durham, N.C.: Duke University Press, 1995.
Mengmeng xiansheng 夢夢先生. *Honglou yuanmeng* 紅樓圓夢. Beijing: Beijing daxue, 1988.
Meyer-Fong, Tobie. "Collecting Knowledge about Women in Early Qing China." Unpublished essay.
Miao Huaiming 苗懷明. "*Sanxia wuyi* chengshu xinkao" 三俠五義成書新考. *Ming Qing xiaoshuo yanjiu* 明清小說研究 49 (1998, no. 3), 209–224, 256.
Miller, Lucien. "Sequels to *The Red Chamber Dream*: Observations on Plagiarism, Imitation, and Originality in Chinese Vernacular Literature." *Tamkang Review* 5. 2 (1974):187–215.
Mingdai xiaoshuo jikan 明代小說輯刊. 3d. Series. Chengdu: Bashu, 1999.
Munro, Donald J. *Images of Human Nature: A Sung Portrait*. Princeton, N.J.: Princeton University Press, 1988.
Murrin, Michael. *The Allegorical Epic*. Chicago: University of Chicago Press, 1980.
Nabokov, Vladimir. *Lectures on Literature*, ed. Fredson Bowers. New York: Harcourt Brace Jovanovich, 1980.
Nie Gannu 聶紺弩. *Zhongguo gudian xiaoshuo lunji* 中國古典小說論集. Shanghai: Shanghai guji, 1981.
Nienhauser, William Jr., ed. *The Indiana Companion to Traditional Chinese Literature*. Bloomington: Indiana University Press, 1986.
Ning Jiayu 寧稼雨. *Shuihu zhuan qutan yu suojie* 水滸傳趣談與索解. Shenyang: Chunfeng wenyi, 1997.
Ogawa Yōichi 小川陽一. "Mingdai xiaoshuo yu shanshu" 明代小說與善書. *Hanxue yanjiu* 漢學研究 6.1 (June 1988):331–340.
Okamoto Sae 岡本. *Shindai kinsho no kenkyū* 清代禁書研究. Tokyo: Tōkyō daigaku Tōyō bunka kenkyūjo, 1996.
Ong, Walter J. *Orality and Literacy: The Technologizing of the Word*. New York: Methuen, 1982.
Ōtsuka Hidetaka 大塚秀高. *Zōho Chūgoku tsūzoku shōsetsu shomoku* 增補中國通俗小說書目. Tokyo: Kyūko shoin, 1987.

Ouyang Jian 歐陽健. "*Dangkou zhi* jiazhi xinshuo" 蕩寇志價值新說. In Ouyang Jian, *Ming Qing xiaoshuo caizheng* 明清小說采正. Taipei: Guanya, 1992, 402–455.

———. "*Shuo Tang*—Pingmin de Sui Tang yingxiong pu" 說唐—平民的隋唐英雄譜. In Ouyang Jian, *Ming Qing xiaoshuo caizheng* 明清小說采正. Taipei, Guanya, 1992, 288–303.

———. "*Sui Tang yanyi* 'zhui ji cheng zhi' kao" 隋唐演義"綴集成帙"考. In Ouyang Jian, *Ming Qing xiaoshuo xinkao* 明清小說新考. Beijing: Zhongguo wenlian, 1992, 353–396.

———. "Wan Qing 'fanxin' xiaoshuo zonglun" 晚清"翻新"小說綜論. In Ouyang Jian, *Guxiaoshuo yanjiu lun* 古小說研究論. Chengdu: Bashu shushe, 1997, 257–282.

———. *Wan Qing xiaoshuo shi* 晚清小說史. Hangzhou: Zhejiang guji, 1997.

Ouyang Jianzhuo 歐陽見拙. "*Dangkou zhi* shi *Shuihu* zuozhe guandian de zaixian" 蕩寇志是水滸作者觀點的再現. *Ming Qing xiaoshuo yanjiu* 明清小說研究 13 (1989, no. 3):21–30.

Ouyang Xiu 歐陽修 and Song Qi 宋祁. *Xin Tangshu* 新唐書, vol. 1. Beijing: Zhonghua, 1975.

Palmer, R. Barton. "Rereading Guillaume de Machaut's Vision of Love: Chaucer's *Book of the Duchess* as *Bricolage*." In David Galef, ed., *Second Thoughts*. Detroit: Wayne State University Press, 1998, 169–195.

Pastreich, Emanuel. "The Reception of Chinese Vernacular Narrative in Korea and Japan." Ph.D. dissertation, Harvard University, 1997.

Pease, Donald E. "Author." In Frank Lentricchia and Thomas McLaughlin, eds., *Critical Terms for Literary Study*. Chicago: The University of Chicago Press, 1990, 105–117.

Peng Zhihui 彭知輝. "Lun *Shuo Tang quanzhuan* de diben" 論說唐全傳的底本. *Ming Qing xiaoshuo yanjiu* 明清小說研究 53 (1999, no. 3):181–187.

Perdue, Peter C. "Culture, History, and Imperial Chinese Strategy: Legacies of the Qing Conquests." In Hans van de Ven, ed., *Warfare in Chinese History*. Leiden: Brill, 2000, 252–287.

Plaks, Andrew H. "After the Fall: *Hsing-shih yin-yüan chuan* and the Seventeenth-Century Chinese Novel." *Harvard Journal of Asiatic Studies* 45.2 (1985):543–580.

———. "Allegory in *Hsi-yu Chi* and *Hung-lou Meng*." In Plaks, ed., *Chinese Narrative: Critical and Theoretical Essays*. Princeton, N.J.: Princeton University Press, 1977, 163–202.

———. *The Four Masterworks of the Ming Novel: Ssu ta ch'i shu*. Princeton, N.J.: Princeton University Press, 1987.

———. "Terminology and Central Concepts." In David L. Rolston, ed., *How to Read the Chinese Novel*, 75–123.

———, trans. "How to Read the *Dream of the Red Chamber*." In David L. Rolston, ed., *How to Read the Chinese Novel*, 323–340.

Pu Andi 普安迪 (Andrew Plaks). *Zhongguo xushixue* 中國敘事學. Beijing: Beijing daxue, 1996.

Qi Yukun 齊裕焜. *Mingdai xiaoshuo shi* 明代小說史. Hangzhou: Zhejiang guji, 1997.

———. *Sui Tang yanyi xilie xiaoshuo* 隋唐演義系列小說. Shenyang: Liaoning jiaoyu, 1993.

Qidong yeren 齊東野人. *Sui Yangdi yanshi* 隋陽帝艷史, ed. Li Huiwu 李悔吾. Wuhan: Qunyitang 群益堂, 1985.

Qin Zichen 秦子忱. *Xu Honglou meng* 續紅樓夢. Beijing: Beijing daxue, 1988.

Qingshi liezhuan 清史列傳. Taipei: Zhonghua, 1962.

Quan Shanggu, Sandai Qin Han San'guo Liuchao wen 全上古三代秦漢三國六朝文. Shijiazhuang: Hebei jiaoyu, 1999.

Roddy, Stephen J. "The Philological Musings of *Jinghua yuan*." In Roddy, *Literati Identity and Its Fictional Representations in Late Imperial China*. Stanford: Stanford University Press, 1998, 171–206.

Rolston, David L. *Traditional Chinese Fiction and Fiction Commentary: Reading and Writing between the Lines*. Stanford: Stanford University Press, 1997.

———, ed. *How to Read the Chinese Novel*. Princeton: Princeton University Press, 1990.

Rose, Margaret A. *Parody: Ancient, Modern, and Post-Modern*. Cambridge: Cambridge University Press, 1993.

———. *Parody/Metafiction: Analysis of Parody as a Critical Mirror to the Writing and Reception of Fiction*. London: Croom Helm, 1979.

Roy, David, trans. "How to Read the *Chin P'ing Mei*." In David L. Rolston, ed., *How to Read the Chinese Novel*, 196–243.

———, trans. *The Plum in the Golden Vase*, vols. 1 and 2. Princeton, N.J.: Princeton University Press, 1993 and 2001.

Rui Heshi 芮和師 et al., eds. *Yuanyang hudie pai wenxue ziliao* 鴛鴦蝴蝶派文學資料. Fuzhou: Fujian renmin, 1984.

Sakai Tadao 酒井忠夫. *Chūgoku zenshō no kenkyū* 中國善書研究. Tokyo: Kobundo, 1960.

Scholes, Robert, and Robert Kellogg. *The Nature of Narrative*. New York: Oxford University Press, 1966.

Seidel, Michael. "Running Titles." In David Galef, ed., *Second Thoughts*, 34–50.

Shadick, Harold, trans. *The Travels of Lao Ts'an*. New York: Columbia University Press, 1990.

Shapiro, Sidney, trans. *Outlaws of the Marsh*. Beijing and Bloomington: Indiana University Press, 1981.

Shen Defu 沈德符. *Wanli yehuo bian* 萬歷野獲編. Beijing: Zhonghua, 1959.

Shen Shanbao 沈善寶. *Hongxuelou shixuan chuji* 鴻雪樓詩選初集 (printed 1836; in Nanjing Library).

Shi Ling 石玲. "*Xu Jin Ping Mei* di zuoqi ji qita" 續金瓶梅的作期及其他. In Jilin daxue Zhongguo wenhua yanjiusuo, ed., *Jin Ping Mei yishu shijie* 金瓶梅藝術世界. Changchun: Jinlin daxue, 1991, 333–337.

Shi Zhengkang 施正康 and Shi Huikang 施惠康. *Shuihu zongheng tan* 水滸縱橫談. Shanghai: Xuelin, 1996.

Shiroaki Naoya 白木直也. "Takizawa Bakin *Suiko gaden* 'kōtei gempon' choroku no kampon ni shu" 瀧澤馬琴水滸畫傳校定原本著錄の刊本二種. *Tōhō gaku* 東方學 47 (1974):87–103.

Shuihu zhuan 水滸傳. Ji'nan: QiLu shushe, 1991.

Shuo Tang houzhuan 說唐後傳, ed. Wu Qiong 吳瓊. Nanjing: Jiangsu guji, 1995.

Shuo Tang quanzhuan 說唐全傳. Beijing: Beijing Shiyue wenyi, 1998.

Shuo Tang zheng xi zhuan 説唐征西傳. Ca. 1900. Rpt. Ningbo: Zhejiangsheng Ningboshi tushuguan wenxian bianjibu, 1985.

Sima Qian 司馬遷. *Records of the Grand Historian,* trans. Burton Watson. Rev. ed., New York: Columbia University Press, 1993.

———. "*Shi ji* 9: The Basic Annals of Empress Lü." In *Records of the Grand Historian,* trans. Burton Watson, 268–284.

———. *Shiji* 史記. Beijing: Zhonghua, 1972.

Siqi zhai 思綺齋. *Nüzi quan* 女子權 [1907]. Rpt. in *Zhongguo jindai xiaoshuo daxi* 中國近代小說大系. Nanchang: Baihua zhou wenyi, 1993.

Song Kefu 宋克夫 and Han Xiao 韓曉. *Xinxue yu wenxue lungao: Mingdai Jiajing Wanli shiqi wenxue gaiguan* 心學與文學論稿: 明代嘉靖萬曆時期文學概觀. Beijing: Zhongguo shehui kexue, 2002.

Stone, Charles R. "The *Ruyijun zhuan* and the Origins of the Chinese Erotic Novel." Ph.D. dissertation, The University of Chicago, 1998.

Su Shi 蘇石. "*Xu Xiyou ji* zuozhe wenti chutan" 續西游記作者問題初探. *Kunming sheke* 昆明社科 (1998, no. 6):44–48.

Su Xing 蘇興. "Shilun *Hou Xiyou ji*" 試論後西游記. In Su Xing, *Xiyou ji ji Ming-Qing xiaoshuo yanjiu,* 117–141.

———. "*Xiyou bu* de zuozhe ji xiezuo shijian kaobian" (shang) 西游補的作者及寫作時間考辨 (上). *Wenshi* 文史 42 (1997):245–264.

———. "*Xiyou bu* de zuozhe ji xiezuo shijian kaobian (xia)" (下). *Wenshi* 43 (1997): 225–239.

———. "*Xiyou bu* zhong po qinggen yu li daogen pouxi" 西游補中破情根與立道根剖析. *Beifang Luncong* 北方論叢 152 (1998, no. 6):45–50.

———. *Xiyou ji ji Ming-Qing xiaoshuo yanjiu* 西游記及明清小說研究. Shanghai: Shanghai guji, 1989.

Sui Tang liangchao zhizhuan 隋唐兩朝志傳. Suzhou: Gong Shaoshan 龔紹山, 1619.

Sun Dianqi 孫殿起. *Liulichang xiaozhi* 琉璃廠小志. Beijing: Beijing chubanshe, 1962.

Sun Kaidi 孫楷第. *Riben Dongjing suo jian Zhongguo xiaoshuo mu* 日本東京所見中國小說目. 1932; rpt. Hong Kong: Shiyong, 1967.

———. "Xia Erming yu *Yesou puyan*" 夏二銘與野叟曝言. In Sun Kaidi, *Cangzhou houji* 滄州後集. Beijing: Zhonghua, 1985, 238–247.

———. *Zhongguo tongsu xiaoshuo shumu* 中國通俗小說書目. Beiping: Guoli Beiping tushuguan, 1932.

———. *Zhongguo tongsu xiaoshuo shumu* 中國通俗小說書目. Rpt., Beijing: Renmin wenxue, 1982.

———. *Zhongguo tongsu xiaoshuo shumu* 中國通俗小說書目. Rpt., Taipei: Fenghuang, 1974.

Sun Wenliang 孫文良, ed. *Manzu da cidian* 滿族大辭典. Shenyang: Liaoning daxue, 1990.

Sun Xidan 孫希旦, anno. and ed. *Liji jijie* 禮記集解. Beijing: Zhonghua, 1989.

Sun Yancheng 孫言誠. "*Xu Jin Ping Mei* de keben, chaoben he gaixieben" 續金瓶梅的刻本、抄本和改寫本. In Jilin daxue Zhongguo wenhua yanjiusuo, ed., *Jin Ping Mei yishu shijie* 金瓶梅藝術世界. Changchun: Jilin daxu, 1991, 319–332.

Taiping guangji 太平廣記, ed. Li Fang 李昉 et al. 10 vols. Beijing: Zhonghua, 1961.

Taiyaku Chūgoku rekishi shōsetsu senshū 對譯中國歷史小說選集. Tokyo: Yumani shobō, 1985.

Takizawa Bakin 瀧澤馬琴. *Chinsetsu yumiharizuki* 椿說弓張月, ed. Gotō Tanji 後滕丹治. Tokyo: Iwanami shoten, 1978.

———. "Hankan sōtan" 半間窗談. Rpt. in *Kokubungaku kenkyū* 國文學研究 27. Waseda daigaku (spring 1952):99–154. In the Seikado bunko.

———. *Nansō satomi hakkenden* 南總里見八犬傳. Tokyo: Kokumin bunko, 1909.

Tan Zhengbi 譚正璧 and Tan Xun 譚尋. *Guben xijian xiaoshuo huikao* 孤本稀見小說匯考. Hangzhou: Zhejiang wenyi, 1984.

Tang Zhesheng 湯哲聲. "Zhongguo xiandai xiaoshuo de yizhong wenti cunzai: Jianlun Lu Shi'e *Xin Shuihu, Xin San'guo, Xin Yesou puyan* 中國現代小說的一種文體存在: 兼論陸士諤新水滸新三國新野叟曝言. *Ming Qing xiaoshuo yanjiu* 明清小說研究 59 (2001, no. 1):85–93.

Taylor, Andrew. "The Curious Eye and the Alternative Ending of the *Canterbury Tales*." In Paul Budra and Betty A. Schellenberg, eds., *Part Two: Reflections on the Sequel*, 34–52.

Tian Pu 田璞. "*Xingshi yinyuan zhuan* zuozhe shi Ding Yaokang" 醒世姻緣傳作者是丁耀亢. *Henan daxue xuebao* (1985, no. 5):77–82.

Tian Shu 田秫. "Xu" 序. In Chen Tianchi, *Ruyijun zhuan*, 1–2.

Tu Lien-chē. "Chēn T'ing-ching." In Arthur Hummel, ed., *Eminent Chinese of the Ch'ing Period*. Washington D.C.: U.S. Government Printing Office, 1943.

Tung Yüeh (Dong Yue). *The Tower of Myriad Mirrors: A Supplement to Journey to the West*, trans. Shuen-fu Lin and Larry F. Schulz. Berkeley: Asian Humanities Press, 1978.

Waley, Arthur. *Three Ways of Thought in Ancient China* [1932]. Stanford: Stanford University Press, n.d.

Wang Ayling 王瑷玲. "Siqing huagong—Ming Qing juzuojia zhi ziwo xuxie yu qi xiju zhanyan" 私情化公—明清劇作家之自我敘寫與其戲劇展演. Paper presented at "Concealing to Reveal: An International Scholarly Conference on the 'Private' and 'Sentiment' in Chinese History and Culture." Taipei: Center for Chinese Studies, August 20–22, 2001.

Wang, David Der-wei. *Fin-de-siècle Splendor: Repressed Modernities of Late Qing Fiction, 1849–1911*. Stanford: Stanford University Press, 1997.

Wang Duanshu 王端淑. *Yinhong* ji 吟紅集 (n.d.; in the Naikaku bunko).

Wang Gang 王崗. *Langman qinggan yu zongjiao jingshen: Wan Ming wenxue yu wenxue sichao* 浪漫情感與宗教精神: 晚明文學與文學思潮. Hong Kong: Tiandi tushu, 1999.

Wang, I-Chun. "Allegory and Allegoresis of the Cave." *Tamkang Review* 22.1–4 (autumn 1991–summer 1992):393–404.

Wang Lanzhi 王蘭沚. *Qilou chongmeng* 綺樓重夢. Beijing: Beijing daxue, 1990.

Wang Liqi 王利器. *Yuan Ming Qing sandai jinhui xiaoshuo xiqu shiliao* 元明清三代禁毀小說戲曲史料. Rev. ed. Shanghai: Shanghai guji, 1981.

Wang Lixing 王立興. "Liu E yu *Lao Can youji*" 劉鶚與老殘遊記. In Wang Lixing, *Zhongguo jindai wenxue kaolun* 中國近代文學考論. Nanjing: Nanjing daxue, 1992, 72–101.

Wang Minqiu 王民求. "*Hou Xiyou* de shehui yiyi" 後西游的社會意義. In *Ming-Qing xiaoshuo luncong* 明清小說論叢. Shenyang: Chunfeng wenyi, 1984, 1:151–158.

Wang Rumei 王汝梅. "Ding Yaokang de *Xu Jin Ping Mei* chuangzuo ji qi xiaoshuo guannian" 丁耀亢的續金瓶梅創作及其小說觀念. In Li Zengbo, ed., *Ding Yaokang yanjiu*, 157–163.

Wang Shaotang 王少堂. *Song Jiang* 宋江. 3 vols. Nanjing: Jiangsu renmin, 1985.

———. *Wu Song* 武松. 2 vols. Nanjing: Jiangsu renmin, 1959; rpt. 1979.

Wang Shouren 王守仁. *Wang Yangming quanji* 王陽明全集, ed. Wu Guang 吳光 et al. 2 vols. Shanghai: Shanghai guji, 1992.

Wang Sucun 王素存. "*Xingshi yinyuan zhuan* zuozhe Xizhou sheng kao" 醒世姻緣傳作者西周生考. *Dalu zazhi* 大陸雜誌 17.3 (1958):7–9.

Wang Tuo 王拓. "Dui *Xiyou bu* de xin pingjia" 對西遊補的新評價. In Xia Zhiqing (C. T. Hsia), et al., eds., *Wenren xiaoshuo yu Zhongguo wenhua* 文人小說與中國文化. Taipei: Jingcao, 1975, 195–213.

Wang Weimin 王為民. "Duiyu *Xiyou ji* de yizhong chanshi: *Xiyou bu* yu *Xiyou ji* de guanxi" 對于西游記的一種闡釋: 西游補與西游記的關係. *Ming Qing xiaoshuo yanjiu* 明清小説研究 59 (2001, no.1):195–201.

Wang Xuejun 王學鈞. "'Ersi chuandao' kaobian: Liu E yu Taigu xuepai guanxi lunkao zhiyi" 二巳傳道考辨: 劉鶚與太谷學派關係論考之一. *Ming Qing xiaoshuo yanjiu* 明清小説研究 17–18 (1990, nos. 3–4):304–331.

———. "Jiang Wentian yu Li Longchuan" 蔣文田與李龍川. *Nanjing ligong daxue xuebao* 南京理工大學學報 13.2 (2000):89–96.

———. "*Lao Can youji* de Chan zhihui: Yiyun shilun" 老殘遊記的禪智慧: 逸雲釋論. *Ming Qing xiaoshuo yanjiu* 明清小説研究 32 (1994, no. 2):81–91.

———. "Liu E de zibian zhuang—*Lao Can youji*" 劉鶚的自辯狀: 老殘遊記. *Ming Qing xiaoshuo yanjiu* 明清小説研究 25 (1992, nos. 3–4):394–408.

———. *Liu E yu Lao Can youji* 劉鶚與老殘遊記. Shenyang: Liaoning jiaoyu, 1992.

Wang Yingzhi 王英志. "Fafen zhushu shuo pingshu" 發憤著書說評述. *Gudai wenxue lilun yanjiu* 古代文學理論研究 11 (1986):125–156.

Wang Zengbin 王增斌 and Tian Tongxu 田同旭. *Zhongguo gudai xiaoshuo tonglun zongjie* 中國古代小說通論綜解. Beijing: Zhongguo wenlian, 1999.

Wang Zhongmin 王重民. *Zhongguo shanben shu tiyao* 中國善本書提要. Shanghai: Shanghai guji, 1983.

Watson, Burton. *Ssu-ma Ch'ien: Grand Historian of China*. New York: Columbia University Press, 1958.

———, trans. *Records of the Grand Historian*. New York: Columbia University Press, 1993.

Watt, Ian. *The Rise of the Novel*. Hammondsworth, England: Penguin, 1985 [1957].

Wayman, Alex. "The Mirror as a Pan-Buddhist Metaphor-Simile." *History of Religions* 13.4 (May 1974):251–269.

Wei Shaochang 魏紹昌. *Niehai hua ziliao* 孽海花資料. Shanghai: Shanghai guji, 1982.

———. *Wan Qing sida xiaoshuo jia* 晚清四大小說家. Taipei: Shangwu yinshuguan, 1993.

Wei Shaochang. *Wo kan Yuanyang wudie pai* 我看鴛鴦蝴蝶派. Hong Kong: Zhonghua shuju, 1990.

———, ed. *Lao Can youji ziliao* 老殘遊記資料. Beijing: Zhonghua, 1962.

Weimojie suoshuo jing 維摩詰所說經 (Vimalakirti Nirdesa sutra). In *Dazheng xinbian Dazang jing* 大正新編大藏經 [*Taishō shinshū Dai-zōkyō* 大正新脩大藏經], vol. 14. Taipei: Xinwenfeng chuban gongsi, 1983.

Wen Kang 文康. *Ernü yingxiong zhuan* 兒女英雄傳. Beijing: Renmin wenxue, 1981.

Widmer, Ellen. "*Honglou meng ying* and Its Publisher, Juzhen Tang of Beijing." *Late Imperial China* 23.2 (2002):33–52.

———. "Island Paradises: Travel and Utopia in Three East Asian Offshoots of *Shuihu zhuan*." *Sino-Japanese Studies* 13.1:20–33.

———. "Ming Loyalism and the Woman's Voice in Fiction after *Honglou meng*." In Ellen Widmer and Kang-I Sun Chang, eds., *Writing Women in Late Imperial China*. Stanford: Stanford University Press, 1997, 366–396.

———. *The Margins of Utopia*: Shui-hu hou-chuan *and the Literature of Ming Loyalism*. Cambridge: Harvard University, Council on East Asian Studies, 1987.

———. "The Trouble with Talent: Hou Zhi (1764–1829) and Her *tanci Zai zaotian* of 1828." *Chinese Literature: Essays, Articles, Reviews* 21(1999):129–148.

Wong, C. Timothy. "Liu E and the *Fang-shih* Tradition." *Journal of the American Oriental Society* 112.2 (1992):302–306.

———. "Notes on the Textual History of the *Lao Ts'an yu-chi*." *T'oung Pao* 69 (1983):23–32.

Wu Cheng'en 吳承恩. *Journey to the West*. Trans. Anthony C. Yu. 4 vols. Chicago: University of Chicago Press, 1977–1983.

———. *Xiyou ji* 西游記. 2 vols. Beijing: Renmin wenxue, 1980.

Wu, H. Laura. "A Fantasy of Perfect Order and Success: The Case of *Ruyijun zhuan*." Paper presented at the 51st Annual Meeting of the AAS, Boston, 1999.

Wu Jianren 吳趼人. *Xin Shitou ji* 新石頭記. Zhengzhou: Zhongzhou guji, 1986.

Wu Liquan 吳禮權. *Zhongguo yanqing xiaoshuo shi* 中國言情小説史. Taipei: Shangwu, 1995.

Wu, Qingyun. "Separation from the Patriarchal World: The *Destiny of the Flowers in the Mirror and Herland*." In Qingyun Wu, *Female Rule in Chinese and English Literary Utopias*. New York: Syracuse University Press, 1995, 82–116.

Wu Shengxi 吳聖昔. *Xiyou xinjie* 西游新解. Beijing: Zhongguo wenlian, 1989.

Xia Xiaohong 夏曉紅. *Wan Qing wenren funü guan* 晚清文人婦女觀. Beijing: Zuojia, 1995.

Xiao, Chi. "Lyric Archi-Occasion: Coexistence of 'Now' and Then." *Chinese Literature: Essays, Articles, Reviews* 15 (1993):17–35.

Xiaoran yusheng 蕭然鬱生. *Xin Jinghua yuan* 新鏡花緣. In *Zhongguo jindai xiaoshuo daxi* 中國近代小説大系. Nanchang: Baihuazhou wenyi, 1996, 6:383–465.

Xiaoyaozi 逍遙子. *Hou Honglou meng* 後紅樓夢. Beijing: Beijing daxue, 1988.

Xiyou ji daxi 西游記大系, ed. Yang Aiqun 楊愛群 et al. 3 vols. Harbin: Heilongjiang renmin, 1996.

Xu Ao 徐敖. "Chen Tianchi *Diyi kuaihuo shu* xu" 陳天池第一快活書序. In Chen Tianchi, *Ruyijun zhuan*, 1–3.

Xu Changling 徐昌齡. *Zetian huanghou Ruyijun zhuan* 則天皇後如意君傳. In *Zhongguo guyan xipin congkan* 中國古艷稀品叢刊. Taipei: n.d., 1:1–50 (individually paginated).

Xu Fuming 徐扶明. "Guanyu *Hou Xiyou*" 關於後西游. In Xu Yuan 徐元, ed., *Hou Xiyou ji*, 1–13.

———. "Guanyu *Xiyou bu* zuozhe Dong Yue de shengping" 關於西遊補作者董説的生平. *Wenxue yichan zengkan* 文學遺產增刊 3 (1956):109–118.

Xu Jiang 徐江. "Dong Yue *Xiyou bu* kaoshu" 董說西游補考述. *Zhongguo shehui kexueyuan yanjiushengyuan xuebao* 中國社會科學院研究生院學報 (1993, no. 4):53–57.

Xu Shuofang 徐朔方. *Xiaoshuo kaoxin bian* 小説考信編. Shanghai: Shanghai guji, 1997.

Xu Xiyou ji 續西遊記 (*Xinbian xiuxiang Xu Xiyou ji* 新編繡像續西遊記, or *Xinbian Xu Xiyou ji* 新編續西遊記, comment. Zhenfu jushi 真復居士). 1805 Jinjiantang 金鑒堂 ed. Rpt. Shanghai: Shanghai guji, 1990.

Xu Xiyou ji 續西游記. Shenyang: Chunfeng wenyi, 1986.

Xu Xiyou ji. Attributed to Ji Gui 季跪. Punctuated and ed. Zhong Fu 鐘夫 and Shi Ping 世平. Shanghai: Shanghai guji, 1993.

Xu Xiyou ji. In *Xiyou ji daxi* 西游記大系 2:1149–1878.

Xu Xiyou ji. Nanjing: Jiangsu wenyi, 1986.

Xu Zhiyan 許指嚴. *Shiye yewen* 十葉野聞. In Wang Shuqing 王樹卿 and Xu Che 徐徹, eds., *Shishuo Cixi* 史說慈禧. Shenyang: Liaoshen shushe, 1994, 1–106.

Yampolsky, Philip, trans. *The Platform Sutra of the Sixth Patriarch*. New York: Columbia University Press, 1967.

Yan Dichang 顏迪昌. *Qing ci shi* 清詞史. Nanjing: Jiangsu guji, 1990.

Yan Dunyi 嚴敦易. "*Shuihu zhuan*" *de yanbian* 水滸傳的演變. Beijing: Zuojia, 1957.

Ye Guitong 葉桂桐. "Cong *Xu Jin Ping Mei* kan *Jin Ping Mei* de banben yu zuozhe" 從續金瓶梅看金瓶梅的版本與作者. *Jilin daxue shehui kexue xuebao* 吉林大學社會科學學報 (1989, no.2):90–96.

Ye Lang 葉朗. *Zhongguo xiaoshuo meixue* 中國小説美學. Beijing: Beijing daxue, 1982.

Yisu 一粟. *Honglou meng shulu* 紅樓夢書錄. Shanghai: Shanghai guji, 1981.

———. *Honglou meng shulu* 紅樓夢書錄. Shanghai: Gudian wenxue, 1958.

———, comp. *Honglou meng juan* 紅樓夢卷. Beijing: Zhonghua, 1963.

Yu, Anthony C. "Heroic Verse and Heroic Mission: Dimensions of the Epic in the *Hsi-yu chi*." *Journal of Asian Studies* 31.3 (1972):879–897.

———. "Narrative Structure and the Problem of Chapter Nine in the *Hsi-yu chi*." *Journal of Asian Studies* 34.2 (Feb. 1975):295–311.

———. "Religion and Literature in China: The 'Obscure Way' of the *Journey to the West*." In Ching-I Tu, ed., *Tradition and Creativity: Essays on East Asian Civilization*. New Brunswick, N.J.: Rutgers University Press, 1987, 109–154.

———. *Rereading the Stone: Desire and the Making of Fiction in Dream of the Red Chamber*. Princeton, N.J.: Princeton University Press, 1997.

———. "Two Literary Examples of Religious Pilgrimage: The *Commedia* and the *Journey to the West*." *History of Religions* 22.3 (Feb. 1983):202–230.

Yu, Anthony C., trans. *Journey to the West*. 4 vols. Chicago: University of Chicago Press, 1977–1983.

Yu Ke 于岢 and Xie Qinglan 解慶蘭. *Jin Ping Mei yu Fo Dao* 金瓶梅與佛道. Beijing: Beijing yanshan, 1998.

Yu Shengting 于盛庭. "Shi Yukun jiqi zhushu chengshu" 石玉崑及其著述成書. *Ming Qing xiaoshuo yanjiu* 明清小説研究 8 (1988, no. 2):145–158.

Yu Wanchun 余萬春. *Dangkou zhi* 蕩寇志, ed. Dai Hongsheng 戴鴻生. Beijing: Renmin wenxue, 1981.

———. *Jie Shuihu quan zhuan* 結水滸全傳. In *Guben xiaoshuo jicheng* series.
Yuan qu xuan waibian 元曲選外編, ed. Sui Shusen 隋樹森. Beijing: Zhonghua, 1959.
Yuan Yuling 袁于令. *Sui shi yiwen* 隋史遺文, ed. Song Xiangrui 宋祥瑞. Beijing: Beijing daxue, 1988.
———. *Sui shi yiwen* 隋史遺文, ed. Liu Wenzhong 劉文忠. Beijing: Renmin wenxue, 1985.
———. *Sui shi yiwen* 隋史遺文. Taipei: Youshi wenhua gongsi, 1975.
Yuanhu Yusou 鴛湖漁叟, collator 校訂. *Shuo Tang quanzhuan* 説唐全傳, ed. Fu Cheng 傅成 and Wu Meng 吳蒙. Shanghai: Shanghai guji, 1985.
Yun Zhu 惲珠. *Guochao guixiu zhengshi ji* 國朝閨秀正始集 (1831; in Harvard-Yenching Library).
———. *Hongxiangguan shicao* 紅香館詩草. In Tao Xiang 陶湘, ed., *Xiyongxuan congshu* 喜永軒叢書, n.p. Rpt., 1927.
Yurui 裕瑞. *Zaochuang xianbi* 棗窗閒筆. In *Lüyan suochuang ji Zaochuang xianbi* 綠煙瑣窗集, 棗窗閒筆. Shanghai: Shanghai guji, 1984.
Zeitlin, Michael. "Donald Barthelme and the Postmodern Sequel." In Paul Budra and Betty A. Schellenberg, eds., *Part Two: Reflections on the Sequel*, 159–173.
Zeng Yongyi 曾永義. "Dong Yue de qingyu shijie: Lüelun *Xiyou bu* de jiegou, zhuti he jiqiao" 董説的鯖魚世界: 略論西遊補的結構、主題和技巧. *Zhongwai wenxue* 中外文學 8.4 (Sept. 1979):18–30.
Zhang Boxing 張伯行. *Zhengyitang quanshu* 正誼堂全書 (*Baibu congshu jicheng* ed.).
Zhang Henshui 張恨水. *Tixiao yinyuan* 啼笑姻緣. In *Zhang Henshui quanji* 張恨水全集, vol. 14. Taiyuan: Beiyue, 1993.
Zhang Hong 張鴻. *Xu Niehai hua* 續孽海花. In *Niehai hua* 孽海花. Beijing: Changcheng, 1999, 195–395.
Zhang Jing'er (Chang Ching-erh) 張靜二. *Xiyou ji renwu yanjiu* 西遊記人物研究. Taipei: Xuesheng, 1984.
Zhang Jinglu 張靜廬. *Zhongguo jindai chuban shiliao: Erbian* 中國近代出版史料: 二編. Shanghai: Qunlian, 1953.
Zhang Juling 張菊玲. *Kuangdai cainü Gu Taiqing* 曠代才女顧太清. Beijing: Beijing chuban she, 2001.
———. *Qingdai Manzu zuojia wenxue gailun* 清代滿族作家文學概論. Beijing: Zhongyang minzuxueyuan, 1990.
Zhang Jun 張俊. *Qingdai xiaoshuo shi* 清代小説史. Hangzhou: Zhejiang guji, 1997.
Zhang Nanquan 張南泉. "Hou Xiyou ji de sixiang yu yishu" 後西游記的思想與藝術. In *Ming Qing xiaoshuo luncong* 明清小説論叢. Shenyang: Chunfeng wenyi, 1984, 1:140–150.
Zhang Qingji 張清吉. *Ding Yaokang nianpu* 丁耀亢年譜. Nanjing: Nanjing daxue, 1996.
———. *Xingshi yinyuan zhuan xinkao* 醒世姻緣傳新考. Zhengzhou: Zhongzhou guji, 1991.
———. "*Xingshi yinyuan* zuozhe shi Ding Yaokang" 醒世姻緣傳作者是丁耀亢. *Xuzhou shifan xueyuanbao* 徐州師範學院報 (1989.3):46–51.
Zhang Xuecheng 章學誠. "*Wenshi tongyi*" *jiaozhu* 文史通義校注, ed. & annot. Ye Ying 葉瑛. Beijing: Zhonghua, 1985.

Zhang Yaosun 張曜孫. *Xu Honglou meng gao* 續紅樓夢稿. Beijing: Beijing daxue, 1990.

Zhang Ying 張穎 and Chen Su 陳速. "Guben *Xiyou* de yibu hanjian xushu" 古本西游的一部罕見續書. In *Xu Xiyou ji*. Shenyang: Chunfeng wenyi, 1986, 778–799.

———. "*Hou Xiyou ji* banben kaoshu" 後西游記版本考述. In *Ming Qing xiaoshuo luncong* 明清小說論叢. Shenyang: Chunfeng wenyi, 1986, 4:235–242.

Zhang Zhang 張章, ed. *Gu Taiqing Yi Hui shici heji* 顧太清奕繪詩詞合集. Shanghai: Shanghai guji, 1998.

Zhao Botao 趙伯陶. "*Honglou meng ying* de zuozhe ji qita" 紅樓影的作者及其他. *Honglou meng xuekan* 紅樓夢學刊 (1989, no. 3):243–251.

Zhao Gang 趙岡 and Chen Zhongyi 陳鍾毅. *Honglou meng yanjiu xinbian* 紅樓夢研究新編. Taipei: Lianjing, 1975.

Zhao Jianzhong 趙建忠. "*Honglou meng* xushu de yuanliu shanbian ji qi yanjiu" 紅樓夢續書的源流嬗變及其研究. *Honglou meng xuekan* 紅樓夢學刊 (1992, no. 4):301–335.

———. *Honglou meng xushu yanjiu* 紅樓夢續書研究. Tianjin: Tianjin guji, 1997.

Zhao Jingshen 趙景深. "*Yesou puyan* zuozhe Xia Erming nianpu" 野叟曝言作者夏二銘年譜. In Zhao Jingshen, *Zhongguo xiaoshuo congkao* 中國小說叢考. Ji'nan: QiLu shushe, 1980, 433–447.

———. "*Yesou puyan* yu Xia shi zongpu" 野叟曝言與夏氏宗譜. In Zhao Jingshen, *Zhongguo xiaoshuo congkao*. Ji'nan: QiLu shushe, 1980, 448–449.

Zhao Shilin 趙士林. *Xinxue yu meixue* 心學與美學. Beijing: Zhongguo shehui kexue, 1992.

Zheng Mingli 鄭明娳. *Xiyou ji tanyuan* 西遊記探源. 2 vols. Taipei: Wenkai, 1982.

Zheng Zhenduo 鄭振鐸. "Zhongguo xiaoshuo tiyao" 中國小說提要. In Zheng Zhenduo, *Zhongguo wenxue yanjiu* 中國文學研究. Beijing, 1957. Rpt., Hong Kong: Guwen, 1961.

Zheng Zhiming 鄭志明. "Gongguoge de lunli sixiang chutan" 功過格的倫理思想初探. *Zhongguo xueshu niankan* 中國學術年刊 10 (1989.2):315–340.

———. *Zhongguo shanshu yu zongjiao* 中國善書與宗教. Taipei: Xuesheng, 1988.

Zheng Zhiyong 鄭智勇. "*Hou Xiyou ji* yu Chaoren" 後西游記與潮人. *Hanshan Shizhuan xuebao* 韓山師專學報 (1993, no. 1):31–34.

Zhongchang 忠昌 (Li Zhongchang). "Lun Zhongguo gudai xiaoshuo de xuyan xianxiang ji chengyin" 論中國古代小說的續衍現象及成因. *Shehui kexue jikan* 社會科學輯刊 (1992, no. 6):124–133.

Zhongguo tongsu xiaoshuo zongmu tiyao 中國通俗小說總目提要, ed. Jiangsu shehui kexue yuan Ming Qing xiaoshuo yanjiu zhongxin. Beijing: Zhongguo wenlian, 1990.

Zhou Cezong (Tse-tsung Chow) 周策縱. "*Honglou meng* yu *Xiyou bu*" 紅樓夢與西游補. *Honglou meng yanjiu jikan* 紅樓夢研究集刊 5 (1980):135–141.

Zhou Juntao 周鈞韜. "*Jin Ping Mei*" sucai laiyuan 金瓶梅素材來源. Zhengzhou: Zhongzhou guji, 1991.

Zhu Meishu 朱眉叔. *Li Ruzhen yu Jinghua yuan* 李汝珍與鏡花緣. Shenyang: Liaoning jiaoyu, 1993.

———. "Lun *Xu Jin Ping Mei* ji qi shan'gai ben *Gelian huaying* he *Jinwu meng*" 論續金瓶梅及其刪改本隔簾花影和金屋夢. In *Ming Qing xiaoshuo luncong* 明清小說論叢. Shenyang: Chunfeng wenyi, 1984, 1:254–257.

Zhu Shenglin 諸聖鄰. *Da Tang Qinwang cihua* 大唐秦王詞話. Beijing: Wenxue guji, 1956.

Zhu Xi 朱熹, ed. and annot. *Sishu zhangju jizhu* 四書章句集注. Bejijing: Zhonghua, 1983.

Zhu Yixuan 朱一玄 and Liu Yuchen 劉毓忱, eds. *Shuihu zhuan ziliao huibian* 水滸傳資料匯編. Tianjin: Baihua wenyi, 1981.

———, eds. *Xiyou ji ziliao huibian* 西游記資料匯編. Zhengzhou: Zhongzhou shuhua she, 1983.

Zolbrod, Leon M. *Takizawa Bakin*. New York: Twayne, 1967.

Zuo Dongling 左東嶺. *Li Zhi yu wan Ming wenxue sixiang* 李贄與晚明文學思想. Tianjin: Tianjin renmin, 1997.

CONTRIBUTORS

ROBERT E. HEGEL is professor of Chinese and comparative literature at Washington University in St. Louis. There he has taught Chinese literature and culture courses for nearly thirty years. His current research involves writing beyond literary creation; he recently convened the first international conference on writing and law in late imperial China.

SIAO-CHEN HU is associate research fellow at the Institute of Chinese Literature and Philosophy, Academia Sinica, Taiwan. She has been working on the female tanci narrative and is the author of *Cainü cheye weimian: Jindai Zhongguo nüxing xushi wenxue de xingqi* (Burning the midnight oil: The rise of female narrative in early modern China, 2003). She is also the editor of *Shibian yu weixin: Wan Ming yu wan Qing de wenxue yishu* (Dynastic decline and literary innovation, 2001).

MARTIN W. HUANG is professor of Chinese at the University of California, Irvine. His publications include *Literati and Self-Re/Representation: Autobiographical Sensibility in the Eighteenth-Century Chinese Novel* (1995) and *Desire and Fictional Narrative in Late Imperial China* (2001). His book on masculinities in late imperial China is forthcoming from University of Hawai'i Press.

QIANCHENG LI is assistant professor of Chinese at Louisiana State University. He is the author of *Fictions of Enlightenment: "Journey to the West," "Tower of Myriad Mirrors," and "Dream of the Red Chamber"* (2004). His research interests include traditional Chinese fiction and drama.

KEITH MCMAHON is professor and chair of East Asian languages and cultures at the University of Kansas. His published work includes *Misers, Shrews, and Polygamists: Sexuality and Male-Female Relations in Eighteenth-century Chinese Fiction* (1995) and *The Fall of the God of Money: Opium Smoking in Nineteenth-century China* (2002). His most recent work is on structures of masculinity and femininity in nineteenth-century China on the verge of modernity.

YING WANG is assistant professor of Asian studies at Mount Holyoke College. Her dissertation is titled "Two Authorial Rhetorics of Li Yu's (1611–1680) Works: Inversion and Auto-Communication." She is the coeditor of *Reflections on Humanity: An Advanced Reader of Contemporary Chinese Short Stories* (2003) and the coeditor of *Literature and Society: Advanced Reader of Modern*

Chinese (1999). She is currently working on two imitative works of *Honglou meng* by the Mongolian Writer Yinzhan naxi (1837–1892).

ELLEN WIDMER is professor of Chinese language and literature at Wesleyan University. Her publications include *The Margins of Utopia: Shui-hu houchuan and the Literature of Ming Loyalism* (1987), *From May Fourth to June Fourth: Fiction and Film in Twentieth Century China* (1993, coedited with David Wang), and *Writing Women in Late Imperial China* (1997, coedited with Kang-i Sun Chang). Her research interests include women's writings of the Ming and Qing, the history of the book in late imperial China, Ming loyalism, and the Christian colleges of China. She is currently finishing a book on women writers of the nineteenth century that centers in part on sequels to *Honglou meng*.

H. LAURA WU is associate professor of Chinese language and culture at Huron University College. She has published articles on traditional Chinese fiction and fiction criticism. Her current research focuses on contemporaneous historical fiction on disorder and its management during the decades of the Ming-Qing transition.

SHUHUI YANG is professor of Chinese at Bates College. He is the author of *Appropriation and Representation: Feng Menglong and the Chinese Vernacular Story* (1998). He also published *Stories Old and New: A Ming Dynasty Collection* (2000), a complete translation of *Gujin xiaoshuo* or *Yushi mingyan* by Feng Menglong. His translation of *Jingshi tongyan* (Stories to caution the world: A Ming dynasty collection II), Feng Menglong's second collection of vernacular stories, is forthcoming.

INDEX

A Ying, 257n6, 258n9
allographic *xushu*, 14–15, 22
anachronism, 214, 232n22
author, 14, 23–30
autographic *xushu*, 13–14, 17n31, 22, 256–257

Ba Jin, 15
Baogong an, 21, 136
Bu Honglou meng, 35, 38, 44n64, 104, 107, 110–111, 114n35, 119, 126, 128, 134
Budra, Paul, 4

Cai Yuanfang, 3
caizi jiaren fiction, 116, 131, 134–135
Can Tang Wudai shi yanyi zhuan, 161, 184n4
Cao Xueqin, 20–21, 36–37, 45n63, 254. See also *Honglou meng*
Castle, Terry, 1
Chanzhen houshi, 13
Chanzhen yishi, 13
Chen Chen, 27, 33, 147
Chen Liao, 259n28
Chen Shaohai, 101
Chen Shiwen, 101
Chen Tianchi, 13, 191
Chen Tingjing, 191
Chen Wenshu, 117, 122
Chen Xianzhang, 60

Chen Xiaolu, 13, 208n68, 211, 214, 226, 228–229, 232n19, 233n34, 235n60. See also *Xu Jinhua yuan*
Cheng Weiyuan, 20, 36–38, 45n63. See also Gao E
Chipozi zhuan, 206n36
chou (clown) characters, 172–74
Christ, 261n55
Chu Renhuo, 3, 10, 12, 162, 165, 177, 189n41
Chunqiu lieguo zhi, 3, 225–226
Cixi (Empress Dowager), 214–215, 225–226, 232n23
Confucius, 25–26, 29, 261n55
continuations, 4, 20, 211, 213–214, 222, 232n19, 229. See also rewritings, sequels, *xushu*

Da Tang Qinwang cihua, 165
Dai Bufan, 45n63
Dangkou zhi, 9–10, 31, 34, 120, 143–158, 232n22
diben (promptbooks), 161, 184n5, 186n21
Ding Yaokang, 6–7, 29–30, 33, 75–94, 95n10; imprisonment of, 29, 94n4; Ming loyalism and, 86. See also *Xu Jing Ping Mei*
Dong Ou nühaojie, 221
Dong Yue, 47. See also *Xiyou bu*

Dong Zhou lieguo zhi, 3
Du Fu, 27

endings of novels, 21, 30–31, 37, 161, 163
Ernü yinxiong zhuan, 30, 43n43, 99–100
Ershi nian mudu zhi guai xianzhuang, 212

Fan Tang yanyi zhuan, 17n31
fanxin xiaoshuo, 12–13, 33, 211–212, 218, 222, 229, 233n32, 234n42
female audience, 127–129, 131–133; in Korea, 130–131
female authors, 124–127
feminine authority, 127, 140n49
Feng Menglong, 3
Fengshen yanyi, 163, 182
Foucault, Michel, 24, 29
Fujian publishers, 160–61, 184n3. See also publishing

Gao E, 20, 36–38, 45n63, 117
Gelian huaying, 94n4,
Genette, Gérard, 4, 16n18, 20, 32, 42n31, 202, 207n48, 230n9
Gu Taiqing, 8, 117–119, 122, 125. See also *Honglou meng ying*
Guanchang xianxing ji, 212
Guichuzi, 24, 124
Guilian meng, 140n37

Haishang chengtianying, 100
Haoqiu zhuan, 163
historical romances, 160–165
Hsia, C. T., 234n40, 247–248
Hong Liangyu, 220
Honglou fumeng, 35, 101–102, 107, 110, 115n57, 119, 125, 127–129, 254
Honglou huanmeng, 101–103, 106–107, 114n33, 126, 130

Honglou juemeng, 139n23
Honglou meng, 2, 143, 230n2, 230n4, 259n20; authorship of, 20–21, 45n63; conclusions of 36–38; *xushu* and, 98–99, 111. See also its *xushu* under individual titles
Honglou meng bu, 38, 105, 119
Honglou meng xinbu, 139n21
Honglou meng ying, 8, 103–104, 110, 120, 122, 125, 135–138; authorship of, 118–119, autobiographic proclivities in, 136–138. See also Gu Taiqing
Honglou yuanmeng, 35, 44n64, 101,102, 105, 107, 114n45, 119–120, 126
Honglou zaimeng, 139n23
Honglou zhenmeng, 119
Hou Honglou meng, 11, 35–37, 100, 102, 106, 117, 119–120, 127–128
Hou Shuihu zhuan, 32, 147
Hou Xiyou ji, 49–50, 58–65; criticism of *Xiyou ji*, 60–61; mistrust of words and texts in, 60, 63; and *Xiyou bu*, 65, 67, 69; and *Xu Xiyou ji*, 62–63
Hou Zhi, 123–125, 127–128
Hu Shi, 13, 211, 221, 230n5
Hua Mulan, 220
Hua Qingshan, 13, 211, 214, 218, 221–222, 225–229, 232n19, 234n42, 234n44, 235n56, 235n60. See also *Xu Jinghua yuan*
Huang Baonian, 249, 259n28
Huang Zhouxing, 47
Huayue hen, 100, 103
Hun Tang houzhuan, 12, 17n29

irony, 169

Jiang Wentian, 249
Jiang Yiyun, 260n41
Jin Ping Mei, 31, 164, 195, 197. See also *Xu Jing Ping Mei*

Jin Shengtan, 23–30, 39, 131, 144–148, 259n28
jing (warrior) characters, 180–181
Jinghua yuan, 120, 128–129, 210–211, 213–216, 218, 220–230, 230nn5–6, 231n16. *See also* its *xushu* under individual titles
Jinwu meng, 94n4

Kang Hai, 193
Kang Youwei, 225

Lao Can youji (chubian), 237–244; and allographic sequels, 261n57, 261n58; dating of, 237–239; journey motif in, 239–244; as travelogue, 239
Lao Can youji erbian, 244–257; autobiographic tendency in, 238, 247–257; journey motif in, 244, 254; textual history of, 237–239
Lee, Leo Ou-fan, 247–248
Li Baojia (Li Boyan), 212, 237–238,
Li Longchuan, 246–247
Li Ruzhen, 210–218, 222–229, 230n5, 231n11, 231n16, 232n19, 232nn. 21–22, 233n34, 234n45, 235n49, 235nn55–56, 235n60. *See also Jinghua yuan*
Li Yu, 1, 131
Li Zhi, 27, 49, 60, 184n4, 258n10
Li Zhongchang, 2, 4, 17n24, 208nn67, 74
Lian Mengqing, 237–238
Liang Qichao, 219
Lin Chen, 3–4, 10, 19, 35, 44n43
Liu Dajun, 261n54
Liu Dashen, 237, 255, 260–261n47, 261nn51, 52, 54, 55
Liu Delong, 238
Liu E, 13, 237–238, 254–257, 258n11, 259n28, 261n55. *See also Lao Can youji*

Liu Guangshi, 261n58
Liu Houze, 238, 257n6, 260nn47, 48
Liu Huisun, 261n58
Liu Tingji, 2, 46, 78
Liu, Xiaolian, 49, 50
Longtu erlu, 21
Longtu gong'an, 21
Lu Jiuyuan, 48
Lu Shi'e, 22–23, 34, 147, 233n32
Lu Xiangshan. *See* Lu Jiuyuan
Lu Xun, 211, 230n5, 237–238, 256, 258n9, 259n29, 261n54
Luo Guanzhong, 28, 144–145

Niehai hua, 22–23, 233n32
Niehai hua xubian, 22
nijiu xiaoshuo, 33–35. *See also fanxin xiaoshuo*
Nongqing kuaishi, 206n36
Nüwashi, 221
Nüyuhua, 221

oral and performing literature, 160, 161, 162, 165, 167–69, 172, 183n1, 186nn17, 19, 20, 21, 187n25, 188n35, 189n42
Ouyang Jian, 12, 17n29, 187n28

parody, 10, 34, 36–37, 108, 159, 160, 169, 182–183, 184n2, 185n9, 213–214, 218, 230n9, 231n15
Pinhua baojian, 100, 103
Plaks, Adnrew, 47, 52, 146, 205n19
Polygamy, 100; in *Honglou meng* sequels, 104–106, 108–111; in *Ruyijun zhuan* (the Qing novel), 198
popular chronicles, 160–161
prequel, 262n58
publishing, 35, 43n34, 120–121, 160–161, 184n3

Qi Yukun, 164, 166–167, 169, 173, 185–186n14, 187nn24, 28, 188n36
qianzhe xiaoshuo, 13, 237
Qilou chongmeng, 99, 101, 102, 107–111, 114n45, 122, 127, 129–131
Qin Zichen, 38, 124, 128
Qinglou meng, 100
Qiu Jin, 221

reading practices, 11–12, 164, 166, 167, 173, 181–183, 185n9, 188n34
re-reading, 210–211, 218, 221, 229–230, 230n1, 230
rewritings, 2, 6, 10–13, 20–21, 30–31, 40, 221, 230n1, 230n1, 230n4, 233n32
Rolston, David, 43n41, 52, 72n55, 208n75, 230n4
Rou putuan, 196
Ruyijun zhuan (Ming novel), 10–11, 190–191, 233; sexuality in, 197–199
Ruyijun zhuan (Qing novel), 10–11, 190–203; parallels with the Ming *Ruyijun zhuan*, 194–197; patriarchy in, 199–201; sexuality in, 197–199; as special *xushu*, 201–203; and *Yesou puyan*, 204n17, 205n31

Sanguo zhi tongsu yanyi, 164
Sanguo zhi yanyi, 164
Sanxia wuyi, 21–22
Schellenburg, Betty A., 4
Sengni niehai, 206n36
sequels, 1, 4, 11–12, 230n9; differences between *xushu* and, 4, 21, 40. See also continuations, prequel, rewritings, and *xushu*
Shao Bao, 193
Shenlou zhi, 115n54
Shi Nai'an, 28, 144
Shi Yukun, 21–22

Shiji, 178, 189n39, 224. See also Sima Qian
Shuihu houzhuan, 27, 33, 122, 133–134
Shuihu zhuan, 8, 28–31,163, 175, 182, 195, 197, 143–158, 230n2, 232n19. See also Jin Shengtan and its *xushu* under individual titles
Shuo Tang houzhuan, 12, 162
Shuo Tang qianzhuan, 162
Shuo Tang quanzhuan, 10–12, 159–189
Shuo Tang sanzhuan, 162
Sima Qian, 26–27, 224, 235n52, 235n55
Su'e pian, 206n36
Sui chao haohan, 166, 168
Sui shi yiwen, 3, 10–12, 161, 163, 165, 166, 170, 177, 184n6, 185n14, 187nn22–23, 188n38
Sui Tang liangchao zhizhuan, 163, 165
Sui Tang yanyi, 3, 10–12, 159, 163, 165, 166, 168–169, 170, 173, 176, 177, 181, 182–183, 185nn6, 8, 14, 186n15, 187nn22–23, 188nn31, 33, 36, 223
Sui Yangdi yanshi, 12

Taigu school, 246–247, 249–250, 252
Taishang ganying pian, 29, 79, 82–83, 85. See also *Xu Jin Ping Mei* and morality books
Takizawa Bakin, 133–134
tanci, 123–125, 127–128
Tang shu zhizhuan tongsu yanyi, 165
Tao Qian, 216
Taohua ying, 206n36
Tixiao yinyuan and *xushu*, 14

vulgar slang, 171, 175, 176, 180, 187n24, 189n41

Wang, David, 44n49, 232n22, 260n46
Wang Duan, 140n37
Wang Duanshu, 140n37

Wang Lan'gao, 124
Wang Lixing, 261n53
Wang Shouren. *See* Wang Yangming
Wang Yangming, 48–49, 52, 192
Watt, Ian, 116–117
Wen Kang, 43n43. See also *Ernü yingxiong zhuan*
Wenming xiaoshi, 212
wenren (literati) novelists, 160–162, 164, 165, 173, 178, 182–183, 185n13
Wu Jianren, 34, 122, 212, 217
Wu Zetian, 190–191, 214–215, 222–226, 228–230
Wu Zetian waishi, 223

Xia Jingqu, 254–255. See also *Yesou puyan*
Xianxingji xiaoshuo, 212–213, 231n12
Xiao wuyi, 21–22
xiaoshuo, 19–20, 23
Xiaoran yusheng, 13, 211–218, 221, 225, 229, 231n11, 213n15, 232n22. See also *Xin Jinghua yuan* (by Xiaoran yusheng)
Xihu jiahua, 207n65
Xin Jinghua yuan (by Chen Xiaolu), 211, 214, 218–229
Xin Jinghua yuan (by Xiaoran yusheng), 211–218, 228–229
Xin jing, 48
Xin Lieguo zhi, 3
Xin Niehai hua, 23
Xin Shitou ji, 34, 122, 217
Xin Shuihu, 147
Xin Xihu jiahua, 207n65
Xinxue (learning of the mind/heart), 48, 69. *See also* Wang Yangming
Xiong Zhonggu, 160
Xiuxiang xiaoshuo, 238, 255
Xiyou bu, 6, 49–50, 65–69, 232n22, 235n49; and desire, 66; and *Hou Xiyou ji*, 65, 67, 69; and *Xin Xiyou ji*, 23n15; and *Xu Xiyou ji*, 68
Xiyou ji, 6, 46, 146. See also its *xushu* under individual titles
Xu Honglou meng, 38, 114n35
Xu Honglou meng gao, 105, 107, 120
Xu Honglou meng xinbian, 107, 110, 132, 134
Xu Jin Ping Mei, 6–7, 32–34, 75–94; and eroticism, 80, 88–92; and misreading of *Jin Ping Mei*, 6, 76–80, 93–94; and morality books, 82–83, 93–94; plot lines of, 76–77, retribution in, 82–88; sexual desire in, 89–90. *See also* Ding Yaokang and *Jin Ping Mei*
Xu Jinhua yuan, 211, 214, 222–228
Xu Niehai hua, 23
Xu Xiyouji, 46–47, 49–58; criticism of *Xiyou ji*, 51, 56, 58; and *Xiyou bu*, 68
xushu, as commentary, 36; as continuum, 12, definitions of, 3–4, 16n17, 32, 40, 201–203, 208n74, 230n9; differences from sequels, 4, 12, 21, 40; and epochal change, 32–35, 228, 236n62; and *fanxin xiaoshuo*, 12–13, 32–35; and interpretation, 5, 27–30, 211; and reader, 11–12; and rewritings, 10–12, 31–32, 40; rise of, 28–30; and textual boundaries of xiaoshuo, 3–4, 19–23; as transitional genre, 5, 32–35. *See also* continuations, prequel, rewritings, sequels, and individual *xushu* titles
xushu anxiety, 5, 38–39

Yesou puyan, 204n17, 205n31, 207n56, 254
Yinhong ji, 140n37
Yu Wanchun, 8, 31, 143–144. See also *Dangkou zhi*

Yu Xiangdou, 161
Yuan Ming yishi, 140n37
Yuan Yuling, 12, 17nn25, 26, 161, 163, 165, 177
Yun Zhu, 116–117, 128, 130; and Gao E, 117

Zai zaotian, 124–125, 127–128
Zhang Henshui, 14–15
Zhang Hong, 23
Zhang Xinzhi, 206n44
Zhang Zhupo, 78, 164

Zhao Jianzhong, 16n6, 44n55, 208n75
Zeng Pu, 22–23
Zengbu Honglou meng, 35, 38, 45n64, 107, 110, 119–121, 128–129, 132
Zhonglie xiao wuyi, 21
Zhonglie xiayi zhuan, 21
Zhongyi (loyalty and righteousness/honor), 42n27, 144–145, 154–155
Zhou Er, 249
Zhou Taigu, 249
Zhu Xi, 25, 48

Production Notes for
Huang / *Snakes' Legs: Sequels, Continuations,
Rewritings, and Chinese Fiction*

Dust jacket and interior designed by Leslie Fitch Design
with text in Minion and display in Meta

Composition by Josie Herr

Printing and binding by The Maple-Vail Book
Manufacturing Group

Printed on 60# Sebago Eggshell, 420 ppi